Proceedings

MW01284846

The Twelfth International Symposium on High-Performance Computer Architecture

HPCA - 12   2006

February 11-15, 2006 • Austin, Texas

Sponsored by

IEEE Computer Society Technical Committee on Computer Architecture

intel.   AMD   IBM Austin Research Lab www.research.ibm.com/arl   Sun. microsystems

IEEE COMPUTER SOCIETY

IEEE

Los Alamitos, California
Washington   ·   Brussels   ·   Tokyo

ISBN 0-7803-9368-6
IEEE Catalog Number 06TH8836

Additional copies may be ordered from:

IEEE Computer Society
Customer Service Center
10662 Los Vaqueros Circle
P.O. Box 3014
Los Alamitos, CA 90720-1314
Tel: + 1 800 272 6657
Fax: + 1 714 821 4641
http://computer.org/cspress
csbooks@computer.org

IEEE Service Center
445 Hoes Lane
P.O. Box 1331
Piscataway, NJ 08855-1331
Tel: + 1 732 981 0060
Fax: + 1 732 981 9667
http://shop.ieee.org/store/
customer-service@ieee.org

IEEE Computer Society
Asia/Pacific Office
Watanabe Bldg. 1-4-2
Minami-Aoyama
Minato-ku, Tokyo 107-0062
JAPAN
Tel: + 81 3 3408 3118
Fax: + 81 3 3408 3553
tokyo.ofc@computer.org

Individual paper REPRINTS may be ordered at: reprints@computer.org

Table of Contents

Twelfth International Symposium on High-Performance Computer Architecture

HPCA-12

Session 9: Hardware/Software Tradeoffs

Session 10: Multi-Threaded Systems

Message from the General Co-Chairs

As General Co-Chairs, we have two very pleasant tasks, (1) to welcome you to the 12th Annual High Performance Computer Architecture Symposium (HPCA-12), and (2) to acknowledge those who contributed greatly to this year's conference.

First, welcome to HPCA. The conference has continued to grow since Dharma Agrawal and Laxmi Bhuyan had the vision back in 1995 that this conference was needed. They were certainly right. Although some of the constraints driving high performance computer architecture have changed since then, the field itself continues to be vibrant and grow in importance. Today we talk a lot about power, energy, and temperature considerations, but at the same time we are not really willing to give up on performance. So, as the field continues to get stronger, likewise the conference gets stronger. This year is no exception. We hope you find the papers thought provoking, and the environment conducive to meaningful interchange.

It is also a pleasure for us to welcome you to Austin, Texas, home to The University of Texas at Austin's Computer Engineering and Computer Science programs that both rank in the top ten in the nation and home to a major chunk of cutting edge computer technology. Austin is also home to a very special ambiance, exemplified by the many "Keep Austin Weird" T-shirts you will see around town. We hope you will make time while you are here to sample Austin fully, its University, its high tech industry, and its live music, parks, and restaurants.

Our second pleasant task is to thank those who have put this conference together. Being General Chairs is a lot easier when there are so many bright and committed people who chip in. First of course is Chita Das, the Program Chair. Much as we talk about ambiance, all would be irrelevant without a strong technical program. Chita and his Program Committee have put in an enormous amount of energy to assemble the HPCA-12 Technical Program. We are fortunate that he has been able to attract two outstanding Keynote speakers, David Elliott Shaw and Per Stenstrom, and what should be a provocative panel, put together by Rich Belgard. We also thank Yan Solihin for organizing the workshops and tutorials, and Mazin Yousif for the industrial session, a practice started last year at HPCA-11.

Behind the scenes, a whole lot needed to get done and we are very grateful to many people. Murali Annavaram and Derek Chiou deserve special thanks for doing much more than their specific duties of Registration and Local Arrangements. Also, Ki Hwan Yum took on both Publicity and the publication of the Proceedings duties and Vijaykrishnan Narayanan served as webmaster. It was a pleasure to work with both of them as well.

Finally, we thank four of Austin's high tech companies for providing financial support to the conference: IBM's Austin Research Lab, AMD, Intel, and Sun Microsystems. Their commitment to HPCA and the research environment HPCA represents is greatly appreciated.

Please enjoy HPCA-12.

Yale Patt, Craig Chase
General Co-Chairs

Message from the Program Chair

On behalf of the Program Committee, I welcome all of you to the Twelfth International Symposium on High Performance Computer Architecture (HPCA-12).

As usual, the technical program for HPCA-12 is very strong covering some of the best research work in Computer Architecture. The program includes 26 regular papers and 3 invited talks from industry, arranged in 10 single-track sessions. The nice mix of papers covering a broad range of topics such as processor architecture, multithreaded systems, memory systems, parallel architectures, Chip multiprocessors (CMPs), energy and power, fault-tolerance/security, and hardware software tradeoffs is testimony to the ever increasing vitality of this field.

The paper selection process for this year's conference was quite rigorous. This was possible because of an outstanding program committee of 39 researchers. We received 172 submissions from 19 countries out of which 32 papers were co-authored by program committee members. Each paper was assigned to at least three program committee members and one external reviewer. We received a total of 693 reviews from 204 reviewers. The reviews were made available to the committee members one week prior to the program committee meeting. The program committee meeting was held on September 24, 2005, at Pittsburgh International airport from 8AM to 6:30PM. 25 committee members and the General Co-Chair, Yale Patt, attended the meeting. A few members could not make it because of the hurricane in the south. The committee discussed the top 60 papers based on their average score. The review process was blind, and the identity of the authors was revealed only after a paper was accepted. Papers co-authored by program committee members were handled with special care without revealing any reviewing information. The papers I had conflict with, were handled by Yale Patt. At the end of the day, after much deliberation, the committee accepted 26 papers for the final program, with 4 papers suggested for shepherding. Out of the 26 papers, 9 papers are co-authored by program committee members. The acceptance rate was 15%, making it one of the most competitive HPCA conferences.

I would like to thank all the program committee members for their hard work in diligently reviewing each paper and selecting a strong program. I am indebted to each one of them. I am thankful to the General Co-Chairs, Craig Chase and Yale Patt, for their help and advice during the entire process. Thanks also to the Web Chair, Vijay Narayanan, and Publication chair, Ki-Hwan Yum, for making my life easier in handing the Web-based submission and publication matters. I would like to thanks Josep Torellas, last year's program chair for his helpful suggestions and for providing the conference software.

I would like to thank all the authors for submitting their high quality work to this conference and all the external reviewers for their detailed and timely reviews. Behind the scene, I received immense help from my Ph.D. students Gyu-Sang Choi, Deniz Ersoz, Jin-Ha Kim, Jongman Kim and Dongkook Park. Gyu-Sang and Deniz were my Web masters and sat through the entire program committee meeting helping me in numerous ways. My thanks to all of them.

I hope you enjoy the program.

Chita R. Das
Program Chair, HPCA-12

Organizing Committee

General Co-Chairs
Yale Patt, UT Austin
Craig Chase, UT Austin

Program Chair
Chita R. Das, Penn State

Industry Liaison Chair
Mazin Yousif, Intel

Local Arrangements Chair
Derek Chiou, UT Austin

Workshop and Tutorial Chair
Yan Solihin, NCSU

Publicity and Publications Chair
Ki Hwan Yum, UT San Antonio

Finance Chair
Craig Chase, UT Austin

Registration Chair
Murali Annavaram, Intel

Web Chair
Vijaykrishnan Narayanan, Penn State

Program Committee

List of Referees

Santosh Abraham
Manuel E. Acacio
Carmelo Acosta
Sarita Adve
Alaa Alameldeen
David Albonesi
Erik Altman
Rajeevan Amirtharajah
Padma Apparao
Chinmay Ashok
David August
Luiz Andre Barroso
Christopher Batten
Laxmi Bhuyan
Ricardo Bianchini
Angelos Bilas
Matthias Blumrich
Pradip Bose
Mic Bowman
David Brooks
Paul D.Bryan
Mihai Budiu
Doug Burger
Martin Burtscher
Brad Calder
Ramón Canal
Rafael Casado
Prashant R.Chandra
Guangyu Chen
Xia chen
Derek Chiou
Sangyeun Cho
Fred Chong
Michael Chu
Douglas Clark
Guojing Cong
Jason Cong
Dan Connors
Tom Conte
Jedidiah Crandall
Adrián Cristal
David Crowe
Chita Das
Srini Devadas
Robert Dick
Jose Duato
Michel Dubois
Carl Ebeling
Itamar Elhanany
Deniz Ersoz
Brian Fahs
Kevin Fan
Jose Flich

Peter A. Franaszek
Diana Franklin
Marco Galluzzi
Jose M. Garcia
Andy Glew
Brian Gold
Madhu S.S. Govindan
Dan Grossman
Rajiv Gupta
Sudhanva Gurumurthi
Frank Hady
Kim Hazelwood
James C. Hoe
Wei Hsu
Jie Hu
Michael Huang
Rameshkumar Illikkal
Balaji Iyer
Matthew Iyer
Ravi Iyer
Nuwan Jayasena
Weihang Jiang
Daniel Jiménez
Erik Johnson
Mahmut Kandemir
Manolis Katevenis
Changkyu Kim
Eun Jung Kim
Jongman Kim
Steve King
Michael Kounavis
Ronny Krashinsky
Manjunath Kudlur
Alok Kumar
Anil Kumar
Sanjeev Kumar
Konrad Lai
Alvin Lebeck
Jooheung Lee
Kai Li
Tao Li
Zhenmin Li
Steve Lieberman
Greg Link
Mikko Lipasti
Chun Liu
Gabriel Loh
David Lombard
Pedro Lopez
Yan Luo
Aqeel Mahesri
Scott Mahlke
Srihari Makineni
José F. Martínez

Margaret Martonosi
Gary McAlpine
Kathryn McKinley
Stephan Meier
Steve Melvin
Gokhan Memik
Maged Michael
Kevin Moore
Tipp Moseley
Randy Moulic
Trevor Mudge
Shubu Mukherjee
Madhu Mutyam
Ashwini Nanda
Vijay Narayanan
Nacho Navarro
Ranjit Noronha
John Oliver
Mark Oskin
Dhabaleswar Panda
Angshuman Parashar
Sanjay Patel
Li-Shiuan Peh
David Penry
Miquel Pericas
Michael Perrone
Fabrizio Petrini
Juan Piernas
Timothy Pinkston
Milos Prvulovic
Valentín Puente
Ravi Rajwar
Alex Ramirez
Marco A. Ramírez
Tanausú Ramírez
Rajiv Ravindran
Glenn Reinman
Jose Renau
Scott Rixner
David Roberts
Chad Rosier
Amir Roth
Ravi Sahita
Julio Sahuquillo
Suleyman Sair
Jose L. Sanchez
Huzefa Sanjeliwala
Oliverio J. Santana
Peter Sassone
Andrew Schwerin
Resit Sendag
Alex Settle
Li Shang
Michael Shebanow

Xiaowei Shen
Tim Sherwood
Cris Simpson
A. Sivasubramaniam
Jared Smolens
Yan Solihin
Seung Woo Son
Francesco Spadini
Evan Speight
Lawrence Spracklen
Per Stenstrom
Stephen Stuart
Lixin Su
Edward Suh
Dam Sunwoo
Steven Swanson
Sheldon Tan
Darshan Thaker
Mithuna Thottethodi
Josep Torrellas
Brian Towles
Dean M. Tullsen
Augustus K. Uht
Theo Ungerer
Manish Vachharajani
Frank Vahid
Mateo Valero
Enrique Vallejo
Stamatis Vassiliadis
Alex Veidenbaum
Jun Wang
Nicholas Wang
Xingfu Wu
Roland Wunderlich
Yuan Xie
Zheng Xu
Jun Yang
Qing Yang
Jingnan Yao
Raj Yavatkar
Pen-Chung Yew
Mazin Yousif
Weikuan Yu
Antonia Zhai
Michael Zhang
Xiangyu Zhang
Xiao Zhang
Zhao Zhang
Li Zhao
Pin Zhou
Yuanyuan Zhou
Qingbo Zhu
Victor Zia

Keynote Address I

New Architectures for a New Biology

David E. Shaw

D. E. Shaw Research and Development and
Center for Computational Biology and Bioinformatics, Columbia University

ABSTRACT

Some of the most important outstanding questions in the fields of biology, chemistry, and medicine remain unsolved as a result of our limited understanding of the structure, behavior and interaction of biologically significant molecules. The laws of physics that determine the form and function of these biomolecules are well understood. Current technology, however, does not allow us to simulate the effect of these laws with sufficient accuracy, and for a sufficient period of time, to answer many of the questions that biologists, biochemists, and biomedical researchers are most anxious to answer. This talk will describe the current state of the art in biomolecular simulation and explore the potential role of high-performance computing technologies in extending current capabilities. Efforts within our own lab to develop novel architectures and algorithms to accelerate molecular dynamics simulations by several orders of magnitude will be described, along with work by other researchers pursuing alternative approaches. If such efforts ultimately prove successful, one might imagine the emergence of an entirely new paradigm in which computational experiments take their place alongside those conducted in "wet" laboratories as central tools in the quest to understand living organisms at a molecular level, and to develop safe, effective, precisely targeted medicines capable of relieving suffering and saving human lives.

Session 1:
Chip Multiprocessors (CMPs)

BulletProof: A Defect-Tolerant CMP Switch Architecture

Kypros Constantinides‡   Stephen Plaza‡   Jason Blome‡   Bin Zhang†
Valeria Bertacco‡   Scott Mahlke‡   Todd Austin‡   Michael Orshansky†

‡Advanced Computer Architecture Lab
University of Michigan
Ann Arbor, MI 48109
{kypros, splaza, jblome, valeria,
mahlke, austin}@umich.edu

†Department of Electrical and Computer Engineering
University of Texas at Austin
Austin, TX, 78712
bzhang@ece.utexas.edu
orshansky@mail.utexas.edu

Abstract

As silicon technologies move into the nanometer regime, transistor reliability is expected to wane as devices become subject to extreme process variation, particle-induced transient errors, and transistor wear-out. Unless these challenges are addressed, computer vendors can expect low yields and short mean-times-to-failure. In this paper, we examine the challenges of designing complex computing systems in the presence of transient and permanent faults. We select one small aspect of a typical chip multiprocessor (CMP) system to study in detail, a single CMP router switch. To start, we develop a unified model of faults, based on the time-tested bathtub curve. Using this convenient abstraction, we analyze the reliability versus area tradeoff across a wide spectrum of CMP switch designs, ranging from unprotected designs to fully protected designs with online repair and recovery capabilities. Protection is considered at multiple levels from the entire system down through arbitrary partitions of the design. To better understand the impact of these faults, we evaluate our CMP switch designs using circuit-level timing on detailed physical layouts. Our experimental results are quite illuminating. We find that designs are attainable that can tolerate a larger number of defects with less overhead than naïve triple-modular redundancy, using domain-specific techniques such as end-to-end error detection, resource sparing, automatic circuit decomposition, and iterative diagnosis and reconfiguration.

1. Introduction

A critical aspect of any computer design is its reliability. Users expect a system to operate without failure when asked to perform a task. In reality, it is impossible to build a completely reliable system, consequently, vendors target design failure rates that are imperceptibly small [23]. Moreover, the failure rate of a population of parts in the field must exhibit a failure rate that does not prove too costly to service. The reliability of a system can be expressed as the mean-time-to-failure (MTTF). Computing system reliability targets are typically expressed as failures-in-time, or FIT rates, where one FIT represents one failure in a billion hours of operation.

In many systems today, reliability targets are achieved by employing a fault-avoidance design strategy. The sources of possible computing failures are assessed, and the necessary margins and guards are placed into the design to ensure it will meet the intended level of reliability. For example, most transistor failures (*e.g.*, gate-oxide breakdown) can be reduced by limiting voltage, temperature and frequency [8]. While these approaches have served manufacturers well for many technology generations, many device experts agree

that transistor reliability will begin to wane in the nanometer regime. As devices become subject to extreme process variation, particle-induced transient errors, and transistor wearout, it will likely no longer be possible to avoid these faults. Instead, computer designers will have to begin to directly address system reliability through fault-tolerant design techniques.

Figure 1 illustrates the fault-tolerant design space we focus on in this paper. The horizontal axis lists the type of device-level faults that systems might experience. The source of failures are widespread, ranging from transient faults due to energetic particle strikes [32] and electrical noise [28], to permanent wearout faults caused by electromigration [13], stress-migration [8], and dielectric breakdown [10]. The vertical axis of Figure 1 lists design solutions to deal with faults. Design solutions range from ignoring any possible faults (as is done in many systems today), to detecting and reporting faults, to detecting and correcting faults, and finally fault correction with repair capabilities. The final two design solutions are the only solutions that can address permanent faults, with the final solution being the only approach that maintains efficient operation after encountering a silicon defect.

In recent years, industry designers and academics have paid significant attention to building resistance to transient faults into their designs. A number of recent publications have suggested that transient faults, due to energetic particles in particular, will grow in future technologies [5, 16]. A variety of techniques have emerged to provide a capability to detect and correct these type of faults in storage, including parity or error correction codes (ECC) [23], and logic, including dual or triple-modular spatial redundancy [23] or time-redundant computation [24] or checkers [30]. Additional work has focused on the extent to which circuit timing, logic, architecture, and software are able to mask out the effects of transient faults, a process referred to as "derating" a design [7, 17, 29].

In contrast, little attention has been paid to incorporating design tolerance for permanent faults, such as silicon defects and transistor wearout. The typical approach used today is to reduce the likelihood of encountering silicon faults through post-manufacturing burn-in, a process that accelerates the aging process as devices are subjected to elevated temperature and voltage [10]. The burn-in process accelerates the failure of weak transistors, ensuring that, after burn-in, devices still working are composed of robust transistors. Additionally, many computer vendors provide the ability to repair faulty memory and cache cells, via the in-

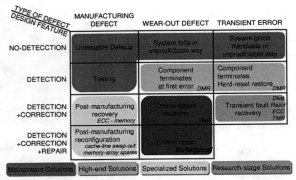

TYPE OF DEFECT / DESIGN FEATURE	MANUFACTURING DEFECT	WEAR-OUT DEFECT	TRANSIENT ERROR
NO-DETECCTION	Untestable Defects	System fails in unpredictable way	System glitch manifests in unpredictable way
DETECTION	Testing	Component terminates at first error *DMR*	Component terminates. Hard-reset restore *DMR*
DETECTION +CORRECTION	Post-manufacturing recovery *ECC - memory*	Online defect recovery *TMR*	Transient fault recovery *Diva Razor ECC TMR*
DETECTION +CORRECTION +REPAIR	Post-manufacturing reconfiguration *cache-line swap-out memory-array spares*	Online repair *Bulletproof*	

| Mainstream Solutions | High-end Solutions | Specialized Solutions | Research-stage Solutions |

Figure 1: *Reliable System Design Space.* **The diagram shows a map of type of device-level faults in a digital system (horizontal axis) vs. protection techniques against these faults (vertical axis). This work addresses the problems/solutions in the dark shaded area of the map.**

clusion of spare storage cells [25]. Recently, academics have begun to extend these techniques to support sparing for additional on-chip memory resources such as branch predictors [6] and registers [22].

1.1 Contributions of This Paper

In this paper, we push forward the understanding in reliable microarchitecture design by performing a comprehensive design study of the effects of permanent faults on a chip-multiprocessor switch design. The goal is to better understand the nature of faults, and to build into our designs a cost-effective means to tolerate these faults. Specifically, we make the following contributions:

- *We develop a high-level architect-friendly model of silicon failures, based on the time-tested bathtub curve.* The bathtub curve models the early-life failures of devices during burn-in, the infrequent failure of devices during the part's lifetime, and the breakdown of devices at the end of their normal operating lifetime. From this bathtub-curve model, we define the design space of interest, and we fit previously published device-level reliability data to the model.

- *We introduce a low-cost chip-multiprocessor (CMP) switch router architecture that incorporates system-level checking and recovery, component-level fault diagnosis, and spare-part reconfiguration.* Our design, called *BulletProof*, is capable of tolerating silicon defects, transient faults, and transistor wearout. We evaluate a variety of Bulletproof switch designs, and compare them to designs that utilize traditional fault tolerance techniques, such as ECC and triple-modular redundancy. We find that our domain-specific fault-tolerance techniques are significantly more robust and less costly than traditional generic fault tolerance techniques.

The remainder of this paper is organized as follows. Section 2 gives additional background on the faults of interest in this study and introduces our architect-friendly fault model based on the bathtub curve. Section 3 presents our fault simulation infrastructure, and examines the exposure of the baseline design to permanent faults. Section 4 introduces the techniques we have employed in our CMP switch designs to provide cost-effective tolerance of transient and permanent faults. In Section 5, we present a detailed trade-off analysis of the resilience and cost of our CMP switch designs,

plus a comparison to traditional fault tolerant techniques, such as ECC and triple-modular redundancy (TMR). Finally, Section 6 gives conclusions and suggestions for future research directions.

2. An Analysis of the Fault Landscape

As silicon technologies progress into the 65nm regime and below, a number of failure factors rise in importance. In this section, we highlight these failure mechanisms, and discuss the relevant trends for future process technologies.

Single-Event Upset (SEU). There is growing concern about providing protection from soft errors caused by charged particles (such as neutrons and alpha particles) that strike the bulk silicon portion of a die [32]. The effect of SEU is a logic glitch that can potentially corrupt combinational logic computation or state bits. While a variety of studies have been performed that demonstrate the unlikeliness of such events [31, 29], concerns remain in the architecture and circuit communities. This concern is fueled by the trends of reduced supply voltage and increased transistor budgets, both of which exacerbate a design's vulnerability to SEU.

Process Variation. Another reliability challenge designers face is the design uncertainty that is created by increasing process variations. Process variations result from device dimension and doping concentration variation that occur during silicon fabrication. These variations are of particular concern because their effects on devices are amplified as device dimensions shrink [20], resulting in structurally weak and poor performing devices. Designers are forced to deal with these variations by assuming worst-case device characteristics (usually, a 3-sigma variation from typical conditions), which leads to overly conservative designs.

Manufacturing Defects. Deep sub-micron technologies are increasingly vulnerable to several fabrication-related failure mechanisms. For example, step coverage problems that occur during the metalization process may cause open circuits. Post-manufacturing test [18] and built-in self-test (BIST) [1] are two techniques to impress test vectors onto circuits in order to identify manufacturing defects. A more global approach to testing for defects is taken by IDDQ testing, which uses on-board current monitoring to detect short-circuits in the manufactured part. During IDDQ testing, any abnormally high current spikes found during functional testing are indicative of short-circuit defects [4].

Gate Oxide Wearout. Technology scaling has adverse effects on the lifetime of transistor devices, due to time-dependent wearout. There are three major failure modes for time-dependent wearout: electromigration, hot carrier degradation (HCD), and time-dependent oxide breakdown. Electro-migration results from the mass transport of metal atoms in chip interconnects. The trends of higher current density in future technologies increases the severity of electromigration, leading to a higher probability of observing open and short-circuit nodes over time [11]. HCD is the result of carriers being heated by strong electrical fields and subsequently being injected into the gate oxide. The trapped carriers cause the threshold voltage to shift, eventually leading to device failure. HCD is predicted to worsen for thinner oxide and shorter channel lengths [14]. Time-dependent oxide breakdown is due to the extensive use of ultra-thin oxide for high performance. The rate of defect generation in the oxide is proportional to the current density flowing through it, and therefore is increasing drastically as a result of relentless down-scaling [27].

Transistor Infant Mortality. Scaling has had adverse effects on the early failures of transistor devices. Traditionally, early transistor failures have been reduced through the use of burn-in. The burn-in process utilizes high voltage and temperature to accelerate the failure of weak devices, thereby ensuring that parts that survive burn-in only possess robust transistors. Unfortunately, burn-in is becoming less effective in the nanometer regime, as deep sub-micron devices are subject to thermal run-away effects, where increased temperature leads to increased leakage current and increased leakage current leads to yet higher temperatures. The end results is that aggressive burn-in will destroy even robust transistors. Consequently, vendors may soon have to relax the burn-in process which will ultimately lead to more early-failures for transistors in the field.

2.1 The Bathtub: A Generic Model for Semiconductor Hard Failures

To derive a simple architect-friendly model of failures, we step back and return to the basics. In the semiconductor industry, it is widely accepted that the failure rate for many systems follows what is known as the bathtub curve, as illustrated in Figure 2. We will adopt this time-tested failure model for our research. Our goal with the bathtub-curve model is not to predict its exact shape and magnitude for the future (although we will fit published data to it to create "design scenarios"), but rather to utilize the bathtub curve to illuminate the potential design space for future fault-tolerant designs. The bathtub curve represents device failure rates over the entire lifetime of transistors, and it is characterized by three distinct regions.

- **Infant Period**: In this phase, failures occur very soon and thus the failure rate declines rapidly over time. These infant mortality failures are caused by latent manufacturing defects that surface quickly if a temperature or voltage stress is applied.

- **Grace Period**: When early failures are eliminated, the failure rate falls to a small constant value where failures occur sporadically due to the occasional breakdown of weak transistors or interconnect.

- **Breakdown Period**: During this period, failures occur with increasing frequency over time due to age-related wearout. Many devices will enter this period at roughly the same time, creating an avalanche effect and a quick rise in device failure rates.

With the respect to Figure 2, the model is represented with the following equations:

$$F(t) = \begin{cases} F_G + \lambda_L \frac{10^9}{t}(1 - \frac{1}{(t+1)^m}), & if \quad 0 \le t < t_A \\ F_G, & if \quad t_A \le t < t_B \\ F_G + (t - t_B)^b, & if \quad t_B \le t \end{cases}$$

(t is measured in hours)
Where the parameters of the model are as follows:

- λ_L: average number of latent manufacturing defects per chip
- m: infant period maturing factor
- F_G: grace period failure rate
- t_B: breakdown period start point
- b: breakdown factor,

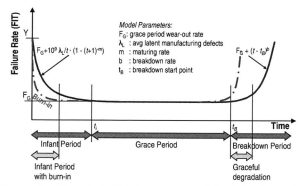

Figure 2: *Simple bathtub curve model of device defect exposure.* **The curve indicates the qualitative trend of failure rates for a silicon part over time. The initial operational phase and the "aged-silicon" phase are characterized by much higher failure rates.**

In an effort to base our experiments off of published empirical fault data, we developed a baseline bathtub model based on published literature. Unfortunately, we were unable to locate a single technology failure model that fully captured the lifetime of a silicon device, so for each period of the bathtub curve we will use reference values from different sources.

Latent Manufacturing Defects per Chip (λ_L): Previous work [3], showed that the rate of latent manufacturing defects is determined by the formula $\lambda_L = \gamma \lambda_K$, where λ_K is the average number of "killer" defects per chip, and γ is an empirically estimated parameter with typical values between 0.01 and 0.02. The same work, provides formulas for deriving the maximum number of latent manufacturing defects that may surface during burn-in test. Based on these models, the average number of latent manufacturing defects per chip ($140mm^2$) for current technologies (λ_L) is approximately 0.005. In the literature, there are no clear trends how this value changes with technology scaling, thus we use the same rate for projections of future technologies.

Grace Period Failure Rate (F_G): For the grace period failure rate, we use reference data by [26]. In [26], a microarchitecture-level model was used to estimate workload-dependent processor hard failure rates at different technologies. The model used supports four main intrinsic failure mechanisms experienced by processors: elegtromigration, stress migration, time-dependence dielectric breakdown, and thermal cycling. For a predicted post-65nm fabrication technology, we adopt their worst-case failure rate (F_G) of 55,000 FITs.

Breakdown Period Start Point (t_B): Previous work [27], estimates the time to dielectric breakdown using extrapolation from the measurement conditions (under stress) to normal operation conditions. We estimate the breakdown period start point (t_B) to be approximately 12 years for 65nm CMOS at 1.0V supply voltage. We were unable to find any predictions as to how this value will trend for fabrication technologies beyond 65nm, but we conservatively assume that the breakdown period will be held to periods beyond the expected lifetime of the product. Thus, we need not address reliable operation in this period, other than to provide a limited amount of resilience to breakdown for the purpose of allowing the part to remain in operation until it can be replaced.

The maturing factor during the infant mortality period

and the breakdown factor during the breakdown period used, are $m = 0.02$ and $b = 2.5$, respectively.

3. A Fault Impact Evaluation Infrastructure

In [7], we introduced a high-fidelity simulation infrastructure for quantifying various derating effects on a design's overall soft-error rate. This infrastructure takes into account circuit level phenomena, such as time-related, logic-related and microarchitectural-related fault masking. Since many tolerance techniques for permanent errors can be adapted to also provide soft error tolerance, the remainder of this work concentrates on the exploration of various defect tolerance techniques.

3.1 Simulation Methodology for Permanent Faults

In this section, we present our simulation infrastructure for evaluating the impact of silicon defects. We create a model for permanent fault parameters, and develop the infrastructure necessary to evaluate the effects on a given design.

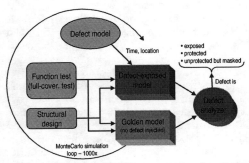

Figure 3: *Simulation infrastructure for permanent faults.* The defect infrastructure uses two models of the system, simulated in parallel. Defects are uniformly distributed in time and space and the input stimuli is a full coverage test that activates each internal circuit node of the system. A fault analyzer classifies defects based on the system response.

Figure 3 shows our simulation framework for evaluating the impact of silicon defects on a digital design. The framework consists of an event-driven simulator that simulates two copies of the structural, gate-level description of the design in parallel. Of these two designs, one copy is kept intact (golden model), while the other is subject to fault injection (defect-exposed model). The structural specification of our design was synthesized from a Verilog description using the Synopsys Design Compiler.

Our silicon defect model distributes defects in the design uniformly in time of occurrence and spatial location. Once a permanent failure occurs, the design may or may not continue to function depending on the circuit's internal structure and the system architecture. The defect analyzer classifies each defect as exposed, protected or unprotected but masked. In the context of defect evaluation, faults accumulate over time until the design fails to operate correctly. The defect that brings the system to failure is the last injected defect in each experiment and it is classified as exposed. A defect may be protected if, for instance, it is the first one to occur in a triple-module-redundant design. An unprotected but masked defect is a defect that it is masked because it occurs in a portion of the design that has already failed, for

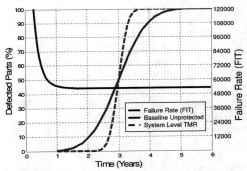

Figure 4: *Baseline design reliability.* The graph superimposes the FIT rates of the bathtub model with the fault tolerance of two variants of the CMP switch design: a baseline unprotected version and a variant with a traditional TMR technique.

example a defect hitting an already failed module of a TMR design.

In the context of defects, we are concerned with studying the potential of a defect to impact the design outputs in any possible future execution. Thus, the input stimuli is a full coverage test, crafted to excite all internal nodes of the design while observing the outputs. If any of the stimuli impact the output correctness, the implication is that there is at least one execution that can expose the defect, and thus such defect is considered exposed.

Finally, to gain statistical confidence of the results, we run the simulations described many times in a Monte Carlo modeling framework.

3.2 Reliability of the Baseline CMP Switch Design

The first experiment is an evaluation of the reliability of the baseline CMP switch design. In Figure 4, we used the bathtub curve fitted for the post-65nm technology node as derived in Section 2. The FIT rate of this curve is 55000 during the grace period, which corresponds to a mean time to failure (MTTF) of 2 years. We used this failure rate in our simulation framework for permanent failures and we plotted the results.

The baseline CMP design does not deploy any protection technique against defects, and one defect is sufficient to bring down the system. Consequently, the graph of Figure 4 shows that in a large parts population, 50% of the parts will be defective by the end of the second year after shipment, and by the fourth year almost all parts will have failed. In this experiment, we have also analyzed a design variant which deploys triple-module-redundancy (TMR) at the full-system level (i.e. three CMP switches with voting gates at their outputs. Designs with TMR applied at different granularities are evaluated at Section 5) to present better defect tolerance.

The TMR model used in this analysis is the classical TMR model which assumes that when a module fails it starts producing incorrect outputs, and if two or more modules fail, the output of the TMR voter will be incorrect. This model is conservative in its reliability analysis because it does not take into account compensating faults. For example, if two faults affect two independent output bits, then the voter circuit should be able to correctly mask both faults. However, the benefit gained from accounting for compensating faults rapidly diminishes with a moderate number of defects because the probabilities of fault independence are multiplied.

Further, though the switch itself demonstrated a moderate number of independent fault sites, submodules within the design tended to exhibit very little independence. Also, in [21], it is demonstrated that even when TMR is applied on diversified designs (i.e. three modules with the same functionality but different implementation), the probability of independence is small. Therefore, in our reliability analysis, we choose to implement the classical TMR model and for the rest of the paper whenever TMR is applied, the classical TMR model is assumed.

From Figure 4, the simulation-based analysis finds that TMR provides very little reliability improvements over the baseline designs, due to the few number of defects that can be tolerated by system-level TMR. Furthermore, the area of the TMR protected design is more than three times the area of the baseline design. The increase in area raises the probability of a defect being manifested in the design, which significantly affects the design's reliability. In the rest of the paper, we propose and evaluate defect-tolerant techniques that are significantly more robust and less costly than traditional defect-tolerant techniques.

4. Self-repairing CMP Switch Design

The goal of the Bulletproof project is to design a defect-tolerant chip-multiprocessor capable of tolerating significant levels of various types of defects. In this work, we address the design of one aspect of the system, a defect tolerant CMP switch. The CMP switch is much less complex than a modern microprocessor, enabling us to understand the entire design and explore a large solution space. Further, this switch design contains many representative components of larger designs including finite state machines, buffers, control logic, and buses.

4.1 Baseline Design

The baseline design, consists of a CMP switch similar to the one described in [19]. This CMP switch provides wormhole routing pipelined at the flit level and implements credit-based flow control functionality for a two-dimensional torus network. In the switch pipeline, head flits will proceed through routing and virtual channel allocation stages, while all flits proceed through switch allocation and switch traversal stages. A high-level block diagram of the router architecture is depicted in Figure 5.

The implemented router is composed of four functional modules: the input controller, the switch arbiter, the crossbar controller, and the crossbar. The input controller is responsible for selecting the appropriate output virtual channel for each packet, maintaining virtual channel state information, and buffering flits as they arrive and await virtual channel allocation. Each input controller is enhanced with an 8-entry 32-bit buffer. The switch arbiter allocates virtual channels to the input controllers, using a priority matrix to ensure that starvation does not occur. The switch arbiter also implements flow control by tallying credit information used to determine the amount of available buffer space at downstream nodes. The crossbar controller is responsible for determining and setting the appropriate control signals so that allocated flits can pass from the input controllers to the appropriate output virtual channels through the interconnect provided by the crossbar.

The router design is specified in Verilog and was synthesized using the Synopsys Design Compiler to create a gate-

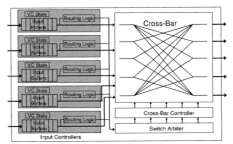

Figure 5: *Baseline CMP switch design.* **A high level block diagram for a wormhole interconnection switch is presented. It consists of 5 input controllers, a cross-bar, a switch arbiter and a cross-bar controller.**

level netlist, which consists of approximately 10k gates. This router design consists of five input controllers which dominate the design's area (86%). Also, the design is heavily dominated by combinational logic, which represents 84% of the total area, making it critical to choose protection techniques that can tolerate errors in logic effectively.

4.2 Protection Mechanisms

A design that is tolerant to permanent defects must provide mechanisms that perform four central actions related to faults: detection, diagnosis, repair, and recovery. Fault detection identifies that a defect has manifested as an error in some signal. Normal operation cannot continue after fault detection as the hardware is not operating properly. Often fault detection occurs at a macro-level, thus it is followed by a diagnosis process to identify the specific location of the defect. Following diagnosis, the faulty portion of the design must be repaired to enable proper system functionality. Repair can be handled in many ways, including disabling, ignoring, or replacing the faulty component. Finally, the system must recover from the fault, purging any incorrect data and recomputing corrupted values. Recovery essentially makes the defect's manifestation transparent to the application's execution. In this section, we discuss a range of techniques that can be applied to the baseline switch to make it tolerant of permanent defects. The techniques differ in their approach and the level at which they are applied to the design.

In [9] the authors present the Reliable Router (RR), a switching element design for improved performance and reliability within a mesh interconnect. The design relies on an adaptive routing algorithm coupled with a link level retransmission protocol in order to maintain service in the presence of a single node or link failure within the network. Our design differs from the RR in that our target domain involves a much higher fault rate and focuses on maintaining switch service in the face of faults rather than simply routing around faulty nodes or links. However, the two techniques can be combined and provide a higher reliability multiprocessor interconnection network.

4.2.1 General Techniques

The most commonly used protection mechanisms are dual and triple modular redundancy, or DMR and TMR [23]. These techniques employ spatial redundancy combined with a majority voter. With permanent faults, DMR provides only fault detection. Hence, a single fault in either of the redundant components will bring the system down. TMR is more effective as it provides solutions to detection, recovery, and repair. In TMR, the majority voter identifies a malfunctioning hardware component and masks its affects on the primary outputs. Hence, repair is trivial since the defective component is always just simply outvoted when it computes an incorrect value. Due to this restriction, TMR is inherently limited to tolerating a single permanent fault. Faults that manifest in either of the other two copies cannot be handled. DMR/TMR are applicable to both state and logic elements and thus are broadly applicable to our baseline switch design.

Storage or state elements are often protected by parity or error correction codes (ECC) [23]. ECC provides a lower overhead solution for state elements than TMR. Like TMR, ECC provides a unified solution to detection and recovery. Repair is again trivial as the parity computation masks the effects of permanent faults. In addition to the storage overhead of the actual parity bits, the computation of parity or ECC bits generally requires a tree of exclusive-ORs. This hardware has moderate overhead, but more importantly, it can often be done in parallel, thus not affecting latency. For our defect-tolerant switch, the application of ECC is limited due to the small fraction of area that holds state.

4.2.2 Domain-specific Techniques

The properties of the wormhole router can be exploited to create domain-specific protection mechanisms. Here, we focus on one efficient design that employs end-to-end error detection, resource sparing, system diagnosis, and reconfiguration.

End-to-End Error Detection and Recovery Mechanism. Within our router design, errors can be separated into two major classes. The first class is comprised of data corrupting errors, for example a defect that alters the data of a routed flit, so that the routed flit is permanently corrupted. The second class is comprised of errors that cause functional incorrectness, for example a defect that causes a flit to be misrouted to a wrong output channel or to get lost and never reach any of the switch's output channels.

The first class of errors, the data corrupting errors, can be addressed by adding Cyclic Redundancy Checkers (CRC) at each one of the switch's five output channels, as shown in Figure 6(a). When an error is detected by a CRC checker, all CRC checkers are notified about the error detection and block any further flit routing. The same error detection signal used to notify the CRC checkers also notifies the switch's recovery logic. The switch's recovery logic logs the error occurrence by incrementing an error counter. In case the error counter surpasses a predefined threshold, the recovery logic signals the need for system diagnosis and reconfiguration.

In case the error counter is still below the predefined threshold, the switch recovers its operation from the last "checkpointed" state, by squashing all inflight flits and rerouting the corrupted flit and all following flits. This is accomplished by maintaining an extra recovery head pointer at the input buffers. As shown in Figure 6(a), each input buffer maintains an extra head pointer which indicates the last flit stored in the buffer which is not yet checked by a CRC checker. The recovery head pointer is automatically incremented four cycles after the associated input controller grants access to the requested output channel, which is the latency needed to route the flit through the switch, once access to the destination channel is granted. In case of a

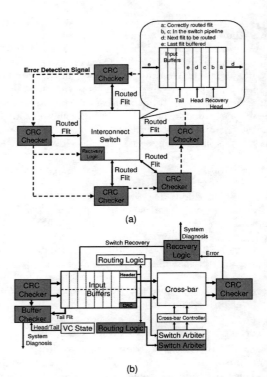

(a)

(b)

Figure 6: *End-to-End error detection and recovery mechanism.* **In part (a) the interconnection switch is enhanced by Cyclic Redundancy Checkers (CRC) and recovery logic for providing data corrupting error detection. The input buffers are enhanced with an extra recovery head pointer to mark the last correctly checked flit. In part (b) a more detailed view of the switch with End-to-End error detection is shown. Flits are split into two parts, which are independently routed through the switch pipeline.**

switch recovery, the recovery head pointer is assigned to the head pointer for all five input buffers, and the switch recovers operations by starting rerouting the flits pointed by the head pointers. Further, the switch's credit backflow mechanism needs to be adjusted accordingly since an input buffer is now considered full when the tail pointer reaches the recovery head pointer. In order for the switch's recovery logic to be able to distinguish soft from hard errors, the error counter is reset to zero at regular intervals.

The detection of errors causing functional incorrectness is considerably more complicated because of the need to be able to detect misrouted and lost flits. A critical issue for the recovery of the system is to assure that there is at least one uncorrupted copy for each flit in flight in the switch's pipeline. This uncorrupted flit can then be used during recovery. To accomplish this, we add a Buffer Checker unit to each input buffer. As shown in Figure 6(b), the Buffer Checker unit compares the CRC checked incoming flit with the last flit allocated into the input buffers (tail flit). Further, to guarantee the input buffer's correct functionality, the Buffer Checker also maintains a copy of the head and the tail pointers which are compared with the input buffer's pointers whenever a new flit is allocated. In the case that the comparison fails, the Buffer Checker signals an allocation retry, to cover the case of a soft error. If the error persists, this means that there is a potential permanent error

8

in the design, and it signals the system diagnosis and reconfiguration procedures. By assuring that a correct copy of the flit is allocated into the input buffers and that the input buffer's head/tail pointers are maintained correctly, we guarantee that each flit entering the switch will correctly reach the head of the queue and be routed through the switch's pipeline.

To guarantee that a flit will get routed to the correct output channel, the flit is split into two parts, as shown in Figure 6(b). Each part will get its output channel requests from a different routing logic block, and access the requested output channel through a different switch arbiter. Finally, each part is routed through the cross-bar independently. To accomplish this, we add an extra routing logic unit and an extra switch arbiter. The status bits in the input controllers that store the output channel reserved by the head flit are duplicated as well. Since the cross-bar routes the flits at the bit-level, the only difference is that the responses to the cross-bar controller from the switch arbiter will not be the same for all the flit bits, but the responses for the first and the second parts of the flit are fitted from the first and second switch arbiters, respectively. If a defect causes a flit to be misrouted, it follows that a single defect can impact only one of the two parts of the flit, and the error will be caught later at the CRC check.

The area overhead of the proposed error detection and recovery mechanism is limited to only 10% of the switch's area. The area overhead of the CRC checkers, the Recovery Logic and the Buffer Checker units is almost negligible. More specifically, the area of a single CRC checker is 0.1% of the switch's area and the area for the Buffer Checker and the Recovery Logic is much less significant. The area overhead of the proposed mechanism is dominated by the extra Switch Arbiter (5.7%), the extra Routing Logic units (5x0.5% = 2.5%), and the additional CRC bits (1.5%). As we can see, the proposed error detection and recovery mechanism has a 10X times less area overhead than a naïve DMR implementation.

Resource Sparing. For providing defect tolerance to the switch design we use resource sparing for selected partitions of the switch. During the switch operation only one spare is active for each distinct partition of the switch. For each spare added in the design, there is an additional overhead for the interconnection and the required logic for enabling and disabling the spare. For resource sparing, we study two different techniques, dedicated sparing and shared sparing. In the dedicated sparing technique, each spare is owned by a single partition and can be used only when the specific partition fails. When shared sparing is applied, one spare can be used to replace a set of partitions. In order for the shared sparing technique to be applied, it requires multiple identical partitions, such as the input controllers for the switch design. Furthermore, each shared spare requires additional interconnect and logic overhead because of its need of having the ability to replace more than one possible defective partitions.

System Diagnosis and Reconfiguration. As a system diagnosis mechanism, we propose an iterative trial-and-error method which recovers to the last correct state of the switch, reconfigures the system, and replays the execution until no error is detected. The general concept is to iterate through each spared partition of the switch and swap in the spare for the current copy. For each swap, the error detection and

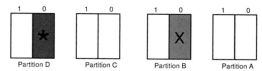

Trial = (Defects + Reconfiguration) ⊕ Configuration ⊕ Defects

Attempt#	Configuration	Reconfiguration	Defects	Trial	Comment
1	0010	0001	0010	0011	Error Detected
2	0010	0010	0010	0010	Iteration Skipped
3	0010	0100	0010	0110	Error Detected
4	0010	1000	0010	1010	Correct Execution

New Configuration = Trial Configuration = 1010
New Defects = Defects + (Configuration ⊕ Trial) = 1010

Figure 7: *Example system diagnosis and reconfiguration.* **This example shows the system with four partitions and one spare for each partition. The first spare of partition B contains a previously detected and corrected defect, thus the latest error in execution is caused by the defect in the first spare of partition D.**

recovery mechanism performs a system replay. Eventually, the partition that happens to possess the current error will be disabled and its corresponding spare enabled. When this occurs, the system diagnosis mechanism will detect correct system behavior and terminate the replay mode. Using this approach, the faulty piece of logic is identified and correctly disabled.

In order for the system diagnosis to operate, it maintains a set of bit vectors as follows:
- Configuration Vector: It indicates which spare partitions are enabled.
- Reconfiguration Vector: It keeps track of which configurations have been tried and indicates the next configuration to be tried. It gets updated at each iteration of system diagnosis.
- Defects Vector: It keeps track of which spare partitions are defected.
- Trial Vector: Indicates which spare partitions are enabled for a specific system diagnosis iteration.

Figure 7, demonstrates an example where system diagnosis is applied on a system with four partitions and two copies (one spare) for each partition. The first copy of partition B has a detected defect (mapped at the Defects Vector). The defect in the first copy of partition D is a recently manifested defect and is the one that caused erroneous execution. Once the error is detected, the system recovers to the last correct state using the mechanism described in the previous section (see error detection and recovery mechanism), and it initializes the Reconfiguration Vector. Next, the Trial Vector is computed using the Configuration, Reconfiguration, and Defects vectors. In case the Trial Vector is the same with the Configuration Vector (attempt 2), due to a defected spare, the iteration is skipped. Otherwise, the Trial Vector is used as the current Configuration vector, indicating which spare partitions will be enabled for the current trial. The execution is then replayed from the recovery point until the error detection point. In case the error is detected, a new trial is initiated by updating the Reconfiguration Vector and recomputing the Trial Vector. In case no error is detected, meaning that the trial configuration is a working configuration, the Trial Vector is copied to the Configuration Vector and the Defects Vector is updated with the located defected copy. If all the trial configurations are exhausted, which are equal to the number of partitions, and no working configuration was found, then the defect was a fatal defect and the system won't be able to recover. The example implementation of the system diagnosis mechanism demonstrated in Figure 7, can be adapted accordingly for designs with more partitions and more spares.

We also consider the Built-In-Self-Test(BIST) technique as an alternative for providing system diagnosis. For each distinct partition in the design we store in ROM automatically generated test vectors. During system diagnosis with BIST, these test vectors are applied to each partition of the system through scan chains to check its functionality correctness and locate the defected partition.

Both the iterative replay and BIST techniques can be implemented as a separate module from the switch and the area overhead for their implementation can be shared by a wide number of switches in a possible chip multiprocessor design.

4.2.3 Level of Protection

The error resiliency achieved by implementing one of the protection techniques (e.g., TMR or sparing) is highly dependent on the granularity of the partitions. In general, the larger the granularity of the partitions, the less robust the design. However, as the granularity of the partition becomes smaller, more logic is required. For TMR, each output for a given partition requires a MAJORITY gate. Since each added MAJORITY gate is unshielded from permanent defects, poorly constructed small partitions can make a design less error resilient than designs with larger partitions.

To illustrate these trade-offs, consider the baseline switch again in Figure 5. Sparing and TMR can be done on the system-level where the whole switch is replicated and each output requires some extra logic like a MUX or MAJORITY gate. A single permanent error makes one copy of the switch completely broken. However, the area overhead beyond the spares is limited to only a gate for each primary output. A slightly more resilient design, considers partitioning based on the components that make up the switch. For instance, each of the five input controllers can have a spare along with the arbiter, cross-bar, and the cross-bar controllers. This partitioning approach leaves the design more protected as a permanent defect in the input controller would make only that small partition broken and not the other four input controllers. There is a small area penalty for this approach as the sum of the outputs for each partition is greater than the switch as a whole. However, the added unprotected logic is still insufficient to worsen the error resiliency of the design. Finally, consider partitioning at the gate-level. In this approach, each gate is in its own partition. In this scheme, the error resiliency for each partition is extremely high because the target is very small. However, the overhead of this approach requires an extra gate for each gate in the switch design. Thus for TMR, the area would be four times the original design. In addition, because each added gate is unprotected, the susceptibility of this design to errors is actually greater than the larger partitions used in the component-based partition.

The previous analysis shows that the level of partitioning effects the error resiliency and the area overheads of the design. In this paper, we introduce a technique called, *Automatic Cluster Decompositions*, that generates partitions that minimizes area overhead while maximizing error resiliency.

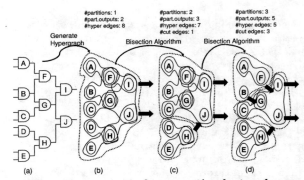

Figure 8: *The process of automatic cluster decomposition.* **In part (a) a sample netlist is shown with 2 primary outputs, along with its corresponding hypergraph in part (b). Part (c) shows the hypergraph after a min-cut bisection creating two unbalanced partitions. Part (d) shows the final 3-way partition resulting from a bisection of the largest partition.**

4.2.4 Automatic Cluster Decomposition

Automatic Cluster Decomposition takes a netlist and creates partitions with the end goal that each partition is approximately the same size and that there is a minimal amount of outputs required for each partition generated. Generating these partitions requires that the netlist be converted into a graph that can then be partitioned using a balanced-recursive min-cut algorithm [15, 12] that has found use in fields like VLSI [2].

Figure 8 shows how these partitions are generated from the netlist of a design. First, the netlist pictured in part (a) is used to generate a *hypergraph* shown in part (b). A hypergraph is an extension of a normal graph where one edge can connect multiple vertices. In the figure, each vertex represents a separate net in the design. A *hyperedge* is drawn around each net and its corresponding fanout. If that net is placed in a different partition than one of its fanout, that net becomes an output for its partition thus increasing the overhead of the partition. Thus the goal of the partitioning algorithm is to minimize the number of hyperedges that are cut. For this example, we show a 3-way partitioning of the circuit. The algorithm in [12] performs a recursive min-cut operation where the original circuit is bisected and then one of these partitions is bisected again. In Figure 8(c), the hypergraph is bisected and the number of hyperedges cut is reported. Notice that one of those pieces is twice the size of the other one. Because 3-way partitioning is desired, one piece is slightly larger so that the final partitions are fairly balanced where each partition has about the same number of vertices/nets. Figure 8(d) shows the final partitioning assignment of the hypergraph along with the number of hyperedges cut which corresponds to the number of total outputs for all the partitions not including the original outputs of the system. In practice, several iterations of [12] are run as the algorithm is heuristically-based and requires many runs for optimal partitions. Also, some imbalance in partition sizes is tolerated if the number of hyperedges cut is significantly smaller as a result.

Once the hypergraph is partitioned, several different replication strategies can be used such as sparing and TMR. In Figure 9, an example of performing 3-way partitioning over an arbitrary piece of logic using one spare per partition is shown. In part (a), sparing is performed at the system-level.

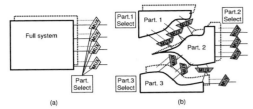

(a)   (b)

Figure 9: *Examples of one spare systems.* In part (a) sparing without any cluster decomposition is shown. In part (b) sparing is applied to a three-way partition. Cluster decomposition increases MUX interconnect overhead, but provides higher protection due to the smaller granularity of the sparing.

The outputs of both identical units are fed into a MUX where a register value determines which unit is active and which one is inactive. In part (b), the circuit is partitioned into three pieces. Notice, that the outputs for each boundary must now have a MUX associated with it. Also, each partition requires a register to determine which copy is active. Thus 3-way partitioning requires a total of three registers and the number of MUXes corresponding to the number of outputs generated by the partitioning.

4.3 Switch Designs

Each configuration providing a defect tolerant switch design is characterized by three parameters: level of protection, techniques applied, and system diagnosis method. For each configuration, we give a name convention as follows: level_technique_diagnosis. The configurations using TMR as the defect tolerance technique do not use the end-to-end error detection, recovery and system diagnosis techniques, since TMR inherently provides error detection, diagnosis and recovery. All other configurations use the end-to-end error detection and recovery technique, along with either iterative replay or BIST for system diagnosis. Table 1, describes the choices that we considered in our simulated configurations for the three parameters, and it gives some example configurations along with their name conventions.

5. Experimental Results

To evaluate the effectiveness of our domain specific defect tolerance techniques in protecting the switch design, we simulated various design configurations with both traditional and domain specific techniques. To assess the effectiveness of the various design configurations in protecting the switch design, we take into account the area and time overheads of the design along with the mean number of defects that the design can tolerate. We also introduce a new metric, the *Silicon Protection Factor (SPF)*, which gives us a more representative notion about the amount of protection that is offered to the system by a given defect tolerance technique. Specifically, the SPF is computed by dividing the mean number of defects needed to cause a switch failure with the area overhead of the protection techniques. In other words, the higher the SPF factor, the more resilient each transistor is to defects. Since the number of defects in a design is proportional to the area of the design, the use of this metric for assessing the effectiveness of the silicon protection techniques is more appropriate.

In Table 2, we list the design configurations that we simulated. The naming convention followed for representing each configuration is described in Table 1. For each simulated

Table 1: *Mnemonic table for design configurations.* For each portion of the naming convention, we show the possible mnemonics with the related description. The last portion provides some example design configurations.

Mnemonic Group	Mnemonic	Description
Level of applying defect tolerance technique	S	System level
	C	Component level
	G	Gate level
	S+CL	System level clusters
	C+CL	Component level clusters
Defect tolerance techniques (can be applied in combinations)	TMR	Triple Modular Redundancy
	#SP	# dedicated spares for each partition
	#SH(X)	# shared spares for partition of type X
	ECC	Error Correction Codes applied at state
System diagnosis technique	IR	Iterative replay
	BIST	Built-In-Self-Test
Example configurations	S+CL_1SP_IR	System level clusters with 1 spare for each partition and iterative replay.
	C_2SH(IC)+1SP_BIST	Component level with 2 shared input controllers and one dedicate spare for the rest of the components. BIST for system diagnosis.
	C+CL_TMR+ECC	Component level clusters TMR with ECC protected state.

design configuration, we provide the area overhead needed for implementing the specific design. This area overhead includes the extra area needed for the spare units, the majority gates, the logic for enabling and disabling spare units, the logic for the end-to-end error detection, recovery and system diagnosis (different configurations have different requirements for the extra logic added). We notice that the design configurations with the higher area overheads are the ones applying BIST for system diagnosis. This is due to the extra area needed for storing the test vectors necessary for self-testing each distinct partition in the design, along with the additional interconnection and logic needed for the scan chains. Even though the area overhead for the test vectors can be shared over the total number of switches per chip, the area overhead of the BIST technique is still rather large. Another design configuration with high area overhead is the one where TMR is applied at the gate level due to the extra voting gate needed for each gate in the baseline switch design. On the other hand, designs with shared spares achieve low area overhead (under two) since not every part of the switch is duplicated. The area overhead for the rest of the design configurations is dependent on the amount of spares per partition.

In the fourth column of the table, we provide the mean number of defects to failure for each design configuration. The design configurations providing high mean number of defects to failure are the ones employing the ACD (Automatic Cluster Decomposition) technique. Another point of interest is that techniques employing ECC even when coupled with automatic cluster decomposition perform poorly. Although state is traditionally protected by ECC, when a design is primarily combinational logic, like our switch, the cost of separating the state from the logic exceeds the protection given to the state elements. In other words, if the state is not considered in the ACD analysis and is therefore not part of any of the spared partitions, the boundary between the state and the spared partitions must have some unprotected interconnection logic. This added logic coupled with the unprotected logic required by ECC makes ECC in a logic dominated design undesirable.

The SPF values for each design are presented in the fifth column of Table 2. The highest SPFs are given by the design configurations that employ automatic cluster decomposition, with the highest being design $S+CL\_2SP\_IR$ at 11.11. Even though design $S+CL\_2SP\_BIST$ uses the same sparing strategies, the area overhead added from BIST decreases the design's SPF significantly. It's interesting that two design configurations have SPFs lower than 1. The first

Table 2: *Results of the evaluated designs.* **For each design configuration we report the mnemonic, the area factor over the baseline design, the number of defects that can be tolerated, the SPF, the number of partitions and an estimate of the impact on the system delay.**

Key	Design Configuration	Area O.head	Defects	SPF	#Part.	%Dly	Key	Design Configuration	Area O.head	Defects	SPF	#Part.	%Dly
1	S_TMR	3.02	2.49	0.82	1	0.00	20	S+CL_2SP+ECC_IR	3.39	8.64	2.55	118	22.22
2	S+CL_TMR	3.08	16.78	5.45	241	22.22	21	C_2SP_IR	3.36	13.07	3.90	12	0.00
3	S+CL_TMR+ECC	3.07	6.92	2.25	185	27.78	22	C_2SP_BIST	3.90	13.07	3.35	12	0.00
4	C_TMR	3.04	4.68	1.54	12	0.00	23	C+CL_2SP_IR	3.44	32.33	9.39	208	18.75
5	C+CL_TMR	3.09	15.86	5.13	223	18.75	24	C_CL_2SP_BIST	4.31	32.33	7.50	208	18.75
6	C+CL_TMR+ECC	3.11	6.25	2.01	298	25.00	25	C+CL_2SP+ECC_R	3.41	7.49	2.20	103	25.00
7	G_TMR	4.00	4.00	1.00	10540	100.00	26	C_2SH(IC)_IR	1.52	3.15	2.07	12	0.00
8	S_1SP_IR	2.22	3.27	1.47	1	0.00	27	C_3SH(IC)_IR	1.71	4.14	2.43	12	0.00
9	S+CL_1SP_IR	2.30	17.53	7.63	206	22.22	28	C_4SH(IC)_IR	1.89	5.02	2.65	12	0.00
10	S+CL_1SP_BIST	3.16	17.53	5.54	206	22.22	29	C_5SH(IC)_IR	2.08	5.90	2.84	12	0.00
11	S+CL_1SP+ECC_IR	2.48	5.96	2.41	183	27.78	30	C_2SH(IC)+1SP_IR	1.74	4.40	2.53	12	0.00
12	S+CL_1SP+ECC_BIST	3.34	5.96	1.78	183	27.78	31	C_3SH(IC)+1SP_IR	1.93	5.79	3.01	12	0.00
13	C_1SP_IR	2.24	5.87	2.62	12	0.00	32	C_4SH(IC)+1SP_IR	2.12	7.10	3.34	12	0.00
14	C_1SP_BIST	2.79	5.87	2.62	12	0.00	33	C_5SH(IC)+1SP_IR	2.41	8.39	3.48	12	0.00
15	C+CL_1SP_IR	2.33	16.04	6.88	223	18.75	34	C_2SH(IC)+2SP_IR	1.93	5.01	2.60	12	0.00
16	C+CL_1SP_ECC_IR	2.51	5.34	2.13	138	25.00	35	C_3SH(IC)+2SP_IR	2.12	6.57	3.09	12	0.00
17	S_2SP_IR	3.32	5.95	1.79	1	0.00	36	C_4SH(IC)+2SP_IR	2.30	8.10	3.52	12	0.00
18	S+CL_2SP_IR	3.42	37.99	11.11	206	22.22	37	C_5SH(IC)+2SP_IR	2.50	9.58	3.84	12	0.00
19	S+CL_2SP_BIST	4.29	37.99	8.86	206	22.22	38	S_ECC	1.18	1.16	0.98	12	0.00

one is TMR applied at the system level, which can tolerate 2.5 defects but the area overhead is more than triple, thus making the new design less defect tolerant than the baseline switch design by 18%. The second one is where the state is protected by ECC. Since our design is logic dominated and the protected fraction of the design is very small, the extra logic required for applying ECC (which is unprotected), is larger than the actual protected area. Thus, this technique makes the specific design less defect tolerant than the baseline unprotected design by 2%.

The sixth column in the table shows the number of distinct partitions for each design configuration. This parameter is very important for the configurations employing ACD. The SPF of a given design configurations, is greatly dependent on the number of partitions in the decomposed design.

Figure 10 shows the dependency of the SPF over the number of decomposed partitions for the design configuration *S+CL_1SP_IR*. We can see that for the given design configuration the peak SPF occurs around 200 partitions. As the per partition size decreases, the SPF value increases, and as the number of cut edges per partition increases, the SPF value decreases. Therefore, the initial rise of the SPF occurs because the area per partition was decreasing as the number of decomposed partitions was getting larger. After the optimal point of 200 partitions, the overhead of the extra unprotected logic required for each cutting edge between partitions causes the SPF to start declining. For each design configuration employing automatic cluster decomposition, we ran several simulations for varying numbers of partitions to achieve an optimal SPF.

The final column in Table 2, %Delay, gives the percentage increase of the critical path delay in the switch. We produce a coarse approximation of the delay overheads that is technology independent by making the delay increase proportional to the number of interconnection gates added to the critical path. Thus, TMR-based designs will achieve the same delay increase as spare-based designs as multiplexers and majority gates are treated the same in the analysis. Our results show that for the best designs, we always achieve a delay increase of less than 25%. The designs that involve ACD involve the greatest increase in delay because the partitions generated frequently split up the critical paths. Designs with minimal amount of clustering, such as

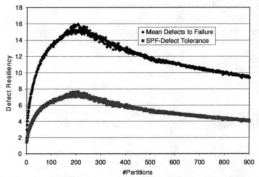

Figure 10: *Defect resiliency as a function of the number of partitions.* **As an example we plot the SPF defect tolerance of configuration *S+CL_1SP_IR* for a varying number of partitions generated by the ACD algorithm.**

the *C_2SH(IC)_IR*, achieve no overhead as no interconnection logic is added to any of the critical paths. In general, our results indicate that achieving high SPF require slight delay penalty; however, in principle the ACD strategy could be used to try to minimize the number of critical paths that are partitioned.

The graph in Figure 11 shows the trade off between defect tolerance and area overhead. The horizontal axis of the graph represents the defect tolerance provided from a design configuration in SPFs, and the vertical axis the area overhead of the design configuration. The further to the right a design configuration lies, the higher the defect tolerance it provides, while the lower it is, the lower the implementation cost.

At the lower left corner, is the design configuration *S_ECC* providing ECC protection to the state. This is the cheapest design configuration, but it does not provide any considerable defect tolerance to the switch design. The rightmost design configuration, *S+CL_2SP_IR*, provides a defect tolerance of 11.11 SPF, by employing automatic cluster decomposition at the system level with 200 partitions and two extra spares for each partition, along with iterative replay for system diagnosis. The area overhead for implementing this design configuration is 3.42X, and provides the better trade-off between area required and offered defect

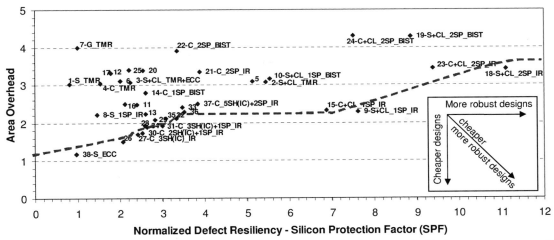

Figure 11: *Pareto chart of the explored solutions.* **The design evaluated are plotted on an area vs. SPF chart. The line across the chart connects the set of optimal solutions. See Table 1 for explanations of design points.**

protection. Design configurations with moderate SPFs but with much less cost in area overhead are: *C_3SH(IC)_IR*, *C_2SH(IC)+1SP_IR*, *C_3SH(IC)+1SP_IR*, and *C_2SH(IC)+2SP_IR*. These design configurations use shared spares of input controllers along with dedicated spares for the other components in the switch design, keeping the area overhead less than 2X, but offering SPFs of 2.5-3 at the same time. Such designs are interesting, since they keep the implementation cost at low levels and provide an attractive solution for defect tolerance.

Other two interesting design configurations are *C+CL_1SP_IR* and *S+CL_1SP_IR*. These two designs use the same technique, automatic cluster decomposition with one spare for each partition, with the difference that design *S+CL_1SP_IR* applies the ACD technique on the system level, and design *C+CL_1SP_IR* at the component level. The area cost of the two designs is almost the same but *S+CL_1SP_IR* provides 11% more SPF. The same argument also holds for designs *S+CL_2SP_IR* and *C+CL_2SP_IR*. This suggests that applying the ACD technique at the system level can offer more effective defect tolerance at the same cost in area.

In Figure 12, we present how some of the design configurations affect the lifetime of the switch design for a future post 65nm technology where the mean time between failures to be manifested on a switch is 2 years (a failure rate of 55000 FITs). The graph's horizontal axis represents the years that the switch design is operating. The vertical axis represent the percentage of defected parts over a population of switches (left axis) and the baseline switch's failure rate (right axis). The baseline switch's lifetime failure rate for the given technology is presented by the darker thick line, forming the bathtub curve. In Figure 12(a), it only forms a part of the bathtub curve since for this graph we assume that the design's breakdown occurs after 30 years. For each design configured presented in the graph, there is a line showing the failing rate of switch parts over time. This line starts from year 1, since we assume that the first year of a parts lifetime is consumed during the accelerated testing (burn-in) procedure, and that shipped parts are already at their first year of lifetime with a constant failure rate.

From the graph in Figure 12(a), we can observe that when applying TMR at the component level, 25% of the shipped parts will be defected by the first year and 75% after the first

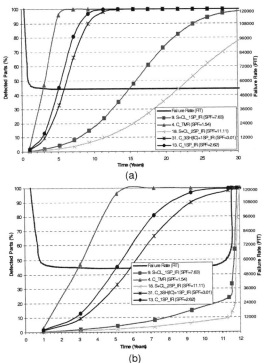

(a)

(b)

Figure 12: *Fault tolerance of some interesting design configurations.* **Part (a) superimposes the FIT rate of the bathtub model with the percentage of defective parts over time. In addition part (b) takes into account the breakdown period.**

three years. On the other hand, when in a design configuration where automated cluster decomposition was applied at the system level with 2 spares for each partition, the 25% of the shipped parts will be defected after 16 years and the 75% after 29 years. If we define the lifetime of a manufactured product as the period of time where 10% of the manufactured parts become defective, then the clustering design configuration *S+CL_2SP_IR* increases the switch's lifetime by 26X over the TMR design configuration *C_TMR*.

System designers, can choose a defect tolerance technique that best matches with their design's specifications. For example the design configuration $S+CL\_1SP\_IR$, where automatic clustering decomposition is applied at system level with one dedicated spare for each partition, where 10% of the parts will get defected after 7 years but with 48% less cost in area than design configuration $S+CL\_2SP\_IR$ might be a more attractive solution.

The same data as in Figure 12(a), is presented in Figure 12(b), with the difference that here we assume that the breakdown for the switch design starts after 10 years of being shipped. For the first three design configurations, there is no difference since by that time all of the parts become defective. For the other two design configurations, what is interesting to observe is that even after the breakdown point where the failure rates increase with an exponential rate, most of the parts will be able to provide the user a warning time window of a month before failure. This is a very important feature for a design configuration, especially for very critical high dependable applications.

6. Conclusions and Future Directions

As silicon technologies continue to scale, transistor reliability is becoming an increasingly important issue. Devices are becoming subject to extreme process variation, transistor wearout, and manufacturing defects. As a result, it will likely be no longer possible to create fault-free designs. In this paper, we investigate the design of a defect-tolerant CMP network switch. To accomplish this design, we first develop a high-level, architect-friendly model of silicon failures based on the time-tested bathtub curve. Based on this model, we explore the design space of defect-tolerant CMP switch designs and the resulting tradeoff between defect tolerance and area overhead. We find that traditional mechanisms, such as triple modular redundancy and error correction codes, are insufficient for tolerating moderate numbers of defects. Rather, domain-specific techniques that include end-to-end error detection, resource sparing, and iterative diagnosis/reconfiguration are more effective. Further, decomposing the netlist of the switch into modest-sized clusters is the most effective granularity to apply the protection techniques.

This work provides a solid foundation for future exploration in the area of defect-tolerant design. We plan to investigate the use of spare components based on wearout profiles to provide more sparing for the most vulnerable components. Further, a CMP switch is only a first step towards the over-reaching goal of designing a defect-tolerant CMP system.

Acknowledgments: This work is supported by grants from NSF and Gigascale Systems Research Center. We would also like to acknowledge Li-Shiuan Peh for providing us access to CMP Switch models, and the anonymous reviewers for providing useful comments on this paper.

7. References

[1] H. Al-Asaad and J. P. Hayes. Logic design validation via simulation and automatic test pattern generation. *J. Electron. Test.*, 16(6):575–589, 2000.

[2] C. J. Alpert and A. B. Kahng. Recent directions in netlist partitioning: a survey. *Integr. VLSI J.*, 19(1-2):1–81, 1995.

[3] T. S. Barnett and A. D. Singh. Relating yield models to burn-in fall-out in time. In *Proc. of International Test Conference (ITC)*, pages 77–84, 2003.

[4] E. Bohl, et al. The fail-stop controller AE11. In *Proc. of International Test Conference (ITC)*, pages 567–577, 1997.

[5] S. Borkar, et al. Design and reliability challenges in nanometer technologies. In *Proc. of the Design Automation Conf.*, 2004.

[6] F. A. Bower, et al. Tolerating hard faults in microprocessor array structures. In *Proc. of International Conference on Dependable Systems and Networks (DSN)*, 2004.

[7] K. Constantinides, et al. Assessing SEU Vulnerability via Circuit-Level Timing Analysis In *Proc. of 1st Workshop on Architectural Reliability (WAR)*, 2005.

[8] J. E. D. E. Council. Failure mechanisms and models for semiconductor devices. *JEDEC Publication JEP122-A*, 2002.

[9] W. J. Dally, et al. The reliable router: A reliable and high-performance communication substrate for parallel computers. In *Proc. International Workshop on Parallel Computer Routing and Communication (PCRCW)*, 1994.

[10] E. Wu, et al. Interplay of voltage and temperature acceleration of oxide breakdown for ultra-thin gate dioxides. *Solid-state Electronics Journal*, 2002.

[11] P. Gupta and A. B. Kahng. Manufacturing-aware physical design. In *Proc. of International Conference on Computer-Aided Design (ICCAD)*, 2003.

[12] hMETIS. *http://www.cs.umn.edu/~karypis*.

[13] C. K. Hu, et al. Scaling effect on electromigration in on-chip Cu wiring. *International Electron Devices Meeting*, 1999.

[14] A. M. Ionescu, M. J. Declercq, S. Mahapatra, K. Banerjee, and J. Gautier. Few electron devices: towards hybrid CMOS-SET integrated circuits. In *Proc. of the Design Automation Conference*, pages 88–93, 2002.

[15] G. Karypis, et al. Multilevel hypergraph partitioning: Applications in VLSI domain. In *Proc. of the Design Automation Conference*, pages 526–529, 1997.

[16] S. Mukherjee, et al. The soft error problem: An architectural perspective. In *Proc. of the International Symposium on High-Performance Computer Architecture*, 2005.

[17] S. Mukherjee, et al. A systematic methodology to compute the architectural vulnerability factors for a high-performance microprocessor. In *Proc. International Symposium on Microarchitecture (MICRO)*, pages 29–42, 2003.

[18] B. T. Murray and J. P. Hayes. Testing ICs: Getting to the core of the problem. *IEEE Computer*, 29(11):32–38, 1996.

[19] L.-S. Peh. *Flow Control and Micro-Architectural Mechanisms for Extending the Performance of Interconnection Networks.* PhD thesis, Stanford University, 2001.

[20] R. Rao, et al. Statistical estimation of leakage current considering inter- and intra-die process variation. In *Proc. of the International Symposium on Low Power Electronics and Design (ISLPED)*, pages 84–89, 2003.

[21] N.R. Saxena, and E.J. McCluskey Dependable Adaptive Computing Systems. *IEEE Systems, Man, and Cybernetics Conf.*, 1998.

[22] P. Shivakumar, et al. Exploiting microarchitectural redundancy for defect tolerance. In *Proc. of International Conference on Computer Design (ICCD)*, 2003.

[23] D. P. Siewiorek, et al. Reliable computer systems: Design and evaluation, 3rd edition. *AK Peters, Ltd Publisher*, 1998.

[24] J. Smolens, et al. Fingerprinting: Bounding the soft-error detection latency and bandwidth. In *Proc. of the Symposium on Architectural Support for Programming Languages and Operating Systems (ASPLOS)*, 2004.

[25] L. Spainhower and T. A. Gregg. G4: A fault-tolerant CMOS mainframe. In *Proc. of International Symposium on Fault-Tolerant Computing (FTCS)*, 1998.

[26] J. Srinivasan, et al. The impact of technology scaling on lifetime reliability. In *Proc. of International Conference on Dependable Systems and Networks (DSN)*, 2004.

[27] J. H. Stathis. Reliability limits for the gate insulator in CMOS technology. *IBM Journal of Research and Development*, 2002.

[28] S. B. K. Vrudhula, D. Blaauw, and S. Sirichotiyakul. Estimation of the likelihood of capacitive coupling noise. In *Proc. of the Design Automation Conference*, 2002.

[29] N. J. Wang, et al. Characterizing the effects of transient faults on a high-performance processor pipeline. In *Proc. of International Conference on Dependable Systems and Networks (DSN)*, pages 61–70, 2004.

[30] C. Weaver and T. Austin. A fault tolerant approach to microprocessor design. In *Proc. of International Conference on Dependable Systems and Networks (DSN)*, 2001.

[31] C. Weaver, et al. Techniques to reduce the soft error rate of a high-performance microprocessor. In *Annual International Symposium on Computer Architecture*, 2004.

[32] J. F. Ziegler. Terrestrial cosmic rays. *IBM Journal of Research and Development*, 40(1), 1996.

CMP Design Space Exploration Subject to Physical Constraints

Yingmin Li[†], Benjamin Lee[‡], David Brooks[‡], Zhigang Hu[††], Kevin Skadron[†]
[†] Dept. of Computer Science, University of Virginia [††] IBM T.J. Watson Research Center
[‡] Division of Engineering and Applied Sciences, Harvard University
{yingmin,skadron}@cs.virginia.edu, zhigangh@us.ibm.com, {dbrooks,bclee}@eecs.harvard.edu

Abstract

This paper explores the multi-dimensional design space for chip multiprocessors, exploring the inter-related variables of core count, pipeline depth, superscalar width, L2 cache size, and operating voltage and frequency, under various area and thermal constraints. The results show the importance of joint optimization. Thermal constraints dominate other physical constraints such as pin-bandwidth and power delivery, demonstrating the importance of considering thermal constraints while optimizing these other parameters. For aggressive cooling solutions, reducing power density is at least as important as reducing total power, while for low-cost cooling solutions, reducing total power is more important. Finally, the paper shows the challenges of accommodating both CPU-bound and memory-bound workloads on the same design. Their respective preferences for more cores and larger caches lead to increasingly irreconcilable configurations as area and other constraints are relaxed; rather than accommodating a happy medium, the extra resources simply encourage more extreme optimization points.

1 Introduction

Recent product announcements show a trend toward aggressive integration of multiple cores on a single chip to maximize throughput. However, this trend presents an expansive design space for chip architects, encompassing the number of cores per die, core size and complexity (pipeline depth and superscalar width), memory hierarchy design, operating voltage and frequency, and so forth. Identifying optimal designs is especially difficult because the variables of interest are inter-related and must be considered simultaneously. Furthermore, trade-offs among these design choices vary depending both on workloads and physical (e.g., area and thermal) constraints.

We explore this multi-dimensional design space across a range of possible chip sizes and thermal constraints, for both CPU-bound and memory-bound workloads. Few prior works have considered so many cores, and to our knowledge, this is the first work to optimize across so many design variables simultaneously. We show the inter-related nature of these parameters and how the optimum choice of design parameters can shift dramatically depending on system constraints. Specifically, this paper demonstrates that:

- A simple, fast approach to simulate a large number of cores by observing that cores only interact through the L2 cache and shared interconnect. Our methodology uses single-core traces and only requires fast cache simulation for multi-core results.

- CPU- and memory-bound applications desire dramatically different configurations. Adaptivity helps, but any compromise incurs throughput penalties.

- Thermal constraints dominate, trumping even pin-bandwidth and power-delivery constraints. Once thermal constraints have been met, throughput is throttled back sufficiently to meet current pin-bandwidth and ITRS power-delivery constraints.

- A design must be optimized with thermal constraints. Scaling from the thermal-blind optimum leads to a configuration that is inferior, sometimes radically so, to a thermally optimized configuration.

- Simpler, smaller cores are preferred under some constraints. In thermally constrained designs, the main determinant is not simply maximizing the number of cores, but maximizing their power efficiency. Thermal constraints generally favor shallower pipelines and lower clock frequencies.

- Additional cores increase throughput, despite the resulting voltage and frequency scaling required to meet thermal constraints, until performance gains from an additional core is negated by the impact of voltage and frequency scaling across all cores.

- For aggressive cooling solutions, reducing power density is at least as important as reducing total power. For low-cost cooling solutions, however, reducing total power is more important.

This paper is organized as follows. Section 2 is the related work. We introduce our model infrastructure and validation in section 3. We present design space exploration results and explanations in section 4. We end with conclusions and proposals for future work in section 5.

2 Related Work

There has been a burst of work in recent years to understand the performance, energy, and thermal efficiency of different CMP organizations. Few have looked at a large numbers of cores and none, of which we are aware, have jointly optimized across the large number of design parameters we consider while addressing the associated methodology challenges. Li and Martínez [17] present the most aggressive study of which we are aware, exploring up to 16-way CMPs for SPLASH benchmarks and considering power constraints. Their results show that parallel execution on a CMP can improve energy efficiency compared to the same performance achieved via single-threaded execution, and that even within the power budget of a single core, a CMP allows substantial speedups compared to single-threaded execution.

Kongetira et al. [12] describe the Sun Niagara processor, an eight-way CMP supporting four threads per core and targeting workloads with high degrees of thread-level parallelism. Chaudhry et al. [4] describe the benefits of multiple cores and multiple threads, sharing eight cores with a single L2 cache. They also describe the Sun Rock processor's "scouting" mechanism that uses a helper thread to prefetch instructions and data.

El-Moursy et al. [6] show the advantages of clustered architectures and evaluate a CMP of multi-threaded, multi-cluster cores with support for up to eight contexts. Huh et al. [10] categorized the SPEC benchmarks into CPU-bound, cache-sensitive, or bandwidth-limited groups and explored core complexity, area efficiency, and pin bandwidth limitations, concluding due to pin-bandwidth limitations that a smaller number of high-performance cores maximizes throughput. Ekman and Stenstrom [5] use SPLASH benchmarks to explore a similar design space for energy-efficiency with the same conclusions.

Kumar et al. [14] consider the performance, power, and area impact of the interconnection network in CMP architecture. They advocate low degrees of sharing, but use transaction oriented workloads with high degrees of inter-thread sharing. Since we are modeling throughput-oriented workloads consisting of independent threads, we follow the example of Niagara [12] and employ more aggressive L2 sharing. In our experiments, each L2 cache bank is shared by half the total number of cores. Interconnection design parameters are not variable in our design space at this time, and in fact constitute a sufficiently expansive design space of their own that we consider this to be beyond the scope of the current paper.

The research presented in this paper differs from prior work in the large number of design parameters and metrics we consider. We evaluate CMP designs for performance, power efficiency, and thermal efficiency while varying the number of cores per chip, pipeline depth and width, chip thermal packaging effectiveness, chip area, and L2 cache size. This evaluation is performed with a fast decoupled simulation infrastructure that separates core simulation from interconnection/cache simulation. By considering many more parameters in the design space, we demonstrate the effectiveness of this infrastructure and show the inter-relatedness of these parameters.

The methodologies for analyzing pipeline depth and width build on prior work by Lee and Brooks [16] by developing first-order models for capturing changes in core area as pipeline dimensions change, thereby enabling power density and temperature analysis. We identify optimal pipeline dimensions in the context of CMP architectures, whereas most prior pipeline analysis considers single-core microprocessors [8, 9, 22], Furthermore, most prior work in optimizing pipelines focused exclusively on performance, although Zyuban et al. found 18FO4 delays to be power-performance optimal for a single-threaded microprocessor [26].

Other researchers have proposed simplified processor models, with the goal of accelerating simulation. Within the microprocessor core, Karkhanis and Smith [11] describe a trace-driven, first-order modeling approach to estimate IPC by adjusting an ideal IPC to account for branch misprediction. In contrast, our methodology adjusts power, performance, and temperature estimates from detailed single-core simulations to account for fabric events, such as cache misses and bus contention. In order to model large scale multiprocessor systems running commercial workloads, Kunkel et al. [15] utilize an approach that combines functional simulation, hardware trace collection, and probabilistic queuing models. However, our decoupled and iterative approach allows us to account for effects such as latency overlap due to out-of-order execution, effects not easily captured by queuing models. Although decoupled simulation frameworks have been proposed in the context of single-core simulation (e.g., Kumar and Davidson [13]) with arguments similar to our own, our methodology is applied in the context of simulating multi-core processors.

3 Experimental Methodology

To facilitate the exploration of large CMP design spaces, we propose decoupling core and interconnect/cache simulation to reduce simulation time. Detailed, cycle-accurate simulations of multi-core organizations are expensive, and the multi-dimensional search of the design space, even with just homogeneous cores, is prohibitive. Decoupling core and interconnect/cache simulation dramatically reduces simulation cost with minimal loss in accuracy. Our simulation approach uses IBM's Turandot/PowerTimer, a cycle-accurate, execution-driven simulator, to generate single-core L2 cache-access traces that are annotated with timestamps and power values. We then feed these traces to Zauber, a cache simulator we developed that models the interaction of multiple threads on one or more shared interconnects and one or more L2 caches. Zauber uses hits and misses to shift the time and power values in the original traces. Generating the traces is therefore a one-time cost, while what would otherwise be a costly multiprocessor simulation is reduced to a much faster cache simulation. Using Zauber, it is cost-effective to search the entire multi-core design space.

3.1 Simulator Infrastructure

Our framework decouples core and interconnect/cache simulation to reduce simulation time. Detailed core simulation provides performance and power data for various

Fetch		Decode	
NFA Predictor	1	Multiple Decode	2
L2 I-Cache	11	Millicode Decode	2
L3 I-Load	8	Expand String	2
I-TLB Miss	10	Mispredict Cycles	3
L2 I-TLB Miss	50	Register Read	1
Execution		Memory	
Fix Execute	1	L1 D-Load	3
Float Execute	4	L2 D-Load	9
Branch Execute	1	L3 D-Load	77
Float Divide	12	Float Load	2
Integer Multiply	7	D-TLB Miss	7
Integer Divide	35	L2 D-TLB Miss	50
Retire Delay	2	StoreQ Forward	4

Table 1. 19FO4 Latencies (cycles).

	8D	4D	2D	1D
Functional Units				
FXU	4	2	1	1
MEM	4	2	1	1
FXU	4	2	1	1
BR	4	2	1	1
CR	2	1	1	1
Pipeline Stage Widths				
FETCH	16	8	4	2
DECODE	8	4	2	1
RENAME	8	4	2	1
DISPATCH	8	4	2	1
RETIRE	8	4	2	1

Table 2. Width Resource Scaling.

Structure	Energy Growth Factor
Register Rename	1.1
Instruction Issue	1.9
Memory Unit	1.5
Multi-ported Register File	1.8
Data Bypass	1.6
Functional Units	1.0

Table 3. Energy Scaling.

core designs, while interconnect/cache simulation projects the impact of core interaction on these metrics.

3.1.1 Core Simulation

Our detailed core simulation infrastructure consists of Turandot, PowerTimer, and HotSpot 2.0. Turandot is a validated model of an IBM POWER4-like architecture [19]. PowerTimer implements circuit-extracted, validated power models, which we have extended with analytical scaling formulas based on Wattch [1, 2]. HotSpot 2.0 is a validated, architectural model of localized, on-chip temperatures [21]. Each of these components in our detailed simulation infrastructure is modular so that any particular simulator can be replaced with an alternative. We extended Turandot and PowerTimer to model the performance and power as pipeline depth and width vary using techniques from prior work [16].

Depth Performance Scaling: Pipeline depth is quantified in terms of FO4 delays per pipeline stage.[1] The performance model for architectures with varying pipeline depths are derived from the reference 19FO4 design by treating the total number of logic levels as constant and independent of the number of pipeline stages. This is an abstraction for the purpose of our analysis; increasing the pipeline depth could require logic design changes. The baseline latencies (Table 1) are scaled to account for pipeline depth changes according to Eq. (1). These scaled latencies account for latch delays ($FO4_{latch} = 3$) and all latencies have a minimum of one cycle. This is consistent with prior work in pipeline depth simulation and analysis for a single-threaded core [26].

$$Lat_{target} = \left\lfloor Lat_{base} \times \frac{FO4_{base} - FO4_{latch}}{FO4_{target} - FO4_{latch}} + 0.5 \right\rfloor \quad (1)$$

Depth Power Scaling: Each factor in the standard equation for dynamic power dissipation, Eq. (2), scales with pipeline depth. The clock frequency f increases linearly with depth as the delay for each pipeline stage decreases. The clock gating factor CGF decreases by a workload dependent factor as pipeline depth increases due

---

[1]Fan-out-of-four (FO4) delay is defined as the delay of one inverter driving four copies of an equally sized inverter. When logic and overhead per pipeline stage is measured in terms of FO4 delay, deeper pipelines have smaller FO4 delays.

to the increased number of cycles in which the shorter pipeline stages are stalled. As the true switching factor α is independent of the pipeline depth and the glitching factor β decreases with pipeline depth due to shorter distances between latches, switching power dissipation decreases with pipeline depth. The latch count, and consequently hold power dissipation, increases linearly with pipeline depth. We refer the reader to prior work for a detailed treatment of these scaling models [26].

$$P_{dyn} = CV^2 f(\alpha + \beta) \times CGF \quad (2)$$

Width Performance Scaling: We quantify the pipeline width in terms of the maximum number of instructions decoded per cycle. Performance data for architectures with varying pipeline widths are obtained from the reference 4-decode design (4D) by a linear scaling of the number of functional units and the number of non-branch instructions fetched, decoded, renamed, dispatched, and retired per cycle (Table 2). All pipelines have at least one instance of each functional unit. As pipeline width decreases, the number of instances of each functional unit is quickly minimized to one. Thus, the decode width becomes the constraining parameter for instruction throughput for the narrower pipelines we consider (e.g., 2D).

Width Power Scaling: We employ a hybrid approach to model the power impact of scaling the width of the pipeline. Our baseline microarchitecture, based on the POWER4, includes a clustered backend microarchitecture for structures like the functional units, issue queues, and register files. This approach is effective at managing complexity, cycle time, and power dissipation in wide-issue superscalar cores [3, 20, 25]. An analogous technique is used to construct the dual-ported data cache. When scaling the width of these structures, we assume that unconstrained hold and switching power increases linearly with the number of functional units, access ports, and any other parameter that must change as width varies.

In certain non-clustered structures, however, linear power scaling may be inaccurate and, for example, does not capture non-linear relationships between power and the number of SRAM access ports since it does not account for the additional circuitry required in a multi-ported SRAM cell. For this reason, we apply superlinear power scaling with exponents (Table 3) drawn from Zyuban's work in estimating energy growth parameters [25]. Since these parameters were experimentally derived through analysis of non-clustered architecture, we only apply this power scaling to the non-clustered components of our architecture.

3.1.2 Interconnection/Cache Simulation

The core simulators are supplemented by Zauber, a much faster simulator that performs interpolation on L2 cache traces provided by the core simulators. Zauber decouples detailed core simulation and the simulation of core interaction. The cores in a CMP architecture usually share one or more L2 caches through an interconnection fabric. Therefore, resource contention between cores occurs primarily in these two resources. We find it possible to simulate cache and fabric contention independent of core simulations without losing too much accuracy. The impact of contention on the performance and power of each core may then be evaluated quickly using interpolation.

First, we collect L2 access traces based on L1 cache misses through one pass of single-core simulations with a specific L2 cache size (0.5MB in our experiment). We found these L2 traces to be independent of the L2 cache size. In these traces we record the L2 cache address and access time (denoted by the cycle) information for every access. We also need to sweep through a range of L2 cache sizes for each benchmark and record the performance and microarchitectural resource utilization every 10k instructions as this information will be used in the interpolation. These L2 traces are fed into an cache simulator and interconnection-contention model that reads the L2 accesses of each core from the traces, sorts them according to time of access, and uses them to drive the interconnection and L2 cache simulation. This interconnection/cache simulator outputs the L2 miss ratio and the delay due to contention for every 10k instruction segment of the thread running on each core.

With this L2 miss ratio and interconnection contention information we calculate the new performance and power number for each 10k instruction segment of all the threads. Since we know the performance and microarchitectural resource utilization for several L2 miss ratio values, we are able to obtain new performance and utilization data for any other L2 miss ratio produced by the cache simulator via interpolation. Power numbers can be derived from the structure utilization data with post-processing.

When we interleave the L2 accesses from each thread, we are using the cycle information attached with each access to sort them by time of access. However, each thread may suffer different degrees of performance degradation due to interconnection and L2 cache contention. Therefore, sorting by time of access may not reflect the real ordering.

In our model, we iterate to improve accuracy. In particular, given the performance impact from cache contention for each thread, we can use this information to adjust the time of each L2 access in each L2 trace and redo L2 cache emulation based on this new L2 access timing information. Iterating to convergence, we find three iterations are typically enough to reach good accuracy.

We validate Zauber against our detailed cycle-accurate simulator, Turandot. Figure 1 shows the average performance and power data from Turandot simulation and Zauber simulation for 2-way and 4-way CMPs. From these figures, the average performance and power difference between Turandot and Zauber is within 1%. For a 2-way CMP, Zauber achieves a simulation time speedup of 40-60x, with detailed Turandot simulations requiring 1-2 hours and the decoupled simulator requiring 1-3 minutes.

Since we are modeling throughput-oriented workloads consisting of independent threads, we consider a relatively high degree of cache sharing Niagara [12]. Each L2 cache bank is shared by half the total number of cores. The interconnection power overheads are extrapolated from [14].

We assume the L2 cache latency does not change when we vary the L2 cache size. We also omit the effects of clock propagation on chip throughput and power when core number increases.

3.2 Analytical Infrastructure

We use formulas to vary and calculate parameters of interest in the CMP design space exploration. The design parameters we consider include core count, core pipeline dimensions, thermal resistance of chip packaging, and L2 cache size. As we vary these parameters, we consider the impact on both power and performance metrics.

3.2.1 Performance and Power Modeling

The analytical model uses performance and dynamic power data generated by Zauber simulation. Leakage power density for a given technology is calculated by Eq. (3), where A and B are coefficients determined by a linear regression of ITRS data and T is the absolute temperature. $A = 207.94$ and $B = 1446$ for 65nm technology.

$$P_{\text{leakage density}} = A \cdot T^2 \cdot e^{-B/T} \qquad (3)$$

3.2.2 Temperature Modeling

We use steady-state temperature at the granularity of each core to estimate the chip thermal effects. This neglects localized hotspots within a core as well as lateral thermal coupling among cores. Addressing these is important future work, but employing a simple analytical temperature formula instead of the more complex models in HotSpot reduces simulation time and allows us to focus on how heat-removal limitations constrain core count and core type.

We observe that the heat spreader is almost isothermal for the range of the chip areas and power values we investigate, so we can separate the global temperature rise across the thermal package due to total chip power dissipation from localized temperature rise above the package

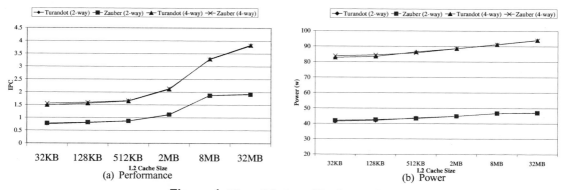

Figure 1. The validation of Zauber model.

due to per-core power dissipation. This is described by Equations 4, 5, and 6. Suppose we want to calculate the temperature of a specific core on the chip, where P_{glo} and P_{core} are the global chip and single core dynamic power, respectively. Similarly, L_{glo} and L_{core} are the global chip and single core leakage power, respectively. The chip's total dynamic power is the sum of the dynamic power dissipated by all the cores on chip, the L2 cache and the interconnect. The chip leakage power is summed in a similar manner. The sum of R_{spread} and R_{hsink} denotes the thermal resistance from the heat spreader to the air and the sum of $R_{silicon}$ and R_{TIM} denotes the thermal resistance from the core. Collectively, these parameters specify the chip's thermal characteristics from the device level to the heat spreader, ignoring the lateral thermal coupling above the heat spreader level.

We categorize the CMP heatup into local and global effects. The former is determined by the local power dissipation of any given core and the effect on its temperature. The latter is determined by the global chip power.

$$H_{glo} + H_{loc} = T_{core} - T_{amb} \quad (4)$$
$$H_{glo} = (P_{glo} + L_{glo}) \cdot (R_{spread} + R_{hsink}) \quad (5)$$
$$H_{loc} = (P_{core} + L_{core}) \cdot (R_{silicon} + R_{TIM}) (6)$$

This distinction between local and global heatup mechanisms is first qualitatively introduced by Li et al. in [18]. They observed that adding cores to a chip of fixed area increases chip temperature. This observation may not be evident strictly from the perspective of per-core power density. Although power density is often used as a proxy for steady-state temperature with each core exhibiting the same power density, core or unit power density is only an accurate predictor of the temperature increases in the silicon relative to the package. Per-unit or per-core power density is analogous to one of the many thermal resistances comprising the entire network that represents the chip.

Adding cores does indeed increase temperature, because it increases the total amount of power that must be removed. The current primary heat removal path is convection from a heat sink. Although accurate expressions for convective heat transfer are complex, a first-order approximation is:

$$q = hA(T_{sink} - T_{air}) \quad (7)$$

where q is the rate of convective heat transfer, h is the convective heat transfer coefficient that incorporates air speed and various airflow properties, A is the surface area for convection, and to first order we can assume T_{air} is fixed. At steady-state, the total rate of heat P generated in the chip must equal the total rate of heat removed from the chip. If we hold h and A constant, then as we add cores and P exceeds q, T_{sink} must rise to balance the rates so that $P = q$. This increases on-chip temperatures because the sink temperature is like an offset for the other layers from the sink-spreader interface through the chip.

Alternative heat removal mechanisms also warrant consideration. For example, fan speed may be increased, but this approach is often limited by acoustical limits and various board-layout and airflow factors that lead to diminishing returns (e.g. increased pressure drop across a larger heat sink). We can lower the inlet air temperature, but this is not an option in many operating environments (e.g. a home office), or may be extremely costly (e.g. in a large data center). We could also increase heat sink area, but this is where Eq. (7) breaks down. That expression assumes that the heat source is similar in size to the conductive surface. In reality, increasing the heat sink surface area does not improve convective heat transfer in a simple way. Increasing fin height and surface area is limited by airflow constraints that dictate an optimal fin configuration. Increasing the total size of the heat sink (i.e. increasing the area of its base), leads to diminishing returns as the ratio of sink to chip area increases due to limitations on how well the heat can be spread. In the limit, the heat source looks like a point source and further increases in the sink area will have no benefit, as heat will not be able to spread at all to the outermost regions of the heat sink.

With regard to the single thermal resistance in the HotSpot model, adding cores is equivalent to adding current sources connected in parallel to a single resistor, the sink-to-air resistance. The increased current leads to a larger IR drop across this resistor and a proportionally larger heat-sink temperature.

Equations 4, 5, and 6, quantify the contributions from global and local heatup. Figure 2 presents results from validating this simple model against HotSpot, varying the heat sink resistance and fixing the power distribution to test different temperature ranges. The temperature difference between these two models is normally within $3°$.

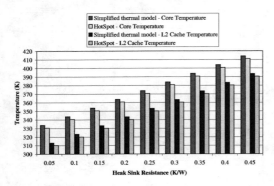

Figure 2. Simplified temperature model validation.

3.2.3 Area Modeling

We assume a 65nm technology. Based on a Power5 die photo, we estimate the baseline core area to be $11.52mm^2$, equivalent to the area of 1MB of L2 cache. We assume each $n/2$ cores share one L2 cache through a crossbar routing over the L2 and estimate the total crossbar area to be $6.25n \cdot mm^2$ [14], where n is the number of cores. As pipeline dimensions vary, we scale the core area to account for additional structures and overhead.

Depth Area Scaling: Given our assumption of fixed logic area independent of pipeline depth, latch area constitutes the primary change in core area as depth varies. Let w_{latch} be the total channel width of all pipeline latch transistors, including local clock distribution circuitry. Let w_{total} be the total channel width for all transistors in the baseline microprocessor, excluding all low-leakage transistors in on-chip memories. Let the latch growth factor (LGF) capture the latch count growth due to logic shape functions. In our analysis, we take the latch ratio (w_{latch}/w_{total}) to be 0.3 and the LGF to be 1.1, assuming superlinear latch growth as pipeline depth increases [26]. Assuming changes in core area are proportional to the total channel width of latch transistors in the pipeline, we scale the portion of core area attributed to latches superlinearly with pipeline depth using Eq. (8).

$$A_{target} = A_{base}\left(1 + \frac{w_{latch}}{w_{total}}\left(\left(\frac{FO4_{target}}{FO4_{base}}\right)^{LGF} - 1\right)\right) \quad (8)$$

Width Area Scaling: Table 4 presents area scaling factors for varying pipeline width. We consider each unit and its underlying macros. To first-order, the core area attributed to the fixed point, floating point, and load store units scale linearly due to clustering. We also assume the area of multi-ported SRAM array structures is wire dominated and scales linearly with the number of ports [23, 24]. This assumption applies to SRAM memories (*e.g.* register files), but may be extended to queues (*e.g.* issue queues), tables (*e.g.* rename mappers), and other structures potentially implemented as an SRAM array.

Note the area of the instruction fetch and decode units (IFU, IDU) are independent of width. Within the fetch unit,

Unit/Macro	2D	4D	8D
FXU	0.5	1.0	2.0
FPU	0.5	1.0	2.0
ISU	0.6	1.0	1.8
IFU	1.0	1.0	1.0
LSU	0.5	1.0	2.0
IDU	1.0	1.0	1.0
Total	**0.7**	**1.0**	**1.7**

Table 4. Pipeline Width Area Scaling.

the instruction cache, instruction TLB, program counter, and branch handling hardware dominate the fetch unit's total power dissipation and, to first-order, these structures are independent of the fetch width. Within the decode unit, the instruction decoder ROM used to crack complex instructions dominates decode power and, to first-order, this ROM is independent of decode width. Also note that only a subset of the macros for the instruction sequencing unit (ISU) scale as width increases, resulting in a sublinear area dependence on width for this unit. For the sequencing unit, only area associated with issue queues and tables for register renaming scale with pipeline width. The total scaling factors, a weighted average of the unit scaling factors, suggest a sublinear relationship between area and width.

3.2.4 DVFS Scaling and Reward Functions

Using a large number of cores may lead to thermal runaway due to high chip power and the positive feedback of leakage power and temperature. We must employ a thermal control mechanism to prevent this behavior and to account for the resulting performance impact. We take this control into consideration by emulating voltage and frequency scaling for steady-state temperature control. Our dynamic simulations do not model the dynamic control aspect of DVFS. Instead, we only simulate workloads in which all cores are occupied — "worst typical-case" workloads that are likely to dictate thermal design. Then, for a given workload, we calculate its steady-state temperature and infer the voltage and frequency settings necessary to prevent the steady-state temperature from pushing the chip above $100°$. These settings could represent the maximum steady-state or nominal settings that are safe for "worst typical-case" workloads, or could represent steady-state V/f values with DVFS when these workloads are running. In reality, the DVFS settings would fluctuate around these values with such workloads, permitting higher settings when fewer cores are occupied.

$$\begin{aligned} T_{thr} - T_{amb} = \; & (P_{global}R_{below} + P_{core}R_{above})V_{sc}^2 F_{sc} \\ & + (L_{global}R_{below} + L_{core}R_{above})V_{sc} \quad (9) \end{aligned}$$

For a given core number n, L2 cache size l, pipeline depth d, and pipeline width w, we obtain the dynamic power consumption and performance from Zauber and the leakage power with Equation 3. For a given temperature threshold, we calculate the voltage and frequency scaling factors from Equation 9, which is deduced from Equation 4, assuming that the leakage power is mainly subthreshold leakage power and is linearly dependent on voltage. Using 0.9V and 2.0 GHz as the nominal voltage and clock frequency and their scaling factors as V_{sc} and F_{sc}, we use a nonlinear voltage/frequency relationship obtained from HSPICE circuit simulation. After determining the voltage and frequency scaling required for thermal control, we calculate our reward functions, BIPS and BIPS^3/W, with Equations 10 and 11.

$$BIPS(n, l, d, w) = BIPS_{base} \cdot F_{sc} \qquad (10)$$

$$\frac{BIPS^3}{W}(n, l, d, w) = \left(\frac{BIPS_{base}{}^3}{P_{dyn} + \frac{P_{leak}}{V_{sc}F_{sc}}} \right) \left(\frac{F_{sc}}{V_{sc}} \right)^2 \quad (11)$$

3.3 Workloads

We characterize all SPEC2000 benchmarks into eight major categories: high IPC(> 0.9) or low IPC(< 0.9), high temperature(peak temperature $> 355K$) or low temperature(peak temperature $< 355K$), floating-point or integer benchmark. We employ eight of the SPEC2000 benchmarks (art, mcf, applu, crafty, gcc, eon, mgrid, swim) as our single thread benchmarks, spanning these categories. We further categorize benchmarks according to their L2 miss ratios, referring to those with high and low miss ratios as memory- and CPU- bound, respectively.

To generate static traces, we compile with the *xlc* compiler and -O3 option. We use Simpoint [7] to identify representative simulation points and generate traces by capturing 100 million instructions beginning at the Simpoint.

For both CPU-bound and memory-bound benchmarks, we use pairs of single-thread benchmarks to form dual-thread benchmarks and replicate these pairs to form multiple benchmark groups of each benchmark category for CMP simulation with more than two cores. We only simulate workloads consisting of a large pool of waiting threads to keep all cores active, representing the "worst typical-case" operation likely to determine physical limits.

4 Results

We present the results from the exploration of a large CMP design space that encompasses core count, pipeline dimensions, and cache size. We consider optimizing for performance (BIPS) and power-performance efficiency (BIPS^3/W) under various area and thermal constraints. In addition to demonstrating the effectiveness of our experimental methodology for exploring large design spaces, our results also quantify significant CMP design trends and demonstrate the need to make balanced design choices.

4.1 Optimal Configurations

Table 5 presents optimal configurations that maximize BIPS and BIPS^3/W for a fixed pipeline depth while Table 6 presents optima for a fixed superscalar width. Configurations are presented for various combinations of area and thermal constraints. The area constraint can take on one of four values: no constraint ("nolimit"), $100mm^2$,

$200mm^2$, or $400mm^2$. Similarly, packaging assumptions and hence thermal constraints can take on one of three values: no constraint (NT), low constraint (LR=0.1, low thermal resistance, i.e. aggressive, high-cost thermal solution), and high constraint (HR=0.5, high thermal resistance, i.e. constrained thermal solution, such as found in a laptop). The tables differentiate between CPU- and memory-bound benchmarks and specify the required voltage and frequency ratios needed to satisfy thermal constraints.

Figures 3–5 present performance trade-offs between core count, L2 cache size, and pipeline dimensions for a $400mm^2$ chip subject to various thermal constraints.

4.1.1 No Constraints

In the absence of area and thermal constraints (no-limit+NT+CPU, nolimit+NT+MEMORY), the throughput maximizing configuration for both CPU- and memory-bound benchmarks employs the largest L2 cache and number of cores. Although the optimal pipeline width for all benchmarks is eight (8W), CPU-bound benchmarks favor deeper pipelines (12FO4) to take advantage of fewer memory stalls and higher instruction level parallelism. Conversely, memory-bound benchmarks favor relatively shallow pipelines (18FO4).

For BIPS^3/W, the optimal depth shifts to shallower pipelines; 18FO4 and 30FO4 delays per stage are optimal for CPU and memory-bound benchmarks, respectively. The optimal width shifts to shallower, narrower pipelines for memory-bound benchmarks due to the relatively high rate of memory stalls and low instruction level parallelism.

4.1.2 Area Constraints

Considering area constraints ($\{100,200,400\}$+NT+*), we find core number and L2 cache size tend to decrease as area constraints are imposed. Although both techniques are applied in certain cases (100+NT+CPU, 100+NT+MEMORY), decreasing the cache size is naturally the most effective approach to meet area constraints for CPU-bound benchmarks, while decreasing the number of cores is most effective for memory-bound benchmarks.

With regard to pipeline dimensions, we find the optimal width decreases to 2W for all area constraints on memory-bound benchmarks (*+NT+MEMORY) except 100+NT+MEMORY. According to the area models in Section 3.2.3, changes in depth scale the latch area (only 30% of total area) whereas changes in width scale the area associated with functional units, queues, and other width-sensitive structures. Thus, shifting to shallower widths provides greater area impact (Table 5). Although pipeline depths may shift from 12 to 18/24FO4 delays per stage, they are never reduced to 30FO4 delays per stage to meet area constraints (Table 6).

As in the case without constraints, the bar plots in Figure 3, which vary pipeline depth, shows CPU-bound

	BIPS					$BIPS^3/W$				
	L2 (MB)	Core Number	Pipeline Width	Voltage Scaling	Frequency Scaling	L2 (MB)	Core Number	Pipeline Width	Voltage Scaling	Frequency Scaling
nolimit+NT+CPU	32	20	8	1.00	1.00	16	20	8	1.00	1.00
nolimit+LR+CPU	8	20	4	0.75	0.63	8	20	4	0.75	0.63
nolimit+HR+CPU	2	18	2	0.59	0.39	2	16	2	0.61	0.43
400+NT+CPU	4	20	4	1.00	1.00	4	20	4	1.00	1.00
400+LR+CPU	4	20	4	0.75	0.64	2	20	4	0.76	0.65
400+HR+CPU	2	18	2	0.59	0.39	2	16	2	0.61	0.43
200+NT+CPU	2	10	4	1.00	1.00	2	10	4	1.00	1.00
200+LR+CPU	2	10	4	0.87	0.80	2	12	2	0.90	0.85
200+HR+CPU	2	12	2	0.67	0.51	2	12	2	0.67	0.51
100+NT+CPU	2	4	4	1.00	1.00	2	4	4	1.00	1.00
100+LR+CPU	2	4	4	0.97	0.96	2	4	4	0.97	0.96
100+HR+CPU	2	4	4	0.79	0.70	2	4	4	0.79	0.70
nolimit+NT+MEMORY	32	20	8	1.00	1.00	32	20	4	1.00	1.00
nolimit+LR+MEMORY	16	20	4	0.73	0.61	16	20	4	0.73	0.61
nolimit+HR+MEMORY	8	10	2	0.62	0.45	8	10	2	0.62	0.45
400+NT+MEMORY	16	16	2	1.00	1.00	16	16	2	1.00	1.00
400+LR+MEMORY	16	12	4	0.81	0.73	16	16	2	0.81	0.72
400+HR+MEMORY	8	10	2	0.62	0.45	8	10	2	0.62	0.45
200+NT+MEMORY	8	8	2	1.00	1.00	8	8	2	1.00	1.00
200+LR+MEMORY	8	6	4	0.93	0.90	8	8	2	0.92	0.88
200+HR+MEMORY	8	8	2	0.66	0.51	8	8	2	0.66	0.51
100+NT+MEMORY	2	4	4	1.00	1.00	4	4	2	1.00	1.00
100+LR+MEMORY	2	4	4	1.00	1.00	4	4	2	0.98	0.98
100+HR+MEMORY	2	4	4	0.81	0.73	4	4	2	0.81	0.73

Table 5. Optimal Configurations with Varying Pipeline Width, Fixed Depth (18FO4)

	BIPS					$BIPS^3/W$				
	L2 (MB)	Core Number	Pipeline Depth	Voltage Scaling	Frequency Scaling	L2 (MB)	Core Number	Pipeline Depth	Voltage Scaling	Frequency Scaling
nolimit+NT+CPU	32	20	12	1.00	1.00	16	20	18	1.00	1.00
nolimit+LR+CPU	8	20	18	0.75	0.63	8	20	18	0.75	0.63
nolimit+HR+CPU	2	14	24	0.62	0.44	2	14	24	0.62	0.44
400+NT+CPU	4	18	12	1.00	1.00	4	20	18	1.00	1.00
400+LR+CPU	4	20	18	0.75	0.64	2	20	24	0.85	0.78
400+HR+CPU	2	14	24	0.62	0.44	2	14	24	0.62	0.44
200+NT+CPU	2	10	18	1.00	1.00	2	10	18	1.00	1.00
200+LR+CPU	2	10	18	0.87	0.80	2	10	24	0.97	0.95
200+HR+CPU	2	10	18	0.63	0.45	2	10	24	0.69	0.55
100+NT+CPU	2	4	18	1.00	1.00	2	4	18	1.00	1.00
100+LR+CPU	2	4	18	0.97	0.96	2	4	18	0.97	0.96
100+HR+CPU	2	4	18	0.79	0.70	2	4	18	0.79	0.70
nolimit+NT+MEMORY	32	20	18	1.00	1.00	32	20	30	1.00	1.00
nolimit+LR+MEMORY	16	20	30	0.85	0.78	16	20	30	0.85	0.78
nolimit+HR+MEMORY	8	10	30	0.65	0.48	8	10	30	0.65	0.48
400+NT+MEMORY	16	12	18	1.00	1.00	16	12	30	1.00	1.00
400+LR+MEMORY	16	12	30	0.94	0.91	8	12	30	1.00	1.00
400+HR+MEMORY	8	10	30	0.65	0.48	8	10	30	0.65	0.48
200+NT+MEMORY	8	6	24	1.00	1.00	8	6	30	1.00	1.00
200+LR+MEMORY	8	6	24	1.00	1.00	8	6	30	1.00	1.00
200+HR+MEMORY	4	6	30	0.83	0.75	4	6	30	0.83	0.75
100+NT+MEMORY	2	4	24	1.00	1.00	2	4	30	1.00	1.00
100+LR+MEMORY	2	4	24	1.00	1.00	2	4	30	1.00	1.00
100+HR+MEMORY	2	4	30	0.96	0.95	2	4	30	0.96	0.95

Table 6. Optimal Configurations with Varying Pipeline Depth, Fixed Width (4D)

benchmarks favor deeper pipelines (4MB/12FO4/4 is optimal) and memory-bound benchmarks favor shallower pipelines (16MB/18FO4/4 or 16MB/24FO4/4 are optimal). The line plots in Figures 3–4 also present performance for varying widths for modest thermal constraints. In this case, the optimal pipeline width is 4W for a fixed depth of 18FO4 delays per stage.

4.1.3 Thermal Constraints

We find thermal constraints (nolimit+{NT,LR,HR}+*), also shift optimal configurations to fewer and simpler cores. The optimal core number and L2 size tends to decrease with heat sink effectiveness. For example, the op-

timum for nolimit+HR+MEMORY is 8MB L2 cache and 10 cores. Again, CPU-bound benchmarks favor decreasing cache size to meet thermal constraints while memory-bound benchmarks favor decreasing the number of cores.

Figure 5 also illustrates the impact of global heating on optimal pipeline configurations. As the number of cores increase for CPU-bound benchmarks, the optimal delay per stage increases by 6FO4 (i.e., from 18 to 24FO4) when twelve cores reside on a single chip. The increasing core count increases chip temperature, leading to shallower pipelines that lower power dissipation, lower global temperature, and meet thermal constraints.

Simpler cores, characterized by smaller pipeline dimensions, tend to consume less power and, therefore, miti-

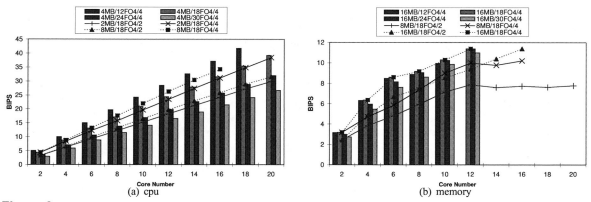

Figure 3. Performance of various configurations with chip area constraint at 400mm^2 (without thermal control).

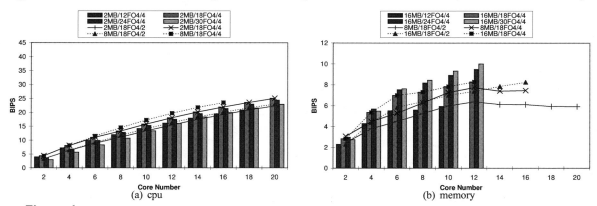

Figure 4. Performance of various configurations with chip area constraint at 400mm^2 (R = 0.1 heat sink).

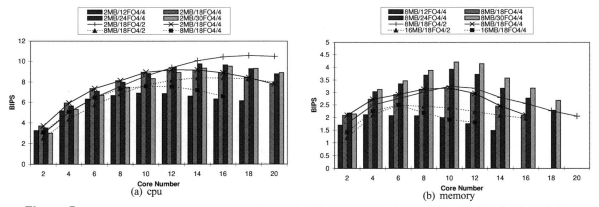

Figure 5. Performance of various configurations with chip area constraint at 400mm^2 (R = 0.5 heat sink).

gate the core's thermal impact. In particular, the optimal pipeline depth shifts to 24 and 30FO4 delays per stage for CPU and memory-bound benchmarks, respectively, when comparing nolimit+NT+* to nolimit+HR+* in Table 6. Similarly, the optimal width shifts to 2W for all benchmarks when comparing the same entries in Table 5.

Figures 4–5 show imposing thermal constraints shifts the optimal depth to shallower design points. The performance for CPU and memory-bound benchmarks are maximized for 18-24 and 24-30FO4 delays per stage, respectively. Pipeline power dissipation increases superlinearly

with depth while pipeline area increases sublinearly according to Section 3.2.3. Thus, growth in power dissipation exceeds area growth and the overall power density increases with depth. Thus, optimal designs must shift to shallower pipelines to meet thermal constraints. Similarly, more aggressive thermal constraints, shown in Figure 5 shifts the optimal width to the narrower 2W, especially as the number of cores increases. These results also suggest thermal constraints will have a greater impact on pipeline configurations than area constraints.

23

4.1.4 Area and Thermal Comparison

Comparing the impact of thermal constraints (no-limit+NT+* versus nolimit+HR+*) to the impact of area constraints (nolimit+NT+* versus 100+NT+*) demonstrates larger shifts towards smaller pipeline dimensions. In general, thermal constraints exert a greater influence on the optimal design configurations.

Applying a more stringent area constraint reduces the trend towards simpler cores. With a smaller chip area, resulting in fewer cores and smaller caches, total power dissipated and the need for thermal control is diminished. As this occurs, pressure towards simpler cores with smaller pipeline dimensions also fades.

4.1.5 Depth and Width Comparison

Consider a baseline configuration 2MB/18FO4/4W. As thermal constraints are imposed, the configuration may either shift to a shallower core (2MB/24FO4/4W) or shift to a narrower core (2MB/18FO4/2W). Since changes in width scale area for both functional units and many queue structures, whereas changes in depth only scale area for latches between stages, width reductions have a greater area impact relative to depth reductions. Thus, the 2MB/24FO4/4W core is a larger core relative to the 2MB/18FO4/2W and exhibits lower dynamic power density. However, the smaller 2MB/18FO4/2W core benefits from less leakage power per core and, consequently, less global power (since dynamic power dissipation is comparable for both cores).

From our temperature models in Section 3.2.2, total power output, P_{global}, has greater thermal impact for a chip with a poor heat sink (i.e., high thermal resistance, $R_{heatsink}$). Similarly, the thermal impact is dominated by the local power density, P_{core}, for a chip with a good heat sink. In this case, the transfer of heat from the silicon substrate to the spreader dominates thermal effects. Thus, to minimize chip heatup, it is advantageous to reduce width and global power in the context of a poor heat sink and advantageous to reduce depth and local power density in the context of a more expensive heat sink.

4.2 Hazards of Neglecting Thermal Constraints

Thermal constraints should be considered early in the design process. If a chip is designed without thermal constraints in mind, designers must later cut voltage and clock frequency to meet thermal constraints. The resulting voltage and frequency, and hence performance, will likely be cut more severely than if a thermally-aware configuration were selected from the beginning. Figure 6 demonstrates the slowdown incurred by choosing a non-thermally optimal design with voltage and frequency scaling over the thermally-optimal design. The y-axis plots the thermal-aware optimal performance minus the performance of the configuration without thermal considerations, normalized to the optimal performance. This figure summarizes the slowdown for all combinations of die sizes, heat-sink configurations, application classes, and for both pipeline depth and width optimizations. The average difference for varying depth is around 12-17% and 7-16% for varying width.

However, we find that for large, $400mm^2$ chips, omitting thermal consideration may result in huge performance degradations. For example, the 400+HR+CPU and 400+HR+MEMORY configurations result in a $40\% - 90\%$ difference in performance for BIPS and BIPS^3/W. As area constraints are relaxed, the optimal point tends to include more cores and larger L2 caches. However, if the chip has severe thermal problems, DVFS scaling must scale aggressively to maintain thermal limits, into a region with significant non-linear voltage and frequency scaling, producing large performance losses. For smaller chips with fewer cores and smaller L2 caches, the difference may be negligible because there are very few configurations to choose from. As future CMP server-class microprocessors target $400mm^2$ chips with more than eight cores, it will be essential to perform thermal analysis in the early-stages of the design process when decisions about the number and complexity of cores are being performed.

4.3 DVFS Versus Core Sizing

In meeting thermal constraints for large CMP machines where global heat-up and total chip power is a concern, designers may be forced to choose among implementing fewer cores, smaller L2 caches, or employing aggressive DVFS scaling. We find DVFS superior to removing cores for CPU-bound applications as long as reductions in frequency are met by at least an equal reduction in dynamic and leakage power. Additional cores for CPU-bound applications provide linear increases in performance with near-linear increases in power dissipation. However, because of the strongly non-linear relationship between voltage scaling and clock frequency at low voltages, voltage scaling at some point stops providing super-linear power savings to make up for the performance (clock-frequency) loss. At this point, designers must consider removing cores and L2 cache from the design to meet thermal constraints.

For example, a chip with 30% leakage power no longer achieves super-linear power-performance benefit from DVFS scaling after roughly 0.55x Vdd scaling; frequency of the chip drops to 0.18x and power dissipation also to 0.18x (dominated by leakage power, which only scales linearly with Vdd). Further reductions in Vdd lead to greater performance loss than power savings. (In future process technologies, more than 0.55x Vdd scaling may also approach reliability limits of conventional CMOS circuits.)

Figure 5 shows an example of this behavior with the 2MB/18FO4/4W design. When this design exceeds 14 cores, further increases in core count lead to performance degradation. Vdd scaling has exceeded 0.55x, and the additional DVFS scaling necessary to meet thermal constraints costs more performance than is gained by adding these additional cores. On the other hand, the 2MB/18FO4/2W design only requires Vdd scaling of

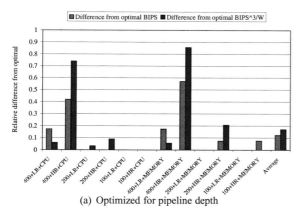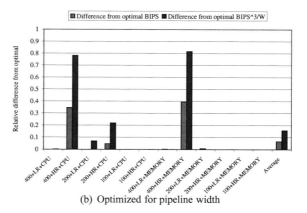

(a) Optimized for pipeline depth   (b) Optimized for pipeline width

Figure 6. The difference from the optimal when no thermal consideration is made in early design.

0.57x out to 20 cores, which is why this design is attractive even with the additional cores.

Similar analyses hold for memory-bound applications. In this case, the tradeoff is more complex, because the performance benefit from adding cores may be non-linear.

4.4 Accommodating Heterogeneous Workloads

Figures 3–5 also highlight the difficulty of accommodating a range of workload types under area constraints. This is less of a concern when looking at a small number of cores like most prior studies. Prior studies have also neglected the role of pipeline dimensions, which we find to play a major role. And for large numbers of cores, radically different configurations are possible.

CPU-bound and memory-bound workloads have different, incompatible optima. The performance loss from using the CPU-bound optimum with the memory-bound workload and vice-versa is severe, 37–41% and 26–53% respectively, depending on thermal constraints. Even if we try to identify compromise configurations, it is surprising how poorly they perform for one or the other workload. Of course, the best compromise depends on how heavily each workload is weighted. We tried to minimize the performance loss on both workloads.

With no thermal limits, the best configuration is 16 4-wide, 18FO4-deep cores with 8MB of cache, incurring an 18% penalty for the CPU-bound workload. If we turn off 8 cores, it incurs 10% penalty for the memory-bound workload. Moving to 16MB improves memory-bound performance, but hurts CPU-bound performance because it sacrifices 8 cores with an area constraint of 400 mm^2.

With thermal limits, the optimal configurations begin to converge, as the maximum possible number of cores and the L2 cache size is constrained, as the BIPS benefit of extra cores is reduced for CPU-bound benchmarks, and as the benefit of additional cache lines is reduced for memory-bound benchmarks. For low thermal resistance, the best compromise is 18 4-wide cores and 8 MB. This incurs only a 4% performance loss for CPU-bound benchmark and a 10% loss for the memory-bound case. With high thermal

resistance, the best compromise is 14 4-wide, 30FO4-deep cores with 8 MB of cache. Turning off 4 cores we reach the optimal configuration for memory-bound case, but this configuration incurs 12% penalty for the CPU-bound case.

Although the discrepancy between the needs of CPU- and memory-bound workloads narrows with increasing thermal constraints, some penalty seems inevitable, because CPU-bound benchmarks prefer more cores while memory-bound benchmarks prefer larger L2 caches. It is interesting to note that we do not see a simple heuristic for identifying good compromise configurations.

5 Conclusions

Our major conclusions include:

- Joint optimization across multiple design variables is necessary. Even pipeline depth, typically fixed in architecture studies, may impact core area and power enough to change the optimal core count. Optimizing without thermal constraints and then scaling to a thermal envelope leads to dramatically inferior designs compared to those obtained from including thermal constraints in the initial optimization.

- Thermal constraints appear to dominate other physical constraints like pin-bandwidth and power delivery. Once thermal constraints are met, at least within the design space we studied, power and throughput have been throttled sufficiently to fall safely within current off-chip I/O bandwidth capabilities and ITRS power-delivery projections.

- Thermal constraints tend to favor shallower pipelines and narrower cores, and tend to reduce the optimal number of cores and L2 cache size. Nevertheless, even under severe thermal constraints, additional cores benefit throughput despite aggressive reductions in operating voltage and frequency. This is true until performance gains from an additional core is negated by the impact of the additional voltage and frequency scaling required of all the cores. This inflection occurs at approximately 55% of the nominal Vdd, well into the range of non-linear frequency scaling (18% of nominal!).

- For aggressive cooling solutions, reducing power density is at least as important as reducing total power. For low-cost cooling solutions, however, reducing total power is more important because raising power dissipation (even if power density is the same) raises a chip's temperature.

These results raise a range of questions for future work, such as the need for adaptive chip architectures that can dynamically accommodate the full range of workloads, from heavily CPU-bound to heavily memory-bound. Examining how our findings here might change with other workloads (e.g., scientific parallel applications or communication-heavy commercial server workloads) and other architectures (e.g., in-order processors) is future work. Further research on L2/L3/Memory interconnect/ hierarchy for CMP and on the impact of clock propagation on CMP throughput and power is also necessary.

While CMPs may optimize for throughput-oriented application workloads at the expense of single-thread performance, single-thread performance will still be an important consideration for many application domains. Addressing single-thread performance will likely require additional design tradeoffs. This does not necessarily require aggressive superscalar cores running at full voltage and frequency. Future research in this direction must consider speculative multithreading, heterogeneous cores, dynamic core adaptation, run-ahead execution/scouting, and so forth.

Acknowledgments

This work was funded in part by the National Science Foundation under grant nos. CAREER CCR-0133634, CAREER CCF-0448313, CCR-0306404, CCF-0429765, a Faculty Partnership Award from IBM T.J. Watson, a gift from Intel Corp., and an Excellence Award from the Univ. Fund for Excellence in Science and Technology. We would also like to thank Dee A. B. Weikle and the anonymous reviewers for their helpful feedback.

References

[1] D. Brooks, P. Bose, V. Srinivasan, M. Gschwind, P. Emma, and M. Rosenfield. Microarchitecture-level power-performance analysis: the powertimer approach. *IBM J. Research and Development*, 47(5), 2003.

[2] D. Brooks, V. Tiwari, and M. Martonosi. Wattch: a framework for architectural-level power analysis and optimizations. In *Proc. of the 27th Int'l Symp. on Computer Architecture*, Jun. 2000.

[3] P. Chaparro, J. Gonzalez, and A. Gonzalez. Thermal-aware clustered microarchitectures. In *Proc. of the Int'l Conf. on Computer Design*, Oct. 2004.

[4] S. Chaudhry, P. Caprioli, S. Yip, and M. Tremblay. High performance throughput computing. *IEEE Micro*, 25(3):32–45, May/June 2005.

[5] M. Ekman and P. Stenstrom. Performance and power impact of issue-width in chip-multiprocessor cores. In *Proc. of the Int'l Conf. on Parallel Processing*, Oct. 2003.

[6] A. El-Moursy, R. Garg, D. Albonesi, and S. Dwarkadas. Partitioning multi-threaded processors with a large number of threads. In *Proc. of the 2005 Int'l Symp. on Performance Analysis of Systems and Software*, Mar. 2005.

[7] G. Hamerly, E. Perelman, J. Lau, and B. Calder. Simpoint 3.0: Faster and more flexible program analysis. In *Proc. of the Wkshp on Modeling, Benchmarking and Simulation*, June 2005.

[8] A. Hartstein and T. R. Puzak. The optimum pipeline depth for a microprocessor. In *Proc. of the 29th Int'l Symp. on Computer Architecture*, pages 7–13, May 2002.

[9] M. S. Hrishikesh et al. The optimal logic depth per pipeline stage is 6 to 8 FO4 inverter delays. In *Proc. of the 29th Int'l Symp. on Computer Architecture*, pages 14–24, May 2002.

[10] J. Huh, D. Burger, and S. W. Keckler. Exploring the design space of future CMPs. In *Proc. of the Int'l Conf. on Parallel Architectures and Compilation Techniques*, Sep. 2001.

[11] T. Karkhanis and J. E. Smith. A first-order superscalar processor model. In *Proc. of the 31st Int'l Symp. on Computer Architecture*, Jun. 2004.

[12] P. Kongetira, K. Aingaran, and K. Olukotun. Niagara: A 32-way multithreaded sparc processor. *IEEE Micro*, 25(2):21–29, Mar./Apr. 2005.

[13] B. Kumar and E. S. Davidson. Computer system design using a hierarchical approach to performance evaluation. In *Communications of the ACM, 23(9)*, Sep. 1980.

[14] R. Kumar, V. Zyuban, and D. M. Tullsen. Interconnections in multi-core architectures: Understanding mechanisms, overheads and scaling. In *The 32nd Int'l Symp. on Computer Architecture*, June 2005.

[15] S. R. Kunkel, R. J. Eickemeyer, M. H. Lipasti, T. J. Mullins, B. O.Krafka, H. Rosenberg, S. P. Vander-Wiel, P. L. Vitale, and L. D. Whitley. A performance methodology for commercial servers. In *IBM J. of Research and Development, 44(6)*, 2000.

[16] B. Lee and D. Brooks. Effects of pipeline complexity on SMT/CMP power-performance efficiency. In *Proc. of the Workshop on Complexity Effective Design*, Jun. 2005.

[17] J. Li and J. F. Martinez. Power-performance implications of thread-level parallelism on chip multiprocessors. In *Proc. of the 2005 Int'l Symp. on Performance Analysis of Systems and Software*, pages 124–34, Mar. 2005.

[18] Y. Li, D. Brooks, Z. Hu, and K. Skadron. Performance, energy and thermal considerations for SMT and CMP architectures: Extended discussion and results. Technical Report CS-2004-32, Univ. of Virginia Dept. of Computer Science, Oct. 2004.

[19] M. Moudgill, J. Wellman, and J. Moreno. Environment for powerpc microarchitecture exploration. *IEEE Micro*, 19(3), May/Jun. 1999.

[20] K. Ramani, N. Muralimanohar, and R. Balasubramonian. Microarchitectural techniques to reduce interconnect power in clustered processors. In *Proc. of the Workshop on Complexity Effective Design*, Jun. 2004.

[21] K. Skadron, K. Sankaranarayanan, S. Velusamy, D. Tarjan, M. R. Stan, and W. Huang. Temperature-aware microarchitecture: Modeling and implementation. *ACM Trans. on Architecture and Code Optimization*, 1(1), Mar. 2004.

[22] E. Sprangle and D. Carmean. Increasing processor performance by implementing deeper pipelines. In *Proc. of the 29th Int'l Symp. on Computer Architecture*, pages 25–34, May 2002.

[23] M. Tremblay, B. Joy, and K. Shin. A three dimensional register file for superscalar processors. In *Proc. of the 28th Hawaii Int'l Conf. on System Sciences*, 1995.

[24] N. Weste and D. Harris. CMOS VLSI design: A circuit and systems perspective. Addison-Wesley, 2005.

[25] V. Zyuban. *Inherently lower-power high-performance superscalar architectures*. PhD thesis, Univ. of Notre Dame, Mar. 2000.

[26] V. Zyuban, D. Brooks, V. Srinivasan, M. Gschwind, P. Bose, P. Strenski, and P. Emma. Integrated analysis of power and performance for pipelined microprocessors. *IEEE Transactions on Computers*, 53(8), Aug. 2004.

Exploiting Parallelism and Structure to Accelerate the Simulation of Chip Multi-processors

David A. Penry[†]   Daniel Fay[‡]   David Hodgdon[‡]   Ryan Wells[†]
Graham Schelle[‡]   David I. August[†]   Dan Connors[‡]

[†]Princeton University
Dept. of Computer Science
35 Olden St.
Princeton, NJ 08540

[‡]University of Colorado at Boulder
Dept. of Electrical and Computer Engineering
Engineering Center
Boulder, CO 80309

Abstract

Simulation is an important means of evaluating new microarchitectures. Current trends toward chip multiprocessors (CMPs) try the ability of designers to develop efficient simulators. CMP simulation speed can be improved by exploiting parallelism in the CMP simulation model. This may be done by either running the simulation on multiple processors or by integrating multiple processors into the simulation to replace simulated processors. Doing so usually requires tedious manual parallelization or re-design to encapsulate processors.

Both problems can be avoided by generating the simulator from a concurrent, structural model of the CMP. Such a model not only resembles hardware, making it easy to understand and use, but also provides sufficient information to automatically parallelize the simulator without requiring manual model changes. Furthermore, individual components of the model such as processors may be replaced with equivalent hardware without requiring repartitioning.

This paper presents techniques to perform automated simulator parallelization and hardware integration for CMP structural models. We show that automated parallelization can achieve an 7.60 speedup for a 16-processor CMP model on a conventional 4-processor shared-memory multiprocessor. We demonstrate the power of hardware integration by integrating eight hardware PowerPC cores into a CMP model, achieving a speedup of up to 5.82.

1. Introduction

Microarchitects develop and use simulators to evaluate their ideas. Developing a simulator requires careful tradeoffs among speed, development time, and accuracy. The on-going trend towards tying multiple processor cores on a single die into a chip multi-processor (CMP) makes determining these tradeoffs even more challenging. As the number of cores and the complexity of their interconnect increases, simulators become larger, more complex, and slower.

One means to accelerate CMP simulation is to exploit the parallelism inherent in the CMP. This can be done in two ways. First, the simulator can be parallelized to run on multiple host processors. Doing so is often difficult, requiring manual parallelization of simulator code not originally written to be parallelized. Second, real processors can be used to replace simulated processors in the CMP simulator. In this case, memory operations from the processors are simulated, while instructions are directly executed. This requires manual re-design of the simulator code to fully encapsulate the processors.

In this paper we show that the difficulties involved in manual parallelization and processor integration can be alleviated if the simulator is not written by a simulator designer, but instead is generated from a concurrent, structural model of the CMP, such as those used in [19] or [8]. Model structure and parallelism may be exploited to achieve automated parallelization and simple replacement of components of the model with actual processors. This ability to exploit parallelism comes in addition to the benefits of reduced development time and reduced modeling error previously shown[19, 16] for such models.

A microarchitectural model in a concurrent structural modeling framework consists of a collection of components. These components execute concurrently and are connected together by signals, which form the principal means of inter-component communication. The user instantiates, parameterizes, and connects components to create the model. The framework then combines the instantiation and connection information with the components' behavioral code to generate a simulator for the model. The concurrent structural modeling framework used and modified in this work is the Liberty Simulation Environment (LSE)[19]. LSE provides explicit support for structural modeling, an extensible library of components, and language features designed to make parameterization, instantiation, and library creation easier. One unusual feature of LSE is that it treats all components as "black boxes": it attempts no analysis of how a component operates, allowing the possibility of the component using hardware to calculate its outputs.

A structural model is a natural candidate for parallelization, as the components in the model are already designed to execute concurrently. This execution must be carefully scheduled to achieve speed improvement. The scheduling problem is similar to that of instruction scheduling, but cache effects and the coordination of accesses to shared state are important additional factors. We describe modifications to parallel scheduling algorithms to deal with these factors. We evaluate automated parallelization on a family of chip multi-processor models and find that automated simulator parallelization achieves a modest speedup of 2.27 with 4 threads for a 4-way CMP model, but a much larger speedup of 7.60 with 4 threads for a 16-way CMP.

The integration of hardware components is made feasible because the structural nature of the system allows portions of the model to be replaced without affecting the remainder of the model. We describe the hardware and software support necessary to integrate an arbitrary piece of hardware into a model. In addition, hardware component integration increases accuracy, obviates the need to model available components, and enables an incremental architecture-to-implementation design flow. We integrate eight PowerPC 405 cores realized in Field-Programmable Gate Arrays (FPGAs) into a CMP model described in LSE, achieving a speedup of 5.82 with perfect caches and 1.31 with a detailed simulated memory hierarchy and interconnect.

Section 2 explains how automated simulator parallelization is carried out, while Section 3 evaluates the parallelization. Section 4 explains integration of hardware components, and Section 5 presents the results of this integration. Section 6 concludes.

2. Automated simulator parallelization

Simulator parallelization is one way to take advantage of parallelism in a CMP simulator. Parallelization, whether manual or automated, requires that the simulator be partitioned into tasks to be run concurrently. It then requires that these tasks be either scheduled or synchronized such that tasks wait for their inputs to become available and that tasks which could simultaneously access shared data do not run concurrently. Furthermore, the scheduling of tasks onto threads must be efficient, minimizing the time threads spend

waiting, if good performance is to be achieved. Meeting these requirements manually is a difficult problem when a simulator's form obscures potential tasks and data sharing. In the following subsections we describe how automated parallel code generation for structural models deals with each of these requirements, obviating the need for manual parallelization.

2.1. Task formation

The general flow of an LSE simulator is shown in Figure 1(a). After an initialization step, control enters the "main loop". For each time step, there are four substeps: PHASE_START, PHASE, PHASE_END, and between-cycle book-keeping. As time steps generally correspond to a single clock cycle of the simulated machine, the substeps can be described in terms of state machine behavior. During PHASE_START, components produce output signals dependent only upon state (i.e., Moore state machine outputs). During PHASE they produce outputs depending on inputs and possibly state (Mealy state machine outputs). During PHASE_END, they update their state.

Within each substep, the framework invokes methods for each substep from each of the component instances. The user does *not* have control of the order in which these invocations are made within the substep and must therefore write components which do not require any particular invocation order to work correctly. The method invocations made during the substeps are the tasks used in the automated parallelization.

The ordering of component method invocations during PHASE_START and PHASE_END is arbitrary as no communication takes place during these substeps. During PHASE, however, signal values may be written and read concurrently, requiring an invocation order that obeys a formal model of computation defining the semantics of communication and concurrent execution. The model used by LSE is known as the Heterogeneous Synchronous Reactive (HSR) model[7]. While the details are beyond the scope of this paper, it is possible to create a static execution schedule of method invocations (possibly repeating some invocations) which guarantees that the collection of signal values reaches a fixed point in each cycle[7, 15]. The resulting schedule is a directed acyclic graph of invocations which may be executed in any valid reverse topological ordering.

2.2. Shared state discovery

There are four ways in which data can be legally shared between component instances in LSE:

Through signals All signals are part of the model structure and can be analyzed by the framework to determine

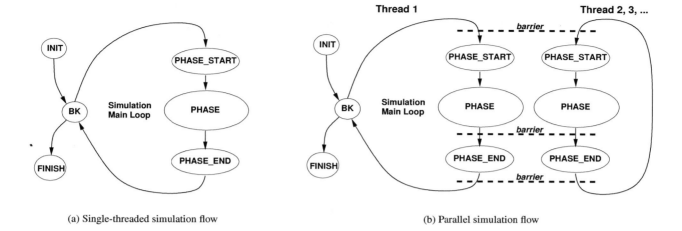

(a) Single-threaded simulation flow

(b) Parallel simulation flow

Figure 1. Simulation flows

data dependencies. Note that components are written with an *atomicity* assumption: no input signals examined by a component method may change while the method is running. This constraint is represented as an automatically generated *conflict* between potential producers and consumers of signals.

Through user-defined "runtime variables" Data dependencies through these variables within PHASE must satisfy the same producer-consumer relationship as some signal and thus need no additional analysis. Data dependencies within PHASE_END and PHASE_START are not allowed.

Through library calls Data dependencies through library calls must obey the same restrictions as data dependencies through runtime variables. Non-thread-safe library calls require that the framework avoid simultaneous calls to the library. As not all library calls are part of the structural description (due to the black-box nature of component code), some minimal user input is required to mark conflicts between the component methods making these calls.

Internally A component instance shares data internally with other invocations of its own methods. This constraint is represented as an automatically generated conflict between method invocations of the same instance.

2.3. Synchronization

The structure of the simulator once automated parallelization has been carried out is shown in Figure 1(b).

The PHASE_START and PHASE substeps are parallelized together, while PHASE_END is parallelized separately; barriers (represented by heavy dashed lines) are used to separate each parallelized section.

Cross-thread data dependencies are respected by automatically adding binary semaphores to indicate when data is available. The framework code waits on these semaphores before invoking consumer component methods and sets the semaphores after invoking producer component methods. Redundant semaphores are removed.

Mutual exclusion of component methods which have a conflict is accomplished by automatically acquiring and releasing locks around the conflicting invocations. Most potential locks are removed through a lock elision algorithm which looks at the cross-thread data dependencies to determine whether two invocations may truly run in parallel.

2.4. Scheduling

The input to the scheduling problem for PHASE_START and PHASE is the directed acyclic graph (DAG) of component instance method invocations produced as the single-thread schedule augmented with nodes for PHASE_START invocations and edges causing PHASE_START method invocations to precede other method invocations in the same component instance. For PHASE_END the input is a simple DAG of invocations with very few edges (there are actually two subsubsteps of PHASE_END which must proceed in order and the edges are used to enforce that).

Scheduling of a task DAG across multiple processors is a well-known problem for which many heuristics have been developed. We describe four strategies for performing this scheduling:

2.4.1 List schedulers

Our first strategy (called **LIST**) is a list scheduler similar to that of Yu[22]. A priority queue of tasks whose predecessor nodes have all been scheduled is maintained. The highest priority task is removed from the queue and scheduled in the earliest available time slot not violating data dependencies in any thread; the queue is then updated. This is repeated until the queue is empty. Priority is the length of the longest directed path originating at the task, where length is the sum of the (estimated) execution times of each task.

List scheduling takes into account load balancing and critical path length. However, it ignores two very important aspects of the scheduling problem for automated parallelization. First, it fails to take into account the potential for conflicts which prevent two tasks from executing concurrently. Second, cache effects on signal values and other data cause the execution times of tasks to depend heavily upon how other tasks accessing the same data (particularly tasks from the same component instance) have been scheduled.

Our second strategy (**LOCKAVOID**) reduces conflicts by actively avoiding locking during the thread selection step of the list scheduler. Tasks are scheduled onto the earliest time available on a thread which does not result in a lock being needed. If all threads would require a lock, the task is *skewed* in time to reduce the likelihood of lock contention; it is purposefully scheduled later than the earliest possible time if that time would be "too close" to a time when the lock is planned to be owned by another thread. Lower priority tasks can then be placed in the resulting schedule hole.

List scheduling has been extended in [22] to include communication costs, but this extension is not appropriate for scheduling around cache misses. The reason is that cache misses require the receiving thread of the communication to initiate the transfer and effectively block the receiving thread. Communication cost extensions to list scheduling assume that the sender initiates the transfer and that useful work may be done by the receiver during the communication time.

2.4.2 Clustering

An alternative to list scheduling is to make thread assignments by trying to *cluster* related tasks together in the same thread. Such an approach can be used to improve cache locality of signal values and other data. After clustering, a list scheduler is run with the thread assignments constrained to those chosen by the clustering strategy; lock skewing as previously described is used to reduce lock conflicts.

Our third strategy (**INSTCLUSTER**) groups all method invocations from the same component instance into one cluster. Clusters are then combined based upon the signal bandwidth between them, starting with the highest band-width pair of clusters. Signal bandwidth between clusters is updated as they are combined. This combination continues until there are either as many clusters as there are threads or a minimum bandwidth value has been reached. The remaining clusters are then mapped onto threads in a load-balanced fashion. Note that this strategy takes into account probable cache effects and load balancing, but not the critical path.

Our final strategy (**IDSC**) is derived from Dominant Sequence Clustering (DSC)[21]. DSC attempts to cluster tasks on the critical path together for an infinitely parallel machine, observing that the critical path changes as decisions are made and threads become utilized. It takes into account communication costs, load balancing, and the critical path. It then assigns clusters to threads. While as noted for list scheduling, communication costs do not model cache effects well for the purpose of determining final schedules, they may be helpful for determining the estimated path lengths required in DSC. We therefore set the communication costs to be the the number of input signals referenced by the task. We also modify the assignment phase to be cache-aware by preferentially assigning clusters to threads which already contain invocations of components in the cluster.

2.5. Related work

Previous efforts to parallelize microarchitecture simulators for multi-processors have used coarse-grain processor-level task granularity with manual or hard-coded assignment of tasks to threads. The Wisconsin Wind Tunnel II[12] uses parallel discrete event simulation to simulate a multi-processor memory hierarchy. Chidester[3] created a parallel multiprocessor simulator by running a modified copy of SimpleScalar in each thread. Barr[1] has created parallel multiprocessor simulators in Asim, another structural modeling system, by defining new port types and changing the models to use these types. While the addition of framework support is similar in spirit to what we have done, it still requires manual thread assignment and model changes to use the new port types.

There is an extensive literature on parallel and distributed discrete event simulation. A good overview is given in [9]. The primary problem addressed is agreement about global time. Parallel HSR simulation is more closely related to multiprocessor scheduling, for which there is again an extensive literature; see [18] for additional references.

3. Evaluation of automated simulator parallelization

We evaluate the effectiveness of automated simulator parallelization for chip multi-processors by using the previously described scheduling strategies to generate parallel simulators for a family of CMP models and measuring their speed.

3.1. Measurement methodology

Our CMP models have a tile-based architecture. Each processing tile contains a processor with its first-level data and instruction caches, a portion of the distributed second-level cache, and a memory controller. The tiles are connected via a standard wormhole routing network organized as a mesh. Five different sizes of CMP are used: 1, 2, 4, 8, and 16 processors. The processor core is an 1-wide in-order core with branch prediction, chosen to be similar to the PowerPC 405 core used in Section 5.

We generate one, two, three, and four-threaded simulators using each of the scheduling strategies. Two to four threads is the number of threads available in today's inexpensive workgroup servers, in particular those becoming available which themselves use CMPs. Task length is predicted from the number of potential input and output signals of the method invocation using a regression-based model derived from measurements upon the 2-core CMP model. In addition, a manually-guided clustering of invocations to threads (called **GUIDED**) is used for comparison; the guided clustering attempts to map complete tiles to threads, though it splits tiles in the 2-way and 1-way CMP models. This clustering should enjoy good cache behavior in addition to being intuitive and similar to previous work. We emphasize that this guided clustering is *not* a manual parallelization of the simulator; it merely overrides the thread assignments of automated clustering.

Each simulator is run on the *FFT* and *Radix* benchmarks from the Splash-2 benchmark suite[20], linked with a mini-OS which provides processor initialization and simple I/O capabilities. The benchmarks were compiled using gcc 3.3 with compiler flags `-g -O2 -msoft-float`. Input sizes and parameters were chosen to use all simulated processors and to provide several minutes of running time. Results are presented for both benchmarks; they are so similar that numbers quoted in the discussion are all from *Radix*.

All experiments were run on a 4-processor server with 6 GB of physical memory running Red Hat Linux Fedora Core 3. The processors used are 2-GHz AMD Opteron processors, which each have 64KB L1 data, 64KB L1 instruction, and 1MB L2 private caches. Memory is partitioned across processor nodes. The oprofile[14] tool is used to profile simulator execution. This tool records the program counter (PC) every N times an event such as a clock cycle or a cache miss occurs, where N can be set by the user. A post-processing step then maps the PC back to instructions, source lines, and functions.

3.2. Results

We begin by looking at the performance scalability of the non-parallelized simulator with increasing CMP model size. Figure 2 shows time per simulated cycle vs. number of simulated processors, normalized to one simulated processor. The speed of the 1-way CMP is 36,130 simulated cycles/sec. As the number of simulated processors grows beyond four, there are large slowdowns. These slowdowns are due to a sharp increase in the number of L2 cache misses as the working set of the simulator increases. The 4-way CMP model incurs only 300 data L2 cache misses per simulated cycle, but the 8-way CMP model incurs 2500 data misses and the 16-way CMP model nearly 5000 data misses per simulated cycle. Such cache behavior has a significant effect upon the effectiveness of automated parallelization.

Figure 3 shows the speedups achieved by automated parallelization. Each panel shows the speedup achieved using each scheduling strategy measured relative to a single-threaded simulator as the model size changes. Note that the baseline single-threaded simulator is different for each model size. Different panels correspond to different benchmarks and numbers of threads.

The most obvious trend visible from Figure 3 is that speedup vs. a single-threaded simulator increases as the size of the model increases. These results can be explained using two factors. First, cache effects should penalize smaller models; when the model is small enough that its working set fits within the L2 cache of a single processor, parallelization will increase cache misses relative to a single-threaded simulator. On the other hand, for larger models whose working sets did not fit within the L2 cache of a single processor but do fit within the combined L2 caches of multiple processors, parallelization can decrease cache misses and boost performance. Second, as the model increases in size, scheduling strategies should have more opportunities to schedule around locks and achieve higher parallelism.

We can separate these two factors by breaking down overall speedup into cache-caused and parallelism-caused speedup. We compute the cache-caused speedup by comparing the number of CPU seconds spent in component method invocations (as reported by oprofile) in the parallelized and single-threaded simulators. The remaining speedup we attribute to parallel execution (though it actually includes and is reduced by all extra overhead due to parallelization). The two speedup components multiply to form the overall speedup. Figure 4 shows the speedup breakdown for *Radix* for two-threaded and four-threaded simulators.

Figures 4(a) and 4(c) show that cache effects are as predicted; smaller models are hurt by cache effects while the largest model is helped by the larger total effective cache size; the tradeoff point appears at around 8 simulated cores

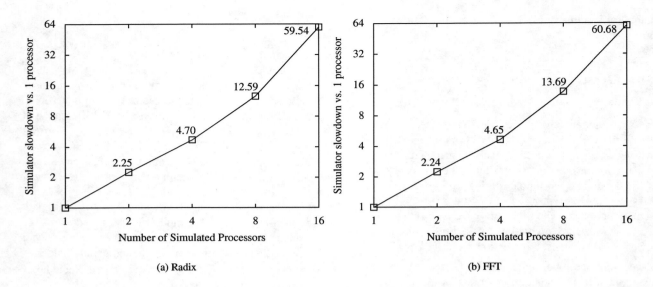

Figure 2. Scalability of single-threaded simulator performance

for 4 threads. This speedup boost due to the larger effective cache size is what leads to superlinear overall speedup. As might be expected, cache effects increase in intensity as the number of threads increases. Both figures also show that clustering strategies are better than non-clustering strategies at handling cache effects; **INSTCLUSTER** is the most effective strategy overall, though **IDSC** is nearly as effective once model size grows beyond four simulated cores. Beyond two simulated cores, both clustering strategies are competitive with manually-guided clustering.

Figures 4(b) and 4(d) indicate how well the strategies find and exploit parallelism. As model size increases, speedup generally increases for most strategies as scheduling opportunities increase. For two threads, there is little difference between the strategies, other than that **LIST** is worse than the rest. However when four threads are used, **IDSC** shows itself to be particularly good at exploiting parallelism, achieving greater than 80% efficiency for four threads. **LOCKAVOID** and **INSTCLUSTER** obtain somewhat lower results. Note also the poor performance of **GUIDED** for smaller models; this is indicative of the difficulty of doing good load-balancing by hand when a good clustering is not obvious to the user.

3.3. Summary of results

Standard list scheduling (**LIST**) is not effective for task scheduling in the simulator because it ignores both cache and locking effects. Locking effects improve when lock avoidance mechanisms are used, but the schedule is still vulnerable to poor cache locality. Locality im-

proves through use of clustering techniques, but there is no clearly preferred clustering strategy. The simpler instance-based strategy (**INSTCLUSTER**) achieves better locality but poorer parallelism than the more complex strategy (**IDSC**) taking into account the critical path. Overall, **INSTCLUSTER** is better when the model is small and there are few threads, but **IDSC** is better when the model is large or there are many threads.

Figure 5 shows the scalability of simulator performance (defined as in Figure 2) as the model size increases for the instance-based strategy scheduler, **INSTCLUSTER**, for different numbers of threads. Ideally, a 4-threaded simulation of a four-way CMP would take as long as a 1-threaded simulation of a 1-way CMP. This is unfortunately not the case; as discussed before, small models do not achieve large parallel efficiency due to the extra L2 data misses implied by parallelization. However, large models do see a large benefit from parallelization due to the increase in effective L2 cache size for data. This benefit is so large that it becomes the primary benefit of parallelization, increasing the range of model sizes for which simulation speed scales approximately linearly with model size.

4. Integrating processors in simulation

While parallelism in a CMP model can be exploited by using multiple processors to parallelize the simulator, these processors can also be integrated as components of the simulation itself. To do so requires that the simulator be explicitly developed in such a way as to encapsulate the hardware, providing input signals to and receiving output signals from

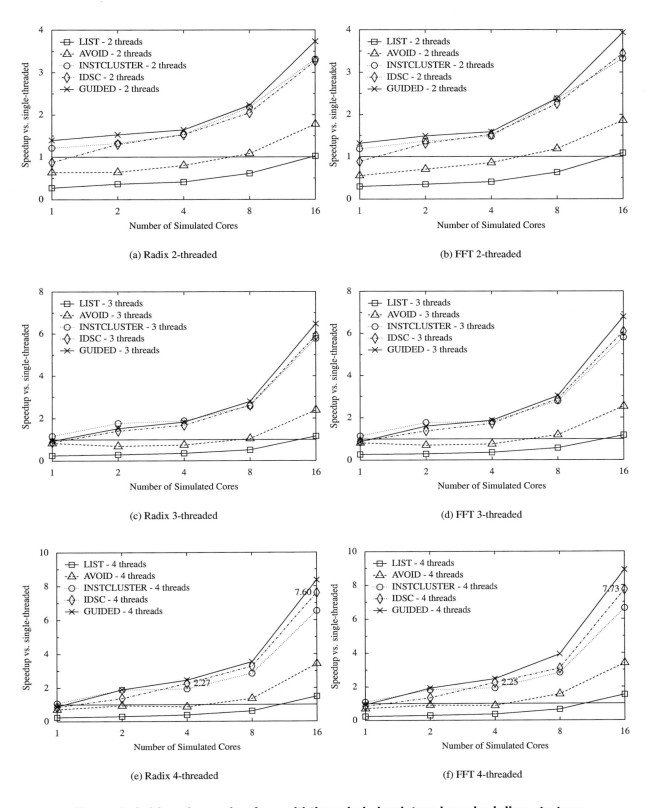

Figure 3. Achieved speedup for multi-threaded simulators by scheduling strategy

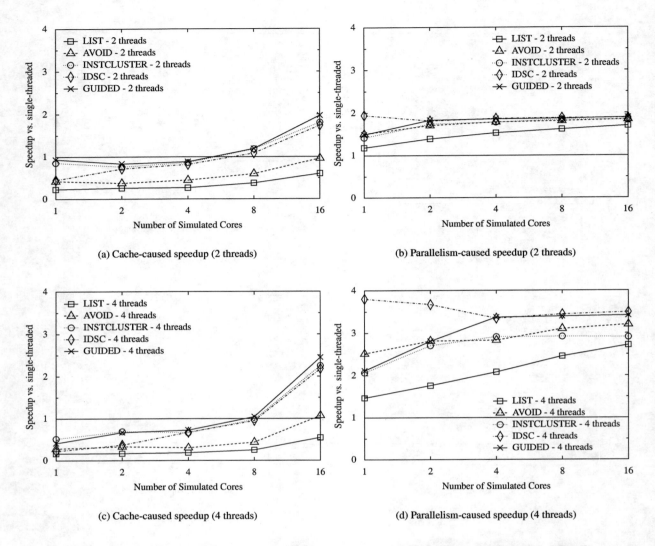

Figure 4. Breakdown of speedup for 2-threaded and 4-threaded simulators on Radix

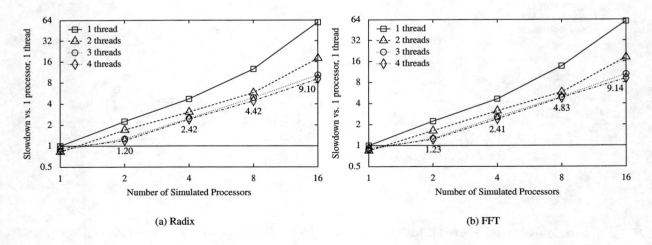

Figure 5. Performance scalability of INSTCLUSTER

the hardware. Concurrent structural simulation frameworks make this process much easier, as this is the normal modeling paradigm: components communicate with each other through signals. As a result, once the hardware component has a corresponding LSE adapter component, integrating the component into the simulator is simply a matter of swapping the software component with the hardware one. No other changes are required to the rest of the simulation model.

Integration of processors (or arbitrary hardware components) can offer additional benefits beyond increases in simulation speed. Two major motivating factors behind the development of structural modeling have been reuse and reduction of error. Using actual hardware can be seen as the ultimate expression of these goals: the component need not be modeled at all and is already completely validated. In addition, simulated components can be incrementally implemented and become hardware components, creating an incremental architecture-to-implementation design flow.

4.1. Integration Requirements

Three requirements must be met when integrating hardware into a structural simulation framework. First, the simulator must control and communicate with the hardware. Second, the hardware must be made to appear as if it obeys the simulator's model of computation. Finally, hardware signals must be translated and mapped to simulator signals.

Control and Communication The simulator must be able to control all of the input signals of the hardware component and to sample all of its output signals. The simulator must also be able to control the hardware clock. We accomplish this by placing hardware input registers, hardware output registers, and a hardware register controlling a clock driver on the interfaces of the hardware component instantiated in a Field-Programmable Gate Array (FPGA), as shown in Figure 6. These registers can be written to and read from via a Linux device driver written for the board upon which the FPGA resides. Device driver methods to write and read these registers are called from an LSE adapter component written specifically for the hardware being integrated.

Model of computation The Hetrogeneous Synchronous Reactive (HSR) model of computation which LSE uses requires that components carefully control when signals are set. An output signal must not be given a value before all inputs needed to compute it are known. An output signal should also be given a value as soon as all of the inputs needed to compute it are known. The essential invariant which an LSE adapter component around a hardware component must maintain, therefore, is to not set a signal value

too early (before it would be set by an HSR model of the component) nor too late.

It is useful to think of the outputs of the hardware to be integrated as being either Moore or Mealy state machine outputs. At the beginning of the simulation timestep, Moore machine outputs should be available from the hardware, and LSE requires that they be driven out of the LSE adapter during the PHASE_START method of the simulation time step. As inputs become available during the timestep, LSE calls the PHASE method of the adapter. The adapter provides its inputs to the hardware and then samples the hardware's outputs. It then drives in LSE those outputs which are known to have resolved to a known value; as the hardware will *not* indicate this, knowledge of the zero-cycle paths through the hardware must be put into the adapter. Finally, during the PHASE_END method, the adapter provides its inputs to the hardware and causes the hardware clock to tick.

Translation and mapping LSE creates three signals for each connection made to a component. These signals – called data, enable, and ack – are used to provide default flow-control behavior across components. Furthermore, data has an implicit "data valid" signal carried with it. Most hardware components will not use precisely the same scheme. To resolve this, the adapter component shown in Figure 6 translates the hardware signals into LSE signals signifying the hardware's flow-control semantics, and vice-versa. It may also translate datatypes; for example, transforming the raw bits off of a command bus into some enumerated type that lists the commands in human-friendly form.

4.2. Related Work

Hardware emulation has been used for microprocessor design and verification in many efforts in the past. Ray and Ho[17] describe using an FPGA prototyping board to verify a synthesizable processor design. Within industry, microprocessors such as the AMD K5[10] and the Sun Ultra-SPARC I[11] have been verified through hardware emulation using specialized emulation systems constructed from FPGAs. These efforts have required that the entire design be emulated, not just portions of it, and that the entire design be described in a hardware-synthesizable language.

Nakamura, et al.[13] present a method for integrating C/C++ simulators with hardware implemented in FPGAs. This is similar in some ways to our work, but the simulators used are written in an ad-hoc fashion and must intersperse driver calls throughout the simulation without the benefit of a structured simulation cycle. Davis, et al.[5] present a prototyping system for multiprocessors built out of FPGA boards with processors. This system does not integrate with simulators, but instead is intended to be used to prototype

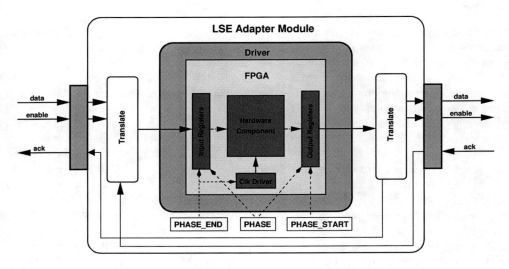

Figure 6. A Hardware Component in LSE

the entire multiprocessor. Chiou[4] partitions simulation between functional and timing simulation and offload the simulation onto FPGAs, but does not present results.

DirectRSIM[6] uses direct execution to model the functionality of processors in a multi-processor system, thus "integrating" them in a sense. The communication mechanism with the processors is not cycle-accurate; the binary being run by the processors is instrumented to call the timing simulator at each memory operation and pass it the execution path taken since the last operation. The timing simulator then performs a timing-only simulation of the processor to determine the time at which the memory operation would actually have been issued.

Finally, integration of different models of computation was one of the goals of the Ptolemy[2] project, out of which the HSR model originated.

5. Evaluation of hardware integration

In this section we demonstrate the feasibility of integrating processors into a concurrent structural simulation model by integrating hardware PPC405 cores into 1-, 2-, 4-, and 8-way chip multi-processor models. This integration is done by simply replacing the PowerPC software LSE component with a PPC405 LSE adapter component. Having swapped the components, we then compare the new simulator's performance to the software-only models.

5.1. Experimental infrastructure

Up to four AMIRIX AP130 PCI boards are used, each board containing one Xilinx Virtex-II Pro XC2VP30 FPGA containing two PPC405 cores implemented as hard macros. 54% of the logic resources (slices) on these mid-size FPGAs

are used. The boards share the host system's single PCI bus, which is 32 bits wide and runs at 33MHz.

The simulations use the minimal number of boards for a given size of CMP model: i.e. the number of cores divided by two. Because the external bus of the PPC405 has no zero-cycle input-to-output paths, a PHASE method is not needed in the adapter. Instead, it simply reads the core's outputs at PHASE_START and drives inputs to the core and toggles the clock at PHASE_END. The adapter translates the core's bus signals to and from cache transactions understood by the simulated cache models. It also handles some special cases of the cache protocol, such as responding to invalidation requests, that the core does not expect to see.

The hardware integration experiments use the same benchmarks and inputs as those used in Section 3. Three families of CMP are considered: the first, **GRID**, is the complex, tiled architecture used in Section 3. The second, **BUS**, has a bus-based architecture and a monolithic L2 cache. The final family, **PERF**, has perfect L1 data and instruction caches and serves to illustrate speedup when nearly all of the simulation has been moved to hardware. The host system, which is also used for software-only speed measurements, has a Pentium 4 630 (3.0 GHz "Prescott" with a 2MB L2 cache) system running the 32-bit version of Red Hat Fedora Core 3.

5.2. Results

Table 1 shows the speed measured in simulated cycles per second of the purely software-based simulators and the hardware-integrated simulators for both *Radix* and *FFT*. Also shown for *Radix* is a profile of the percentage of time spent in the adapter component and the board driver in the hardware-integrated models.

Model	Radix					FFT		
	Speed (cycles/sec)			% time spent in		Speed (cycles/sec)		
	SW-only	HW	Speedup	driver	adapter	SW-only	HW	Speedup
1-way PERF	37314	160978	4.31	68.7	10.8	37461	162920	4.35
2-way PERF	17277	71316	4.13	56.5	17.8	17312	72329	4.18
4-way PERF	7496	38363	5.12	46.7	22.7	7481	39049	5.22
8-way PERF	3136	17930	5.72	40.8	27.3	3130	18229	5.82
1-way BUS	24720	41860	1.69	12.7	7.0	24858	41974	1.69
2-way BUS	11544	21494	1.86	12.7	7.7	11731	21664	1.85
4-way BUS	5074	9759	1.92	11.5	9.9	5154	9873	1.92
8-way BUS	2205	4278	1.90	9.4	11.6	2146	4359	2.03
1-way GRID	22210	31692	1.43	9.4	5.3	22348	31898	1.43
2-way GRID	9551	12341	1.29	7.5	5.3	9584	12408	1.29
4-way GRID	3951	4761	1.21	5.7	6.1	3983	4767	1.20
8-way GRID	1649	2092	1.27	4.7	6.3	1604	2101	1.31

Table 1. Hardware-integrated vs. software-only simulators

Large speedups are seen for the **PERF** models. Integration of hardware has accelerated simulation by moving most of the computation into efficient, highly-parallel hardware. Up to 69% of simulation time is spent within the driver; of this time, nearly all of it is spent waiting for PCI read transactions to complete. Notice also that the proportion of time spent in the adapter relative to the driver increases as the number of cores increases. We believe this is because the frequency with which memory transactions occurs increases as the number of cores increases due to the increased amount of time spent in synchronization constructs such as locks in the target benchmarks. As a result, the adapter must spend proportionally more time translating signals, as the driver's time to provide the signals to and from the hardware each cycle remains relatively constant.

We stress that the simulation model of the PPC405 core is a very simple parameterized generic core model which does not model the PPC405 particularly accurately. A more detailed and accurate core model would likely be much slower, causing the speed benefit of hardware integration to be even higher. This effect would be even more pronounced for more complex cores. Thus these speedup results should be considered to be very conservative.

The **BUS** and **GRID** models show less speedup. This is a consequence of Amdahl's Law. As the memory hierarchy becomes more complex and takes up a much larger proportion of simulation time, the potential speedup due to reducing the time spent in the processors is reduced. The large reduction in speedup seen implies that implementation and integration of portions of the memory hierarchy (for example, first-level caches) in hardware could be worthwhile.

6. Conclusion

We have shown that the use of structural concurrent models for CMPs allows simulators to exploit structure and parallelism in the CMP model. This can be achieved either through automated parallelization of the simulator or by integrating processors into the simulation itself. Structural models make it possible to use either technique without requiring the user to manually parallelize or re-design the simulator.

Automated parallelization is possible because the structural, concurrent nature of the model provides a rich assortment of tasks which can then be automatically scheduled. We show that shared data access and cache behavior are important to consider while scheduling and demonstrate an automatic scheduler which can achieve moderate (2.27) speedup on a 4-way CMP model and large (7.60) speedup on a 16-way CMP model. Future work will focus on further improving the data cache locality of the parallelized simulator.

We have also demonstrated that processors can be integrated into a structural CMP model without requiring re-design of the model, achieving a speedup of 5.82 for an 8-way CMP model with perfect caches and 1.31 for an 8-way CMP model with a complex tiled memory architecture. Besides this speed advantage, hardware component integration offers advantages of accuracy, reduced model development time, and incremental architecture-to-implementation design flow possibilities. Future work will improve board communication overhead with the driver and explore the performance issues involved in simulating multiple microarchitectural components on multiple FPGAs and FPGA boards as well as the effects of various hardware parameters and configurations on performance.

7. Acknowledgements

This work has been supported by the National Science Foundation (CAREER CCF-0133712, NGS-0305617). Opinions, findings, conclusions, and recommendations expressed throughout this work are not necessarily the views of the National Science Foundation. We would also like to acknowledge Krista Marks and Glenn Steiner of Xilinx Corporation for the donation of FPGA prototyping equipment and software.

References

[1] K. C. Barr, R. Matas-Navarro, C. Weaver, T. Juan, and J. Emer. Simulating a chip multiprocessor with a symmetric multiprocessor. In *Boston Area Architecture Workshop*, January 2005.

[2] J. Buck, S. Ha, E. A. Lee, and D. G. Messerschmitt. Ptolemy: A framework for simulating and prototyping heterogeneous systems. *International Journal in Computer Simulation*, 4:155–182, 1994.

[3] M. Chidister and A. George. Parallel simulation of chip-multiprocessor architectures. *ACM Transactions on Modeling and Computer Simulation*, 12(3):176–200, July 2002.

[4] D. Chiou. FAST: FPGA-based acceleration of simulator timing models. In *In Workshop on Architecture Research Using FPGA Platforms*, February 2005.

[5] J. D. Davis, L. Hammond, and K. Olukotun. A flexible architecture for simulation and testing (FAST) multiprocessors systems. In *In Workshop on Architecture Research Using FPGA Platforms*, February 2005.

[6] M. Durbhakula, V. S. Pai, and S. Adve. Improving the accuracy vs. speed tradeoff for simulating shared-memory multiprocessors with ILP processors. In *Proceedings of the Fifth International Symposium on High Performance Computer Architecture*, January 1999.

[7] S. A. Edwards. *The Specification and Execution of Heterogeneous Synchronous Reactive Systems*. PhD thesis, University of California, Berkeley, 1997.

[8] J. Emer, P. Ahuja, E. Borch, A. Klauser, C.-K. Luk, S. Manne, S. S. Mukherjee, H. Patil, S. Wallace, N. Binkert, R. Espasa, and T. Juan. Asim: A performance model framework. *IEEE Computer*, 0018-9162:68–76, February 2002.

[9] A. Ferscha. Parallel and distributed simulation of discrete event system. In A. Y. Zomaya, editor, *Parallel and Distributed Computing Handbook*, pages 1003–1041. McGraw-Hill, 1996.

[10] G. Ganapathy, R. Narayan, G. Jorden, D. Fernandez, M. Wang, and J. Nishimura. Hardware emulation for functional verification of K5. In *Proceedings of the 33rd Design Automation Conference (DAC)*, pages 315–318, 1996.

[11] J. Gateley, M. Blatt, D. Chen, S. Cooke, P. Desai, M. Doreswamy, M. Elgood, G. Feierbach, T. Goldsbury, D. Greenley, R. Joshi, M. Khosraviani, R. Kwong, M. Motwani, C. Narasimhaiah, S. J. N. Jr., T. Ozeki, G. Peterson, C. Salzmann, N. Shayesteh, J. Whitman, and P. Wong. UltraSPARC-I emulation. In *Proceedings of the 32nd Annual Design Automation Conference (DAC)*, pages 13–18, 1995.

[12] S. S. Mukherjee, S. K. Reinhardt, B. Falsafi, M. Litzkow, S. Huss-Lederman, M. D. Hill, J. R. Larus, and D. A. Wood. Wisconsin Wind Tunnel II: A fast and portable architecture simulator. In *Workshop on Performance Analysis and its Impact on Design (PAID)*, June 1997.

[13] Y. Nakamura, K. Hosokawa, I. Kuroda, K. Yoshikawa, and T. Yoshimura. A fast hardware/software co-verification method for system-on-a-chip by using a C/C++ simulator and FPGA emulator with shared register communication. In *Proceedings of the 41st Annual Design Automation Conference (DAC)*, pages 299–304, 2004.

[14] OProfile. Web site: http://oprofile.sourceforge.net/.

[15] D. Penry and D. I. August. Optimizations for a simulator construction system supporting reusable components. In *Proceedings of the 40th Design Automation Conference (DAC)*, June 2003.

[16] D. A. Penry, M. Vachharajani, and D. I. August. Rapid development of a flexible validated processor model. In *Proceedings of the 2005 Workshop on Modeling, Benchmarking, and Simulation (MOBS)*, June 2005.

[17] J. Ray and J. C. Hoe. High-level modeling and FPGA prototyping of microprocessors. In *FPGA '03: Proceedings of the 2003 ACM/SIGDA Eleventh International Symposium on Field Programmable Gate Arrays*, pages 100–107, 2003.

[18] S. Sriram and S. S. Bhattacharyya. *Embedded Multiprocessors: Scheduling and Synchronization*, chapter 5. Marcel Dekker, Inc., New York, NY, 2000.

[19] M. Vachharajani, N. Vachharajani, D. A. Penry, J. A. Blome, and D. I. August. Microarchitectural exploration with Liberty. In *Proceedings of the 35th International Symposium on Microarchitecture (MICRO)*, pages 271–282, November 2002.

[20] S. C. Woo, M. Ohara, E. Torrie, J. P. Singh, and A. Gupta. The SPLASH-2 programs: Characterization and methodological considerations. In *Proceedings of the 22nd Annual International Symposium on Computer Architecture (ISCA)*, pages 24–36, June 1995.

[21] T. Yang and A. Gerasoulis. DSC: Scheduling parallel tasks on an unbounded number of processors. *IEEE Transactions on Parallel and Distributed Systems*, 5(9):951–967, September 1994.

[22] W. H. Yu. *LU Decomposition on a Multiprocessing System with Communication Delay*. PhD thesis, University of California at Berkeley, Berkeley, CA, 1984.

Session 2:
Processor Architecture

An Approach for Implementing Efficient Superscalar CISC Processors

Shiliang Hu [†]   Ilhyun Kim [‡ *]   Mikko H. Lipasti [‡]   James E. Smith [‡]

shiliang@cs.wisc.edu, ilhyun.kim@intel.com, mikko@engr.wisc.edu, jes@ece.wisc.edu

Departments of [†]Computer Sciences & [‡]Electrical and Computer Engineering
University of Wisconsin - Madison

Abstract

An integrated, hardware / software co-designed CISC processor is proposed and analyzed. The objectives are high performance and reduced complexity. Although the x86 ISA is targeted, the overall approach is applicable to other CISC ISAs. To provide high performance on frequently executed code sequences, fully transparent dynamic translation software decomposes CISC superblocks into RISC-style micro-ops. Then, pairs of dependent micro-ops are reordered and fused into macro-ops held in a large, concealed code cache. The macro-ops are fetched from the code cache and processed throughout the pipeline as single units. Consequently, instruction level communication and management are reduced, and processor resources such as the issue buffer and register file ports are better utilized. Moreover, fused instructions lead naturally to pipelined instruction scheduling (issue) logic, and collapsed 3-1 ALUs can be used, resulting in much simplified result forwarding logic. Steady state performance is evaluated for the SPEC2000 benchmarks,, and a proposed x86 implementation with complexity similar to a two-wide superscalar processor is shown to provide performance (instructions per cycle) that is equivalent to a conventional four-wide superscalar processor.

1. Introduction

The most widely used ISA for general purpose computing is a CISC – the x86. It is used in portable, desktop, and server systems. Furthermore, it is likely to be the dominant ISA for the next decade, probably longer. There are many challenging issues in implementing a CISC ISA such as the x86, however. These include the implementation of complex, multi-operation instructions, implicitly set condition codes, and the trap architecture.

A major issue with implementing the x86 (and CISC ISAs in general) is suboptimal internal code sequences. Even if the original x86 binary is optimized, the many micro-ops produced by decomposing (*"cracking"*) the CISC instructions are not optimized [39]. Furthermore,

performing runtime optimization of the micro-ops is non-trivial. In this paper, we propose and study an overall paradigm for the efficient and high performance implementation of an x86 processor. The design employs a special implementation instruction set based on micro-ops, a simplified but enhanced superscalar microarchitecture, and a layer of concealed dynamic binary translation software that is co-designed with the hardware.

A major optimization performed by the co-designed software is the combination of *dependent* micro-op pairs into fused "macro-ops" that are managed throughout the pipeline as single entities. Although a CISC ISA already has instructions that are essentially fused micro-ops, higher efficiency and performance can be achieved by first cracking the CISC instructions and then re-arranging and fusing them into different combinations than in the original code. The fused pairs increase effective instruction level parallelism (ILP) for a given issue width and reduce inter-instruction communication. For example, collapsed 3-1 ALUs can be employed to reduce the size of the result forwarding network dramatically.

Because implementing high quality optimizations such as macro-op fusing is a relatively complex task, we rely on dynamic translation software that is concealed from all conventional software. In fact, the translation software becomes part of the processor design; collectively the hardware and software become a *co-designed virtual machine* (VM) [10, 11, 29, 42] implementing the x86 ISA.

We consider an overall x86 implementation, and make a number of contributions; three of the more important are the following.

1) The co-designed VM approach is applied to an enhanced out-of-order superscalar implementation of a CISC ISA, the x86 ISA in particular.

2) The macro-op execution pipeline combines collapsed 3-1 ALU functional units with a pipelined 2-cycle macro-op scheduler. This execution engine achieves high performance, while also significantly reducing the pipeline backend complexity; for example, in the result forwarding network.

---

[*] Currently: *Intel Corporation*, Hillsboro, OR

40

3) The advanced macro-op fusing algorithm both prioritizes critical dependences and ALU ops, and also fuses more dynamic instructions (55+ %) than reported in other work [5, 8, 27, 38] (40% or less on average) for the common SPEC2000int benchmarks.

The paper is organized as follows. Section 2 discusses related work. The co-designed x86 processor is outlined in section 3 from an architectural perspective. Section 4 elaborates key microarchitecture details. Section 5 presents design evaluation and analysis. Section 6 concludes the paper.

2. Related Work

2.1 x86 Processor Implementations

Decoder logic in a typical high performance x86 implementation decomposes instructions into one or more RISC-like micro-ops. Some recent x86 implementations have gone in the direction of more complex internal operations in certain pipeline stages, however. The AMD K7/K8 microarchitecture [9, 23] maps x86 instructions to internal Macro-Operations that are designed to reduce the dynamic operation count in the pipeline front-end. The front-end pipeline of the Intel Pentium M microarchitecture [16] fuses ALU operations with memory stores, and memory loads with ALU operations as specified in the original x86 instructions. However, the operations in each pair are still individually scheduled and executed in the pipeline backend.

The fundamental difference between our fused macro-ops and the AMD/Intel coarse-grain internal operations is that our macro-ops combine pairs of operations that (1) are suitable for processing as single entities for the entire pipeline, and (2) can be taken from different x86 instructions -- as our data shows, 70+% of the fused macro-ops combine operations from different x86 instructions. In contrast, AMD K7/K8 and Intel Pentium M group only micro-operations already contained in a single x86 instruction. In a sense, one could argue that rather than "fusing", these implementations actually employ "reduced splitting." In addition, these existing x86 implementations maintain fused operations for only part of the pipeline, e.g. individual micro-operations are scheduled separately by single-cycle issue logic.

2.2 Macro-op Execution

The proposed microarchitecture evolved from prior work on coarse-grained instruction scheduling and execution [27, 28] and a dynamic binary translation approach for fusing dependent instruction pairs [20]. The work on coarse-grained scheduling [27] proposed hardware-based grouping of pairs of dependent RISC (Alpha) instructions into macro-ops to achieve pipelined instruction scheduling. Compared with the hardware approach in [27, 28], we remove considerable complexity from the hardware

and enable more sophisticated fusing heuristics, resulting in a larger number of fused macro-ops. Furthermore, we propose a new microarchitecture in which the front-end features dual-mode x86 decoders and the backend execution engine uniquely couples collapsed 3-1 ALUs with a 2-cycle pipelined macro-op scheduler and simplified operand forwarding network. The software fusing algorithm presented here is more advanced than that reported in [20]; it is based on the observations that it is easier to determine dependence criticality of ALU-ops, and fused ALU-ops better match the capabilities of a collapsed ALU. Finally, a major contribution over prior work is that we extend macro-op processing to the *entire* processor pipeline, realizing 4-wide superscalar performance with a 2-wide macro-op pipeline.

There are a number of related research projects. Instruction-level distributed processing (ILDP)[25] carries the principle of combining dependent operations (strands) further than instruction pairs. However, instructions are not fused, and the highly clustered microarchitecture is considerably different from the one proposed here. Dynamic Strands [38] uses intensive hardware to form strands and involves major changes to superscalar pipeline stages, e.g. issue queue slots need more register tags for potentially *(n+1)* source registers of an *n*-ops strand. The Dataflow Mini-Graph [5] collapses multiple instructions in a small dataflow graph and evaluates performance with Alpha binaries. However, this approach needs static compiler support. Such a static approach is very difficult for x86 binaries because variable length instructions and embedded data lead to extremely complex code "discovery" problems [19]. CCA, proposed in [8] either needs a very complex hardware fill unit to discover instruction groups or needs to generate new binaries, and thus will have difficulties in maintaining x86 binary compatibility. The fill unit in [15] also collapses some instruction patterns. Continuous Optimization [12] and RENO [34] present novel dynamic optimizations at the rename stage. By completely removing some dynamic instructions (also performed in [39] by a hardware-based frame optimizer), they achieve some of the performance effects as fused macro-ops. Some of their optimizations are compatible with macro-op fusing. PARROT [1] is a hardware-based x86 dynamic optimization system capable of various optimizations. Compared with these hardware-intensive optimizing schemes, our software-based solution reduces hardware complexity and provides more flexibility for optimizations and implementation of subtle compatibility issues, especially involving traps [30].

2.3 Co-designed Virtual Machines

The Transmeta Crusoe and Efficeon processors [29, 42] and IBM DAISY and BOA [10, 11] are examples of co-designed VMs. They contain translation/optimization software and a *code cache*, which resides in a region of

41

physical memory that is completely hidden from all conventional software. In effect, the code cache [10, 11, 29] is a very large trace cache. The software is implementation-specific and is developed along with the hardware design. The co-designed VM systems from Transmeta and IBM use in-order VLIW hardware engines. As such, considerably heavier software optimization is required for translation and reordering instructions than our superscalar implementation, which is capable of dynamic instruction scheduling and dataflow graph collapsing.

3. Processor Overview

There are two major components in a co-designed VM implementation -- the *software binary translator/optimizer* and the supporting *hardware microarchitecture*. The interface between the two is the x86-specific *implementation instruction set*.

A new feature of the proposed architecture, targeted specifically at CISC ISAs, is a two-level decoder, similar in some respects to the microcode engine in the Motorola 68000 [40]. In the proposed implementation (Figure 1), the decoder first translates x86 instructions into "vertical" micro-ops -- the same fixed-format micro-ops we use as the implementation ISA (refer to the next subsection). Then, a second level decoder generates the decoded "horizontal" control signals used by the pipeline. A two-level decoder is especially suited to the x86 ISA because complex x86 instructions need to be cracked into micro-ops and then decoded into pipeline control signals. Compared with a single-level monolithic decode control table, the two-level decoder is smaller [40] by breaking the single monolithic decode table into two much smaller decode tables. It also yields decode logic that is not only more regular and flexible, but also more amenable to a fast clock.

With the two-level decoder, the pipeline can process both x86 instructions (x86-mode) and fused macro-ops (macro-op mode). When in x86-mode, instructions pass through both decode levels; this would be done when a program starts up, for example. In x86-mode, performance will be similar to a conventional x86 implementation (there is no dynamic optimization). Profiling hardware such as that proposed by Merten et al. [32] detects frequently-used code regions ("hotspots"). As hotspots are discovered, control is transferred to the VM software which organizes them into superblocks [21], translates and optimizes them as fused macro-ops, and places them in the concealed code cache. When executing this hotspot code in macro-op mode, the first level of decode in Figure 1 is bypassed, and only the second (horizontal) decode level is used. Then, the full benefits of the fused instruction set are realized. While optimized instructions are executed from the code cache, the first-level decode logic can be powered off.

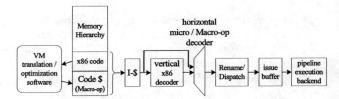

Figure 1. Overview of the proposed x86 design

As the processor runs, it will switch back and forth between x86 mode and macro-op mode, under the control of co-designed VM software. In this paper, *we focus on the macro-op mode of execution*; our goal is to demonstrate the steady-state performance benefits of the proposed x86 design. The x86 mode is intended to provide very good startup performance to address program startup concerns regarding dynamic translation. The full dual mode implementation and performance tradeoffs are the subject of research currently underway; this is being done in conjunction with our migration to a 64-bit x86 research infrastructure.

3.1 The Implementation ISA

Core 32-bit instruction formats	Add-on 16-bit instruction formats for code density

F	10b opcode	21-bit Immediate / Displacement		
F	10b opcode	16-bit immediate / Displacement	5b Rds	
F	10b opcode	11b Immediate / Disp	5b Rsrc	5b Rds
F	16-bit opcode		5b Rsrc	5b Rsrc	5b Rds

F	5b op	10b Immd / Disp
F	5b op	5b Rsrc	5b Rds
F	5b op	5b Rsrc	5b Rds

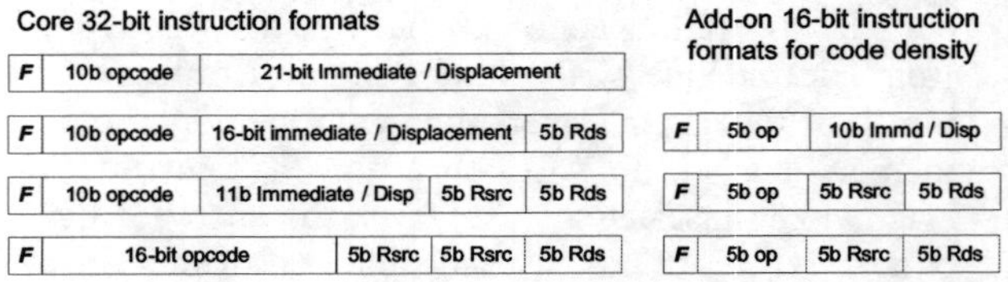

Figure 2. Formats for fusible micro-ops

The implementation instruction set (the fusible ISA) is shown in Figure 2 and contains RISC-style micro-ops that target the x86 instruction set.

The fusible micro-ops are encoded in 16-bit and 32-bit formats. Using a 16/32-bit instruction format is not essential, but provides a denser encoding of translated instructions (and better I-cache performance) than a 32-bit only format as in most RISCs (the Cray Research and CDC machines [4, 36, 41] are notable exceptions). The 32-bit formats encode three register operands and/or an immediate value. The 16-bit formats use an x86-like 2-operand encoding in which one of the operands is both a source and a destination. This ISA is extended from an earlier version [20] by supporting 5-bit register designators in the 16-bit formats. This is done in anticipation of implementing the 64-bit x86 ISA, although results presented here are for the 32-bit version.

The first bit of each micro-op indicates whether it should be fused with the immediately following micro-op to form a single macro-op. The *head* of a fused macro-op is the first micro-op in the pair, and the *tail* is the second, dependent micro-op which consumes the value produced by the head. To reduce pipeline complexity, e.g., in the rename and scheduling stages, fusing is performed only for dependent micro-op pairs that have a combined total of two or fewer unique input register operands. This assures that the fused macro-ops can be easily handled by conventional instruction rename/issue logic and an execution engine with a collapsed 3-1 ALU.

3.2 Dynamic Binary Translator

The major task of the co-designed dynamic binary translation software is to translate and optimize hotspot x86 instructions via macro-op fusing. Clearly, as exemplified by existing designs, finding x86 instruction boundaries and then cracking individual x86 instructions into micro-ops is lightweight enough that it can be performed with hardware alone. However, our software translation algorithm not only translates, but also finds critical micro-op pairs for fusing and potentially performs other dynamic optimizations. This requires an overall analysis of the micro-ops, reordering of micro-ops, and fusing of pairs of operation taken from different x86 instructions.

Many other runtime optimizations could also be performed by the dynamic translation software, e.g. performing common sub-expression elimination and the Pentium M's "stack engine" [16] cost-effectively in software, or even conducting "SIMDification" [1] to exploit SIMD functional units. However, in this work we do not perform such optimizations.

3.3 Microarchitecture

The co-designed microarchitecture has the same basic stages as a conventional x86 superscalar pipeline. Consequently, it inherits most of the proven benefits of such designs. A key difference is that the proposed microarchitecture can process instructions at the coarser macro-op granularity throughout the entire pipeline.

Because of the two-level decoders, there are two slightly different pipeline flows – one for executing x86 code and the other for executing optimized, macro-op code (see Figure 3). For x86 code, the pipeline operates just as a conventional dynamic superscalar processor except that the instruction scheduler is pipelined for a faster clock cycle. After the decode stage, some adjacent micro-ops cracked from x86 instructions are re-fused as in some current x86 implementations, but no reordering or optimizations are done. Note that even without optimized fusing of macro-ops, the pipeline is still a high performance superscalar processor for x86 instructions.

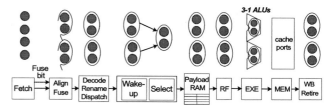

Figure 4. Macro-op execution overview

For the optimized macro-op code, paired dependent micro-ops are placed in adjacent memory locations in the code cache and are identified via a special "fuse" bit. After they are fetched the two fused micro-ops are immediately aligned and fused. From then on, macro-ops are processed throughout the pipeline as single units (Figure 4). Macro-ops contain dependent micro-ops at a granularity comparable to the original x86 CISC instructions; however, fused macro-ops are streamlined and appear as RISC-like operations to the pipeline. By processing fused micro-op pairs as a unit, processor resources such as register ports and instruction dispatch/tracking logic are reduced or better utilized. Perhaps more importantly, the dependent micro-ops in a fused pair share a single issue queue slot and are awakened and selected for issue as a single entity. The number of issue buffer slots and issue width can then be reduced without affecting performance.

After fusing, there are very few isolated single-cycle micro-ops that generate register results. Consequently, key pipeline stages can be designed as if the minimum instruction latency is two cycles. The instruction issue stage is one of the more difficult pipeline stages in a conventional design, because of the need to execute single cycle back-to-back instructions. In the proposed x86 processor design, instruction issue can be pipelined in two stages, simply and without performance loss.

Another critical stage in a conventional design is the ALU and result forwarding logic. In our design, these two operations can be performed in two cycles. In the first cycle, two dependent ALU micro-ops in a macro-op are executed by using a combination of a collapsed three-input ALU [31, 35, 37] and a conventional two-input ALU. There is no need for an expensive and time-consuming ALU-to-ALU operand forwarding network during the same cycle. Rather, the results only need to be sent to the register file (or ROB) at the end of the ALU execution cycle, and register file (or ROB) hardware can take care of providing results to dependent instructions during the next cycle as in a conventional design.

The co-designed VM CISC implementation has other advantages. For example, unused legacy features in the architected ISA can be largely (or entirely) emulated by software. A simple microarchitecture reduces design risks and cost and yields a shorter time-to-market. Although it is true that the translation software must be validated for correctness, this translation software does not require

x86-mode Pipeline					2-cycle Issue								
Fetch	Align	x86 Decode 1 2 3			Re-name	Dis-patch	Wake-up	Se-lect	Pay-load	RF	Exe	WB	Retire
Macro-op Pipeline	Fetch	Align	De-code	Re-name	Dis-patch	Wake-up	Se-lect	Pay-load	RF	Exe	WB	Retire	

Figure 3. x86-mode and macro-op mode pipelines

43

physical design checking, does not require circuit timing verification, and if a bug is discovered late in the design process, it does not require re-spinning the silicon.

4. Microarchitecture Details

The major features to support our efficient x86 processor are the software runtime macro-op fusing algorithm, and macro-op processing in the co-designed superscalar pipeline. We elaborate on technical details regarding hotspot x86 code optimization and generated macro-op code execution.

4.1 The Dynamic Translator: Macro-op Fusing

Once a hot superblock is detected, the dynamic binary translator performs translation and fusing steps. We use registers R0-R15 to map the x86 state (R0-R7 for 32-bit code), registers R16- R31 are used mainly for temporary/scratch values, x86 hotspot optimization, code cache management, precise state recovery, etc. The fusing algorithm substantially improves on the algorithm in [20]; the critical improvements will be summarized following the description of the algorithm.

Two main heuristics are used for fusing. (1) Single-cycle micro-ops are given higher priority as the head of a pair. It is easier to determine dependence criticality among ALU-ops. Furthermore, a non-fused multi-cycle micro-op will cause no IPC loss due to pipelined scheduling logic, so there is reduced value in prioritizing it. (2) Higher priority is given to pairing micro-ops that are close together in the original x86 code sequence. The rationale is that these pairs are more likely to be on the program's critical path and should be scheduled for fused execution in order to reduce the critical path latency. Consecutive (or close) pairs also tend to be less problematic with regard to other issues, e.g., extending register live ranges to provide precise x86 state recovery [30] when there is a trap. An additional constraint is maintaining the original ordering of all memory operations. This avoids complicating memory ordering hardware (beyond that used in a conventional superscalar design).

A *forward two-pass scan* algorithm creates fused macro-ops quickly and effectively (Figure 5). After constructing the data dependence graph, the first forward scan considers single-cycle micro-ops one-by-one as tail candidates. For each tail candidate, the algorithm looks backwards in the micro-op stream to find a head. This is done by scanning from the second micro-op to the last in the superblock, attempting to fuse each not-yet-fused single-cycle micro-op with the nearest preceding, not-yet-fused single-cycle micro-op that produces one of its input operands. The fusing rules favor dependent pairs with condition code dependence. And the fusing tests make sure that *no* fused macro-ops can have more than two distinct source operands, break any dependence in the original code, or break memory ordering.

```
1. for(int pass = 1; pass <=2; pass++){
2.    for(each micro-op from 2nd to last) {
3.       if(micro-op already fused)continue;
4.       if (pass == 1 and micro-op multi-cycle,
            e.g. mem-ops) continue;
5.       look backward via dependence edges for
          its head candidate;
6.       if (heuristic fusing tests pass)
            mark as a new fused pair;
7.    }
8. }
```

Figure 5. Two-pass fusing algorithm

After the first scan, a second scan is performed; the second scan allows multi-cycle micro-ops as fusing candidate tails. The lines of pseudo-code specific to the two-pass fusing algorithm are highlighted in Figure 5.

```
1. lea       eax, DS:[edi + 01]
2. mov       [DS:080b8658], eax
3. movzx     ebx, SS:[ebp + ecx << 1]
4. and       eax, 0000007f
5. mov       edx, DS:[eax + esi << 0 + 0x7c]
```
(a) x86 assembly
```
1. ADD     Reax, Redi, 1
2. ST      Reax, mem[R18]
3. LDzx    Rebx, mem[Rebp + Recx << 1]
4. AND     Reax, 0000007f
5. ADD     R21, Reax, Resi
6. LD      Redx, mem[R21 + 0x7c]
```
(b) micro-operations
```
1. ADD  R20, Redi, 1  ::AND Reax,R20, 7f
2. ST   R20, mem[R18]
3. LDzx Rebx, mem[Rebp + Recx << 1]
4. ADD  R21, Reax,Resi::LD Redx, mem[R21 + 0x7c]
```
(c) Fused macro-ops

Figure 6. Two-pass fusing algorithm example

Figure 6 illustrates fusing of dependent pairs into macro-ops. Figure 6a is a hot x86 code snippet taken from 164.gzip in SPEC2000. The translator first cracks the x86 binary into the micro-ops, as shown in Figure 6b. Reax denotes the native register to which the x86 eax register is mapped. The long immediate 080b8658 is allocated to register R18 due to its frequent usage. After building the dependence graph, the two-pass fusing algorithm looks for pairs of dependent single-cycle ALU micro-ops during the first scan. In the example, the AND and the first ADD are fused. (Fused pairs are marked with double colon, :: in Figure 6c). Reordering, as is done here, complicates precise traps because the AND overwrites the value in register eax earlier than in the original code. Register assignment resolves this issue [30]; i.e., R20 is assigned to hold the result of the first ADD, retaining the original value of eax. During the second scan, the fusing algorithm considers multi-cycle micro-ops (e.g., memory ops) as candidate tails. In this pass, the last two dependent micro-ops are fused as an ALU-head, LD-tail macro-op.

The key to fusing macro-ops is to fuse more dependent pairs on or near the critical path. The two-pass fusing algorithm fuses more single-cycle ALU pairs on the critical path than the single-pass method in [20] by observing that the criticality for ALU-ops is easier to model and that fused ALU-ops better match the collapsed ALU units. The single-pass algorithm [20] would fuse the first ADD aggressively with the following store, which typically would not be on the critical path. Also, using memory instructions (especially stores) as tails may sometimes slow down the wakeup of the entire pair, thus losing cycles when the head micro-op is critical for another dependent micro-op. Although this fusing algorithm improvement comes with slightly higher translation overhead and slightly fewer fused macro-ops overall, the generated code runs significantly faster with pipelined issue logic.

Fused macro-ops serve as a means for re-organizing the operations in a CISC binary to better match state-of-the-art pipelines, e.g. most x86 conditional branches are fused with the condition test instructions to dynamically form concise branches and reduce much of the x86 condition code communication. The x86 ISA also has limited general purpose registers (especially for the 32-bit x86) and the ISA is accumulator-based, i.e. one register operand is both a source and destination. The consequent dependence graphs for micro-ops tend to be narrow and deep. This leads to good opportunities for fusing and most candidate dependent pairs have no more than two distinct source registers. Additionally, micro-ops cracked from x86 code tend to have more memory operations than a typical RISC binary; fusing some memory operations can effectively improve machine bandwidth.

4.2 The Pipeline Front-End: Macro-op Formation

The front-end of the pipeline (Figure 7) is responsible for fetching, decoding instructions, and renaming source and target register identifiers. To support processing macro-ops, the front-end fuses adjacent micro-ops based on the fuse bits marked by the dynamic binary translator.

Fetch, Align and Fuse

Each cycle, the fetch stage brings in a 16-byte chunk of instruction bytes from the L1 instruction cache. After fetch, an align operation recognizes instruction boundaries. x86-mode instructions are routed directly to the first level of the dual-mode decoders.

The handling of optimized macro-op code is similar, but the complexity is lower due to dual-length 16-bit granularity micro-ops as opposed to arbitrary multi-length, byte-granularity x86 instructions. The effective fetch bandwidth, four to eight micro-ops per cycle, is a good match for the pipeline backend. Micro-ops bypass the first level of the decoders and go to the second level directly. The first bit of each micro-op, the fuse bit, indicates that it should be fused with the immediately following micro-op. When a fused pair is indicated, the two micro-ops are aligned to a single pipeline lane, and they flow through the pipeline as a single entity.

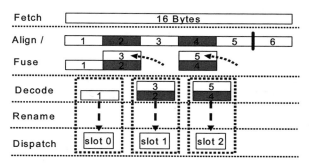

Figure 7. Front-end of macro-op execution

Instruction Decode

The x86 instructions pass through both decode levels and take three or more cycles (similar to conventional x86 processors [9, 17, 23]) for x86 cracking and decoding. RISC-style micro-ops only pass through the second level and take one cycle to decode. For each pipeline lane, decoders for micro-ops have two simple level-two micro-op decoders that can handle pairs of micro-ops (a fused macro-op pair in macro-op mode or two micro-ops in x86 mode). These micro-op decoders decode the head and tail of a macro-op pair independently of each other. Bypassing the level-one decoders results in an overall pipeline structure with fewer front-end stages when in macro-op mode than in x86 mode. The biggest performance advantage of a shorter pipeline for macro-ops is reduced branch misprediction penalties.

Rename and Macro-op Dependence Translation

Fused macro-ops do not affect register value communication. Dependence checking and map table access for renaming are performed at the individual micro-op level. Two micro-ops per lane are renamed. Using macro-ops simplifies the rename process (especially source operand renaming) because (1) the known dependence between macro-op head and tail does not require intra-group dependence checking or a map table access, and (2) there are two source operands per macro-op, which is the same for a single micro-op in a conventional pipeline.

Macro-op dependence translation converts register names into macro-op names so that issue logic can keep track of dependences in a separate macro-op level name space. In fact, the hardware structure required for this translation is identical to that required for register renaming, except that a single name is allocated to two fused micro-ops. This type of dependence translation is already required for wired-OR-style wakeup logic that specifies register dependences in terms of issue queue entry numbers rather than physical register names. This process is performed in parallel with register renaming and hence does not require an additional pipeline stage. Fused macro-ops need fewer macro-op names, thus reducing the power-intensive wakeup broadcasts in the scheduler.

Dispatch

Macro-ops check the most recent ready status of source operands and are inserted into available issue buffer and ROB entries at the dispatch stage. Because the two micro-ops in a fused pair have at most two source operands and occupy a single issue buffer slot, complexity of the dispatch unit can be significantly reduced; i.e. fewer dispatch paths are required versus a conventional design. In parallel with dispatch, the physical register identifiers, immediate values, opcodes as well as other information are stored in the payload RAM [6].

4.3 The Pipeline Back End: Macro-op Execution

The back-end of the pipeline performs out-of-order execution by scheduling and executing macro-ops as soon as their source values become available.

Instruction (Macro–op) Scheduler

The macro-op scheduler (issue logic) is pipelined and can issue back-to-back dependent *macro-ops* every two cycles. However, because each macro-op contains two dependent *micro-ops*, the net effect is the same as a conventional scheduler issuing back-to-back micro-ops every cycle. Moreover, the issue logic wakes up and selects at the macro-op granularity, so the number of wakeup tag broadcasts is reduced for energy efficiency.

Because the macro-op execution pipeline processes macro-ops throughout the *entire* pipeline, the scheduler achieves an extra benefit of higher issue bandwidth. (Macro-op execution eliminates the sequencing point at the payload RAM stage [27] that blocks the select logic for macro-op tail micro-ops).

Operand fetch: Payload RAM Access & Register File

An issued macro-op accesses the payload RAM to acquire the physical register identifiers, opcodes and other information needed for execution. Each payload RAM line has two entries for the two micro-ops fused into a macro-op. Although this configuration increases the number of bits to be accessed by a single request, the two operations in a macro-op use only a single port for both reads (the payload stage) and writes (the dispatch stage), increasing the effective bandwidth. For example, a 3-wide dispatch machine configuration has three read and three write ports that support up to six micro-ops in parallel.

A macro-op accesses the physical register file for the source values of the two fused operations. Because the maximum number of distinct source registers in a macro-op is limited to two by the dynamic binary translator, the read bandwidth is the same as for a single micro-op in a conventional implementation. Fused macro-ops better utilize register read ports by fetching an operand only once if it appears in both head and tail, and increasing the probability that both register identifiers of a macro-op are actually used. Furthermore, because we employ collapsed 3-1 ALU units at the execution stage the tail micro-op does not need the result value produced by the macro-op

head to be passed through either the register file or an operand forwarding network.

Macro-op mode does not improve register write port utilization, however, and requires the same number of write ports as a conventional machine with an equivalent number of functional units. However, macro-op execution can be extended to reduce write port requirements by analyzing the liveness of register values at translation time. We leave this to future work.

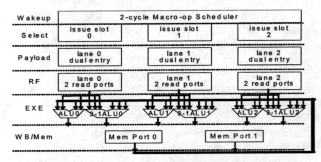

Figure 8. Datapath for macro-op execution

Execution and Forwarding Network

Figure 8 illustrates the datapath of a 3-wide macro-op pipeline. When a macro-op reaches the execution stage, the macro-op head is executed in a normal ALU. In parallel, the source operands for both head and tail micro-ops are routed to a collapsed 3-1 ALU [31, 35, 37] to generate the tail value in a single cycle. Although it finishes execution of two dependent ALU operations in one step, a collapsed 3-1 ALU increases the number of gate levels by at most one compared with a normal 2-1 ALU [31, 35]. On the other hand, modern processors consume a significant fraction of the ALU execution cycle for operand forwarding [14, 33]. As we have already observed, the macro-op execution engine removes same-cycle ALU-ALU forwarding logic, which should more than compensate for the extra gate level for the collapsed 3-1 ALUs. Thus, the overall cycle time should not be affected by the collapsed 3-1 ALU.

To better appreciate the advantages of forwarding logic simplification, first observe that for a conventional superscalar execution engine with *n* ALUs, the ALU-to-ALU forwarding network needs to connect all *n* ALU outputs to *2*n* ALU inputs. Each forwarding path therefore needs to drive at least *2*n* loads. Typically there are other forwarding paths from other functional units such as memory ports. The implications are two-fold. (1) The many input sources at each input of the ALUs necessitate a complex MUX network and control logic. (2) The big fan-out at each ALU output means large load capacitance and wire routing that leads to long wire delays and extra power consumption. To make matters worse, when operands are extended to 64-bits, the areas and wires also increase significantly. In fact, wire issues related to forwarding led the designers of the Alpha EV6 [24] to adopt a clustered microarchitecture. There is also a substantial body of related work (e.g. [13, 26, 33]) that attempts to address such wiring issues.

Functional units that have multiple cycle latencies, e.g. cache ports, still need a forwarding network as illustrated in Figure 8. However, the complexity of the forwarding paths for macro-op execution is much less than a conventional processor. In macro-op execution, the forwarding network only connects multi-cycle functional unit outputs to ALU inputs. In contrast, a conventional superscalar design having a full forwarding network needs to connect all input and output ports across all functional units.

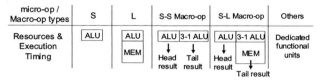

Figure 9. Resource demands and execution timing

Figure 9 illustrates resources and effective execution timings for different types of micro-ops and macro-ops; S represents a single-cycle micro-op; L represents a multi-cycle micro-op, e.g., a load, which is composed of an address generation and a cache port access. Macro-ops combining the test with the branch resolve the branch one cycle earlier than a conventional design. Macro-ops with fused address calculation ALU-ops finish address generation one cycle earlier for the LD/ST queues. These are especially effective for the x86 where complex addressing modes exist and conditional branches need separate test or compare operations to set condition codes.

Instruction Retirement

The reorder buffer performs retirement at macro-op granularity, which reduces the overhead of tracking the status of individual instructions. This retirement policy does not complicate branch misprediction recovery because a branch cannot be fused as a macro-op head. In the event of a trap, the virtual machine software is invoked to assist precise exception handling for any aggressive optimizations by reconstructing the precise x86 state (using side tables or de-optimization) [30]. Therefore, the VM runtime software enables aggressive optimization without losing intrinsic binary compatibility.

5. Evaluation

5.1 Evaluation Methodology

The proposed x86 processor is evaluated for performance via timing simulation models. The dynamic binary translator/optimizer is implemented as part of the concealed co-designed virtual machine software. The co-designed processor pipeline as described is modeled with a much modified version of SimpleScalar [7, 26] that

incorporates a macro-op execution pipeline. A number of alternative x86 microarchitecture models were also simulated for comparison and performance analysis. Details regarding the microarchitecture parameters are given in Section 5.2, along with the performance results.

SPEC2000 integer benchmarks are simulated. Benchmark binaries are generated by the Intel C/C++ v7.1 compiler with SPEC2000 –O3 base optimization. Except for 253.perlbmk, which uses a small reference input data set, all benchmarks use the test input data set to reduce simulation time. All programs are simulated from start to finish. The entire benchmark suite executes more than 35 billion x86 instructions.

As stated earlier, in this work we focus on evaluating the performance of optimized macro-op code. The detailed evaluation of mixed mode x86/macro-op operation is the subject of our on-going research. Startup IPC performance in x86-mode will likely be slightly degraded with respect to conventional designs because the design is slanted toward optimized macro-op execution; results given below support this observation. The hotspot optimization overhead is negligible for most codes (including the SPEC benchmarks). With a straightforward translator / optimizer written in C++, we measure slightly more than 1000 translator instructions per single translated instruction. The SPEC benchmarks typically have hot code regions of at most a few thousand static instructions; benchmark *gcc* has the most hot code with almost 29,000 static instructions. The total translation overhead is thus measured in the few millions of instructions; about 30 million in the case of *gcc*. Most of the benchmarks contain over a billion instructions even for the relatively small test input set. Hence, the overhead is a fraction of one percent for all but two of the benchmarks. Overhead is largest for *gcc*, where it is two percent. With the larger reference input data, we estimate the overhead to be much smaller than one percent (.2 percent for *gcc*). This observation regarding translation overheads of under one percent is qualitatively supported by other related works in dynamic translation for SPEC2000 [3] and dynamic optimization at the x86 binary level for a set of Windows applications [32].

5.2 Performance

Pipeline models

To analyze and compare our design with conventional x86 superscalar designs, we simulated two primary microarchitecture models. The first, *baseline*, models a conventional dynamic superscalar design with single-cycle issue logic. The second model, *macro-op*, is the co-designed x86 microarchitecture we propose. Simulation results were also collected for a version of the baseline model with pipelined, two-cycle issue logic; this model is very similar to the proposed pipeline when in x86-mode. Figure 3 also serves to compare the pipeline models.

Table 1. Microarchitecture configuration

	BASELINE	BASELINE PIPELINED	MACRO-OP
ROB Size	128	128	128
Retire width	3,4	3,4	2,3,4 MOP
Scheduler Pipeline Stages	1	2	2
Fuse RISCops ?	No	No	Yes
Issue Width	3,4	3,4	2,3,4 MOP
Issue Buffer Size	Variable. Sample points: from 16 up to 64 Effectively larger for Macro-op execution.		
Register File	128 entries, 8,10 Read ports, 5,6 Write ports		128 entries, 6,8,10 Read & Write ports
Functional Units	4,6,8 INT ALU, 2 MEM R/W ports, 2 FP ALU		
CacheHierarchy	4-way 32KB L1-I, 32KB L1-D, 8-way 1 MB L2		
Cache/Memory Latency	L1 : 2 cycles + 1 cycle AGU, L2 : 8 cycles, Mem: 200 cycles for the 1st chunk, 6 cycles b/w chunks		
Fetch width	16-Bytes x86 instructions		16B fusible RISC-ops

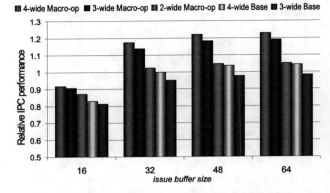

Figure 10. IPC performance comparison

The *baseline* design is intended to capture the performance characteristics of a Pentium-M-like implementation although it only approximates the Pentium-M approach. First, it uses our cracked micro-ops instead of Pentium-M micro-ops (which are not available to us for obvious reasons). Second, it does not fuse the micro-ops, but has significantly wider front-end resources to provide a performance effect similar to Pentium-M micro-op fusion. In the baseline design, an "*n*-wide" baseline front-end can crack up to *n* x86 instructions per cycle, producing up to 1.5 * n micro-ops which are then passed up a width 1.5n pipeline. For example, the four-wide baseline can crack four x86 instructions into up to six micro-ops, which are then passed through a six-wide front-end pipeline. The micro-ops in the baseline are scheduled and issued separately as in current x86 processors.

Resources for the three microarchitectures are listed in Table 1. Two register read ports are reserved for stores and two write ports are reserved for loads We simulated two pipeline widths (3,4) for the baseline models and three widths (2,3,4) for the co-designed x86 processor model featuring macro-op execution.

Performance

Figure 10 shows the relative IPC performance for issue buffer sizes ranging from 16 to 64. Performance is normalized with respect to a 4-wide baseline x86 processor with a size 32 issue buffer[1]. Five bars are presented for configurations of 2-, 3-, and 4-wide *macro-op* execution model; 3- and 4-wide *baseline* superscalar.

---

[1] The normalized values are very close to the absolute values; the harmonic mean of absolute x86 IPC is 0.95 for the four-wide baseline with issue buffer size 32.

If we first focus on complexity effectiveness, we observe that the two-wide co-designed x86 implementation performs at approximately the same IPC level as the four-wide baseline processor. However, the two-wide macro-op model has approximately same level of complexity as a conventional two-wide machine. The only exceptions are stages where individual micro-ops require independent parallel processing elements, i.e. ALUs. Furthermore, the co-designed x86 processor has a pipelined issue stage. Hence, we argue that the macro-op model should be able to support either a significantly higher clock frequency or a larger issue buffer for a given frequency, thus giving the same or better performance as a conventional four-wide processor. It assumes a pipeline no deeper than the baseline model, and in fact it reduces pipeline depth for hot code by removing the complex first-level x86 decoding and cracking stages from the critical branch misprediction path. On the other hand, if we pipeline the issue logic in the baseline design for a faster clock, there is an IPC performance loss of about 6~9%.

If we consider the performance data in terms of IPC alone, a four-wide co-designed x86 processor performs nearly 20% better than the baseline four-wide superscalar primarily due to its runtime binary optimization and the macro-op execution engine that has an effectively larger issue buffer and issue width. As will be illustrated in subsection 5.3, macro-op fusing increases operation granularity by 1.4. We also observe that the four-wide co-designed x86 pipeline performs no more than 4% better than the three-wide co-designed x86 pipeline and the extra complexity involved, for example, in renaming and register ports, may make the three-wide configuration more desirable for high performance.

5.3 Performance Analysis: Software Fusing

In the proposed co-designed x86 processor, the major performance-boosting feature is macro-op fusing performed by the dynamic translator. The degree of fusing, i.e., the percentage of micro-ops that are fused into pairs determines how effectively the macro-op mode can utilize the pipeline bandwidth. Furthermore, the profile of non-fused operations implies how the pipelined scheduler may affect IPC performance. Figure 11 shows that on average, more than 56% of all dynamic micro-ops are fused into macro-ops, more than the sub-40% coverage reported in the related work [5, 8, 27, 38]. Most of the non-fused operations are loads, stores, branches, floating point, and NOPs. Non-fused single-cycle integer ALU micro-ops are only 6% of the total, thus greatly reducing the penalty due to pipelining the issue logic.

The nearly 60% fused micro-op pairs lead to an effective 30% bandwidth reduction throughout the pipeline. This number is lower than the ~65% reported in [20] because the improved fusing algorithm prioritizes critical single-cycle ALU-ops for fusing. Previous experiments with the single-pass fusing algorithm [20] actually show average IPC slowdowns because the greedy fusing algorithm does not prioritize critical dependences and single-cycle ALU operations.

Additional fusing characterization data are also collected on the SPEC 2000 integer benchmarks to evaluate the fusing algorithm and its implications on the co-designed pipeline. About 70% of the fused macro-ops are composed of micro-ops cracked from two different original x86 instructions, suggesting that inter-x86 instruction optimization is important. Among the fused macro-ops, more than 50% are composed of two single-cycle ALU micro-ops, about 18% are composed of an ALU operation head and a memory operation tail, about 30% are dynamically synthesized powerful branches, i.e. either a fused condition test with a conditional branch (mostly), or a fused ALU operation with an indirect jump in some cases.

After fusing, 46% of the fused macro-ops access two unique source registers for operands, and only 15% of fused macro-ops (about 6% among all instruction entities) write two unique destination registers. Therefore, there exist opportunities to reduce register file write ports, and further reduce pipeline complexity. Other experimental data indicate that fused micro-ops are usually close together in the micro-op sequence cracked from x86 binary.

Profiling the dynamic binary translator code indicates that, because the fusing scans are not the dominant part of the translation overhead, the two-pass fusing algorithm increases binary translation overhead slightly (<10%) over a single-pass fusing algorithm.

5.4 Performance Analysis: HW Microarchitecture

In the co-designed x86 microarchitecture, a number of features all combine to improve performance. The major reasons for performance improvement are:

1) Fusing of dependent operations allows a larger effective window size and issue width, as has been noted.

2) Re-laying out code in profile-based superblocks leads to more efficient instruction delivery due to better cache locality and increased straight-line fetching. Superblocks are an indirect benefit of the co-designed VM approach. The advantages of superblocks may be somewhat offset by the code replication that occurs when superblocks are formed.

3) Fused operations lead naturally to collapsed ALUs having a single cycle latency for dependent instruction pairs. Due to pipelined (two cycle) instruction issue, the primary benefit is simplified result forwarding logic, not performance. However, there are performance advantages because the latency for resolving conditional branch outcomes and the latency of address calculation for load / store instructions is sometimes reduced by a cycle.

4) Because the macro-op mode pipeline only has to deal with RISC-like operations, the pipelined front-end is shorter due to fewer decoding stages.

Because speedups come from multiple sources, we simulated a variety of microarchitectures in order to separate the performance gains from each of the sources.

o *Baseline:* as before
o *M0:* Baseline plus superblock formation and code caching (but no translation)
o *M1:* M0 plus fused macro-ops; the pipeline length is unchanged.
o *M2:* M1 with a shortened front-end pipeline to reflect the simplified decoders for the macro-op mode.
o *Macro-op:* as before – M2 plus collapsed 3-1 ALU.

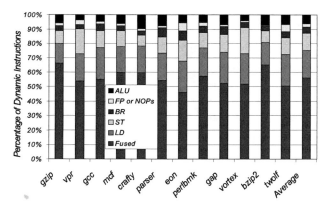

Figure 11. Macro-op fusing profile

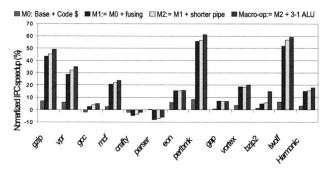

Figure 12. IPC improvement factors

All of these configurations were simulated for the four-wide co-designed x86 processor configuration featuring the macro-op execution engine, and results are normalized with respect the four-wide baseline (Figure 12). The M0 configuration shows that a hotspot code cache helps improve performance via code re-layout. The improvement is nearly 4% on average. Of course, one could get similar improvement by static feedback directed re-compilation, but this is not commonly done in practice, and with the co-designed VM approach, it happens automatically for all binaries.

The performance of M1 (when compared with M0) illustrates the gain due to macro-op fusion. This is the major contributor to IPC improvements and is more than 10% on average. The gain due to a shortened decode pipeline is nearly 1% on average. However, this gain is projected to be higher for applications where branches are less predictable. Finally, the benefit due to a collapsed ALU is about 2.5%; as noted earlier these gains are from reduced latencies for some branches and loads because the ALU result feeding these operations is sometimes available a cycle sooner than in a conventional design.

Fused macro-ops generally increase ILP by collapsing the dataflow graph. However, fusing may also cause extra cycles in some cases, e.g. when the head result feeds some other operation besides the tail, and the head is delayed because an input operand to the tail is not ready. Additionally, the pipelined scheduler may sometimes introduce an extra cycle for the 6% non-fused single-cycle ALU-ops. Figure 12 shows that our simple and fast runtime fusing heuristics may still cause slowdowns for benchmarks such as *crafty* and *parser*. The speedup for a benchmark is determined by its runtime characteristics and by how well the fusing heuristics work for it.

5.5 Discussion

Without a circuit implementation of the proposed x86 processor, some characteristics are hard to evaluate. One example is the faster clock potential that results from pipelined issue logic, removed ALU-to-ALU forwarding network, and two-level x86 decoders.

At the same pipeline width, the proposed pipeline needs more transistors for some stages, for example, ALUs, the Payload RAM and some profiling support. However, we reduce some critical implementation issues (e.g. forwarding, issue queue). Fused macro-ops reduce instruction traffic throughout the pipeline and can reduce pipeline width, leading to better complexity effectiveness and power efficiency.

6. Conclusion

Efficient and high performance x86 processors can be implemented in a co-designed virtual machine paradigm. With cost-effective hardware support and co-designed runtime software optimizers, the VM approach achieves higher performance for macro-op mode with minimal performance loss in x86-mode (during startup). This is important for the x86 (and CISC in general) where cracking generates many micro-ops that are not optimized.

The proposed co-designed x86 processor design improves processor efficiency by reducing pipeline stage complexity for a given level of IPC performance. For complexity effective processor designs, the two-wide co-designed x86 processor significantly reduces pipeline complexity without losing IPC performance when compared with a four-wide conventional x86 superscalar pipeline. The biggest complexity savings are in the reduced pipeline width, pipelined instruction issue logic, and the removal of ALU-to-ALU forwarding paths. This reduced complexity will lead to a higher frequency clock (and higher performance), reduced power consumption, and shorter hardware design cycles.

Alternatively, with similar design complexity, the co-designed x86 macro-op execution engine improves x86 IPC performance by 20% on average over a comparable conventional superscalar design on integer benchmarks. From the IPC perspective, the largest performance gains come from macro-op fusing which treats fused micro-ops as single entities throughout the pipeline to improve ILP and reduce communication and management overhead. Our data shows that there is a high degree of macro-op fusing in typical x86 binaries after cracking, and this improves throughput for a given macro-op pipeline "width" and issue buffer size. Other features also add performance improvements of 1% to 4% each. These include superblock code re-layout (byproduct of dynamic translation), a shorter decode pipeline for optimized hotspot code, and the use of a collapsed 3-1 ALU which results in reduced latency for some branches and loads.

This study explores a CISC ISA implementation that couples the co-designed virtual machine approach with an enhanced superscalar microarchitecture. It demonstrates that this is a promising approach that addresses many of the thorny and challenging issues that are present in a CISC ISA such as the x86. The co-designed x86 processor enables efficient new microarchitecture designs while maintaining intrinsic binary compatibility.

Acknowledgements

We thank Dr. Michael Shebanow and anonymous reviewers for helpful feedback. We appreciate Dr. Ho-Seop Kim's help with the microarchitecture timing model. This work was supported by NSF grants CCF-0429854, CCR-0133437, CCR-0311361 and the Intel Corporation.

References

1. Y. Almog *et al.* "Specialized Dynamic Optimizations for high-performance Energy-Efficient Microarchitecture", *2nd Int'l Symp. on Code Generation and Optimization*, 2004.

2. Vasanth Bala, *et al.* "Dynamo: A Transparent Dynamic Optimization System", *Int'l Symp. on Programming Language Design and Implementation*, pp. 1-12, 2000.

3. Leonid Baraz, *et al.* "IA-32 Execution Layer: a two phase dynamic translator designed to support IA-32 applications on Itanium®-based systems" *36th Int'l Symp. on Microarchitecture* pp 191-202 Dec. 2003.

4. P. Bonseigneur, "Description of the 7600 Computer System", *Computer Group News*, May 1969, pp. 11-15.

5. A. Bracy, P. Prahlad, A. Roth, "Dataflow Mini-Graph: Amplifying Superscalar Capacity and Bandwidth", *37th Int'l Symp. on Microarchitecture*, Dec. 2004.

6. Mary D. Brown, Jared Stark, and Yale N. Patt, "Select-Free Instruction Scheduling Logic", *34th Int'l Symp. on Microarchitecture*, pp. 204-213, Dec. 2001.

7. D. Burger, T. M. Austin, and S. Bennett, "Evaluating Future Microprocessors: The SimpleScalar ToolSet", *University of Wisconsin – Madison, Computer Sciences Department, Technical Report* CS-TR-1308, 1996.

8. N. Clark, *et al.* "Application-Specific Processing on a General-Purpose Core via Transparent Instruction Set Customization", *37th Int'l Symp. on Microarchitecture*, 2004.

9. Keith Diefendorff "K7 Challenges Intel" *Microprocessor Report*. Vol.12, No. 14, Oct. 25, 1998

10. Kemal Ebcioglu *et al.* "Dynamic Binary Translation and Optimization", *IEEE Transactions on Computers*, Vol. 50, No. 6, pp. 529-548. June 2001.

11. Kemal Ebcioglu, Eric R. Altman, "DAISY: Dynamic Compilation for 100% Architectural Compatibility", *24th Int'l Symp. on Computer Architecture*, 1997.

12. Brian Fahs, *et al.* "Continuous Optimization", *32nd Int'l Symp. on Computer Architecture*, 2005.

13. K. I. Farkas, *et al.* "The Multicluster Architecture: Reducing cycle time through partitioning." *30th Symp. on Microarchitecture (MICRO-30)*, Dec. 1997

14. E. Fetzer, J. Orton, "A fully bypassed 6-issue integer datapath and register file on an Itanium-2 microprocessor", *Int'l Solid State Circuits Conference*, Nov. 2002.

15. D. H. Friendly, S. J. Patel, Y. N. Patt, "Putting the fill unit to work: Dynamic optimizations for trace cache microprocessors", *31st Int'l Symp. on Microarchitecture*, Dec. 1998.

16. Simcha Gochamn *et al.* "The Intel Pentium M Processor: Microarchitecture and Performance", *Intel Technology Journal*, vol7, issue 2, 2003.

17. L. Gwennap, "Intel P6 Uses Decoupled Superscalar Design", *Microprocessor Report*, Vol. 9 No. 2, Feb. 1995

18. Glenn Hinton *et al.* "The Microarchitecture of the Pentium 4 Processor", *Intel Technology Journal*. Q1, 2001.

19. R. N. Horspool and N. Marovac. "An Approach to the Problem of Detranslation of Computer Programs", *Computer Journal*, August, 1980.

20. Shiliang Hu and James E. Smith, "Using Dynamic Binary Translation to Fuse Dependent Instructions", *2nd Int'l Symp. on Code Generation and Optimization,* March 2004.

21. Wen-Mei Hwu, *et al.* "The Superblock: An Effective Technique for VLIW and Superscalar Compilation", *The Journal of Supercomputing*, 7(1-2) pp. 229-248, 1993.

22. Quinn Jacobson and James E. Smith, "Instruction Pre-Processing in Trace Processors", *5th Int'l Symp. on High Performance Computer Architecture*. 1999

23. C. N. Keltcher, *et al.*, "The AMD Opteron Processor for Multiprocessor Servers", *IEEE MICRO*, Mar.-Apr. 2003.

24. R. E. Kessler, "The Alpha 21264 Microprocessor", *IEEE Micro* Vol 19, No. 2. pp 24-36, March/April, 1999.

25. Ho-Seop Kim and James E. Smith, "An Instruction Set and Microarchitecture for Instruction Level Distributed Processing", *29th Int'l Symp. on Computer Architecture*, 2002.

26. Ho-Seop Kim, "A Co-Designed Virtual Machine for Instruction Level Distributed Processing", Ph.D. Thesis, http://www.cs.wisc.edu/arch/uwarch/theses

27. Ilhyun Kim and Mikko H. Lipasti, "Macro-op Scheduling: Relaxing Scheduling Loop Constraints", *36th Int'l Symp. on Microarchitecture*, pp. 277-288, Dec. 2003.

28. Ilhyun Kim "Macro-op Scheduling & Execution", Ph.D. Thesis, http://www.ece.wisc.edu/~pharm. May, 2004

29. A. Klaiber, "The Technology Behind Crusoe Processors", *Transmeta Technical Brief*, 2000.

30. Bich C. Le, "An Out-of-Order Execution Technique for Runtime Binary Translators", *8th Int'l Symp. on Architecture Support for Programming Languages and Operating System*, pp. 151-158, Oct. 1998.

31. Nadeem Malik, Richard J. Elchemeyer, Stamatis Vassilladis, "Interlock collapsing ALU for increased instruction-level parallelism", *ACM SIGMICRO Newsletter* Vol. 23, pp: 149 – 157, Dec. 1992

32. Matthew Merten, *et al.* "An Architectural Framework for Runtime Optimization". *IEEE Trans. Computers* 50(6): 567-589 (2001)

33. S. Palacharla, N. P. Jouppi, J. E. Smith, "Complexity-Effective Superscalar Processors", *24th Int. Symp. on Computer Architecture*, pp. 206-218, Jun, 1997

34. Vlad Petric *et al.* Tingting Sha, Amir Roth, "RENO – A Rename-based Instruction Optimizer", *32nd Int'l Symp. on Computer Architecture*, 2005.

35. J. E. Phillips, S. Vassiliadis, "Proof of correctness of high-performance 3-1 interlock collapsing ALUs", *IBM Journal of Research and Development*, Vol. 37. No. 1, 1993.

36. R. M. Russell, "The CRAY-1 Computer System" *Communications of the ACM*, Vol.21, No.1, Jan. 1978, pp.63--72.

37. Y. Sazeides, S. Vassiliadis, J. E. Smith, "The performance potential of data dependence speculation and collapsing", *29th Int'l Symp. on Microarchitecture*, 1996

38. P. Sassone, S. Wills, "Dynamic Strands: Collapsing Speculative Dependence Chains for Reducing Pipeline Communication", *37th Int'l Symp. on Microarchitecture*, Dec. 2004

39. Brian Sletchta, *et al.* "Dynamic Optimization of Micro-Operations", *9th Int'l Symp. on High Performance Computer Architecture*. Feb. 2003.

40. E. P. Stritter, H. L. Tredennick, "Microprogrammed Implementation of a Single chip Microprocessor", *11th Annual Microprogramming Workshop*, Nov. 1978.

41. J. E. Thornton, "The Design of a Computer: the Control Data 6600", *Scott, Foresman, and Co.*, Chicago, 1970

42. Transmeta Corp. website. Transmeta Efficeon Processor.

A Decoupled KILO–Instruction Processor

Miquel Pericàs[†*], Adrian Cristal[†*], Ruben González[†], Daniel A. Jiménez[‡] and Mateo Valero[†*]

[†]Departament d'Arquitectura de Computadors, Universitat Politècnica de Catalunya
{mpericas,adrian,gonzalez,mateo}@ac.upc.edu

[*]Barcelona Supercomputing Center   [‡]Department of Computer Science, Rutgers University
djimenez@acm.org

Abstract

Building processors with large instruction windows has been proposed as a mechanism for overcoming the memory wall, but finding a feasible and implementable design has been an elusive goal. Traditional processors are composed of structures that do not scale to large instruction windows because of timing and power constraints. However, the behavior of programs executed with large instruction windows gives rise to a natural and simple alternative to scaling. We characterize this phenomenon of execution locality and propose a microarchitecture to exploit it to achieve the benefit of a large instruction window processor with low implementation cost. Execution locality is the tendency of instructions to exhibit high or low latency based on their dependence on memory operations. In this paper we propose a decoupled microarchitecture that executes low latency instructions on a Cache Processor and high latency instructions on a Memory Processor. We demonstrate that such a design, using small structures and many in-order components, can achieve the same performance as much more aggressive proposals while minimizing design complexity.

1 Introduction

The most important impediment to improving single-threaded processor performance is the memory wall [1]. Due to improvements in process technology and microarchitecture, modern microprocessors are clocked in the gigahertz range and can reach peak performances of several billion instructions per second. Unfortunately, improvements in memory systems have not kept pace with improvements in microprocessors. As these rates of improvement continue to diverge, we reach a point where some instructions can execute in just a few cycles while others may take hundreds or even thousands of cycles because they depend on uncached data. Critical high-latency instructions caused by cache misses can slow a processor well below its peak potential.

We present an efficient and practical proposal to address this problem. We observe that programs exhibit *execution locality*. That is, instructions tend to exhibit regular behavior in terms of their ability to be classified as either high or low latency depending on their dependence on uncached data. Just as caches were proposed to exploit data locality, we propose a decoupled Cache/Memory microarchitecture to exploit execution locality. One pipeline, the out-of-order Cache Processor (CP), handles low latency instructions and exploits as much traditional instruction-level parallelism (ILP) as possible. A second pipeline, the in-order Memory Processor (MP), handles high latency instructions and enables memory-level parallelism (MLP). The two pipelines are connected by a simple queue that gives the effect of a large instruction window without the need for a large content-addressable memory (CAM). Our decoupled approach fully exploits the parallelism available in the instruction stream by maintaining an effective window of thousands of in-flight instructions with much less complexity than competing proposals.

1.1 Our Contribution

Rather than address the limitations of each processor structure, we exploit the behavior of programs with respect to long memory latencies to produce a holistic approach to building a large instruction window processor.

This analysis allows establishing an important relationship between the memory hierarchy and the number of cycles instructions must wait for issue. This relationship gives rise to the new concept of execution locality, enabling us to build a new decoupled architecture that has many design advantages over a centralized architecture.

Config	L1 access time	L1 size	L2 access time	L2 size	memory access time
L1-2	2	∞	-	-	-
L2-11	2	32KB	11	∞	-
L2-21	2	32KB	21	∞	-
MEM-100	2	32KB	11	512KB	100
MEM-400	2	32KB	11	512KB	400
MEM-1000	2	32KB	11	512KB	1000

Table 1. Configurations for quantifying the effect of memory wall

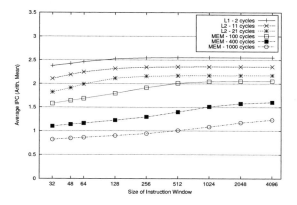

Figure 1. Effects of memory subsystem on SpecINT

2 Execution limits and Execution Locality

The memory wall itself is not necessarily a limitation to the ability to exploit instruction-level parallelism. Processor characteristics and program characteristics play an important role in the effect of the memory wall on execution.

We quantify this effect by observing the impact of several memory subsystems on a range of out-of-order cores. Out-of-order execution is necessary to evaluate the ability of these cores to hide latencies of independent instructions, usually loads. The resources of all out-of-order cores evaluated are sized such that stalls can only occur due to shortage of entries in the ROB. Thus, providing the number of ROB entries is enough to describe these 4-way speculative processors. Using SPEC2000 as the workload, six different memory subsystems are evaluated for IPC. Table 1 details their configurations. In this table, memory access times are given in processor clock cycles.

Figures 1 and 2 show the effects on IPC of using these six memory subsystems. In these figures *Size of Instruction Window* is the same size as the Reorder Buffer.

An analysis of SpecFP benchmarks shows that even for the slowest memory subsystems it is possible to recover the lost IPC simply by scaling the processor to support thousands of in-flight instructions. With an ROB of 4K entries

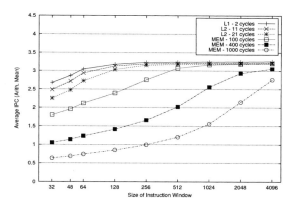

Figure 2. Effects of memory subsystem on SpecFP

almost all architectures perform similarly to the perfect L1 cache configuration. The reason behind this IPC recovery is that load misses are not on the critical path on SpecFP when enough instructions can be kept in–flight.

For SpecINT benchmarks the analysis is somewhat different. These workloads sometimes misbehave in two ways that can put a high latency load on the critical path: pointer chasing behavior and branch mispredictions depending on uncached data. The latter will force a complete squash of the instructions of the processor with a devastating effect on performance. Note that branch mispredictions depending on short latency events can be recovered from quickly and thus have little impact on IPC. Figure 1 shows how in this case recovering IPC by using large instruction windows is not an effective solution. Thus, different techniques need to be researched for these cases [2]. In any case, large-instruction windows are not detrimental to integer codes. They simply do not help as much as they do for floating point workloads.

2.1 Exploiting Execution Locality

Clearly, one way to build an architecture capable of overcoming the memory wall is to produce a chip with resources to handle thousands of in-flight instructions. This is analogous to the design methodology used for current out-of-order chips with respect to handling L1 cache miss latencies. These latencies are quite small. An L2 hit normally takes around 5-20 cycles. As new technologies have been used to implement chips, the cache distance has slowly increased. To hide this new latency, the resources on the chip (instruction queue, register file, load/store queue and reorder buffer) must be increased commensurately to maintain the previous IPC rates. This approach is feasible for dealing with increasing L1 miss latencies. However, increasing the structures more than 1000% to support thousands of in-flight instructions is totally impractical due to

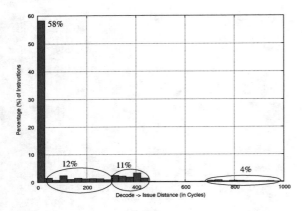

Figure 3. Average Distance between Decode and Issue/Writeback

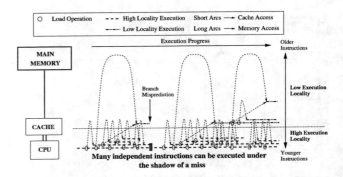

Figure 4. Execution Progress and Execution Locality

power and timing issues. Thus, most research on large-window processors has focused on replacing non-scalable resources with new resources that scale much better using a variety of techniques ranging from virtualization to hierarchical implementations, etc. Unfortunately, the design complexity of such approaches is still high.

To propose innovative designs with reduced complexity we wanted to collect more information about the execution of programs. To this end, the following instruction-centric analysis was performed. Using an out-of-order architecture with a memory latency of 400 cycles and an unlimited processor we focused on SpecFP and analyzed the average number of cycles a correct–path instruction waits in the instruction queue until it is issued. The results, shown in Figure 3, indicate that there is considerable regularity in the *issue latency* of instructions. This regularity is highly correlated with the parameters of the memory subsystem.

Several groups/peaks can be seen in the figure. Most instructions (about 70%) execute in fewer than 300 cycles while about 11% of all instructions execute around 400 cycles and about 4% execute around 800 cycles. This distribution is highly correlated with the memory access type of loads present in the instruction slices. The front-end normally advances at full speed, fetching 4 instructions per cycle. Thus the whole instruction slice is fetched in a relatively small number of cycles. We can conclude that the 70% of instructions that execute in fewer than 300 cycles are instructions that depend on a cache hit or are instructions whose source registers will all be computed in a short amount of time. The small peak around 400 cycles corresponds to instructions that depend on a single cache miss. The same applies to the small peak around 800 cycles which is made of instructions that depend on a chain of 2 cache misses. The provided numbers add up to 85%. The remaining 15% belongs to instructions where it is not clear if they depend on 1 or 2 misses, or are instructions that depend on more than 2 misses. For SpecINT applications, almost

all correct–path instructions are issued shortly after decode. The reason is that long latency events are often on a mispredicted path. After recovery, long latency loads have been turned into prefetches and most of correct-path code ends up having short issue latency.

This phenomenon can be given an interesting interpretation in terms of register availability. Once an instruction enters the instruction window, its source registers can be in 1 of 4 states: 1) READY, ie, with computed value; 2) NOT READY, depending on cache events; 3) NOT READY, waiting for other instructions to writeback; and 4) NOT READY, depending on long-latency memory events. In terms of execution, cases 2 and 3 have a very similar behavior. We are now ready to establish a new classification of instructions: Those instructions that have at least one long–latency register (ie, in state 4) are classified as having *low execution locality*. The remaining instructions, which will be issued quickly, have *high execution locality*. Execution locality is a property that describes instructions as a function of the number of cycles they wait in the queues until they issue. This distance is called the *Issue Latency*. In general, instructions depending on cache misses will have low execution locality while instructions that depend only on cache hits will have high execution locality. This concept is exemplified in Figure 4 where it is shown that different execution groups are clearly disjoint. This figure also represents one of they key properties of programs which is Karkhanis' observation that *many independent instructions can be executed under the shadow of a load miss* [3]. Large window processors, such as KILO-Instruction processors [2], profit from this characteristic to hide the latencies of long-latency misses. Figure 4 also shows the detrimental effects of mispredictions depending on cache misses. Therefore, to establish a relationship between execution locality and performance it is necessary to take into account the criticality of loads. In general, loads get very critical when they drive a low-confidence branch. These cache accesses will strongly determine performance [4].

3 A Decoupled KILO-Instruction Processor

It is interesting to take a second look at Figure 4. As the processor advances execution, the gap between the youngest and the oldest instruction tends to increase. Some events, like mispredictions or stores that end long-latency slices, will reduce this gap. Two features provide the most benefit to an architecture with an unlimited window:

1. The Fetch Unit never stalls. Thus, high locality code continues to execute in the presence of several high latency loads and loads that miss can be executed early.

2. Low locality instructions can be executed in parallel with recently fetched high locality instructions.

Execution of low locality code deserves one more look. As Karkhanis *et al.* point out [3], most instructions that are fetched under the shadow of a miss are independent of it. Thus, *The amount of low locality code is small when compared to high locality code*. Most of the execution bandwidth is consumed by high locality code. Nevertheless, current architectures have to stall every time they encounter a memory access. Thus, the small amount of low locality code present in the instruction stream causes stalls that significantly reduce performance.

The following guidelines can be derived from the analysis of execution locality:

- *Never Stall in Fetch*: It is important to continue fetching instructions and executing them because a large part of the execution bandwidth will be used for short issue latency instructions. Also, this permits executing `load` operations as soon as possible. This is the same motivation behind Continual Flow Pipelines [5].

- *Large Storage is Important but a Large CAM is Not*: We will need to store many non-executable instructions during a cache miss. However, there will be plenty of time to execute them and they do not require high execution bandwidth. Therefore it is not necessary to have all of these instructions in an issuable queue based on CAM logic. This concept has been exploited before in the Waiting Instruction Buffer [6].

- *Distributed Execution*: Low execution locality code is very decoupled from high execution locality code. There is no need to communicate back values as low locality code feeds only low locality code.

3.1 A Decoupled KILO-Instruction Processor

Using these insights we will now introduce the main contribution of this paper: the *Decoupled KILO-Instruction Processor* (D-KIP). The D-KIP is the result of exercising

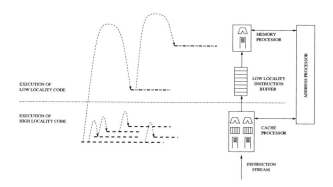

Figure 5. 2-Level Decoupled Processor

the simplest implementation of the presented guidelines; we have 1) two different execution points, 2) unidirectional communication from high locality to low locality code and 3) high latency tolerance in the low locality code. The direct implementation of these ideas is to use one processor for each locality type linked by an unidirectional instruction buffer. This structure, shown in Figure 5, complies with all design guidelines.

We will now describe the details of this microarchitecture before analyzing its performance and complexity characteristics.

3.2 Implementation of a D-KIP processor

The two-level D-KIP processor is based mostly on structures for which implementations already exist, allowing it to be built reusing standard modules and focusing on the interfaces. Thus most of the work consists in adapting the structures to comply with the interfaces. In Section 5, we analyze D-KIP from a design perspective.

Figure 5 shows that the microarchitecture consists of two processors, a simple, non-issue-capable instruction buffer and an address processor that handles all memory operations. The small and fast *Cache Processor* can be efficiently implemented using the MIPS R10000 as starting point [7]. It is useful to use a register-mapped architecture because it is important to provide fast branch recovery in the front-end. Because this processor assumes a perfect L2 Cache it can be smaller than current generation processors. The *Memory Processor* can be even simpler since it does not require much execution bandwidth. Thus in this study we have modeled it using a simple Future File architecture [8].

We target the following execution model: Instructions are fetched by the Cache Processor (CP). They stay there, waiting to be executed until they are issued to the functional units or they are determined to have long issue latency, i.e., they belong to a low execution locality slice. In this case they are moved from the CP into a Low Locality Instruction Buffer (LLIB) and wait until all long-latency events they depend on have finished. There is one LLIB for floating point and another LLIB for integer instructions.

When the long-latency load completes it simply keeps the value in the address processor. When the depending instructions arrive at the head of the LLIB and the load value is available, both the instructions and the value are inserted into the corresponding Memory Processor (MP). Execution can now proceed in the MP.

The LLIB Queues do not provide global issue capabilities. In addition, they use a FIFO policy which greatly simplifies the register management.

We will now discuss some of the modifications necessary to implement the decoupled processor.

Aging-ROB. The Cache Processor contains a ROB like other processors but in addition to allowing recovery from mispredictions and exceptions, the CP's ROB is also used to determine if instructions belong to a low execution locality group or not. For this task the ROB cannot wait until writeback because this is too late.

The D-KIP proposes using a scheme known as the *Aging-ROB*, which improves and supersedes the pseudo-ROB scheme introduced in [9]. The Aging-ROB is a ROB structure in which instructions progress at a constant pace. This allows checking whether instructions are short latency or not using a timer. In general the size of the ROB will be the number of aging cycles multiplied by the commit width, which in our study is 4. The Aging-ROB is implemented as a circular FIFO with a `head` and a `tail` pointer that is moved forward at the same speed as decode but with a constant delay.

LLIB Insertion and Wake-up. The Aging-ROB will force analysis of an instruction after a certain number of cycles. This operation is called *Analyze* in our pipeline and it determines if the instruction is long–latency. There are two instruction types that behave differently. Loads are special and they are analyzed first here. When a load arrives at *Analyze* it must be determined if it has missed; thus, the ROB timer should be large enough that it can detect a miss. To detect whether a load has missed in the L2 cache it is necessary to wait until the tag array has been accessed and the hit/miss information returns. This imposes a minimal size on the ROB timer. If the load missed, then this information is recorded in a bit vector that identifies long–latency registers (the Low Locality Bit Vector, LLBV). Otherwise the register is marked as short latency. In any case, the analysis of instructions does not stall unless the current situation of the load is still unknown. When a generic (non-load) instruction arrives at *Analyze* it is first checked whether it has already executed (this information is stored in the ROB). In that case the destination register is marked as short latency. Otherwise the sources are analyzed. If one of the sources is

long-latency then the instruction is also classified as long-latency and is therefore inserted in the LLIB. If none of the two situations applies, then the instruction is still in-flight, but will be executed soon. In this case the architecture stalls in the *Analyze* stage until the instruction writeback. The reason to stall and not continue at this point is due to the way checkpoints work, which we explain shortly. The impact of these stalls is minimal, averaging 0.7% IPC loss.

As instructions source long-latency registers, new registers are marked as long-latency in the LLBV. It is theoretically possible that, after a while, all registers are marked as long–latency, an undesirable situation that would not improve performance as all instructions would be processed by the potentially slower memory processor. However, it has been measured that this does not happen during steady state. There are various reasons for this:

- Checkpoint recovery restores the full state to the cache processor. This operations clears the LLBV completely.

- Short–latency operations, which represent more than 65% of all executed code (see section 2.1), will redefine registers that were marked as long–latency. After completion, the corresponding bit in the LLBV will be cleared.

Long-latency loads are executed in the address processor, where the LSQ is located. Upon completion, the load value is stored in a FIFO buffer, one per LLIB. Each entry in this FIFO is associated to a long latency load. When the first depending instruction is about to enter the Memory Processor, and the load value is available, the value is first inserted from this buffer into the Future File of the Memory Processor from where the operation will then obtain the value.

Registers. Register management is a critical issue. We want to keep a minimum number of registers while having a simple and implementable management algorithm. The D-KIP architecture provides a solution for both goals using a distributed organization of registers allowing for distributed and independent register management.

The Cache Processor does not need any modification. The traditional algorithm of freeing registers once the renaming instruction is *analyzed* can be used here. The Memory Processor uses a Future File architecture. It requires a logical register file in the front-end plus the associated space in the reservation stations. The low requirements of the MP enable it to have a very small number of reservation stations, so register management is very efficient in this part of the architecture.

The only structure that requires more attention is the LLIB since it may need to store many registers. However, the LLIB has some helpful properties. First, this

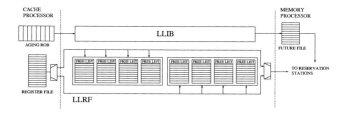

Figure 6. Schematic of the LLRF

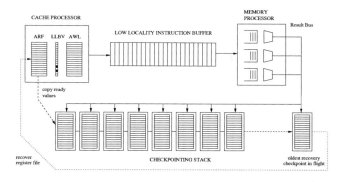

Figure 7. Schematic of checkpoints

structure is in-order, so the order in which registers are inserted/extracted is known before-hand. The LLIB register storage (called LLRF, *Low Locality Register File*) works as follows. During *Analyze* it is determined if a long-latency instruction has READY operands. These operands are then inserted into the LLRF. In the Alpha ISA, which we are using, there will never be more than one READY operand per instruction. Thus we need to preallocate at most one register per instruction. The commit width of the processor we are modeling is 4. This will require an insertion rate of 4 registers per cycle in the worst case. The same applies to the instruction extraction rate. However, the serial FIFO nature of the LLIB allows storing each register in a different bank. We model our LLRF as a banked register file with 8 banks. LLIB Insertion and LLIB Extraction always operates on a disjoint group of 4 banks. If a value to be read happens to be in a bank that is being written, the reading instruction is simply stalled for one cycle. This avoids conflicts in their access and allows to implement these banks as single-ported structures. The result is that each bank occupies minimal area and has minimal size. We calculated that the data array would be 6.6 times smaller than a centralized register file with 4 read ports and 4 write ports and the same number of entries [10]. Each bank has a free list that works independently of the other banks. The instruction in the LLIB records the position of the READY operand during insertion. Actually, not all instructions have a READY register. There are many integer instructions that have a single operand and there are instructions with two long-latency sources. These will not require an additional operand. We will analyze how to exploit this property to further reduce the size of the LLRF. A schematic showing the LLRF and the associated machinery is shown in Figure 6.

Checkpoints. The processor can recover mispredictions in the Cache Processor using the ROB structure there or a rename stack. In the memory processor, these events, although less likely, also occur. Recovery in the MP is supported by using selective checkpointing [11]. Full state checkpoints are taken at specific points during the analyze stage in the CP. At this point the instruction sees a register file composed of READY registers and some long-latency registers. Taking a checkpoint involves copying the ready

values from the architectural register file (ARF) at *Analyze* into a free entry of the Checkpointing stack. In addition, all operations that generate a long-latency register must be informed that they should writeback their destination values into this entry of the stack. This implementation is aided by keeping a small RAM parallel to the long-latency bit vector (LLBV). For each active bit in this vector, the RAM contains the position in the LLIB of the instruction that generates the value or a pointer to a previous checkpoint from which to copy the value. Having at least one checkpoint in-flight in the LLIB before wakeup assures that no inconsistencies occur. This scheme is shown in Figure 7 where the small RAM structure is referred to as the *Architectural Writers Log* (AWL). The number of ports of the Checkpointing Stack is not a problem as this structure is not frequently accessed.

In the LLIB paragraph it was mentioned that *Analyze* needs to wait for short latency instructions that have not written back their values. This simplifies checkpoint management as it makes sure that all short latency values have written into the ARF when a checkpoint is taken.

3.3 Load/Store Queues

We do not directly address a very important component of the microarchitecture: the load/store queues. A large window processor requires a scalable structure capable of supporting hundreds of in–flight loads and stores. In the D-KIP, the LSQ is decoupled from the remaining structures of the processor and it requires only small modifications to comply with the new interfaces. The reader can assume that D-KIP integrates the hierarchical queue designs presented in [12] or one of the several scalable LSQ designs that have been recently proposed [13] [14].

The LSQ is decoupled from the D-KIP in the same sense as a Decoupled Access-Execute Architecture [15]. In the D-KIP, the Address Processor needs to interface the Cache Processor and the Memory Processor. Load and Store ports can be asymmetrically partitioned – with more capacity for

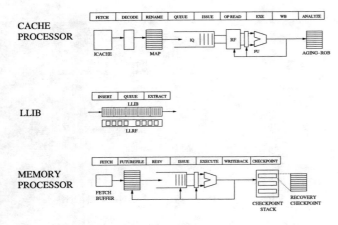

CACHE PROCESSOR

| FETCH | DECODE | RENAME | QUEUE | ISSUE | OP READ | EXE | WB | ANALYZE |

ICACHE   MAP   IQ   RF   FU   AGING-ROB

LLIB

| INSERT | QUEUE | EXTRACT |

LLIB
LLRF

MEMORY PROCESSOR

| FETCH | FUTUREFILE | RESV | ISSUE | EXECUTE | WRITEBACK | CHECKPOINT |

FETCH BUFFER

CHECKPOINT STACK   RECOVERY CHECKPOINT

Figure 8. Full Pipeline of the D-KIP

the CP – to support both cores. As was already mentioned, the address processor also needs to keep a FIFO buffer, one per LLIB, to store the results of long latency loads.

3.4 Pipeline

To conclude this section we show the full pipeline of the architecture in Figure 8. The three pipelines (Cache Processor, LLIB, Memory Processor) are chained. Most instructions only traverse the CP pipeline. Instructions will enter the LLIB when the *Analyze* stage determines that they belong to a low locality slice. Finally, insertion into the Memory Processor happens when the oldest instruction in the LLIB depends on a long-latency load that has completed. For other instructions insertion is performed without additional checks.

4 Performance Evaluation

The evaluation of the D-KIP is oriented toward verifying the introduced concept of execution locality and analyzing the efficiency of the architecture itself.

4.1 Simulation Infrastructure

Our simulation infrastructure is designed to execute Alpha binaries and traces. We rely on Simplescalar-3.0 [16] for the loading and execution of these programs. The simplescalar cycle accurate simulator is replaced by a KILO-Instruction Processor simulator capable of simulating a decoupled KILO-Instruction processor. The workbench consists of all benchmarks of the SPEC2000 benchmarking suite. We simulate 200 million committed instructions selected using the SimPoint methodology [17].

We will be evaluating several sizes for structures in the architecture. Table 2 summarizes architectural parameters

Cache Processor	
Architecture	Merged Register File [7]
Fetch/Decode/Analyze Width	4
Branch Predictor	Perceptron [18]
ROB Timer	16 cycles
ROB Capacity	64 entries
ALU Units	4
Integer Multipliers	1
FP Adders	4
FP Multipliers/Divisors	1
LLIB	
Architecture	FIFO Queue
Number of Entries	2048 each
Insertion/Extraction Rate	4
Register Storage	8 banks, 256 regs each (max)
Integer Memory Processor	
Architecture	Future File [8]
Decode Width	4
ALU Units	4
Integer Multipliers	1
FP Memory Processor	
Architecture	Future File [8]
Decode Width	4
FP Adders	4
FP Multipliers/Divisors	1
Address Processor	
Architecture	Hierarchical [12]
Load/Store Queue Size	512 entries
Number of Memory Ports	2 R/W ports (global)
L1 Cache Size	32 KB
L1 Cache Hit Latency	2 (1+1) cycles
L2 Cache Hit Latency	11 (1+10) cycles
Memory Access Latency	400 cycles

Table 2. Parameters of the architecture

that are invariant throughout this evaluation. Table 3 summarizes parameters that are going to be analyzed throughout the paper. The provided values are the defaults and are used when not specified otherwise.

L2 Cache Size	512 KB
CP Integer Queue Size	40
CP FP Queue Size	40
CP Scheduler	Out-of-Order
MP Integer Queue Size	20
MP FP Queue Size	20
MP Scheduler	In-Order

Table 3. Default values for variable parameters

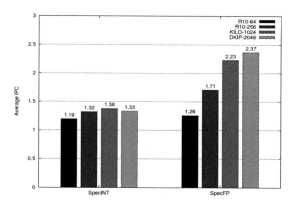

Figure 9. Performance of the D-KIP compared to baselines and a traditional KILO processor

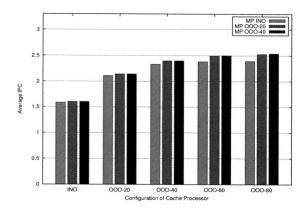

Figure 10. Impact of Scheduling Policy and Queue Sizes in SpecFP

4.2 Performance Comparison

First of all we want to test the performance of our architecture against other existing and experimental architectures. For this test we will use all the default values shown in Table 3. All LSQs are identical and have 512 entries. We will compare against three architectures:

R10-64 An Out-of-Order processor that models a MIPS R10000 processor. It has a ROB size of 64 entries and 40-entry issue queues. It is thus identical to the default Cache Processor.

R10-256 Another R10000-style processor, but with futuristic ROB and Queue sizes. The ROB here has 256 entries and the queues have 160 entries.

KILO-1024 This is an implementation of [9]. The pseudo–ROB has 64 entries and the Slow Lane Instruction Queue is Out-of-Order with 1024 entries. The issue queues have 72 entries.

D-KIP-2048 This is the implementation described here. It features two LLIBs (integer + FP) of 2048 entries each. Note that these queues are FIFOs, which allows them to be larger than the SLIQ. However, as will be shown, this has no impact on performance.

Figure 9 shows the IPC that these configurations yield. The figure shows dramatic speed-ups achievable from the two large window processors. The floating point benchmarks in particular achieve a considerable performance benefit. The reason is simple: Branch prediction in these architectures is highly accurate. Thus, long latency instructions are almost never discarded and are simply processed later after being reinserted from the long latency buffering system. Note that for integer benchmarks the performance of the D-KIP is less than that of the traditional KILO processor. The reason is that integer codes feature a lot of chasing pointers which will profit from an out-of-order instruction buffer such as the SLIQ [9]. Therefore it achieves better

performance. It does so, however, at the cost of high complexity and requires a very complex mechanism for register storage [19]. The performance advantage of the D-KIP in SpecFP compared to the KILO stems from the fact that the D-KIPs simple implementation supports trivially to implement two LLIBs and two memory processors which allows it to exploit more parallelism and adds a minimal out-of-order capability to the LLIBs which now can progress out-of-order, but only with respect to each other.

Looking at Figure 2 we see that the D-KIP-2048 achieves a SpecFP performance similar to that of the R10-768, with the difference that the D-KIP-2048 processor has no out-of-order structure larger than 40 entries.

We will analyze now which parameters are most important in these speed–ups.

4.3 Impact of Scheduler Policies and Queue Sizes

In this section we will evaluate the impact of the instruction queue sizes and impose a more severe restriction by forcing the queues to be in-order.

We find that, for integer benchmarks, the D-KIP configuration is only sensitive to the scheduling policy in the Cache Processor. Being out-of-order instead of in-order in this part of the pipeline increases the IPC by 29%. The D-KIP is insensitive to the configuration of the MP. This is reasonable as the MP processes only about 5% of all instructions during integer codes. The speed-ups are a sign that integer benchmarks profit from the D-KIP prefetching capabilities, but not from the additional processing capacity.

An analysis of SpecFP benchmarks shows that there is more potential here. Figure 10 shows the impact of the processor configurations on the execution speed for SpecFP. In this figure, *INO* means "In-Order", while *OOO-XX* means "Out-of-Order" and *XX* refers to the size of the queue.

First, the difference of in-order execution versus out-of-order execution in the Cache Processor again produces a speedup of 32%. However, in this case there are still performance increases as we go to larger processors. With an in-order MP, there is a 13% speed–up when going from an OOO CP with 20 entries to an OOO CP with 80 entries. In addition, as we go to larger CP processors, the configuration of the MP also has more impact. Going from an in-order MP to an out-of-order MP with 40 entries in the queues gives a speed-up of 1% when the Cache Processor is in-order. The same variation produces a speed-up of 6.3% when the Cache Processor is out-of-order with 80 queue entries. Figure 10 also shows that the OOO MP with 20 entries achieves almost the same IPC as the OOO MP with 40 entries. Thus, while OOO in the MP can be useful for aggressive configurations, the number of entries required can be very small in general. The most aggressive configuration achieves an IPC of 2.54, up from the 2.37 achieved by our baseline D-KIP in Figure 9.

4.4 Impact of Cache Sizes

Our next analysis focuses on the memory subsystem. We want to see how the D-KIP behaves under a subset of different sized caches. Smaller caches result in higher miss rates which in the context of the D-KIP means that more instructions are going to be executed in the memory processor. If more instructions are executed in the MP, the scheduling policy there could be of higher importance.

Based on the previous section we select a subset of configurations: *Config–CacheProc/Config–MemProc*. The configurations are: INO/INO (as the worst behaving), OOO-20/INO, OOO-80/INO and OOO-80/OOO-40. We will modify the size of the L2 Cache from 64KB to 4MB, maintaining all other parameters, and analyze the behavior of the architecture under different cache sizes. We also add the R10-256 processor to show the differences with traditional OOO–based processors. The average IPC is shown in Figure 11 and Figure 12 for SpecINT and SpecFP.

The behavior of the D-KIP under cache variations in integer benchmarks is quite common. Each duplication of size in the L2 cache produces more or less a linear speed-up in the IPC. This is very similar to the single-core out-of-order processor. The interesting properties of the D-KIP do show itself in the SpecFP figure. IPC variations are much smaller here. The capacity of the D-KIP to process correct-path long-latency instructions without stalls allows it to be more cache insensitive. The difference between using a 64KB cache and a 2MB cache is less than 15%. It is only when a 4MB Cache is added that a considerable speed-up can be perceived. In any case, the maximum speed–up is still only about 24% (INO–INO configuration).

From the figure it seems that the scheduling policy in the memory processor does not have that much influence on the IPC variations. Thus we expect that even for the small-

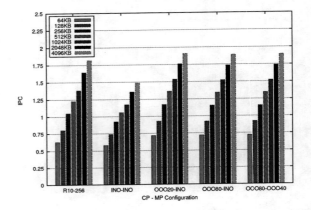

Figure 11. Impact of L2 Cache Size on SpecINT)

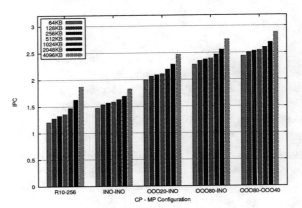

Figure 12. Impact of L2 Cache Size on SpecFP

est cache of 64KB there is still enough execution locality so that the cache processor still processes most of the instruction stream. Our simulations confirm this hypothesis. Even for the 64KB cache, the OOO-80/OOO-40 CP still processes 67% of all committed instructions in the cache processor (for SpecFP). When a 4MB cache is in use, the total number of high locality instructions increases to 77%. This difference is not so large considering that the cache size differs by about two orders of magnitude. It also explains why the D-KIP configuration is so tolerant to variations of the cache size. Compare this with the single-core R10-256 configuration. For the range of caches observed the R10-256 configuration sees a total speed-up of 1.55 while the most aggressive D-KIP configuration sees only a speed–up of 1.18. This shows the tolerance of the decoupled architecture to different cache sizes when executing numerical codes.

4.5 Storage Requirements

The LLIB requires an associated register buffer that can be very large. However, not all instructions in the LLIB

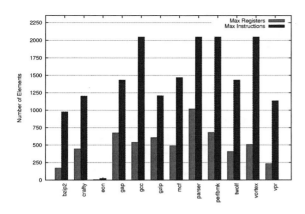

Figure 13. Maximum number of registers and instructions in the LLIB for SpecINT

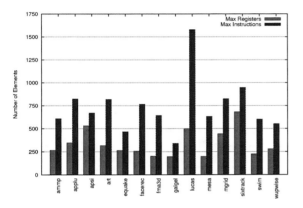

Figure 14. Maximum number of registers and instructions in the LLIB for SpecFP

have an associated READY register. They can be single-source instructions or both sources may be long latency. If a large number of instructions do not require additional storage it may be possible to reduce the size of the register storage by not allocating a register.

Figures 13 and 14 show the maximum number of simultaneous instructions and registers in the LLIB during execution in our D-KIP architecture. Each LLIB can accommodate up to 2048 instructions and an equal number of registers.

The figures show that the real number of necessary registers can be much smaller. The worst case corresponds to integer registers/instructions during SpecINT benchmarks. Many of these benchmarks contain large and irregular load chains. This results in LLIB stalls due to fill-ups for four integer benchmarks. On the other side, none of the SpecFP benchmarks required to fill the LLIB. Note that in Figure 13 we are considering the integer LLIB while in Figure 14 only the floating point LLIB is being considered.

These results suggest that the LLIB can probably be reduced considerably without significantly degrading IPC.

For the code regions executed, an LLRF with only 1000 entries would have been enough. This number is large, however there is only a single benchmark that required more than 750 registers. The average number is much smaller, fewer than 500 registers. In any case, it must not be forgotten that the LLRF is a very regular structure with 8 single-ported banks. This makes it clear that a structure such as the LLRF would not be a bottleneck, for neither area nor energy reasons.

5 Design Issues

The D-KIP processor is an attempt to provide the benefits of KILO–Instruction Processing at moderate cost. This section will focus on design issues and comment on the complexity of the approach.

The main technique that we have focused on using to reduce the complexity is decoupling [15]. While *decoupling* does not reduce the amount of hardware that has to be designed, it does limit the interaction between the two modules. The idea is to maintain only very narrow interfaces. Exploiting this property allows designer groups to work almost in isolation, with only little efforts to verify cross-module interaction correctness.

The following interfaces must be considered between the four structures:

CP→LLIB During the *Analyze* stage instructions may be sent to the LLIB as if it were a functional unit. The LLIB must synchronize with the CP and provide entries for the instruction and possibly an associated register. Moreover, when a checkpoint is taken there needs to be a path into the LLIB to inform instructions that create checkpointed registers that they have to writeback into the checkpoint stack.

LLIB→MP When an instruction slice is ready it must be sent to the MP. This is simple considering that the LLIB is a FIFO. In addition, some registers may need to be fetched from the LLRF.

LSQ→MP When long latency loads complete their values are temporarily stored in a FIFO buffer. When the depending instruction arrives at the head of the LLIB it checks if the value is available. In that case, the value needs to be written into the Future File of the MP.

CHPT→CP When the architecture returns to a checkpoint the CP's register file has to be recovered and the LLBV cleared.

CP→CHPT Checkpointed registers must be copied from the ARF in the CP to the Checkpoint Stack when a Checkpoint is taken.

MP→CHPT Checkpointed instructions must write their results into the Checkpointing Stack. Note that MP→CHPT→CP is the only way back–communication can happen in the D-KIP.

6 Related Work

Recently, there has been much research conducted to design microarchitectures able to overcome the memory wall by introducing techniques for the ROB, register files, instruction queues and load/store queues. The basic difference between these techniques and the proposal introduced here is that the D-KIP approaches the memory wall problem from the point of view of the execution locality concept, while previous efforts have concentrated on individually overcoming the scalability problem of complex processor structures.

Several modern techniques try to improve the accuracy of prefetching by actually pre–executing the program but without committing the results. *Assisted threads* [20] [21] [22] rely on pre–executing future parts of the program, selected at compile time or generated dynamically at run time. *Runahead Execution* [23] [24] pre–executes future instructions while an L2 cache miss is blocking the ROB.

Processor behavior in the event of L2 Cache misses has been studied in detail in [3]. Karkhanis *et al.* showed that many independent instructions can be fetched and executed in the shadow of a cache miss. This observation has fueled the development of microarchitectures to support thousands of in–flight instructions.

Many suggestions have been proposed for overcoming the ROB size and management problem. Cristal *et al.* propose virtualizing the ROB by using a small sequential ROB combined with multicheckpointing [25] [9] [26]. Akkary *et al.* have also introduced a checkpointing approach [12] which consists in taking checkpoints on low–confidence branches. *Cherry* [27] uses a single checkpoint outside the ROB to divide the ROB into two regions: a speculative region and a non–speculative region. *Cherry* is then able to early release physical registers and LSQ entries for instructions in the non–speculative ROB section.

Instruction queues have also received attention. The *Waiting Instruction Buffer* (WIB) [6] is a structure that holds all the instructions dependent on a cache miss until it is resolved. The *Slow Lane Instruction Queue* (SLIQ) [9] is similar in concept to the WIB but is designed as an integral component of an overall KILO–instruction microarchitecture. Recently, Akkary *et al.* have proposed the *Continual Flow Pipelines* (CFP) architecture [5] in which they propose the efficient implementation of a two–level instruction queue. It contains a Slice Data Buffer (SDB) which is similar in concept with the SLIQ. As with the SLIQ, the SDB is tightly integrated in a complete microarchitecture designed to overcome the memory wall.

Register Management has also been studied extensively. Several techniques have been developed in the context of out-of-order processors with centralized register storage. *Virtual Registers* [28] is a technique to delay the allocation of physical registers until the issue stage. On the other hand, *Early Release* [29] tries to release register earlier by keeping track of the number of consumers. An aggressive technique consists in combining both approaches. This technique is known as *Ephemeral Registers* [19]. The CFP architecture [5] stores long-lived registers along with the instructions in the Slice Data Buffer. Thus, each entry in the SDB is increased with the space to hold a register value. If the instruction has no READY registers, then the space is wasted. The D-KIP stores long-lived registers through an additional level of indirection and is thus able to save register storage.

7 Conclusions

Our main conclusion is that traditional out–of–order (OOO) execution is not a cost–effective way to handle code that depends on long–latency events. We showed that this technique is effective only to handle code dependent on cache hits, where it provides around 30% IPC improvement (see Figure 10).

Studying program behavior, we observed that over 70% of all instructions are executed a short time after they are fetched. Making an analogy with memory subsystems we described program execution using the concept of execution locality. Instructions depending on short latency events are said to have high execution locality while instructions which depend on off-chip memory accesses are said to have low execution locality.

Exploiting this idea we propose building a decoupled KILO–Instruction processor at moderate cost. We showed that high locality instructions are best processed by an out–of–order *Cache Processor* while low locality instructions can be efficiently processed by a simple in–order *Memory Processor*. Our basic implementation of the architecture featuring out–of–order queues in the Cache Processor with 40 entries and an in–order Memory Processor obtains a speed–up for SpecFP of 40% compared to a futuristic out–of-order processor with 256 entries in the issue queues and an 88% speed–up when compared to a smaller, Cache Processor–like, out–of–order processor. For SpecINT the gains are limited by the irregular branch behavior and by the presence of load chains. In future work we plan to address the impact of these load chains as well as to investigate a decentralized load/store queue organization.

The nature of the decoupled design offers the promise for reduced design complexity. Both the Cache Processor and the Memory Processor are based on well known designs such as the R10000 [7] or the Future File [8]. In addition the Low Locality Instruction Buffer uses a FIFO architecture with a simple register management algorithm.

Acknowlegements

This work has been supported by the Ministerio de Educación y Ciencia of Spain under contract TIN–2004–07739–C02–01, the HiPEAC European Network of Excellence under contract IST-004408, and by the Barcelona Supercomputing Center (BSC-CNS). Daniel A. Jiménez is supported by NSF Grant CCR-0311091 as well as a grant from the Ministerio de Educación y Ciencia of Spain, SB2003-0357. In addition, we would like to thank James C. Hoe, Francisco J. Cazorla, Oliverio J. Santana and the anonymous reviewers for the extensive comments that were helpful to improve the quality of this paper.

References

[1] W. A. Wulf and S. A. McKee, "Hitting the memory wall: Implications of the obvious," *Computer Architecture News*, March 1995.

[2] A. Cristal, O. J. Santana, F. Cazorla, M. Galluzzi, T. Ramirez, M. Pericas, and M. Valero, "Kilo-Instruction Processors: Overcoming the Memory Wall," *IEEE Micro*, vol. 25(3), pp. 48–57, May/June 2005.

[3] T. Karkhanis and J. E. Smith, "A day in the life of a data cache miss," in *Proc. of the Workshop on Memory Performance Issues*, 2002.

[4] S. T. Srinivasan and A. R. Lebeck, "Load latency tolerance in dynamically scheduled processors," *Journal of Instruction Level Parallelism*, vol. 1, pp. 1–24, 1999.

[5] S. T. Srinivasan, R. Rajwar, H. Akkary, A. Gandhi, and M. Upton, "Continual flow pipelines," in *Proc. of the 11th Intl. Conf. on Architectural Support for Programming Languages and Operating Systems*, 2004.

[6] A. R. Lebeck, J. Koppanalil, T. Li, J. Patwardhan, and E. Rotenberg, "A large, fast instruction window for tolerating cache misses," in *Proc. of the 29th Intl. Symp. on Computer Architecture*, 2002.

[7] K. C. Yeager, "The MIPS R10000 superscalar microprocessor," *IEEE Micro*, vol. 16, pp. 28–41, Apr. 1996.

[8] J. E. Smith and A. R. Pleszkun, "Implementation of precise interrupts in pipelined procceFsors," *Proc. of the 12th Intl. Symp. on Computer Architecture*, pp. 34–44, 1985.

[9] A. Cristal, D. Ortega, J. Llosa, and M. Valero, "Out-of-order commit processors," in *Proc. of the 10th Intl. Symp. on High-Performance Computer Architecture*, 2004.

[10] S. Rixner, W. J. Dally, B. Khailany, P. R. Mattson, U. J. Kapasi, and J. D. Owens, "Register organization for media processing," in *Proc. of the 6th Intl. Symp. on High Performance Computer Architecture*, 2000, pp. 375–386.

[11] W. mei W. Hwu and Y. N. Patt, "Checkpoint repair for out-of-order execution machines," in *Proc. of the 14th Intl. Symp. on Computer Architecture*, 1987, pp. 18–26.

[12] H. Akkary, R. Rajwar, and S. T. Srinivasan, "Checkpoint processing and recovery: Towards scalable large instruction window processors," 2003.

[13] S. Sethumadhavan, R. Desikan, D. Burger, C. R. Moore, and S. W. Keckler, "Scalable hardware memory disambiguation for high ILP processors," in *Proc. of the 36th Intl. Symp. on Microarchitecture*, 2003.

[14] I. Park, C. L. Ooi, and T. N. Vijaykumar, "Reducing design complexity of the load/store queue," in *Proc. of the 36th Intl. Symp. on Microarchitecture*, 2003.

[15] J. E. Smith, "Decoupled state/access computer architectures," in *Proc. of the 9th annual Intl. Symp. on Computer Architecture*, 1982.

[16] T. Austin, E. Larson, and D. Ernst, "Simplescalar: an infrastructure for computer system modeling," *IEEE Computer*, 2002.

[17] T. Sherwood, E. Perelman, G. Hamerly, and B. Calder, "Automatically characterizing large scale program behavior," in *Proc of the 10th Intl. Conference on Architectural Support for Programming Languages and Operating Systems*, 2002.

[18] D. A. Jimenez and C. Lin, "Dynamic branch prediction with perceptrons," in *Proc. of the 7th Intl. Symp. on High Performance Computer Architecture*, January 2001, pp. 197–206.

[19] A. Cristal, J. Martinez, J. LLosa, and M. Valero, "Ephemeral registers with multicheckpointing," Tech. Rep., 2003, technical Report number UPC-DAC-2003-51, Departament d'Arquitectura de Computadors, Universitat Politecnica de Catalunya.

[20] Y. H. Song and M. Dubois, "Assisted execution," Tech. Rep., 1998, technical Report #CENG 98-25, Department of EE-Systems, University of Southern California.

[21] R. S. Chappell, J. Stark, S. P. Kim, S. K. Reinhardt, and Y. N. Patt, "Simultaneous subordinate microthreading (SSMT)," in *Proc. of the 26th. Intl. Symp. on Computer Architecture*, 1999.

[22] A. Roth and G. Sohi, "Speculative data-driven multithreading," in *Proc.of the 7th Intl. Symp. on High-Performance Computer Architecture*, 2001.

[23] J. Dundas and T. Mudge, "Improving data cache performance by pre-executing instructions under a cache miss," in *Proc. of the 11th Intl. Conf. on Supercomputing*, 1997, pp. 68–75.

[24] O. Mutlu, J. Stark, C. Wilkerson, and Y. N. Patt, "Runahead execution: An alternative to very large instruction windows for out-of-order processors," in *Proc. of the 9th Intl. Symp. on High Performance Computer Architecture*, 2003, pp. 129–140.

[25] A. Cristal, M. Valero, A. Gonzalez, and J. LLosa, "Large virtual ROBs by processor checkpointing," Tech. Rep., 2002, technical Report number UPC-DAC-2002-39. [Online]. Available: http://www.ac.upc.edu/recerca/reports/DAC/2002/index,en.html

[26] A. Cristal, O. J. Santana, J. F. Martinez, and M. Valero, "Toward kilo-instruction processors," *ACM Transactions on Architecture and Code Optimization (TACO)*, pp. 389 – 417, December 2004.

[27] J. Martinez, J. Renau, M. Huang, M. Prvulovic, and J. Torrellas, "Cherry: Checkpointed early resource recycling in out-of-order microprocessors," in *Proc. of the 35th Intl. Symp. on Microarchitecture*, 2002, pp. 3–14.

[28] A. Gonzalez, M. Valero, J. Gonzalez, and T. Monreal, "Virtual registers," in *Proc. of the 4th Intl. Conf. on High-Performance Computing*, 1997.

[29] M. Moudgill, K. Pingali, and S. Vassiliadis, "Register renaming and dynamic speculation: an alternative approach," in *Proc. of the 26th. Intl. Symp. on Microarchitecture*, 1993, pp. 202–213.

Store Vectors for Scalable Memory Dependence Prediction and Scheduling

Samantika Subramaniam   Gabriel H. Loh

Georgia Institute of Technology

College of Computing

{samantik,loh}@cc.gatech.edu

Abstract

Allowing loads to issue out-of-order with respect to earlier unresolved store addresses is very important for extracting parallelism in large-window superscalar processors. Blindly allowing all loads to issue as soon as their addresses are ready can lead to a net performance loss due to a large number of load-store ordering violations. Previous research has proposed memory dependence prediction algorithms to prevent only loads with true memory dependencies from issuing in the presence of unresolved stores. Techniques such as load-store pair identification and store sets have been very successful in achieving performance levels close to that attained by an oracle dependence predictor. These techniques tend to employ relatively complex CAM-based designs, which we believe have been obstacles to the industrial adoption of these algorithms. In this paper, we use the idea of dependency vectors from matrix schedulers for non-memory instructions, and adapt them to implement a new dependence prediction algorithm. For applications that experience frequent memory ordering violations, our "store vector" prediction algorithm delivers an 8.4% speedup over blind speculation (compared to 8.5% for perfect dependence prediction), achieves better performance than store sets (8.1%), and the store vector algorithm's matrix implementation is considerably simpler.

1. Introduction

Each successive technology generation provides more transistors to processor designers. However, an increase in the device count does not automatically result in an increase in performance. Processor microarchitectures evolve with each process generation to convert exponential device scaling into exponential performance scaling.

Microarchitecture contributes to performance scaling through hardware algorithms for extracting instruction level parallelism (ILP) [7, 22, 25]. A frequently studied technique for exposing more ILP is to increase the number of instructions in-flight in the processor. This may come from implementing very large instruction windows [4, 15, 18], creating large *effective* instruction windows [1, 26], or using non-conventional processor organizations [24, 27]. The effectiveness of a large instruction window for mining ILP is quickly limited by memory level parallelism (MLP) [9]. To maximize the effectiveness of a large instruction window, loads must be able to execute out-of-order with respect to unresolved store addresses.

Out-of-order load instruction scheduling is a non-trivial problem. Load instructions may have data dependencies through memory where an earlier store instruction writes a value to an address and the load instruction reads that value from the same memory location. Unfortunately, the effective addresses of all load and store instructions may not be available because the corresponding address computations may not have issued. This leads to a dependency ambiguity: depending on the result of a store's address computation, a later load instruction may or may not actually be data-dependent. If the load is actually independent, then it should be scheduled for execution to maximize performance. If the load is data-dependent, then it must wait for the store instruction.

Memory dependence prediction is a technique for speculatively disambiguating the relationship between loads and stores. However, a load instruction that issues too early due to a dependence misspeculation will load a stale value from the data cache and propagate this incorrect value to its dependent instructions. Many cycles may pass between when the load instruction issues and when the processor finally detects the ordering violation. At this point, a large number of instructions from the load's forward slice [28] may have already executed. Tracking down and rescheduling all of these instructions is a very difficult task, and so a memory dependence misspeculation is typically handled by flushing the pipeline. Overly aggressive load scheduling combined with the high cost of pipeline flushes can therefore result in a net performance decrease.

The most accurate memory dependence predictors rely on identifying relationships between load instructions and one or more earlier stores that are likely data-flow predecessors. Before a load instruction can issue, it must wait until these predicted dependencies have been resolved. The communication of this dependency resolution typically requires hardware-intensive CAM logic. The load-store queue (LSQ) is already a very complex circuit with a full set of CAMs for detecting load-store ordering violations as well as supporting store-to-load data forwarding; adding a second set of CAMs to support memory dependence prediction is not practical because of the negative consequences on critical path latency of the LSQ and overall processor clock frequency.

Conventional implementations of non-memory instruction schedulers are also CAM-based. The associative logic causes the scheduler to be a timing critical path [21]. Dependency-vector/matrix scheduler organizations have been proposed for faster and more scalable implementations [5, 10]. In this paper, we propose a new memory dependency prediction and scheduling algorithm based on this idea of dependency vectors. Besides providing a more scalable hardware implementation, our "store vector" prediction algorithm also results in higher overall performance than the previous state-of-the-art CAM-based store sets approach.

The next section discusses prior work on memory dependence prediction, and in particular it reviews the store sets algorithm in greater detail. Section 3 explains our proposed store vector approach, providing a step-by-step description and example of the technique. Section 4 presents the performance results of our store vector algorithm compared to naive speculation, store sets, and perfect dependence prediction. Section 4 also provides more detail on why store vectors perform better than store sets. Section 5 concludes the paper with a discussion on possible design alternatives if microarchitectural parameters were changed.

2. Background

2.1. Memory Dependence Predictors

Like many other properties in microprocessors, memory dependencies exhibit a form of temporal locality. The concept of *memory dependence locality* was introduced by Moshovos [19]. In his thesis work, Moshovos characterized two forms of locality: memory dependence status locality, and memory dependence set locality. Memory dependence status locality makes the observation that when a load experiences a store dependency, subsequent instances of the same load will likely experience a dependency as well. Status locality makes no statement about *which particular stores* a load may or may not be dependent on. Memory dependence set locality makes the observation that if a load is dependent on a set of store instructions, then future instances of that load will likely be dependent on the same set of stores.

Previously proposed memory dependence predictors typically predict the *dependence status* of a load: whether a dependence currently exists or not which determines if the load can issue. The basic dependence predictors do not attempt to exploit the dependence set locality property. The most basic predictor is a *naive* or *blind* predictor that simply predicts all load instructions to not have any store dependencies. A blind predictor will never cause a load to wait when store dependencies are not present, but it will always cause a costly misprediction if a dependency exists. The Alpha 21264 employed a "store wait table" that tracks all loads that experienced ordering violations [13]. When a store executes and exposes a load ordering violation, the load's address indexes into the store wait table where a bit is set. On subsequent instances of the load, the store wait table will indicate that the load previously caused a memory ordering violation and the scheduler will force the load to wait until all earlier store addresses have been resolved. The processor periodically clears the table to avoid permanently preventing loads from speculatively issuing.

Status-based prediction schemes do not take instruction timing into account. A load that is predicted to have a dependency will wait for *all* previous store instructions before issuing. In practice, the load will only be dependent on one or a few of the previous stores. Even if all of these store dependencies have computed their addresses, the load must conservatively wait until the non-dependent stores have resolved as well. A status-based predictor may correctly predict the status of a load and avoid a pipeline flush, but potential ILP may still be lost from preventing a "timely" issuing of the load. Memory dependence predictors based on observing the exact sets of stores that a load collides with have shown to provide better prediction accuracy and overall performance. Moshovos proposed a dependence history tracking technique that identifies load-store pairs known to have memory dependencies [19, 20]. When a load speculatively issues and violates a true dependency with an older store, the program counters (PC) of the load and the store are recorded in a table. Subsequent executions of the load instruction will check the table to see if they have conflicted with a store in the past. If so, the load will also check the store queue (using the store PC recorded in the table) to see if that store is present. If the store is present in the store queue, then the load must wait until the store has issued. This load-store pair approach has the advantage that mis-speculations can be avoided, but at the same time the dependent loads are not delayed longer than necessary.

Different dynamic invocations of a load may have memory dependencies with different static stores. Moshovos also proposed an extension to load-store pair identification that associates a bounded number of stores with each load [19]. Chrysos and Emer generalized this approach with their "store sets" algorithm that allows one or more load in-

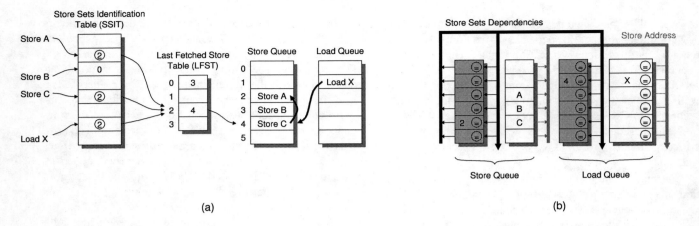

Figure 1. (a) Store sets data structures, (b) LSQ hardware modifications (shaded) required to support store sets.

structions to be associated with one or more stores [6]. Previous work showed that a store sets memory dependence predictor provides performance close to that of an oracle predictor. From our own simulations we observed that store sets delivers about 94% of the benefit that an oracle predictor provides over blind speculation. We use store sets as our baseline for comparison in this paper, and therefore we describe the algorithm in greater detail in the next section.

2.2. Store Sets

The store sets algorithm groups a load's conflicting stores into one logical group or a *store set* [6]. Each store set has a unique identifier, called the store set identifier (SSID). Each load and each store may belong to one store set. Figure 1(a) shows the hardware organization of the store sets data structures. The store sets identification table (SSIT) is a PC-indexed, tagless table that tracks the current store set assignment for each load and store instruction. The example in the figure shows Stores A and C and Load X belonging to store set number 2, while Store B belongs to store set number 0. This means that in the past, Load X has had memory ordering violations with Stores A and C. The SSIT combined with proper SSID assignment track the active store sets in the program.

To prevent memory ordering violations, a load instruction must wait on any unresolved store instructions that belong to the load's store set. To determine if any such stores are present in the store queue (STQ), each store updates the last fetched store table (LFST) which indicates the store queue index of the most recent in-flight store. At dispatch, a load instruction consults the LFST and if an active store is present, a dependency is established between the two instructions. In Figure 1(a), the most recently fetched store (from the load's store set) resides in STQ entry 4 as indi-

cated by the LFST and the dependency is illustrated by the bold arrow. To make a load wait on *all* active stores in its store set, all stores within the same set are also serialized. This is represented by the dependency arc between Store A and Store C in Figure 1(a). As described, each store can only belong to a single store set determined by the value in the single SSIT entry corresponding to the store. This means that if there are two different loads that are dependent on the same store, then the store will "ping-pong" back and forth between the two loads. To address this problem, Chrysos and Emer proposed a modified SSID assignment rule called store sets merging that allows more than one load to share the same store set.

The store sets algorithm introduces new dependencies from stores to stores, and from stores to loads. These dependencies prevent costly memory ordering violations while allowing independent loads to aggressively issue out-of-order. However, the load and store queues must incorporate new hardware to track and enforce the store sets dependencies. The load and store queues are already very complex structures, requiring a large amount of content addressable memory (CAM) logic for the detection of memory ordering violations and to support store-to-load data forwarding. Compared to a non-memory instruction scheduler, the load and store queue CAMs are much larger because they must deal with 64-bit addresses rather than 7-8 bit physical register identifiers. Furthermore, the load and store queues must also employ some form of age or order-tracking information because a load must be able to distinguish between an older (in program order) store and a younger store to the same address. In situations where there exist multiple older stores to the same address, a load needs the age information to make sure that it receives its data from the more recent store. Implementing store sets requires a second set of

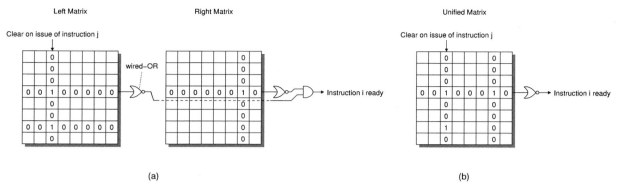

Figure 2. (a) Two-matrix scheduler, (b) single-matrix unified scheduler.

CAM logic and the associated broadcast buses to track the store sets dependencies, as illustrated by the shaded blocks in Figure 1(b).

Conventional non-memory instruction scheduling logic is already a timing critical path in modern processors [21]. The load and store queue circuits have similar complexity[1], and therefore adding even more logic to implement store sets will likely have severe negative consequences on the processor clock frequency or the maximum load and store queue sizes. As processors increase the number of instructions in flight, the load and store queues will not scale well [8] and a CAM-based store sets implementation would only make the poor scaling worse. Furthermore, the LFST creates a new critical loop similar to the register renamer. It is possible that multiple stores need to update the LFST in the same cycle. If all of these stores belong to the same store set, then some sort of dependency checker is required to correctly set up the intra-group dependencies, and a prioritized write logic is needed to make sure that only the last store in the store set updates the corresponding LFST entry.

2.3. Scheduling Structures

Instruction schedulers typically use content addressable memory (CAM) organizations. Each issuing instruction broadcasts a unique identifier to notify its dataflow children that the dependency has been resolved. Each instruction must monitor all of the broadcast buses, constantly comparing the identifiers of its inputs with the broadcast traffic. Palacharla analyzed the structure of CAM-based schedulers and found that the critical path delay increases quadratically with the issue width and the number of entries [21].

The dependency vector or dependency matrix scheduler organization is an alternative scheduler topology designed to be significantly more scalable. Goshima et al. proposed

to replace the left and right CAM banks of a conventional scheduler with left and right dependency matrices as illustrated in Figure 2(a). For a W-entry scheduler, each matrix has W rows and W columns; one for each instruction. If instruction i is data-dependent on instruction j, then the matrix entry at row i and column j is set to one. So long as instruction i has a bit set in its row, then the corresponding input dependency has not been resolved. When instruction j issues, it clears *all* bits in column j, thus notifying any dependents in the window that the parent instruction has been scheduled. The critical path logic is significantly reduced as compared to a CAM-based scheme. The tag comparison for computing readiness has been replaced by a single wired-NOR and an AND gate to check that both left and right inputs are ready. The multi-bit tag broadcast has been replaced by a single bit latch-clear signal. The matrix structures only contain one bit per entry which makes the total area significantly smaller than a CAM-based scheduler that contains registers for the dependency tags, comparators, large broadcast buses, and additional logic. Figure 2(b) illustrates a single-matrix implementation, suggested by Brown et al. Each matrix row can contain multiple non-zero entries to denote all of the dependencies [5], which halves the matrix area and removes the AND gates for detecting both left-and-right input readiness. Our store-vector dependence predictor's hardware implementation is based on this compact, scalable single-matrix scheduler structure.

3. Store Vector Dependence Prediction

We propose a new algorithm for memory dependence prediction based on *store vectors*. Store vectors are different than the load-store pair and store set approaches in that store vectors do not explicitly track the program counters (PC) of stores that collide with loads. Instead, we implicitly track load-store dependencies based on the relative *age* of a store. Consider the example in Figure 3. The five load and store instructions are listed in program order, and Load

---

[1]The previous discussion would make it seem like the load and store queues are *significantly* more complex, but the issue width of these structures tend to be less than that of non-memory instruction schedulers which somewhat balances out the complexity.

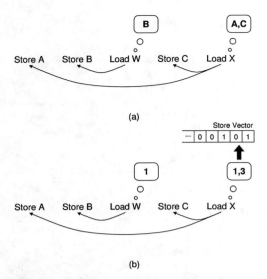

Figure 3. (a) Store-address tracking of dependencies, and (b) store position or age tracking of dependencies.

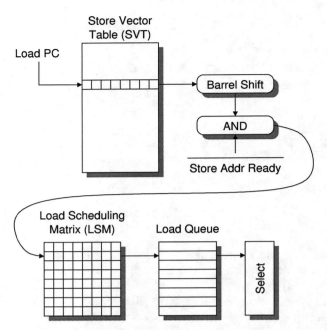

Figure 4. Store vectors data structures and interaction with a conventional load queue.

W has had ordering violations with Store B in the past, and Load X has had ordering violations with both Stores A and C. Figure 3(a) illustrates the PC-based dependency information used by previous pair or set-based approaches. In contrast, an age-based approach illustrated in Figure 3(b) stores the relative age or positions of the stores. Load X remembers that it had previous conflicts with the most recent store and the third most recent store.

A load's *store vector* records the relative positions or ages of all stores that were involved in previous memory ordering violations. The store vector for Load X is illustrated in Figure 3(b). In the general case, the length of the store vector will be equal to the number of store queue entries. The store vector could be optimized to only track store dependencies if the violating store was one of the k most recent stores with respect to the misspeculating load.

3.1. Step-by-Step Operation

The store vector algorithm has three main steps: lookup/prediction, scheduling, and update due to ordering violations. These are described in turn below, followed by an example.

Lookup/Prediction — The primary data structure for recording load-store dependencies is the store vector table (SVT). For each load, the least significant bits of the load's PC provides an index into the SVT, shown in Figure 4. The corresponding store vector is then rotated and copied into the load scheduling matrix (LSM or simply the *matrix*). The process for setting a load's store vector is described later. The LSM consists of one row for each load queue entry,

and one column for each store queue entry (the matrix need not be square).

An SVT entry records a load's store vector in a format where the least significant bit corresponds to the most recent store before the load. The rightmost column of the LSM may not correspond to the most recently fetched store. A barrel shifter must rotate the vector such that the least significant bit is aligned with the column of the most recent store. Any bits in the vector that correspond to already resolved stores must be cleared to prevent the load from waiting on an already resolved dependency (which could result in deadlock). This is accomplished by taking a bitwise AND of the store vector with the bits from each store queue entry that indicates if the store's address is *not* ready. Finally, the vector is written into the matrix.

Note that for both the store sets and store vector techniques, the prediction lookup latency can be overlapped with other front-end activities. Both approaches use PC-based table lookups which could in theory be initiated as early as the fetch stage, although for power reasons one would likely defer the lookup to the decode stage to avoid unnecessary predictions for non-load instructions.

Scheduling — After the prediction phase has written a load's store vector into the LSM, there may be some bits in the vector that are set. The position of the bits indicate the stores that this load is predicted to have a dependency with. While any of the bits are still set, the load will not be considered as ready. The hardware implementation of the

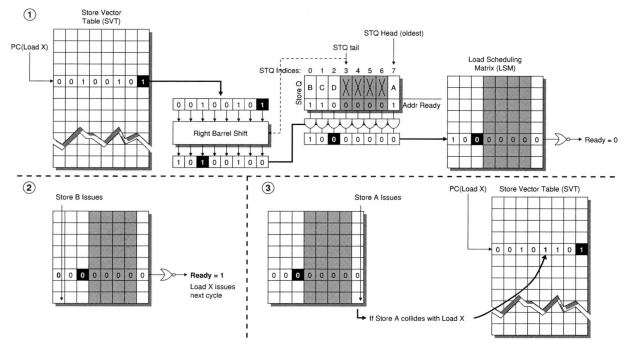

Figure 5. Example store vector operation for the ② prediction phase, ③ scheduling phase, and ④ update phase.

matrix is identical to the single-matrix scheduler described earlier in Figure 2(b). A wired-NOR determines if any unresolved predicted dependencies remain.

Each store queue entry is uniquely mapped to a column of the matrix. When the store issues, it simply clears all of the bits in its corresponding column. Note that stores in the same vector can issue in any order, whereas with store sets all of the stores are serialized. Furthermore, a store can be a predicted input dependence for any number of load instructions (more than one entry per column may be set), whereas with store sets the LFST forces each store to belong to only a single store set.

Update — Initially, vectors in the SVT are initialized to all zeros. In this fashion, all load instructions will initially execute as if under a naive/blind speculation policy. When a load-store ordering violation occurs, the store's relative position/age is determined. The position of the most recent store with respect to the offending load is easily determined because the processor already keeps this information for tracking the ordering of all load and stores. The difference between the store queue indexes of the most recent store and the store involved in the ordering violation provides the relative age of the offending store. This bit is then set in the load's SVT entry.

Eventually, all bits in the vector may get set, thus making the processor behave as if it was incapable of any memory

speculation at all. Similar to the 21264 store wait table and store sets, we periodically reset the contents of the SVT to clear out predicted dependencies that may no longer exist due to changes in program phases, dynamic data values, or other reasons.

3.2. Example

This section provides a detailed example of predicting a load's dependencies, scheduling the load, and updating the load's store vector when an ordering violation occurs. The different steps of the example are illustrated in Figure 5.

① **Prediction:** After decoding the instruction Load X, a hash of the load's PC is used to select a vector from the Store Vector Table. The store vector bit that corresponds to the most recent store fetched before this load is indicated with shading. The 1's in the vector indicate that Load X is predicted to be dependent on the most recent store (shaded), the third most recent store, and the sixth most recent store.

In this example, the most recent store is Store D which has been allocated to store queue (STQ) entry 2. The STQ-head points to the oldest STQ entry, and the STQ-tail points to the next available STQ entry. If we right barrel shift (least significant bits wrap around to the most significant positions) by an amount equal to the STQ-tail, the store vector bit for the most recent store will now be properly aligned with the most recent STQ entry. In this case, the right barrel shift is by three; note that the position of the shaded bit has moved to reflect the location of the most-recent store.

Corresponding to the non-zero bits in load's store vector, the most recent store is Store A, the third most recent is Store C, and a sixth most recent does not exist. The store vector predicts that Load X is dependent on the most recent store, but at the time of dispatch, Store A had already issued and so Load X should not wait on Store A. Each entry of the store queue has a bit that indicates whether the corresponding store address is unknown. In the case of invalid entries, the bit is cleared to indicate that the address is known. By taking a bitwise AND, we clear the store vector bit that corresponded to the invalid store (the sixth most recent store) as well as a store that had already been resolved (Store A). This final store vector is written into the Load Scheduling Matrix in the row specified by the load's Load Queue entry index.

② **Scheduling:** In this example, Load X only has one remaining dependency in its store vector. At some point in the future, Store B will issue. At this point, Store B clears its column in the Load Scheduling Matrix. Each STQ entry can simply have a single hardwired connection to the clear signal for the corresponding column. Load X's store vector no longer contains any 1's, and so the wired-NOR will raise its output to indicate that Load X's predicted store dependencies have all been satisfied. Assuming that Load X's address has already been computed, it will proceed to bid for a memory port and then issue.

③ **Update:** If Load X issued and the load and store queues do not eventually detect any memory ordering violations, then no other actions are required. If after Load X speculatively issues and Store A ends up writing to the same address as Load X, then there will be a memory ordering violation. In this case, Load X and all instructions afterward are flushed from the pipeline and re-fetched. Store A is the fourth most recent store with respect to Load X, although it may not be the fourth most recent store in the store queue because other store instructions may have been fetched since Load X was dispatched. To prevent future memory-ordering violations between Store A and Load X, the store updates Load X's store vector in the SVT, setting the bit for the fourth most recent store.

4. Results

This section presents the performance evaluation of our Store Vector dependence prediction algorithm.

4.1. Evaluation Methodology

We use cycle-level simulation to evaluate the performance of memory dependence predictors. In particular,

Processor Width	6	IL1 Cache	16KB, 4-way, 3-cycle
Scheduler Size (RS)	64	DL1 Cache	16KB, 4-way, 3-cycle
Load Queue Size	32	L2 Cache	512KB, 8-way, 10-cycle
Store Queue Size	32	L3 Cache	4MB, 16-way, 30-cycle
ROB Size	256	Main Memory	250 cycles
Integer ALU/Mult	4/1	ITLB	64-entry, FA
FP ALU/Mult	2/1	DTLB	64-entry, FA
Memory Ports	2	L2 TLB	1024-entry, 8-way, 7-cycle

Table 1. Simulated processor configuration.

we use the MASE simulator [14] from the SimpleScalar toolset [2] for the Alpha instruction set architecture. We made several modifications related to memory dependence prediction and scheduling, including support for separate load and store queues (as opposed to a unified load-store queue), store sets and the store vector algorithms.

Our experiments use a 6-wide superscalar processor. Table 1 lists the processor parameters which were loosely based on the Intel Netburst microarchitecture (Pentium 4) [12]. We are not trying to model an Intel processor with an Alpha-based simulator; rather, we use Netburst as a configuration starting point to baseline the aggressiveness of our microarchitecture. The minimum latency from fetch to execution is twenty cycles, and we simulate a full in-order front-end pipeline as opposed to the default SimpleScalar behavior of simply stalling fetch for some number of cycles.

We simulated a variety of applications from SPEC2000, MediaBench [16], MiBench [11], Graphics applications including 3D games and ray-tracing, and pointer-intensive benchmarks [3]. All SPEC applications use the reference inputs, where applications with multiple reference inputs are listed with different numerical suffixes. To reduce simulation time, we used the SimPoint 1.2 toolset to choose representative samples of 100 million instructions [23]. Using SimPoint avoids simulating non-representative portions of an application such as start-up and initialization code which can sometimes take up the first several billion instructions of a program's execution. All "average" IPC speedups are computed using the geometric mean.

4.2. Performance Results

Our baseline processor configuration uses naive/blind speculation. We also use a perfect oracle dependence predictor as an "upper bound." The oracle guarantees perfect dependency prediction, but this does not necessarily result in maximum performance because misspeculated loads can still have performance benefits due to prefetching effects or early branch misprediction detection. Table 2 lists the raw IPC rates for all of the benchmarks with blind speculation, and the relative performance impact of the different memory dependence predictors.

Note that the IPC rates of several applications are not sensitive to memory dependence prediction. In most of

70

Benchmark Name			Base IPC	St.Sets	St.Vectors	Perfect
adpcm-dec	M		3.83	0.0%	**0.0%**	0.0%
adpcm-enc	M		1.58	0.0%	**0.0%**	0.0%
ammp	F		1.32	0.0%	**0.0%**	0.0%
anagram	P	x	2.06	11.6%	**11.7%**	11.7%
applu	F		0.72	0.0%	**0.0%**	0.0%
apsi	F	x	2.14	1.8%	**1.9%**	1.9%
art-1	F		1.53	0.0%	**0.0%**	0.0%
art-2	F		1.49	0.0%	**0.0%**	0.0%
bc-1	P	x	2.17	6.0%	**6.8%**	6.0%
bc-2	P	x	1.11	3.2%	**3.6%**	3.5%
bc-3	P		1.15	0.2%	**0.2%**	0.3%
bzip2-1	I		1.56	0.5%	**0.5%**	0.6%
bzip2-2	I		1.59	0.1%	**0.0%**	0.1%
bzip2-3	I		1.70	-0.3%	**-0.3%**	0.4%
crafty	I	x	1.24	6.3%	**6.2%**	6.3%
crc32	E		2.62	0.0%	**0.0%**	0.0%
dijkstra	E		2.15	0.0%	**0.0%**	0.1%
eon-1	I	x	1.23	19.9%	**18.8%**	19.4%
eon-2	I	x	0.91	3.6%	**3.4%**	3.9%
eon-3	I	x	1.00	7.1%	**7.4%**	8.1%
epic	M		1.86	0.0%	**0.0%**	0.0%
equake	F		0.83	0.0%	**0.0%**	0.0%
facerec	F	x	2.06	6.7%	**6.7%**	6.7%
fft-fwd	E		1.98	0.0%	**0.0%**	0.0%
fft-inv	E		1.98	0.0%	**0.0%**	0.0%
fma3d	F	x	0.97	1.9%	**2.1%**	2.0%
ft	P		2.12	0.3%	**0.4%**	0.4%
g721decode	M	x	1.76	1.5%	**1.6%**	1.6%
g721encode	M	x	1.64	1.1%	**1.2%**	1.2%
galgel	F		3.31	0.0%	**0.0%**	0.0%
gap	I		1.27	0.6%	**-0.2%**	0.7%
gcc2k-1	I	x	2.31	0.7%	**1.0%**	1.0%
gcc2k-2	I	x	0.76	4.3%	**4.1%**	4.8%
gcc2k-3	I	x	0.82	2.6%	**2.7%**	2.8%
gcc2k-4	I	x	0.96	2.5%	**2.5%**	2.6%
ghostscript-1	E	x	1.40	15.0%	**15.1%**	14.8%
ghostscript-2	M	x	1.40	15.5%	**16.0%**	15.5%
ghostscript-3	E	x	1.67	11.2%	**12.5%**	12.7%
glquake-1	G	x	1.04	4.1%	**4.2%**	4.3%
glquake-2	G	x	1.17	3.3%	**3.5%**	3.6%
gzip-1	I		1.79	0.0%	**0.0%**	0.1%
gzip-2	I		1.37	0.3%	**0.3%**	0.3%
gzip-3	I	x	1.49	1.2%	**1.2%**	1.3%
gzip-4	I		1.80	0.0%	**0.0%**	0.0%
gzip-5	I		1.34	0.3%	**0.3%**	0.3%
jpegdecode	M		2.12	0.5%	**0.7%**	0.7%
jpegencode	M	x	1.72	3.7%	**3.8%**	3.7%
ks-1	P		1.22	0.0%	**0.0%**	0.0%
ks-2	P		0.78	0.0%	**0.0%**	0.0%
lucas	F		1.00	0.0%	**0.0%**	0.0%
mcf	I		0.58	0.0%	**0.0%**	0.0%

Benchmark Name			Base IPC	St.Sets	St.Vectors	Perfect
mesa-1	M		1.49	0.0%	**0.0%**	0.0%
mesa-2	F	x	1.50	18.0%	**18.2%**	18.4%
mesa-3	M	x	1.06	1.3%	**1.3%**	1.3%
mgrid	F		1.26	0.1%	**0.1%**	0.1%
mpeg2decode	M		2.26	0.2%	**0.3%**	0.4%
mpeg2encode	M		3.12	0.1%	**0.1%**	0.1%
parser	I	x	1.26	6.9%	**6.9%**	7.1%
patricia	E		1.09	0.1%	**0.3%**	0.1%
perlbmk-1	I	x	0.95	10.5%	**11.6%**	11.3%
perlbmk-2	I	x	1.22	1.8%	**2.4%**	1.9%
perlbmk-3	I	x	2.37	2.1%	**2.6%**	2.7%
povray-1	G	x	0.76	18.6%	**18.7%**	19.1%
povray-2	G	x	0.98	8.7%	**9.1%**	9.3%
povray-3	G	x	1.01	20.8%	**20.8%**	21.3%
povray-4	G	x	1.03	11.8%	**11.5%**	12.0%
povray-5	G	x	0.84	10.9%	**11.0%**	11.2%
rsynth	E		1.62	0.1%	**0.1%**	0.1%
sha	E	x	2.88	9.0%	**8.8%**	9.0%
sixtrack	F		1.30	0.2%	**0.2%**	0.3%
susan-1	E		2.27	0.2%	**0.2%**	0.2%
susan-2	E		1.64	0.0%	**0.0%**	0.0%
swim	F		0.80	0.0%	**0.0%**	0.0%
tiff2bw	E		1.51	0.0%	**0.0%**	0.0%
tiff2rgba	E		1.63	0.2%	**0.2%**	0.2%
tiffdither	E	x	1.59	3.7%	**3.7%**	3.9%
tiffmedian	E		2.46	0.1%	**0.1%**	0.1%
twolf	I	x	0.83	1.2%	**1.3%**	1.3%
unepic	M		0.40	0.0%	**0.0%**	0.0%
vortex-1	I	x	1.56	30.4%	**31.7%**	32.4%
vortex-2	I	x	1.06	37.6%	**41.0%**	39.9%
vortex-3	I	x	1.45	35.2%	**36.7%**	37.2%
vpr-1	I	x	1.06	5.0%	**5.2%**	5.2%
vpr-2	I	x	0.65	3.5%	**3.5%**	3.6%
wupwise	F		2.29	0.5%	**0.5%**	0.5%
x11quake-1	G	x	1.44	4.4%	**4.2%**	4.7%
x11quake-2	G		2.74	-0.1%	**-0.2%**	0.1%
x11quake-3	G	x	1.42	4.5%	**4.3%**	4.9%
xanim-1	G		3.27	0.0%	**0.0%**	0.0%
xanim-2	G	x	2.86	0.9%	**1.0%**	1.0%
xdoom	G	x	2.06	4.9%	**5.3%**	5.4%
yacr2	P	x	2.10	2.5%	**2.6%**	2.5%

Benchmark Group		Base IPC	St.Sets	St.Vectors	Perfect
ALL		1.44	4.0%	**4.2%**	4.2%
SpecINT	I	1.22	6.1%	**6.3%**	6.5%
SpecFP	F	1.37	1.9%	**1.9%**	1.9%
MediaBench	M	1.69	0.7%	**0.7%**	0.7%
MiBench	E	1.84	2.5%	**2.6%**	2.6%
Graphics	G	1.41	7.0%	**7.0%**	7.3%
PtrDist	P	1.49	2.9%	**3.1%**	3.0%
Dep. Sensitive	x	1.31	8.1%	**8.4%**	8.5%

Table 2. The performance of the memory dependence predictors. The base IPC is for a blind/naive predictor, and the IPC speedups of the remaining configurations are all relative to blind speculation. The letter after each benchmark denotes its application group, and an 'x' signifies that the benchmark is dependency sensitive ($>$ 1% performance change between blind and perfect).

these cases, even blind speculation only results in a few (single digits) ordering violations over the course of 100 million instructions. We call an application *dependence-sensitive* if perfect dependence prediction results in at least a 1% IPC speedup over blind speculation. Each dependence-sensitive application is marked with an 'x'.

Table 2 lists the performance of the store sets and store vector algorithms over blind speculation. Both predictors use 2KB of state in their prediction tables; we do not count the storage for the LFST against store sets. The bottom of Table 2 lists the overall speedups by application group as well as the speedup for those benchmarks categorized as being dependence-sensitive. The non-sensitive applications are not of great interest in this context because even perfect dependence prediction does not have any significant impact. Perfect prediction achieves an 8.5% speedup over blind speculation on the dependence-sensitive programs. Consistent with previously reported results, the store sets algorithm's speedup of 8.1% is very close to the performance of perfect speculation. However, this performance comes with the price of complex hardware support. Our store vector prediction algorithm has a simpler implementation, and it also attains a speedup of 8.4% which is better than store sets.

On a per-group basis, there are clearly some program classes that are more sensitive to ordering violations than others. For example, the floating point and media programs typically have very regular data access patterns (vector/matrix or streaming) that result in few store-to-load forwardings. It may be surprising that the pointer-intensive benchmarks are not more sensitive to memory dependencies, however, these applications spend much more time traversing pointer-based data structures (loads) rather than modifying the structures (stores).

There are a few applications where store sets performs slightly better than the store vector algorithm. In these cases, there were more memory ordering violations overall in the blind speculation case. Store sets' set merging heuristics cause store sets to be slightly more conservative, which is why it results in slightly better performance than store vectors for these applications. For a small number of other applications, both store sets and store vectors are too aggressive and actually cause performance to be slightly worse than the baseline case. There are also a few cases where either store sets or store vectors outperform perfect dependence prediction due to the prefetching and early branch mispredict detection effects mentioned earlier.

The performance speedup of store sets and store vectors is very close to that of perfect dependence prediction. To make it easier to distinguish between the algorithms, we define the *performance effectiveness* of a memory dependence

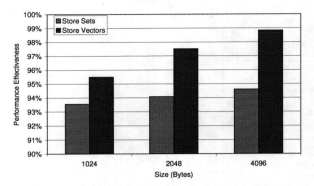

Figure 6. Percent of perfect prediction's performance achieved by store sets and store vectors for 1KB, 2KB and 4KB hardware budgets.

predictor P as:

$$\text{Performance Effectiveness}(P) = \left(\frac{1 - \frac{\text{IPC}_P}{\text{IPC}_{\text{blind}}}}{1 - \frac{\text{IPC}_{\text{perfect}}}{\text{IPC}_{\text{blind}}}} \right)$$

This metric has no physical significance; it simply measures the performance benefit of a prediction algorithm P as a fraction of what is achievable with perfect dependence prediction. For example, if $\text{IPC}_{\text{blind}} = 1.0$, $\text{IPC}_{\text{perfect}} = 1.2$ and $\text{IPC}_P = 1.15$, then P's performance effectiveness is 75%. Figure 6 shows the performance effectiveness of store sets and store vectors for three different predictor sizes on the SPECint benchmarks. As the hardware budget increases from 1KB to 4KB, the performance effectiveness of store sets ranges from 93.5% up to 94.7%. For our store vector algorithm, the performance effectiveness ranges from 95.5% to almost 99%. For both algorithms, further increases in predictor hardware budgets do not result in any significant increases in performance.

4.3. Why Do Store Vectors Work?

In this section, we explain the advantages of store vectors over store sets. In particular, we will discuss scenarios where the store sets algorithm results in overly conservative predictions or unnecessary delays.

The first reason why store sets can delay a load from issuing actually stems from delaying the issuing of stores. The desired behavior of a load with a predicted set of store dependencies is that the load waits for all of the dependencies to be resolved. Figure 7(a) shows a load instruction with four predicted store input dependencies. Ideally, the stores should be able to execute independently since memory write-after-write false dependencies are already properly handled by the store queue. To prevent loads

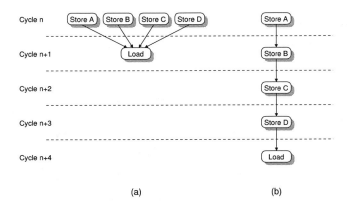

(a)   (b)

Figure 7. (a) Ideal load synchronization against predicted store dependencies, and (b) actual serialization with store sets.

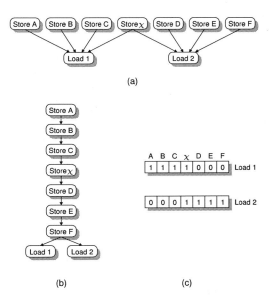

(b)   (c)

Figure 8. (a) Ideal load synchronization for two loads against their predicted store dependencies, (b) actual serialization of merged store sets, and (c) the store vector values which avoid unnecessary serialization.

and stores from having multiple direct input dependencies (which would require more CAMs), the store sets algorithm serializes execution of stores within the same store set. This is illustrated in Figure 7(b) where the load's execution has now been delayed by three extra cycles. With the store vector approach, individual stores have no knowledge about dependency relationships with other stores; in fact, the store does not even explicitly know if any loads are dependent on it. Stores may issue in any order, and they just obliviously clear their respective columns in the LSM.

The store sets merging update rules allow two or more different loads to be dependent on the same store. Consider the loads in Figure 8(a), where both loads have several predicted store dependencies, and both loads are predicted to be dependent on Store-χ. Without store sets merging, Store-χ can only belong to the store set of Load-1, for example. In this situation, Load-2 will not wait for Store-χ which results in ordering violations. With store sets merging, all of the stores associated with both loads will be merged into the same store set. Now Load-1 and Load-2 will serialize behind Store-χ. This prevents the ordering violation. Unfortunately, this can introduce substantial additional store dependencies. Load-1 must wait for all stores in Load-2's store set, and visa-versa. If all Stores A through F, and Store-χ are simultaneously present in the store queue, then Loads 1 and 2 will be considerably delayed as illustrated in Figure 8(b). With the store vector approach, each load may have its own store vector that is capable of tracking dependencies independent of all other loads (modulo aliasing effects in the SVT). Figure 8(c) shows the corresponding store vectors for Loads 1 and 2 which do not result in the spurious serializations induced by store sets.

4.4. Design Alternatives

As described, the store vector length is tied to the number of entries in the store queue. While we found that this configuration performed well, it is possible to reduce the store vector length to decrease the hardware cost. For example, reducing the store vector length to only track the 16 most recent stores (as opposed to 32 as assumed in the rest of the paper) would reduce the space requirements of the Store Vector Table (SVT) by one half. However, the sizes of the remaining hardware structures are still tied to the store queue size. The Load Scheduling Matrix still requires one column per store, and therefore the barrel shifter must also produce a bit vector matched to the number of store queue entries.

For our processor configuration, the benefit of store vectors drops off relatively quickly with shorter store vector lengths. Figure 9 shows the relative performance for different store vector sizes, where zero is the performance of blind speculation and 1.0 is the performance of the baseline store vector technique. From these results, we conclude that the less recent stores have a greater impact on load ordering violations. This intuitively makes sense as the compiler should choose to spill registers that will not be soon reused. If a data dependency exists between two nearby instructions, it is likely that the value will be kept in a register as opposed to being pushed out to memory. Even for subroutine calls, most functions have only a few argu-

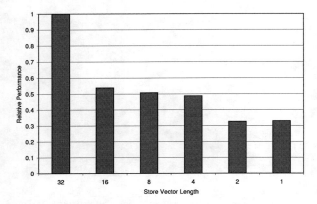

Figure 9. The relative performance impact of reducing the length of the store vectors (dependence-sensitive applications only). Zero represents the performance with blind speculation, and 1.0 is the performance of the baseline store vector predictor.

ments which can be passed through the registers. However, our evaluation was conducted on the Alpha ISA which has a relatively large number of registers. The results and optimal memory dependence predictor configuration are likely to be different for an ISA like x86 where spills/fills and memory traffic in general is much more frequent.

For our simulations, the effects of control flow on dependence prediction performance were negligible. In theory, store sets should have some more tolerance to memory dependence predictions that vary depending on the control path leading up to a load because the stores are all explicitly tracked by their PCs. With store vectors, a load might have a conflict with the third previous store when the program traverses one path, and the load might conflict with the fourth oldest store on another path. The store vector will mark bits three and four as conflicts, which may in turn cause the load to be overly conservative. There are a few reasons why this effect does not have a great impact on performance. First, the load is only unnecessarily delayed if the non-conflicting store address resolves after the real store dependency. Second, even if delayed, the load only impacts performance if it is on the critical path. Third, aggressive compiler optimization may reduce the effects of control flow on dependence prediction. A load aggressively hoisted and duplicated to both paths leading up to a control flow "join" effectively assigns the load to two different PCs which allows the predictor to identify the different control flow cases. If programs other than SPEC exhibit a high-degree of memory dependences within very branchy code, the store vector table can be modified in a gshare fashion [17] to make use of some branch or path history information.

5. Summary

Out-of-order load execution is necessary to realize the potential of large-window superscalar processors. Blindly allowing loads to execute however will result in ordering violations which may cancel out the benefits of supporting a large number of in-flight instructions. We have proposed a new memory dependence prediction and scheduling algorithm based on dependency vectors and scheduling matrices. Our store vectors approach yields performance results better than the state of the art store sets algorithm while maintaining a simpler implementation.

The results presented in this study are for a specific microarchitecture configuration. The performance benefits of store vectors (and store sets) may change given different assumptions about the underlying microarchitecture. A larger instruction window may increase the potential cases for ordering violations. A deeper pipeline increases the penalty for misspeculating load-store dependencies. However, if the relative performance cost of being too conservative or too aggressive changes, the store vector algorithm can be easily modified and re-tuned for a new microarchitecture. For example, adding tags or partial tags to the SVT could improve prediction accuracy. In the case of a SVT miss, the default prediction could be set to blind speculation, no speculation (wait on all unresolved stores), or the predictor could even dynamically choose the default prediction based on the recent frequency of mispredictions. For our microarchitecture, the 2KB store vector predictor was able to deliver 97.5% of the performance benefit of an oracle dependence predictor, and so we did not place too much effort into further optimizing the prediction algorithm.

Acknowledgments

This research was sponsored in part by equipment and funding donations from Intel Corporation. We are grateful for the constructive feedback provided by the anonymous reviewers.

References

[1] Haitham Akkary, Ravi Rajwar, and Srikanth T. Srinivasan. Checkpoint Processing and Recovery: Towards Scalable Large Instruction Window Processors. In *Proceedings of the 36th International Symposium on Microarchitecture*, pages 423–434, San Diego, CA, USA, May 2003.

[2] Todd Austin, Eric Larson, and Dan Ernst. SimpleScalar: An Infrastructure for Computer System Modeling. *IEEE Micro Magazine*, pages 59–67, February 2002.

[3] Todd M. Austin, Scott E. Breach, and Gurindar S. Sohi. Efficient Detection of All Pointer and Array Access Errors. In *Proceedings of the SIGPLAN Conference on Programming Language Design and Implementation*, pages 290–301, Orlando, FL, USA, June 1994.

[4] Edward Brekelbaum, Jeff Rupley II, Chris Wilkerson, and Bryan Black. Hierarchical Scheduling Windows. In *Proceedings of the 35th International Symposium on Microarchitecture*, pages 27–36, Istanbul, Turkey, November 2002.

[5] Mary D. Brown, Jared Stark, and Yale N. Patt. Select-Free Instruction Scheduling Logic. In *Proceedings of the 34th International Symposium on Microarchitecture*, pages 204–213, Austin, TX, USA, December 2001.

[6] George Z. Chrysos and Joel S. Emer. Memory Dependence Prediction Using Store Sets. In *Proceedings of the 25th International Symposium on Computer Architecture*, pages 142–153, Barcelona, Spain, June 1998.

[7] Adrián Cristal, Oliverio J. Santana, Mateo Valero, and José F. Martínez. Toward Kilo-Instruction Processors. *Transactions on Architecture and Code Optimization*, 1(4):389–417, December 2004.

[8] Amit Gandhi, Haitham Akkary, Ravi Rajwar, Srikanth T. Srinivasan, and Konrad Lai. Scalable Load and Store Processing in Latency Tolerant Processors. In *Proceedings of the 32nd International Symposium on Computer Architecture*, pages 446–457, Madison, Wisconsin, June 2005.

[9] Andy Glew. MLP Yes! ILP No! Memory Level Parallelism, or, Why I No Longer Worry About IPC. In *Proceedings of the ASPLOS Wild and Crazy Ideas Session*, San Jose, CA, USA, October 1997.

[10] Masahiro Goshima, Kengo Nishino, Yasuhiko Nakashima, Shin ichiro Mori, Toshiaki Kitamura, and Shinji Tomita. A High-Speed Dynamic Instruction Scheduling Scheme for Superscalar Processors. In *Proceedings of the 34th International Symposium on Microarchitecture*, pages 225–236, Austin, TX, USA, December 2001.

[11] Matthew R. Guthaus, Jeffrey S. Ringenberg, Dan Ernst, Todd M. Austin, Trevor Mudge, and Richard B. Brown. MiBench: A Free, Commerically Representative Embedded Benchmark Suite. In *Proceedings of the 4th Workshop on Workload Characterization*, pages 83–94, Austin, TX, USA, December 2001.

[12] Glenn Hinton, Dave Sager, Mike Upton, Darrell Boggs, Doug Carmean, Alan Kyler, and Patrice Roussel. The Microarchitecture of the Pentium 4 Processor. *Intel Technology Journal*, Q1 2001.

[13] R. E. Kessler. The Alpha 21264 Microprocessor. *IEEE Micro Magazine*, 19(2):24–36, March–April 1999.

[14] Eric Larson, Saugata Chatterjee, and Todd Austin. MASE: A Novel Infrastructure for Detailed Microarchitectural Modeling. In *Proceedings of the 2001 International Symposium on Performance Analysis of Systems and Software*, pages 1–9, Tucson, AZ, USA, November 2001.

[15] Alvin R. Lebeck, Jinson Koppanalil, Tong Li, Jaidev Patwardhan, and Eric Rotenberg. A Large, Fast Instruction Window for Tolerating Cache Misses. In *Proceedings of the 29th International Symposium on Computer Architecture*, pages 59–70, Anchorage, AK, USA, May 2002.

[16] Chunho Lee, Miodrag Potkonjak, and William H. Mangione-Smith. MediaBench: A Tool for Evaluating and Synthesizing Multimedia and Communication Systems. In *Proceedings of the 30th International Symposium on Microarchitecture*, pages 330–335, Research Triangle Park, NC, USA, December 1997.

[17] Scott McFarling. Combining Branch Predictors. TN 36, Compaq Computer Corporation Western Research Laboratory, June 1993.

[18] Pierre Michaud and André Seznec. Data-Flow Prescheduling for Large Instruction Window in Out-of-Order Processors. In *Proceedings of the 7th International Symposium on High Performance Computer Architecture*, pages 27–36, Monterrey, Mexico, January 2001.

[19] Andreas Moshovos. *Memory Dependence Prediction*. PhD thesis, University of Wisconsin, 1998.

[20] Andreas Moshovos, Scott E. Breach, T. N. Vijaykumar, and Gurindar S. Sohi. Dynamic Speculation and Synchronization of Data Dependences. In *Proceedings of the 24th International Symposium on Computer Architecture*, pages 181–193, Boulder, CO, USA, June 1997.

[21] Subbarao Palacharla. *Complexity-Effective Superscalar Processors*. PhD thesis, University of Wisconsin, 1998.

[22] Yale N. Patt, Sanjay J. Patel, Marius Evers, Daniel H. Friendly, and Jared Stark. One Billion Transistors, One Uniprocessor, One Chip. *IEEE Computer*, pages 51–57, September 1997.

[23] Erez Perelman, Greg Hamerly, and Brad Calder. Picking Statistically Valid and Early Simulation Points. In *Proceedings of the 2003 International Conference on Parallel Architectures and Compilation Techniques*, pages 244–255, New Orleans, LA, USA, September 2004.

[24] Karthikeyan Sankaralingam, Ramadass Nagarajan, Haiming Liu, Changkyu Kim, Jaehyuk Huh, Doug Burger, Stephen W. Keckler, and Charles R. Moore. Exploiting ILP, TLP, and DLP with the Polymorphous TRIPS Architecture. In *Proceedings of the 30th International Symposium on Computer Architecture*, pages 422–433, San Diego, CA, USA, May 2003.

[25] Gurindar S. Sohi, Scott E. Breach, and T. N. Vijaykumar. Multiscalar Processors. In *Proceedings of the 22nd International Symposium on Computer Architecture*, pages 414–425, Santa Margheruta Liguire, Italy, June 1995.

[26] Srikanth T. Srinivasan, Ravi Rajwar, Haitham Akkary, Amit Gandhi, and Mike Upton. Continual Flow Pipelines. In *Proceedings of the 11th Symposium on Architectural Support for Programming Languages and Operating Systems*, pages 107–119, Boston, MA, USA, October 2004.

[27] Steve Swanson, Ken Michelson, Andrew Schwerin, and Mark Oskin. WaveScalar. In *Proceedings of the 36th International Symposium on Microarchitecture*, pages 291–302, San Diego, CA, USA, May 2003.

[28] Craig B. Zilles and Gurindar S. Sohi. Understanding the Backward Slices of Performance Degrading Instructions. In *Proceedings of the 27th International Symposium on Computer Architecture*, pages 172–181, Vancouver, Canada, June 2000.

Session 3:
Parallel Architecture

Dynamic Power-Performance Adaptation of Parallel Computation on Chip Multiprocessors

Jian Li and José F. Martínez

Computer Systems Laboratory
Cornell University
Ithaca, NY 14853 USA

http://m3.csl.cornell.edu/

ABSTRACT

Previous proposals for power-aware thread-level parallelism on chip multiprocessors (CMPs) mostly focus on multiprogrammed workloads. Nonetheless, parallel computation of a single application is critical in light of the expanding performance demands of important future workloads. This work addresses the problem of dynamically optimizing power consumption of a parallel application that executes on a many-core CMP under a given performance constraint. The optimization space is two-dimensional, allowing changes in the number of active processors and applying dynamic voltage/frequency scaling. We demonstrate that the particular optimum operating point depends nontrivially on the power-performance characteristics of the CMP, the application's behavior, and the particular performance target. We present simple, low-overhead heuristics for dynamic optimization that significantly cut down on the search effort along both dimensions of the optimization space. In our evaluation of several parallel applications with different performance targets, these heuristics quickly lock on a configuration that yields optimal power savings in virtually all cases.

1 INTRODUCTION

Chip multiprocessors (CMPs) have emerged as a promising way to deliver sustained performance growth while relying less on raw circuit speed, and thus power [1]. That parallelism may bring power-performance advantages is not new: earlier VLSI works have discussed the trade-offs that sequential vs. parallel circuits present in silicon area and power consumption [6, 37]. Yet even as researchers have investigated extensively the power-performance issues of uniprocessor and, to a lesser extent, multiprogrammed CMP architectures [10, 14, 26, 32, 41, 42], to date there is still little understanding of the specific power-performance challenges involving parallel applications executing on CMPs.

In a parallel run, for example, the overall performance ultimately depends on all the processors; however, at any point in time, the critical path may depend on only a few of them. In that case, slowing down processors not in the critical path to save power may not affect the overall performance at all. Conversely, slowing down processors in the critical path will negatively impact perfor-mance, and the local savings may be easily negated by the extra waste on other processors due to longer execution time. Furthermore, the available parallelism and parallel efficiency may depend nontrivially on the problem size and execution environment. Moreover, it is viable to change the number of concurrent processors/threads at run-time [5, 16] to optimize execution across program regions, or to accommodate changes in the execution environment; however, the power-performance trade-offs that appear as a result of such run-time adaptive parallelism cannot be easily explained without considering the parallel application behavior.

As the number of cores per CMP increases and the opportunities for performance growth of single-threaded codes dwindle, we anticipate that many important future applications—as many as 80% by some industry projections [3, 25]—will be parallelized to utilize the potential of these CMP cores. With future CMPs likely support many threads on the same die, and its cores in turn supporting a number of voltage and frequency levels, the amount of possible power-performance configurations of a CMP is bound to be large, making it hard to find an optimal power-performance operating point for a parallel application, in particular at run-time.

In this work, we target run-time power-performance adaptation of future CMPs that run shared-memory parallel applications. This run-time adaptation takes place in the two-dimensional space constituted by (1) the possible number of active processors (2) the different voltage-frequency levels available. Specifically, in this paper, we explore one typical scenario—maximizing power savings while delivering a specified level of performance. This scenario essentially reduces energy cost per application, as energy is the integral of power over execution time. It aims to prolong battery life for embedded systems, or to reduce power supply capacity for high-end systems, as long as performance is satisfactory. We show that the optimum operating point depends nontrivially on the particular performance target, the application, and the hardware's power-performance characteristics. However, we demonstrate that the arrangement of the possible operating points generally allows for an efficient pruning of the search space, which enables low-overhead dynamic optimization. In that context, we present simple heuristic mechanisms that are able to quickly converge to a con-

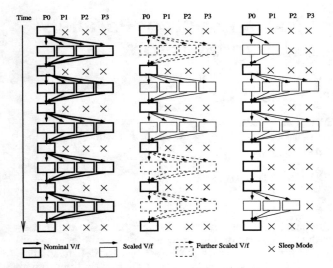

Figure 1: Execution of an imaginary parallel code on a CMP with four processors under three different scenarios: full throttle parallel execution (left), power-aware parallel execution regulated with DVFS exclusively (center), and power-aware parallel execution regulated with DVFS and adaptive parallelism (right). Regions are not drawn to scale with respect to each other.

figuration in the search space that achieves near-optimal power consumption and complies with the performance requirement in virtually all the cases that we study.

Our mechanism is implemented at the granularity of parallel regions, with a combination of modest software and hardware support. It does not change the application semantics, and can be made largely transparent to the application by encapsulating the code in a typical parallelization macro or directive.

The rest of the paper is organized as follows: Section 2 describes the scope of our study; Section 3 characterizes the search space and describes our proposed mechanisms; Section 4 lays out our experimental setup; Section 5 analyzes the results of our evaluation; and Section 6 discusses related work.

2 SCOPE

This section lays out the scope of our work. We use an imaginary execution of a parallel code on a CMP with four processors as an example. The code contains a series of interleaved serial and parallel regions. Figure 1 shows the execution of a fragment of such code under three different scenarios. In the figure, regions are not drawn to scale with respect to each other. In fact, we expect parallel regions to be dominant in many future applications, and thus the focus of our paper.

The left diagram represents a conventional parallel run at full throttle. The code runs on all four cores during parallel sections, all at nominal voltage/frequency levels—no dynamic voltage/frequency scaling (DVFS) is applied in any case.

The central diagram represents a power-aware execution where power can be regulated using whole-chip

DVFS. In the example, parallel sections are slowed down by applying DVFS to all processors. This presents us with a power-performance trade-off, which we can exploit, for example, to reduce power consumption and still meet a predetermined performance target.

Unfortunately, this one-dimensional trade-off limits the power-performance optimization options. Specifically, no matter how relaxed the performance constraint, it is not possible to reduce power consumption in a parallel region below the static power consumption of all four cores at room temperature, since all of them remain active. Notice that if the chip's power budget is tight, executing in all cores may result in a very limited number of feasible DVFS levels. In the worst case, if the application's parallel efficiency degrades significantly at that degree of parallelism, the chip's limited power budget may make it simply impossible to meet the performance target [29].

The right diagram tries to address this limitation, by allowing parallel regions to execute on a variable number of processors. In this scenario, a parallel region executes on possibly a subset of the available processors, with DVFS properly adjusted to meet the performance target, and unused processors are brought down to sleep mode. (Naturally, we assume that the application does support execution of parallel regions with different number of processors. We address this assumption later in Section 3.3.)

On the one hand, this scenario is highly desirable, as it allows much greater flexibility in trading off power and performance. On the other hand, such a two-dimensional space can be quite large, especially as CMPs incorporate more cores, making the task of finding the optimal operating point a challenging one, particularly if the number of instances of a parallel region at run-time is such that a brute-force search could not be amortized easily. This motivates the need to explore whether a reasonably quick and easy procedure exists that can find an acceptable operating point at run time, such that power consumption is reduced significantly but the performance target is still met. Our work shows that this is feasible.

In our study, we limit ourselves to a homogeneous CMP that has chip-wide DVFS capability, and focus on power optimization at the granularity of a parallel region that must meet a certain performance target. We generally define our performance target as a steady-state rate (e.g., frames per second in a multimedia application). Finally, we generally assume a CMP in which each processor executes at most one application thread, and leave overthreading issues to future work.

3 DYNAMIC POWER-PERFORMANCE ADAPTATION

In this section, we first explain the general characteristics of the two-dimensional power-performance optimization space, using one of the applications from our experimental setup as an example (Section 4.3). Then, in the context of dynamic power optimization given a certain performance constraint, we describe simple run-time heuristics that cut down on the optimization space search significantly, and justify intuitively that such heuristics should

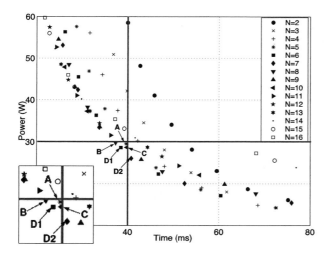

Figure 2: Power consumption and execution time of CMP configurations with varying number of processors N and voltage/frequency levels for an instance of BSOM's parallel region (a parallel data mining application). Target execution time and power are 40ms and 30W, respectively.

generally converge to an operating point that is reasonably close to the global optimum, which is later confirmed in our evaluation (Section 5.2). Finally, we comment on some hardware/software implementation issues of our mechanism.

3.1 Power-Performance Characterization

In this section, we build a case study around BSOM, the parallel data mining application (Section 4.3), to illustrate the power-performance trade-offs of parallel computation on a CMP. Fig. 2 shows the power consumption and execution time of an iteration of the main (parallel) loop, or *epoch*. Each point in the plot represents one CMP configuration, using a certain number of processors N (shown in the legend), and a particular DVFS level (not indicated directly in the plot). We vary N between two and sixteen processors, and for each N we explore sixteen different DVFS levels, distributed regularly along the allowable range (Section 4.1). In the figure, we limit our discussion to a window of power ranging from 10 to 60W, and execution time of an epoch ranging from 20 to 80ms. (Naturally, we are using a reduced input set to make simulation time affordable; execution time of each epoch is longer with realistic input sizes.)

In general, as expected, points for a fixed N move right and down as we apply DVFS, as it takes more time to execute one epoch, but on the other hand the power consumption is lower. The plot shows two well differentiated operating areas: On the one hand, operating points toward the upper-left corner lie in a *performance-oriented* (or *power-sensitive*) area. In this area, power consumption is generally high, but small reductions in voltage/frequency levels translate into significant savings in power consump-

tion, at a relatively small performance cost. On the other hand, operating points toward the lower-right corner lie in a *power-oriented* or (*performance-sensitive*) area. In this area, while performance is generally low, small voltage/frequency increases result in large performance gains, at a relatively small power cost.

If we try to make sense of the curves depending on the performance target that we impose, we can again find two well differentiated areas. As we move left (strict performance target), configurations with a small number of processors need to operate at high DVFS levels to meet the performance target, thus consuming significant power. If, as it is the case in BSOM, parallel efficiency is generally high, a higher number of processors allows the CMP to meet the performance target while achieving significant power savings, by aggressively throttling voltage and frequency. On the other hand, toward the right end of the plot (relaxed performance target), most configurations can meet or exceed the performance target with very low voltage and frequency levels. In that case, the static power consumption of configurations with a high number of processors puts them at a disadvantage with respect to smaller configurations.

If we assume the target execution time for one epoch is 40ms (vertical line), and we consider 30W as the maximum allowable power dissipation (horizontal line), our search for valid configurations is confined, in principle, to the quadrant left of and below such bounds, respectively. Only a few operating points reside in this quadrant, which we label A, B, C, and D1 in the plot. Any of these points satisfy both performance and power constraints; the actual choice depends on a number of possible factors.

Configuration C in the plot, for example, yields acceptable performance and maximum power savings. Configuration D1 yields better performance at the same power cost, and thus would seem a better choice in terms of overall power-performance behavior. Configurations A and B consume a little more power, but they are still within the allowed limit.

One difference between these operating points lies in the number of processors required by each case, which varies widely—between five (configuration A) and ten (configuration C) in our experiment. If the application is also expected to minimize the number of allocated processors (for example, in a multiprogrammed environment), configuration C may prove too costly at $N = 10$. On the other hand, configuration A, which uses half as many processors, may constitute an attractive choice in this case, even as it consumes slightly more power. The opposite may be true if, for example, power density is a concern.

Finally, if we define our performance target as a rate (e.g., frames per second in MPEG decoder/encoder), and allow epochs to borrow leftover time from previous "fast" instances to execute slower and save more power while still meeting the target rate, further power savings opportunities may be possible. For example, we can alternate runs with $N = 6$ for one epoch, and $N = 7$ for the following epoch (configurations D1 and D2 in the plot, respectively). These configurations result, as the plot shows, in per-epoch execution times that are slightly under and over target, respectively. However, alternating between these two states is likely to meet or exceed the target rate (with D2 borrowing time from the slack created by D1). And the combination D1-D2 consumes, on average, less power than any other valid configuration by itself. Therefore, it can be argued that configuration D1 controls execution time as configuration D2 lowers power consumption, resulting in a favorable net balance.

3.2 Dynamic Power Optimization

When optimizing for power, the operating point that meets the performance requirement and minimizes power consumption lies, generally speaking, at the intersection of the performance target and the lower envelope of the power-performance curves for the different number of processors and DVFS levels. Unfortunately, such lower envelope is not generally known at run-time, and must be constructed or approximated.

If the number of instances of the parallel region is large enough that an exhaustive search is feasible, an easy way to construct such lower envelope at run-time is to try all possible number of processors and (legal) DVFS levels: For each number of processors, starting with the maximum DVFS level allowable by the chip's power budget (which we assume known), we gradually decrease DVFS levels (one step per instance of the parallel region) until the desired performance is no longer met. The DVFS level immediately before is the local minimum for that number of processors. Among all the local minima, a global minimum can be picked. The cost of an exhaustive search is $L \cdot N$ steps, with L being the number of DVFS levels and N the number of processors on the CMP.

Often times, however, an exhaustive search may not be possible, or its overhead prove prohibitive, because the parallel region is not invoked enough times as to amortize the search phase. In that case, search heuristics that can converge toward the global optimum much faster are highly desirable.

After the search has concluded, the algorithm enters steady state. In this mode, the goal is to minimize power consumption while making sure that the target rate (e.g., frames per second) is met. In this mode, as we finish execution of one instance, we compute the distance to the next target (since we may have under- or overshot the current target). Then we select, among the operating points recorded during our search phase, the one whose execution time constitutes the tightest upper bound. This gives us the processor count and DVFS level to use next. If we undershot the current target, this constitutes an opportunity to save extra power. If we overshot, we may now pick a more aggressive operating point, which will allow us to catch up.

Reducing Search Space: Processor Dimension

We propose to use a combination of binary search and hill-climbing optimization to prune the search space along the processor dimension. In hill-climbing optimization, search continues until a local optimum is observed — i.e., the immediate proximity of that point in any allowed search direction yields a less optimal operating point. Hill-climbing is limited in the sense that it may get "stuck" at a local optimum that is significantly worse than the global optimum in the search space. Three main factors influence the quality of hill-climbing algorithms: (1) the general shape of the search space; (2) whether the search algorithm generally conforms to such shape; and (3) possible heuristics to overcome local optima situations, such as the use of "jitter" or "momentum." In this paper, we choose to focus on the first two factors, and do not explore the third one.

From the insights developed in Section 3.1, we can build a search heuristic around the observed general trends in the search space, namely: (1) On tight performance constraints, configurations with more processors are generally favored, provided the application exhibits enough parallel efficiency, since they can meet the requirement at lower DVFS levels. (2) On loose performance constraints, configurations with fewer processors are generally preferable, since they can meet the requirement with low DVFS levels and they do not constitute as large an aggregation of static power; (3) on middle-ground performance constraints, multiple configurations that yield similar power-performance levels may be possible.

Cases (1) and (2) are likely to yield good operating points, since configurations are generally arranged in a monotonic fashion along the time constraint, which a hill-climbing algorithm can exploit well. In Case (3), the chances of getting "stuck" at a local optimum may be higher, however our evaluation empirically shows that the local optima found by our algorithm are generally close to the global optima in that scenario.

We conduct the hill-climbing optimization using a binary search along the dimension of the number of processors. Generally speaking, the hill-climbing algorithm starts at some mid-point number of processors p, and gradually decreases DVFS levels until the performance target is missed, as it is the case of the exhaustive search explained above. The DVFS level immediately above is the optimum for that p. Then, another p' half-way between the current configuration and either of the active endpoints is chosen, and the process is repeated. If the optimum for that p' is better, the other side is disregarded, and the binary search continues on that side. Otherwise, the algorithm switches to the other side, disregarding further attempts on the first side. When neither side is better, or we run out of options, the search ends.

The choice of which side to explore first may be important in cases where local optima may exist on both sides of the search, and thus the final number of processors may depend on the order in which they are searched. On the other hand, in the "monotonic" areas of the search space described above, the search is likely to converge toward the optimum. In any case, the cost of this heuristic is $L \cdot \lg N$ steps — a significant improvement.

Reducing Search Space: DVFS Dimension

An orthogonal way to prune the search space is to exploit, along the DVFS dimension, the strong correlation between performance and frequency in many applications. The formula for execution time proposed by Hennessy and Patterson [17] is $t = IC \cdot CPI \cdot f^{-1}$, where IC is the dynamic instruction count, CPI is the average number of cycles per instruction, and f is the operating frequency. If we make the simplifying assumption that CPI is independent of the clock frequency, then the the ratio between the actual and target execution times of a parallel region should be approximately equal to the ratio of the target and actual clock frequency.

This is a powerful result that would allow us, theoretically, to execute the parallel region once at clock frequency f, measure execution time t, and in one shot derive the target frequency f_{target} that would yield our performance target t_{target} (which is a known value of course).

In practice, however, neither is frequency in DVFS scaling a continuous function, nor is CPI independent of the clock frequency.[1] While the former limitation would still allow us to pick the optimum frequency in one shot (the closest legal frequency above the exact solution), the latter introduces some inaccuracy that may result in over- or undershooting the performance target. Nevertheless, observe that we can now apply a new iteration of the procedure, this time using execution time and frequency of the latest run. The key insight is that, with each additional iteration, the ratio should be much smaller than before, and thus convergence should be fast (unless the application exhibits erratic behavior, in which case none of the proposed heuristics is likely to work anyway).

As before, we start with the highest DVFS level allowable by the chip's power budget for the number of processors currently under consideration by the hill-climbing algorithm. If the execution time is unfavorable (i.e., the performance target is stricter than the measured performance), we cannot meet the required performance at the current number of processors, and thus we move on to another number of processors. If, on the other hand, the execution time is favorable, we can apply the formula to compute the new target frequency. The new *legal* target frequency maybe at the same DVFS level, in which case we stop searching, or at a lower DVFS level, in which case we iterate once more.

If we eventually miss the performance target, applying the formula again results in a target frequency that is necessarily faster, and since we always pick the closest legal frequency *above* the exact solution, this is guaranteed to move to a higher DVFS level. In the general case where this DVFS level has not been tried before, we iterate once more.

Notice that we may have already tried this DVFS level. Because of the general convergence property of the algorithm, the execution time at this DVFS level was most likely favorable the last time around, and thus we may stop searching. However, it might occur that this DVFS level was also recorded as unfavorable. In this (empirically rare) case, we simply select the closest recorded DVFS level above that yielded a favorable execution time and stop searching.

When combined with the hill-climbing heuristic, we estimate the expected cost to be $\alpha \lg N$ steps, where α is a function that grows much slower than L. In our evaluation (Section 5), where the number of DVFS levels is 16, the above procedure converges in about three iterations in most cases.

Thus, intuitively, the combination of the search reduction heuristics along each axis of the two-dimensional search space should converge quickly to an operating point that is reasonably close to the global optimum.

3.3 Implementation Issues

We envision implementing our proposed mechanism as a combination of modest hardware and software support. On the hardware side, we mainly require support to measure power and performance directly, chip-wide DVFS, and the ability to put cores to sleep. On the software side, we need support to execute parallel regions with different processor counts. We address each one in turn.

Hardware Support

Our mechanism obviously requires the ability to apply DVFS, although we limit our study to simple chip-wide DVFS, leaving potentially more versatile mechanisms such as core-level DVFS for future work.[2] Moreover, because the relative power-performance characteristics across different operating points may not be easily correlated to indirect metrics (e.g., IPC or cache miss rates), we would like to *directly* measure both power and performance to characterize such operating points, and thus we need to provide such support as well. While measuring performance can be achieved using well-known mechanisms based on programmable hardware counters, the hardware support to directly measure and regulate power is not as obvious.

In a recent publication [35], Intel describes its upcoming Foxton technology for Itanium Montecito. It utilizes on-chip sensors and an embedded microcontroller attached to the processor core to directly measure power and temperature, and apply DVFS to maximize the processor's performance while abiding by power/temperature constraints. We believe this microcontroller-based approach offers great potential and flexibility for our purposes, and thus propose that our mechanism be supported with similar hardware.

The Foxton-like microcontroller should be properly interfaced with the software, so that the choices of DVFS

---

[1]In memory-bound applications, for example, CPI may improve with lower frequencies, as off-chip memory accesses may become effectively faster in terms of processor clock cycles.

[2]In a multiprogrammed scenario, where the application receives a partition of the entire chip, our mechanism may require *partition*-wide DVFS. In that case, each partition may operate under different, interdependent power/temperature budgets. For the sake of simplicity, in this work we intentionally ignore this scenario.

CMP Size	16-way
Processor Core	Alpha 21264 [8]
Process Technology	65nm
Nominal Frequency	3.2GHz
Nominal V_{dd}	1.1v [21]
V_{th}	0.18v [21]
Ambient Temperature	45°C
Die Size	244.5mm^2 (15.6mm × 15.6mm)
L1 I-, D-Cache	64kB, 64B line, 2-way, 2-cycle RT
Unified L2 Cache	Shared on chip, 4MB, 128B line, 8-way, 12-cycle RT
Memory	75ns RT

Table 1: The CMP configuration modeled in the experiments. In the table, RT stands for round-trip.

and number of cores can be communicated and/or agreed upon properly. In that respect, an intermediate layer is needed to identify a parallel region (monitoring instruction addresses) and, based on past history and progress, decide on the appropriate course of action in terms of number of processors and DVFS level to apply to the execution of the next instance of such a region. The particular decision of which parts to map onto hardware or software libraries is more of an engineering issue that falls out of the scope of this paper. One definite requirement, however, is the ability to execute a parallel region on different number of processors. We address this next.

Software Support

In our proposed mechanism, both system and application should be able to support different processor counts on different instances of a parallel region.

On the system side, the operating system could assign a (probably oversized) partition to the application, which would basically determine the processor count range at the application's disposal. During the search phase, our mechanism would pick different number of processors and put the rest of the partition in a low-power sleep mode. Once the mechanism converges to a local optimum and enters steady state, any excess of processors could be given back to the operating system, or put in a low-power sleep mode for the duration of the program. (Notice that processors in a low-power sleep mode may still be required to respond to snoop requests if their cached updates have not been written back [30].)

On the application side, the parallel region should be written to support different processor counts. Fortunately, this is often supported (in fact, it is frequently the default mode) by widely used APIs for shared-memory programming, most notably OpenMP [36]. (Notice that some applications do restrict the possible number of processors to certain values, e.g. powers of two. While any search heuristic could be easily adapted to this scenario, we do not explicitly address it.) Furthermore, we envision the software-side support to be encapsulated in the existing parallel directives of such APIs, making it virtually transparent to the programmer or compiler.

4 SIMULATION ENVIRONMENT

4.1 Architecture

Our study uses a detailed model of a 16-processor CMP. CMP cores are modeled after the Alpha 21264 (EV6) processor [8]. Each processor core has private L1 instruction and data caches. All cores share a 4MB on-chip L2 cache through a common bus, and implement a MESI cache coherence protocol [9]. Table 1 lists relevant cache and memory parameters.

We choose a 65nm process technology. The original EV6 ran at 600MHz on a 350nm process technology; by proceeding similarly to [26], we determine the clock frequency of our 65nm EV6 cores to be 3.2GHz. We set nominal supply and threshold voltages at 1.1v and 0.18v, respectively [21], and in-box ambient air temperature at 45°C [33, 43]. Using CACTI [44], we obtain an estimated chip area of 244.5mm^2 (15.6mm × 15.6mm), using a scaling method similar to [27].

For the sake of simplicity, we assume global voltage/frequency scaling for the entire chip. (While it is conceivable to allow each core to run at a different frequency, the applicability and performance impact in the context of a parallel execution is nontrivial and beyond the scope of this paper.) Frequency can scale from 3.2GHz down to 200MHz, and we resort to [20] to establish the relationship between frequency and supply voltage. Notice that, because voltage/frequency scaling is applied at the chip level, on-chip latencies (e.g., on-chip cache hit time) do not vary in terms of cycles. However, a round trip to (off-chip) memory takes the same amount of time regardless of the voltage/frequency scaling applied on chip, and thus the round-trip memory latency in processor cycles goes down as we downscale frequency.

4.2 Power Model

We use Wattch to model the switching activity and dynamic power consumption of the on-chip functional blocks. As for static power consumption, we approximate it as a fraction of the dynamic power consumption [7, 43]. In our model, this fraction is exponentially dependent on the temperature [7]. The average operating temperature (over the chip area) in our model ranges from in-box ambient air temperature (45°C) to a maximum operating temperature of 100°C, in agreement with multiple contemporary processor chip designs. We use the HotSpot thermal model [43] for chip temperature estimation.

Wattch is reasonably accurate in relative terms; however, the absolute power values can be off by a nontrivial amount [26]. Because we use power values to communicate across two different tools (Wattch and HotSpot), we ought to ensure we do so in a meaningful way. We achieve this by renormalizing power values as follows.

We use HotSpot to determine the maximum operational power consumption (dynamic plus static), which is the one that yields the maximum operating temperature of 100°C. Then, using the dynamic/static ratio that corresponds to that temperature [7], we derive the dynamic component.

We now need to establish the connection with Wattch. To do so, we use a compute-intensive microbenchmark to recreate a quasi-maximum power consumption scenario at nominal voltage and frequency levels in our simulation model, and obtain Wattch's dynamic power value. This number is often different from the one obtained through HotSpot using the method explained above. To overcome this gap, we calculate the ratio between Wattch and HotSpot's dynamic power values, and use it throughout the experiments to renormalize wattage obtained with Wattch in our simulations as needed. This makes it possible for both tools to work together. While the absolute power may again not be exact, the results should be meaningful in relative terms. Using both tools, plus the power ratio/temperature curve, we are able to connect dynamic and static power consumption with temperature for any voltage and frequency scaling point.

Finally, we notice that the temperature and power density of the shared L2 cache is significantly lower than the rest of the chip across all the applications studied. Reasons include: much less switching activity; aggressive clock gating in the model [4]; and large L2 cache dissipation area. This observation is in agreement with published work by others [7, 10]. To obtain meaningful temperature figures, we exclude L2 from the temperature calculation. However, we do include the power consumption of L2 in the reported power consumption.

4.3 Applications

We select six parallel applications from different problem domains: MPGdec and MPGenc, two popular video decoding/encoding applications, from ALPBench [31]; FMM, Volrend, and Water-Ns, which represent N-body, rendering, and molecular dynamics applications, respectively, from the SPLASH-2 suite [45]; and BSOM, a parallelized data mining application [28]. The execution time in all these applications is spent mostly on one single parallel region, which suits our purpose. In our experiments, we do not change the problem sizes as we change the number of cores. Table 2 lists the applications and their execution parameters. The number of instances in the parallel regions of FMM (steps of an N-body problem), Volrend (rendering from different viewpoints), and Water-Ns (steps of a molecular dynamics problem) as included in the SPLASH-2 benchmark suite are only a handful, and thus we increase that number to obtain a sufficient number of samples for our evaluation (50 for Volrend and Water-Ns, only 10 for FMM given the extended simulation time of each region). On the other hand, in MPGdec/MPGenc we simulate 60 frames (out of the original 150) to get resonable simulation times. In all cases, we skip initialization and then simulate to completion.

We assume all processors are available to the application, and that unused processors are put to sleep. We also do not model the overhead of switching among DVFS levels, as we reasonably assume that real-world parallel instances of interest would each run for much longer than the typical tens of microseconds for DVFS switching.

Application	Description	Problem Size
BSOM	Batched Self-Organizing Maps of neural network	16k records, 104 dim., 16-node network, 50 epochs
FMM	Fast Multipole Method	16k particles, 10 steps
MPGdec	MPEG-2 decoder	flowg.mpg (Stanford) 352 × 240, 60 frames
MPGenc	MPEG-2 encoder	flowg.mpg (Stanford) 352 × 240, 60 frames
Volrend	Volume rendering using a ray casting technique	head 50 viewpoints
Water-Ns	Forces and potentials of water molecules	512 molecules 50 steps

Table 2: Applications used in the experiments.

Because these applications are generally not written to change the number of processors dynamically, we approximate this behavior by simulating in two phases: In the first phase, we execute each application once for every combination of processor number and DVFS level, and collect the measured execution time and power consumption for each instance of the parallel region. In the second phase, for each application, we simulate the different optimization mechanisms with Matlab, using the processor count and DVFS level selected by the optimization mechanisms in each step to pick the execution time and power consumption of the appropriate instance from the first phase, which in turn serve to determine the next step in the optimization mechanism. In the case of FMM, whose simulation time was particularly long, we traverse its ten instances five times to come up with a total number similar to the other applications.

5 EVALUATION

In Section 3.2, we discuss the extent to which our combined heuristics may cut down on the two-dimensional space search of processor count and DVFS. We predict this to be important for parallel applications for which the number of instances or steps is moderate, particularly as we scale up the number of processors on a CMP. For our proposed mechanisms to be useful, however, we need to address two additional questions: (1) For a parallel region and a particular performance target, is the choice of operating point(s) that minimize power consumption a non-trivial one that makes a space search useful? (2) In spite of the reduced knowledge about the search space, do the proposed mechanisms achieve optimum power savings and still meet the performance requirement? Our evaluation shows that the answer to these two questions is Yes. In what follows, we address each question in turn.

In all our experiments, we set the chip's total power budget to that of one processor running at peak performance.

5.1 Optimization Space

In our first experiment, we assess the power optimization opportunities for each processor count within range (1 to 16). Specifically, for a particular processor count, we measure power and performance for each possible operating point within budget. Then, in steady state, we pick

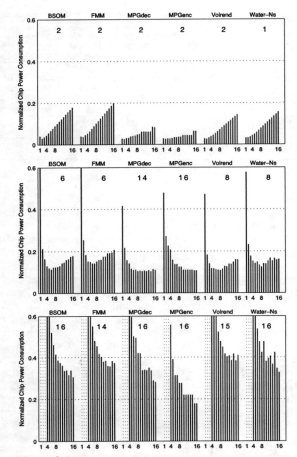

Figure 3: Optimal chip power consumption, normalized to the power budget, of configurations with different processor counts [1,16] for all the applications under study, for loose (top), intermediate (middle), and tight (bottom) performance targets. Dotted bars indicate configurations that cannot meet the specified performance target within the power budget. The numbers on top of bar groups correspond to the number of processors that yields the lowest power consumption.

at each instance the DVFS level whose recorded execution time is the tightest upper bound to our next target. (Recall that, in steady state, as a result of variability in the execution time across instances, we accummulate any deviation from the target into the next instance's). Our goal is to see whether there exists a "universal pick" of processor count regardless of the performance target. To do that, for each application, we pick three deadlines: (1) a "loose" performance target, roughly equivalent to one fourth of the fastest possible execution on one processor within the power budget; (2) an intermediate deadline, roughly equivalent to the fastest possible execution on one processor within the power budget; and (3) a "tight" performance target, roughly equivalent to the fastest possible execution on four processors, still within the power budget. We normalize all power measurements to the chip's power budget. Fig. 3 shows the results.

The plots show that significant (and often nonlinear) differences exist in the optimized power consumption for each processor count, even as the performance of all plotted configurations are within 2-3% of the target (not

shown). Generally speaking, given a particular performance target, an increase in the number of processors allows for DVFS downscaling. This may initially result in overall power savings, however as we keep increasing the number of processors and we run out of DVFS levels, static power starts to dominate, eventually reversing the power savings trend.

With a loose performance target (top), configurations with low processor count can downscale DVFS aggressively, consuming little power, but leaving little room for further DVFS reduction to higher processor counts, which soon experience increased (static) power consumption. On the other hand, a tight performance target (bottom) requires configurations with low processor count to use high DVFS levels (and thus power) in order to meet the performance constraint, which allows a prolonged trend of power savings as we increase the processor count (provided the application scales well [29].)

Notice that, with greater static power consumption in future process technologies, the differences in power consumption for the scenarios with loose and intemediate performance targets (top and middle plots, respectively) are bound to increase, as static power will be more dominant in configurations with high processor count.

Moreover, across the plots, it becomes evident that the optimum processor count shifts depending on the performance target. Each plot shows, on top of the bars for each application, the number of processors of the configuration that minimizes power consumption.

Thus, to find the configuration that minimizes power consumption, it is generally necessary to connect the particular performance target to the power and performance characteristics of the application and the hardware, which is precisely what our proposed mechanisms try to do at run time.

5.2 Effectiveness of Optimization Mechanisms

We now investigate the effectiveness of the proposed optimization mechanisms. We combine the DVFS search heuristic and the hill-climbing binary processor count search heuristic; this we call HC (for Hill Climbing). HC starts with eight processors, and initially veers toward a lower number of processors (four). After that, and for the duration of the search phase, HC reuses the last profitable direction in determining which new processor count to try first. Once in steady state, HC uses the operating points visited during the search phase to try and match the target rate.

We also try a variant of HC which we call HC-Fixed, in which, once in steady state, we can only use the operating points visited during the search phase whose processor count is that of the local optimum found by the hill-climbing heuristic. This represents a scenario in which, for whatever reason, we do not want to use a variable number of processors in steady state.

We use the same power budget and performance targets as before. For comparison purposes, for each application

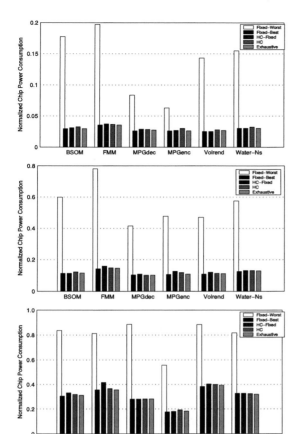

Figure 4: Chip power consumption of two proposed mechanisms (HC and HC-Fixed) against the best (Fixed-Best) and worst (Fixed-Worst) configurations of the earlier experiment, and a configuration with full knowledge of the search space (Exhaustive), for loose (top), intermediate (middle), and tight (bottom) performance targets. All bars are normalized to the power budget. Notice the different scales on the Y axes.

and performance target, we plot the power consumption of the best (Fixed-Best) and worst (Fixed-Worst) configurations from the earlier experiment. (Recall that Fixed-Best and Fixed-Worst can use *any* legal DVFS level for their processor count. This is unlike HC and, in particular, HC-Fixed.)

Finally, we also compare against a configuration that has full knowledge of the execution time and power consumption of every operating point for each instance of the parallel region under study. We call this optimistic configuration Exhaustive.

Fig. 4 shows the power consumption for each configuration, all normalized to the power budget. As in the case of the earlier experiments, all configurations successfully execute within 2-3% of the performance target in steady state (not shown). The results are very encouraging: In virtually all cases, our proposed mechanisms (HC and HC-Fixed) are capable of achieving the same level of power savings of not only the best configuration from the earlier experiment (Fixed-Best), but even Exhaustive, which has full knowledge of the power-performance behavior of all possible operating points at each moment.

This result is quite remarkable, considering that HC can only leverage the approximately 12 operating points visited during the search phase in most cases (about four steps along the processor dimension, with around three steps along the DVFS dimension each time). Even more remarkable is HC-Fixed which, with only about three visited operating points along the range of the final processor count, closely tracks the performance of the more powerful configurations, with the possible exception of FMM on a fast performance target (bottom plot), in which HC-Fixed trails the other optimization mechanisms somewhat (but HC does not).

Overall, the results of our evaluation show that, indeed:

- For a parallel region and a particular performance target, the choice of operating point(s) that minimize power consumption in our experimental setup is nontrivial, which makes optimization space search useful.

- In spite of the reduced knowledge about the optimization space, the proposed mechanisms HC and HC-Fixed, based on the presented heuristics for space search reduction, achieve virtually optimum power savings for the applications under study.

6 RELATED WORK

There is a rich collection of literature on power- and thermal-aware simultaneous multithreading (SMT) and CMP designs (or similar architecture configurations), most of which focuses on multiprogrammed workloads [10, 14, 26, 32, 41, 42]. In contrast, our work focuses on power-performance issues of CMPs in the context of parallel applications.

Huh et al. [19] conduct an in-depth exploration of the design space of CMPs. However, they do not address power. More recently, Ekman and Stenström [11] conduct a design-space study of CMPs in which they address some power issues. Assuming a certain silicon budget, they compare chips with different numbers of cores, and correspondingly different core sizes. They argue that parallel applications with limited scalability but some instruction-level parallelism may run better on CMPs with few, wide-issue cores. They also argue that CMPs with few, wide-issue cores and with many, narrow-issue cores consume roughly the same power, as cache activity offsets savings at the cores. Our work assumes a given chip design, and explores the issues of minimizing power consumption by judiciously applying the optimum number of processors and voltage/frequency levels to a parallel region, given certain performance constraints.

Grochowski et al. [15] discuss trade-offs between microprocessor processing speed vs. throughput in a power-constrained environment. They postulate that a microprocessor that can achieve both high scalar performance and high throughput performance ought to be able to dynamically vary the amount of energy expended to process each instruction, according to the amount of parallelism available in the software. To achieve this, they survey four techniques: dynamic voltage/frequency scaling (DVFS), asymmetric cores, variable-sized cores, and speculation control, and conclude that a combination of DVFS and asymmetric cores is best.

More recently, Annavaram et al. [2] use an asymmetric CMP to maximize the performance of a multithreaded application, by assuming that nontrivial serial regions exist in the application. They use the notion of energy per instruction (EPI) throttle to orchestrate the application's execution on its sequential and parallel portions under a fixed power budget. For the sequential portions, they assign a faster but more power-hungry processor. For the parallel portions, depending on the number of threads that are inherent in the application's parallelization and the number of available processors, they assign multiple slower but power-thrifty processors. In our work, we study dynamic optimization on a parallel region running on a symmetric CMP with a large configuration space.

Kaxiras et al. [24] compare the power consumption of an SMT and a CMP digital signal processing chip for mobile phone applications. They do not explicitly study parallel applications in the "traditional" sense. For example, they approximate a parallel encoder with four independent MPEG encoder threads, each thread processing one quarter of the original image size. A speech encoder and a speech decoder are connected in a pipelined fashion to a channel encoder and decoder, respectively. The issues that we address in our work cannot be easily conveyed in this context.

Kadayif et al. [22] propose to shut down idle processors in order to save energy when running nested loops on a CMP. The authors also study a pre-activation strategy based on compiler analysis to reduce the wake-up overhead of powered-off processors. Although they address program granularity and power, they do not exploit DVFS in their solution, which is fundamental in our work.

In a different work, Kadayif et al. [23] propose to use DVFS to slow down lightly loaded threads, to compensate for load imbalance in a program and save power and energy. They use the compiler to estimate the load imbalance of array-based loops on single-issue processor cores. The authors also mention the opportunity for further energy savings by using less than the number of available processor cores using profile information. However, the connection of DVFS to parallelization granularity of the code is not fleshed out.

In the context of cache-coherent shared-memory multiprocessors, Moshovos, et al. [34] reduce energy consumption by filtering snoop requests in a bus-based parallel system. Saldanha and Lipasti [40] observe significant potential of energy savings by using serial snooping for load misses. Li, et al. [30] propose saving energy wasted in barrier spin-waiting, by predicting a processor's stall time and, if warranted, forcing it into an appropriate ACPI-like low-power sleep state. This work is complementary to ours in that it does not consider the number of processors, and does not attack power consumption during useful activity by the parallel application.

In an environment of loosely-coupled web servers running independent workloads, several studies evaluate different policies to control the number of active servers (and thus their performance level) to preserve power while maintaining acceptable quality of service [12, 13, 38, 39]. Elnozahy et al [12] evaluate policies that employ various combinations of independent and coordinated dynamic voltage/frequency scaling, and node vary-on/vary-off, to reduce the aggregated power consumption of a web server cluster during periods of reduced workload. They evaluate the policies with simulations, and show that the combination of coordinated voltage/frequency scaling and node vary-on/vary-off obtains the largest power savings. They only consider dynamic power in their simulations.

In the context of micro-architectures, Heo and Asanović [18] study the effectiveness of pipelining as a power-saving tool in a uniprocessor. They examine the relationship between the logic depth per stage and the supply voltage in deep submicron technology under different conditions. This is complementary to our work, since we study power-performance issues of using multiple cores on a CMP.

7 CONCLUSIONS

In this work, we have addressed the problem of dynamic power optimization of parallel execution on many-core, DVFS-capable CMPs under given performance restrictions. We have shown that the number of available processors and DVFS levels may constitute a considerable search space, and the particular optimum depends nontrivially on the power-performance CMP characteristics, the application's behavior, and the specific performance target. To attack this problem, we have proposed simple heuristics that can be used to cut down on the search effort along both dimensions of the optimization space. Our evaluation shows that these heuristics produce near-optimum results in virtually all cases considered.

ACKNOWLEDGMENTS

We thank Engin İpek and the anonymous reviewers for valuable feedback. This work is supported in part by NSF awards CNS-0509404 and CCF-0429922, and gifts from Intel.

REFERENCES

[1] T. Agerwala. Computer architecture: Challenges and opportunities for the next decade. In *International Symposium on Computer Architecture*, München, Germany, June 2004. (Keynote presentation).

[2] M. Annavaram, E. Grochowski, and J. Shen. Mitigating Amdahl's Law through EPI throttling. In *International Symposium on Computer Architecture*, pages 298–309, Madison, Wisconsin, June 2005.

[3] S. Y. Borkar. Platform 2015: Intel processor and platform evolution for the next decade. Technical report, Intel White Paper, Mar. 2005.

[4] D. Brooks, V. Tiwari, and M. Martonosi. Wattch: A framework for architectural-level power analysis and optimizations. In *International Symposium on Computer Architecture*, pages 83–94, Vancouver, Canada, June 2000.

[5] N. Carriero, E. Freeman, D. Gelernter, and D. Kaminsky. Adaptive parallelism and Piranha. *IEEE Computer*, 28(1):40–49, Jan. 1995.

[6] A. Chandrakasan, S. Sheng, and R. W. Brodersen. Low-power CMOS digital design. *IEEE Journal of Solid-State Circuits*, 27(4):473–484, Apr. 1992.

[7] P. Chaparro, J. González, and A. González. Thermal-effective clustered microarchitectures. In *Workshop on Temperature-Aware Computer Systems*, München, Germany, June 2004.

[8] Compaq Computer Corporation, Shrewsbury, Massachusetts. *Alpha 21264 Microprocessor Hardware Reference Manual*, July 1999.

[9] D. E. Culler and J. P. Singh. *Parallel Computer Architecture: A Hardware/Software Approach*. Morgan Kaufmann, 1999.

[10] J. Donald and M. Martonosi. Temperature-aware design issues for SMT and CMP architectures. In *Workshop on Complexity-Effective Design*, München, Germany, June 2004.

[11] M. Ekman and P. Stenström. Performance and power impact of issue-width in chip-multiprocessor cores. In *International Conference on Parallel Processing*, pages 359–368, Kaohsiung, Taiwan, Oct. 2003.

[12] E. N. Elnozahy, M. Kistler, and R. Rajamony. Energy-efficient server clusters. In *Workshop on Power Aware Computing Systems*, pages 179–196, Cambridge, MA, Feb. 2002.

[13] E. N. Elnozahy, M. Kistler, and R. Rajamony. Energy conservation policies for web servers. In *USENIX Symposium on Internet Technologies and Systems*, Seattle, WA, Mar. 2003.

[14] S. Ghiasi and D. Grunwald. Design choices for thermal control in dual-core processors. In *Workshop on Complexity-Effective Design*, München, Germany, June 2004.

[15] E. Grochowski, R. Ronen, J. Shen, and H. Wang. Best of both latency and throughput. In *International Conference on Computer Design*, pages 236–243, San Jose, CA, Oct. 2004.

[16] M. Hall and M. Martonosi. Adaptive parallelism in compiler-parallelized code. In *SUIF Compiler Workshop*, Stanford University, CA, Aug. 1997.

[17] J. L. Hennessy and D. A. Patterson. *Computer Architecture: A Quantitative Approach*. Elsevier Science Pte Ltd., third edition, 2003.

[18] S. Heo and K. Asanović. Power-optimal pipelining in deep submicron technology. In *International Symposium on Low Power Electronics and Design*, Newport Beach, CA, Aug. 2004.

[19] J. Huh, D. Burger, and S. W. Keckler. Exploring the design space of future CMPs. In *International Conference on Parallel Architectures and Compilation Techniques*, pages 199–210, Barcelona, Spain, Sept. 2001.

[20] Intel Corporation. *Intel Pentium M Processor on 90nm Process with 2-MB L2 Cache Datasheet*, June 2004.

[21] The ITRS Technology Working Groups. *International Technology Roadmap for Semiconductors (ITRS)*, http://public.itrs.net.

[22] I. Kadayif, M. Kandemir, and U. Sezer. An integer linear programming based approach for parallelizing applications in on-chip multiprocessors. In *IEEE/ACM Design Automation Conference*, pages 703–708, New Orleans, LA, June 2002.

[23] I. Kadayif, M. Kandemir, N. Vijaykrishnan, and M. J. Irwin. Exploiting processor workload heterogeneity for reducing energy consumption in chip multiprocessors. In *Design, Automation and Test in Europe*, pages 1158–1163, Paris, France, Feb. 2004.

[24] S. Kaxiras, G. Narlikar, A. D. Berenbaum, and Z. Hu. Comparing power consumption of an SMT and a CMP DSP for mobile phone workloads. In *International Conference on Compilers, Architecture, and Systhesis for Embedded Systems*, pages 211–220, Atlanta, Georgia, Nov. 2001.

[25] D. J. Kuck. Platform 2015 software: Enabling innovation in parallelism for the next decade. Technical report, Intel White Paper, Mar. 2005.

[26] R. Kumar, K. I. Farkas, N. P. Jouppi, P. Ranganathan, and D. M. Tullsen. Single-ISA heterogeneous multi-core architectures: The potential for processor power reduction. In *International Symposium on Microarchitecture*, pages 81–92, San Diego, CA, Dec. 2003.

[27] R. Kumar, D. M. Tullsen, P. Ranganathan, N. P. Jouppi, and K. I. Farkas. Single-ISA heterogeneous multi-core architectures for multithreaded workload performance. In *International Symposium on Computer Architecture*, pages 64–75, München, Germany, June 2004.

[28] R. D. Lawrence, G. S. Almasi, and H. E. Rushmeier. A scalable parallel algorithm for self-organizing maps with applications to sparse data mining problems. *Data Mining and Knowledge Discovery*, 3(2):171–195, Sept. 1999.

[29] J. Li and J. F. Martínez. Power-Performance implications of thread-level parallelism on chip multiprocessors. In *International Symposium on Performance Analysis of Systems and Software*, Austin, TX, Mar. 2005.

[30] J. Li, J. F. Martínez, and M. C. Huang. The Thrifty Barrier: Energy-aware synchronization in shared-memory multiprocessors. In *International Symposium on High-Performance Computer Architecture*, pages 14–23, Madrid, Spain, Feb. 2004.

[31] M.-L. Li, R. Sasanka, S. V. Adve, Y.-K. Chen, and E. Debes. The ALPBench benchmark suite for complex multimedia applications. In *IEEE International Symposium on Workload Characterization*, Austin, TX, Oct. 2006.

[32] Y. Li, D. Brooks, Z. Hu, and K. Skadron. Performance, energy, and temperature considerations for SMT and CMP architectures. In *International Symposium on High-Performance Computer Architecture*, San Francisco, CA, Feb. 2005.

[33] R. Majan. Thermal management of CPUs: A perspective on trends, needs and opportunities. In *International Workshop on Thermal Investigations of ICs and Systems*, Madrid, Spain, Oct. 2002. Keynote presentation.

[34] A. Moshovos, G. Memik, B. Falsafi, and A. Choudhary. JETTY: Filtering snoops for reduced energy consumption in SMP servers. In *International Symposium on High-Performance Computer Architecture*, pages 85–96, Nuevo Leone, Mexico, Jan. 2001.

[35] S. Naffziger, B. Stackhouse, and T. Grutkowski. The implementation of a 2-core multi-threaded itanium-family processor. In *IEEE International Solid-State Circuits Conference*, San Francisco, CA, Feb. 2005.

[36] OpenMP Architecture Review Board. *OpenMP Specifications*, http://www.openmp.org.

[37] K. K. Parhi. *VLSI Digital Signal Processing Systems*. John Wiley and Sons, Inc., New York, NY, 1999.

[38] E. Pinheiro, R. Bianchini, E. Carrera, and T. Heath. Load balancing and unbalancing for power and performance in cluster-based systems. In *International Workshop on Compilers and Operating Systems for Low Power*, Barcelona, Spain, Sept. 2001.

[39] K. Rajamani and C. Lefurgy. On evaluating request-distribution schemes for saving energy in server clusters. In *International Symposium on Performance Analysis of Systems and Software*, pages 111–122, Austin, TX, Mar. 2003.

[40] C. Saldanha and M. Lipasti. Power efficient cache coherence. In *Workshop on Memory Performance Issues*, Göteborg, Sweden, June 2001.

[41] R. Sasanka, S. V. Adve, Y. Chen, and E. Debes. Comparing the energy efficiency of CMP and SMT architectures for multimedia workloads. In *International Conference on Supercomputing*, pages 196–206, Malo, France, June–July 2004.

[42] J. S. Seng, D. M. Tullsen, and G. Z. N. Cai. Power-sensitive multithreaded architecture. In *International Conference on Computer Design*, pages 199–208, Austin, Texas, Sept. 2000.

[43] K. Skadron, M. Stan, W. Huang, and S. Velusamy. Temperature-aware microarchitecture: Extended discussion and results. Technical Report CS-2003-08, University of Virginia, Apr. 2003.

[44] S. Wilton and N. Jouppi. CACTI: An enhanced cache access and cycle time model. *IEEE Journal of Solid-State Circuits*, 31(5):677–688, May 1996.

[45] S. C. Woo, M. Ohara, E. Torrie, J. P. Singh, and A. Gupta. The SPLASH-2 programs: Characterization and methodological considerations. In *International Symposium on Computer Architecture*, pages 24–36, Santa Margherita Ligure, Italy, June 1995.

Last Level Cache (LLC) Performance of Data Mining Workloads On a CMP — A Case Study of Parallel Bioinformatics Workloads

Aamer Jaleel

Intel Corporation, VSSAD
aamer.jaleel@intel.com

Matthew Mattina[*]

Tilera Corporation
mmattina@tilera.com

Bruce Jacob

University of Maryland, College Park
Dept. of Electrical and Computer Engineering
blj@eng.umd.edu

Abstract

With the continuing growth in the amount of genetic data, members of the bioinformatics community are developing a variety of data-mining applications to understand the data and discover meaningful information. These applications are important in defining the design and performance decisions of future high performance microprocessors. This paper presents a detailed data-sharing analysis and chip-multiprocessor (CMP) cache study of several multi-threaded data-mining bioinformatics workloads. For a CMP with a three-level cache hierarchy, we model the last-level of the cache hierarchy as either multiple private caches or a single cache shared amongst different cores of the CMP. Our experiments show that the bioinformatics workloads exhibit significant data-sharing—50–95% of the data cache is shared by the different threads of the workload. Furthermore, regardless of the amount of data cache shared, for some workloads, as many as 98% of the accesses to the last-level cache are to shared data cache lines. Additionally, the amount of data-sharing exhibited by the workloads is a function of the total cache size available—the larger the data cache the better the sharing behavior. Thus, partitioning the available last-level cache silicon area into multiple private caches can cause applications to lose their inherent data-sharing behavior. For the workloads in this study, a shared 32MB last-level cache is able to capture a tremendous amount of data-sharing and outperform a 32MB private cache configuration by several orders of magnitude. Specifically, with shared last-level caches, the bandwidth demands beyond the last-level cache can be reduced by factors of 3–625 when compared to private last-level caches.

1. Introduction

Recent trends in industry show that the future of high performance computing will be defined by the performance of multi-core processors [1, 4, 5]. Additionally, *recognition, mining, and synthesis* (RMS) workloads in the fields of medicine, investment, business and gaming are emerging as the memory intensive workloads that will run on these CMPs [21]. Within these fields, one of the most important and growing application domains is the field of bioinformatics, where workloads mine enormous amounts of genetic data to discover knowledge [14]. This motivates investigating the performance

characteristics of these data-mining workloads to help define the suitable microarchitectural parameters of future CMPs.

As multi-core processors become pervasive and the number of on-die cores increases, a key design issue facing processor architects will be the hierarchy and policies for the on-die last-level cache (LLC). The most important application characteristics that drive this cache hierarchy and design are the amount and type of sharing exhibited by important multi-threaded applications. For example, if the target multi-threaded applications exhibit little or no sharing, and the threads have similar working set sizes, a simple "SMP on a chip" strategy may be the best approach. In such a case, each core has its own private cache hierarchy. Any memory block that is shared by more than one core is replicated in the hierarchies of the respective cores, thereby lowering the effective cache capacity. On a cache miss, the hierarchies of all the other cores' caches must be snooped (depending on the specifics of the inclusion policy). On the other hand, if the target multi-threaded applications exhibit a significant amount of sharing, or the threads have varying working set sizes, a shared-cache CMP is more attractive. In this case, a single, large, last-level cache—which may be centralized or distributed depending on bandwidth requirements—is shared by all the on-die cores. Cache blocks that are referenced by more than one core are not replicated in the shared cache. Furthermore, the shared cache naturally accommodates variations in the working set sizes of the different threads. In essence (and at the risk of oversimplifying), the CMP design team, building a chip with C cores and having silicon area for N bytes of last-level cache, must decide between building C private caches of N/C bytes each, or one large shared cache of N bytes. Of course, there is a large solution space between the two extremes, including replication of read-only blocks, migration of blocks, and selective exclusion to name just a few. However, the key application characteristics concerning the amount of data-sharing and the type of sharing is important for the entire design space, and thus we focus on these characteristics independently of the specific techniques used in the last-level cache. Since we have focused on the miss-analysis of shared caches on CMPs, we also ignore the impact of latency on overall performance.

Having alluded to the fact that future high-performance processors are tending towards CMPs, the question now is: *What are the important workloads of the future that will run on these CMPs?*

Recent studies have shown that the amount of data in the world is increasing by 30% each year [21]. Of the many different contributors to this growing mass of data, the biotechnology community is playing a major role via contribution of enormous amounts of genetic data

---

[*]Matthew Mattina's contribution to this work was while he was an architect at Intel Massachusetts Microprocessor Design Center (MMDC).

into GenBank, a database of all publicly known biological sequences. With the amount of genetic data more than doubling each year [14], members of the bioinformatics community have developed a variety of data-mining applications to gather meaningful information from the data and discover knowledge. With the completion of the sequencing of the human genome in 2001, the focus in bioinformatics has now shifted from gathering and sequencing data to developing intelligent algorithms that mine the massive amounts of known DNA, RNA, and protein data, with the intent of discovering previously unknown relationships, structures, and insights. These algorithms are high performance computing challenges and will help define the design and performance decisions of future high performance microprocessors.

Thus, for the purpose of this study, we chose the emerging class of bioinformatics applications as our target application set. With this in mind and with the industry transition towards CMPs, this paper makes the following contributions:

- We perform a detailed analysis of the sharing behavior of bioinformatics workloads and show that most of them exhibit a tremendous amount of data-sharing. With a shared cache, we show that 50–95% of the data cache is shared by different threads of the workload and as many as 98% of the accesses to the last-level cache are to shared cache lines. Furthermore, application sharing behavior is a function of the total size of the data cache— the larger the data cache the more an application is able to exploit its sharing behavior. For example, an application with a 4MB shared last-level data cache can exhibit 10% data-sharing; however, increasing the data cache size to 32MB shows that the workload actually exhibits 90% data-sharing. We show that for most of the workloads studied, a shared 32MB last-level cache is able to capture the bulk of an application's data-sharing. Furthermore, for these workloads, a shared 32MB last-level cache can reduce the bandwidth demands beyond the last-level cache by a factor of 3–625 when compared to a private last-level cache configuration. This implies that such workloads need the maximum cache size possible to exploit their inherent data-sharing behavior. Reducing the cache size or partitioning the cache into multiple private caches can cause a degradation in overall cache performance.

- We show that there is a direct correlation between the amount of data-sharing and the performance of shared caches. The time varying behavior of our workloads show multiple phases of execution where some phases exhibit significant data-sharing and some phases that do not. For such workloads, we observe that a shared last-level cache offers tremendous benefits during the data-sharing phase. To our knowledge, there is no prior study that correlates the data-sharing behavior of workloads with the performance of shared or private caches.

- We also investigate the impact of scaling the number of threads of the workload on cache performance. By scaling the number of workload threads from 4 to 8 and 16, and assuming CMPs of 8 and 16 cores each, we observe that shared last-level caches outperform a private last-level cache by 40-60% when comparing overall cache miss-rate.

The rest of the paper is organized in the following manner. Section 2 provides a brief description of the parallel bioinformatics workloads. Section 3 describes our methodology and the metrics used to measure application data-sharing. Section 4 provides the sharing characteristics of the workloads and presents the cache performance of private and shared caches. Section 5 presents related work. Finally in Section 6 we provide conclusions of this study.

2. Background

In this section, we provide a brief description of the OpenMP parallel bioinformatics workloads studied by Chen et al. [16]. Interested readers are referred to the original article on the description and scalability of these workloads [16].

- **GeneNet**: This application is used to measure the regulatory relationship between genes. One of the main goals of molecular biology is to understand the regulation of protein synthesis and its relation to internal and external signals. In the GeneNet application, each gene is represented as a variable of a Bayesian network, and the gene expression problem is formulated as a Bayesian network structure-learning problem. GeneNet uses hill-climbing as its main search algorithm. The algorithm is written in C++ with some details implemented using Intel's open source Probabilistic Networks Library (PNL). The training data input is the cell cycle data of Yeast (173 sequences) [16]. The total memory working set size of this application is 350MB.

- **SNP**: This application is used to measure and understand the patterns of Single Nucleotide Polymorphisms (SNPs). SNPs are a small genetic change or substitution in the nucleotides of an individual's DNA sequence. An important goal here is to understand the reasoning behind these substitutions. In the SNP application, each possible nucleotide is represented as a random variable, and all possible relations between the different nucleotides are modeled using a Bayesian network structure. Like GeneNet, the SNP application also uses hill-climbing as its main search algorithm. The algorithm is written in C++ with some details implemented using the Probabilistic Networks Library (PNL). The training input is a 30MB freely downloadable data set from the HGBASE (Human Genic Bi-Alletic Sequences), a database of SNPs [3]. There are a total of 616,179 SNPs sequences in the training data set and each sequence has a length of 50 [16]. The total memory working set size of this application is 170MB.

- **SEMPHY:** This application is a tool for constructing phylogenetic trees. Phylogenetic trees are used to represent the relationship among different species and possibly describe the course of evolution. The construction of a phylogenetic tree is a high performance computing problem, especially with the growing mass of biological data. The SEMPHY application uses the structural expectation maximization (SEM) algorithm [22] as its main search algorithm [8]. The algorithm is written in C++ and handles both DNA and protein sequences. The input data set are sequences from the Pfam database [6]. The total memory working set size of this application is 90MB.

- **Support Vector Machines Recursive Feature Elimination (SVM-RFE):** This application is used to eliminate gene redundancy from a given input data set in order to provide compact gene subsets. It uses Support Vector Machines (SVM) as the means to classify genes into different subsets. The SVM-RFE algorithm is written in C++ and uses the Intel Math Kernel Library (MKL) to enhance performance. The input data set to the application is a microarray data set involving ovarian cancer.

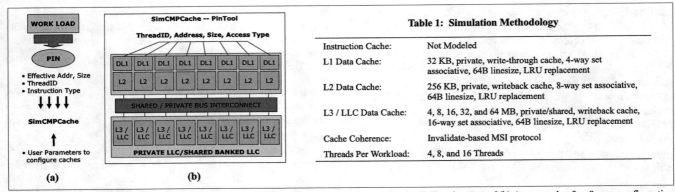

Figure 1: Simulation Methodology. (a) The relationship between the workload, Pin, and the simCMPcache *pin tool* (b) An example of an 8-core configuration of simCMPcache (c) Configuration parameters for the study in this paper.

Table 1: Simulation Methodology

Instruction Cache:	Not Modeled
L1 Data Cache:	32 KB, private, write-through cache, 4-way set associative, 64B linesize, LRU replacement
L2 Data Cache:	256 KB, private, writeback cache, 8-way set associative, 64B linesize, LRU replacement
L3 / LLC Data Cache:	4, 8, 16, 32, and 64 MB, private/shared, writeback cache, 16-way set associative, 64B linesize, LRU replacement
Cache Coherence:	Invalidate-based MSI protocol
Threads Per Workload:	4, 8, and 16 Threads

The ovarian data set contains 253 (tissue samples) x 15154 (genes) expression values. The total memory working set size of this application is 300MB.

- **Parallel Linear Space Alignment (PLSA):** This application is used to identify the similarities or differences between two genetic sequences, e.g. DNA/protein sequences. The similarity between two sequences (or the lack of it) can provide insight on understanding the functionality, structure, and evolutionary relationship of the two sequences. The application uses a dynamic programming approach to solve the sequence similarity problem, with the main algorithm being the Smith-Waterman algorithm [29]. The application is written in C++ and takes as inputs two sequences each 30,000 letters long. The total memory working set size of this application is 14MB.

3. Methodology

We now describe the tools and the hardware platform used to simulate the cache memory hierarchy.

3.1. Pin

Pin[7, 28] is a tool for the dynamic instrumentation of application binaries. It supports Linux executables for Intel® Xscale®, IA-32 (32-bit), IA-32E (64-bit), and Itanium® processors. Pin is similar to the ATOM[31] toolkit for Compaq's Tru64 Unix on Alpha processors. Like ATOM, Pin provides an infrastructure for writing program analysis tools called *pin tools*. The two main components of a Pin tool are instrumentation and analysis routines. Instrumentation routines utilize the rich API provided by Pin to insert calls to user defined analysis routines. These calls are inserted by the user at arbitrary points in the application instruction stream. Instrumentation routines are useful in defining what characteristics of an application to instrument. Analysis routines are called by the instrumentation routines at application run time. Besides instrumenting single-threaded applications, Pin also supports the instrumentation of multi-threaded applications. Pin automatically detects the creation of threads and internally creates contexts for the newly created threads without any additional user support. The scheduling of different threads of the application is controlled by the operating system.

3.2. SimCMPcache — A CMP cache simulator

For the purpose of our memory-characterization study, we implement *simCMPcache*, a pin tool that simulates the cache hierarchy of a CMP. Figure 1a provides an overview of how workload binaries, Pin, and simCMPcache interact with each other. The workload essentially runs on top of Pin; Pin captures relevant information from the workload and passes it to the simCMPcache pintool. Specifically, for every memory instruction in the workload, Pin passes to simCMPcache the associated thread ID, effective address, data size, and instruction type (load/store). SimCMPcache then takes the incoming memory instruction information and simulates cache performance using its internal cache model.

The cache model in simCMPcache is fully configurable based on parameters provided by the user. Figure 1b provides an illustrative view of simCMPcache configured as an 8-core CMP. We model a three level cache hierarchy—L1, L2, and L3 (last-level cache). The different levels of the cache can either be private or shared amongst the CMP cores. We enforce inclusion between all levels of caches. We model an MSI invalidate-based cache coherence protocol where the states for the cache line are *Modified*, *Shared*, and *Invalid*. On a write request, invalidates are sent to the relevant private caches to invalidate any matching entries. Similarly, when read requests miss in the private caches, remote dirty lines (if any) are required to perform a write-back to lower levels of memory before servicing the miss.

SimCMPcache is capable of gathering a variety of statistics. On a per-application-thread basis, the simulator tracks the application instruction profile, cache statistics in terms of accesses and misses, sharing characteristics of the last-level cache, and statistics on the coherence traffic between caches. These statistics can be written to a logfile when the program has finished execution. However, to characterize the time varying behavior of the application, cache statistics are logged to file every 10 million instructions committed by any thread of the application.

Table 1 presents the methodology for studying the cache performance of our workloads. For the purpose of this study, we assume a perfect instruction cache. The L1 data cache is 32KB in size, 4-way set associative, with 64-byte linesize and a write-through policy. The L2 cache is 256KB in size, 8-way set associative, with 64-byte linesize and write-back policy. For the purpose of this study we do not consider changing the parameters of the L1 and L2 caches. Finally, the last-level cache is either 4/8/16/32/64 MB, 16-way set

Table 2: Dynamic Application Instruction Distribution

	Instruction Count (Billions)	%Memory Instructions	% ALU Instructions	%Memory Read Instructions
PLSA	418.53 B	85.05%	14.95%	49.40%
GeneNet	1,491.49 B	65.54%	34.46%	48.89%
SEMPHY	811.96 B	61.15%	38.85%	46.33%
SNP	59.59 B	45.19%	54.81%	36.85%
SVM	40.91 B	43.52%	56.48%	38.75%

Table 3: First and Second Level Cache Statistics

	DL1 Accesses / 1000 Inst	DL1 Misses / 1000 Inst	DL1 Miss-rate	DL2 Misses / 1000 Inst	DL2 Read Misses / 1000 Inst	DL2 Miss-rate
PLSA	850	0.85	0.10	0.04	0.02	0.01
GeneNet	656	4.50	0.68	3.73	3.55	2.21
SEMPHY	611	7.25	1.18	6.83	3.96	4.49
SNP	452	11.57	2.56	11.57	11.33	10.50
SVM	435	97.20	22.30	51.90	50.34	48.05

associative, with 64-byte linesize and write-back policy. All caches allocate on a store miss and use the LRU cache-line replacement policy. The L1 and L2 cache are modeled as private caches and the last-level cache can either be private or shared.

3.3. Hardware platform

To capture the memory-access characteristics of multi-threaded workloads, our experiments are run on 4-way or 8-way shared memory multi-processor (SMP) systems of Intel® Pentium® 4 processors. The systems all run the RedHat Linux 7.1 operating system with hyper-threading enabled. Such systems allow us to run our workloads with 1 to 16 threads. The workloads are compiled using the *icc* compiler with optimization flags -O3. For the purpose of this study our workloads are executed with 4, 8, and 16 threads.

3.4. Metrics

To understand the sharing behavior of parallel workloads, we define the following metrics to measure the degree of data-sharing existent in parallel applications.

- **Shared Cache Line:** Cache lines in a shared data cache can either be private or shared. When executing parallel applications, an important workload characteristic is a measure of how much data is shared between threads. One way of measuring the degree of sharing is to measure the number of cache lines that are touched by different cores of a CMP. Assuming that the threads of an application execute on different cores of a CMP, and threads do not migrate between cores, we define a *shared cache line* as one that is accessed by more than one core of a CMP during its *lifetime* in the cache. For the purpose of this study, we classify a shared cacheline as either read-only shared or read-write shared. Read-only shared cache lines are those cache lines that are only read from and not written to. For example, while searching a database in parallel, more than one thread of a workload can read the same cache line. A read-write shared cache line is a shared cache line that is used as a means of

communication between threads. A producer thread writes to a cache line and a consumer reads data from the same cache line. The shared cache line metric is useful in determining the shared data footprint of a workload and the type of sharing the workload exhibits.

- **Shared Access:** An access to a shared cache line is defined as a *shared access*. This metric is useful in determining the variation and frequency of accesses to shared or private cache lines. Such a metric not only indicates the amount of data-sharing prevalent in an application, but it also provides intuition for the choice of cache design for parallel applications. For example, if most of the cache accesses are to shared data, then perhaps shared caches may provide better cache performance than private caches.

- **Active-Shared Access:** An active shared access is an access to a shared cache line with the condition that the last core that accessed the shared cache line is *not* the same as the current core. For example, if the accesses to a shared cache line is represented by the following core ids: ...1, *2*, 2, 2, *1*, *3*, *4*, *3*, *2*, 2, 2, *3*, *2*..., the accesses by the underlined core IDs are *active-shared accesses*. Such a metric is useful in identifying and characterizing whether workloads share cache lines interactively or in a serial fashion. Such information can be useful for determining the benefits of data migration to cache banks closer to the accessing cores.

4. Characterization results

The OpenMP implementation of the bioinformatics workloads in this study typically start with a serial initialization or training phase where only the main thread is active. After the serial phase, threads are created to perform work during the parallel phase. Even though data is gathered over the entire run of each workload, unless otherwise mentioned, we present the behavior of the workloads during the parallel phase of execution, which dominates overall execution time. The data presented is averaged over the periodic logs generated by our cache simulator.

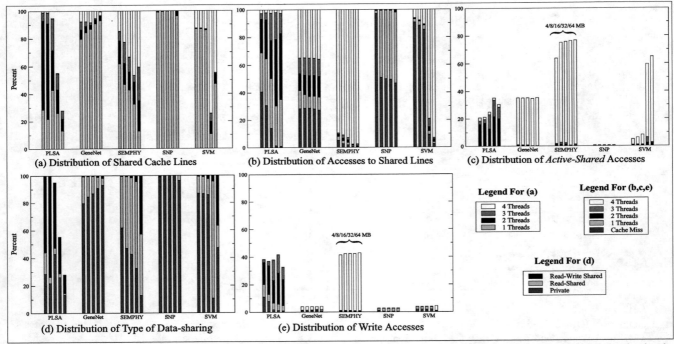

Figure 2: Sharing Behavior with a Shared Last-Level Cache. Distribution of (a) shared data in last-level cache (b) cache accesses to data in last-level cache (c) cache accesses to actively shared data in last-level cache (d) classification of data-sharing in last level cache (e) write accesses to data in last-level cache.

4.1. Application instruction profile

Table 2 presents the dynamic instruction profile for the different workloads when run with 4 threads. For each application we present the total number of instructions executed across all threads and the distribution of instructions categorized into memory instructions and ALU instructions. With the CISC nature of the x86 ISA, instructions can perform arithmetic or logic computation based on operands that reside either in memory or the register file. Accordingly, we define memory instructions as those instructions that have one or more operands in memory and ALU instructions as those instructions that have all their operands in the register file. We also provide the breakdown of total instructions that were memory read instructions.

Based on the application instruction profile, we observe that the workloads consist of roughly 43–65% memory instructions, with as many as 85% for the PLSA workload. We also observe that memory read instructions constitute 60–90% of total memory instructions. The large share of memory instructions, especially memory read instructions, is to be expected as these workloads work through large amounts of data in attempts to discover meaningful patterns or relationships between data.

4.2. Workload L1/L2 cache behavior

Table 3 presents the L1 and L2 cache statistics for the different workloads. For each level of the cache, we present the number of accesses and misses per 1000 instructions (committed) as well as the overall cache miss-rate. From the table, PLSA has the lowest L1 data cache miss-rate and SVM has the largest L1 and L2 data cache miss-rates. With the exception of PLSA and SVM, comparing the L1 and L2 misses per 1000 reveals that 80–95% of read accesses that miss in the L1 data cache usually also miss in the L2 data cache. This implies

that these workloads have two different data sets: one that is small and frequently used and another that is large and does not fit into the L2 data cache.

4.3. Cache utilization and data-sharing

We now present the workload cache utilization as well as data-sharing behavior for five last-level cache sizes: 4/8/16/32/64 MB. With four threads per workload, Figure 2a illustrates, on the y-axis, the percent of cache utilized as well as the distribution of cache lines shared amongst different threads. In the figure, for each workload, the five bars represent the different last-level cache sizes in increasing order with the left most bar representing the 4MB last-level cache. Each bar is split into four categories: the bottommost portion represents those cache lines that are private, the next one up represents those cache lines shared by 2 threads, the next one up represents those cache lines shared by 3 threads, and finally the topmost portion represents those cache lines that are shared by 4 threads. From the figure, with the exception of PLSA, these workloads fully utilize a 64MB last-level cache (last bar graph for each workload). PLSA's entire memory foot print fits in a 16MB last-level cache. Unlike SPEC workloads (that barely utilize a 2-8MB last-level cache), the large memory working-set sizes of these workloads will continue to put pressure on processor and DRAM architects to reduce the ever growing "memory gap".

Figure 2a also illustrates that the workloads present a varying amount of data-sharing. Some workloads exhibit very little data-sharing, as in the case of SNP where only 2% of a 64MB cache is shared by two threads. GeneNet, SEMPHY, and SVM demonstrate a cache with data that is either private or shared amongst two to four threads. On the other hand, PLSA demonstrates data that is either private or shared amongst two or three threads. This behavior goes to show that even though workloads are run with four threads, workloads need not share data cache lines amongst all four threads. For example, based on PLSA's dynamic programming algorithm, data can only be shared by a maximum of three threads. However, there is one caveat: even though algorithmically data can not be shared by all threads of a parallel workload, data-sharing between all threads may still exist for purposes of synchronizing between all the threads of the workload.

Based on Figure 2a, it can be seen that the amount of sharing varies with the size of the data cache. Increasing the size of the data cache can either increase or decrease the percent of shared data in the cache. A decrease in the percent of shared data with increasing cache sizes implies that an application's shared data footprint is smaller than the private data footprint. For example, in GeneNet, increasing the data cache size beyond 4MB causes the amount of shared data in the cache to decrease from 20% in a 4MB cache to 5% in a 64MB cache. Similarly, increasing the cache size beyond 32MB for SVM causes the amount of shared data in the cache to decrease from 90% in a 32MB cache to 55% in a 64MB cache. Such behavior provides a good indication of the total shared working-set of these workloads.

Alternatively, increasing the size of the cache can also increase the ratio of shared data in the cache. This is because conflict and capacity misses in smaller caches can result in the eviction of potential shared data. For example, a cache line that is actually shared amongst four cores of a CMP can be evicted due to a cacheline conflict immediately after the first core brings the cacheline into the cache. Increasing the cache capacity reduces the number of conflict misses and provides opportunity for both private and shared data to co-exist in the cache. This behavior is evident in the workloads PLSA, SEMPHY, SNP, and SVM and can be better explained by the distribution of accesses to the shared cache.

Figure 2b illustrates, on the y-axis, the distribution of accesses to the shared last-level cache. In the figure, the five bars represent the different last-level cache sizes. Each bar graph is split into five categories based on the type of cache access. Cache accesses are divided into accesses that miss in the data cache and accesses that are either to private or shared (by two, three, or four threads) cache lines. From the figure, for all workloads besides GeneNet, increasing the data cache size reduces the percent of cache misses in the last-level cache. For these workloads, a direct correlation exists between the reduction in cache misses and the increase in the amount of shared data in the cache. Particularly with SVM, almost 90% of cache accesses in a 4 or 8 MB last-level cache result in a cache miss. However, reducing the number of conflict misses by increasing the data cache size reveals that SVM, which initially exhibited very little data-sharing with a 4MB cache, *actually* exhibits a tremendous amount of data-sharing with a larger cache size (compare with Figure 2a). Based on this behavior, we can conclude that workloads require the maximum possible cache space available to exploit their inherent data-sharing behavior. We will show that attempting to reduce the size of the cache or partition the cache into multiple smaller independent caches proves detrimental to cache performance.

Figure 2b shows an interesting behavior in terms of the cache access patterns for several of the workloads. For workloads that share their data cache lines, most of the cache accesses to the last-level cache are to the shared data. For example, with a 64MB shared last-level cache, 62% of PLSA's cache accesses (in some phases of execution as much as 100%) are to its 8MB shared footprint, 60% of GeneNet's cache accesses are to its 4MB shared footprint, and 98% of

SEMPHY and SVM's cache accesses are to their 56MB and 32MB shared footprints respectively. Furthermore, Figure 2c shows, on the y-axis, the distribution of active-shared accesses to the last-level cache. Recall that an *active-shared* access is an access to a shared data cache line by core C_i and the last access to the same cache line was not C_i. For the workloads, 30–80% of cache accesses are to data shared that is interactively shared by two to four threads. Thus, from Figure 2b and 2c, we conclude that workloads not only access shared data frequently, but they also access the shared data interactively rather than in a per-thread serial fashion.

Based on the data presented in this section, we observe that most of the workloads exhibit a significant amount of data-sharing. Sharing is not only exhibited by the existence of shared data in the cache but also by the large distribution of interactive accesses to the shared data. We show that sharing is exposed when other factors such as cache misses are removed from the scene. Hence, reducing or partitioning last-level caches can cause an application to lose its sharing behavior. We show later in the paper that the loss of sharing can place unnecessary demands for bandwidth on the memory subsystem, or could require extensive last-level cache snoop bandwidth if such an implementation technique is employed.

4.4. Data-sharing classification

Having demonstrated that these applications exhibit large amounts of data-sharing, we now analyze the type of data-sharing. Figure 2d illustrates, on the y-axis, the distribution of cache lines categorized into those that are private, read-only shared, and read-write shared. From the figure, 30–50% of PLSA, SEMPHY, and SVM's cache lines are read-write shared while GeneNet and SNP's cache lines are mostly private. To better understand the type of data-sharing in these workloads, Figure 2e illustrates, on the y-axis, the percent of write accesses to the shared last-level cache. From the figure, GeneNet, SNP, and SVM exhibit negligible write-accesses, hence we can classify them as read-shared workloads. Even though SVM exhibits 30% read-write shared cache lines, the negligible amount of write-accesses to the last-level cache classifies SVM as a read-shared workload. On the other hand, roughly 30–40% of SEMPHY and PLSA's write accesses are to shared data. This implies that both PLSA and SEMPHY are read-write shared workloads. This motivates investigation into the coherence traffic behavior of these workloads. Based on the type of data sharing exhibited, we conclude that even though some workloads exhibit negligible write accesses to the shared last-level cache, the fact that the workloads exhibit extensive read sharing emphasizes the need for shared caches to avoid unnecessary duplication of data.

4.5. Performance of private and shared last-level caches

Figure 3 presents the cache metrics for the private and shared last-level cache configurations for the different workloads. In each figure, the first five bars represent private last-level caches, and the last five bars represent shared last-level caches. The performance of the private cache is plotted as the average of the performance of all private caches. We remind the reader that when using private caches, the total on-die last-level cache is partitioned equally amongst different cores of the CMP. Thus, with 4 cores, and with on-die last-level cache sizes of 4/8/16/32/64 MB, the private last-level cache sizes are 1/2/4/8/16 MB each. For each cache, we present accesses per

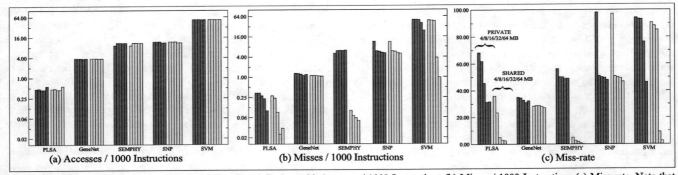

Figure 3: Performance of Private and Shared Last-Level Caches. (a) Accesses / 1000 Instructions (b) Misses / 1000 Instructions (c) Miss-rate. Note that figures (a) and (b) are on a logarithmic scale to accommodate the varying behavior of the different workloads.

1000 instructions, misses per 1000 instructions, and cache miss-rate. The accesses and misses per 1000 are presented on a logarithmic scale to accommodate the varying behavior of the workloads.

As expected, from Figure 3a, the cache access rates for both the private and shared last-level cache are identical. Furthermore, varying the last-level cache size does not affect the cache access rate. This is to be expected as we do not vary the sizes of the first and second level caches. We note that minor variations are expected, and are due to the already known repeatability problem [13] of running workloads multiple times on real machines with real operating systems.

As expected, Figure 3c shows that increasing the size of the private last-level cache aids in reducing the overall cache miss-rate by 3–50%. GeneNet and SNP show no significant improvements in cache performance with larger private (or shared) caches, most likely due to little data reuse and frequent misses in the last-level cache (one-third to one-half of accesses to the last-level cache result in cache misses). We observe that all workloads, besides PLSA, require heavy memory bandwidth, with 4–50 misses per 1000 instructions (GeneNet has execution phases with 4–5 misses per 1000 instructions). PLSA fits well in the private L2 cache as the core of the dynamic programming algorithm works on small blocks of a matrix before moving onto the next block.

We now compare the performance of shared last-level caches to that of private caches. From figure 3b, we observe that with small shared last-level caches, a shared last-level cache in general performs as well or better than the same sized partitioned private last-level cache. For example, a shared 8 MB last-level cache has similar cache performance as a 32 MB private last-level cache configuration (i.e. each of the four cores has an allotted private 8MB cache). This can be explained by the fact that accesses to shared data causes only one miss in a shared cache. However, with a private cache configuration, an access to uncached shared data results in a cache miss in the private cache of each core. For example, in a four-core CMP, an access to data (that is initially not present in the last-level cache) shared by all four cores results in a 100% overall cache miss-rate with the use of a private cache and a 25% overall cache miss-rate with the use of a shared cache. This is because, with a shared cache, the access by the first core fills the cache with the missing data, hence all successive requests for the same data from other cores of the CMP hit in the cache. On the other hand, with a private cache, all cores miss in their respective private caches.

We observe that the reduction in miss-rate translates into reductions in the bandwidth demands beyond the last-level cache by as much as a factor of 625. Based on Figure 3b, the number of last-

level cache misses (per 1000 instructions) for a 64MB cache reduces from 0.1 to 0.03 for PLSA, 6.27 to 0.01 for SEMPHY and 24.2 to 0.98 for SVM when the last-level cache is changed from private to shared. Furthermore, these workloads benefit the most from a shared last-level cache as 98% of their last-level cache accesses were to shared data. This reinforces the fact that workloads that frequently access shared data tend to benefit the most from shared caches.

From the figure, we also observe that GeneNet and SNP receive little or no benefit with a shared last-level cache. Both these workloads exhibit little data-sharing and have poor last-level cache performance. For the different last-level cache sizes that we simulated, independent of the size of the last-level cache, roughly 30–50% of all accesses result in a cache miss (see Figure 2b). This is perhaps the primary reason for these workloads not exhibiting significant data sharing—potential shared cache lines are evicted from the cache due to conflict misses before other threads have a chance to access them. Based on such behavior, data-sharing parameters may need to be considered in cache allocation and eviction policies. This is discussed as part of our future work.

PLSA, SEMPHY, SNP, and SVM all present a constant behavior during the course of execution—they either share or do not share their data. However, workloads can have multiple phases of execution where some phases exhibit significant data-sharing while other phases exhibit a lesser degree of data-sharing. For such workloads, a shared last-level cache can offer tremendous benefits in the data-sharing phase. Of the five workloads, GeneNet displays this behavior. Figure 5b (in the appendix) shows the detailed cache behavior of GeneNet over its entire run. From the figure, during the first 1/8th phase of execution, GeneNet exhibits a tremendous amount of data-sharing—close to 80% of cache accesses are to shared data. During this phase, a shared last-level cache has roughly one-third the miss-rate of a private last-level cache (22% vs. 78%). For other phases of execution, 50–60% of cache accesses are to shared cache lines, and during this phase the shared last-level cache performs better than the private last-level cache by 5–10% on average. Thus, the time-varying sharing behavior of GeneNet further reinforces the fact that a shared last-level cache is highly beneficial when workloads exhibit a large amount of data-sharing.

Based on the data presented, we conclude that workloads or phases of execution that heavily access shared data tend to benefit the most with shared last-level caches. Since the workloads in this study display a large amount of data-sharing, a shared last-level cache can provide tremendous opportunity to reduce the bandwidth demands beyond the last-level cache. Furthermore, with parallel applications in

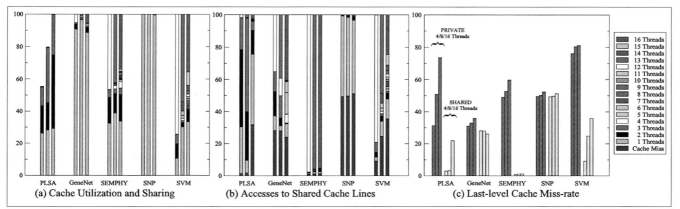

Figure 4: Cache Performance of Workloads Executed With 4, 8, and 16 Threads With a 32MB Last-Level Cache. (a) Distribution of data in shared last-level cache (b) Distribution of accesses to data in shared last-level cache (c) Performance comparison of private and shared last-level caches.

other emerging domains [9, 12], extensive data-sharing may force shared last-level caches to be a necessity in future CMPs.

4.6. Performance of private and shared last-level caches in larger CMPs (8 and 16 cores)

Based on the performance of the different caches, we observe that maximum cache performance is achieved while moving from a 16MB cache to a 32MB cache. Beyond a 32MB cache size, all workloads, other than SVM, receive marginal improvements in terms of cache performance. Based on this data, we chose to determine the cache performance of these workloads with a 32MB last-level cache while varying the core count from 4 to 8 and 16 cores (i.e. the workloads are run with 8 and 16 threads). Note that our purpose for scaling the workloads is to quantify the impact on miss-rate with an increasing core count while keeping the cache size fixed. Figure 4 illustrates the amount of data-sharing, distribution of cache accesses, and a comparison of private and last-level cache performance for the different workloads. In Figures 4a and 4b, the three bar graphs for each workload represent the 4, 8, and 16 threaded runs. The legend of each individual bar graph is similar to the legends of Figure 2b except that additional legend entries are present for the 8 and 16 thread configurations to represent cache lines that are shared amongst 5, 6, 7,..., 14, 15, and 16 threads.

Based on Figure 4a and 4c, scaling the number of threads for the workloads increases the cache utilization as well as the cache miss-rate. The increase in cache utilization can be explained by the fact that the working sets of these workloads are not entirely shared. Each additional worker thread adds its own private data to the workload data footprint, hence increasing the overall data footprint of the workload. Consequently, the increase in footprint translates into an increase in the overall cache miss-rate. Furthermore, we also point out that an increase in cache miss-rate with private caches can also be explained by the fact that the size of the private partitions of each core decreases when the number of on-chip cores increases. For example, with a 32MB last-level cache, each private cache in a 4-core CMP is 8MB in size, while in a 8 and 16-core CMP each private cache is 4MB and 2MB in size respectively. Thus, the reductions in the sizes of the private cache partitions per core also contributes to an increase in the overall cache miss-rate with private last-level caches.

Figure 4c compares the cache performance of private and shared caches. In the figure, the first three bars represent the workloads run with 4, 8 and 16 threads with a private cache, and the last three represent those that are run with shared caches. For the workloads in this study, with larger CMPs a shared cache configuration reduces the overall miss-rate by 40–60% when compared to a private cache configuration. Additionally, the performance of shared caches varies as the core count of the CMP is scaled up to 8 and 16 cores. PLSA and SVM experience a 20–30% increase in the over-all cache miss-rate while GeneNet, SNP, and SEMPHY experience marginal increases in the over-all cache miss-rate. With 4 threads, SVM and PLSA fit well into a 32MB cache, however scaling them to 8 and 16 threads increases the cache miss-rate. This can be explained by the fact that both PLSA and SVM's data footprint is not entirely shared, each new thread adds additional private data footprint. As a result, Figure 4b illustrates that the additional per-thread private data footprint causes as many as 30% of cache accesses to miss in the data cache. The increase in the number of cache misses results in potential shared lines to be evicted from the data cache hence reducing the total amount of shared data in the last-level cache. On the other hand, for the workloads GeneNet and SEMPHY, the additional per-thread private data portion of the total working set is relatively small, hence the marginal increase in the over-all cache miss-rate. This implies that such workloads can potentially achieve *super-linear speedup* with the scaling up of the number of threads as cache performance is unaffected.

Based on the data presented in this paper, the key point is that shared last-level caches are essential for the workloads in this study to have good cache performance. By scaling the number of CMP cores, we conclude that the performance of a shared last-level cache can out-perform a private last-level cache by 40–60% in terms of over-all cache miss-rate. Hence, given the option of designing private or shared last-level caches, we conclude that shared last-level caches are a necessity for this emerging class of data-mining workloads.

5. Related work

Bioinformatics has emerged as an important application domain for future high performance microprocessors. Consequently, industry has invested resources in characterizing the scalability and performance of common bioinformatics applications. Cheng et al. looked at the scalability of bioinformatics applications like BLAST, FASTA, HMMER, etc. on the IBM eServer pSeries 690 [18]. Chen et al. looked at the scalability and performance of data mining bioinformatics applications [16, 17]. Sun Microsystems presented a whitepaper on the challenges faced and the opportunities available in the field of computational biology [10]. Furthermore, the Informatics Benchmarking Toolkit (IBT) provided by *BioTeam* compares the performance of common bioinformatics applications [2]. In academia, Albayraktaroglu et al. compiled the BioBench suite of bioinformatics applications and characterized their behavior and differences from the SPEC benchmark suite [14].

Recent studies have investigated the design for the cache-hierarchy of CMPs. Liu et al. discussed the tradeoffs of implementing shared and private caches and proposed a mechanism of allocating multiple last-level private caches to one core of a CMP [25]. Chishti et al. presented novel mechanisms of optimizing replication, coherence communication, and exploiting unused cache space in CMPs [19]. Zhang et al. proposed victim replication to achieve the benefits of private caches with shared caches [33]. Speight et al. looked at CMP performance through intelligently handling writebacks [30].

Characterizing the memory behavior and performance of parallel workloads is an area of ongoing research. Abandah et al. proposed a configuration-independent approach to analyze the working set, concurrency, and communication patterns, as well as sharing behavior of shared memory applications [11]. They present the *Shared-Memory Application Instrumentation Tool* (SMAIT) to measure different sharing characteristics of the NAS shared-memory applications [12]. Barroso et al. characterized the memory system behavior of commercial workloads such as Oracle, TPC-B, TPC-D, and the AltaVista search engine [15]. They performed their characterization of the memory system behavior using ATOM [31], performance counters on an Alpha 21164, and the SimOS simulation environment. Woo et al. characterized several aspects of the SPLASH-2 benchmark suite [32]. They used an execution-driven simulation with the Tango Lite [23] tracing tool. Perl et al. studied Windows NT applications on Alpha PCs and characterized application bandwidth requirements, memory access patterns, and application sensitivity to cache size [27]. Chodneker et al. analyzed the time distribution and locality of communication events in some message-passing and shared-memory applications [20]. Nurvitadhi et al. used an FPGA-based cache model (PHA$E) that connects directly to the front-side bus to analyze the shared vs. private L3 cache behavior of SPECjAppServer and TPC-C [26].

Our work differs from prior work in that it performs a detailed last-level cache characterization of the emerging class of bioinformatics data-mining workloads. We perform a detailed data-sharing analysis of these workloads over their entire execution without using any tracing mechanisms, performance counters, or "bus sniffers". Contrary to existing trace driven and execution driven methodologies, we use the binary instrumentation approach to characterize the cache performance of workloads over their entire run. We believe this to be the first study that characterizes the cache performance of data-mining workloads from the perspective of a CMP. Additionally, we also believe this to be the first study that clearly correlates cache sizes and cache performance with workload-sharing behavior.

6. Conclusions and future work

The study in this paper gives important insight into workloads that will be very important in future high-performance machines, and this insight is valuable to architects of new CMPs. We show that the bioinformatics data-mining workloads used in this study exhibit a tremendous amount of data-sharing—50–95% of the data cache is shared by different threads of the workload. Furthermore, regardless of the amount of data cache shared, for some workloads, as many as 98% of the accesses to the last-level cache can be to the shared data. Additionally, the amount of data-sharing exhibited by the workloads is a function of the total cache size available; the larger the data cache the better the sharing behavior. Thus, rather than partitioning the last-level cache into multiple private caches, we show that a shared last-level cache is important for improving the performance of these workloads on future high performance machines. With a shared last-level cache, the bandwidth demands beyond the last-level cache can be reduced by factors of 3–625 when compared to a private last-level cache configuration. Thus, we conclude that, given the option of designing shared or private last-level caches in future CMPs, a shared last-level cache is the logical choice of implementation as it allows workloads to exploit their data-sharing behavior and significantly reduce the bandwidth demands beyond the last-level cache.

Looking ahead, our on-going work focuses on investigating the performance bottlenecks of these workloads using performance models. Additionally, we are also studying the sensitivity of the sharing behavior of these workloads to varying data input sizes. Furthermore, we are also exploring the use of novel cache allocation and replacement policies that can allow applications to exhibit the sharing behavior observed in large last-level caches with smaller last-level caches.

Acknowledgements

The authors would like to acknowledge the following individuals for their contribution to this work: Robert Cohn and C. K. Luk for their help in developing the simCMPcache pin tool, Carole Dulong for her support with the bioinformatics applications, and Joel Emer, Brinda Ganesh, Srilatha Manne, Moinuddin Qureshi, Jason Papadapolous, and Simon Steely for reviewing the paper. We would also like to thank the reviewers for their comments and suggestions.

References

[1] AMD MultiCore Technology: http://multicore.amd.com

[2] The BioTeam: Infomatics Benchmarking Toolkit (IBT), AMD Funded, http://bioteam.net/ibt/

[3] HGBase: http://hgvbase.cgb.ki.se/

[4] IBM Cell Processor: http://www-306.ibm.com/chips/techlib/ techlib.nsf/products/Cell

[5] Intel Pentium Processor Extreme Edition: http://www.intel.com/ products/processor/pentiumXE/index.htm

[6] PFam Database: http://www.sanger.ac.uk/Software/Pfam/

[7] PIN home page: http://rogue.colorado.edu/Pin/.

[8] SEMPHY Download Page: http://www.cs.huji.ac.il/~nir/ SEMPHY/

[9] SPECOMP2001 http://www.spec.org/

[10] "Sun Briefing In Computational Biology", White Paper, December, 2003.

[11] G. A. Abandah, and E. S. Davidson. "Configuration Independent Analysis for Characterizing Shared-Memory Applications." In *Proceedings of the 12th. International Parallel Processing Symposium (IPPS)*, Orlando, Florida, 1998.

[12] G. A. Abandah. "Characterizing Shared-Memory Applications: A Case Study of the NAS Parallel Benchmarks." Technical Report, HPL-97-24, Hewlett Packard.

[13] A. R. Alameldeen and D. A. Wood. "Variability in Architectural Simulations of Multi-threaded Workloads." In *Proceedings of the 3rd International Conference on High Performance Computer Architecture (HPCA)*, Anaheim, California, 2003.

[14] K. Albayraktaroglu, A. Jaleel, X. Wu, M. Franklin, B. Jacob, C. Tseng, and D. Yeung, "BioBench: A Benchmark Suite of Bioinformatics Applications." In *the 5th International Symposium on Performance Analysis of Systems and Software (ISPASS)*, Austin, Texas, 2005.

[15] L. A. Barroso, K. Gharachorloo, and E. Bugnion. "Memory System Characterization of Commercial Workloads." In *Proceedings of the 25t International Symposium on Computer Architecture (ISCA)*, Barcelona, Spain, 1998.

[16] Y. Chen, Q. Diao, C. Dulong, C. Lai, W. Hu, E. Li, W. Li, T. Wang, and Y. Zhang. "Performance Scalability of Data-Mining Workloads in Bioinformatics." Intel Technology Journal, Volume 09, Issue 02, May 19, 2005.

[17] Y. Chen, Q. Diao, C. Dulong, C. Lai, W. Hu, E. Li, W. Li, T. Wang, and Y. Zhang. "Performance Scalability of Data-Mining Workloads in Bioinformatics." Technical Report.

[18] Y. Cheng, J. Mark, C. Skawratananond, and T. K. Tzeng. "Scalability Comparison of Bioinformatics for Applications on AIX and Linux on IBM eServer pSeries 690." Redbooks Paper, August 2004.

[19] Z. Chishti, M. Powell, and T. N. Vijaykumar. "Optimizing Replication, Communication, and Capacity Allocation in CMPs." In *Proceedings of the 32nd International Symposium on Computer Architecture (ISCA)*, Wisconsin, Madison, 2005.

[20] S. Chodnekar, V. Srinivasan, A. Vaidya, A. Sivasubramaniam, and C. Das. "Towards a Communication Characterization Methodology for Parallel Applications." In *Proceedings of the 3rd International Conference on High Performance Computer Architecture (HPCA)*, San Antonio, Texas, 1997.

[21] P. Dubey. "Recognition, Mining and Synthesis Moves Computers to the Era of Tera." Intel Technology Journal, February 2005.

[22] N. Friedman, M. Ninio, I. Pe'er, and T. Pupko. "A Structural EM Algorithm for Phylogenetic Inference". In *Journal of Computational Biology*, 2001.

[23] S. Goldschmidt and J. Hennessey. "The Accuracy of Trace-Driven Simulations of Multiprocessors." Tech Rep. CSL-TR-92-546, Stanford University, Sept. 1992.

[24] N. Friedman, M. Linial, I. Nachman, and D. Pe'er. "Using Bayesian Networks to Analyze Expression Data." Journal of Computational Biology, 7:601-620, 2000.

[25] C. Liu, A. Sivasubramaniam, M. Kandemir. "Organizing the Last Line of Defense before Hitting the Memory Wall for CMPs." In *Proceedings of the 6th International Conference on High Performance Computer Architecture (HPCA)*, Madrid, Spain, 2004.

[26] E. Nurvitadhi, N. Chalainanont, and S. L. Lu. "Characterization of L3 Cache Behavior of SPECjAppServer2002 and TPC-C." In *Proceedings of the 19th International Conference on Supercomputing (ICS)*, Boston, Massachusetts, 2005.

[27] S. E. Perl and R. L. Sites. "Studies of Windows NT performance using dynamic execution traces." In *Proceedings of the 2nd International Symposium on Operation Systems Design and Implementation (OSDI)*, Seattle, Washington, 1996.

[28] V. Reddi, A. M.Settle, D. A. Connors and R. S. Cohn. "Pin: A Binary Instrumentation Tool for Computer Architecture Research and Education." In *Proceedings of the Workshop on Computer Architecture Education*, June 2004.

[29] T. F. Smith and Michael S. Waterman. "Identification of Common Molecular Subsequences." In *Proceedings of the Journal of Molecular Biology*, 147:195-197, 1981.

[30] E. Speight, H. Shafi, L. Zhang, R. Rajamony. "Adaptive Mechanisms and Policies for Managing Cache Hierarchies in CMPs." In *Proceedings of the 32nd International Symposium on Computer Architecture (ISCA)*, Wisconsin, Madison, 2005.

[31] A. Srivastava and A. Eustace, "ATOM: A System for Building Customized Program Analysis Tools", Programming Language Design and Implementation (PLDI), 1994, pp. 196-205.

[32] S. Woo, M. Ohara, E. Torrie, J. Singh, and A. Gupta. "The SPLASH-2 Programs: Characterization and Methodology Considerations." In *Proceedings of the 22nd International Symposium on Computer Architecture (ISCA)*, Santa Margherita Ligure, Italy, 1995.

[33] M. Zhang and K. Asanovic. "Victim Replication: Maximizing capacity while Hiding Wire Delay in Tiled CMPs." In *Proceedings of the 32nd International Symposium on Computer Architecture (ISCA)*, Wisconsin, Madison, 2005.

Appendix

This section presents the time varying behavior of the workloads. We present the distribution of private and shared data in the cache, the distribution of accesses to private and shared data, and the private and shared last-level cache miss-rates. The data is presented for the 4MB, 16MB, and 64MB last-level cache sizes. Each graph illustrates the total instruction count (in billions) on the x-axis and the appropriate metric represented as a percent on the y-axis.

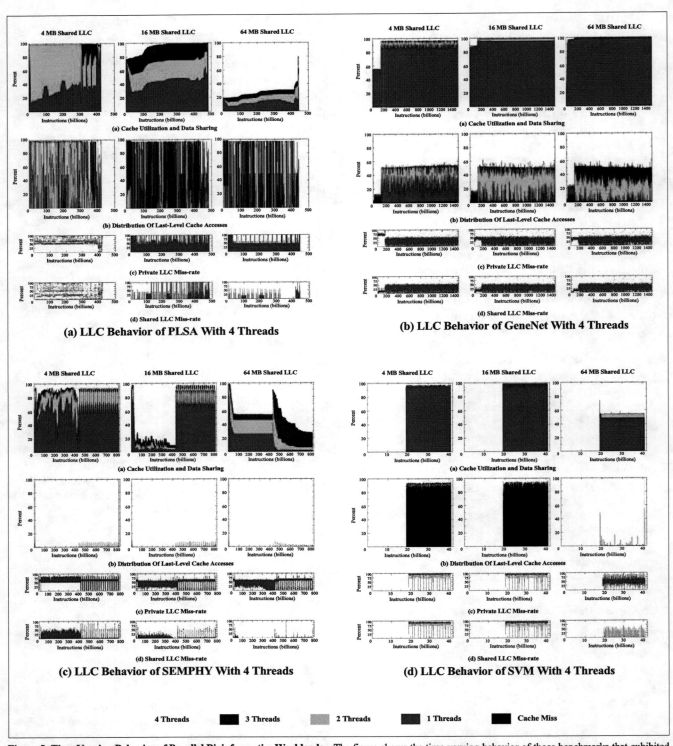

Figure 5: Time Varying Behavior of Parallel Bioinformatics Workloads. The figure shows the time varying behavior of those benchmarks that exhibited data sharing (SNP exhibited no sharing hence is not displayed). The x-axis represents the total number of instructions executed (in billions) and the y-axis represents the appropriate metric presented as a percent. The private last level cache miss-rate is presented as the average miss-rate of all private caches. This figure is best viewed as a soft copy or a color printout.

Construction and Use of Linear Regression Models for Processor Performance Analysis

P. J.Joseph   Kapil Vaswani   Matthew J. Thazhuthaveetil

Department of Computer Science & Automation
Indian Institute of Science, Bangalore, India.
E-mail: {peejay,kapil,mjt}@csa.iisc.ernet.in

Abstract

Processor architects have a challenging task of evaluating a large design space consisting of several interacting parameters and optimizations. In order to assist architects in making crucial design decisions, we build linear regression models that relate processor performance to micro-architectural parameters, using simulation based experiments. We obtain good approximate models using an iterative process in which Akaike's information criteria is used to extract a good linear model from a small set of simulations, and limited further simulation is guided by the model using D-optimal experimental designs. The iterative process is repeated until desired error bounds are achieved. We used this procedure to establish the relationship of the CPI performance response to 26 key micro-architectural parameters using a detailed cycle-by-cycle superscalar processor simulator. The resulting models provide a significance ordering on all micro-architectural parameters and their interactions, and explain the performance variations of micro-architectural techniques.

1. Introduction

Modern processors are evolving at a rapid pace and in the quest for better performance architects introduce sophisticated micro-architectural enhancements in each new generation of processors. However, the increasing complexity of modern architectures has direct consequence on the process of designing processors. To arrive at optimal design points, architects are expected to evaluate a large design space consisting of several micro-architectural parameters such as cache sizes and associativities, queue sizes, branch predictor configuration, pipeline depth etc., each with a wide range of potential settings. Complex interactions between these parameters make it hard to gain an intuitive understanding of their impact on performance.

Designers in many disciplines of science and engineering deal with design complexity by building abstract models of the system that relate input parameters to the response. The models help designers gain a better understanding of the system and answer several key questions; for instance, which input parameters have the largest impact on response? How does a particular parameter interact with the others? What is the expected benefit of an enhancement? Although there have been several attempts to build models for processor performance over the past years [6, 9], they rely on prior knowledge about the significant parameters, fail to model the design space in sufficient detail, and their validity across a larger design space is unknown.

The aim of our research is to develop empirical models for processors that characterize the relationship between processor response and micro-architectural parameters. As a first step in building such models we quantify the *significance* of micro-architectural parameters and their interactions. Quantifying the interactions between micro-architectural parameters is important, and is best illustrated through a simple experiment. We measured the improvement in average instructions issued per cycle (IPC) due to out-of-order issue over in-order issue for different L1 data cache configurations. Improvements in IPC for the SPEC *twolf* benchmark are plotted in Figure 1. The impact of out-of-order issue varies with data cache size, and the variation depends on cache latency. Such significant interactions need to be included in the model. In this paper, we show that precise estimates of the significance of all parameters and interactions can be obtained by building *linear regression models* using simulation-based experiments. We show how the parameters of the regression model, which reflect the significance of the corresponding terms, can be empirically computed without any prior knowledge or understanding of processor dynamics. Since these significant factors have a large impact on performance and are usually small in number, they are ideal candidates for further analysis.

In this paper, we draw from past research in the field of design of experiments and linear model construction and propose an iterative process for constructing accurate regression models of processor performance consisting of all significant main effects and interaction terms using a rea-

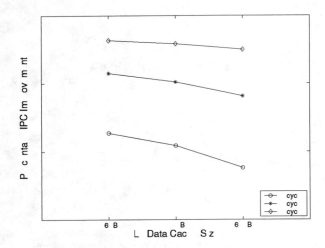

Figure 1. IPC performance improvement of out-of-order issue over in-order issue.

sonable number of simulations. We use this procedure to build a linear model relating superscalar processor performance to 26 key micro-architectural parameters. We also show how parameters that were originally not a part of the experiment can be added to the linear model using few additional simulations.

The rest of the paper is organized as follows. In Section 2, we discuss the basic concepts of linear regression models. We describe our iterative procedure for building the linear model in Section 3, and the experimental framework in Section 4. Section 5 presents the results of model construction. We present an overview of existing processor modeling techniques in Section 6 and conclude in Section 7 with a discussion of future work.

2. Linear Regression Models

A regression model is a compact mathematical representation of the relationship between the response variable and the input parameters in a given design space [8]. Linear regression models are widely used to obtain estimates of parameter significance as well as predictions of the response variable at arbitrary points in the design space. One of the simpler forms of such models is

$$y = \beta_0 + \sum_{i=1}^{m} \beta_i x_i + \epsilon \qquad (1)$$

where y is the dependent or response variable, $\{x_i | 1 \leq i \leq m\}$ are the independent or *regressor* variables and ϵ is the *residual* - the error due to lack of fit. β_0 is interpreted as the intercept of the response surface with the y-axis and $\{\beta_i | 1 \leq i \leq m\}$ are known as the *partial regression co-efficients*. The co-efficient values represent the expected

change in the response y per unit change in x_i and indicate the relative significance of the corresponding terms.

It is often the case that the regressor variables interact i.e. the effect of a change in x_i on y depends on the value of x_j. In such cases, the simple model in Eq. 1 is not sufficient. It is necessary to introduce terms that explicitly model *two-factor interactions* as shown below.

$$y = \beta_0 + \sum_{i=1}^{m} \beta_i x_i + \sum_{i=1}^{m} \sum_{j=i+1}^{m} \beta_{i,j} x_i x_j + \epsilon \qquad (2)$$

Eq. 3 represents a complete model that include *three-factor*, *four-factor* and all higher order interactions. There are 2^m terms in this model and an equal number of unknown regression co-efficients.

$$y = \beta_0 + \sum_{i=1}^{m} \beta_i x_i + \sum_{i=1}^{m} \sum_{j=i+1}^{m} \beta_{i,j} x_i x_j + \\ \sum_{i=1}^{m} \sum_{j=i+1}^{m} \sum_{k=j+1}^{m} \beta_{i,j,k} x_i x_j x_k + \ldots \\ \cdots + \beta_{1,2,\ldots m} x_1 x_2 \ldots x_m \qquad (3)$$

The linear regression models we develop in this paper can be represented as a sum of k terms from this complete linear model, expressed in a generic form as

$$y = \beta_0 + \beta_1 x_{i^1} + \beta_2 x_{i^2} \cdots + \beta_{k-1} x_{i^{k-1}} + \epsilon \qquad (4)$$

where each x_{ij} is a distinct term from the complete model, and can be single factor, two factor, three factor or of any higher order. The collection of terms chosen for a given linear model will be referred to as the *model terms*.

In matrix terms, Eq. 4 can be written as

$$\mathbf{y} = \mathbf{X}\beta + \epsilon \qquad (5)$$

where β is the vector of regression coefficients and X is the *model matrix*. The model matrix has columns corresponding to the regressor variables $x_1, x_2, \ldots, x_m$, columns for interaction terms of any order, and a column of ones defining the intercept.

Our goal in this paper is to accurately estimate all significant micro-architectural parameters and interactions affecting processor performance. We achieve this by performing simulation-based experiments in which the regressor variables are set to different values and the resulting performance metric is fitted as per Eq. 4, minimizing the number of terms k and the residual error ϵ simultaneously. As a by-product, we obtain precise estimates of the partial regression co-efficients and hence estimates and an ordering of the significant factors and interactions affecting processor performance.

There are a few guidelines that an architect must keep in mind while planning and designing the simulation experiments. The guidelines help in the selection of the response variable, the set of factors to be included in the experiment, their ranges and the levels at which each factor is varied during the experiments.

Factor selection: A designer must initially identify a set of factors that can potentially influence the system response. For our experiments, we assume no prior knowledge of factor effects and select factors conservatively i.e. factors are included in the experiments even though their impact on performance may not be significant.

Factor ranges and levels: The choice of factor ranges and levels is primarily governed by technological constraints and the objective of the experiment. If the primary objective is to determine significant coefficients in a linear model, as is the case with our study, wide factor ranges are preferred. We choose a range consisting of values just lower and higher than potential factor settings under current technology. During our experiments, each factor is varied at two levels (encoded as -1 and 1) corresponding to the low and high value of its range.

Response variable and output transformations: Our simulator reports simulated processor performance measured in IPC. However, to build a linear model, it is often beneficial to use a transformation of the response variable instead of the response variable itself [8]. Such transformations might result in response surfaces that are more linear and easier to fit. We evaluate a family of such transformations in the context of processor modeling in the following section.

2.1. A Case Study on Building a Linear Model

We illustrate our approach by building a linear regression model that relates the IPC of SPEC CPU2000 integer benchmarks to six micro-architectural parameters – namely the pipeline depth, reorder buffer size, issue queue size, L2 cache size, out-of-order capability, and the memory configuration. We limit the number of factors to six so that all regression co-efficients in the complete linear model can be exactly determined using a reasonable number of simulations. The factor ranges were chosen based on experimental design guidelines. During the experiment, simulations were conducted for the 2^6 possible combinations of factor levels and the regression co-efficients were obtained by solving Eq. 3 for the measured IPC. The experiment led to the following observations.

Output transformations: We measured the effect of output transformations on the accuracy of linear models. We considered a family of transformations $y^t, t = -2, -1, -0.5, 0.5, 1, 2$ and $log(y)$ as potential candidates. For each transformation, we computed the regression coefficients and sorted them in decreasing order of magnitude. We then built linear models incorporating the first k terms, for different values of k and used the models to predict the IPC of 64 processor configurations mentioned above. We then computed the residuals by subtracting the actual IPC from the predicted IPC and used the maximum residual

Terms	
intercept	1.230
pipe_depth	-0.566
ROB_size	-0.480
pipe_depth*ROB_size	0.378
IQ_size	-0.347
ROB_size*IQ_size	0.289
pipe_depth*IQ_size	0.274
pipe_depth*ROB_size*IQ_size	-0.219
mem_config	-0.037
L2_size	-0.033
issue_order	-0.026
L2_size*mem_config	0.023
ROB_size*issue_order	-0.015
pipe_depth*issue_order	-0.009
IQ_size*issue_order	-0.007
pipe_depth*ROB_size*IQ_size*L2_size	0.006

Table 1. The most significant terms from the 6-factor model for the weighted mean CPI of benchmarks. * denotes interaction.

value as an indicator of the accuracy of the model.

Figure 2 plots the maximum residual value against the number of terms incorporated in the model. We observe that for all output transformations, the maximum residual reduces to acceptable levels even when many terms have been excluded from the models. Further, the inverse transformation (y^{-1}) results in the lowest maximum residuals. We observe similar behavior for all benchmarks. Hence, using the inverse transformation allows the construction of accurate linear models with the least number of terms. Note that the inverse transformation of IPC results in the CPI metric. CPI is an intuitive metric expressible as a dot product of event frequencies and event penalties within a processor [2] and it is most amenable for linear model construction. We use CPI as the performance metric in the rest of this paper.

Sparsity of effects: Our experiment reveals that processors exhibit the principle of *sparsity of effects* — system response is largely governed by a few main factors and low order interactions and the influence of higher order interactions on response is marginal. As a consequence, terms corresponding to higher order interactions can be excluded from the model. Table 1 lists the 16 terms, out of the 64 terms in our experiment, that we identified for inclusion in a simplified model of the processor's CPI performance. This observed sparsity of significant effects has a large bearing on the feasibility of our simulation-based model building process. We discuss this further in section 2.2.

Significance of factors: Table 1 shows the most significant factors and interactions in our regression model. Some of the two-factor interaction terms are also critical, as is the three-factor interaction between pipeline depth, ROB size and issue queue size. These observations highlight the im-

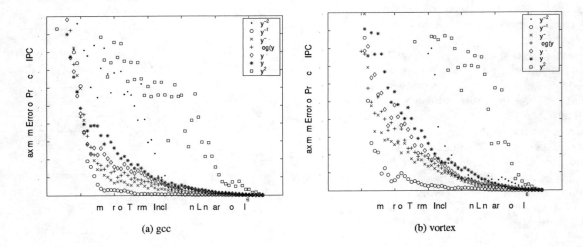

(a) gcc

(b) vortex

Figure 2. Number of terms required in linear model under different data transformations.

portance of incorporating second and third order interactions in models.

2.2. Linear Models Incorporating All Factors

Our aim is to build a linear model involving all processor parameters. For this purpose it is infeasible to experiment with all combinations of factor levels as was done in the previous section. However, sparsity of effects makes it possible to have accurate and compact linear models of the type specified in Eq. 4 incorporating only significant effects. Coefficients of the k most significant parameters can usually be estimated from processor's response at n different factor level combinations using least square fitting, where $n > k$ and $n << 2^m$. The least square estimates of the k-dimensional coefficient vector $\beta = (\beta_0, \beta_1.., \beta_{k-1})$ in Eq. 5 is

$$\hat{\beta} = (\mathbf{X'X})^{-1}\mathbf{X'y} \qquad (6)$$

where X is the model matrix for the experimented factor settings. The variance of the error term in Eq. 5 can be estimated as

$$\hat{\sigma}^2 = \frac{\sum_{i=1}^{n}(y_i - \hat{y}_i)^2}{n - k} \qquad (7)$$

where $\hat{y} = X\hat{\beta}$ is the fitted response. This least square fitting method provides useful approximations with simulations reduced close to the number of significant effects.

The coefficients computed as above are only estimates of the actual linear model coefficients. However, we can compute a bound on this error. Under the simplifying assumption that errors due to non-incorporated terms are normally distributed, a $100(1-\alpha)$ percent confidence error bound for β_j is

$$|\beta_j - \hat{\beta}_j| \leqslant t_{\alpha/2, n-k}\sqrt{C_{jj}\hat{\sigma}^2} \qquad (8)$$

where $t_{\alpha/2, n-k}$ is the upper $\alpha/2$ percentage point of the t distribution with $n - k$ degrees of freedom, and C_{jj} is the $(j, j)^{th}$ entry of $(X'X)^{-1}$ matrix [8]. It follows that the accuracy of our estimates depend on:

- *Error Degree of Freedom:*.

  Increasing $n - k$, the degree of freedom for the error term, reduces $t_{\alpha/2, n-k}$ in Eq. 8. However, this reduction decreases as $n - k$ is increased beyond a point.

- *Experimental Design:*

  The specific set of factor level combinations used for the experiment determine the C_{jj} term in Eq. 8. Hence appropriate experimental designs are critical to achieving good accuracy. We chose D-optimal experimental designs[8], which maximize det($X'X$) for a set of model terms, for our model construction process[5].

- *Error Variance:*

  Minimization of the error variance, $\hat{\sigma}^2$, in Eq. 8 requires all significant terms to be in the model. However, since the significant terms are not known *a priori* they need to be identified from experimental data. We next describe the procedure we use to identify and include all significant effects.

3. Procedure for Model Construction

Our aim in model construction is to obtain accurate estimates of all significant coefficients with minimum number of simulations. Since the significant effects are not known *a priori*, this information has to be extracted from experimental data. However, designing the best experimental strategy requires knowledge of significant terms; D-optimal designs are optimized for an identified set of model terms. Hence, in order to obtain the best experimental designs having minimal simulations we use an iterative procedure where initial small D-optimal designs are used to learn significant effects, and this information is used to guide further simulation using augmented D-optimal designs, until an adequate model is achieved. Each of the required steps and the complete iterative procedure are described in the following subsections.

3.1. Obtaining the Best Model

Given an experimental design and simulation results we have to determine the best model that fits the data well. We use Akaike's Information Criteria (AIC) [11] to select a model that fits well and has a minimum number of parameters, resulting in the most significant effects being included in the model, and thus reducing the model over-fitting problem. In our procedure we use the corrected version of AIC (AIC_c) developed for small experimental samples [4] since it allows us to keep the simulation count low. AIC_c for linear regression models can be written as

$$AIC_c = nlog(\hat{\sigma}^2) + 2k + \frac{2(k+1)(k+2)}{(n-k)} + constant \quad (9)$$

where n is the number of simulations, k is the number of terms in the linear model, and $\hat{\sigma}^2$ is the error variance. This measure accounts for model accuracy using error variance, and model simplicity using the count of model terms. Amongst several models possible for fixed experimental data, the best model has the lowest AIC_c [11].

Arriving at the best model involves searching for the set of model terms producing the lowest AIC_c. Since an exhaustive search of all model combinations is computationally expensive we used a procedure which stepwise refines an initial model. This procedure is based on our observation that the more significant higher order terms are typically composed of the significant lower order terms and is detailed in [5].

3.2. Determining Model Adequacy

We use the maximum error of estimated coefficients as the main measure of model adequacy, since our aim is to get accurate estimates of all significant effects. This error bound can be obtained from Eq. 8 as $t_{\alpha/2, n-k}\sqrt{\hat{\sigma}^2 maxC_{jj}}$, where $maxC_{jj}$ is the maximum C_{jj} value of the model. We follow the iterative model construction scheme until a prescribed maximum bound on error is achieved. We also check for violations of the basic assumptions in estimating regression coefficients and their bounds by examining the *residuals*.

3.3. The Iterative Procedure

Our model construction procedure takes as inputs m (the number of experimented factors), θ (the prescribed maximum error), and α (the confidence level required on the error), and outputs Error Bounded Linear Models (EBLMs). We describe it below.

1. Design an initial D-optimal experimental design S with $2m$ runs for an initial linear model having all main effects. Obtain the best linear model L.

2. Measure the error variance $\hat{\sigma}^2$ of model L, and the maximum error in estimated coefficients. Stop and finalize the model if the error is less than θ, and residual plots are free from gross deviations.

3. Augment the experimental design S with additional D-optimal experiments ensuring the following: (i) the new design is D-optimal for a model containing union of terms in L and the main effect terms, (ii) there are sufficient number of additional experiments such that the maximum C_{jj} value is reduced by half.

4. Obtain the best linear model L for the new augmented design S. Go to step 2.

The above procedure can be used to obtain linear models at any specified level of accuracy. We implemented this procedure as a MATLAB script which takes the required inputs and completed simulation experimental data, and provides either the accurate coefficient estimates or a prescription for further experimentation.

4. Experimental Framework

4.1. Processor Simulator and Benchmarks

We developed and validated a detailed superscalar processor simulator for use in our experimentation. Our simulation framework - FAFSIM - models pipelined, multiple-issue, dynamically scheduled, speculative execution processors. It models all the performance critical micro-architectural events and structures in superscalar processors and is detailed in [5]. The pipeline, caches, branch direction and target predictors, various micro-architectural queues, functional units, DRAM device timing, queuing at the memory controller, and contention for the memory bus are all modeled. We verified the functionality of each component, and in addition validated the summary statistics against another similarly configured verified simulator, *alphasim* [1]. This validation was done for several design points to verify the simulator's accuracy across the design space.

We used our simulator to run all SPEC CPU2000 integer benchmarks using the *lgred* data set in MinneSPEC [7] reduced data sets. This was done using traces generated with

Pipeline Depth	pipe_depth
Reorder Buffer Size	ROB_size
Issue Queue Size	IQ_size
L2 Cache Size	L2_size
L2 Cache Associativity	L2_assoc
L2 Cache Block Size	L2_bsize
L2 Cache Latency	L2_lat
Instruction Cache Size	il1_size
Instruction Cache Associativity	il1_assoc
Instruction Cache Block Size	il1_bsize
Instruction Cache Latency	il1_lat
Data Cache Size	dl1_size
Data Cache Associativity	dl1_assoc
Data Cache Block Size	dl1_bsize
Data Cache Latency	dl1_lat
FTB entries	ftb_ent
FTB associativity	ftb_assoc
Operation Latency	op_lat
Issue Order	issue_order
Load-Store Queue Size	LSQ_size
Number of Functional Units	num_units
DRAM Memory Configuration	mem_config
Predictor Type	pred_type
Predictor Size	pred_size
Processor Width	width
Return Address Stack Size	RAS_size

Table 2. Micro-architectural parameters.

Parameter	Low Value	High Value
pipe_depth	24	7
ROB_size	24	128
IQ_size	$(1/4)* x_2$	x_2
L2_size	256KB	8MB
L2_assoc	1	8
L2_bsize	64	256
L2_lat	20	5
il1_size	8KB	128KB
il1_assoc	1	8
il1_bsize	16	64
il1_lat	2	1
dl1_size	8KB	128KB
dl1_assoc	1	8
dl1_bsize	16	64
dl1_lat	4	1
ftb_ent	128	8192
ftb_assoc	1	8
issue_order	In-order	Out-of-order
LSQ_size	$(1/4)*x_2$	x_2
pred_type	*gshare*	*perceptron*
pred_size	2KB	16KB
width	4	8
RAS_size	4	64

Table 3. Parameter ranges.

IBM PowerPC executables, compiled with xlc compiler applying the -O3 option.

4.2. Micro-architectural Parameters and Ranges

We experimented with the 26 key micro-architectural parameters listed in Table 2. The range of parameters are chosen to include the complete range of settings possible under current technology, and is listed in Table 3. Some parameters like issue order have only two potential settings and the low and high values correspond to these. Some of the parameters - operation latency, number of functional units, and the DRAM configuration - combine several parameters for ease of experimentation and their settings are reported in Tables 4, 5 and 6.

5. Results

5.1. Results of Model Construction

Table 7 presents the most significant terms in the constructed error bounded linear models. The significance ordering in the table is based on an EBLM of the weighted mean CPI response computed from the EBLMs constructed for all benchmarks. Apart from providing an ordering of the performance significance of effects, the models also provide

Functional unit	Settings			
	Low Width		High Width	
	Low	High	Low	High
Integer ALU	1	4	2	8
Integer mult/div	1	2	1	4
Float	1	4	2	8
Float mult/div	1	2	1	4
Branch	1	2	1	4
Load/store	1	2	1	4

Table 4. Number of functional units (*num_units*).

Operation	Latency		Func. Unit
	Low	High	
Int. arith./logic	2	1	Integer ALU
Int. mult.	15	2	Integer mult/div
Simple float	5	1	Float
Float. mult.	5	2	Float mult/div
Float. div.	35	10	Float mult/div
Branch	3	1	Branch
Load	Cache latency		Load/store
Store	NIL		Load/store

Table 5. Operation latencies (*op_lat*).

Terms	Weighted Mean	crafty	eon	gap	gcc	gzip	vortex
intercept	1.974	2.279	2.085	2.325	2.304	1.664	1.885
pipe_depth	-0.517	-0.563	-0.501	-0.542	-0.574	-0.494	-0.511
ROB_size	-0.444	-0.399	-0.477	-0.408	-0.385	-0.456	-0.458
pipe_depth*ROB_size	0.346	0.317	0.351	0.317	0.315	0.367	0.317
IQ_size	-0.280	-0.291	-0.247	-0.283	-0.270	-0.307	-0.302
ROB_size*IQ_size	0.264	0.268	0.233	0.274	0.270	0.283	0.260
L2_lat	-0.233	-0.409	-0.312	-0.195	-0.314	-0.113	-0.249
pipe_depth*IQ_size	0.232	0.227	0.208	0.277	0.221	0.251	0.236
pipe_depth*ROB_size*IQ_size	-0.209	-0.216	-0.191	-0.156	-0.209	-0.227	-0.202
il1_size	-0.177	-0.466	-0.287	-0.164	-0.294	0.014	-0.319
dl1_lat	-0.153	-0.081	-0.150	-0.201	-0.170	-0.152	-0.126
il1_size*L2_lat	0.120	0.293	0.210	0.107	0.168	–	0.175
dl1_size	-0.100	-0.102	-0.093	-0.039	-0.124	-0.102	-0.060
op_lat	-0.092	-0.095	-0.130	-0.113	-0.077	-0.072	-0.047
issue_order	-0.082	-0.060	-0.066	-0.111	-0.056	-0.113	-0.042
il1_bsize	-0.079	-0.222	-0.170	-0.007	-0.099	0.011	-0.079
ftb_ent	-0.075	-0.239	-0.082	-0.068	-0.160	–	-0.151
il1_size*il1_bsize	0.074	0.206	0.162	–	0.072	–	0.071
L2_size	-0.071	-0.070	-0.013	-0.155	-0.134	-0.076	-0.078
dl1_size*L2_lat	0.064	0.049	0.066	0.017	0.057	0.077	0.028
L2_size*mem_config	0.059	0.050	–	0.201	0.099	0.069	0.092
dl1_assoc	-0.059	-0.041	-0.065	-0.158	-0.035	-0.059	-0.062
il1_bsize*L2_lat	0.059	0.156	0.137	–	0.053	–	0.031
mem_config	-0.058	-0.053	–	-0.260	-0.100	-0.063	-0.069
il1_size*il1_bsize*L2_lat	-0.053	-0.140	-0.109	–	-0.063	–	-0.040
ROB_size*LSQ_size	0.052	0.034	0.082	–	0.038	0.042	0.061
IQ_size*LSQ_size	-0.051	-0.034	-0.085	–	-0.021	-0.046	-0.051
LSQ_size	-0.049	-0.038	-0.070	-0.060	-0.023	-0.050	-0.023
pipe_depth*LSQ_size	0.045	0.033	0.076	–	0.017	0.041	0.044
L2_assoc	-0.044	-0.030	-0.019	-0.068	-0.053	-0.054	-0.085
ROB_size*IQ_size*LSQ_size	0.043	0.030	0.055	–	0.029	0.046	0.049
num_units	-0.042	-0.047	-0.061	-0.014	-0.034	-0.036	-0.016
ROB_size*issue_order	-0.038	-0.043	-0.036	-0.056	-0.022	-0.049	-0.022
pipe_depth*ROB_size*LSQ_size	-0.037	-0.024	-0.060	–	-0.030	-0.027	-0.039
L2_size*L2_assoc	0.036	0.035	–	0.046	0.058	0.049	0.058
L2_assoc*mem_config	0.034	0.024	–	0.060	0.052	0.047	0.057
pipe_depth*IQ_size*LSQ_size	0.034	–	0.071	–	0.002	0.029	0.027
pipe_depth*ROB_size*IQ_size*LSQ_size	-0.031	–	-0.044	–	-0.017	-0.034	-0.033
icache_assoc	-0.028	-0.074	-0.025	-0.088	-0.052	–	-0.089
L2_size*L2_assoc*mem_config	-0.028	-0.017	–	–	-0.046	-0.031	-0.048
issue_order*dl1_lat	0.027	0.013	–	–	0.050	0.038	0.033
issue_order*dl1_size	0.024	0.012	0.048	–	0.002	0.022	–

Table 7. The most significant terms and their co-efficients in the EBLMs of the CPI performance response of superscalar processors.

Diagnostics	crafty	eon	gap	gcc	gzip	vortex
Number of simulations	364	217	158	287	222	222
Number of terms	193	108	93	139	94	119
Error variance	0.001	0.002	0.001	0.002	0.001	0.002
Max. C_{jj}	0.007	0.011	0.019	0.008	0.009	0.012
Error bound (95% confidence)	0.006	0.009	0.008	0.008	0.006	0.008

Table 8. Diagnostics of the EBLMs with error bound of 0.01 at 95% confidence level.

DRAM parameter	Low	High
CPU clock:DRAM clock ratio	24	6
Module read latency	5	3
Module burst length	4	8
Module page size	512 bytes	
Bus width in bytes	8	16
CPU clock:Bus clock ratio	12	3
No. of DRAM channels	1	2
No. of banks	1	8

Table 6. mem_config parameter settings.

information on the interdependence of parameter settings on processor response. For example, the terms involving issue order provide the complete set of parameters which determine the performance variation of out-of-order issue. From the wealth of information provided by these EBLMs we summarize a few important observations below:

- Pipeline depth, reorder buffer size, and issue queue size are the three most important parameters influencing CPI performance of superscalar processors. The two-factor interactions, and the three-factor interaction involving these three parameters are highly significant. The load store queue size and its interactions with these three parameters are also significant, though at a lower level. Hence, a processor architect should simultaneously tune these parameters for optimum system performance.

- L2 cache size and latency have high impact on performance. L2 latency interacts with instruction cache size and block size, and with data cache size and associativity. L2 cache size interacts with instruction cache size and DRAM configuration. Since for a given implementation technology, L2 latency is primarily determined by L2 cache size, the processor architect should choose an optimal L2 cache size in conjunction with these interacting parameters.

- The performance with out-of-order issue is largely dependent on reorder buffer size, data cache size, and data cache latency.

- Operation latency has high significance, but it has no significant interactions. Hence, there is performance to be gained by reducing operation latency irrespective of the other processor settings.

- Amongst the predictor related parameters, the number of fetch target buffer (FTB) entries has the highest significance and the branch predictor size and type are less significant.

- The processor width has negligible impact on performance. However, the functional unit settings chosen

for a given width is important. Hence, providing an adequate number of functional units is likely to be more beneficial than increasing the issue width beyond 4 instructions.

Our error bounding procedure makes it feasible to produce a complete list of such effects to any desired level of significance.

5.2. Diagnostics of Model Construction

Our model construction process constructs the EBLMs with number of simulations close to the minimum required. Table 8 reports the number of simulations and other diagnostics of the construction process of the EBLMs reported in the previous section. Note that the simulation count is approximately twice the number of extracted significant terms for each model. The table also reports the maximum C_{jj} values for constructed experimental designs, the error variance of the EBLMs, and the actual error bounds achieved by the models.

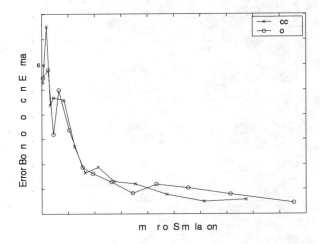

Figure 3. Tightening of error bounds.

Achieving better error bounds is possible at the cost of increased simulation. Figure 3 plots simulation counts against achieved error bounds. The error bounds globally decrease with increased simulation, though there are some local increases in the estimated error bounds. While we have used an error bound of 0.01 to obtain our EBLMs, better bounds are necessary to accurately estimate effects with values near and less than 0.01. In order to understand actual CPI variations caused by effects at this range, we studied them with all other parameters kept at suitably chosen center points. We observe that they contribute less than 2% of CPI variation. Hence, error bounds smaller than 0.01 are necessary only for studying performance variations at a finer level. The error bounding procedure can be used to construct models at any level of accuracy.

Benchmark	gcc			vortex		
Model type	$EBLM$	PB	PB/AIC_c	$EBLM$	PB	PB/AIC_c
Number of simulations	287	56	56	222	56	56
Number of model terms	139	26	22	119	26	24
Error bound (95% confidence)	0.008	0.231	0.072	0.008	0.238	0.078

Table 9. Chief characteristics of the linear models constructed using different procedures.

	eon	gzip	vortex
Additional simulations	70	40	64
Error Bound	0.010	0.006	0.009

Table 10. The number of additional simulations to include a new factor in model.

Terms	eon	gzip	vortex
il1_bsize*across_taken	-0.023	–	-0.039
L2_assoc*across_taken	-0.017	–	–
ROB_size*across_taken	–	–	0.025
ftb_ent*across_taken	–	–	-0.021
ftb_assoc*across_taken	–	–	0.017
across_taken	0.010	–	0.005

Table 11. The additional terms in new model involving fetch across taken branch.

In other work [12, 13], foldover Plackett-Burman experimental designs have been used to obtain a significance ordering of micro-architectural parameters. Hence, we next compared the simulation costs and estimation error of using such designs against that of our approach. We ran simulations for the foldover Plackett-Burman designs and computed the coefficients in a main effects model as done in [12] (PB model), and also extracted the best model from the results using the AIC_c based model extraction procedure (PB/AIC_c model). Table 9 presents the simulation count, number of model terms, and error bounds for $PB, PB/AIC_c$, and $EBLM$ for *gcc* and *vortex*. Though the required simulation count is approximately four times lower for PB and PB/AIC_c, the achieved error bounds are much higher. PB/AIC_c achieves lower error bounds with a small number of simulations. However, these bounds still preclude the correct estimation of many significant effects. More simulations are clearly required to extract all the significant effects.

5.3. Evaluating Enhancements

We used our error bounding procedure to rebuild the model after incorporating a micro-architectural enhancement. An additional parameter was introduced into the model, with the absence of the enhancement as its low value and its presence as the high value. We conduct augmented experiments using our error bounding procedure, after ensuring that the base model without the parameter is *stable* - i.e. increased simulations do not increase the error bound. The augmented experiments typically have the enhancement, and our procedure uses the result data from the additional simulations to extract the significant parameter estimates under the enhancement. It produces a new set of significant terms and estimates, and typically some terms with the new factor.

The enhancement we examined is the capability to fetch beyond taken branches up to the processor width, which was the motivation behind the design of trace caches [10]. Table 10 gives the number of additional simulations that were required to produce the 27 factor model with coefficient error bounds less than 0.01. The number of experiments is always less than thrice the total number of experimented factors. Table 11 gives the terms involving the new factor which account for the performance variations of the enhancement. The instruction cache block size has the highest variational effect for both *eon* and *vortex*. The main effect term has low significance, showing that the benefit of this optimization is heavily dependent on other parameter settings. *gzip*'s performance is almost unaffected by the enhancement.

6. Related Work

Much of the early research in the area of modeling and analysis of processors focused on deriving performance limits imposed by programming model constraints such as data and control dependencies while assuming infinite hardware resources. Subsequent modeling techniques have used these limits to estimate performance for realistic processor configurations by accounting for slowdowns due to various hardware limitations [6, 9]. For instance, Karkhanis and Smith [6] propose an analytical model in which performance is composed of two components, a constant idealistic throughput in the absence of any miss events and the loss in throughput due to branch mispredictions and cache misses. The impact of individual miss events on performance is modeled and estimates of the loss in throughput are obtained using various branch misprediction and cache miss statistics collected via trace driven simulations. In another approach, Fields et al. [3] model program execution using a dynamic dependence graph and measure the significance of micro-architectural events and their interactions by the change in the length of the critical path through the dependence graph brought by idealizing these events. Perhaps the approach closest to our work is the experimental methodology proposed by Yi et al. [12, 13]. Here, the significance of the main micro-architectural parameters is obtained using experiments based on the Plackett-Burman design.

Our approach overcomes several drawbacks of these techniques. 1) In existing modeling schemes, the designer is assumed to have prior knowledge or must make simplifying assumptions about the relative significance of micro-architectural parameters and their interactions. For instance, experimentation based on the PB design inherently assumes that all parameter interactions are negligible, and Karkhanis and Smith [6] assume a set of significant miss events. Our procedure for building linear models does not require any prior knowledge or assumptions; all parameters and interactions are assumed to be significant until experiments prove otherwise. 2) Instead of modeling the effect of micro-architectural events, our approach directly captures the impact of individual micro-architectural parameters on performance. The model therefore enhances the designer's understanding of the influence of hardware changes on performance. 3) Adding parameters to the model is a matter of a few additional simulations.

7. Conclusion and Directions of Work

We have developed an algorithmic procedure to determine accurate estimates of all significant micro-architectural parameters and interactions using data from a reasonable number of simulations. This procedure builds linear models relating a processor's performance response to the micro-architectural parameters. Further, it allows the impact of micro-architectural enhancements to be included in the model with a small number of additional simulations. Thus, our procedure provides a cost effective way to experiment with all relevant parameters. The constructed error bounded linear models explain the variability in performance of micro-architectural techniques.

Our use of the reduced MinneSPEC data inputs, motivated by the need to reduce simulation time, does influence the estimated coefficients and especially the data memory hierarchy related coefficients [13]. We have used the reduced inputs since our primary aim was to show the efficacy of the linear model construction procedure. The same procedure can be used to build models for full or sampled simulations using realistic data inputs.

The constructed linear models can be used to predict the response at other parameter settings. We are continuing our work to use these models to predict the response at combinations of any chosen parameter levels in the experimented range.

References

[1] R. Desikan, D. Burger, and S. W. Keckler. Measuring Experimental Error in Microprocessor Simulation. In *Proceedings of 28th Annual International Symposium on Computer Architecture*, July 2001.

[2] P. G. Emma. Understanding Some Simple Processor-Performance Limits. *IBM Journal of Research and Development*, 41(3), 1997.

[3] B. A. Fields, R. Bodik, M. D. Hill, and C. J. Newburn. Using Interaction Costs for Microarchitectural Bottleneck Analysis. In *Proceedings of the 36th International Symposium on Microarchitecture*, December 2003.

[4] C. M Hurvich and C-L Tsai. Regression and Time Series Model Selection in Small Samples. *Biometrika*, 76:297–307, 1989.

[5] P. J. Joseph, K. Vaswani, and M. J. Thazhuthaveetil. Construction and Use of Linear Regression Models for Processor Performance Analysis. Technical Report IISc-CSA-TR-2005-16, Department of Computer Science & Automation, Indian Institute of Science, November 2005.

[6] T. Karkhanis and J. E. Smith. A First-order Model of Superscalar Processors. In *Proceedings of the 31st Annual International Symposium on Computer Architecture*, June 2004.

[7] A. J. KleinOsowski and D. J. Lilja. MinneSPEC: A new SPEC Benchmark Workload for Simulation-Based Computer Architecture Research. *Computer Architecture Letters*, June 2002.

[8] D. C. Montgomery. *Design and Analysis of Experiments*. Wiley, 5th edition, 2001.

[9] D. B. Noonburg and J. P. Shen. Theoretical Modeling of Superscalar Processor Performance. In *Proceedings of the 27th International Symposium on Microarchitecture*, December 1994.

[10] E. Rotenberg, S. Bennett, and J. E. Smith. Trace Cache: A Low Latency Approach to High Bandwidth Instruction Fetching. In *Proceedings of the 29th International Symposium on Microarchitecture*, December 1996.

[11] Y. Sakamoto, M. Ishiguro, and G. Kitagawa. *Akaike Information Criterion Statistics*. Kluwer Academic Publishers, 1987.

[12] J. J. Yi, D. J. Lilja, and D. M. Hawkins. A Statistically Rigorous Approach for Improving Simulation Methodology. In *Proceedings of the 9th International Symposium on High Performance Computer Architecture*, February 2003.

[13] J. J. Yi, D. J. Lilja, R. Sendag, S. V. Kodakara, and D. M. Hawkins. Characterizing and Comparing Prevailing Simulation Techniques. In *Proceedings of the 11th International Symposium on High Performance Computer Architecture*, January 2005.

Keynote Address II

Chip-multiprocessing and Beyond

Per Stenstrom

Chalmers University of Technology
Goteborg, Sweden

ABSTRACT

At a point in time when it is harder to harvest more instruction-level parallelism and to push the clock frequency to higher levels, industry has opted for integrating multiple processor cores on a chip. It is an attractive way of reducing the verification time by simply replicating moderately complex cores on a chip, but it introduces several challenges. The first challenge is to transform the processing power of multiple cores to a high application performance. The second challenge is to bridge the increasing speedgap between processor and memory by more elaborate on-chip memory hierarchies. Related to the second challenge is how to make more effective use of the limited bandwidth out of and into the chip. A third cross-cutting challenge is how we can move forward and yet manage the complexity of billion transistor chips.

In this talk I will elaborate on the opportunities that chip-multiprocessing offers along with the research issues that it introduces. Even if multiprocessing has been studied for more than two decades, the tight integration of cores and their on-chip memory subsystems opens up new unexplored terrains. I will discuss and reflect upon approaches to explore new forms of parallelism as well as approaches to manage the on-chip cache hierarchies in the pursuit of making multi-core chips deliver higher performance.

Session 4:
Energy and Power

Probabilistic Counter Updates for Predictor Hysteresis and Stratification

Nicholas Riley   Craig Zilles

Department of Computer Science
University of Illinois at Urbana-Champaign
{njriley, zilles}@uiuc.edu

Abstract

Hardware counters are a fundamental building block of modern high-performance processors. This paper explores two applications of probabilistic counter updates, in which the output of a pseudo-random number generator decides whether to perform a counter increment or decrement. First, we discuss a probabilistic implementation of counter hysteresis, whereby previously proposed branch confidence and criticality predictors can be reduced in size by factors of 2 and 3, respectively, with negligible impact on performance. Second, we build a frequency stratifier by making increment and decrement probabilities functions of the current counter value. The stratifier enables a 4-bit counter to classify an instruction's Likelihood of Criticality with sufficient accuracy to closely approximate the performance of an unbounded precision classifier. Because probabilistic updates are both simple and effective, we believe these ideas hold great promise for immediate use by industry, perhaps enabling the use of structures such as branch confidence predictors which may have previously been viewed as too expensive given their functionality.

1. Introduction

Hardware counters are a fundamental component of modern high-performance processors. As many techniques for improving single-thread performance—especially in non-numeric programs—exploit repetition in program behavior, they require the means to characterize this behavior. Processors employ hardware counters to perform efficient on-line aggregation of multiple observations and identify dominant behavior in recent execution.

In most designs, counters are deterministically updated, *e.g.*, every observed positive feedback event triggers a counter value increment. We explore only performing counter updates in response to a subset of observations. Specifically, we propose inserting a simple pseudo-random number generator—a linear feedback shift register (LFSR)—whose output determines if a given observation

should result in a counter update. LFSRs and the design of hardware counters with probabilistic updates are further discussed in Section 2.

We identify two applications of probabilistic updates. First, we show how probabilistic updates provide probabilistic hysteresis. As we discuss in Section 2, a number of proposed hardware counters use many bits per counter for hysteresis. By substituting probabilistic hysteresis, we can often significantly reduce counter sizes with little effect on predictor behavior. We demonstrate this application in two previously studied contexts: Section 3 introduces a 2-bit branch confidence predictor that performs similarly to a previously proposed 4-bit predictor, and Section 4 describes a 2-bit criticality predictor that performs similarly to a previously proposed 6-bit one.

Second, probabilistic updates can stratify instructions into different classes according to the frequency with which they exhibit a particular behavior. Not only can we make a binary prediction of whether an instruction will be critical, but we can classify an instruction based on its likelihood of being critical, allowing us to treat always-critical instructions differently than sometimes-critical instructions. The key enabler for instruction stratification is the use of different update probabilities at different counter values. Lower counter values are associated with a much higher probability of incrementing on positive feedback and a much lower probability of decrementing on negative feedback. We thereby select an operating point (ratio of positive to negative feedback) for each counter value; instructions tend to hover around the counter values that most closely approximate their operating point. In Section 5, we motivate the utility of such a stratification and demonstrate how a 4-bit counter can stratify an instruction's Likelihood of Criticality with performance comparable to an approach employing an unbounded-precision likelihood representation.

We conclude by discussing the limits of probabilistic updates. It appears at least one bit of real hysteresis, in addition to the bit(s) encoding the information being stored, is required to closely approximate a multi-bit predictor. Branch confidence and criticality predictor behavior noticeably changes between 2-bit and 1-bit counters, though the lost accuracy is not commensurate with the 50% storage reduction. Regardless, this limits the benefit of probabilistic updates applied to 2-bit counters, especially in aggressive branch predictors that have been scaled well past the point of linear reduction of misprediction rate with increased table size.

2. Hardware counter design

This section presents the organization of a hardware counter with probabilistic updates. We start by reviewing the design of traditional hardware counters and explaining why multi-bit counters can be useful. In Section 2.2, we introduce a notation for describing counters and how probabilistically-updating counters can approximate deterministic counters while requiring fewer bits of storage. Section 2.3 details the components of our probabilistically-updated hardware counter design.

2.1. Traditional hardware counters

Predictors of instruction behavior employ arrays of hardware counters because, while multiple executions of the same static instruction are generally similar, we want to independently track the behavior of different static instructions. To select a counter from an array, a hash function is applied to the instruction's address, perhaps including some historical information. A counter is updated by incrementing (decrementing) on positive (negative) feedback, and predictions are made by comparing the current counter value against a threshold. For example, each counter in Smith's 2-bit branch predictor [17] increments when a corresponding branch is resolved as taken and decrements when not taken; a branch is predicted as taken when the counter value exceeds a threshold of 1. Counter updates use saturating arithmetic to prevent values from wrapping.

While a branch predictor outputs a single bit of information (*taken* or *not taken*), 2-bit counters are used to provide hysteresis. One bit of hysteresis is generally sufficient for branch prediction, because it prevents a second misprediction when a branch occasionally executes against its bias direction—including the important case of a loop exit.

Some more complicated predictors can benefit from larger counters. Consider predictors used to decide whether to speculate, such as one proposed to control selective value prediction [3]. Unlike branch predictors, these predictors have inherently asymmetric misprediction penalties: the performance lost by speculating with an incorrect value (often incurring a pipeline flush) is significantly greater than the opportunity cost of not speculating if the suggested prediction would have been correct. This imbalance motivates a *biased* counter design, which conservatively prefers a cheaper false negative to a more expensive false positive.

Two attributes typify existing biased counter designs. First, the magnitudes of counter increment (I) and decrement (D) differ in order to adjust the minimum ratio of positive to negative (or negative to positive) feedback that saturates a counter in one direction. For an unbiased counter, this ratio is 50%. But by setting $I = 1$ and $D = 2$, we can require positive feedback at a rate above 66% ($\frac{D}{I+D}$) for the counter to saturate at its maximum value. Second, additional bits per counter store more history, enabling a moving average to be computed with a larger window. In this way, occasional feedback in the minority direction can be filtered out. Both of these attributes can be observed in the previously mentioned selective value prediction counter, which uses 4 bits of storage, $I = 1$ and $D = 7$.

2.2. Notation and probabilistic updates

We represent counters by 4-tuples, $\langle n, I, D, T \rangle$. An n-bit saturating counter's value increments by I on a positive outcome, decrements by D on a negative outcome, and predicts true if greater than the threshold value T, where possible values range from 0 to $2^n - 1$. Table 1 presents several previously proposed counters in this notation.

Table 1. Some proposed multi-bit hardware counters.

Predictor	Counter
Smith's 2-bit branch [17]	$\langle 2, 1, 1, 1 \rangle$
Calder *et al.*'s biased 4-bit value confidence; low, medium and high confidence thresholds T, respectively [3]	$\langle 4, 1, 7, \{2, 6, 14\} \rangle$
Jacobsen *et al.*'s 4-bit resetting branch confidence estimator [7]	$\langle 4, 1, 15, T \rangle$
Fields *et al.*'s biased 6-bit criticality [4]	$\langle 6, 8, 1, 8 \rangle$
Torres *et al.*'s Non-Forwarding Store [18]	$\langle 3, 1, 1, 6 \rangle$

Deterministic updates constrain the elements of the 4-tuple to integral values. With probabilistic updates, we can set fractional values for I and/or D. For example, $D = \frac{1}{4}$ gives the counter a 25% chance of being decremented on negative feedback. We can proportionally scale down a predictor by reducing its size by one bit and halving I, D and T (*e.g.*, $\langle 4, 1, 15, 14 \rangle \rightarrow \langle 3, \frac{1}{2}, 7, 6 \rangle \rightarrow \langle 2, \frac{1}{4}, 3, 2 \rangle$). In Sections 3 and 4, we show that this proportional scaling can be applied with little impact on predictor behavior.

2.3. Designing with probabilistic counter updates

Multi-bit counters are updated in a read-modify-write sequence. In traditional, deterministic counters, the current value of the counter is read, incremented by I or decremented by D (using saturating arithmetic) depending on the type of event, and written back to the counter, as depicted in Fig. 1(a). To implement probabilistic updates, *e.g.*, a 25% chance of decrementing on negative feedback denoted by

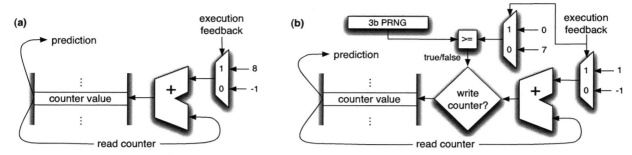

Figure 1. The update path for deterministic and probabilistic multi-bit counters with the same increment and decrement ratio. The deterministic counter (a) increments by eight and decrements by one; the probabilistic counter (b) increments by one and uses a 3-bit value read from a PRNG to decrement by one 12.5% of the time.

$D = \frac{1}{4}$, we introduce randomness into the counter update sequence.

Fig. 1(b) illustrates a probabilistic counter update mechanism. For fractional values of I and D, the counter write is conditional. If the value read from a pseudo-random number generator (PRNG) exceeds a threshold value—if I and D differ and are both fractional, two separate threshold values are required—the counter is updated. Note that there is a single PRNG for the whole array, not one for each counter. While not shown in the figure, it may be possible to gate the entire read-modify-write process, saving power by reducing the frequency of counter reads and writes.

Our probabilistic counters require a source of pseudo-random numbers, but it does not have to be a particularly good one. Some applications may obtain a 12.5% probability by simply using a counter to select every eighth update. Using a PRNG with such a short period increases the likelihood of matching periodicity in the instruction stream, potentially always updating some instructions and never updating others. As a result, we believe a linear feedback shift register, whose period scales logarithmically with its size, represents a good cost-benefit tradeoff.

A linear feedback shift register (LFSR) [5] is a sequential shift register with logic that causes it to cycle through a pseudo-random sequence of values. The feedback in a LFSR is generated by the output of a set of its stages, called *taps*, which are XORed into a value shifted into the register. When optimally configured, an n-bit LFSR sequences through every bit pattern except all zeros, yielding a period of $2^n - 1$. To achieve this maximal period, an LFSR needs an even number of taps; the oldest bit is always tapped. An 8-bit LFSR with taps in a configuration with maximal period is shown in Fig. 2. If the LFSR exceeds the size of the required random number (*e.g.*, only a 3-bit number is needed in Fig. 1), any subset of the LFSR's bits can be used.

While LFSR behavior is extremely predictable, it is adequate for our purposes. A 32-bit Mersenne Twister-based PRNG [11] produced results that did not differ substantially from those obtained with a 16-bit LFSR. Given this result,

we did not explore more sophisticated PRNG hardware.

3. Branch confidence

Our first set of experiments explores probabilistic variants of branch confidence estimators. These predictors classify a fetched branch as *high confidence* if it is likely to be correctly predicted, or *low confidence* otherwise. Applications of branch confidence predictors include pipeline gating [9]—trying to save power by reducing the number of wrong-path instructions fetched—and selecting low confidence branches at which to checkpoint processor state in large-window processors [1].

Branch confidence estimators exploit a key observation about branch predictor behavior: a branch which has been consistently predicted correctly is likely to continue to be predicted correctly. In light of this observation, Jacobsen *et al.* proposed a predictor—subsequently referred to as the JRS estimator—that tracks the number of correct branch predictions since the last misprediction [7]. The estimator's saturating counters increment on every correct prediction and *reset* on a branch misprediction; a 4-bit version is represented in our notation as $\langle 4, 1, 15, T \rangle$. In practice, the JRS estimator works quite well, isolating almost 90% of the mispredictions to just 25% of the dynamic branches.

An important consideration in the design of a branch confidence estimator is the tradeoff between accuracy and coverage. Increasing the high-confidence threshold (the number of correct predictions that must be observed before a branch is considered predictable) increases the fraction of high-confidence branches predicted correctly, but reduces the number of correctly-predicted branches labeled as high

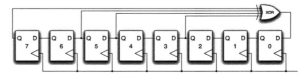

Figure 2. An 8-bit LFSR. Bits 2, 4, 5 and 7 are tapped.

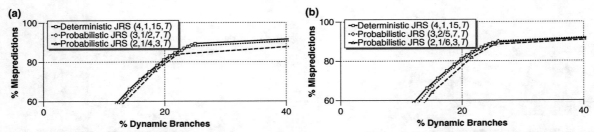

Figure 3. Proportionally scaled probabilistic branch confidence counters have similar behavior to deterministic versions; non-proportionally scaled predictors can match their behavior. Points correspond to different values of T.

confidence. With deterministic updates, increasing T requires larger counters to store a larger number of correct predictions since the last misprediction. For example, the 2-bit determinstic JRS estimator $\langle 2, 1, 3, 2 \rangle$ is only able to isolate about 60% of the branch mispredictions in the low confidence set.

Probabilistic updates allow us to decouple T from the amount of storage allocated. We can approximate a branch confidence estimator that requires 15 correct predictions by ignoring half the correct predictions and requiring only 7 correct predictions. Results of applying this strategy are shown in Fig. 3, analogous to Jacobsen's Fig. 8 [7].

Here, we implemented branch confidence estimators for a *gshare* branch predictor with 16 bits of global history in a SimpleScalar-based functional simulator [2]. The simulated execution includes the first 4 billion instructions of each of the SPEC CINT2000 benchmarks. After each branch execution, we record the branch predictor correctness with the corresponding counter value for each estimator. From this information, we reconstruct the number of correct and incorrect high and low confidence predictions at each possible threshold T.

Fig. 3(a) includes linearly scaled 3-bit and 2-bit probabilistic counter variants of the 4-bit JRS estimator. While these variants closely track the deterministic estimator, the rightmost point falls somewhat short of the 4-bit version. This stems from two effects: we are forced to scale the threshold superlinearly ($\frac{14}{2} = 7$ but the highest threshold for a 3-bit counter is 6), and some imprecision is introduced by the probabilistic updates (*i.e.*, with $I = \frac{1}{2}$, a branch would need an average of 14 correct predictions, but could saturate with as few as 7). Nevertheless, nonlinearly scaled probabilistic counters can closely approximate the 4-bit predictor, as shown in Fig. 3(b). The nondeterministic versions require roughly 0.25% more dynamic branches to reach the same level of misprediction coverage.

We can also observe the behavior of probabilistic counters using the metrics introduced by Grunwald *et al.* [6]: sensitivity (SENS), the fraction of correct predictions identified as high confidence; predictive value of a positive test (PVP), the probability a high confidence estimate is correct; specificity (SPEC), the fraction of incorrect predictions iden-

tified as low confidence; and predictive value of a negative test (PVN), the probability a low confidence estimate is correct.

Different applications seek to optimize different metrics: consumers of branch confidence data use either PVP or PVN, and place varying importance on SENS and SPEC. Grunwald identifies PVN and SPEC as critical for pipeline gating, to avoid stalling the processor unnecessarily while maximizing power-saving opportunities. In contrast, selection of branches for checkpointing benefits from optimizing PVP and SENS, to minimize the likelihood that a misprediction happens at a non-checkpointed branch and to avoid running out of checkpoints (which would occur if we predicted too many branches as low confidence).

In Fig. 4(a), we plot PVP versus SENS for a range of predictors. We now use Grunwald *et al.*'s enhanced JRS estimator, which improves accuracy by appending the currently predicted branch outcome to the branch history used to index into the counter array. A point in the upper right-hand corner of this graph would correspond to an ideal predictor. Lines connect predictors of the same size, demonstrating a tradeoff between PVP and SENS. Probabilistic updates enable this tradeoff independent of predictor size. Only the topmost point on each line represents a deterministic predictor; the others represent predictors with probabilistic increments. A deterministic predictor with half the number of entries is shown for reference; it uses the same amount of space as the 2-bit predictors.

The "iso-size" curves in the figure shift slightly to the right (increased PVP) as the counter size increases from 1 to 4 bits. This trend enables estimators with 2- and 3-bit probabilistic counters to perform almost as well as the 4-bit (deterministic) predictor. Specifically, 2- and 3-bit counters with the same SENS as the 4-bit counter respectively exhibit only 0.08% and 0.02% reduction in PVP. The probabilistic 2-bit predictor significantly outperforms an equivalently-sized 4-bit deterministic predictor with half as many counters. There is a significant performance gap between the 1-bit and 2-bit counters, though both outperform deterministic counter arrays using an equivalent or lesser amount of storage.

Fig. 4(b) plots PVN versus SPEC, demonstrating the

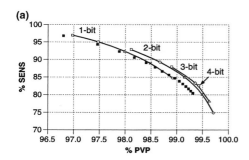 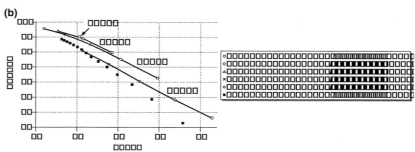

Figure 4. Probabilistic updates endow smaller predictors with performance equivalent to that of larger deterministic predictors and decouples threshold from size. Curves connect predictors using approximately the same area.

tradeoffs important to a class of applications including pipeline gating. Predictor behavior is similar to the PVP versus SENS data, with the relative positions of the various counter sizes reversed.

4. Critical path prediction

Our second set of experiments was performed in the context of Fields *et al.*'s critical path predictor [4]. In this model, a token-passing criticality analyzer updates biased 6-bit counters. The binary (*critical*, *non-critical*) output of the predictor directs optimizations. Because a relatively small number of instructions are indeed critical, predicting a few non-critical instructions as critical does not greatly affect performance, but missed critical instructions represent a significant loss of optimization opportunity. The counters are therefore biased to predict an instruction as critical if it has recently been measured as critical at least $\frac{1}{9}$ of the time.

Optimizing a predicted critical instruction might make it non-critical in the optimized dynamic instance. Nevertheless, it is desirable to continue predicting the instruction as critical, because if it is not optimized, it will remain truly critical, and the optimization can expose a secondary critical path which can also be optimized. As a result, Fields's criticality predictor is designed with a significant amount of hysteresis to ensure these instructions continue to be predicted critical. We experimented with reducing the size and/or bias of these deterministically updated counters and observed reductions in prediction accuracy that justify Fields's selection of counter parameters. For comparison, we include the best deterministic 3-bit predictor we found, $\langle 3, 4, 1, 4 \rangle$.

The following experiments evaluate 3-, 2- and 1-bit probabilistic counters which represent linear scalings of Fields's 6-bit deterministic counter: $\langle 3, 1, \frac{1}{8}, 1 \rangle$, $\langle 2, \frac{1}{2}, \frac{1}{16}, 0 \rangle$, and $\langle 1, \frac{1}{4}, \frac{1}{32}, 0 \rangle$[1]. Fractional values of T were rounded down to 0, as this provided better performance. The 1-bit probabilistic counter is not suggested as a practical

alternative—its behavior exhibits the graceful degradation of our method.

We describe two sets of experiments performed using critical path predictors. The first demonstrates that our proposed probabilistically-updating counter designs have the same qualitative behavior as deterministically updated counters that are two to three times larger. The second demonstrates that this behavior translates into equivalent performance for criticality-based scheduling in a clustered microarchitecture.

Experimental method: To perform experiments similar to those of Fields *et al.*, we simulated an 8-wide dynamically-scheduled superscalar processor with a 128-entry instruction window, 13-stage pipeline, and a *gshare* branch predictor using 16 bits of global history. We assume a perfect instruction cache, a 32 KB, 4-way L1 data cache with 2-cycle access latency, a 1 MB, 8-way L2 data cache with 10-cycle access latency, and memory with a 100-cycle latency and 4-cycle interconnect occupancy for 32-byte blocks. Simulated 16-bit LFSRs are initialized at the start of each experiment; one shift occurs per value read from the register, not per CPU cycle.

The SPEC CINT2000 benchmarks were compiled using the Digital Alpha compiler with full traditional optimization (no profile feedback). Speedups are calculated by averaging three 10 million instruction runs of the benchmarks after skipping 3, 5, and 8 billion instructions, after warming up predictors and caches for one million instructions.

4.1. Predictor behavior

To evaluate the behavior of alternative counter designs in isolation, we examined simulation-generated traces of Fields's model-based criticality results grouped by static instruction. We demonstrate the prediction accuracy of probabilistic counters in the context of an alias-free predictor with immediate updates—a best-case scenario for the predictors.

The accuracy of each predictor is plotted in Fig. 5. As accurate identification of critical instructions is the greater performance contributor, the reader should focus on the bottom and top segments of each column, labeled "correctly

---

[1]As part of this work, we explored a variety of counter parameters. Among them, we found a 2-bit configuration $\langle 2, 1, \frac{1}{16}, 0 \rangle$ whose average performance slightly exceeds that of the baseline 6-bit predictor.

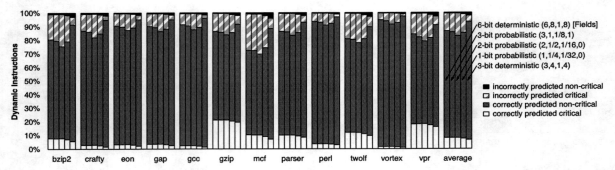

Figure 5. The behavior of probabilistic predictors qualitiatively resembles that of larger deterministic ones. Predictions from Fields's deterministic, three LFSR-based probabilistic, and a 3-bit deterministic counter trained on model-based criticality results, one static instruction at a time, using traces of 19 million dynamic instruction executions per benchmark.

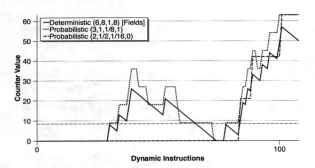

Figure 6. Fields's deterministic and two approximating probabilistic counters, predicting model-based criticality of a single static instruction over a partial execution of *crafty*. The dashed line indicates the threshold of Fields's counter; probabilistic counter values are scaled such that their thresholds coincide.

predicted critical" and "incorrectly predicted non-critical". There is no visibly discernible difference among the 6-bit deterministic, 3-bit and 2-bit probabilistic predictor results for these segments. The 1-bit predictor is noticeably less accurate, though its behavior is quite similar.

All the predictors can trivially classify instructions which exhibit consistent behavior over the duration of program execution—those which are always critical or never critical. More interesting cases, where instructions are occasionally critical or go through phases of criticality, distinguish the predictors' performance.

Fig. 6 illustrates probabilistic counters approximating Fields's deterministic counter design in such a case. The scales of the counters have been normalized to that of the baseline counter, from 0 to 63 ($2^6 - 1$). Plateaus indicate periods when criticality feedback is being ignored by probabilistic counters.

As the 3-bit counter is deterministically incremented, its upward movements match those of the 6-bit counter. It has proportionally fewer intermediate steps than the 6-bit counter and so must periodically—one-eighth of the time—

make correspondingly larger jumps downward.

To demonstrate differing probabilistic and deterministic counter behavior, the trace in Fig. 6 was selected such that the 2-bit counter—which, unlike the 3-bit counter, has a fractional value for I—experiences bad luck. It effectively receives "tails" on flips of five coins in a row, completely missing the initial critical behavior of the instruction. These occurrences are rare, as demonstrated by Fig. 5, but lead to a slight reduction in accuracy relative to the 6-bit predictor.

4.2. Performance

We measure the performance impact of using a reduced-size probabilistic counter on Fields's applications of criticality-based scheduling in clustered architectures. Our baseline machine includes eight 1-wide clusters, each with 16-entry instruction windows, and uses a dependence-based steering policy. The criticality predictors employ 16K-entry tables trained using Fields's criticality model.

Fig. 7 plots speedups over executions without critical scheduling. Consistent with the idealized predictor accuracy, performance degrades slowly with reduced predictor storage. On average, the 2- and 3-bit counters achieve speedups only slightly smaller than the 6-bit counter: 7.75% and 7.91% compared to 7.94%. For some benchmarks, the probabilistic counter "gets lucky" and outperforms the 6-bit deterministic predictor: see *bzip2*, *gzip* and *twolf*. Even the 1-bit counter is competitive in several benchmarks, achieving 6.4% speedup on average. Notably, the 1-bit probabilistic predictor outperformed the deterministic 3-bit predictor, which achieved an average speedup of 5.1%.

Alternatively, keeping the predictor size constant, non-determinism can be used to increase performance. For any predictor size, a probabilistic predictor exists which outperforms Fields's 6-bit deterministic one (Fig. 8). The best probabilistic counter varies with size: the 2-bit predictor performs better at smaller sizes where conflicts from aliasing are more significant than the loss in resolution.

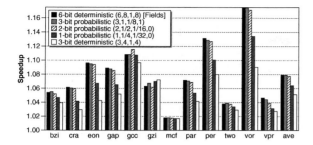

Figure 7. The performance achieved by 3- and 2-bit probabilistic predictors closely approximates that of a 6-bit deterministic predictor. Speedups over a clustered microarchitecture without critical scheduling, using predictions from model-based criticality results.

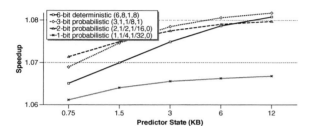

Figure 8. Probabilistic predictors outperform deterministic ones of the same size. Probabilistic predictors are less sensitive to size. The 3-bit deterministic predictor (not shown) always offers less than 6% speedup.

5. A Likelihood of Criticality tracker

The previous section demonstrated how probabilistic updates can increase the storage efficiency of a binary predictor whose outputs are (*critical, non-critical*). We now show that it can be useful to go beyond a binary notion of criticality to a *Likelihood of Criticality* (described in Section 5.1). We demonstrate a counter design in Section 5.2 that can stratify instructions into groups based on the frequency at which they are critical. This design includes probabilistic updates where the probabilities of incrementing and decrementing depend on the current counter state. As few as four bits of storage can thereby be used to predict Likelihood of Criticality almost as well as a predictor with unbounded precision (Section 5.3). While demonstrated in the context of criticality, the proposed counter design is equally applicable for tracking other program behaviors.

5.1. Likelihood of Criticality

Previous work [15] has shown, when giving preferential scheduling priority to critical instructions, it can be desirable to have more than a binary notion of criticality. With multiple levels of criticality, we can distinguish between two predicted critical instructions, and two predicted non-critical instructions. A motivating example is the fragment

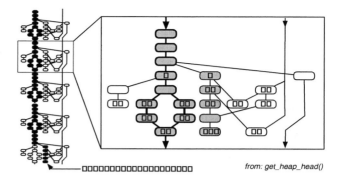

Figure 9. A code example demonstrating the source of contention-related stalls. The critical path, ending in a mispredicted branch (**BR***), is highlighted. Both instructions **a** (on the rib) and **b** (on the spine) are predicted critical, but instructions on the spine are more often critical.

from the benchmark *vpr* shown in Fig. 9, which exhibits a "spine and ribs" structure commonplace in programs. In this loop, the dominant spine (including instruction **b**) computes a loop-carried dependence used by ribs which periodically diverge from the spine and do not reconverge.

The rib that starts with instruction **a** includes a hard-to-predict branch. As a result, both the static instructions labeled **a** and **b** are frequently predicted as critical: they are regularly on the critical backward slice of the mispredicted branch. If we need to make a choice between these instructions, as we have to do on a clustered microarchitecture with single-issue clusters—where only one of the two instructions can issue immediately after their predecessor, and the other has to be steered away or stalled—binary predictions of criticality are insufficient.

If we choose to break ties by preferring the older instruction, in this case instruction **a**, we make the wrong choice for every iteration but the last, because only in the last iteration is **a** critical. If we instead predict *how likely an instruction is to be critical*—**b** is much more likely to be critical than **a**—and prioritize instructions based on their likelihood to be critical, we can achieve a better schedule than with a prediction of critical/not-critical. In practice, an instruction's *Likelihood of Criticality* (LoC) is well predicted by the fraction of occurrences—a real number between 0 and 1—that an instruction has been critical in the past.

While each instance where LoC improves performance only saves a few cycles, such instances are common enough to significantly impact overall performance. In the 8-wide single-issue clustered machine described in Section 4, a LoC-based scheduler offers a 5% speedup over binary criticality scheduling, as shown in Fig. 10. These results include an "unlimited precision" or "infinite" LoC tracker which records the number of critical and non-critical instances of a given instruction. When a prediction is needed, it computes the fraction of critical instances and assigns the instruction

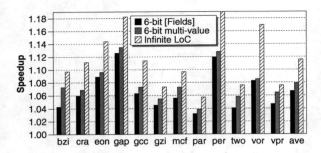

Figure 10. True Likelihood of Criticality (LoC) information enables effective resource allocation.

one of eight priority levels for scheduling (rather than criticality scheduling's two [4]).

Empirically, we find little benefit in providing more than eight priority levels. With eight levels, we can correctly prioritize instructions unless they have very similar LoCs, in which case the penalty of incorrectly prioritizing them—which only happens half the time—is negligible. As a result, the results in the remainder of this section use eight priority levels.

5.2. A LoC estimator

Clearly, tracking LoC by keeping a count of critical and total instances is not feasible, as it requires too many bits of state per instruction. In this section, we describe a feasible approach to estimating LoC, but first demonstrate that merely reinterpreting the existing counter states of Fields's predictor poorly approximates a true LoC tracker.

Fig. 10 shows that interpreting a Fields multi-bit criticality predictor's value to create a continuum of criticality, encoding eight criticality levels in the top three bits, provides only a 1% average speedup over binary criticality. This traditional predictor organization does not improve performance much because it tends to saturate at the ends of the spectrum. Fig. 11 shows a Fields predictor's behavior when fed random bit streams with a variable fraction of 1's, from 0 to 100% on the x axis. For each stream, we plot the fraction of time spent in each of the eight priority levels. While the Fields predictor is effective at distinguishing between instructions with LoC above and below 11%, as the predictor increments by 8 and decrements by 1 ($\frac{1}{8+1} \approx 11\%$), it is really only able to distinguish whether an instruction is above or below that threshold.

The key to distinguishing multiple thresholds throughout the LoC continuum is a collection of increment and decrement ratios, each of which distinguishes one stratum from the next. We now describe how this can be implemented. The first step is to associate each counter encoding with a LoC. In demonstrating this idea, we consider a 3-bit counter and initially distribute the encodings equally throughout the range of LoCs (Table 2). More bits provide better resolu-

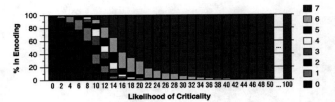

Figure 11. Traditional saturating counters effectively encode a binary threshold. The Fields predictor only uses the intermediate encodings for LoCs in a small transition region around 11%.

tion. The goal is for our predictor to be in a state that closely approximates the LoC of the instruction being tracked (*i.e.*, an instruction that is critical 40% of the time should have a counter value of 2 or 3 most of the time).

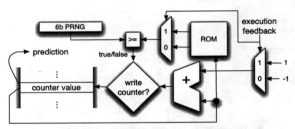

Figure 12. A probabilistic stratifier.

Counters track likelihoods by probabilistically incrementing (decrementing) on positive (negative) feedback with different probabilities for each value. Fig. 12 depicts a design where the current counter value indexes into a ROM, retrieving a threshold applied to the PRNG output. LoCs above the threshold are more likely to increment, and those below it are more likely to decrement.

Using different probabilities at each state lets us partition the range of likelihoods into multiple segments. Specifically, we decrease the probability of incrementing with increasing counter values (and correspondingly increase the probability of decrementing), as shown in Table 2, to create the desired operating points. These probabilities will create a tendency for an instruction to move toward an encoding that matches its LoC.

Equation 1 shows how to compute the bias direction for a given LoC at a particular counter value.

$$\text{bias direction} = \text{LoC} \times (\text{increment probability}) - \quad (1)$$
$$(1 - \text{LoC}) \times (\text{decrement probability})$$

The bias direction is positive when the LoC exceeds the counter value's operating point and negative otherwise. Thus, instructions tend to find an equilibrium point, oscillating between the operating points immediately above and below the LoC. In our example, an instruction with an LoC of 40% will tend to oscillate between counter values 2 and

118

Table 2. A 3-bit LoC tracker associates a different operating point with each encoding. Increment probabilities are (100%−operating point); decrement probabilities match the corresponding operating points.

counter value	0	1	2	3	4	5	6	7
operating point	11%	22%	33%	44%	55%	66%	77%	88%
increment probability	89%	78%	67%	56%	45%	34%	23%	0%
decrement probability	0%	22%	33%	44%	55%	66%	77%	88%

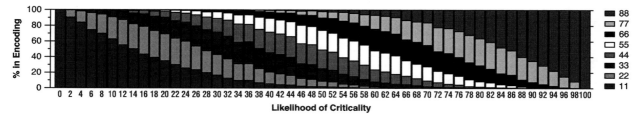

Figure 13. The probabilistic stratifier more evenly distributes encodings. We again use randomly generated streams with fractions of ones between 0 and 100%.

3, as shown by equations 2 and 3.

when counter = 2:

$$0.4 \times 0.67 - 0.6 \times 0.33 = 0.268 - 0.198 = +0.07 \quad (2)$$

when counter = 3:

$$0.4 \times 0.56 - 0.6 \times 0.44 = 0.224 - 0.264 = -0.04 \quad (3)$$

Using this style of counters, we can more evenly distribute encodings across the space of LoCs to construct a *probabilistic stratifier*. Figure 13 shows how long each LoC spends in each of the 3-bit counter encodings. Instructions in the middle of the LoC range spend non-trivial amounts of time in as many as six encodings. While we achieve the correct encodings on average, the statistical nature of the counters leads to some "jitter" in the value. The amount of jitter does not scale with the size of the counter, but does present a lower bound on the size of effective counters, as we show below.

Despite the jitter, the counter values can effectively distinguish two instructions of different criticality. Fig. 14 shows the probability of correctly selecting the more critical instruction as a function of the difference in criticality. For a 6-bit counter, instructions that differ in criticality by 20% can be distinguished almost 100% of the time, and even differences of only 10% can be distinguished 90% of the time. This is encouraging, as our previous experiments showed that it was only necessary to distinguish 8 levels of LoC.

We can tailor our probabilistic stratifier to the LoC domain by considering the distribution of LoC values. In the above examples, we distributed counter encodings evenly throughout the LoC space. Observed instruction LoCs are not evenly distributed, however: as shown in Fig. 15, more than half of dynamic instructions correspond to static instructions that are on average critical less than one percent of the time. We have found empirically that the best performance is achieved by distributing encodings in proportion

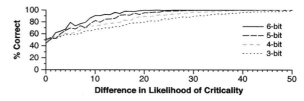

Figure 14. Likelihood trackers can consistently distinguish instructions with differing criticality.

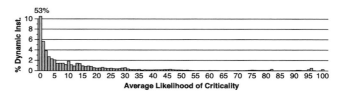

Figure 15. Likelihoods of criticality are not equally distributed. 53% of instructions are critical less than 1%; almost 75% are critical less than 10% of the time.

to the distribution of LoCs, *i.e.*, allocating more encodings to lower criticality values[2]. While it may seem counter-intuitive to allocate many encodings to differentiate many levels of "non-criticalness," it is important to correctly prioritize between rarely critical instructions because of the overwhelming frequency with which such comparisons are made.

5.3. Results

With this approach, we find that as small as a 4-bit counter, mapped down to 8 priority levels, can closely approximate the performance of the unbounded precision LoC tracker. In Fig. 16, we compare the performance of, from

---

[2]For example, our 4-bit counters use the following set points: 0, 0.002, 0.005, 0.01, 0.02, 0.03, 0.05, 0.07, 0.10, 0.13, 0.16, 0.21, 0.29, 0.40, 0.50, 0.60. Thus the 0000 encoding is meant to encode instructions with LoC between 0% and 0.2%.

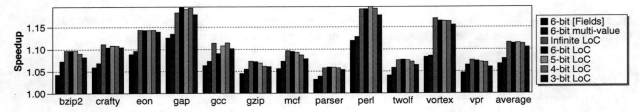

Figure 16. A 4-bit Likelihood of Criticality (LoC) predictor approximates one of infinite size.

left to right in each group, Fields's binary criticality predictor (using 6-bit counters), a multi-level criticality predictor implemented by using the top 3 bits of the Fields predictor, a LoC tracker with unbounded precision, and LoC trackers with 6, 5, 4, and 3 bits of precision.

The LoC trackers significantly outperform the traditional saturating counter implementations. Four bits provide sufficient precision; with fewer than four bits, there is a perceptible loss of performance as the jitter becomes non-negligible relative to the number of available encodings. Nevertheless, this probabilistic scheme, like those shown in previous sections, degrades gracefully; the 3-bit version loses only 1% of performance with respect to the ideal of unbounded precision.

Interestingly, in some benchmarks the probabilistic stratifiers occasionally outperform the infinite precision one. We do not believe this to be an important phenomenon, just "dumb luck" where elided updates happen to yield better predictions than the deteriministically updated version.

6. Related work

Probabilistic event counter updates and nonuniform update probabilities were previously proposed by Morris [12]. Morris's counter encoding was logarithmic, as opposed to the linear and discrete encodings we use.

Loh *et al.* observe that 2-bit counters remain in the *strongly taken* or *strongly not taken* states for 90% of the predictions made by an 8K entry *gshare* branch predictor on the SPEC CINT2000 benchmarks [8]. Instead of fractional values for I and D, Loh *et al.* implement fractional values for n by sharing a hysteresis bit among multiple counters. Reductions in area of 25% or 37.5% can be achieved with only 2.8% or 8.3% increase in mispredictions with a single hysteresis bit shared among two or four counters, respectively.

The Alpha EV8 branch predictor design [16] employed four sets of separated prediction and hysteresis arrays. In two of these hysteresis arrays, implementing the meta-predictor and part of an *e-gskew* predictor, each hysteresis bit is shared between two counters. A partial update strategy, in which the hysteresis table is not written on every prediction, somewhat alleviates the aliasing effects caused by the shared hysteresis.

The Bandwidth Adaptive Snooping Hybrid (BASH) cache coherence protocol [10] uses a saturating policy counter $\langle 8, 1, 1, T \rangle$, where T is a randomly generated 8-bit integer, to determine whether to unicast or broadcast based on the bandwidth utilization. Pseudo-random numbers are generated by an LFSR and compared to the policy counter off the critical path, though the amount of logic required to implement a LFSR (as shown earlier) is negligible. Region-Scout [13] is an cache coherence optimization which uses an array of LFSRs to record locally-cached regions.

A portion of this work appeared in [14].

7. Conclusion

We have demonstrated how probabilistic updates—implemented by introducing a pseudo-random number generator into the counter update path—can reduce hardware predictor sizes by providing probabilistic hysteresis. Branch confidence and criticality predictors' counters can be reduced to 2 bits from 4 and 6 bits, respectively, with little impact on performance. Probabilistic updates can also be used to build probabilistic stratifiers: predictors that classify an instruction based on the frequency a given behavior is observed. A 4-bit stratifier can represent eight levels of Likelihood of Criticality (LoC) with sufficient accuracy to achieve performance closely approximating that of an unbounded-precision mechanism.

While these results are significant, it is important to observe the limitations of probabilistic updates. Specifically, it should be noted that all of the above cases required at least one bit of "real" hysteresis provided by counter state to approximate the behavior of a larger counter. For branch confidence and criticality, which make binary predictions, 2-bit predictors were required; for LoC with 3-bit resolution, a 4-bit predictor was required. Below this point, with 1-bit binary predictors and 3-bit LoC stratifiers, we observed a more noticeable drop in performance. Some real hysteresis appears necessary to smooth out the randomness-introduced jitter. Demonstrating that one bit of hysteresis is both necessary and sufficient for approximating any multi-bit counter would be interesting future work.

More practically, this requirement for real hysteresis limits the applicability of probabilistic updates. It appears that probabilistic updates have little to offer counters of two or

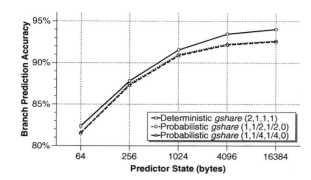

Figure 17. Probabilistic updates are not effective for 2-bit counter-based branch predictors.

fewer bits, including those used in most branch predictors. We confirmed this intuition with experiments comparing equal-resource *gshare* branch predictors using probabilistically updated 1-bit counters with those using deterministically updated 2-bit counters, as shown in Fig. 17. With 1-bit probabilistic counters, we can use twice as many with similar hardware cost, but the benefit of using additional counters (and increasing the history length by one) always failed to balance the penalty introduced by probabilistic updates. This is especially true in large branch predictors where additional history bits achieve diminishing returns.

Nevertheless, probabilistic updates can significantly reduce the cost—both in area and power—of other proposed predictors. By reducing the barrier to entry, probabilistic updates potentially enable inclusion of predictors whose function could not otherwise be justified. In particular, 1-bit probabilistic predictors present an interesting design point, as they are even simpler than deterministic predictors: they do not require a read-modify-write update sequence. Overall, we are optimistic that the simplicity and effectiveness of probabilistic updates will lead to their inclusion in future microprocessors.

Acknowledgments

This research was supported in part by NSF CAREER award CCR-03047260 and a gift from the Intel corporation. We thank Pierre Salverda, Luis Ceze, Paul Sack, Naveen Neelakantam and the anonymous reviewers for their feedback on this work.

References

[1] H. Akkary, R. Rajwar, and S. T. Srinivasan. Checkpoint processing and recovery: Towards scalable large instruction window processors. In *Proc. 36th Annual IEEE/ACM International Symposium on Microarchitecture*, 2003.

[2] T. Austin, E. Larson, and D. Ernst. SimpleScalar: An infrastructure for computer system modeling. *IEEE Computer*, 35(2):59–67, Feb. 2002.

[3] B. Calder, G. Reinman, and D. M. Tullsen. Selective value prediction. In *Proc. 26th International Symposium on Computer Architecture*, pages 64–74, 1999.

[4] B. A. Fields, S. Rubin, and R. Bodik. Focusing processor policies via critical-path prediction. In *Proc. 28th International Symposium on Computer Architecture*, pages 74–85, 2001.

[5] S. W. Golomb. *Shift Register Sequences*. Aegean Park Press, Laguna Hills, CA, 2nd edition, 1982.

[6] D. Grunwald, A. Klauser, S. Manne, and A. Pleszkun. Confidence estimation for speculation control. In *Proc. 25th International Symposium on Computer Architecture*, pages 122–131, 1998.

[7] E. Jacobsen, E. Rotenberg, and J. E. Smith. Assigning confidence to conditional branch predictions. In *Proc. 29th Annual International Symposium on Microarchitecture*, pages 142–152, 1996.

[8] G. H. Loh, D. S. Henry, and A. Krishnamurthy. Exploiting bias in the hysteresis bit of 2-bit saturating counters in branch predictors. *The Journal of Instruction-Level Parallelism*, 5, June 2003.

[9] S. Manne, A. Klauser, and D. Grunwald. Pipeline gating: Speculation control for energy reduction. In *Proc. 25th International Symposium on Computer Architecture*, pages 132–141, 1998.

[10] M. M. K. Martin, D. J. Sorin, M. D. Hill, and D. A. Wood. Bandwidth adaptive snooping. In *Proc. 8th Annual International Symposium on High-Performance Computer Architecture*, pages 251–262, 2002.

[11] M. Matsumoto and T. Nishimura. Mersenne Twister: a 623-dimensionally equidistributed uniform pseudo-random number generator. *ACM Trans. Model. Comput. Simul.*, 8(1):3–30, 1998.

[12] R. Morris. Counting large numbers of events in small registers. *Communications of the ACM*, 21(10):840–842, 1978.

[13] A. Moshovos. RegionScout: Exploiting coarse grain sharing in snoop-based coherence. In *Proc. 32nd International Symposium on Computer Architecture*, pages 234–245, 2005.

[14] N. Riley and C. Zilles. Probabilistic counter updates for predictor hysteresis and bias. *Computer Architecture Letters*, August 2005.

[15] P. Salverda and C. Zilles. A criticality analysis of clustering in superscalar processors. In *Proc. 38th Annual International Symposium on Microarchitecture*, 2005.

[16] A. Seznec, S. Felix, V. Krishnan, and Y. Sazeides. Design tradeoffs for the Alpha EV8 conditional branch predictor. In *Proc. 29th Annual International Symposium on Computer Architecture*, pages 295–306, 2002.

[17] J. E. Smith. A study of branch prediction strategies. In *Proc. 8th Annual International Symposium on Computer Architecture*, pages 135–148, 1981.

[18] E. F. Torres, P. Ibanez, V. Vinals, and J. M. Llaberia. Store buffer design in first-level multibanked data caches. In *Proc. 32nd Annual International Symposium on Computer Architecture*, pages 469–480, 2005.

Phase Characterization for Power:
Evaluating Control-Flow-Based and Event-Counter-Based Techniques

Canturk Isci and Margaret Martonosi
Department of Electrical Engineering
Princeton University
{canturk,mrm}@princeton.edu

Abstract

Computer systems increasingly rely on dynamic, phase-based system management techniques, in which system hardware and software parameters may be altered or tuned at runtime for different program phases. Prior research has considered a range of possible phase analysis techniques, but has focused almost exclusively on performance-oriented phases; the notion of power-oriented phases has not been explored. Moreover, the bulk of phase-analysis studies have focused on simulation evaluation. There is need for real-system experiments that provide direct comparison of different practical techniques (such as control flow sampling, event counters, and power measurements) for gauging phase behavior.

In this paper, we propose and evaluate a live, real-system measurement framework for collecting and analyzing power phases in running applications. Our experimental framework simultaneously collects control flow, performance counter and live power measurement information. Using this framework, we directly compare between code-oriented techniques (such as "basic block vectors") and performance counter techniques for characterizing power phases. Across a collection of both SPEC2000 benchmarks as well as mainstream desktop applications, our results indicate that both techniques are promising, but that performance counters consistently provide better representation of power behavior. For many of the experimented cases, basic block vectors demonstrate a strong relationship between the execution path and power consumption. However, there are instances where power behavior cannot be captured from control flow, for example due to differences in memory hierarchy performance. We demonstrate these with examples from real applications. Overall, counter-based techniques offer average classification errors of 1.9% for SPEC and 7.1% for other benchmarks, while basic block vectors achieve 2.9% average errors for SPEC and 11.7% for other benchmarks respectively.

1 Introduction

In recent years, phase behavior of applications has drawn a growing research interest for two main reasons. First, the increasing complexity and power demand of processor architectures mandate workload dependent dynamic management techniques. These techniques extensively benefit from tracking application phases to optimize power/performance tradeoffs and to identify critical execution regions for management actions [1, 3, 9]. Second, in parallel with increasing processor complexities, architectural simulation studies have a growing need to research long execution timescales to capture the increasingly variable behavior of applications. These studies benefit from phase characterizations that summarize application behavior with representative execution regions, alleviating the prohibitively high computational costs of large-scale simulations [32, 36].

Various prior studies demonstrated that phase behavior can be observed via different features of applications. Most of these approaches fall into two main categories: In the first category application phases are determined from the control flow of the applications or the program counter (PC) signatures of the executed instructions [9, 18, 24, 27, 32, 35, 36, 37]. In the second category, phases are determined based on the performance characteristics of the applications [3, 7, 12, 20, 39, 40].

Although there have been some previous efforts to compare or evaluate phase characterization techniques [2, 8, 26], they do not perform a direct comparison of the two main approaches. Moreover, there is generally a missing link between phase characterizations and their ability to represent power behavior, especially with real-system experiments. Such power characterization is very important for real systems, as a primary goal of phase characterization is dynamic power management of running systems.

Following from these motivations, in this work, we compare phase characterizations based on PC signatures and performance behavior of applications. Our study primarily evaluates these techniques for accurate power behavior characterization on a real-system. We compare these with respect to the actual, measured runtime power dissipation behavior of applications. Specifically, we look at phase analysis based on basic block vector (BBV) features of an application [36] to determine regions of similar power behavior. We compare this to phases determined by a particular set of performance monitoring counter (PMC) events that are chosen to reflect power dissipation [21]. We test the power characterization accuracy of these methods on 21 benchmarks from SPEC2000 suite and 9 other benchmarks derived from commonly used desktop and multimedia applications. We show that, in general, tracking performance metrics performs better than tracking control flow in identifying power phase behavior of applications. Additionally, we present specific examples from real applications demonstrating cases where power phase behavior cannot be deduced from code signatures.

There are three primary contributions of this work. First, we have designed an accurate, real-system method for synchronizing BBV signatures, performance events, and power measurements on running machines. This method allows us to study large-scale application behavior on running systems rather than being limited to simulation approaches. Second, utilizing this experimental framework, we evaluate how BBV and PMC based approaches perform from a real power characterization point of view. Compared to an uninformed phase characterization, both phase based techniques achieve significantly higher accuracies in identifying power phases, leading to 2-6X less errors for benchmarks with significant power variations. Last, we compare control flow (BBV) and performance (PMC) based approaches against each other for their power phase classification abilities. Overall tracking performance behavior leads to 30-40% fewer errors than tracking control flow in representing real power phase behavior.

The rest of the paper is organized as follows. Section 2 describes the goals of our phase analysis research and discusses the reasons why control flow and performance phases can differ. Section 3 describes our experimentation platform. Section 4 explains the collection of BBV and PMC information with our experimental setup. Section 5 describes our phase classification methods. Section 6 describes our quantitative evaluation and presents the power phase characterization results. Section 7 provides detailed observations from performed experiments. Section 8 provides a final discussion of BBV and PMC based approaches and presents recommendations for future research. Section 9 summarizes related work and Section 10 offers our conclusions.

2 Goals and Challenges of Phase Analysis

2.1 Phase Overview

Regardless of whether the phase characterization of an application is geared towards summarizing its execution behavior or towards identifying periods with different power/performance implications, the underlying goal is fundamentally the same. The principle purpose of phase characterization is to accurately classify execution behavior into self-similar operation regions based on the observed features. However, the choice of tracked features can be different for different endgoals. It might be desirable to have architecturally independent metrics to summarize execution for architectural exploration studies. In other cases, it is preferable to have metrics that reflect the different behavior under different architectures so that resulting phases closely track different power/performance behavior and correspond to different dynamic management opportunities.

In our research perspective, phase analysis lies as a layer between the architecture and the applications that make use of phase information. Based on the target application, there also exists a processing layer between phase analysis and the application, which helps interpret the phase behavior for application specific goals. An application can simply match observed phases with appropriate adaptive responses or can further process phase information to engage different dynamic management actions. For example, phase patterns can be used to detect recurrent behavior [22, 37] or to predict durations for certain modes of operation to amortize mode transition costs [23, 27]. Several system-level or architectural methods can benefit from phase information to guide dynamic management actions. Temperature aware scheduling [3] can benefit from detecting repetitive power phases to select among tasks with different power/temperature behavior to reduce performance degradation due to idling or throttling. Multicore power balancing and activity migration [16, 33] rely on application behavior to distribute or transfer activity among different components. Phases can provide both history and phase change information to decision policies of these techniques. Dynamic voltage and frequency scaling approaches [6, 30, 41] can evaluate costs and benefits of switching among operation modes at

runtime based on diversity and duration of different phases.

Specifically in this study, our focus is how well different phase characterizations—based on different features—represent workload power characteristics. We look at how previous control-flow based approaches perform for power characterization and compare this to our—power oriented—PMC based approach.

2.2 What Control Flow Information Does Not Show

Before delving into the details of our experimentation and phase characterization methodology, here we discuss the reasons why control flow and power/performance behavior of an application may disagree.

There are multiple aspects of application behavior that can cause the control flow and performance based approaches to reach different phase characterization conclusions. *Dynamic change in data locality* during an application's execution can cause the power behavior to significantly change. While this change can be easily recovered from memory performance metrics, code signatures cannot reflect this as execution footprints are not altered. *Effectively same execution* represents the converse of the above effect. In various applications, multiple procedures or code segments perform similar processes, leading to practically identical power behavior. These are considered as fairly different phases in terms of control flow, which may result in many different phase clusters that do not reflect actual changes in program power. Typical examples for these are scientific or other iterative processing applications performing different tasks on an input with similar power/performance implications. *Operand dependent behavior* may result in similar effects as the first case, where power and latency of a unit depends on the input operands, despite the same control flow. Typical cases for these are overflow handling and scaling of execution based on the input operand values or widths [4].

We revisit these effects after presenting our power phase characterization study. In Section 7, we show the differences that can arise between control flow and performance based phase tracking for power, with observations from real experimented applications.

3 Software and Hardware Measurement Platform

To collect synchronous PC, PMC and power information during an application's execution, we use dynamic instrumentation via Pin [29]. Pin provides several flexible methods to dynamically instrument the binary at different granularities. This first step, *instrumentation*, simply decides where in the native code the additional procedures to analyze the application behavior should be inserted. Afterwards, whenever one of these instrumentation checkpoints are reached, Pin gains the control of the application and injects corresponding analysis routines. During execution, each time the instrumented locations are visited, their injected analysis routines also execute, providing the dynamic application information. This second phase of operation is called *analysis*. Pin utilizes a single executable, *Pintool*, to perform instrumentation and analysis on an application.

Figure 1 presents an overview of our experimental setup for power phase analysis with Pin. In our Pintool, we use trace level instrumentation to keep track of executed code traces.

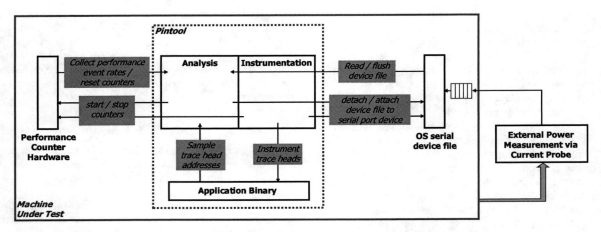

Figure 1. Experimental setup for power phase analysis with Pin.

Our analysis routine consists of three levels of hierarchy. The first level simply provides an account of executed instructions. This is implemented as an inlined conditional to improve performance and to avoid overwhelming power behavior. The second level samples one PC address approximately every 1 million instructions. The highest level analysis is invoked every 100 million instructions. This routine generates one BBV from the 100 PC samples, reads performance statistics from PMCs and logs the measured power history from the serial device file. These three sources of data collection are shown with the three incoming arrows to the analysis routine of our Pintool.

It is important to isolate application behavior from Pin operation. Pin provides application exclusive control flow information, however, performance monitoring and power measurements are out of Pin's control. Therefore, we provide handles to our Pin routines to disable the logging of data for power and performance at routine entries, and to reenable data logging at routine exits. Under Pin execution, instrumentation and analysis are temporally intermixed. Therefore, we use these handles during both instrumentation and analysis.

We provide real power behavior feedback to our power phase characterizations via external, live power measurements. We perform power measurements by measuring the current flow into the processor with a current probe. This measurement information is then fed back to the measurement system over the serial port interface.

To isolate the application power behavior from Pin analysis and instrumentation, we use certain controls within the instrumentation and analysis routines of our Pintool. These handles detach/attach serial device driver from the device file at routine entries/exits via `termios` flags. This approach allows us to preserve previous application power history, while preventing further logging while inside an instrumentation or analysis routine. At the end of a 100 million instruction sampling period, the highest level analysis routine halts logging and reads the logged power history for the past sampling period. This history is then averaged and is assigned as the observed power for the past sampling quantum. Afterwards, the buffer is flushed and reenabled for logging at the start of the next sampling interval.

Similar to the power measurement method, we developed several handles to control PMC monitoring from within our Pintool. At Pintool initialization, we first configure the events to be monitored. This is the most heavyweight operation, and is applied only once, before application execution commences. We selectively halt/start performance monitoring at instrumentation and analysis routine entries/exits. This is used to avoid polluting the PMC information with Pin execution. Although we provide the start/stop handles to all routines, after our initial experiments, we do not invoke them for instrumentation and the second level analysis routines, as their costs are comparable. Note that, this trade-off only affects PMC information without any effect on control flow information and power measurements. During the highest level analysis routine we read the past PMC statistics and reset the counters for the following sampling period.

With this experimental framework, we provide a valid matching between application execution flow, performance statistics and application specific power behavior. Inevitably, there can be error due to measurements, and due to transient operations that perform the control functions for selective logging and asynchronous operation of different data sources. However, in the experimented cases, our selective power collection and PMC sampling process produces power/performance information with good fidelity. Acquired power behavior and performance statistics are similar, both temporally and in terms of delta variations, to native executions of applications.

All of our experiments described in this paper are performed on a 1.4GHz Pentium 4 processor with Linux operating system, kernel 2.4.7-10. The experiments are carried out with the SPECCPU 2000 benchmarks using reference datasets and other benchmarks derived from well-known suites and desktop applications. All benchmarks are compiled with gcc and g77 compilers with base compiler flags.

4 Generating BBV and Performance Information from Pin/Hardware Structure

4.1 Program Counter Sampling and BBV Generation

To track control flow based application phases, we use the basic block vector (BBV) approach [36]. BBVs summarize application execution by tracking both which basic blocks of the application are touched and how many times each basic block is visited during a sampling interval. BBVs represent application execution behavior by providing both working set information and execution frequencies for different basic blocks [8]. BBVs are constructed from execution flow by mapping executed PC addresses to the basic blocks of an application binary. Originally, each component of a BBV is a specific basic block, and the magnitude of the component represents how often the corresponding basic block has been executed for a past sampling period. For practical purposes, BBVs are generally mapped into smaller dimensional vectors via random projection/hashing, component analysis or eliminating least significant dimensions [2, 13, 26, 36, 37].

In our implementation, we use Pin to sample the PC addresses at trace heads. As each trace head is also a basic block start address, each sampled PC actually corresponds to a specific basic block. Consequently, different sampled PCs represent different elements of the BBV and number of samples for a specific PC represents the execution frequency of the corresponding block. For sampling periods, we use previously published granularities [2]. We sample one PC every 1 million instructions and construct a BBV at every 100 million instructions. Thus, each BBV has an $L1$-norm—sum of vector components—of 100. We perform static instrumentation of our experimented applications with gcc compiler to determine the dimensions of basic block profiles. Even after eliminating untouched basic blocks and libraries, applications exhibit large BBV dimensions ranging from 33000 (gcc) to 100 (swim). These lead to highly sparse and impractical to implement BBVs. Therefore, we also apply dimension reduction. For the reduced dimensions, we choose 32 buckets based on previous work [37]. We use a variation of Jenkins' 32 bit integer hash function [25] to reduce the large and variable BBV dimensions into common 32 dimensional vectors.

As has been discussed in previous studies [26], sampling always incurs some amount of information loss. However, for any practical implementation of runtime control flow tracking, sampling is inevitable. Our observations show that our sampled PC information offers good similarity information for large scale control flow behavior. We compare full-blown BBVs, constructed from complete PC information, to our sampled BBVs with similarity matrices [36]. Both methods reflect the major phase content in terms of execution flow similarity and lead to similar phases for small numbers of target phase clusters.

4.2 Using Performance Counters to Generate PMC Vectors

In order to track power phases, we use a set of 15 performance counters that are good proxies for power estimation. The chosen counters track metrics such as CPU instruction counts, L1 and L2 access rates and and bus utilizations for memory behavior. The complete list of chosen performance counters are shown in Table 1 together with the applied mask configurations that define the particular event subsets we choose to track. The performance monitoring method is similar to prior research [21], but streamlined to avoid counter rotations. The final set of 15 PMC events can be monitored simultaneously without conflicts. Therefore, no PMC configuration is required except at the initial Pintool startup.

Every 100 million instructions, we collect the performance event counts and cycle count for the past sampling period. We then convert these event counts into per-cycle rates. These 15 event rates are then used to construct a 15 dimensional *PMC*

PMC Event	Mask	Description
IOQ_allocation	0x0EFE1	I/O Queue and Bus Sequence Queue allocations from all agents
BSQ_cache_ref	0x0507	L2 cache read and write accesses
FSB_data_activity	0x03F	Front Side Bus utilization for reading, driving or reserving the bus.
ITLB_reference	0x07	ITLB translations performed
uop_queue_writes	0x07	All μops written to the μop queue
TC_deliver_mode	0x038	Number of cycles the processor is buiding traces from instruction decode
uop_queue_writes	0x04	μops written to the μop queue by microcode ROM
x87_FP_uop	0x08000	All x87 floating point μops executed
LD_port_replay	0x02	Number of replays at the load port
x87_SIMD_moves	0x018	Executed x87, MMX, SSE and SSE2 load, store and register move μops
ST_port_replay	0x02	Number of replays at the store port
branch_retired	0x0F	All branches retired
uops_retired	0x03	Number of μops retired
front_end_event	0x03	Number of loads and stores retired
uop_type	0x06	Tags load and stores (Does not count)

Table 1. The set of chosen performance counter events and mask configurations.

vector, which gauges the similarity of execution samples in a similar manner as BBVs.

5 Phase Classification

We cluster BBV and PMC vector samples into phases with multiple clustering algorithms. First, we develop a fast, but less accurate method based on the descriptions of previous work [20]. This method is more suitable for runtime analysis as it assigns samples to phases as they are observed. We call this method *First Pivot Clustering*. To corroborate the observed characterization results are not due to the choice of clustering, we also experiment with a very computationally expensive method, *Agglomerative Clustering* [11]. We use two variations of this method: *complete linkage* and *average linkage*. Patil et al. [32] show that SPECint and SPECfp lead to on average 4 and 5 phases respectively. Therefore, in this study, to provide consistent results and error metrics across all applications, we target towards 5 final phases for all benchmarks. Afterwards, we show that observed results are consistent as the target number of phases changes.

5.1 First Pivot Clustering

First Pivot Clustering uses *pivot* samples to represent different phases. In the original description of this method, a new gathered sample is compared to all previous pivots, i.e. starters of different phases. If the current sample is within a specified threshold distance of a pivot, it is assigned to that phase. If it is not within the similarity distance of any of the pivots, it starts a new phase and is added to the list of pivots as the representative sample for the new phase. By this way, The original description can assign samples to phases at runtime. This approach provides an upper bound to the distance within each phase, but it does not guarantee a fixed number of phases.

We change this to an iterative process, where the threshold is changed dynamically based on both the acquired and target number of phases. With this modification, we classify both BBVs and PMC vectors into 5 final phases after a few iterations.

5.2 Agglomerative Clustering

Agglomerative clustering is a tedious bottom-up approach to clustering samples into phases. In this approach, clustering algorithm starts with an initial clustering solution of N clusters, where N is the number of samples. At each iteration, the algorithm compares all pairwise combinations of the current set of clusters and finds the best candidate pair of clusters to combine into a single cluster. The pairs are compared based on a *linkage* criterion, which determines the best candidates. This iterative process continues until a final target number of clusters are reached or a distance threshold among clusters is exceeded. For agglomerative clustering, we experiment with two types of linkages, complete and average linkage. We describe these below.

5.2.1 Average Linkage

Average linkage compares the average distance between all sample pairs belonging to two different clusters. For two clusters with i and j samples respectively, it computes the distance between all the $i \cdot j$ pairs and finds the average distance between the clusters. Performing this operation for all cluster combinations, it chooses to combine two clusters with the minimum average distance. This leads to clusters with similar ranges in all dimensions, but can result in significantly different ranges for different clusters.

5.2.2 Complete Linkage

Complete linkage does similar comparisons as average linkage. However, it compares the maximum pairwise sample-distance among clusters. It combines the clusters with the least maximum distance among all their pairs. Consequently, the final set of clusters have similar ranges among most of their samples, although the range across each dimension can be different.

In all our analyses we use $L1$—Manhattan—distance, as our measure of distance between two samples. For BBV based clustering, we compute the $L1$-distance between the two corresponding 32 dimensional BBVs. For PMC based clustering, we use the two 15 dimensional PMC vectors to gauge the similarity between points. We apply the above three clustering methods and evaluate clustering criteria based on these distances.

6 Power Phase Characterization: Evaluation of Techniques and Results

We apply our described power phase classification methods to several benchmarks. Using both control flow and performance features, we cluster each benchmark into 5 phases with multiple clustering methods. Here, we discuss first how we evaluate the fidelity of these phases in terms of power behavior characterization. Afterwards, we provide the complete set of results based on these evaluations. With the demonstrated results, we show how code signatures and PMC phases perform in identifying power behavior characteristics with respect to a "gold standard" phase classification as our lower bound and an "uninformed" classification as the upper bound. We also present a direct comparison between BBV phases and PMC phases for power characterization.

6.1 Evaluating the Error of Power Phase Characterization

We evaluate the quality of generated phase clusters by comparing the measured power at each sample to the aggregate power for the whole cluster the sample belongs to. For a benchmark with N samples, each sample i ($i = 1, \ldots, N$) is an element of one of the final phase sets P_j ($j = 1, \ldots, 5$). Each sample has a corresponding set of data $[bbv_i, pmc_i, pwr_i]$, where bbv_i and pmc_i are the corresponding BBV and PMC vectors used during phase clusterings, and pwr_i is the measured power value during sample i's execution. For each phase P_j, we compute a "representative power", R_j, as the arithmetic average of the power values for the total N_j samples belonging to that phase. Then, for each sample i, we compute the squared difference between the sample's actual power value pwr_i and the representative power R_j for its owner phase P_j. We denote R_j values corresponding to each sample i with Rj_i. Afterwards, we compute the rooted average of these squared differences over all samples for our final RMS error figure E_{RMS}. We summarize this error computation in Equation 1.

$$R_j = \frac{\sum_{i \in P_j} pwr_i}{N_j} \qquad (j = 1, \ldots, 5)$$

$$E_{RMS} = \sqrt{\frac{\sum_{i=1}^{N} (pwr_i - Rj_i)^2}{N}} \qquad (1)$$

This error value represents the quality of power phase characterization for a given phase classification method on the evaluated benchmark. The methods are the combinations of tracked feature (BBVs or PMCs) and clustering algorithm (first pivot, agglomerative with average or complete linkage). We use this error measure to gauge the effectiveness of BBV and PMC based features in representing power phase behavior of applications in our experiments with various benchmarks.

6.2 Error Boundaries

To gauge the ability of the phase classification techniques in discerning application power behavior, we also provide the error boundaries that can be achieved with perfect knowledge of power information—lower bound—as well as without any knowledge of application behavior—upper bound.

To compute lower error bounds, we look directly at the measured power, which is the independent target experiment parameter in all other analyses. We apply all three clustering algorithms to each benchmark's power information and for each case choose the smallest error value achieved. We refer to this "gold standard" measure as *baseline error* in our results.

For the upper error bounds, we design a separate clustering method, which assigns each sample to any of the final target phases randomly, without using any application behavior information. We refer to the results of this "uninformed" phase characterization as *random error*. We show the results achieved with these approaches for each benchmark. These demonstrate opportunities for improvement that remain and how much improvement each tested phase analysis feature brings to power characterization.

6.3 Experimented Benchmarks

For our power phase analysis experiments, we obtain control flow, performance and power characteristics for several benchmarks on our test machine. We look at 11 SPECint benchmarks—all except perlbmk due to compilation problems—and 10 SPECfp benchmarks—excluded are F90 benchmarks. We experiment with all reference datasets for the 21 SPEC benchmarks leading to a total of 37 different experiments.

In addition to SPEC, we also use 9 other benchmarks from previous studies and derived from well-known applications. These benchmarks are ghostscript, dvips, gimp, lame, cjpeg, djpeg, mesh, stream and mdbnch. For some cases, we alter the dataset or iterations for the benchmarks to achieve longer execution times. We describe these benchmarks and any modifications here.

In the first category, ghostscript and dvips are conversion utilities commonly used in document creation. Their behavior depends on the nature and layout of the input document. Next, gimp, lame, cjpeg and djpeg are media processing tools used to convert among formats or manipulate media files. Last, mesh, stream and mdbnch are iterative applications with multiple sequential functions similar to many scientific computation tools.

For ghostscript and dvips we use a large document of 190 pages, with different size images in the middle of the document. ghostscript converts a postscript input to pdf, and dvips converts dvi input to postscript.

Gimp is an image manipulation tool [15]. We use gimp in batch mode to perform several image processing operations such as blurring, filtering and applying digital effects. Depending on the computation and memory intensity of the applied functions, they can lead to different power behavior. We use the lame MP3 encoder [38] to encode a wave file under varying quality settings. Both power levels and the total execution increase with the quality settings. Cjpeg and djpeg are image compression and decompression programs from MediaBench [28]. We use cjpeg to encode a very large (110 MB) ppm image file into jpeg and djpeg to decode the jpeg file into ppm. Their power behavior also changes during execution and with input data.

Mesh is a well-known program used in dynamic program optimization studies [10, 34]. It performs various computations over the input mesh edges and faces, with sequentially executed repetitive functions. Our mesh input consists of 10K nodes and 60K edges, leading to very quick iterations. To emphasize the execution of separate functions, we alter the original mesh code to repeat each function 100-200 times. Mdbnch is a relatively older, scalar molecular dynamics benchmark [14]. It performs seven different molecular dynamics tasks with different sizes or complexities. To extend its execution, we increase the number of time steps for each task by 4-50x. Both mesh and mdbnch have similar iterative properties of scientific computation. Although they iterate within different control paths, each task usually has similar computation properties—except for changes in memory intensity. These lead to fairly flat behavior with small data footprints. Stream is actually a synthetic benchmark, commonly used to measure sustainable memory bandwidth [31]. It iterates over four small tasks doing different computations. Similar to the above two applications, stream also exhibits a stable power behavior during normal operation. However, it has a loop carried positive feedback that eventually overflows the inputs for its tasks, resulting in a drastic change in power behavior. For our stream experiments, we use an iteration count of 275 and data size of 2 million entry arrays.

6.4 Power Phase Characterization Results

We show the overall results for our experiments in Figures 2-4. Three figures show phase characterization errors for the three clustering algorithms. In each figure, we show the upper—*random*—and lower—*baseline*—error bounds for each application and the achieved error with BBV and PMC based approaches. We also show the average accuracies for SPECint, SPECfp and other experimented benchmarks.

First, obtained characterization results are consistent, independent of the applied clustering algorithm. In general Figure 2 shows relatively higher errors due to the cheaper clustering method. However, the general accuracy relation between BBVs and PMCs are preserved.

Comparing among the three sets of applications, SPECfp applications lead to relatively low errors even with random phase clustering for some cases. This is due to the generic flat power behavior of these benchmarks (applu, art, sixtrack, wupwise). In some other cases, benchmarks go through specific initialization (i.e. equake) or periodic (i.e. ammp) phases with significant changes in all control flow, performance and power features. In these cases, both BBVs and PMCs achieve very good power characterizations approaching baseline errors.

SPECint shows significantly higher errors for all approaches due to higher variations in behavior. In many of the shown cases, BBVs and PMCs are seen to have significant improvement over random clustering. This shows the benefits of phase tracking for power behavior characterization.

Most of the other experimented benchmarks show significantly higher error ranges due to their high power variability based on input data characteristics and functional behavior. In these cases, applying phase analysis, especially with PMCs, proves to be very useful in identifying similar power behavior.

Overall, for the three benchmark sets, BBVs achieve errors that are on average 48% less than random clustering errors, for benchmarks with non-flat power behavior. PMC phases lead to 66% less errors than random clustering. For PMC based approach, power characterization accuracies vary between 2-6X improvements over random clusterings for these benchmarks. Performing same comparisons with respect to baseline errors show, BBVs on average achieve 2.9X higher errors compared to baseline, while PMC errors are 1.8X of baseline figures. These comparisons show, BBV and PMC phase analyses have significant benefit in characterizing power behavior. However, there still exist opportunities to improve power phase behavior characterization of applications.

As above measures also indicate, in almost all experimented cases, PMC based phase analysis performs better than BBV based approach for representing power behavior. PMCs lead to 2.2% and 1.4% errors for SPECint and SPECfp, while BBVs achieve 3.4% and 1.5% errors. For the other experimented benchmarks, PMCs and BBVs have 7.1% and 14.7% average errors respectively. For most of the benchmarks PMCs achieve 30-40% less errors than BBVs with an average

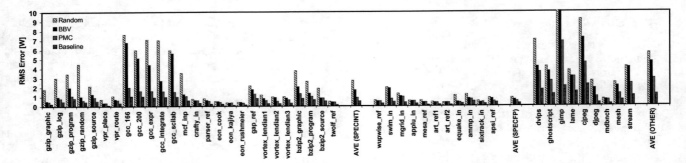

Figure 2. Power characterization errors (absolute) for BBV and PMC phases with first pivot clustering.

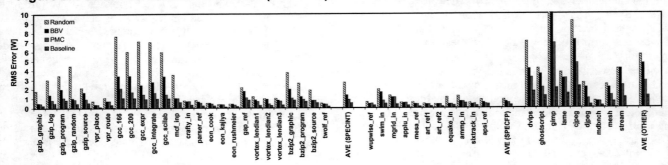

Figure 3. Power characterization errors (absolute) for BBV and PMC phases with agglomerative clustering-average linkage.

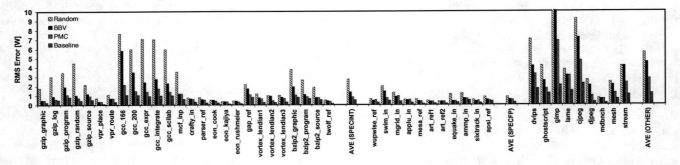

Figure 4. Power characterization errors (absolute) for BBV and PMC phases with agglomerative clustering-complete linkage.

of 33%. This direct comparison between BBVs and PMCs shows, although both techniques provide useful features to identify power phase behavior, in general PMCs features are better candidates for identifying power phases.

6.5 Sensitivity to Different Target Number of Phases

We have presented our complete analysis for a fixed target number of 5 phases for consistency. However, we have also experimented with different numbers of target phases to verify the reliability of our results. We show these in Figure 5.

Here, we show the effect of target phases with agglomerative clustering/complete linkage. For all the benchmarks, we perform clusterings for final phase numbers varying from 1 to 5000. We show the achieved errors as both RMS and maximum observed values. For each benchmark, we compute the RMS and maximum error figure for each target phase count. Afterwards, we average these values over all benchmarks to reach a single error figure for each target phase count.

Intuitively, for a single final phase, both BBVs and PMCs will reach the same error, equivalent to the standard deviation of all the power samples of the benchmark. Afterwards, as the number of phases increase, errors for both methods will decrease with different slopes. As number of target final phases grows towards infinity, both error curves will converge to 0, i.e. where each phase is a singleton sample.

In Figure 5, we show the behavior up to 100 phases for demonstration purposes. As phase counts grow beyond 100, both curves approach 0. For all practical purposes, PMC based phases perform consistently better, independent of the number of final phase clusters.

7 Observations from Experimented Applications

Initially we discussed some of the possible reasons that can cause control flow information and performance statistics to arrive at different conclusions about application power behav-

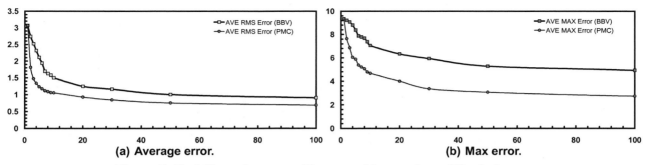

Figure 5. Variation of errors with respect to number of final phases.

(a) Average error.

(b) Max error.

ior. Here, we show our observations from actual applications that we experimented on. We demonstrate the effects for two of the sources of disagreement, *operand dependent behavior* and *effectively same execution*.

7.1 Operand Dependent Behavior

Here, we show an example of operand dependent behavior with the `stream` benchmark. `Stream` performs four repetitive operations with simple vector kernels. It operates on three vectors, a, b and c. The four operations are *copy* ($c[j] = a[j]$), *scale* ($b[j] = scalar * c[j]$), *add* ($c[j] = a[j] + b[j]$) and *triad* ($a[j] = b[j] + scalar * c[j]$). It targets at measuring sustainable memory bandwidth with vectors larger than cache sizes and by avoiding data reuse. We use this application to show operand dependent behavior and its implications on power. There exists a positive feedback between each iteration of the four described operations. This causes the the FP operations to overflow at iteration 261, where first vector a overflows at *triad*. This is then propagated to vectors b and c in the next iteration. This overflow causes the three FP kernels to experience a slowdown larger than 10x, while the *copy* operation is not significantly effected. Consequently, power dissipation experiences a drastic phase change, while execution path is still conserved.

In Figure 6, we show the resulting behavior in terms of power, BBV signatures and PMC signatures. Figure 6(a) shows, the power (top) and BBV signatures (bottom) with respect to executed instructions. We show BBV signatures as stacked vector sample bars, where magnitude of each vector component adds on top of the stack. Here, we see the repetitive BBV vector patterns throughout the execution, corresponding to the 4 different operations repeated 275 times. As the control flow is repetitive, the sudden power drop goes undetected with BBVs. In Figure 6(b), we show the same execution with power (top) and few of the PMC vector samples (bottom). Shown PMC metrics represent instructions per cycle (IPC), L2 cache access rates (L2) and memory access rates (MEM). Here, we show the execution with respect to cycles, to emphasize the actual effect of overflow on elapsed time in different power phases. While, the lower power phase occupies less than 6% of executed instructions, the time spent in this phase is more than half of the total execution. Tracking PMCs easily identifies this power phase change resulting from operand dependent behavior of `stream`.

7.2 Effectively Same Execution

Phase characterizations of applications have two related outcomes. First, phase characterizations provide feedback for identifying phase changes in program behavior. Second, they classify applications into similar regions of execution. These two aspects have an inverse relation, which can be considered in terms of *similarity* and *granularity* [17]. Dictating more restrictive similarity features within each phase results in higher number of phases with smaller granularity. These may, then, lead to numerous false alarms for spurious phase transitions, as many of the small variations in tracked features do not reflect in application (power) behavior. Thus, a desired property for phase characterization is to lead to high granularity phases that capture major application behavior; balancing similarity and granularity.

Effectively same execution represents a characteristic behavior when PMC and BBV approaches perform differently in achieving this balance. In many occurrences, applications walk through different code paths, while performing similar computational tasks. These lead to different code signatures, indicating different phases, while actual power phase behavior is similar.

We demonstrate the impact of this effect with the `mesh` benchmark. During its execution, `mesh` first reads an input mesh configuration and performs various tasks on the input mesh. Most of these tasks have computationally similar properties, leading to effectively same execution behavior—while in different execution address spaces. In Figure 7, we show part of the execution characteristics for `mesh`. In the figure, we first show the measured power behavior. We can easily separate `mesh` execution into three power phases by observing the power trace. We label these "actual" power phases as *H*, *L* and *M* on the power trace, representing phases with high, low and medium power consumption. Underneath the power trace, we show the corresponding BBV vector patterns for each sample. Again, we present the 32 dimensional BBVs as stacked bars, where each vector component adds up to the stack based on its magnitude. Several distinct control flow phases are observable from the BBV patterns. We separate each of these regions with vertical dotted lines. These correlate well with `mesh` tasks. The first high power phase corresponds to the sorting task after reading nodes and initialization. This task sorts nodes based on their types. It operates mainly in L1 cache and performs several arithmetics. The following low power phase, results from *SetBoundaryData* task which sets the values for boundary nodes. This task mostly accesses L2, and has low overlapping computation, which leads to less power. After this task, `mesh` repetitively operates on three computation tasks, namely, *ComputeForces()*, *ComputeVelocityChange()* and *SmoothenVelocity()*. These constitute the medium power phase of `mesh`. All these tasks also make significant L2 accesses. However,

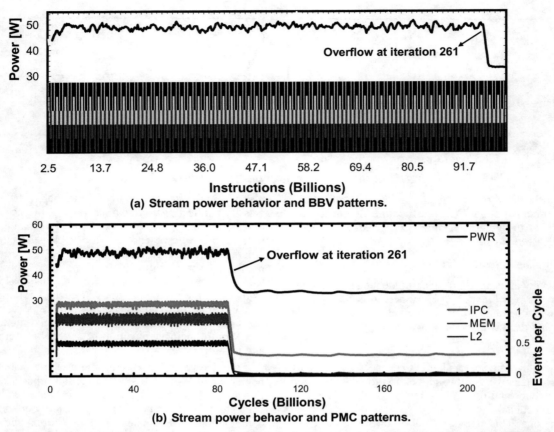

(a) Stream power behavior and BBV patterns.

(b) Stream power behavior and PMC patterns.

Figure 6. Power phase change at overflow condition for `stream` benchmark. (a) shows BBV signatures, unable to detect the phase change, (b) shows PMCs detecting the change. (b) is drawn with respect to elapsed cycles to show the actual time behavior.

their overlapping FP computations lead to relatively higher power.

In the lower two plots of Figure 7, we show the phase classifications performed by BBVs and PMCs. We apply agglomerative clustering with complete linkage and use target phase numbers, N, of 5—our base choice—and 3 for a more restrictive case. In these plots, y axis shows different phases ranging from 1 to 5 for the first case and 1 to 3 for the second. For each sample, we add a tick mark above the horizontal line corresponding to its phase assigned by BBV classification. We also add a tick mark below the horizontal line that corresponds to each sample's PMC phase. These marks then form the bands of phases seen in these plots. For example, for the case with 5 phases, low power phase of `mesh` is classified into phase "1" by BBVs and phase "3" by PMCs.

These plots show the significant impact of effectively same execution in phase classification. For $N = 5$, PMCs correctly identify the three actual power phases. BBVs on the other hand, collapse the high and low power phases into a single phase, leading to a false characterization. This is because, BBVs identify several different large-scale control flow phases. Clustering starts to overlap these based on their $L1$-distances, and these result in combining the high and low phases of power. The three repetitive control flow phases with effectively same power behavior are seen as the more different phases by BBVs, and are assigned to different clusters. These

indicate several false alarms of spurious phase changes. For $N = 3$, BBV phases still show more sensitivity to the three repetitive tasks of medium power phase and assign them to three different phases. In this case, all high, low and parts of medium power phases are assigned to same phase ("1") by BBVs. In contrast, PMCs show very good fidelity. They successfully identify three power regions and assign them to different phases.

This example demonstrates the clear impact of effectively same execution on control-flow-based phase characterization. It is important to note that, this effect has implications for not only phase characterizations, but also runtime phase detection. Various control-flow phases with similar power behavior can cause a detection framework to produce several false alarms for phase transitions.

There are also other cases where differences between PMC and BBV approaches arise including some SPEC benchmarks such as `mcf`. We do not present these here for brevity. Nonetheless, overall both BBV and PMC phases provide a good account of application power phase behavior; in many cases showing good correlation between power and both control flow and performance measures. PMCs usually show a better mapping to power behavior due to both their proximity to the actual flow of power in the processor, as well as due to these discussed sources of disagreement between power and code signatures.

130

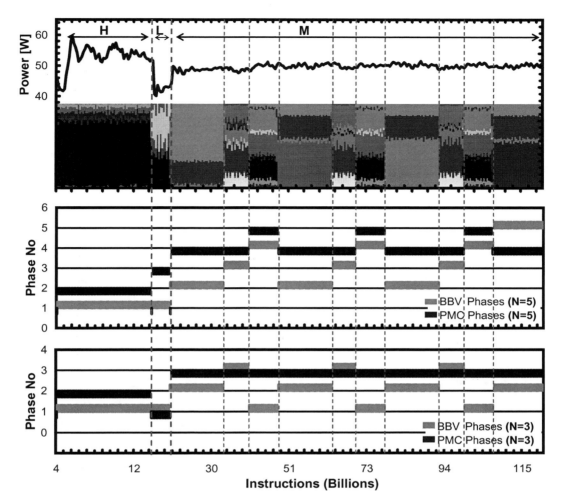

Figure 7. `Mesh` **power and BBV signatures (top) and generated PMC and BBV phases with target cluster numbers of 5 (middle) and 3 (bottom). Multiple control flow phases with effectively same power characteristics disguise actual power phases in BBV based classification. Actual power phases are labeled as** H, L **and** M, **for high, low and medium power dissipation regions.**

8 Summary and Recommendations for Future Research

Here, we first make a final comparison of BBVs and PMCs for power phase characterization. We summarize different pros and cons of the two approaches. Afterwards, we discuss how the strengths of these two features can be conceptually combined for application to dynamic management techniques. Finally, we present the directions for future research following from these discussions.

BBVs are known to have several benefits for summarizing application performance or tracking application phases. The most important advantage of BBVs is the repeatability of the observed phase behavior. Tracked code signatures do not change due to system effects or with the application of dynamic management actions that affect system power and performance.

The biggest disadvantage of BBVs lies in runtime applicability. It is impractical to collect full blown BBV information during application runtime. Sampling methods, as applied in this study, provide acceptable resolution, but BBV generation

still requires mapping PC samples into control flow blocks. Another related issue is the high dimensionality of BBVs that requires processing for dimension reduction. In addition to these, false alarms due to changes only in control flow are an important consideration for a runtime detection system. Finally, the indifference of BBVs to varying data locality and operand dependent behavior can be a significant impediment in power/performance phase characterizations for some real applications [2].

The important advantages of PMCs are their straightforward runtime applicability and their proximity to processor power consumption. PMCs are easily accessible at runtime with lightweight interfaces, which makes them good candidates for dynamic applications on real systems. Several PMCs show good correlations with processor power behavior, so they don't suffer significantly from false alarms. Also as the number of simultaneously monitored PMCs is less than 20, they require no dimension reduction during phase characterizations.

The most important issue with PMCs is repeatability. As PMC data comes from several event counts over the proces-

131

sor, the values are not identical among repetitions of phases. A phase detection method that utilizes PMCs is required to consider event count ranges or has to track deltas together with events to detect phases or phase changes. Our previous studies show quantization can be unreliable, while tracking changes produces higher fidelity [22]. The PMC based approach also requires range considerations. Different dimensions of PMC vectors are not of similar strength. For example, memory access counts and instructions issued have different orders of magnitude. Therefore, scaling of vector components or normalizations may be necessary to match the impact of certain events.

Our quantitative results show that PMCs have relatively higher fidelity in characterizing power phase behavior. However, we believe a better solution can be achieved by combining the strengths of BBVs with the PMC approach. For a general phase tracking method, we envision a hierarchical approach between BBVs and PMCs. We consider using PMC based phase tracking as the global mechanism to identify phase changes and using BBVs to track the repetitive execution progress. In terms of decision hierarchy, PMCs provide confidence to phase changes detected from control flow and provide the final decision whether this is an actual or spurious phase change. On the other hand, BBVs enhance the repeatability of observed PMC phases, by informing the PMC method when a repetitive control flow is detected.

As future research, we consider application of control-flow feedback to PMC-based phase tracking for runtime dynamic management. For example, we plan to use a DVFS enabled system and process phase information to detect repetitive behavior under different DVFS settings. Using both PMC and control flow features, we expect to achieve better power/performance trade-offs than a simple reactive response. In addition to this, other future research avenues include applying these power phase analysis methods to global CMP power management and to dynamic thermal management as mentioned in Section 2.

9 Related Work

Several previous studies investigate phase behavior of applications for adaptation and characterization purposes. Most of these research studies focus on either control flow or performance characteristics of applications. Iyer and Marculescu [24], Dhodapkar and Smith [9], Sherwood et al. [36, 37], Huang et al. [19] and Lau et al. [27] analyze control flow behavior of applications via different features such as subroutines, working sets and basic block profiles. These studies use simulation based methods to identify application phases for summarizing performance and architectural studies. Patil et al. [32] also look at control flow phases with real-system experiments. They use similar dynamic instrumentation to identify BBV phases of applications. Their work uses basic block profiles of applications to find representative execution points, while we look at power characterizations with BBV and PMC phases.

Cook et al. [7] show the repetitive performance phase characteristics of different applications using simulations. Todi [39], Weissel and Bellosa [40] and Duesterwald et al. [12] utilize performance counters to identify performance based phases. They use performance statistics to guide dynamic optimizations and metric predictions. These works do not con-

sider power behavior of applications. Our earlier work [20] employed runtime power measurements and power estimation with performance counters to identify phases of applications. Chang et al. [5] apply process power profiling to determine software power breakdowns. While these studies also look at power behavior, they do not investigate control flow approaches. Hu et al. [18] describe a compile time methodology to find basic block phases at runtime for power studies. This study looks at control flow information from a compiler perspective, while we investigate runtime power phase behaviors of both control flow and performance statistics.

There are also previous studies that compare or evaluate phase characterization techniques. Dhodapkar and Smith [8], perform a comparison between different control flow techniques, working set signatures and BBVs. Annavaram et al. [2] sample executed program counters as a proxy to control flow and show the correlations between code signatures and application performance. They show that, control flow does not always correlate well with application performance. Lau et al. [26] also look at control flow and performance of applications to show a strong correlation can be established by linking program counter to procedures and loops of applications via profiling. In comparison, our work looks at the direct comparison of two phase characterization features, BBVs and PMCs with runtime measurement feedback for real power evaluation on a real-system.

10 Conclusion

Phase analysis is increasingly important for computer systems first because simulation-based techniques rely on phase-directed sampling to reduce simulation time, and second, because real-life adaptive hardware and software mechanisms rely on dynamic phase-directed readjustments.

With power being such a pressing constraint in current processors, it becomes important to understand not just the phases of performance metrics, but also of their related power counterparts. Observing power phase behavior on real systems is particularly important because the real-system phases show the impact of a comprehensive range of systems effects typically excluded from simulations.

This work has explored methods for real-system power phase generation. Drawing on prior work, we have developed an experimental framework for comparing both control-flow-based and performance-monitoring-based phase techniques, and for comparing against live power measurements. Our results show that both control-flow and performance statistics provide useful hints to power phase behavior. In general, performance-based phase tracking leads to approximately 33% less power characterization errors than code signatures.

In some cases where power behavior depends on aspects other than control flow (e.g. data locality, operand values, or other characteristics), phases based on control flow can "miss" some transitions. In other cases, control flow phase classification can result in "extra" phases, where applications perform different tasks with effectively the same execution characteristics. These effects lead to both false alarms for phase changes and incorrect power phase classifications.

Overall, the results presented here show a roadmap to effective power phase analysis in real systems. Control-flow techniques offer a good base, but may well be best applied as hybrid techniques together with performance counters that can more closely track the details of program behavior, needed for detection of power phases with high fidelity.

Acknowledgments

We would like to thank Gilberto Contreras, Belma Dogdas, James Donald, Qiang Wu and the members of the Pin mailing group for their help during the development of this work and for several useful discussions. We also thank Chen Ding for his help with the benchmarks, and the anonymous reviewers for their useful suggestions. This research was supported by NSF grants CCR-0086031 (ITR) and CNS-0410937. Martonosi's work is also supported in part by Intel, IBM, and SRC.

References

[1] D. Albonesi, R. Balasubramanian, S. Dropsho, S. Dwarkadas, E. Friedman, M. Huang, V. Kursun, G. Magklis, M. Scott, G. Semeraro, P. Bose, A. Buyuktosunoglu, P. Cook, and S. Schuster. Dynamically Tuning Processor Resources with Adaptive Processing. *IEEE Computer*, 36(12):43–51, 2003.

[2] M. Annavaram, R. Rakvic, M. Polito, J.-Y. Bouguet, R. Hankins, and B. Davies. The Fuzzy Correlation between Code and Performance Predictability. In *Proceedings of the 37th annual International Symp. on Microarchitecture*, 2004.

[3] F. Bellosa, A. Weissel, M. Waitz, and S. Kellner. Event-Driven Energy Accounting for Dynamic Thermal Management. In *Proceedings of the Workshop on Compilers and Operating Systems for Low Power (COLP'03), New Orleans*, Sept. 2003.

[4] D. Brooks and M. Martonosi. Dynamically exploiting narrow width operands to improve processor power and performance. In *Proceedings of the 5th International Symposium on High Performance Computer Architecture*, Jan. 1999.

[5] F. Chang, K. Farkas, and P. Ranganathan. Energy driven statistical profiling: Detecting software hotspots. In *Proceedings of the Proceedings of the Workshop on Computer Systems*, 2002.

[6] K. Choi, R. Soma, and M. Pedram. Dynamic Voltage and Frequency Scaling based on Workload Decomposition. In *Proceedings of International Symposium on Low Power Electronics and Design (ISLPED)*, Aug. 2004.

[7] J. Cook, R. L. Oliver, and E. E. Johnson. Examining performance differences in workload execution phases. In *Proceedings of the IEEE International Workshop on Workload Characterization (WWC-4)*, 2001.

[8] A. Dhodapkar and J. Smith. Comparing Program Phase Detection Techniques. In 36th International Symp. on Microarchitecture, 2003.

[9] A. Dhodapkar and J. Smith. Managing multi-configurable hardware via dynamic working set analysis. In 29th Annual International Symposium on Computer Architecture, 2002.

[10] C. Ding and K. Kennedy. Improving Cache Performance in Dynamic Applications through Data and Computation Reorganization at Run Time. In *Proceedings of ACM SIGPLAN Conference on Programming Language Design and Implementation*, 1999.

[11] R. O. Duda, P. E. Hart, and D. G. Stork. *Pattern Classification. Second Edition.* Wiley Interscience, New York, 2001.

[12] E. Duesterwald, C. Cascaval, and S. Dwarkadas. Characterizing and Predicting Program Behavior and its Variability. In *IEEE PACT*, pages 220–231, 2003.

[13] L. Eeckhout, R. Sundareswara, J. Yi, D. Lilja, and P. Schrater. Accurate Statistical Approaches for Generating Representative Workload Compositions. In *Proceedings of the IEEE International Symposium on Workload Characterization*, Oct. 2005.

[14] F. Ercolessi. MDBNCH - A molecular dynamics benchmark. International School for Advanced Studies in Trieste. www.fisica.uniud.it/ ercolessi/mdbnch.html.

[15] GIMP. GNU Image Manipulation Program. http://www.gimp.org/.

[16] S. Heo, K. Barr, and K. Asanovic. Reducing Power Density through Activity Migration. In *Proceedings of International Symposium on Low Power Electronics and Design (ISLPED), Seoul, Korea*, Aug. 2003.

[17] M. J. Hind, V. T. Rajan, and P. F. Sweeney. Phase Shift Detection: A Problem Classification. IBM Research Report RC-22887, IBM T. J. Watson, Aug. 2003.

[18] C. Hu, D. Jimenez, and U. Kremer. Toward an Evaluation Infrastructure for Power and Energy Optimizations. In *Workshop on High-Performance, Power-Aware Computing*, 2005.

[19] M. Huang, J. Renau, and J. Torrellas. Positional Adaptation of Processors: Application to Energy Reduction. In *Proceedings of the International Symp. on Computer Architecture*, 2003.

[20] C. Isci and M. Martonosi. Identifying Program Power Phase Behavior using Power Vectors. In *Proceedings of the IEEE International Workshop on Workload Characterization (WWC-6)*, 2003.

[21] C. Isci and M. Martonosi. Runtime Power Monitoring in High-End Processors: Methodology and Empirical Data. In *Proceedings of the 36th International Symp. on Microarchitecture*, Dec. 2003.

[22] C. Isci and M. Martonosi. Detecting Recurrent Phase Behavior under Real-System Variability. In *Proceedings of the IEEE International Symposium on Workload Characterization*, Oct. 2005.

[23] C. Isci, M. Martonosi, and A. Buyuktosunoglu. Long-term Workload Phases: Duration Predictions and Applications to DVFS. *IEEE Micro: Special Issue on Energy Efficient Design*, 25(5):39–51, Sep/Oct 2005.

[24] A. Iyer and D. Marculescu. Power aware microarchitecture resource scaling. In *Proceedings of Design Automation and Test in Europe, DATE*, Mar. 2001.

[25] R. Jenkins. Hash functions. *Dr. Dobb's Journal*, 9709, Sept. 1997.

[26] J. Lau, J. Sampson, E. Perelman, G. Hamerly, and B. Calder. The Strong Correlation between Code Signatures and Performance. In *IEEE International Symposium on Performance Analysis of Systems and Software*, Mar. 2005.

[27] J. Lau, S. Schoenmackers, and B. Calder. Transition Phase Classification and Prediction. In *11th International Symposium on High Performance Computer Architecture*, 2005.

[28] C. Lee, M. Potkonjak, and W. H. Mangione-Smith. MediaBench: A Tool for Evaluating and Synthesizing Multimedia and Communicatons Systems. In *Proceedings of the 30th annual International Symposium on Microarchitecture*, 1997.

[29] C. Luk, R. Cohn, R. Muth, H. Patil, A. Klauser, G. Lowney, S. Wallace, V. Reddi, and K. Hazelwood. Pin: Building Customized Program Analysis Tools with Dynamic Instrumentation. In *Programming Language Design and Implementation (PLDI)*, June 2005.

[30] G. Magklis, M. L. Scott, G. Semeraro, D. H. Albonesi, and S. Dropsho. Profile-based Dynamic Voltage and Frequency Scaling for a Multiple Clock Domain Processor. In *Proceedings of the 30th International Symposium on Computer Architecture*, June 2003.

[31] J. McCalphin. STREAM: Sustainable Memory Bandwidth in Current High Performance Computers. Technical report, University of Virginia, 1995.

[32] H. Patil, R. Cohn, M. Charney, R. Kapoor, A. Sun, and A. Karunanidhi. Pinpointing Representative Portions of Large Intel Itanium Programs with Dynamic Instrumentation. In *Proceedings of the 37th annual International Symp. on Microarchitecture*, 2004.

[33] M. Powell, M. Gomaa, and T. N. Vijaykumar. Heat-and-run: Leveraging SMT and CMP to manage power density through the operating system. In *Eleventh International Conference on Architectural Support for Programming Languages and Operating Systems (ASPLOS XI)*, 2004.

[34] X. Shen, Y. Zhong, and C. Ding. Locality Phase Prediction. In *Eleventh International Conference on Architectural Support for Programming Languages and Operating Systems (ASPLOS XI)*, Oct. 2004.

[35] T. Sherwood, E. Perelman, and B. Calder. Basic block distribution analysis to find periodic behavior and simulation points in applications. In *International Conference on Parallel Architectures and Compilation Techniques*, Sept. 2001.

[36] T. Sherwood, E. Perelman, G. Hamerly, and B. Calder. Automatically characterizing large scale program behavior, 2002. In Tenth International Conference on Architectural Support for Programming Languages and Operating Systems, October 2002. http://www.cs.ucsd.edu/users/calder/simpoint/.

[37] T. Sherwood, S. Sair, and B. Calder. Phase tracking and prediction. In *Proceedings of the 28th International Symposium on Computer Architecture (ISCA-30)*, June 2003.

[38] Sourceforge.net. The LAME Project. http://www.mp3dev.org/.

[39] R. Todi. Speclite: using representative samples to reduce spec cpu2000 workload. In *Proceedings of the IEEE International Workshop on Workload Characterization (WWC-4)*, 2001.

[40] A. Weissel and F. Bellosa. Process cruise control: Event-driven clock scaling for dynamic power management. In *Proceedings of the International Conference on Compilers, Architecture and Synthesis for Embedded Systems (CASES 2002), Grenoble, France,*, Aug. 2002.

[41] Q. Wu, V. Reddi, Y. Wu, J. Lee, D. Connors, D. Brooks, M. Martonosi, and D. W. Clark. A Dynamic Compilation Framework for Controlling Microprocessor Energy and Performance. In *Proceedings of the 38th annual International Symp. on Microarchitecture*, 2005.

DMA-Aware Memory Energy Management *

Vivek Pandey, Weihang Jiang, Yuanyuan Zhou, and Ricardo Bianchini[†]

Department of Computer Science,
University of Illinois at Urbana Champaign
{pandey1,wjiang3,yyzhou}@cs.uiuc.edu

[†]Department of Computer Science
Rutgers University
ricardob@cs.rutgers.edu

Abstract

As increasingly larger memories are used to bridge the widening gap between processor and disk speeds, main memory energy consumption is becoming increasingly dominant. Even though much prior research has been conducted on memory energy management, no study has focused on data servers, where main memory is predominantly accessed by DMAs instead of processors.

In this paper, we study DMA-aware techniques for memory energy management in data servers. We first characterize the effect of DMA accesses on memory energy and show that, due to the mismatch between memory and I/O bus bandwidths, significant energy is wasted when memory is idle but still active during DMA transfers. To reduce this waste, we propose two novel performance-directed energy management techniques that maximize the utilization of memory devices by increasing the level of concurrency between multiple DMA transfers from different I/O buses to the same memory device.

We evaluate our techniques using a detailed trace-driven simulator, and storage and database server traces. The results show that our techniques can effectively minimize the amount of idle energy waste during DMA transfers and, consequently, conserve up to 38.6% more memory energy than previous approaches while providing similar performance.

1 Introduction

As shown in many previous studies [16, 17, 18], main memory is one of the largest energy consumers in high-end servers, such as *data servers* (including file, storage, and database servers) in data centers. Measurements from real server systems show that memory can consume 50% more power than processors [17]. In fact, memory energy consumption will become increasingly dominant as increasingly larger memories are used to bridge the widening gap between processor and disk speeds. For example, the most recent EMC Symmetrix DMX3000 storage system can be configured to have up to 256 GB of main memory [8], and the IBM eSeries p5 595 server (the one that provides the best TPC-C performance in the world) is configured with *2 TB* of main memory [13] to avoid accessing disks. As a result, memory energy consumption will soon become dominant in data servers.

Even though much research has been conducted on memory energy management [1, 6, 15, 16, 18, 25], most of the previous works studied only computation-centric applications, such as SPEC benchmarks or multimedia applications. To the best of our knowledge, no prior studies have considered the memory accesses generated by network and disk DMAs, which are the dominant accesses in data servers.

The memory accesses made by DMAs are different from those made by processors and therefore have different implications for memory energy management. Most DMA transfers usually have large size such as multiple data blocks of size 512 bytes (disk sector size) or 8 KBytes (page size), whereas each memory access from processors involves a single cache line. As a result, a DMA transfer requires the accessed memory device to be in active mode for a relatively long period of time, as compared to processor-generated accesses. Consequently, the memory energy consumption due to DMA accesses is less sensitive to the length of idleness thresholds and the energy and time overheads of power mode transitions, which have been the main topics of previous research on memory energy management. The energy wasted waiting and then transitioning power modes is only a small fraction of the total memory energy consumption, as shown in Figure 2(b).

In contrast, DMA accesses have a different type of energy waste as each DMA operation is broken into a large number of small memory accesses, which are referred to in this paper as *DMA-memory requests* for simplicity. Due to the mismatch between I/O bus and memory transfer rates, DMA-memory requests cannot arrive at the memory device at the rate at which a modern memory device can serve them. Further, the time gap between any two DMA-memory requests is too short to justify transitioning the memory device into low-power mode to conserve energy. As a result, energy is wasted when the memory device stays in high-power mode waiting between every two DMA-memory requests during a large DMA transfer.

To address this problem, we conduct the first study of DMA-aware memory energy management. More specifi-

---
*This research has been supported by NSF CAREER Awards CNS-0347854 and CCR-0238182, NSF CCR-03-12286, NSF EIA 02-24453, IBM SUR grant, and IBM Faculty award.

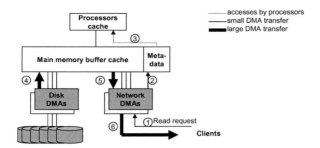

Figure 1. Path of a read request in a typical storage server.

Power State/Transition	Power	Time
Active	300mW	-
Standby	180mW	-
Nap	30mW	-
Powerdown	3mW	-
Active → Standby	240mW	1 memory cycle
Active → nap	160mW	8 memory cycle
Active → powerdown	15mW	8 memory cycle
Standby → Active	240mW	+6ns
Nap → Active	160mW	+60ns
Powerdown → Active	15mW	+6000ns

Table 1. Power consumption and transition time for different power modes.

cally, we first characterize the effect of DMA accesses on memory energy consumption. To minimize memory energy waste caused by DMA accesses, we propose two novel performance-directed DMA-aware memory energy management techniques. Both techniques strive to maximize the *utilization* of the memory active energy. The first technique does this by temporally aligning DMA operations from different I/O buses to the same memory device to sequence these operations in lockstep, whereas the second technique lays pages out in memory according to the logarithmic page popularity curve commonly found in data server workloads to increase the opportunity to temporally align DMA transfers.

We evaluate our techniques using a detailed trace-driven simulator, and both synthetic traces and real traces collected from a commercial database server (IBM DB2) and a real storage server. The results show that our techniques can effectively minimize the amount of idle energy waste during DMA transfers and, consequently, conserve up to 38.6% more energy than previous techniques while still providing similar performance. Our results also show the effect of workload and hardware characteristics on memory energy conservation.

The rest of the paper is organized as follows. Section 2 briefly describes the background behind the paper. Section 3 discusses the effect of DMA transfers on memory energy consumption. Section 4 describes our two techniques for DMA-aware memory energy management. Section 5 presents our evaluation methodology and simulation results. Section 6 discusses the difference between our techniques and prior related work. Section 7 concludes the paper.

2 Background

In this section, we detail the path of different types of requests in data servers, as well as the memory power model and power management mechanisms we assume.

2.1 Access Path in a Data Server

Figure 1 shows the path of a read request for an 8-Kbyte data block in a typical data server, using a storage server as an example. When a read request arrives from the storage area network (SAN), the processor first parses the request and checks the index table of the main-memory buffer cache to see

if the requested block is currently cached. If it is, the processor initiates a network DMA operation to transfer the data out directly from main memory to the SAN. If it is not, the processor initiates a disk DMA operation to read the data from disk to the main-memory buffer cache and then initiates a network DMA operation to send the data out. The path of a write request is similar but data flows in the reverse direction.

For every request, the main memory needs to service one or two large DMA data transfers of 8 Kbytes. In many cases, especially in storage servers, processors only access meta-data, such as index tables and requests, and does little processing of the actual data. Since the meta-data is usually orders of magnitude smaller than the actual data and can be placed in a separate memory device managed using previous dynamic energy management strategies, our work does not consider memory accesses to meta-data.

Interestingly, in database servers, data in the buffer cache are accessed by the processor as well as the DMA engines. However, the granularity of accesses by the DMA engines is significantly larger than that by processors. As previous memory energy management strategies [16, 18] can handle accesses by processors, our discussion will focus on memory energy management for DMA operations, even though we still discuss the coordination with processor-initiated accesses and evaluate our ideas using traces that contain accesses by both processors and DMAs.

2.2 Memory Power Model and Management

The power model we assume for the memory subsystem is based on memory chips capable of operating in multiple power modes. In particular, our model follows the specifications for Rambus DRAM (RDRAM) [22]. In RDRAM, each memory chip can be independently set to an appropriate power state: active, standby, nap, or powerdown. In active state, all parts of the chip are active, whereas each low-power mode only activates certain parts of the memory circuitry [22]. Data is preserved in all power modes. More details about the workings of these modes can be found elsewhere [22, 23].

An RDRAM chip must be in active mode to perform a read or write operation. Accesses to chips in low-power operating modes incur additional delay and energy for bringing the chip back to active state. The delay varies from several cycles to several thousand cycles, depending on which low-power state the chip is in. Table 1 lists the power states, their power consumptions, as well as their transition costs back to active mode. These numbers are the same as those in [18], which were obtained from the latest RDRAM specifications [22].

Previous research on memory energy management [16, 18] has explored when to send memory devices to which low-power modes. These techniques can be divided into two classes: static and dynamic. Static techniques always put a device in a fixed low-power mode. The device only transitions back into full-power mode if it needs to service a request. After a request is serviced, it immediately transitions back to the original mode, unless there is another request waiting. In contrast, dynamic techniques transition a device from the current power mode to the next lower power mode, after being idle for a specified threshold amount of time (different thresholds are used for different power modes). The threshold is usually set based on the break-even time [16] or dynamically adjusted based on the memory accesses from processors.

As previous studies [16, 18] show that dynamic schemes can conserve more energy than static schemes, our study focuses on dynamic management in our evaluation, even though our DMA-aware memory energy management techniques can be applied to both static and dynamic management.

3 Energy Implications of DMA Transfers

In a data server, DMA transfers are usually very large. As mentioned in Section 1, each transfer is broken down into many small DMA-memory requests whose sizes depend on the transfer rate of the I/O bus.

The most popular I/O bus for high-end servers is the PCI-X bus, which is the enhanced version of the standard PCI bus. PCI-X allows a maximum frequency of 133 MHz and is 8 bytes wide, giving a maximum data transfer rate of 1.064 GB/s. In contrast, modern memory chips are capable of transferring data at much higher rates. For example, transfer rates of DDR SDRAMs are up to 2.1 GB/s, and those for RDRAMs are up to 3.2 GB/s.

The mismatch between I/O bus and memory transfer rates is likely to continue, as the main memory transfer rate has been increasing at a steady pace to address the gap between processor and memory speeds, while the I/O bus transfer rate is improving at a lower rate.

Due to this mismatch, a DMA engine cannot place DMA-memory requests on the I/O bus at the rate at which a memory chip can serve them. As a result, the memory chips need to stay in high-power mode for more cycles than necessary to serve a DMA-memory request and thereby waste energy.

Figure 2(a) shows this phenomenon. The most recent RAMBUS chip [22] runs at 1600 MHz frequency and each memory module is capable of transferring 2 bytes per cycle, thus providing a peak transfer rate of 3.2 GB/s (a factor of three more than the bandwidth of a PCI-X bus). The RAM-BUS memory bus is also able to provide this peak bandwidth. Since a large DMA transfer is broken into DMA-memory requests of 8 bytes each, a memory chip can serve each request in only 4 memory cycles. As the PCI-X bus runs at a lower speed, the next request for 8 bytes arrives at the memory chip 8 cycles later. During these 8 cycles, the memory chip is idle but cannot transition to a low-power mode since the idle period is too short to justify the transition [16, 18]. As a result, two-thirds (8 out of 12 cycles) of the active memory energy are wasted. The analysis with other modern memory technologies such as SDRAM is similar but with different absolute numbers (because current DDR SDRAM technology can only provide a 2.1GB/s transfer rate), and Section 5.4 will discuss the effects of memory architecture differences.

Many high-end servers use several I/O buses to achieve a higher I/O transfer rate. For example, Intel's chipsets E8870 and E7500 [14] have support for multiple PCI buses. When DMAs on multiple I/O buses access the same memory chip simultaneously, the waste of active memory cycles is reduced because the memory chip can multiplex between the various I/O buses.

However, since the various I/O devices do not coordinate with each other in accessing the memory bus, having several I/O buses does not fully eliminate the cycle waste. In fact, even when multiple DMA transfers from different I/O buses are directed to the same memory chip, they are typically skewed in time and do not create enough overlap to maximize the utilization of the memory active cycles.

This observation is confirmed in Figure 2(b), which shows the distribution of memory energy spent in various modes in a system with *three* PCI-X buses, according to our detailed trace-driven simulations. For energy management, our simulations assume the dynamic scheme described by Lebeck et al [16]. (We have also tried other schemes, such as the self-tuning dynamic schemes proposed in our previous work [18], but the results were similar since the large size of DMA transfers makes memory energy consumption almost insensitive to the threshold setting.) The details of the workloads and the simulation infrastructure are described in Section 5.1.

The memory energy breakdown shows that a significant amount (48-51%) of the energy is spent when idle in active mode between successive DMA-memory requests of a large DMA transfer operation. In fact, this energy waste is larger than the amount of energy (26-27%) spent when actually accessing memory. In contrast, the energy waste due to waiting for the specified threshold of idle time is only 3-4%.

These results are intuitive since each DMA transfer keeps the accessed memory chip active for a long period of time, a significant fraction of which is wasted between successive DMA-memory requests as shown in Figure 2(a). For example, a 512-byte DMA transfer over a PCI-X bus keeps a 1600-MHz RDRAM memory chip active for 768 (64 × 12) memory cycles. In contrast, the best setting of the threshold value

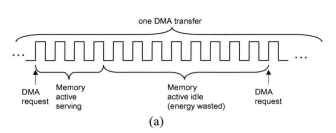

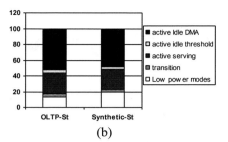

(a)   (b)

Figure 2. (a) Time line showing that the accessed memory chip is idle for two-thirds of the time when serving a DMA transfer. (b) Memory energy breakdown for two workloads. The up-downs denote memory cycles, not power mode transitions. "Active Serving" denotes that the memory is actively serving DMA-memory requests; "Active Idle DMA" denotes that the memory is in active mode but idle between two DMA-memory requests, because the DMA cannot issue requests as fast as the memory chip can serve them; "Active Idle Threshold" denotes that the memory is idle in active mode until a threshold of idle time passes before transitioning into low power modes; "Transition" denotes the energy consumed in transitioning between power modes; "Low Power Modes" denotes the energy consumed in low-power modes.

for transitioning a memory chip from active into low-power modes is usually around 20-30 memory cycles. As a result, the energy waste between successive DMA-memory requests due to the transfer rate mismatch is much larger than that due to idle thresholds.

4 DMA-Aware Memory Energy Management

We propose two techniques to reduce the amount of active idle energy wasted between DMA-memory requests. Both techniques exploit the multiple I/O buses in modern data servers to maximize the *utilization* of the memory-active energy without excessively degrading performance, even in the presence of processor-initiated requests as well. In essence, their goal is to make the DMA-initiated memory accesses more energy-efficient. However, it is still the responsibility of the lower level memory energy management policy, such as the dynamic policy from [16], to manage the actual memory power states.

Note also that both techniques operate on physical pages and, therefore, do not affect the page-fault ratios of data servers. Additionally, as they work at a time granularity that is much smaller than the request service time or the power-mode transition overhead of disk and network devices, they do not increase the energy consumed by these devices.

The next two subsections describe our techniques in detail. For simplicity of our description, when describing each technique, we first present it assuming DMA transfers only, then discuss the coordination with processor-initiated accesses, and finally discuss their complexity and overheads.

4.1 Temporal Alignment of DMA Transfers

4.1.1 Main Idea

The first technique, called *Temporal Alignment (DMA-TA)*, reduces the amount of active energy waste between DMA-memory requests by temporally aligning requests from different I/O buses to the same memory chip. Specifically, the memory controller delays DMA-memory requests directed to

a memory chip in low-power mode, trying to gather enough requests (from other I/O buses) to fully utilize the memory chip active cycles, instead of avoiding power-mode transitioning as previous works on request batching to reduce disk or network energy consumption [7, 11]. When enough DMA-memory requests have been gathered or the access delay exceeds a threshold value, the controller allows the requests through, enabling the memory chip to service the requests back-to-back. Since the first request of a DMA transfer may be delayed and not immediately acknowledged by the memory controller to the DMA engine, subsequent requests of the same DMA transfer operation will not be issued.

Interestingly, after this first gathering of requests, all subsequent requests from the different I/O buses to the chip will be sequenced in *lockstep*; until the end of the entire DMA transfers, the chip will remain active and requests will not be delayed again. (Similarly, when a new DMA transfer starts while others are already in progress, its requests are not delayed at all.) The reason is that the time gap between any two adjacent DMA-memory requests of the same DMA transfer is usually fixed as the corresponding DMA engine moves data from or to the memory. As a result, all the DMA transfers become properly aligned (interleaved) with each other. This is one of the key differences between DMA-TA and traditional request batching [7, 11].

Figure 3 illustrates the case in which the controller is able to gather enough requests to fully utilize the memory chip. In this example, the first three DMA-memory requests, namely DMA_{11}, DMA_{21} and DMA_{31}, that arrive from different I/O buses are not serviced right away; the chip remains in whatever low-power mode it currently is. When the fourth request, DMA_{41}, arrives, the memory chip is activated and allowed to start servicing one request right after the other, wasting no memory cycles. For all these four DMA transfers, subsequent DMA-memory requests, DMA_{ij} ($i = 1 \ldots 4$ and $j > 1$), are in lockstep and are not delayed at all.

The delaying of DMA-memory requests to a memory chip

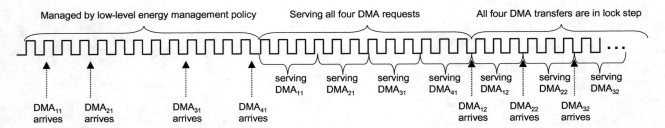

Figure 3. DMA-TA time line for four DMA-memory requests arriving from DMA engines in four different I/O buses to the same memory chip.

in a low-power mode can be implemented by temporarily buffering the requests in the memory controller. As described later, DMA-TA does not delay too many requests for performance reasons, so the space requirement to temporarily buffer these delayed requests is very small. For example, for a system with 1 GB of main memory consisting of 32 32-MB memory chips and the same memory and I/O bus bandwidths as in Figure 2, the memory controller requires at most 768 ($3 \times 8 \times 32$) bytes of buffer space to support request delays.

In contrast to DMA-TA, a simple alternative that only buffers requests on the I/O-device side of PCI bus would not suffice to meet our goals. First, buffering DMA-memory requests to different memory chips is not useful to conserve memory energy. Second, buffering depends on the current mode of the target memory chip. If the target chip is already actively serving one or more DMA transfers, there is no need to delay new DMA-memory requests. Due to these reasons, DMA-memory request buffering should be done by the memory controller and for each memory chip.

4.1.2 Performance Guarantees

Having described the main idea behind DMA-TA, we now determine how long the memory controller can delay the DMA-memory requests directed to a memory chip. Obviously, there is no need to collect more DMA-memory requests to each memory chip than necessary to achieve full utilization of the chip. More interestingly, due to performance concerns, we cannot delay a DMA-memory request (and its corresponding DMA transfer) indefinitely in order to achieve full utilization.

To address this problem, DMA-TA provides a soft performance guarantee for each DMA-memory request. Specifically, it takes an application-specified performance-degradation parameter μ, such that if the average service time for a DMA-memory request is T *without* temporal alignment and power management, it should be no worse than $(1 + \mu)T$ *with* temporal alignment and power management. T can be determined from the memory manufacturer or measured off-line on a real system that uses the same memory chips. The value of μ can be computed by the application designer based on the end-user service-level agreement, which specifies the client-perceived average response time for each client request. For example, the application designer can conduct various measurements (using a method similar to that in [2]) to find

out the correlation between DMA-memory request service time and the client-perceived average response time. For the purposes of this paper, we assume that μ is a user-provided input parameter.

For the sake of describing the performance-guarantee algorithm, let us assume that the sustained transfer rate of main memory is R_m, and that the transfer rate for each I/O bus is R_b. Let the number of I/O buses be r. Further, assume that there are more than R_m/R_b I/O buses, i.e. $r > R_m/R_b$. This assumption is not essential to our algorithm and we make it only for simplicity of description. Let k be the number of I/O buses that can achieve the same bandwidth as the main memory, i.e. $k = \lceil R_m/R_b \rceil$. If the memory controller can group requests from k I/O buses to the same chip, all of its active cycles will be utilized in transferring data. Thus, the memory controller does not need to delay any longer than the time to gather k DMA-memory requests for the same memory chip.

However, it may take excessively long for k such requests to arrive. DMA-TA dynamically determines how long it can wait based on the available total delay, $Slack$, which denotes the total sum of the delays that all requests are allowed without violating the performance guarantee. For example, if l requests have been received so far, we would have $l\mu T$ as the total slack in order to guarantee that the average DMA-memory request service time is within the specified limit $(1 + \mu)T$. A negative value of $Slack$ denotes that the desired performance level is not being maintained. Note that $Slack$ is not meant to represent a level of degradation to end-performance, which would require consideration of request parallelism. Instead, $Slack$ is just the sum of the slacks for each request to provide a performance guarantee for the average DMA-memory request service time.

The amount of slack currently available is updated as follows. Upon the arrival of a new DMA-memory request, the memory controller adds an amount μT of credits to the slack. The controller reduces the slack as requests are delayed by DMA-TA, power-mode transitions, or processor-initiated memory accesses (we discuss these accesses in the next subsection). The slack reductions due to DMA-TA are done by dividing the execution into time intervals or epochs. At the beginning of each epoch, $Slack$ is reduced by $epochLength \times n$, where n is the number of pending DMA-memory requests that are waiting to be serviced and $epochLength$ is the length of the epoch. (As we only use *epochLength* for delay accounting instead of energy management, we find that our results are insensitive to this parameter setting as long as it is not too large.) Intuitively, this approach pessimistically decreases *Slack* assuming that all requests will be delayed by the entire duration of the epoch. Although a worst-case assumption, it makes sure that DMA-TA will not violate the performance guarantee. Furthermore, this approach obviates the need for the controller to update *Slack* after every request. The slack reductions due to power-mode transitions are done by decreasing *Slack* by the time overhead of activating each memory chip (different chips might be in different power modes) times the number of requests pending for it.

Given the current available slack, DMA-TA can dynamically calculate how long a DMA-memory request that finds the corresponding memory chip in low-power mode can wait. Suppose that there are n_i pending DMA-memory requests from the ith I/O bus for $i = 1, 2, \ldots, r$ (each pending request coming from an I/O bus has been issued by a different DMA engine attached to the bus). Let $m = max\{n_i \mid 1 \leq i \leq r\}$. Under these assumptions, $U = mT\lceil r/k \rceil$ represents an upper bound on the time taken to service all the pending requests. To see this more clearly, recall that each DMA-memory request takes T time when no alignment or power management is performed. Since k requests from different I/O buses can be performed in the way shown in Figure 3, k such requests will also take time T. Next, we can divide all pending DMA-memory requests into $\lceil r/k \rceil$ groups such that requests in each group are from different I/O buses. Since each group has at most mk requests, each group can be served in mT time.

Given the value for U, if the memory started to service requests now, the average *additional* delay per pending request would be $U/2$. (Note that early delays are charged via the epoch-based scheme. Here, we only need to charge the queuing delay.) The reason is that the first request serviced would incur zero additional delay, the second one would incur T additional delay, and so on. Based on this observation, a simple mathematical calculation computes the average additional delay of $U/2$. Thus, the total delay for all n pending requests would be $nU/2$. Therefore, the memory chip should start serving requests when $nU/2$ is close to the current *Slack* to avoid exceeding the acceptable performance degradation.

Our extensive simulations confirm that this approach enforces our performance guarantees. In fact, none of the simulations discussed in Section 5 violates such guarantees.

4.1.3 Interaction with Accesses from Processors

DMA-TA may interfere with accesses from processors only when the memory chip is servicing DMA-memory requests. More specifically, when requests are aligned to achieve maximum utilization of the memory-active cycles, there are no cycles left to handle accesses from processors. There are at least a couple of possible solutions to this problem. A simple solution is to always allow accesses from processors to take priority over DMA accesses. In other words, a memory chip always services accesses from processors first, before servicing accesses from DMAs. Another solution is to keep the active memory cycles at most $x\%$ (e.g. 75%) utilized for DMA-memory requests so that the remaining $1 - x\%$ (e.g. 25%) is reserved for accesses from processors. In our evaluation, we use the first method.

Regardless of the solution, processor accesses need to be reflected in the remaining amount of available slack for DMA-memory requests. The way we perform these updates is to decrease *Slack* by the time it takes for the processor accesses to be serviced times the number of DMA-memory requests pending for the corresponding memory chip.

4.1.4 Complexity and Overheads

DMA-TA can be implemented in memory controllers with even little processing power. Many memory controllers (e.g., the Impulse memory controller [24]) already contain low-power processors. Specifically, DMA-TA needs to count the number of pending DMA-memory requests for each memory chip, which requires only one counter per chip. DMA-TA also needs to maintain a counter for the total available slack, which is updated at the beginning of each epoch and after processor-initiated accesses. Whenever a DMA-memory request arrives that finds the corresponding memory chip in low-power mode, DMA-TA needs to compare $nU/2$ with the current value of *Slack* to decide whether the memory chip should start servicing all pending DMA-memory requests. Such an operation requires only one addition and one comparison, since $U/2$ can be pre-computed and $nU/2$ can be computed incrementally using one addition every time a new request arrives. Furthermore, this overhead is amortized over the large DMA transfer; subsequent DMA-memory requests do not perform this comparison, since they are serviced right away when the memory chip is already in active mode. Finally, the controller needs a little buffer space for delayed requests.

4.2 Popularity-based Layout

4.2.1 Main Idea

To increase the opportunity for DMA-TA to reduce memory energy waste, our second technique, called *Popularity-based Layout (PL)*, exploits a common access pattern, namely the "20-80 rule" of many data server workloads. Specifically, many of these workloads exhibit considerable skew of accesses towards a small fraction of the blocks. In other words, a majority of accesses are made to a small fraction of the data. For example, Figure 4 shows the access distribution for an OLTP storage DMA transfer trace collected from a real storage server. As shown in the figure, around 20% of the pages account for 60% of the DMA accesses to the main memory of the storage server.

We can exploit this access pattern in workloads by clustering frequently accessed pages in a small subset of the memory chips, so that more concurrent DMA transfers can arrive at such memory chips and the number of isolated transfers at

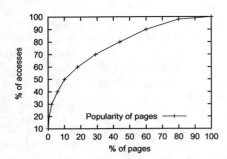

Figure 4. CDF of the popularity of pages in an OLTP storage DMA transfer workload. A point (x, y) in the curve indicates that $x\%$ of the pages receive $y\%$ of the DMA accesses.

other chips can be reduced. The reason this layout increases the DMA-TA energy savings is that the memory controller can temporally align more DMA-memory requests directed towards the "hot" memory chips. Further, the number of DMA-memory requests to "cold" chips is reduced, allowing them to stay in low-power modes for a longer period of time. As a result, the overall memory energy consumption is reduced.

To identify hot pages, our PL technique uses a few bits to keep track of the DMA reference counts (number of accesses by DMAs instead of processors) for each memory page. The reference counts can be maintained either inside the memory controller or as a part of the page table. To adapt to workload changes, these reference bits should be "aged" periodically by either resetting them to zero or right-shifting them by one.

Dynamically, the memory controller can build statistical access distribution histograms to record the percentage of pages with different popularity and the percentage of accesses to pages with different popularity. Based on such histograms, pages can be placed into memory chips according to their popularity values. For example, let N be the total number of memory chips. We divide the memory chips into multiple groups. Let N_{hot} be the fraction of chips such that if the most popular pages are put in the N_{hot} chips, they account for p percentage (e.g. 60%) of the total number of DMA-memory requests in the last epoch (time period), where p is a tunable parameter. The remaining $N - N_{hot}$ chips comprises the last group, the "cold" group.

For the N_{hot} hot chips, we can further divide them into $K-1$ groups, namely G_1 with only 1 memory chip, G_2 with 2 chips, G_3 with 4 chips,..., G_{K-1} with $2^{\lfloor \log(pN_{hot}) \rfloor - 2}$ chips. The K-th group G_K is the cold group. PL associates a popularity ordering among these K groups. We designate that group G_i is more popular than G_j if $i < j$. Pages are placed into groups according to their popularity values. Our grouping of pages in PL is a key difference between ours and previous popularity-based layout approaches, e.g. [21].

To adapt to workload changes, memory pages are reorganized periodically by the memory controller via page migration. Page migration is based on dividing the execution of the

application into intervals (multiple epochs). At the beginning of each interval, the layout is recomputed to maintain the same invariant. The memory controller follows a simple algorithm to perform the shuffling, such that the number of swaps required is less than or equal to the number of pages which are in a group that does not match their popularity value. Pages that are in the wrong group are migrated to the correct group based on the new layout. For each page migration, its content is first copied into a free page in the destination chip.

To avoid affecting the application, the memory controller and the operating system need to cooperate. A simple method would be for the memory controller to interrupt the processor whenever a page was migrated. The operating system would then update the page table accordingly. However, this approach would involve excessive overhead. To avoid this overhead, the memory controller must store a small table of $< old\_location, new\_location >$ page translations. Before the page table is modified, the memory controller simply redirects accesses to the old location of a migrated page to its new location. In this approach, the page table would only be modified when the translation table is completely filled or at the end of the current interval. Thus, the cost of the interrupts and the page table updates can be amortized across a number of migrations. In fact, the amount of overhead can be adjusted by increasing/decreasing the size of the translation table or the length of the intervals. By adjusting these parameters, we believe that this overhead can be made negligible, so our simulations do not account for it.

Since page migration incurs energy and time overheads, maintaining a perfectly accurate popularity ordering would be excessively expensive, offsetting the benefit of popularity-based layout. This is one of the reasons that groups are not of equal size. Instead, the sizes of the first $K - 1$ groups follow an exponential curve in order to accommodate the popularity distribution shown in Figure 4. The rationale is that pages accessed 8 times are not necessarily "hotter" than pages that have been accessed 10 times, for example.

Interestingly, we find that using only 2 groups provides the best result in energy conservation given a specified performance goal, making the PL technique simple to implement with minimum page-migration traffic. The reason is that, with only 2 groups, there are only a hot group for the pages that contribute to a p percentage of accesses and a cold group for all remaining pages.

4.2.2 Hiding Migration Energy and Time Overheads

Page migration may interfere with memory accesses from DMAs and processors. One possible optimization is to perform page migration in small chunks, such as cache-line or 8-byte chunks. The small granularity can leverage those memory cycles during which the involved memory chips are idle in active mode either waiting for DMA-memory requests or waiting to go down to low-power mode, so that they incur no extra energy and time overhead. Furthermore, the page accesses can be performed by the memory controller itself with-

Trace	Content	Description
OLTP-St	Memory accesses from network and disk DMAs	Collected from a real storage server that is connected to a database server running IBM DB2 with a TPC-C benchmark.
Synthetic-St	Memory accesses from network and disk DMAs	Synthetically generated based on distribution observed in real systems.
OLTP-Db	Memory accesses from processors and network DMAs	Collected from a real database server (IBM DB2) running on the Simics simulator [19] with Gems timing model [20], running a TPC-C benchmark.
Synthetic-Db	Memory accesses from processors and network DMAs	Synthetically generated based on distribution observed in real systems.

Table 2. Traces used in our evaluation.

out involving the processor or any DMA engine. Currently, these optimizations are still being implemented in our simulator. When such optimizations are implemented, we expect our results will be better than those we present in Section 5.

4.2.3 Complexity and Overhead

Similar to DMA-TA, PL can also be implemented in a simple way by smart memory controllers. The memory controller needs to use a counter to record the number of DMA-memory requests for each page during an interval. To reduce the space requirement of these counters, we can increase the granularity from a page to a memory region which may consist of tens (e.g. 32) of pages. Also, we can remember the access counter for only those recently accessed pages. These methods are likely to work well since DMA transfers are usually at large granularity with good temporal locality in memory addresses. Each DMA-memory request requires a hash-based lookup by the memory controller to find and increment the corresponding page's reference counter. Since subsequent requests of the same DMA transfer are typically for the same page, a few recently accessed counters can be kept in a small cache as shortcuts for fast lookups and increments.

Finally, the memory controller needs to implement the migration algorithm and the table of page translations. The algorithm only runs at the beginning of an interval. The table of translations is similar to equivalent structures in previously proposed smart memory controllers [24].

5 Evaluation Results

5.1 Methodology

We evaluate our DMA-aware memory energy management techniques using an accurate trace-driven simulator that integrates several component-based simulators including: (1) the widely used disk-array simulator DiskSim [10], which models disk accesses very accurately; (2) a trace-driven main memory simulator that models both timing and energy based on the latest 512-Mb 1600-MHz RDRAM specification shown in Table 1; and (3) a network and disk DMA simulator. The simulated system has 32 memory chips. We simulate three 133-MHz 64-bit PCI-X buses attached to the memory bus. The default DMA-memory request size is 8 bytes, whereas the default number of groups for PL is 2. Our simulator is driven by

memory access traces that include accesses from both processors and DMAs.

We use two sets of traces, each set representing a different type of workload. The first set includes two memory access traces representing memory workloads of storage servers. These traces contain accesses from network and disk DMAs only, because the processor in a typical storage server does not do any processing of the data requested by clients. The second set includes two memory access traces representing memory workloads of database servers, which contain memory accesses from both processors and network DMAs. The processor accesses are for 64-byte cache lines. Each set includes a trace collected from a real system and a synthetically generated trace. The OLTP-St trace contains network and disk DMA operations at average rates of 45.0 transfers/ms and 16.7 transfers/ms, respectively. The OLTP-Db trace has network DMA operations and processor accesses at average rates of 100.0 transfers/ms and 23,300 accesses/ms, respectively. The synthetic traces assume a Zipf distribution of page popularity with $\alpha = 1$, a Poisson DMA transfer arrival rate with an average of 100 transfers/ms, and a Poisson processor access rate with an average of 10000 accesses/ms (Synthetic-Db only). The synthetic traces allow us to easily vary the characteristics of the workloads, as we do in Section 5.4. Table 2 summarizes the characteristics of the four traces.

In our simulations, the dynamic memory energy management scheme [16] is always used as the low-level memory energy management policy. Most of our results show the energy savings when this low-level policy is enhanced with our DMA-aware energy management techniques. For this reason, we refer to the system using the low-level policy only as the "baseline" in this section.

Our results show the behavior of our techniques with respect to the baseline, focusing on the effect of the acceptable performance degradation, the workload intensity, the number of processor-initiated memory accesses per DMA transfer, and the ratio between memory and I/O transfer rates.

It is important to note that from now on we express the acceptable performance degradation as the limit on the client-perceived average response time degradation. As such, we refer to it as CP-Limit. CP-Limit is a more intuitive and meaningful value than μ (the acceptable degradation in the

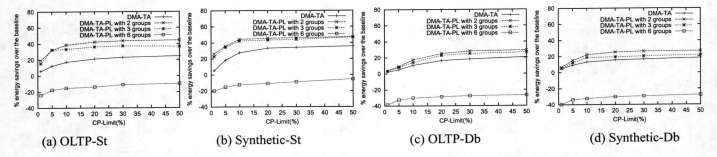

(a) OLTP-St	(b) Synthetic-St	(c) OLTP-Db	(d) Synthetic-Db

Figure 5. Memory energy savings by the DMA-aware techniques compared to the baseline low-level energy management. The X-axis denotes the maximum *client-perceived* average response time degradation, whereas the Y-axis shows the percentage of energy saving over the baseline (the dynamic energy management scheme [16]). The curves labeled "DMA-TA" show the results for DMA-TA only, whereas those labeled "DMA-TA-PL" show the results when both of our techniques are used.

average response time of each DMA-memory request), the actual parameter that DMA-TA takes. We transform CP-Limit into μ off-line by determining how much each DMA-memory request would have to be slowed down to achieve a client-perceived degradation of CP-Limit. Our results show that our techniques never violate CP-Limit.

5.2 Overall Results

Figure 5 shows the percentage energy savings of our DMA-aware techniques as a function of CP-Limit, compared to a system that only uses the baseline policy. The graphs show results for DMA-TA-PL (the combination of DMA-TA and PL schemes) using various numbers of popularity groups. All results for the DMA-TA and PL schemes provide performance degradation within the specified CP-Limit limit. (Due to space limitations, we do not show the actual performance degradation results here.) Because baseline does not provide any performance guarantees, our techniques' results are always compared to the same baseline result.

From these graphs, it is clear that our DMA-aware techniques can conserve significantly more energy than a memory energy management policy that is oblivious to DMA transfers. For example, DMA-TA-PL (with 2 groups) results in 38.6% less energy consumption than the baseline for a maximum 10% client-perceived response time degradation for the OLTP-St workload. The reason is that DMA-TA-PL is very effective at temporally aligning DMA transfers, thereby reducing the amount of memory energy waste.

The results also show that DMA-TA-PL is very effective at increasing the energy savings with respect to DMA-TA alone. Take the OLTP-St workload as an example. DMA-TA alone can achieve only moderate (6-24.8%) energy savings over the baseline, whereas DMA-TA-PL can provide high (19.4-44.5%) energy savings. The reason is that PL significantly increases the opportunity for DMA-TA to gather more DMA-memory requests to "hot" chips.

Interestingly, our results indicate that PL behaves best with just 2 groups. Considering the OLTP-St workload and a CP-Limit of 10% for example, we can see that DMA-TA-PL with 2 groups provides 38.6% energy savings over the baseline,

whereas it achieves only 33.4% and -15.2% savings with 3 and 6 groups, respectively. This effect is caused by the energy and time overheads of page migration. With more groups, the amount of page shuffling increases, offsetting the benefit of PL. For this reason, from now on we only present DMA-TA-PL results for 2 groups.

It is also important to note that, as CP-Limit increases, both DMA-TA and DMA-TA-PL conserve increasingly more energy. This result was expected, since DMA-TA can delay DMA-memory requests for a longer time, trying to gather more of them. The increases in energy savings are substantial up to 10% performance degradation. Beyond this point, the energy savings increase much more slowly. The reason is that, after enough requests have been gathered to achieve maximum memory utilization, there is no benefit in delaying requests longer. This behavior is actually quite different from those of the request batching approaches studied in previous work for processor or disk energy management.

Finally, these results show that our techniques behave well regardless of whether the workload includes processor-initiated memory accesses. In particular, the results for OLTP-Db and Synthetic-Db show lower but still significant energy savings, especially for DMA-TA-PL with 2 groups. Energy savings are lower for database servers than for storage servers, because processor-initiated accesses in the former servers consume some of the idle cycles when the memory is active between DMA-memory requests. Overall, the trends we see are exactly the same in both types of servers. For this reason, the following subsections focus only on storage servers.

5.3 Analysis of Results

To further understand the reasons behind the energy savings produced by our techniques, we compare the memory energy breakdowns of the baseline, DMA-TA, and DMA-TA-PL schemes for 10% CP-Limit. As shown in Figure 6, while the active energy spent on serving requests remains the same, there is a significant reduction in the energy wasted when chips are active but idle between successive DMA-memory requests. As an additional benefit from our DMA-TA and PL

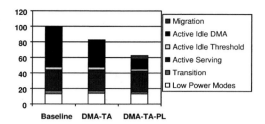

Figure 6. Energy breakdowns of OLTP-St with 10% CP-Limit. Each energy component has the same meaning as in Figure 2(b), except for the migration energy of DMA-TA-PL.

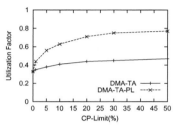

Figure 7. Utilization factors of DMA-TA and DMA-TA-PL for OLTP-St with 10% CP-Limit.

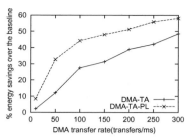

Figure 8. Energy savings as a function of workload intensity for Synthetic-St.

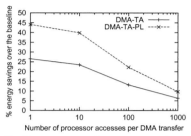

Figure 9. Energy savings as a function of number of processor accesses per DMA transfer for Synthetic-Db.

techniques, the number of power-mode transitions is also decreased, which leads to reduced transition energy. However, this effect is essentially negligible in our results.

Comparing DMA-TA-PL with DMA-TA, we can see that the former technique reduces the waste of active energy further than the latter one. In fact, it is interesting to see that the energy overhead of migration is more than offset by the reduction in active energy waste.

As the main benefit of DMA-TA and PL comes from increased concurrency and improved utilization of active memory cycles, we introduce a metric to measure these effects explicitly, the utilization factor (uf):

$$uf = \frac{T_{useful}}{T_{tot}}$$

where T_{tot} is the total amount of time during which some DMA transfer is in progress and so the accessed memory chips are in the active mode. This includes the time between successive DMA-memory requests for a given transfer operation. T_{useful} is the time during which the memory is actually serving some DMA-memory request. For example, if the memory transfer rate is three times the transfer rate of the I/O bus and no two DMA-memory requests are interleaved, $uf = 0.33$. Clearly, the maximum value of uf is 1.

Figure 7 shows the utilization factors of DMA-TA and DMA-TA-PL, as a function of CP-Limit. Without our DMA-aware techniques, the utilization factors are only around 0.33, which means that 67% of the active memory energy is wasted. In contrast, with DMA-TA-PL, the utilization factors of OLTP-St are improved to 0.63 with 10% CP-Limit and 0.75 with 30% CP-Limit. These results indicate an improved uti-

lization of active cycles. Similar to the energy savings of Figure 5, the utilization factors increase rapidly with CP-Limit at first, but more slowly for CP-Limits larger than 10%.

5.4 Sensitivity Analysis

This subsection evaluates the sensitivity of our techniques to workload and hardware characteristics. We use 10% CP-Limit and our default parameters, unless otherwise specified.

Workload intensity. Figure 8 shows the effect of varying the workload intensity of the Synthetic-St trace. We vary the intensity by varying the average DMA transfer arrival rate. Recall that our default average arrival rate in this synthetic trace is 100 transfers/ms. The results show that DMA-TA and DMA-TA-PL can save more energy over the baseline for more intensive workloads. The reason is that more intensive workloads provide more opportunity for request aligning to reduce active energy waste. As one would expect, the benefit of DMA-TA and PL increases more slowly at higher intensities, since some DMA transfers are already naturally aligned in the baseline system at those intensities.

Intensity of processor accesses. A comparison between the storage and database server results in Figure 5 shows that processor-initiated accesses reduce the energy savings achievable by our techniques. These accesses consume some of the active idle energy that our techniques seek to eliminate.

Figure 9 illustrates this effect more clearly. The figure shows the energy savings produced by DMA-TA and DMA-TA-PL, as a function of the number of processor accesses

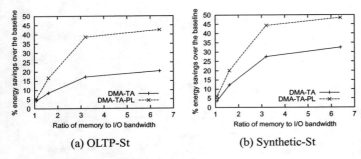

(a) OLTP-St   (b) Synthetic-St

Figure 10. Energy savings as a function of the ratio between memory and I/O bus bandwidth.

(each to a 64-byte cache line) per DMA transfer. To generate the figure, we injected different numbers of processor accesses per DMA transfer into Synthetic-Db. The figure shows that indeed energy savings drop significantly with an increase in processor accesses. However, even when the number of accesses is in the hundreds, the energy savings are still significant. For comparison, the OLTP-Db trace collected from a commercial database server (IBM DB2) has an average of 233 processor accesses per DMA transfer.

Ratio of memory and I/O transfer rates. Finally, we study the effect of the ratio between memory and I/O transfer rates. Recall that the results above assume that the I/O bus bandwidth is 1 GB/s (the bandwidth of the PCI-X bus), and that memory can transfer data at rate of 3.2 GB/s (the data rate of RDRAM). So the ratio between the two is around 3.

Figure 10 shows the results for OLTP-St and Synthetic-St. To vary the ratio, we kept the memory bandwidth fixed at 3.2 GB/s and varied the I/O bus bandwidth (0.5 GB/s, 1 GB/s, 2GB/s, and 3 GB/s). When the ratio is close to 1, i.e. the memory and the I/O bus have about the same transfer rate, DMA-TA and PL provide small (around 5%) energy savings, which is expectable. As we increase the ratio, the amount of energy conserved by DMA-TA and DMA-TA-PL also quickly increases, since the active energy waste starts to dominate. Because PL provides greater opportunities to align requests, DMA-TA-PL improves faster than DMA-TA for higher ratios.

6 Related Work

This section discusses closely related works that are not detailed in earlier sections. The discussion is divided into works that relate to memory energy management in general, temporal alignment, and popularity-based layouts in the main memory and disks.

Memory energy management. In addition to the works described in Sections 1 and 2, Fan et al. have investigated memory controller policies for determining chip power states based on the estimated idle time between accesses [9]. Delaluz et al. have studied compiler-directed [5] and operating-system-based approaches [3] to conserve memory energy. Recently, Huang et al. proposed a power-aware virtual memory imple-

mentation to conserve memory energy [12]. Li et al. considered performance-directed memory energy management [18]. Zhou et al. proposed using applications' miss ratio curves to direct memory energy management [25].

Our work differs from these prior works in that it focuses on DMA-aware memory energy management, which is necessary to conserve memory energy in data servers.

Temporal Alignment. Our DMA-TA technique shares some similarity to request batching used in disk energy management [11] and processor energy management [7]. For example, in [7], the requests sent to a Web server are batched by the network interface card to increase host processor idle times. DMA-TA differs from these works in two respects: (1) Previous works batch request to minimize the energy and time spent in powering devices up and down, whereas our techniques increase the level of concurrency in DMA transfers by sequencing multiple DMA operations in lockstep to reduce the amount of energy waste due to the mismatch between memory and I/O bus bandwidths; and (2) In previous works, it is typically beneficial to batch as many requests as possible as long as performance is not significantly affected. In our techniques, batching more requests than the maximum level of concurrency supported by the memory device has little benefit, since the energy cost for transitioning between power modes is negligible compared to the energy consumption of a large DMA operation, as we explain in Section 3.

Popularity-based Layout. Lebeck et al. have conducted a preliminary investigation of popularity-based layouts to allow some memory devices to stay in low-power modes for a longer time [16]. Their results for SPEC benchmarks showed that a popularity-based layout is not very helpful. Therefore, they did not propose or evaluate a realistic popularity-based layout strategy. Delaluz et al. have studied compiler and operating-system-based strategies to place frequently accessed data together in a few memory modules again for scientific applications [3, 4, 5, 6]. A similar idea has been explored by Pinheiro and Bianchini in the context of disk array energy management [21], where popular files are migrated to a subset of disks to skew the workload, and thus allow the remaining disks to conserve energy.

Unlike the works that use popularity-based layouts to create skewed loads on devices, we use such layouts for a different purpose: to increase the opportunity for temporal alignment of DMA operations for data servers. As such, our PL technique can be relatively simple and incur only small overheads. Further, while previous work on popularity-based memory layouts follows a strict popularity-based ordering, our PL technique uses a logarithmic order based on the popularity distribution characteristics of real workloads.

7 Conclusion

To the best of our knowledge, this paper is the first to study memory energy management for DMA-initiated memory accesses. These accesses have different characteristics and implications for energy management than processor-initiated accesses. We characterized the effect of DMA accesses on memory energy and showed that, due to the mismatch between memory and I/O bus bandwidths, significant energy is wasted when memory is idle but still active during large DMA transfers. To reduce this waste, we proposed two novel performance-directed energy management techniques, temporal alignment and popularity-based layout, which increase the level of concurrency between multiple DMA transfers from different I/O buses to the same memory chip. Our results on a detailed trace-driven simulator with storage and database server traces showed that our techniques can effectively minimize the amount of idle energy waste during DMA transfers and, consequently, conserve as much as 38.6% more memory energy than previous approaches for only a small degradation in performance.

Since memory accesses from DMAs are dominant in data servers such as storage and database servers, our work takes a significant step forward in memory energy management for these servers, an important class of applications in which energy consumption is one of the major concerns.

We envision several directions for future work. First, we plan to conduct run-time cost-benefit analysis before page migration, so that migration is performed only when it is beneficial. Second, we will explore other workloads, such as TPC-H workloads, and evaluate them in a whole-system simulator that can run a real commercial database server. Third, we are in the process of investigating the optimizations described in Section 4.2 to reduce migration overheads.

References

[1] F. Catthoor, S. Wuytack, E. D. Greef, F. Balasa, L. Nachtergaele, and A. Vandecappelle. Custom memory management methodology exploration of memory organization for embedded multimedia systems design. In *Kluwer Academic Publishers*, 1998.

[2] I. Cohen, J. S. Chase, M. Goldszmidt, T. Kelly, and J. Symons. Correlating instrumentation data to system states: A building block for automated diagnosis and control. In *Proceedings of the International Symposium on Operating Systems Design and Implementation (OSDI)*, pages 231–244, December 2004.

[3] V. Delaluz, M. Kandemir, and I. Kolcu. Automatic data migration for reducing energy consumption in multi-bank memory systems. In *Proceedings of the 39th Design Automation Conference*, pages 213–218, June 2002.

[4] V. Delaluz, M. Kandemir, N. Vijaykrishnan, and M. J. Irwin. Energy-oriented compiler optimizations for partitioned memory architectures. In *Proceedings of the International Conference on Compilers, Architecture, and Synthesis for Embedded Systems*, pages 138–147, August 2000.

[5] V. Delaluz, M. Kandemir, N. Vijaykrishnan, A. Sivasubramniam, and M. J. Irwin. Hardware and software techniques for controlling dram power modes. *IEEE Transactions on Computers*, 50(11), 2001.

[6] V. Delaluz, A. Sivasubramaniam, M. Kandemir, N. Vijaykrishnan, and M. J. Irwin. Scheduler-based dram energy management. In *Proceedings of the 39th Design Automation Conference*, pages 697–702, June 2002.

[7] E. Elnozahy, M. Kistler, and R. Rajamony. Energy conservation policies for web servers. In *Proceedings of the 4th USENIX Symposium on Internet Technologies and Systems*, March 2003.

[8] EMC Symmetrix DMX 3000 Specification Sheet. http://www.emc.com/products/systems/symmetrix/symmetri _DMX1000/pdf/DMX3000.pdf, April 2005.

[9] X. Fan, C. Ellis, and A. Lebeck. Memory controller policies for dram power management. In *Proceedings of the International Symposium on Low Power Electronics and Design*, pages 129–134, August 2001.

[10] G. R. Ganger, B. L. Worthington, and Y. N. Patt. The DiskSim simulation environment - version 2.0 reference manual, December 1999.

[11] T. Heath, E. Pinheiro, J. Hom, U. Kremer, and R. Bianchini. Application transformations for energy and performance-aware device management. In *Proceedings of the International Conference on Parallel Architectures and Compilation Techniques*, pages 121–130, September 2002.

[12] H. Huang, P. Pillai, and K. G. Shin. Design and implementation of power-aware virtual memory. In *Proceedings of the USENIX Annual Technical Conference*, pages 57–70, June 2003.

[13] IBM eServer p5 595 Model 9119-595 Executive Summary. http://www.tpc.org/results/individualresults/IBM/IBM _595_64_20041118_ES.pdf, May 2005.

[14] Intel chipsets. http://www.intel.com/products/server/chipsets/index.htm.

[15] M. T. Kandemir, N. Vijaykrishnan, M. J. Irwin, and W. Ye. Influence of compiler optimizations on system power. In *Proceedings of the 37th Design Automation Conference*, June 2000.

[16] A. R. Lebeck, X. Fan, H. Zeng, and C. S. Ellis. Power aware page allocation. In *Proceedings of the International Conference on Architectural Support for Programming Languages and Operating Systems (ASPLOS)*, pages 105–116, November 2000.

[17] C. Lefurgy, K. Rajamani, F. Rawson, W. Felter, M. Kistler, and T. W. Keller. Energy management for commercial servers. *IEEE Computer*, 36(12):39–48, December 2003.

[18] X. Li, Z. Li, F. M. David, P. Zhou, Y. Zhou, S. V. Adve, and S. Kumar. Performance directed energy management for main memory and disks. In *Proceedings of the 11th International Conference on Architectural Support for Programming Languages and Operating Systems (ASPLOS)*, pages 271–283, October 2004.

[19] P. S. Magnusson, M. Christensson, J. Eskilson, D. Forsgren, G. Hallberg, J. Hogberg, F. Larsson, A. Moestedt, and B. Werner. Simics: A full system simulation platform. *IEEE Computer*, 35(2):50–58, 2002.

[20] M. M. Martin, D. J. Sorin, B. M. Beckmann, M. R. Marty, M. Xu, A. R. Alameldeen, K. E. Moore, M. D. Hill, and D. A. Wood. Multifacet's general execution-driven multiprocessor simulator (gems) toolset. In *Computer Architecture News*, 2005.

[21] E. Pinheiro and R. Bianchini. Energy conservation techniques for disk array-based servers. In *Proceedings of the International Conference on Supercomputing*, July 2004.

[22] Rambus. RDRAM. http://www.rambus.com, 1999.

[23] Storage Systems Division. Adaptive power management for mobile hard drives. IBM White Paper, 1999.

[24] L. Zhang, Z. Fang, M. Parker, B. Mathew, L. Schaelicke, J. Carter, W. Hsieh, and S. McKee. The impulse memory controller. *IEEE Transactions on Computers, Special Issue on Advances in High Performance Memory Systems*, pages 1117–1132, November 2001.

[25] P. Zhou, V. Pandey, J. Sundaresan, A. Raghuraman, Y. Zhou, and S. Kumar. Dynamic tracking of page miss ratio curve for memory management. In *Proceedings of the 11th International Conference on Architectural Support for Programming Languages and Operating Systems (ASPLOS)*, October 2004.

Session 5:
Memory Systems

Increasing the Cache Efficiency by Eliminating Noise

Prateek Pujara and Aneesh Aggarwal
Department of Electrical and Computer Engineering
Binghamton University, Binghamton, NY 13902
{prateek,aneesh}@binghamton.edu

Abstract

Caches are very inefficiently utilized because not all the excess data fetched into the cache, to exploit spatial locality, is utilized. We define cache utilization as the percentage of data brought into the cache that is actually used. Our experiments showed that Level 1 data cache has a utilization of only about 57%. In this paper, we show that the useless data in a cache block (cache noise) is highly predictable. This can be used to bring only the to-be-referenced data into the cache on a cache miss, reducing the energy, cache space, and bandwidth wasted on useless data. Cache noise prediction is based on the last words usage history of each cache block. Our experiments showed that a code-context predictor is the best performing predictor and has a predictability of about 95%. In a code context predictor, each cache block belongs to a code context determined by the upper order PC bits of the instructions that fetched the cache block. When applying cache noise prediction to L1 data cache, we observed about 37% improvement in cache utilization, and about 23% and 28% reduction in cache energy consumption and bandwidth requirement, respectively. Cache noise mispredictions increased the miss rate by 0.1% and had almost no impact on instructions per cycle (IPC) count. When compared to a sub-blocked cache, fetching the to-be-referenced data resulted in 97% and 44% improvement in miss rate and cache utilization, respectively. The sub-blocked cache had a bandwidth requirement about 35% of the cache noise prediction based approach.

Keywords: Cache Noise, Block Size, Cache Organization, Spatial Locality, Hardware Prefetching

1. Introduction

Caches exploit spatial locality by also fetching the words adjacent to the word for which the miss occurred. This can result in considerable noise (words that are not required) being brought into the cache. *We define cache utilization as the percentage of the useful words out of the total words brought into the cache.* Our studies show that with a block size of 32 bytes, cache utilization for the Level 1 data cache is only about 57% for the SPEC 2K benchmarks (a result also observed previously by Burger et. al. [2] and others). Lower cache utilization results in energy, bandwidth, and precious cache space being spent for useless words. Improving cache utilization, by fetching only the to-be-referenced words can lower energy consumption (by avoiding wastage of energy on useless words), improve performance (by making more cache space available for compression), and facilitate complexity-effective bus design (by reducing the bandwidth requirement between different levels of cache).

Spatial locality in programs can be further exploited by increasing the cache block size. Larger cache blocks also reduce the tag overhead. However, they increase the bandwidth requirement (between the different levels of cache) and the cache noise. On the other hand, smaller cache blocks reduce the cache noise, however,

at the expense of larger tag overheads and lower spatial locality exploitation. Sub-blocking is used to mitigate the limitations of larger blocks. In sub-blocked caches, sub-blocks (which are portions of the larger cache block) are fetched on demand. However, sub-blocking can result in significant increase in cache miss rate and cache noise if words are accessed from different sub-blocks. Other alternatives [18, 20] are to dynamically adapt the block size to the spatial locality exhibited by the application, still bringing in contiguous words. In this paper, we investigate prediction techniques (called cache noise prediction) that fetch only the to-be-referenced words (which may be in non-contiguous locations) in a cache block. This technique is an attractive alternative to sub-blocking for larger cache blocks because it has the benefit of reducing the bandwidth requirement, while avoiding the miss rate and cache noise impact of sub-blocking.

Cache noise predictor considers the usage history of the words (defined by the offsets of the words that are actually used) in the cache blocks. We investigated three different kinds of cache noise predictors. The first predictor – *phase context predictor (PCP)* – bases its prediction on the words usage history in the most recently evicted cache block. The second predictor – *memory context predictor (MCP)* – bases its prediction on the words usage history of the most recently evicted cache block in a particular memory context, defined as contiguous memory locations. The third predictor – *code context predictor (CCP)* – bases its prediction on the words usage history of the most recently evicted cache block that was fetched by a program code context, defined as a contiguous set of instructions. Even though the cache noise predictor can be used for any cache, we focus on Level 1 data cache. Our experiments showed that, even a simple last words usage CCP predictor (which we found to be the best performing predictor) gives a correct cache noise predictability of about 95%. We implemented the *CCP* cache noise predictor for L1 data cache and observed that its utilization increased by about 37% and the bandwidth requirement between the L1 and L2 cache reduced by about 28%. Cache noise mispredictions increased the miss rate by only about 0.1%, resulting in almost zero reduction in IPC.

The contributions of this paper are:

1. Illustrating the high predictability of cache noise, proposing efficient cache noise predictor implementations, and showing the benefits of cache noise prediction based fetching of words in terms of cache utilization, cache power consumption, and bandwidth requirement.
2. Illustrating the benefits of cache noise prediction based fetching of words in reducing the bandwidth requirement and cache pollution effects of hardware prefetching mechanisms.
3. Investigating cache noise prediction based fetching of words as an alternative to sub-blocking.
4. Investigating profiling to further improve the prediction capabilities of the predictors.

The rest of the paper is organized as follows. Section 2 presents the motivation behind increasing the cache utilization and discusses the intuition behind the prediction mechanisms proposed in this paper.

147

Section 3 discusses the implementation of the *CCP* predictor. Section 4 presents the related work. Section 5 presents the experimental setup and the results. Section 6 presents the application of cache noise prediction to hardware prefetching. Section 7 investigates cache noise prediction based fetching of words as an alternative to sub-blocking. Section 8 presents the results of profiling to improve predictor efficiency. Section 9 presents the prediction accuracy results for different sized cache blocks. Finally, we conclude in Section 10.

2. Cache Utilization and Cache Noise Prediction

2.1 Cache Utilization

We define cache utilization as the percentage of words brought into the cache that is actually used. To motivate why techniques increasing the cache utilization should be investigated, we present the level 1 data cache (in this paper, we focus only on level 1 data cache) utilization statistics for the SPEC 2K benchmarks. For the experiments, we ran trace-driven simulations for 500M instructions after skipping the first 3B instructions, for a 32-bit PISA architecture. We used a 4-way set associative, 16KB L1 data cache with a block size of 32 bytes. To measure cache utilization, we divide the total number of unique words touched in the cache by the total words brought into the cache. Figure 1 presents the results of the cache utilization measurement. Figure 1 shows that the cache utilization is bad for almost all the benchmarks (except gcc, applu, wupwise, and mgrid). The average cache utilization is about 42% for the integer benchmarks and about 69% for the floating point benchmarks. Overall, the average cache utilization is only about 57%. An interesting point to be noted in Figure 1 is that the average cache utilization is noticeably lower for integer benchmarks than the floating point benchmarks. This is because the floating point benchmarks access data more sequentially than integer benchmarks and because the floating point benchmarks load and store a considerable number of *doubles* (which occupy two words), resulting in more words being accessed and a better cache utilization.

2.2 Cache Noise Prediction

We predict the cache noise based on the history of words accessed in the cache blocks, assuming that programs may repeat the pattern of memory references. This is the same intuition behind the various memory address predictors [1, 6]. First, we discuss the advantages and the disadvantages of the two different words usage histories that can be used for prediction – *eviction time history* and *current history*. In *eviction time history*, the words usage history used for prediction is the words accessed in the cache block that was most recently evicted. In the *current history* method, the words usage history used for prediction is the words currently accessed in the cache block that was most recently fetched. *Eviction time history* has the advantage that the entire words usage history for a cache block is available before a prediction is made. However, the disadvantage of *eviction time history* is that the cache blocks brought into the cache may use a stale history for prediction – because a long time may have passed since the last cache block eviction, or may use an outdated history – because the cache blocks being evicted currently have a words usage pattern that is no longer valid. *Current history* has the advantage of more up-to-date words usage history, but suffers from not knowing the entire set of words that will be used in a cache block. Our experiments showed that an *eviction time history* predictor performed better than a *current history* predictor.

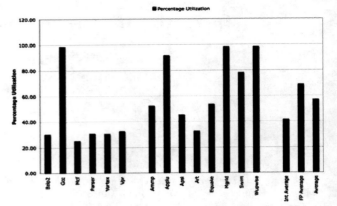

Figure 1: Level 1 Data Cache Utilization for Spec 2K benchmarks

In *eviction time history* predictors, the words usage of the cache blocks is recorded as they are accessed and the predictor is updated when a cache block is evicted. We experimented with three cache noise predictors. The first predictor – *phase context predictor (PCP)* – records the words usage history of the most recently evicted cache block and makes the prediction based on that. The second predictor – *memory context predictor (MCP)* – bases its prediction on the assumption that the data accessed from a contiguous location of memory (called memory context) will always be accessed in the same fashion. C*ode context predictor (CCP)* – bases its prediction on the assumption that any instruction in a particular portion of code (called code context) will always access the data in the same pattern. A code context is defined by the upper order bits of the instruction PC, and a memory context is defined by the upper order bits of the memory address. Here, we explain the functioning of the CCP predictor, which can be easily modified for other predictors.

Figure 2 shows the working of the *CCP* predictor for 3 code contexts X, Y, and Z, given by the upper address bits 100110, 101001, and 101110, respectively. A cache block belongs to a code context if it was fetched into the cache (on a cache miss) by a memory instruction in that code context. For instance, any cache block fetched due to a cache miss generated by an instruction with higher order PC bits as 100110 will belong to code context X. *CCP* predictor records the words usage history of the most recently evicted cache block in a code context, and uses it to make predictions for any cache misses originating out of that code context. For instance, in Figure 2, when instruction I_n (which belongs to code context X) generates a miss, the words usage history of the code context X is checked. Accordingly, only the first two words of the cache block A are fetched into the cache. However, the cache block A evicts a cache block in the code context Z. Hence, the words usage history of the evicted cache block is used to update the predictor table for code context Z. Subsequently, when instruction I_x (which belongs to code context Z) misses in the cache, only the first word in the block is fetched.

To measure predictabilities of the predictor, the predicted words usage history for a cache block is remembered when it is brought into the cache. Words usage history may not be available if no cache blocks have been evicted in a particular context, resulting in "no predictions". We observed that the average "no prediction" was almost zero for all the benchmarks. When a cache block is evicted, the words accessed for the block are compared with the remembered words usage history. If the words accessed in a cache block are a subset of the predicted words in the cache block (for instance the prediction is 1011, and the usage is 1001), then we consider it as correct prediction because no additional misses are incurred for that cache block. Figure 3 gives the predictability of the CCP predictor for context sizes of 26, 28, and 30 bits. Figure 4 gives the predictability of the PCP predictor and the MCP predictor with context sizes of 20 and 22 bits. We experimented with many different context sizes. For the *CCP* predictor, the predictability reduced further as the number of bits defining the context is reduced (beyond 26 bits). The *MCP* predictor (with a maximum context size of 27 bits for a 32 byte cache block and 32 bit addresses), on the other hand, behaved differently for different benchmarks. As also observed in Figure 4, as the context size is increased for the *MCP* predictor, the predictability increases for some benchmarks, whereas remains the same or decreases for others. Not much difference is observed in the predictabilities of the CCP predictor with context sizes of 28 and 30 bits because not all the instructions are memory instructions. The predictability of the CCP predictor for floating point benchmarks (an average of about 90% for 28 bits) is much higher than that for the integer benchmarks (an average of about 50% for 28 bits). An average prediction accuracy (correct predictions out of all the new cache blocks fetched) of about 70% is observed. Overall, the CCP predictor has a better predictability than the MCP and the PCP predictors. Next, we discuss techniques to further improve the predictability.

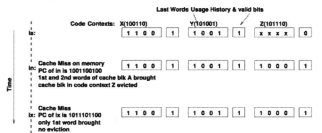

Figure 2: Working of the CCP cache noise predictor

2.3 Improving Predictability

Here, we discuss 2 techniques that can be employed to improve the predictability of the predictors.

Miss Initiator Based History (MIBH): The *MIBH* technique further records the words usage history of cache blocks based on the offset (in the cache block) of the word that initiated the cache miss. We call the word that initiated the miss as the *miss initiator word*. For instance, the words usage history for the same code context in the *CCP* predictor may differ if the offset of the word that initiated the miss is different. The *MIBH* technique will further improve the predictability if the relative position of the words accessed in a cache block remains the same, however, the location of the words in the block may differ. For instance, a loop may be accessing all the elements of an array, where each element of the array is a *struct*, and all loop iterations access only the first field in the *struct*. To measure the predictabilities in the *MIBH* technique, a maximum of 8 (for an 8-word cache block) different words usage histories are recorded. When a cache block is evicted, the words usage history that is updated depends not only on its code context but also on the miss initiator word for the cache block. Similarly, on a cache miss, cache noise prediction is made based on the context of the cache access and also on the word offset of the access.

ORing Previous Two Histories (OPTH): In the *OPTH* technique, words usage histories of two, instead of one, previously evicted cache blocks are recorded for each context. The prediction is then made by bitwise oring the two words usage histories. The intuition behind the *OPTH* technique is that there may be multiple valid words usage histories for a context, and basing the prediction on just one history can result in a misprediction. The *OPTH* technique will result in better predictability because more words will be brought into the cache for each cache block. However, the *OPTH* technique may reduce the cache utilization by still bringing in more words than required. In fact, we observed that if the number of previous histories that is "ored" for prediction is increased beyond 2, the improvement in utilization reduces significantly.

Results: Figure 5 shows the predictabilities of the 28 and 30 bits *CCP* predictor with the *MIBH* and the *OPTH* techniques. Figure 5 shows that the *MIBH* technique performs much better than the *OPTH* technique. The average prediction accuracy for the *CCP* predictor with the *MIBH* technique is about 90% for the integer benchmarks and almost 100% for the floating point benchmarks (the total average is about 95%). The best average prediction accuracy for the *PCP* predictor with both the *OPTH* and the *MIBH* techniques was about 68% and for the *MCP* predictor was about 75%, compared to 95% for the *CCP* predictor. Henceforth, we only consider the *CCP* predictor. Combination of the *MIBH* and the *OPTH* techniques gives the best performance, but only slightly higher than the *MIBH* technique. Henceforth, we only consider the 28-bit CCP predictor with the MIBH technique, as *OPTH + MIBH* results in lower cache utilization than just *MIBH*. With this high prediction accuracy, we observed that the cache utilization can potentially increase from about 57% to about 92%.

3. CCP Cache Noise Predictor Implementation

With the cache noise predictors, the cache miss request is also accompanied by the pattern of words (if available) in the cache block to be fetched. If the words usage history is not available, then all the words in the cache block are fetched. Each cache block in the cache is provided with 2 bit-vectors (of sizes equal to the number of words in the cache block). The *valid words* bit-vector indicates the valid words in the cache block, and the *words usage* bit-vector records the words accessed in the cache block. For every cache block access, the bit corresponding to the offset of the access is set in the *words usage* bit-vector. In addition, each cache block is also provided with space to store the code context and the miss initiator word offset (for the MIBH technique) for the cache block. When the cache is accessed, the hit or a miss depends on the validity of the cache block, the result of the tag comparison, and also the validity of the word accessed. If the cache access is a miss because the word is invalid, then only the remaining words are brought into the cache. The rest of the discussion only considers cache misses due to invalid cache blocks or due to tag mismatch. In a writeback cache, only the valid words are written back into the lower level cache. In a write through cache, cache miss on a write to an invalid word can be implemented with a write-allocate or with a write-no-allocate policy. Our L1 data cache uses writeback with write allocate policy. In the predictor, the most recently seen code contexts and their words usage histories are maintained in a predictor table. On a cache miss the words usage history (if available) of the code context is read from the table and sent to the lower level memory. When a

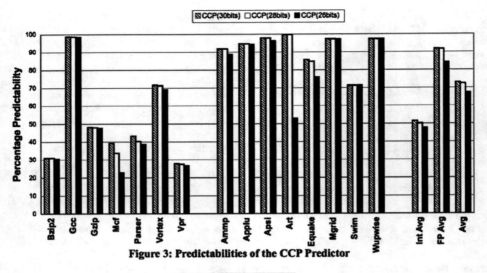

Figure 3: Predictabilities of the CCP Predictor

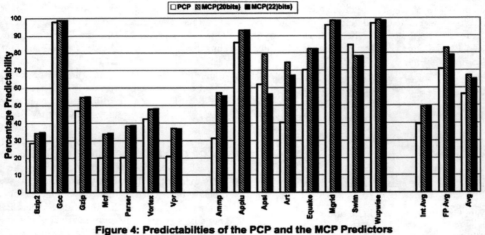

Figure 4: Predictabilties of the PCP and the MCP Predictors

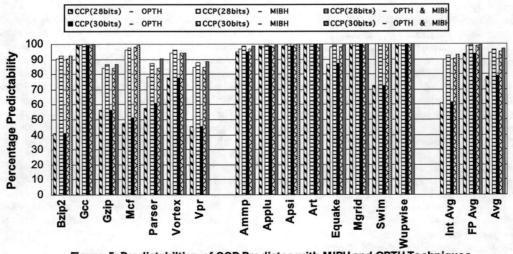

Figure 5: Predictabilties of CCP Predictor with MIBH and OPTH Techniques

valid block is evicted from the cache, the table is updated with the words usage history of the evicted cache block. The code context table can be implemented as a direct-mapped, set associative, or a fully associative CAM/RAM structure.

The CAM portion stores the code contexts, and the RAM structure stores the words usage histories. The code context of the cache miss or of the evicted cache block is broadcast in the CAM structure. This is followed by comparisons of the valid code contexts. On a match, the corresponding words usage history is either used or updated. The replacement policy used is the Least Recently Used (LRU) policy. The *CCP* predictor can be alternately implemented by storing the code context along with the instruction cache.

For the *MIBH* technique, each entry in the context table stores multiple words usage histories for the different *miss initiator words*. However, if space is provided for the histories of only a few *miss initiator words*, then each history also stores the initiator word offset. In this case, *miss initiator word offsets (MIWOs)* are also compared along with the code contexts to determine a hit in the table. Figure 6(a) shows the structure of the predictor table entry for the base case, and Figure 6(b) with the *MIBH* technique (with space for just two *miss initiator words*). In Figure 6(b), each CAM portion of the entry has a single broadcast tag, which is used to broadcast the context and the *MIWO*. The comparison result and the validity of the entry drive the word-line of the RAM portion of the structure, which has a single read/write port. If the word-line is activated, then either the history on the port is written into the entry or the history is read from the entry. The context table requires only a single broadcast tag and a single read/write port, because the table is accessed only on a cache miss and on eviction of a cache block. This also prevents the access to the context table from being in the critical path. On a rare case that there are multiple accesses to the table in a single cycle, either the requests can be arbitrarily dropped or a small buffer can be maintained to serialize the requests. We observed that a 2-entry buffer is enough to avoid any loss of requests. Additionally, we did not observe any variation in the performance of the predictor with the two alternatives.

Better Space Utilizing *MIBH* Predictor: In the *MIBH* predictor of Figure 6(b), predictor space will be wasted if a code context has only a few *miss initiator words*. To avoid wastage of predictor space, we discuss a novel code context predictor shown in Figure 6(c), where each table entry is provided with space for two *MIWOs*. In this predictor, each context is divided into two parts: *common context* and *different context*. *Common context* is the upper order bits of the context, and *different context* is the remaining lower order bits. In Figure 6(c), each context table entry can hold histories of two contexts provided that they have the same common context. For a hit in the table, the *common context*, the *different context*, and the *MIWO* of a cache block should match with the values in an entry. The number of bits required to implement this MIBH predictor will be slightly more than that required for the predictor in Figure 6(b), which will depend on the size of the *common context*. The replacement policy replaces the least recently used entry, and if the LRU entry has the same common context, then the least recently used history in that entry is replaced.

Predictor size: A larger table will have a lower "no prediction" rate resulting in better cache utilization and lower cache energy, however at the expense of a higher predictor table energy consumption. Note that performance is only impacted by the misprediction rate and not by the "no prediction" rate. We only use small predictors in our experiments that may increase the "no prediction" rate, but will limit the energy consumption in the predictor. We measured the percentage of correct, mis, and no

predictions (out of the cache blocks fetched) for predictor tables with 16 entries with 4 MIWOs (16/4), 16 entries with 8 MIWOs (16/8), and 32 entries with 4 MIWOs (32/4). The better utilizing MIBH predictor uses a common context of 25 bits and a different context of 3 bits. The experimental parameters are given in Table 1. We observed that, for the 16/4 predictor, the percentage of cache misses for which prediction is made by the better space utilizing predictor of Figure 6(c) is about 10% more than that by the conventional predictor of Figure 6(b). The 16/4 predictor predicted the pattern for almost 80% of the cache misses. We also observed that a 64/4 predictor is enough to predict for almost all the cache misses.

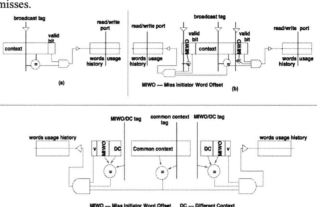

Figure 6: Predictor Table Entry for (a) Base Case; (b) MIBH; (c) Better Space Utilizing MIBH

First Access Check (FAC): To further reduce the misprediction rate, the *FAC* checks whether the *miss initiator word* (for which a cache miss has occurred) is in the predicted words usage history for the block. If the miss initiator word is not in the history, then either all words in the cache block are fetched or the words indicated by the predicted history plus the miss initiator word are fetched. We follow the first alternative where all the words in the cache block are brought into the cache. For instance, if the predicted words usage history for a block is "0110" and the miss initiator word is the first word in the block then the entire cache block is brought.

Early Misprediction Detection (EMD): Another alternative to reduce the misprediction rate is to avoid successive mispredictions due to stale or outdated words usage history. Since the predictor table is updated at eviction time, the words usage history in the table could be stale or outdated, as discussed in Section 2. The EMD technique is implemented on top of the FAC technique. In the EMD technique, once a misprediction is detected (which could be for the miss initiator word), the words usage history for that context and *MIWO* is invalidated in the predictor table to prevent other cache misses from using the outdated/stale history. However, in this technique a single glitch in the words usage history can result in converting correct predictions to "no predictions".

We experimented with the CCP predictors with both FAC and FAC/EMD techniques, and observed that the EMD technique does not result in significant reduction in misprediction rate. However, the FAC reduced the misprediction rate by more than 50%. Figure 7 presents the prediction accuracy results of the CCP predictor with the FAC technique for the 16/4, 16/8, and 32/4 CCP predictors. Figure 7 shows that the 16/4 and 16/8 techniques are able to predict for almost 75% of the cache misses, and the correct predictions are about 97% (out of the total predicted). In the rest of the paper, we experiment with the 16/4 predictor table.

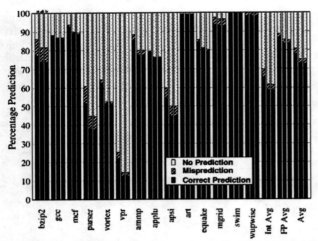

Figure 7: Prediction accuracies with (a) 32/4; (b) 16/8; (c) 16/4 CCP predictors

4. Related Work

Sub-blocked caches reduce the cost of tagging a cache with small blocks at cache block granularity by associating a single tag with a cache block consisting of multiple sub-blocks. The sub-blocks have their own status bits. With sub-blocking, memory traffic is reduced by transferring only a single sub-block on a cache miss. Seznec [16] proposed decoupled sectored caches (DSC), where the address tag location associated with a cache sub-block is dynamically chosen among several possible tag locations, emulating variable cache block sizes. However, the non-fetched sub-blocks within a cache block result in higher miss rates. With our prediction mechanisms, the cache can be designed as a single-word sub-blocked cache. However, the important difference is that all (and only) the required sub-blocks are brought into the cache simultaneously.

Veidenbaum et al. [18] propose adapting the cache line size to application behavior by using the words usage history of a cache line. However, unlike our scheme, their scheme still brings contiguous words (which can result in cache noise in the cache), the cache line size can only be halved or doubled, and only uses the words usage history of a cache line when bringing the same cache line again. Zhang et al. [20] propose a different implementation of a sub-blocked cache, where each cache line is of size equal to the sub-block and a counter in the cache controller specifies the number of contiguous sub-blocks to be read from the memory. Inoue et al. [9] propose a sub-blocks usage history based fetching of sub-blocks forming a cache line. Their scheme is somewhat similar to our PCP predictor, with the major difference being that they use the sub-block usage history of the cache block that is currently being evicted. For this, on a cache miss, they first determine which cache block will be replaced, and then send the sub-block usage pattern for that block to bring the corresponding sub-blocks in the new cache block. This can increase the cache miss penalty. Dubnicki and Leblanc [5] proposed adjustable block size caches to prevent false sharing in shared memory multiprocessor systems.

Johnson et al. introduce the notion of a macroblock of memory where the memory access pattern is consistent across the macroblock. This concept is somewhat similar to the memory context discussed in this paper. However, they use the access pattern within a macroblock for optimal placement of data in the memory hierarchy (for instance bypassing the data cache) [10], and for varying the size of the cache block [11], where multiple adjacent cache blocks are fetched if the adjacent cache blocks in a macroblock are accessed simultaneously. The main purpose of their study was to reduce the conflict misses. Their techniques can still result in lower cache utilization as they still bring contiguous data into the cache. Kumar and Wilkerson [12] reduce the miss rate of the decoupled sectored cache by prefetching cache lines based on the spatial footprint of a sector. Chen et al. [21] use prediction of to-be-referenced sub-blocks to save leakage energy by turning off the sub-blocks that will not be referenced. They extend the prediction mechanism to also selectively prefetch cache lines based on the usage history of these lines.

Nicolaescu [14] uses profile information to guide a compiler in inserting line size configuration information into a program. Witchel [19] proposed a software-controlled cache line size, where the compiler specifies how much data to fetch on a data cache miss. Several studies [7, 8, 15, 17] have also been performed to measure the trade-offs between miss ratio and traffic ratio by varying block and sub-block sizes. McNiven et al. [13] also looked at reducing traffic between adjacent levels of the memory hierarchy.

In summary, to our knowledge, no techniques have been proposed that attempt to reduce the cache noise by predicting and fetching all and only the required words in a cache block. Techniques have been proposed that vary the cache line size to match the spatial locality of an application, but the main difference compared to our approach is that they still bring in contiguous words into the cache which can still result in cache pollution. In addition, the techniques can only increase the cache line size if the adjacent sub-blocks (smaller cache lines) are accessed simultaneously.

5. Experimental Setup and Results
5.1 Experimental Setup

We use a modified version of the SimpleScalar simulator [3], simulating a 32-bit PISA architecture. For benchmarks, we use a collection of 6 integer (vpr, mcf, parser, bzip2, vortex, and gcc), and 8 FP (equake, ammp, mgrid, swim, wupwise, applu, apsi, and art) benchmarks, using ref inputs, from the SPEC2K benchmark suite. The statistics are collected for 500M instructions, after skipping the first 3B instructions. In our experiments, we focus only on L1 data cache. Table 1 gives the hardware parameters for the experiments. Our *CCP* predictor has a *common context* of 25 upper order PC bits for a context of 28 bits. The results are only for a fully associative predictor table with 16 entries with 4 *MIWO*s.

5.2 Results

We present the L1 data cache miss rates, the bandwidth requirement in terms of the average number of words fetched per cache block, Instructions per cycle (IPC) count, and the cache utilization of the L1 data cache in Table 2. Table 2 shows that the miss rate increases minimally due to mispredictions (an average of about 0.1%), resulting in almost zero reduction in IPC. On the other hand, the bandwidth requirement in terms of average number of words fetched per cache block reduces by about 28%, and the L1 cache utilization increases by about 37%. Words fetched per cache block reduce significantly for benchmarks (such as art, mcf, and bzip2) that have lower cache utilization for the base case and significantly higher utilization with cache noise prediction. In addition, for benchmarks such as vpr, a large percentage of no prediction results in almost no improvement in cache utilization.

5.3 Power Measurements

By fetching only the to-be-referenced words in a cache block, cache energy consumption can be reduced, by reducing the energy consumed in reading the words from the lower level caches, in the bus to transfer the words to the upper level caches, and in writing the words in the upper level cache. Furthermore, writing only the

Parameter	Value	Parameter	Value
Fetch/Commit Width	8 instructions	Floating-point FUs	3 ALU, 1 Mul/Div
Unified Register File	128 Int/128 FP 1 cycle inter-subsys. Lat	Integer FUs	4 ALU, 2 AGU, 1 Mul/Div
Issue Width	5 Int/ 3 FP	Issue Queue Size	96 Int/64 FP
Branch Predictor	4K Gshare	BTB Size	4K entries, 2 way assoc.
L1 Icache	16K direct mapped 2 cycle latency	L1 Dcache	16K, 4-way assoc., 2 cycle latency
Memory Latency	100 cycles 1st word, 2 cycle inter-word	L2 cache	Unified 512K 8-way assoc. 10 cycle lat.
ROB Size	256 instructions	Load/store buffer	64 entries

Table 1: Default Experimental Parameters

valid words back into the lower level cache for a dirty cache block, and shutting down invalid portions of cache blocks will also result in reducing the energy consumption. The disadvantage of this method is the additional energy consumption in the predictor and additional bits in the cache. This is in addition to the savings in leakage energy consumption obtained due to a reduction in the number of active transistors. In this section, we only measure the savings obtained in dynamic energy consumption. Figure 8 shows the percentage reduction in dynamic energy consumption of the new cache + predictor as compared to the conventional cache. We use a modified version of the cacti tool [22](0.18um) to perform the energy consumption of each access to the cache and the predictor table. Note that Figure 8 also includes the energy consumption on cache hits and in the additional bits. Figure 8 shows that an average of about 23% savings in dynamic energy consumption can be obtained with cache noise prediction. Higher energy savings is obtained for benchmarks (such as bzip2, mcf, and art) whose cache utilization increases significantly with the use of a cache noise prediction. On the other hand, negative energy savings are obtained for benchmarks (such as gcc, applu, mgrid, and wupwise) that are using most of the words in a cache block and have higher cache utilization for the base case. Hence, the prediction overhead results in higher energy consumption in these benchmarks.

	IPC		Miss Rate		Words/Block		Utilization	
	Base	CCP	Base	CCP	Base	CCP	Base	CCP
Bzip2	1.029	1.02	4.1	4.4	8	3.6	27.9	61.3
Gcc	0.942	0.94	10.4	10.4	8	7.9	98.4	98.5
Mcf	0.733	0.73	24.5	24.7	8	2.6	25.1	76.1
Parser	0.935	0.93	4.3	4.6	8	5.6	29.	42.2
Vortex	0.994	0.99	1.7	1.7	8	5.1	30.3	47.0
Vpr	0.957	0.95	5.7	5.8	8	7.2	31.4	34.8
Ammp	1.048	1.04	7.2	7.3	8	4.7	50.6	85.0
Applu	1.081	1.08	3.0	3.0	8	7.8	90.8	92.0
Apsi	1.100	1.10	1.5	1.	8	6.1	41.8	54.4
Art	1.006	1.00	45.9	45.9	8	2.6	32.6	98.1
Equake	1.058	1.05	6.5	6.6	8	5.2	53.1	80.6
Mgrid	1.068	1.06	3.7	3.8	8	7.6	94.0	98.3
Swim	1.062	1.06	1	14.0	8	6.2	77.7	99.8
Wupwise	1.052	1.05	0.5	0.5	8	7.9	96.6	99.2
Int Avg	0.93	0.93	8.50	8.6	8	5.38	40.5	60.03
FP Avg	1.05	1.05	10.32	10.38	8	6.067	67.19	88.47
Average	1.00	1.00	9.54	9.64	8	5.77	55.76	76.28

Table 2: IPC, Miss rate; Bandwidth in terms of words per cache block; and cache utilization for the 16/4 CCP predictor

6 Hardware Prefetching

Processors employ hardware prefetching to improve the cache miss rates of L1 caches. The most common hardware prefetching mechanism is to also fetch the next cache block on a cache miss to exploit more spatial locality. Prefetching reduces the miss rate, however at the expense of increased cache pollution and increased pressure on the bandwidth. Cache noise prediction can alleviate these two limitations of the prefetching mechanisms. When applying cache noise prediction to a prefetching mechanism, only

the required words are fetched from the prefetched cache block. Note that this is different from predicting and prefetching only the to-be-referenced cache blocks as discussed in [21].

With prefetching, the prefetched cache block has not been accessed in the current cache miss. Hence, its code context and its *MIWO* are not known. One alternative is to also predict the word pattern for the prefetched cache block, either using a separate predictor table or using the same predictor table with minor modifications. In our current implementation, the fetched and the prefetched cache blocks are predicted to have the same pattern of words. We experiment with two variants. In one approach, the prefetched cache block does not update the predictor table when it is evicted. In the other approach, the prefetched cache block is updated with its code context and *MIWO* when it is accessed for the first time. The cache block then updates the predictor table on eviction benefiting future misses in its code context. We experiment with prefetching all the words of the next cache block (base case) and cache noise prediction based prefetching with the above two variants.

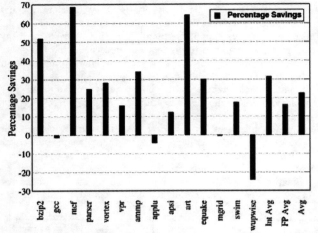

Figure 8: Percentage dynamic energy savings of predictor + cache wrt to the traditional cache

Figure 9 shows the prediction accuracy results for the cache noise based hardware prefetching along with the prediction accuracies without hardware prefetching. The results are for the 16/4 predictor. It can be observed that the prediction rate reduces with prefetching. This is because cache misses reduce with hardware prefetching. We observed that the reduction in cache misses that hit in the predictor table is more than the cache misses that miss, resulting in lower prediction rate. Nevertheless, the prediction accuracy of cache noise prediction is still very high, an average of about 93% when the prefetched cache block does not update the predictor table and about 96% when the prefetched cache block updates the predictor table. When comparing the two variants of prediction, the prediction rate usually increases and the misprediction rate usually decreases when the prefetched cache block updates the predictor table. This is because a more up-to-date words usage history for the context of the prefetched cache block is now available. In some benchmarks, especially gcc, the prediction rate decreases when the prefetched cache block updates the predictor because the updated history evicts critical history and never gets used. Figure 10 gives percentage decrease in energy consumption and percentage increase in cache utilization with respect to the base case prefetching mechanism. It can be observed that, when the prefetched cache block updates the predictor, cache energy consumption reduces by about 22% and the cache utilization increases by about 70%. We also observed that the miss rate increased by only about 2% with respect to the base cache prefetching mechanism.

7 Cache noise prediction as an alternative to sub-blocking
Sub-blocking is used to have the lower tag overhead and higher spatial locality exploitation benefits of a larger cache block, while reducing the higher cache noise and bandwidth requirements associated with them. These are also the benefits of cache noise prediction based fetching of words. In this section, we investigate the use of cache noise prediction based fetching of words as an

alternative to sub-blocking. For this, we compare the miss rates, cache utilization, bandwidth requirements, and energy consumption of a cache using the cache noise predictor with that of a sub-blocked cache. We use the 16/4 prediction for the prediction based fetching of words, and sub-blocks of two words for the sub-blocked cache. Table 3 gives the results of our measurements. The energy measurements in Table 3 are percentage reduction in energy with respect to a conventional non-sub-blocked 32-byte cache. Table 3 shows that the average bandwidth requirement of the sub-blocked cache is about 35% of that of the prediction based approach. However, the energy consumption and the miss rate of sub-blocked cache is about 44% and 97% more, respectively, than the prediction based approach. In addition, the cache utilization of the prediction based approach is about 10% more than the sub-blocked cache. This suggests that cache noise prediction based approach can be a good alternative to sub-blocking if slightly higher bandwidth is available.

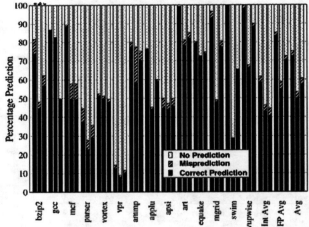

Figure 9: Prediction accuracies with (a) no prefetching; (b) no updates for prefetched block; and (c) updates for prefetched block; for the 16/4 predictor with 32-byte block size

8 Profiling to improve total prediction
For some of the benchmarks, especially vpr, parser, vortex, and apsi, the number of predictions is significantly low, inspite ot their higher predictabilities as shown in Figure 3. The primary reason for this decrease in prediction rate is that the predictor table is too small to accommodate all the words usage histories. An alternative to increasing the predictor table size to alleviate this limitation of small predictor tables is to use the table more efficiently. In particular, there may be many word usage histories in the predictor that are evicted without getting used. However, when the predictor table is updated with these histories, they could replace histories that may be required in the future (even with LRU replacement policy). In this section, we investigate using profiling to improve the efficiency of the predictor table. Figure 11(x) shows the distribution of histories based on its usage for a 32-byte cache block and the 16/4 predictor table. The figure shows that there are a significant percentage of histories that are evicted either without getting used or with getting used only a few times, especially for benchmarks with lower prediction rates. Hence, we explore using profile information to avoid allocation of predictor table entries to those histories that are not used. For this, we run the benchmarks once to collect the combination of code contexts and *MIWO*s for the histories that are not used and utilize the collected information to prevent them from updating the predictor table in another run. The prediction results are shown in Figure 11 (y). Figure 11(y) shows

154

that profiling improves the prediction rate by about 7%. However, the improvement in prediction rate is not as high as expected, suggesting that the predictor table may have to be increased to get better prediction rates.

9 Sensitivity

In this section, we present the prediction accuracy results of the 16/4 *CCP with FAC* predictor as the cache block size is increased to 64 bytes and 128 bytes. The increase in cache block size can have two implications on the prediction accuracy: (i) the predictor misprediction rate can increase because of an increase in the probability that a word is used that is not present in the predicted words usage history, (ii) the predictor "no prediction rate" can increase because of an increase in the probability that a new cache block brought into the cache has a *miss initiator word* for which the words usage history has not been recorded. Figure 12 gives the prediction results for the different sized cache blocks. As expected, the "no prediction" rate increases with an increase in the cache block size, suggesting that larger predictor tables may be required for larger block sizes. This also suggests that profiling will be much more beneficial for larger cache blocks. On the other hand, the increase in misprediction rate is negligible, an average of about 1%, with wupwise being the only benchmark with a noticeable increase in misprediction rate (by about 20% for 128-byte block size). Hence, cache miss rate will remain largely unaffected because the

miss rate is only affected by the misprediction rate of cache noise prediction. Even with decreased prediction rate of the cache noise predictor, the cache utilization increased by about 79% for 64-byte cache block and by about 91% for 128-byte cache block.

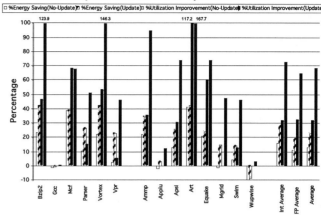

Figure 10: Percentage reduction in energy consumption and percentage improvement in cache utilization for hardware prefetching with 16/4 CCP cache noise predictor

	Energy		Miss Rate		Words/Block		Utilization	
	Sub-block	CCP	Sub-block	CCP	Sub-block	CCP	Sub-block	CCP
Bzip2	46.92	52.01	8.96	4.48	2	3.64	60.8	61.36
Gcc	26.14	-1.17	27.81	10.41	2	7.99	74.13	98.52
Mcf	56.69	68.59	45.85	24.79	2	2.64	54.95	76.19
Parser	35.44	24.56	10.63	4.67	2	5.66	60.99	42.27
Vortex	34.57	28.15	4.27	1.76	2	5.16	49.36	47.03
Vpr	37.03	15.91	14.14	5.85	2	7.23	61.99	34.85
Ammp	45.16	34.02	15.2	7.37	2	4.76	75.11	85.08
Applu	-12.87	-4.29	13.17	3.09	2	7.89	77.98	92.08
Apsi	42.54	12.36	3.33	1.6	2	6.15	87.65	54.44
Art	64.01	64.36	61.24	45.95	2	2.66	80.57	98.19
Equake	39.31	29.93	14.35	6.61	2	5.28	69.42	80.61
Mgrid	-19.04	-0.32	17.56	3.88	2	7.65	73.62	98.31
Swim	47.31	17.64	27.05	14.02	2	6.23	69.31	99.86
Wupwise	13.58	-23.92	1.88	0.59	2	7.92	73.82	99.25
Int Avg	39.47	31.34	18.61	8.66	2	5.387	60.37	60.037
FP Avg	27.5	16.22	19.22	10.389	2	6.0675	75.94	88.478
Average	32.63	22.7	18.96	9.648	2	5.776	69.26	76.289

Table 3: Miss rate; Bandwidth in terms of words per cache block; power consumption overhead and cache utilization for the 16/4 CCP predictor compared with a sub-blocked cache

10 Conclusion

In this paper, we proposed prediction mechanisms to reduce the number of words that are fetched into the cache and never used. The prediction mechanism uses the words usage history of the last evicted cache block. We experimented with three different kinds of predictors – *PCP*, *MCP*, and *CCP* – and observed that the predictability of the code context predictor (*CCP*) is the best. With the help of predictability improving techniques such as *MIBH*, the

CCP predictor had about 95% correct prediction for an infinite predictor. We also explored techniques to improve the prediction rate of smaller predictor tables (better space utilizing *MIBH*), and reduce the misprediction rate of cache noise prediction (*FAC*). With all these techniques, even a small predictor CCP predictor with 16 entries and space for only four miss initiator words' usage histories (16/4 predictor), achieved a prediction rate of 75% with correct prediction of about 97% out of the total predictions.

The 16/4 predictor improved the cache utilization of the L1 data cache by about 37%, reduced the bandwidth requirement between the L1 and the L2 caches by about 28%, and reduced the cache energy consumption (including the consumption in the additional hardware) by about 23%. All these benefits were obtained with a minimal 0.1% increase in cache miss rate and almost zero impact on IPC. We also investigated the applicability of cache noise prediction mechanisms for hardware prefetching, and observed that prediction accuracy of about 96%(out-of total prediction) was achieved with hardware prefetching as well. However, about 70% cache utilization improvement is observed for the hardware prefetching mechanism. When compared to sub-blocking with two word sub-blocks, cache noise prediction based fetching of words improves miss rate and cache utilization by 97% and 10%, respectively, and reduces energy consumption by 44%. We also explored using profiling to improve the cache noise predictor efficiency.

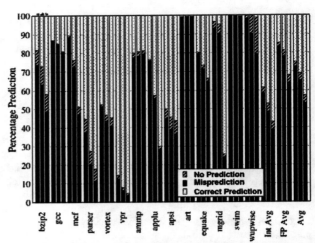

Figure 12: Prediction results for a 16/4 CCP predictor for cache block size of (a) 32 bytes; (b) 64 bytes; and (c) 128 bytes

[3] D. Burger and T. Austin, The SimpleScalar Tool Set, Version 2.0, Computer Arch. News, 1997.

[4] A. Dhodapkar and J. Smith, Comparing Program Phase Detection Techniques, Proc. Micro-36, 2003.

[5] C. Dubnicki and T. LeBlanc, Adjustable block size coherent caches, Proc. ISCA-19, 1992.

[6] J. Gonzalez and A. Gonzalez, Speculative execution via address prediction and data prefetching, Proc. ICS, 1997.

[7] M. Hill and A. Smith, Experimental evaluation of on-chip microprocessor cache memories, Proc. ISCA-11, 1984.

[8] A. Huang and J. Shen, A limit study of local memory requirements using value reuse profiles, Micro-28, 1995.

[9] K. Inoue, et. al., Dynamically Variable Line-Size Cache Exploiting High On-Chip Memory Bandwidth of Merged DRAM/Logic LSIs, Proc. HPCA, 1999.

[10] T. Johnson and W. Hwu, Run-time adaptive cache hierarchy management via reference analysis, Proc. ISCA-24, 1997.

[11] T. Johnson, et. al., Run-time spatial locality detection and optimization, Proc. Micro-30, 1997.

[12] S. Kumar and C. Wilkerson, Exploiting spatial locality in data caches using spatial footprints, Proc. ISCA-25, 1998.

[13] G. McNiven and E. Davidson, Analysis of memory referencing behavior for design of local memories, Proc. ISCA-15, 1988.

[14] D. Nicolaescu, et. al., Compiler-directed Cache Line Size Adaptivity, IMS, 2000.

[15] S. Przybylski, The performance impact of block sizes and fetch strategies, Proc. ISCA-20, 1993.

[16] A. Seznec, Decoupled sectored caches: Conciliating low tag implementation cost and low miss ratio, Proc. ISCA-21, 1994.

[17] A. Smith, Line(block) size choice for cpu cache memories, ACM Transactions on Computer Systems, C-36:1063-1075, 1987.

[18] A. Veidenbaum, et. al., Adapting Cache Line Size to Application Behavior, Proc. ICS, 1999.

[19] E. Witchel and K. Asanovic, The Span Cache: Software Controlled Tag Checks and Cache Line Size, Proc. ISCA-28, 2001.

[20] C. Zhang, et. al., Energy Benefits of a Configurable Line Size Cache for Embedded Systems, Proc. Int'l Symp. on VLSI, 2003.

[21] C. F. Chen et al., Accurate and complexity-effective spatial pattern prediction, *Proc. HPCA-10*, 2004.

[22] P. Shivakumar and N. Jouppi, CACTI 3.0: An Integrated Cache timing, Power, and Area Model, *Technical Report, DEC Western Lab*, 2002.

(x)

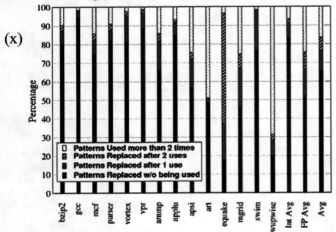

(y)

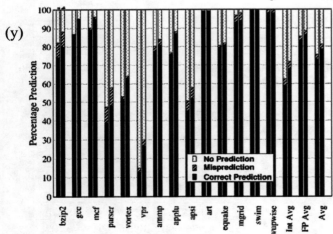

Figure 11: (x) Percentage distribution of histories in the predictor w.r.t their usage; (y) Prediction accuracies (a) w/o profiling; (b) with profiling w/o updates for not used histories

References

[1] M. Bekerman, et. al., Correlated Load Address Predictors, Proc. ISCA-26, 1999.

[2] D. Burger, et. al., Memory bandwidth limitations of future microprocessors, Proc. ISCA-23, 1996.

Retention-Aware Placement in DRAM (RAPID):
Software Methods for Quasi-Non-Volatile DRAM

Ravi K. Venkatesan, Stephen Herr, Eric Rotenberg
ECE Department, Center for Embedded Systems Research, North Carolina State University
{rkvenkat, sdherr, ericro}@ece.ncsu.edu

Abstract

Measurements of an off-the-shelf DRAM chip confirm that different cells retain information for different amounts of time. This result extends to DRAM rows, or pages (retention time of a page is defined as the shortest retention time among its constituent cells). Currently, a single worst-case refresh period is selected based on the page with the shortest retention time. Even with refresh optimized for room temperature, the worst page limits the safe refresh period to no longer than 500 ms. Yet, 99% and 85% of pages have retention times above 3 seconds and 10 seconds, respectively.

We propose Retention-Aware Placement in DRAM (RAPID), novel software approaches that can exploit off-the-shelf DRAMs to reduce refresh power to vanishingly small levels approaching non-volatile memory. The key idea is to favor longer-retention pages over shorter-retention pages when allocating DRAM pages. This allows selecting a single refresh period that depends on the shortest-retention page among populated pages, instead of the shortest-retention page overall. We explore three versions of RAPID and observe refresh energy savings of 83%, 93%, and 95%, relative to the best temperature-compensated refresh. RAPID with off-the-shelf DRAM also approaches the energy levels of idealized techniques that require custom DRAM support.

1. Introduction

Dynamic Random Access Memory (DRAM) is predicted to displace Static Random Access Memory (SRAM) as the primary volatile memory in next-generation mobile devices, as future applications increase memory requirements [22]. For example, Micron recently introduced DRAMs targeting mobile devices, called CellularRAM™ [3]. Nodes in sensor networks with unpredictable recharging capability, e.g., environmental energy harvesting [8,14], could also benefit from deep storage capacity, enabling uninterrupted data gathering while waiting for favorable recharging circumstances for wireless transmission.

However, DRAM refresh (needed to preserve stored information) continuously drains battery energy even in standby operation. Detailed power analysis of the prototype ITSY computer [20] shows that, in the deepest standby mode that still preserves the DRAM contents ("sleep"), DRAM consumes a third of total power and this fraction will increase with more DRAM and even lower power conservation modes.

DRAM refresh power can be reduced by exploiting variations in retention times among different memory cells, rows (pages), or arbitrary blocks of cells within a single DRAM chip. Process variations cause leakage to differ from one cell to another. Therefore, different cells retain information for longer or shorter periods of time [7]. Currently, a single worst-case refresh period (typically 64 milliseconds) is selected based on the cell with the shortest retention time. The worst-case refresh period also accounts for worst-case temperature (leakage increases with temperature). Limited support for temperature-compensated refresh (TCR) is now being deployed in some DRAMs [3]. However, TCR does not exploit retention-time variations among different cells, i.e., all cells are still treated uniformly with a single temperature-dependent refresh period, determined by the worst cell. Several researchers have recognized the opportunity presented by retention-time variations, proposing custom DRAM support for refreshing different cells or blocks of cells at different refresh rates [21,9,10,15]. However, to our knowledge, this approach has not been implemented in commodity DRAMs.

Instead of custom DRAM support, we propose *Retention-Aware Placement in DRAM* (RAPID), software methods for exploiting retention-time variations among different pages to minimize refresh power in off-the-shelf DRAMs. The key idea is to allocate longer-retention pages to application programs before allocating shorter-retention pages. This allows selecting a single refresh period that depends on the shortest-retention page among pages that are actually populated, rather than the shortest-retention page overall. Note that all pages are refreshed, as usual, but the extended refresh period (lower refresh rate) selected by RAPID is only safe for populated pages, which is sufficient for overall correctness.

Three versions of RAPID are explored in this paper, described below in order of increasing complexity.

- *RAPID-1*: Our retention-time measurements of a real DRAM chip reveal a handful of outlier pages with atypically short retention times, consistent with previous retention time characterizations [7]. For example, if the worst 1% of pages are not populated, then a refresh period of 3 seconds (s) is sufficient for the remaining 99% of pages at room temperature (25°C). Likewise, a 1 s refresh period is sufficient at the industry-standard worst-case temperature of 70°C. In contrast, the worst outlier page requires a 500 millisecond (ms) refresh period at room temperature and 150 ms at 70°C. RAPID-1 is a static approach in which the handful of outlier pages are discarded, i.e., never populated, yielding a very reasonable refresh period (e.g., 3 s at room temperature and 1 s at 70°C) with only a negligible reduction in DRAM capacity (e.g., 1%). Since the approach is static, the refresh period is independent of actual DRAM utilization.

- *RAPID-2*: Pages are placed into bins according to their retention times. Longer-retaining pages are allocated before shorter-retaining pages. Thus, the refresh period starts out at the highest setting corresponding to the best bin. The refresh period is decreased when no more free pages are available in the best bin because we begin populating pages in the second-best bin, and so on. The refresh period may only be increased back again if all pages in the lowest populated bin become free. Thus, once the refresh period has been decreased, increasing it again is a matter of "chance" since it depends on which pages happen to be freed by application programs. Note that outlier pages are discarded so that RAPID-2 refresh power is at least as good as RAPID-1 refresh power.

- *RAPID-3*: RAPID-3 builds on RAPID-2. When a free page becomes available in a higher bin, the contents of a populated page in a lower bin can be migrated to the newly freed page in the higher bin. Thus, RAPID-3 continuously reconsolidates data into the longest-retention pages possible. As a result, the refresh period selected by RAPID-3 more closely reflects actual DRAM utilization than RAPID-2. Migration can be naturally implemented as part of our proposed allocation/deallocation routines. A downside is extra power consumption due to migration, which must be weighed against extra refresh power savings. This hints at a deep design space, in terms of designing good criteria and timing for migrating pages.

The contributions of this paper include (1) three versions of RAPID, the first software-only techniques for exploiting retention-time variations in off-the-shelf DRAMs, (2) an interrupt-driven technique for coupling RAPID with arbitrary DRAMs in the context of commonly available refresh options, and (3) a test algorithm for determining page retention times and insights regarding its run-time and other costs.

The remainder of this paper is organized as follows. Section 2 discusses related work. Section 3 presents our test algorithm, discusses on-line/off-line testing trade-offs, and presents measured page retention times for a real DRAM chip. Section 4 presents the RAPID techniques and discusses how RAPID can be coupled with off-the-shelf DRAMs. Section 5 and Section 6 present our evaluation methodology and results, respectively. Section 7 summarizes the paper.

2. Related Work

Yanagisawa [21], Kim and Papaefthymiou [9,10], and Ohsawa et al. [15] propose custom hardware support in the DRAM chip itself, to refresh different cells at different refresh rates and thereby exploit retention-time variations among memory cells. Yanagisawa [21] classifies DRAM cells into two types – cells with long retention times and cells with short retention times. He proposes modifications to conventional counter-based refresh circuitry to refresh cells with long retention times less frequently than cells with short retention times. Kim and Papaefthymiou [9,10] propose a block-based multiperiod refresh approach, where a custom refresh period is selected for each block, i.e., group of cells. They also provide an algorithm to compute the optimal number of blocks. Ohsawa et al. [15] propose a hardware technique to exploit retention-time variations among DRAM pages, where each DRAM page is refreshed at a tailored refresh period that is a multiple of the shortest refresh period among all pages.

Our approach is unique, in that it does not require custom hardware modifications to the DRAM. The underlying reason is that a single refresh period is used at any given time. RAPID software populates longer-retention pages before shorter-retention pages, enabling a single refresh period at any given moment that correlates with the shortest-retention page among only populated pages rather than the shortest-retention page overall. A single refresh period, selected and possibly adjusted by RAPID as DRAM utilization changes, can be used to refresh contemporary off-the-shelf DRAMs for practical exploitation of retention-time variations. We also contribute a software testing method for characterizing page retention times, and discuss the factors that determine the run time, power activity, and precision of the test algorithm.

Hamamoto et al. [7] characterize retention-time variations among individual cells and provide insight into contributing factors, although no techniques to exploit retention-time variations are proposed. Our retention time measurements corroborate those of Hamamoto et al. and extend their results by showing significant variations even at the page granularity, an important result for practical exploitation of retention time variations at the level of pages instead individual cells, since pages are the natural refresh granularity.

Murotani [13] and Pelley et al. [16] propose modifications to DRAM refresh circuitry, to automatically tune a single refresh period with temperature. Burgan [2] proposes monitoring the leakage of test cells, representative of the entire memory, for automatically detecting a suitable refresh period for the DRAM as a whole. Test cells monitor leakage of both logic "1" and logic "0". These inventions do not appear to exploit retention-time variations across cells, so the shortest-retention cell among all DRAM cells still limits the refresh period.

Hsu et al. [4] and Cho et al. [5] propose monitoring the leakage of four test cells, one for each bank, thus automatically selecting a refresh period for each bank of the DRAM. The shortest-retention cell in a bank still limits the refresh period of the bank as a whole. That is, the granularity is only slightly finer than that of the whole DRAM, and it is not clear if there will be much separation among per-bank refresh periods.

Lebeck et al. [12] exploit low-level support for transitioning DRAM chips among four power modes. Their power-aware page allocation polices attempt to maximize use of lower power modes while minimizing performance overhead of transitioning back to higher power modes. None of the modes appear to disable a chip entirely, i.e., refresh is always present and RAPID techniques can be applied to reduce refresh power.

RAPID can be classified among techniques that exploit the principle of better-than-worst-case design [1,6,18]. Due to future variation-limited technology, better-than-worst-case design has recently received significant attention in the context of microprocessors [1,6,18], for example. Variation-oriented low-power memory techniques such as RAPID complement these variation-oriented low-power microprocessor techniques.

The ITSY prototype is a source of information regarding power consumption in next-generation mobile devices [20]. On-line technology news sources forecast the displacement of SRAM in mobile devices with DRAM [22]. Micron's CellularRAM™ and Samsung's UtRAM™, which are specially tailored DRAMs for mobile devices and marketed as pseudo-SRAMs, seem to corroborate these forecasts [3][19].

3. Testing Methods

This section discusses strategies for testing page retention times and presents test results for a real DRAM chip. We use the DRAM of an embedded systems development board donated by Ubicom [17]. Ubicom develops embedded microprocessors for wireless applications, including some of the first multithreaded embedded microprocessors, such as the IP3023 with 8 hardware threads. Among other components, the board has an IP3023 microprocessor (which has on-chip 64KB instruction and 256KB data scratchpad SRAM, an on-chip SDRAM memory controller, and numerous other on-chip peripheral devices and interfaces), 16MB of synchronous DRAM (IS42S16800A SDRAM manufactured by ISSI), and Flash memory.

The ISSI DRAM supports both auto-refresh and self-refresh. When auto-refresh is enabled, the external memory controller issues auto-refresh commands at regular intervals to the DRAM. The DRAM refreshes the next row in sequence (as kept track of, by the DRAM) when it receives an auto-refresh command. The external memory controller's auto-refresh period is programmable. When self-refresh is enabled, the DRAM refreshes rows autonomously, always at the fixed self-refresh period of 64 ms. Self-refresh can only be used when the DRAM is in standby operation. Both auto-refresh and self-refresh can be disabled, a useful feature for testing page retention times.

Figure 1. Experimental setup for testing page retention times.

The experimental setup for testing page retention times is pictured in Figure 1. The four parts are labeled 1-4 in the picture: (1) the Ubicom board with DRAM under test, (2) a PC workstation with Ubicom software development environment for compiling and downloading programs to the Flash memory via an ethernet connection to the board, (3) a multimeter with attached thermistor for temperature readout, and (4) a heat gun for varying ambient temperature.

3.1. Testing Algorithm

To characterize retention times of DRAM pages, auto-refresh and self-refresh are disabled in the memory controller and DRAM, respectively, so that pages are not refreshed. Testing a single page consists of writing all 1's or all 0's to the page, waiting a specified amount of time, and reading the pattern back to see if it remains intact. If the pattern is retained for a wait time of T, the test is repeated for a wait time of T + Δt. If this next attempt fails (one or more bit errors), the retention time for the page is recorded as T (since it worked for a wait time of T but not T + Δt).

Some DRAM technologies may leak to all 0's, all 1's, or a mixture of 0's and 1's. For the ISSI DRAM, we observed that half the cells in a row decay to 1's and half the cells decay to 0's. We have not yet explored the underlying reason. Whatever the reason, we must test a page's retention of all 1's and all 0's. Ten trials of all 1's and ten trials of all 0's are performed. The minimum among the twenty trials is recorded as the retention time of the page.

We measured retention times of some pages approaching a minute at room temperature. Assuming an initial wait time T of 1 second and proceeding in increments Δt of 1 second, it takes 22 minutes (1 + 2 + … + 51 seconds) for just one trial of a page that retains information for 50 seconds. Testing pages one at a time would take far too long. Fortunately, all pages can be tested in parallel. The test program writes the entire DRAM with 1's (or 0's), waits for the next wait interval T + Δt, checks the contents of every page, and records a retention time of T for any page that retained for T but not for T + Δt. One trial is completed for all pages collectively before attempting other trials.

The time to write and check the entire ISSI DRAM is about 74 ms and 250 ms, respectively. A recorded retention time reflects only the wait time after writing and before checking, therefore, the overheads can only mean that the actual retention time for a page is slightly longer than recorded, a safe margin of error as it will ensure that the page is refreshed slightly more often than required.

It is interesting to note that the test time for a trial is insensitive to the number of pages tested in parallel. We stop testing pages whose retention times become known midway through the trial, only as a matter of power efficiency for on-line testing (more on this in the next section). Rather, test time is dominated by the long wait times.

Specifically, the test time for one trial depends directly on the wait time increment Δt, the initial wait time, and the final wait time (either the longest measured retention time or an imposed maximum wait time). The granularity Δt has a dramatic effect on test time, moreover, it is the more flexible parameter of the three. Therefore, we used a non-uniform approach. We used a granularity of 1 second for tests above 3 seconds, 100 ms for tests between 1 and 3 seconds, and 10 ms for tests below 1 second. Moreover, we first test above 3 seconds, so that only pages that do not retain above 3 seconds are considered in the finer tests (the overhead of writing and checking the entire DRAM would skew the finer tests). Likewise, we test

between 1 and 3 seconds before testing below 1 second so that only residual outlier pages are tested at the finest granularity. This testing strategy allows for precise measurements of the shortest-retention pages while keeping the test time reasonable. However, these parameters can be adjusted in the interest of test time or precision, as desired. At room temperature, we found it necessary to set the maximum wait time to 50 seconds.

Table 1 summarizes the test time and the number of page writes/checks for one complete trial of the DRAM. Retention times from the first trial can be exploited to reduce the number of page writes/checks in subsequent trials. Subsequent trials can begin at the median of the distribution and spiral outward from the median, eliminating the greatest number of pages earliest in the trial. Thus, the number of page writes/checks in Table 1 is a worst-case number for the first trial. The test time is not reduced for subsequent trials because we still cycle through all the same wait times.

Table 1. One complete trial of the DRAM.

test time	22.3 minutes
# page writes/reads (worst-case – first trial)	274,000

3.2. Off-line vs. On-line Testing

Page retention times can be tested off-line by the DRAM manufacturer, off-line by the system designer, or on-line during actual use of the system.

Currently, the DRAM manufacturer only tests chips at the worst-case refresh period (e.g., 64 ms) to confirm correct operation of the chip. This basic test is much faster than our generalized test algorithm due to its single short wait time. Applying our test algorithm would increase DRAM tester time, causing an unwanted increase in price. Furthermore, conveying chip-specific page retention times to DRAM customers poses unusual logistics problems – a small Flash table coupled with the DRAM in a multi-chip package or a web-accessible database are improbable.

Alternatively, system designers (e.g., cell phone designers, sensor network researchers) could run the tests off-line for their particular applications. Since extreme energy efficiency is needed for these applications, this form of off-line testing is potentially justifiable from a business standpoint.

In the case of on-line testing, trials are performed gradually, opportunistically, and overall as non-intrusively as possible, e.g., while recharging the batteries of a mobile device or during extensive idle periods. (Or, for mobile devices, a Windows-style installation wizard could give users the option of testing the device upon first use or at some later time.) Multiple trials are collected over days, weeks, or even months. Testing time and power overheads recede over time as the DRAM is mapped. RAPID is only employed when the trials are

160

complete. Correct operation is assured because the system safely reverts to the default refresh policy when trials are incomplete.

3.3. Testing and Temperature

Conventional DRAMs use a single worst-case refresh period (typically 64 ms), safe for the highest rated temperature and all lower temperatures. CellularRAM™ temperature-compensated refresh (TCR) provides four refresh settings, corresponding to four temperature ranges. A given refresh setting is safe for the highest temperature in its range and all lower temperatures. Exploiting TCR requires an external temperature sensor or *a priori* knowledge of the peak operating temperature, to guide selection of the lowest safe refresh setting.

Temperature can be accommodated in RAPID similarly, using either a single or multiple temperature ranges. The only difference is the use of page-dependent information instead of page-independent information.

However, the testing method – off-line vs. on-line – affects temperature options. A key advantage of off-line testing is that temperature can be explicitly controlled. Thus, testing can be done for the highest rated temperature and possibly several lower temperatures. If a temperature sensor is available, we can select page retention times corresponding to the current temperature. If a temperature sensor is not available, we can at least select page retention times corresponding to the highest rated temperature.

On-line testing is less flexible in two ways. First, a temperature sensor is mandatory, to tag each trial with the maximum temperature for which the trial is safe. The sensor is likewise needed to select safe page retention times corresponding to the current temperature. Second, temperature cannot be controlled during testing. It is possible for the current temperature to exceed the maximum recorded temperature among trials, in which case a RAPID refresh period cannot be determined and we must downgrade to either of the two conventional refresh policies (worst-case refresh period or lowest safe refresh setting of TCR).

3.4. Page Retention Times

This section presents page retention times using the testing algorithm described in Section 3.1. Note that the DRAM under test implements a "close page" policy, meaning the page is not held open in the row buffer. Therefore, the row buffer is not used as a cache, guaranteeing reads and writes always truly access the memory cells.

The graph in Figure 2 shows retention times of the 16,384 pages in the chip. These measurements were taken at the particular room temperature (24°C). The y-axis shows retention time in milliseconds (ms) and the x-axis shows all 16,384 pages, labeled by "page #".

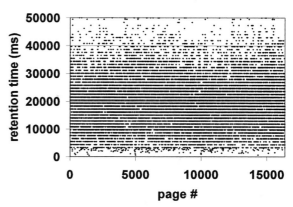

Figure 2. Measured retention times of different pages (rows) of DRAM at 24°C.

The first observation is that retention time varies noticeably among different pages, from 500 ms to slightly over 50 seconds.

The second observation is that most pages have longer retention times than the default 64 ms refresh period or even the longest temperature-compensated refresh period (TCR), which is at most 500 ms according to our results in Figure 2. For example, a refresh period of 1,400 ms covers 99.9% of all pages and a refresh period of 3,100 ms covers 99% of all pages. For a 99% DRAM bank utilization, RAPID-1 can consolidate data into the longest-retention 99% of the DRAM bank, permitting a refresh period as long as 3,100 ms without losing information.

As mentioned earlier, we observed some cells in the ISSI DRAM leaked to 0 and others to 1. However, leaking to 1 seems to be a much slower process, as the average page retention time for 1's is only 17 seconds compared to an average page retention time of 50 seconds for 0's (at room temperature for pages in the first bank).

The distribution of page retention times follows a bell curve, as shown on the left-hand side of Figure 3. The corresponding cumulative distribution on the right-hand side of Figure 3 shows the percent usable DRAM for a given target refresh period. For example, a 10 second refresh period covers about 85% of the DRAM pages.

Temperature is known to have a significant effect on leakage and, therefore, retention time in DRAM. We measured the page retention times of only the first bank at two higher temperatures, 45°C and 70°C (the latter is the maximum operating temperature for the chip). The temperature was raised using the heat gun pictured in Figure 1 (labeled 4). The temperature was monitored during testing, using a multi-meter with temperature-sensing thermistor (labeled 3) placed in contact with the DRAM package, and was kept within two degrees of the desired temperature. The results are shown in Figure 4 and Figure 5. Retention times decrease with increasing temperature as expected.

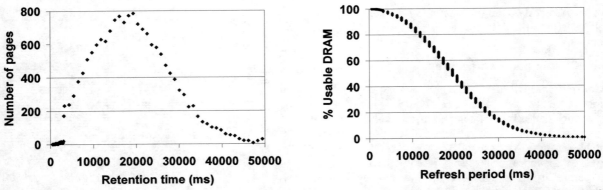

Figure 3. Distribution (left) and cumulative distribution (right) of page retention times for entire DRAM at room temperature (24°C).

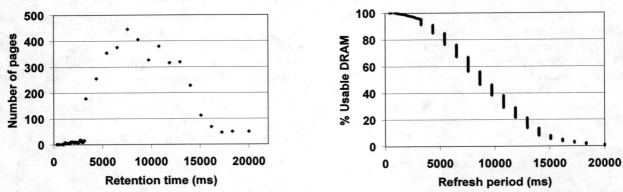

Figure 4. Distribution (left) and cumulative distribution (right) of page retention times for first DRAM bank at 45°C.

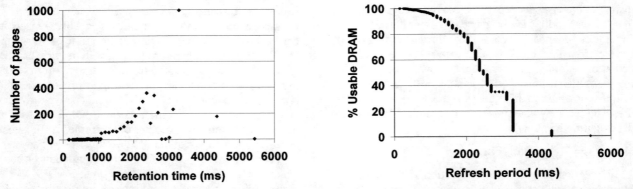

Figure 5. Distribution (left) and cumulative distribution (right) of page retention times for first DRAM bank at maximum operating temperature (70°C).

4. Retention-Aware Placement in DRAM (RAPID)

RAPID is a software-only solution for exploiting retention-time variations among different pages to minimize the refresh power in contemporary off-the-shelf DRAMs, a major component of power consumption in standby operation. The key idea is that longer-retention pages are preferred for allocation over shorter-retention pages. This enables selecting a global refresh period that is the longest possible, based on the shortest retention time among occupied pages instead of the shortest retention time among all DRAM pages.

The primary software support is modifications to routines which allocate and deallocate physical pages in memory. For example, the Linux kernel's virtual memory manager maintains a free-list of inactive physical pages – pages not touched for extended periods of time and deemed inactive – called the Inactive List. The Inactive List contains pages marked as "Inactive Dirty" or "Inactive Clean" (inactive dirty pages have yet to be flushed to their corresponding pages in the backing non-volatile storage). The RAPID-1 allocation/deallocation routines merely exclude outlier pages from the initial Inactive List. The RAPID-2 and RAPID-3 allocation/deallocation routines transform the single Inactive List into multiple Inactive Lists, one for each retention time bin. For systems with a virtual memory manager, existing Inactive List management routines would be adapted for RAPID as just described. Many embedded systems do not implement virtual memory, in which case equivalent user routines would be adapted or substituted with the RAPID allocation/deallocation routines.

The three RAPID versions are described in Sections 4.1 through 4.3. Some of the software implementation costs, in terms of software tables, are summarized in Section 4.4. Section 4.5 gives background on common refresh options available in off-the-shelf DRAMs, and explains how the single refresh period selected by RAPID can be applied to these DRAMs without custom hardware support.

4.1. RAPID-1

RAPID-1 is a static approach in which shortest-retention pages, constituting a small fraction of the overall DRAM, are made unavailable for use by application programs. They are made unavailable by excluding these pages from the Inactive List when it is initialized.

In this paper, for room temperature, we excluded all pages with retention times below 3,118 ms, a total of 168 pages (out of 16,384 pages). This yields a static refresh period of 3.2 s with 99% DRAM availability.

4.2. RAPID-2

Pages are placed into bins according to their retention times. Initial studies show 10 bins provide most of the benefit so 10 bins are used in this paper. The 10 bins are equally spaced between 3.2 s and 49 s. The shortest retention time is 3.2 s because the 168 pages below 3.2 s are excluded, like in RAPID-1. In the future, we plan to explore bins that are balanced in terms of page count. Also, note that using only 10 bins can be exploited *a priori* to reduce the run time of the testing algorithm described in Section 3.1.

The original Inactive List is split into 10 Inactive Lists, one per bin. Pages within each Inactive List are unordered, as usual, so allocating and deallocating pages from a given list remains an O(1) operation.

The bins are ordered from longest to shortest retention time. When none of the DRAM pages are populated, i.e., all Inactive Lists are full, the RAPID refresh period corresponds to the retention time of the highest bin.

A page allocation request is satisfied from the highest bin that has a non-empty Inactive List. If no more free pages are available in any of the bins that have populated pages, a page is allocated from the next lower bin. However, before the page is given over to the application program, the RAPID refresh period is decreased to accommodate the shorter retention time of the fresh bin.

When a page is deallocated, the page is returned to the Inactive List corresponding to its retention time. The page's entry in the page bin table (see Section 4.4) indicates the RAPID-2 bin to which the page belongs, to facilitate returning it to the correct Inactive List. Each bin knows how many pages (active plus inactive) belong to it. Thus, if an Inactive List becomes full when a page is returned to it, and the corresponding bin was previously the lowest bin with populated pages, then the RAPID refresh period is increased to the next higher bin that still has populated pages.

4.3. RAPID-3

RAPID-3 builds on RAPID-2. It uses the same allocation/deallocation routines described in Section 4.2, enhanced with page migration to reconsolidate data from lower to higher bins when higher bins become fragmented, i.e., underutilized. This causes the RAPID refresh period to respond faster to decreases in DRAM utilization, compared to RAPID-2.

Many migration policies are possible, from migrating immediately when a page in a higher bin becomes free, to periodically reconsolidating pages *en masse*. For our experiments, we migrate immediately when an opportunity presents itself.

4.4. RAPID Software Storage Costs

There are three major software data structures. The first is unique to RAPID. The last two have counterparts in existing page-managed systems.

- *Page bin table*. This table indicates which RAPID-2 bin each page belongs too. For 16K DRAM pages, there are 16K 4-bit entries (to encode up to 16 bins) for a storage cost of 8KB.
- *Logical-to-physical address translation table*. This is the page table in traditional virtual memory systems. The RAPID allocation routine does not change the structure or management of the traditional page table, it only affects which DRAM pages are otherwise sequentially or randomly allocated. For 16K DRAM pages, a one-to-one mapping of logical to physical

pages requires 16K 14-bit entries for a storage cost of 28KB.

- *Inactive list*. Although the single Inactive List is divided into multiple Inactive Lists for RAPID-2 and RAPID-3, the total storage cost remains the same as in traditional page-managed systems. For 16K DRAM pages, 16K list nodes are needed when no pages are populated. Assuming 8-byte nodes, the storage cost is 128KB.

4.5. Using RAPID Refresh Period with Off-the-shelf DRAMs

Off-the-shelf DRAMs typically provide one or both of the following conventional refresh options.

- *Self-refresh*. Self-refresh is implemented solely within the DRAM chip itself.
- *Auto-refresh*. The external memory controller issues regularly timed auto-refresh commands and the DRAM chip refreshes the next row in sequence. The memory controller does not send an address since the DRAM keeps track of the next row to be refreshed in sequence.

Self-refresh is significantly more power-efficient than auto-refresh, both in terms of DRAM power and external memory controller power. However, our search of DRAM datasheets reveals no DRAMs with a programmable self-refresh period. It is either 64 ms or temperature compensated, neither of which approaches the quasi-non-volatile RAPID refresh periods. If there exists a DRAM with a programmable self-refresh period, RAPID can exploit self-refresh directly by setting the self-refresh period to the RAPID refresh period.

An external memory controller typically supports a single programmable auto-refresh period. While directly compatible with the RAPID refresh period, this is not a good general solution because auto-refresh is too inefficient during long standby periods, i.e., it is better to power down the memory controller and DRAM leaving only self-refresh on. Auto-refresh may make sense during active periods. In fact, some DRAMs (like our ISSI DRAM) only support auto-refresh during active periods and self-refresh during standby periods, to explicitly avoid conflicts between internal self-refresh and external requests.

The CellularRAM™ [3] for ultra-low-power systems only supports the efficient self-refresh option. Self-refresh is used during both active and standby periods. However, the self-refresh period is not programmable except for limited temperature compensation support. As is typical, self-refresh can be enabled/disabled via a configuration register. Thus, we propose the following approach for coupling RAPID with CellularRAM™:

- When RAPID is in use, self-refresh is disabled by default.

- RAPID sets up a periodic timer interrupt, its period equal to the RAPID refresh period.
- When the interrupt occurs, a lightweight handler enables the DRAM's self-refresh and sets up a near-term interrupt for 64 ms in the future. During the 64 ms interval, self-refresh transparently refreshes the entire DRAM. The near-term interrupt invokes a second lightweight handler that disables the DRAM's self-refresh.
- In this way, the entire DRAM is refreshed only once – in a burst fashion – every RAPID refresh period.

While we discussed the above approach in the context of DRAMs with only self-refresh, the approach can be adapted to exploit programmable auto-refresh during active periods and self-refresh during standby periods, for the ISSI DRAM and others with a similar refresh dichotomy.

5. Evaluation Methodology

Mobile devices often exhibit short bursts of activity (active mode) followed by long idle periods (standby mode) [23][9]. During active mode, DRAM refresh may be a small component of overall system power, whereas, during standby mode, DRAM refresh may be the largest power component.

Obtaining activity traces of a real mobile device or sensor node is beyond the scope of this paper. We use the above bimodal active/standby characterization to guide a simplified evaluation technique for comparing refresh optimizations. This evaluation technique focuses on DRAM utilization over long tracts of time. We divide the long timeline into consecutive 100-second intervals and randomly inject 100-second active periods in place of otherwise standby periods, with a random probability that yields a typical active utilization, e.g., 5%. During active periods, we inject a random number of page requests. A request is equally probable to be an allocation vs. a deallocation so that DRAM utilization remains on average what the initial utilization was, making it possible to target a particular average DRAM utilization while still having significant utilization fluctuations during the timeline. Different refresh techniques may or may not exploit fluctuations in DRAM utilization, yielding a means for comparing techniques in a generic way. We compare the following refresh techniques:

- *TCR* (TCR): Optimal temperature-compensated refresh (TCR), i.e., the self-refresh period is based on the shortest retention time among all pages for the current temperature, as measured in Section 3.4. We use this as the baseline since the default 64 ms self-refresh is overly pessimistic and TCR is available in some current DRAMs.
- *RAPID-1* (R-1), *RAPID-2* (R-2), *RAPID-3* (R-3): These are the new RAPID methods.

- *HW-Multiperiod* (HW-M): A custom hardware solution, in which each page is refreshed at a tailored refresh period that is a multiple of the shortest refresh period among all pages in the DRAM.
- *HW-Multiperiod-Occupied* (HW-M-O): Same as HW-Multiperiod, but only pages that are currently occupied are refreshed.
- *HW-Ideal* (HW-I): An ideal custom hardware solution, in which each page is refreshed at its own tailored refresh period.
- *HW-Ideal-Occupied* (HW-I-O): Same as HW-Ideal, but only pages that are currently occupied are refreshed.

The simulated timeline is 24 hours. All simulations are configured for 5% activity and 95% standby operation. Average DRAM utilizations of 25%, 50%, and 75% are targeted. Three operating temperatures are simulated, 25°C (room temperature), 45°C, and 70°C.

The Micron CellularRAM™ [3] is the basis for refresh power. Given the CellularRAM™ refresh power at its default self-refresh period, refresh power can be calculated for an arbitrary refresh period via simple scaling.

6. Results

Figure 6 shows the refresh energy consumption (in mW·hours) for an average DRAM utilization of 75% at three different temperatures. TCR uses the worst-case refresh period at a given temperature (500 ms at 25°C, 323 ms at 45°C, and 151 ms at 70°C). By simply discarding 1% of outlier pages, RAPID-1 yields 83% (25°C), 80% (45°C), and 70% (70°C) energy savings with respect to TCR. RAPID-2 yields 93% (25°C and 45°C) and 92% (70°C) energy savings with respect to TCR. RAPID-3 yields 95% (25°C and 45°C) and 93% (70°C) energy savings with respect to TCR. Another positive result is that RAPID-2 and RAPID-3 are nearly as effective as the custom hardware approaches.

Energy savings of RAPID-1 decreases only moderately as temperature increases, from 83% to 70% over the full temperature range. One factor contributing to this decline is that, some pages that lie above the RAPID-1 retention-time threshold at 25°C, lie below this threshold at 70°C. These pages become "outliers" with respect to the 25°C RAPID-1 standard, yet they are not excluded.

In contrast, energy savings of RAPID-2 and RAPID-3 hardly decline with increasing temperature. At 75% average DRAM utilization, typical RAPID-2 and RAPID-3 refresh periods are substantially long even at 70°C.

Energy consumption of RAPID-1 at 70°C (worst-case RAPID-1) is comparable to energy consumption of TCR at 25°C (best-case TCR). This implies that a worst-case, non-temperature-adjusted RAPID-1 implementation yields the same or better energy than TCR, suggesting a potentially simpler alternative to temperature-aware DRAM design. The same case can be made in even stronger terms, for non-temperature-adjusted RAPID-2 and RAPID-3 implementations.

Figure 7 shows refresh energy at 25°C for average DRAM utilizations of 75%, 50%, and 25%. A key observation is that, as the DRAM utilization decreases, both RAPID-2 and RAPID-3 yield more energy savings than the two hardware techniques HW-M and HW-I. At 75% average utilization, the energy consumption of RAPID-2 and RAPID-3 are slightly higher than HW-M and HW-I. Yet, at 50% and 25% average utilizations, both RAPID-2 and RAPID-3 consume less energy than HW-M and even HW-I. At lower DRAM utilizations, many lines are unoccupied and RAPID's refresh period exceeds the "average" period of the hardware techniques.

The ideal hardware technique, HW-I-O, provides a more reliable lower bound on energy because it does not refresh unoccupied pages. For 25% average utilization, RAPID-3 (and even RAPID-2) approaches this lower bound.

However, even HW-I-O does not necessarily provide a lower bound on refresh energy. For non-RAPID implementations, pages are allocated without regard to page retention times. Thus, HW-I-O energy can differ for the same DRAM utilization, depending on which pages are allocated. For example, for 25% utilization, the energy of HW-I-O can vary from 0.01 mW·hours to 0.023 mW·hours, depending on whether the best or worst 25% of the DRAM pages are occupied. Energy of RAPID-3 at 25% utilization is 0.018 mW·hours. Therefore, it is possible for RAPID-3 to outperform HW-I-O.

7. Summary and Future Work

DRAM is predicted to displace SRAM in future embedded systems as functionality evolves. This future can be better met by dealing with the DRAM refresh problem and thereby reap the capacity benefits of DRAM without impacting battery life.

The key lies with exploiting dramatic variations in retention times among different DRAM pages. We proposed Retention-Aware Placement in DRAM (RAPID), novel software approaches that can exploit off-the-shelf DRAMs to reduce refresh power to vanishingly small levels approaching non-volatile memory. The key idea is to favor longer-retention pages over shorter-retention pages when allocating DRAM pages. This allows selecting a single refresh period that depends on the shortest-retention page among populated pages, instead of the shortest-retention page overall. We explore three versions of RAPID and observe refresh energy savings of 83%, 93%, and 95%, relative to conventional temperature-compensated refresh. RAPID with off-the-shelf DRAM also approaches the energy levels of

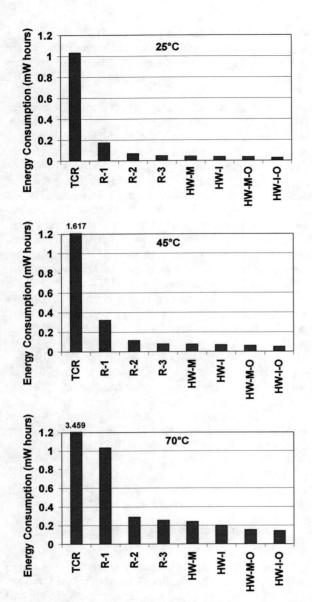

Figure 6. Refresh energy for 75% average DRAM utilization, at 25°C, 45°C, and 70°C.

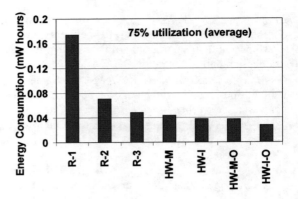

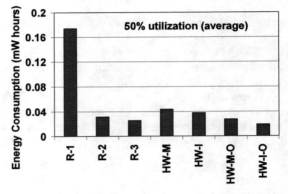

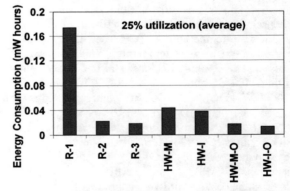

Figure 7. Refresh energy at 25°C for average DRAM utilizations of 75%, 50%, and 25%.

idealized techniques that require custom DRAM support. This ultimately yields a software implementation of quasi-non-volatile DRAM.

Much future work remains. In the area of testing, we plan to extend retention-time measurements to multiple chips from different vendors, develop rigorous testing methods with a statistical basis, apply arbitrary test patterns to identify potential cross-cell retention-time degradation or other interactions, and explore formulas for automatically scaling retention times with temperature. In the area of RAPID software, we plan to explore modifications for handling differing O/S and DRAM page sizes, sub-page retention-aware placement

(e.g., padding data structures to skip over sub-par cells), and binning strategies in RAPID-2/RAPID-3. We may also explore novel interactions between RAPID and ECC, for example, defining a page's retention time according to its second-worst bit and leveraging ECC to repair the worst bit. Finally, we plan to develop a prototype embedded system with RAPID, to demonstrate extended battery life, conveniences of instant-on/instant-off computing, enhanced resilience to power outages, and other benefits traditionally afforded by non-volatile memory.

8. Acknowledgments

We would like to thank the anonymous reviewers for their valuable comments. This research was supported in part by NSF grants CCR-0207785, CCR-0208581, and CCR-0310860, NSF CAREER grant CCR-0092832, and funding and equipment donations from Intel and Ubicom.

9. References

[1] T. Austin, D. Blaauw, T. Mudge, K. Flautner. Making Typical Silicon Matter with Razor. IEEE Computer, Volume 37 Number 3, March 2004.

[2] J. Burgan. Variable Refresh Control for a Memory. US Patent #6,778,457, Aug. 2004.

[3] CellularRAM™ – Micron website: http://download.micron.com/pdf/flyers/cellularram_flyer.pdf.

[4] L.L. Chen Hsu, G. Frankowsky, O. Weinfurtner. Dynamic DRAM Refresh Rate Adjustment Based on Cell Leakage Monitoring. US Patent #6,483,764, Nov. 2002.

[5] H.Y. Cho, J.K. Oh. Self-Refresh Apparatus for a Semiconductor Memory Device. US Patent #6,229,747, May 2001.

[6] D. Ernst et al. Razor: A Low Power Pipeline Based on Circuit-Level Timing Speculation. MICRO-36, IEEE CS Press, 2003, pp.7-18.

[7] T. Hamamoto, S. Sugiura, S. Sawada. On the Retention Time Distribution of Dynamic Random Access Memory (DRAM). IEEE Transactions on Electron Devices, Volume 45 Issue 6, June 1998, pp.1300-1309.

[8] M. Hempstead, N. Tripathi, et al. An Ultra Low Power System Architecture for Sensor Network Applications. 32nd Int'l Symp. on Computer Architecture, June 2005.

[9] J. Kim, M. Papaefthymiou. Block-Based Multiperiod Dynamic Memory Design for Low Data-Retention Power. IEEE Transactions on Very Large Scale Integration (VLSI) Systems, Vol. 11, No. 6, Dec. 2003, pp.1006-1018.

[10] J. Kim, M. Papaefthymiou. Block-Based Multi-Period Refresh for Energy Efficient Dynamic Memory. 14th ASIC/SOC Conference, Sept. 2001, pp 193-197.

[11] T. Komatsu. Self-Refreshing of Dynamic Random Access Memory Device and Operating Method Therefor. US Patent #4,943,960, July 1990.

[12] A. Lebeck, X. Fan, H. Zeng, C. Ellis. Power Aware Page Allocation. ASPLOS IX, Nov. 2000.

[13] T. Murotani. Temperature Responsive Refresh Control Circuit. US Patent #4,393,477, June 1983.

[14] L. Nazahandali, B. Zhai, et al. Energy Optimization of Subthreshold-Voltage Sensor Network Processors. 32nd Int'l Symp. on Computer Architecture, June 2005.

[15] T. Ohsawa, K. Kai, K. Murakami. Optimizing the DRAM Refresh Count for Merged DRAM/Logic LSIs. ISPLED98, pp. 82-87, August 1998.

[16] P. Pelley, J. Burgan. Memory Having Variable Refresh Control and Method Therefor. US Patent #6,781,908, Aug. 2004.

[17] Ubicom. http://www.ubicom.com

[18] A. Uht. Going Beyond Worst-Case Specs with TEAtime. IEEE Computer, Volume 37 Number 3, March 2004.

[19] UtRAM™ - Samsung website http://www.samsung.com/Products/Semiconductor/SRAM.

[20] M. Viredaz, D. Wallach. Power Evaluation of a Handheld Computer: A Case Study. Compaq-WRL Research Report 2001/1, 2001. http://www.hpl.hp.com/research/papers/2003/handheld.pdf

[21] K. Yanagisawa. Semiconductor Memory. US Patent #4,736,344, April 1988.

[22] S. Fyffe. DRAMatic Cell Phone Showdown. Electronic News, 2/12/2001. M. Kanellos, B. Charny. Phone makers copy PCs. CNET News.Com, 4/2/2002. Dram Makers Prep Multichip Cell Phone Memories. ElectroSpec, 1/3/2003.

[23] Infineon – Mobile-RAM, Specialty DRAMs. Application Note, V 1.1, Feb. 2002.

Completely Verifying Memory Consistency of Test Program Executions

Chaiyasit Manovit
Sun Microsystems / Stanford University, CA, USA
chaiyasit.manovit@sun.com

Sudheendra Hangal
Magic Lamp Software, Bangalore, India[†]
hangal@magiclampsoftware.com

Abstract

An important means of validating the design of commercial-grade shared memory multiprocessors is to run a large number of pseudo-random test programs on them. However, when intentional data races are placed in a test program, there may be many correct results according to the memory consistency model supported by the system. For popular memory models like SC and TSO, the problem of verifying correctness of an execution is known to be NP-complete. As a result, analysis techniques implemented in the past have been incomplete: violations of the memory model are flagged if provable, otherwise the result is inconclusive and it is assumed optimistically that the machine's results are correct.

In this paper, we describe for the first time a practical, new algorithm which can solve this problem with certainty, thus ensuring that incorrect behavior of a large, complex multiprocessor cannot escape. We present results of our analysis algorithm on test programs run on a newly designed multiprocessor system built by Sun Microsystems. We show that our algorithm performs very well, typically analyzing a program with 512K memory operations distributed across 60 processors within a few minutes. Our algorithm runs in less than 2.6 times the time taken by an incomplete baseline algorithm which may miss errors. Our approach greatly increases the confidence in the correctness of the results generated by the multiprocessor, and allows us to potentially uncover more bugs in the design than was previously possible.

1. Introduction

This paper deals with the problem of verifying whether the outcome generated by a shared memory multiprocessor on executing a test program with data races is correct. Correctness of the result is defined by the memory consistency model [1]. Examples of common memory consistency models (also referred to as memory models in the rest of this paper) are Sequential Consistency (SC), Total Store Order (TSO), Relaxed Memory Order (RMO) [16] and Release Consistency (RC) [7]. While the focus of our discussion in this paper is the TSO memory model, our general methodology can be extended relatively easy to other memory models as well.

Our work is motivated by the challenges we have encountered in verifying large, complex multiprocessor systems. While pseudo-random testing is the backbone of microprocessor design validation efforts, it is difficult to employ this methodology effectively for multiprocessors, since a simple "golden reference model" cannot be used to check the result of a test program unless it is free of data races [13]. This is a severe limitation because tests with aggressive data races tend to expose multiprocessor bugs much faster. This is proved by the fact that verification teams often run such tests "blind", even if they are unable to check correctness of program results. They hope to expose bugs by hitting obvious problems such as a machine hang, system panic, or an unexpected program crash. However, such testing cannot hope to expose subtle multiprocessor issues such as illegal instruction ordering or atomicity violations. Even if an analysis methodology does exist to check for such violations, its efficiency is an important consideration, since test throughput is an important factor in pseudo-random testing. The more test cycles run, the higher the confidence in the design, and it is not uncommon for verification teams to be required to run several trillions of pseudo-randomly generated test instructions correctly before shipping a new processor or system [2].

Our overall multiprocessor validation flow is like this:
1. Random generator creates programs with data races
2. Each test program is run on a multiprocessor
3. Analysis algorithm verifies if program results are legal

In step 1, a multiprocessor test program is generated, which may also include instructions to store programmer visible results of its load instructions for further analysis, depending on the available observability (if the system under test is simulated, for example, we may be able to directly observe the results of load instructions). In step 2, the program is run on a test platform and the results are collected. This paper assumes the dynamic program description and its results are available, and focuses on efficient algorithms to be used in step 3. Any testing-based approach has the limitation that it is only as good as the tests employed. (Of course, we continuously tune our test-program generator to better expose corner-cases in the design). However, it has the advantage that it can be employed on a real system and not just on an abstract model. Checking end-to-end correctness on real systems is very important given the disparate elements involved –

[†] This work was carried out while the author was affiliated with Sun Microsystems India Private Limited.

e.g. multi-core, multi-threaded processors, various caches in the memory hierarchy, the coherency protocol, the system interconnect, software emulation routines in the kernel, etc. – and the complexities and corner cases in their interaction. In addition, our test methodology has the advantage that it runs on commercial multiprocessor hardware, running stock operating systems, and can even be run as a user-mode process at a customer site, since it requires no additional probes into the system, such as logic analyzers and oscilloscopes. The analysis algorithms rely only on programmer-visible results of the program and do not inherently need additional information from the system; of course, any additional ordering information is used if it is available.

Not requiring extra observability is a key attribute affecting overall test throughput, since maintaining observability often involves slowing down the system and reducing test throughput. Even in pre-silicon validation environments, hardware accelerators can simulate designs orders of magnitude faster if observability is sacrificed.

Unlike previous work [8][11], our goal in this paper is to develop a sound *and* complete algorithm (i.e. no false errors reported and no consistency errors left undetected) which is practically applicable. Instead of assuming a machine innocent unless proved guilty, we aim to determine exactly whether or not the system obeys the memory model guarantees available to the programmer, for a given test execution result.

Our paper makes the two following important contributions:

1. We describe a set of efficient algorithms for verifying TSO compliance of a test program execution. We also introduce an efficient way to perform backtracking in order to make the analysis complete.

2. We implement these algorithms and report results of applying them on large multiprocessor server systems currently under test. We show that a complete analysis incorporating edges inference with backtracking, while being theoretically exponential in the number of processors, actually runs in very reasonable time and requires minimal backtracking. Our algorithm also suggests a potential technique to solve the view serializability problem in databases, which is reducible to the VSC-read problem (see definition in Section 2.)

Paper Outline: Section 2 discusses related work and existing approaches to verifying compliance of a test execution with the memory consistency model. Section 3 presents a formal specification for TSO, and the equivalence of two variants which are necessary for correctness of the analysis algorithms. Section 4 presents a baseline algorithm, and then describes three increasingly precise extensions. Section 5 describes our results on running these analysis algorithms on large

multiprocessor configurations of up to 60 processors. Section 6 concludes the paper.

2. Related work

The problem of verifying whether a multiprocessor test program execution complies with a memory consistency model was first studied by Gibbons and Korach for the SC memory model [6]. They called the problem VSC (Verifying Sequential Consistency) and proved that the basic VSC problem is NP-complete with respect to the number of operations in the program, as are several variations of the problem, when the number of processors is unbounded. In particular, the VSC-read problem, which assumes the presence of a mapping function of every read to the operation which wrote the value it read, is also NP-complete. The VSC and VSC-read problems were originally proven NP-complete by a reduction from the 3SAT and the database view serializability problem respectively [14]. The VSC-conflict problem, which is the VSC-read problem augmented with the total write order per-location, however, is in P (and similarly, so is the conflict serializability problem in databases). Similar results have been shown for the corresponding problems for the TSO memory model; VTSO and VTSO-read are NP-complete, while the VTSO-conflict problem can be solved in linear time [8][11]. The Verifying Memory Coherence (VMC) problem, which is like VSC, but involves only one memory location, is also NP-complete; however, VMC-read is in P [4]. The most interesting variants of the problem for our purpose are the VTSO and VTSO-read (or VSC and VSC-read), since pseudo-randomly generated tests can easily be mapped to these problems and the analysis is performed on architectural results visible to the program. The VSC-conflict problem, though easier to solve, is not very useful on real systems, since write ordering per location is not easily observable in general. Gibbons and Korach also propose an algorithm for VSC-read based on searching a frontier graph which has a worst case running time of $O(n^p)$ for n operations and a fixed number of processors p [5]; however, this algorithm is impractical for realistic values of p.

Our previous work describes an incomplete algorithm which makes a best effort to determine if there is a valid ordering of operations which can justify the results of the test program [8]. We also developed a simple heuristic to determine if an order satisfying all the axioms of the memory model exist [11]. However, in the many cases (up to 80% of 16 processor program runs) that the heuristic failed to determine this, we had to optimistically assume an order exists though it had not been found. This runs the risk of letting illegal results go undetected. In contrast, our new algorithm finds out exactly whether an order satisfying all the axioms of the memory model exists, and if it does, it finds the valid order as well.

169

Cain and Lipasti have proposed a distributed algorithm to verify correctness of program execution with respect to SC [3]; however, their techniques employs online vector clocks for each processor and at each shared memory location and assumes additional hardware logic is available for keeping these clocks updated. In our technique, in contrast, vector clocks are offline, imposing no overhead on the test program or hardware implementation. Plakal et al statically verify that a directory-based protocol implements Sequential Consistency [15], while Meixner and Sorin use their proofs to propose addition of verification hardware to the processor, cache and memory controller which can dynamically verify Sequential Consistency [12].

Microprocessor design verification teams often use the additional observability present in simulation to reason about ordering and correctness [9]. However, these techniques are heavily microarchitecture dependent, and are not usable when additional observability is absent. Taylor et al use a set of informal rules to reason about ordering of events in test execution [17]; however the completeness or efficiency of their algorithm is not described.

Finally, the generic notion of embedding memory ordering relations in a graph (and performing cycle detection on the graph to flag inconsistencies) has been used often and is originally attributed to Landin et al [10].

3. TSO specification

The axioms of the TSO memory model have been formally described by Sindhu et al [16]. We briefly discuss the notation and the axioms below. The notation used is as follows:

L_a^i	a Load to location a by processor i
S_a^i	a Store to location a by processor i
$[L_a^i; S_a^i]$	a Swap to location a by processor i
$Val[L_a^i]$	the value read by L_a^i
$Val[S_a^i]$	the value written by S_a^i
Op_a^i	either a load or a store
M	a memory barrier
;	a per processor program order
$\leq$	the global memory order

An order is defined as a relation that is reflexive, anti-symmetric and transitive. The per processor program order is denoted by the character ; and the global memory order is denoted by the character $\leq$. The following are the TSO axioms per Sindhu et al, augmented with an additional axiom for Memory barriers.

Order: There is a total order over all stores.

$$\forall S_a^i, S_b^j : (S_a^i \leq S_b^j) \vee (S_b^j \leq S_a^i)$$

Atomicity: No stores can intervene between the load and store components of an atomic swap.

$$[L_a^i; S_a^i] \Rightarrow (L_a^i \leq S_a^i) \wedge (\forall S_b^j : S_b^j \leq L_a^i \vee S_a^i \leq S_b^j)$$

Termination: If one processor does a store and another processor repeatedly does loads to the same location, there will eventually be a load that succeeds S in $\leq$.

$$S_a^i \wedge (L_a^j;) \infty \Rightarrow \exists L_a^j \in (L_a^j;) \infty \text{ such that } S_a^i \leq L_a^j$$

LoadOp and **StoreStore**: The only reordering allowed between operations on the same processor is that loads can overtake preceding stores.

$$L_a^i; Op_b^i \Rightarrow L_a^i \leq Op_b^i$$

$$S_a^i; S_b^i \Rightarrow S_a^i \leq S_b^i$$

Value: The value returned by a load is the value written to it by the last store in global order, amongst the set of stores preceding it in either global order or program order.

$$Val[L_a^i] = Val[\underset{\leq}{Max}[\{S_a^k | S_a^k \leq L_a^i\} \cup \{S_a^i | S_a^i; L_a^i\}]]$$

Membar: Membars order operations on the issuing processor.

$$Op_1; M; Op_2 \Rightarrow Op_1 \leq Op_2$$

Note that the definition of the value axiom permits implementations with store buffers to locally bypass data from a store to a load, before the store is globally visible. For the SC memory model, the only difference from TSO is that this is disallowed; all relations in program order must also appear in global order.

The TSO memory model as defined in SPARC V9 [18] is slightly different from the above axioms in 2 points:

1. Memory order is total on all memory operations. (The Order axiom above only defines it to be total on all stores.)
2. Atomic swaps do not allow any other memory operation to intervene the load and the store components at all. (The Atomicity axiom above only prevents intervening stores.)

Formally:

Order: There is a total order over all operations.

$$\forall Op_a^i, Op_b^j : (Op_a^i \leq Op_b^j) \vee (Op_b^j \leq Op_a^i)$$

Atomicity: No operations can intervene between the load and store components of an atomic swap.

$$[L_a^i; S_a^i] \Rightarrow (L_a^i \leq S_a^i) \wedge (\forall Op_b^j : Op_b^j \leq L_a^i \vee S_a^i \leq Op_b^j)$$

It can be shown, however, that these 2 seemingly different definitions of the TSO model are essentially equivalent for verification purposes, i.e. any execution trace which satisfies the axioms of either system also satisfies the other. For ease of understanding and designing analysis algorithms, we will use the stricter versions of the Order and Atomicity axioms.

4. Algorithms for verifying TSO

Our main focus in this section is algorithms for the VTSO-read problem. We impose the constraint on test programs that each store in a test program writes a different value. This allows us to map each load to the store which created the value it read, and thus gives us the read-mapping function.

The following features are common to all algorithms described in this section. A program and its execution result are represented by a directed graph, whose nodes represent dynamic operations (loads or stores) in the program. Edges represent ordering relations in the global memory order $\leq$. Since $\leq$ is transitive, any path in the graph implies the existence of the $\leq$ relation between the source and destination of the path. We ignore reflexivity of $\leq$ by not explicitly adding an edge from each node to itself. A legal outcome should not cause cycles in the graph, since this would violate the anti-symmetry property of $\leq$.

A synthetic node at the root of the graph acts like a set of stores writing initial values to all memory locations. A set of atomic operations is modeled in the graph by forcing incoming edges incident to any node in the set to point to its first node; similarly, outgoing edges from any node in the set are redirected to leave from its last node. This automatically ensures that the (stronger version of the) Atomicity axiom holds for all relations embedded in the graph at all times. A read-mapping function $w(L)$ maps each load to the store which wrote that value. A failure is directly signaled if there exists a load reading a value never written to that memory location. An inverse of the read-mapping is also computed and cached in each store node; it represents the set of all loads that read the value written by that store.

4.1. Baseline algorithm for VTSO-read

The baseline algorithm (reproduced from our previous work [11]) adds edges to the graph using following rules:

Static Edges: Program order edges are added to the graph according to the following 3 rules. These edges are independent of execution results:

R1: $L;Op \Rightarrow L \leq Op$ (LoadOp axiom)

R2: $S;S' \Rightarrow S \leq S'$ (StoreStore axiom)

R3: $S;M;L \Rightarrow S \leq L$ (Membar axiom)

Note that we can redirect our verification from TSO to the SC memory model just by changing the above rules to ensure that program order between two operations also implies global order between them. The rest of the rules for all the algorithms in this section can remain exactly the same.

For the remaining rules, let S, S', and L be accesses to the same location; where $S = w(L)$ and $S' \neq S$.

Observed Edges: For all loads, the edges specified by the following 2 rules are added based on the load results.

R4: $\neg S;L \Rightarrow S \leq L$ (Value axiom)

This follows because S must be in one of the two store sets in the Value axiom for L.

R5: $S';L \Rightarrow S' \leq S$ (Value axiom)

This must be true because if both $S \leq S'$ and $S';L$ are true, L cannot read the value written by S according to the Value axiom. We only need to consider the latest store S' preceding L, because prior stores from the same thread are ordered before S'.

Inferred Edges: The last 2 rules follow from the Value axiom:

R6: $S' \leq L \Rightarrow S' \leq S$ (Value axiom)

Assuming otherwise, $S \leq S'$ (and given $S' \leq L$) will lead to a contradiction because L cannot read the value written by S as it would have already been overwritten by S'.

R7: $S \leq S' \Rightarrow L \leq S'$ (Value axiom)

Assuming otherwise, $S' \leq L$ (because there is a total order on all operations, according to the stronger version of the Order axiom), it would be illegal for L to read the value written by S as it would have already been overwritten by S'.

Note that we use the order $\leq$, which is still being derived, to determine the condition to infer more edges in rules R6 and R7. To solve this circular dependency, we iterate over these two rules until no further edges can be added to the graph and a fixed point is reached.

Intuitively, this algorithm tries to efficiently infer as much information about ordering as possible. The rules in this algorithm are selected such that they can be efficiently implemented; they are not necessarily complete. Nevertheless, if we also have available the total write order per location for the test case, the VTSO-read problem is transformed into an instance of the VTSO-conflict problem, for which this algorithm is complete [11].

A key performance enhancement for the above algorithm is the employment of vector clocks. The use of vector clocks is popular in the area of distributed computing, where they are used on each processing element to track the perceived time at other processing elements. In a similar way, we associate offline vector clocks with each operation in the program to reason about what operations on other processors must succeed this operation. These vector clocks are present only during analysis; they do not involve any maintenance by the hardware or the test program as it is running.

Using vector clocks, we avoid being exhaustive in applying rules R6 and R7 to every pair $S' \leq L$ and $S \leq S'$ in the program in each iteration. It is sufficient to start at each store node and search only for its earliest successors, either loads or stores, that access the same location but with different values. For the SC model, we only need to find the earliest such successor per thread as program order in SC implies global order. For the TSO model, a load can overtake preceding stores on the same processor, and therefore, we split the instruction stream of one TSO processor into two *virtual SC* processors; one contains only loads and the other contains the rest (stores, atomics, and membars). In the TSO model $L;S$ also implies $L \leq S$, and $S;M;L$ implies $S \leq M \leq L$, and we shall represent these ordering requirements with an edge between such operations which are now separated in the two *virtual SC* processors. We attach to each node a data structure based on reverse time vector clocks to track its earliest successors in other *virtual SC* processors. This data structure helps limit the number of edges per node to the number of *virtual SC* processors. Figure 1 outlines the algorithm for rules R6 and R7.

Time Complexity: Although the total number of edges in the graph at a given point in time is bounded by $O(pn)$ where p is the number of processors and n is the number of nodes, the number of iterations in the worst case is actually bounded by the total number of possible edges, which is $O(n^2)$. This is because an edge inferred in one iteration may be rendered redundant and removed due to a stronger edge inferred in a later iteration. In each iteration, there are $O(n)$ stores whose vector clocks will be traced with $O(p)$ time complexity each. This totals to $O(pn^3)$.

4.2. Completely verifying TSO

We now turn our attention to algorithms which can completely verify TSO. The baseline algorithm presented in the previous section is incomplete because even when the graph is acyclic, it does not explicitly ensure that the Order axiom is satisfied. Figure 2a illustrates a case where an existing relation is not inferred by the algorithm; the edges in the graph are depicted at the point when the fixed point has been reached (edges from a store to corresponding loads reading its value are omitted to not overcrowd the graph). The notation here is: S[A]#1 refers to a store which writes value 1 to location A, while L[B]=11 refers to a load to address B which reads value 11; Pn denotes operations on processor n. Notice that S[A]#1 and S[A]#2 are left unordered by the baseline analysis. However, we can reason that S[A]#1 $\leq$ S[A]#2 must be true. If not, S[A]#2 $\leq$ S[A]#1 by the Order axiom; but with this order and the fact that only one of the two values, either 11 or 12, can survive in location B after S[A]#2, both loads from location B must read the same value. This example illustrates a missing relation, but not yet a missed TSO violation; simply adding a similar, mirrored set of nodes to a different location C

Input: A per virtual SC processor instruction sequence consisting of loads, stores, and membars. A swap is considered to be both a load and a store. A function w, which maps a load to the store which created its value:

Data Structure: An offline Reverse Time Vector Clock at each node x, $x.rtvc[i]$ points to the first node in virtual SC processor i such that $x \leq x.rtvc[i]$. Initial $rtvc[]$ for all nodes are precomputed with backward topological sort.

Apply **rules R1-R5**

[rule R6 and R7] - done in iterations

do
  for each store S whose $rtvc[]$ has been changed
    for each virtual SC processor i
     $x := S.rtvc[i]$
     if x is a load (virtual SC processor i contains only loads) then
      $L :=$ first load that accesses same location as S, $x;L$, and $w(L) \neq S$
      [rule R6]
      add edge $S \rightarrow w(L)$ if not already $S \leq w(L)$
      update $S.rtvc[]$ (and propagate to its predecessors recursively)
     else (virtual SC processor i contains stores, atomics and membars)
      $S' :=$ first store/atomic that accesses same location as S and $x;S'$
      [rule R7]
      for all loads L such that $w(L)=S$
       add edge $L \rightarrow S'$ if not already $L \leq S'$
       update $L.rtvc[]$ (and propagate to its predecessors recursively)
      end for
     end if
    end for
  end for
until no more edges can be added

Figure 1. High level description of the iteration over R6 & R7 with Vector Clocks

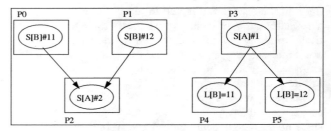

Figure 2a.

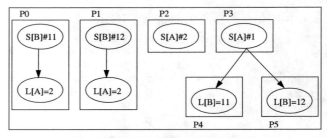

Figure 2b. (Membars are omitted)

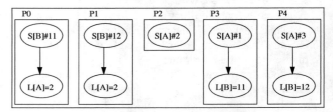

Figure 2c. (Membars are omitted)

Figure 2. Examples of incompleteness

(two stores to C ordered before S[A]#1, and two loads to C ordered after S[A]#2) creates an instance of a real TSO violation. In this case, the two stores S[A]#1 and S[A]#2 cannot be ordered, but such a violation would be missed by the incomplete algorithm in the previous section.

One may attempt to design a rule to infer the missing edge in this example. Consider the following hypothetical rule:

R8: *CommonPred(L, L') ≤ CommonSucc(S, S')*

L and *L'* are loads to the same location reading different values written by *S* and *S'* respectively. *CommonPred(L, L')* is the latest node that precedes both *L* and *L'* in the current snapshot of the global order being derived, while *CommonSucc(S, S')* is conversely defined. While this rule will catch the missing edge in the example shown in Figure 2a, it still misses the edge in a slightly modified scenario shown in Figure 2b because there is no common successor between S[B]#11 and S[B]#12. Note that Membars between the store and the load in the same processor are omitted from the picture (or readers may assume the SC model). S[A]#1 ≤ S[A]#2 is a missing edge because, assumed the opposite order, both L[A]=2 nodes will be ordered before S[A]#1 by rule R7, making S[A]#1 the common successor of S[B]#11 and S[B]#12 and, hence, only one value, either 11 or 12, can survive in location B.

Figure 2c illustrates that missing edges are not the only form of incompleteness. One can reason that S[A]#2 cannot be ordered before both S[A]#1 *and* S[A]#3 because that would lead to the same contradiction seen earlier with Figure 2b (when we incorrectly order S[A]#2 ≤ S[A]#1). However, such a constraint cannot be captured in our graph representation where we only draw an edge to order 2 operations when such an order is certain. Despite knowing that S[A]#1 ≤ S[A]#2 *or* S[A]#3 ≤ S[A]#2 (or both) in this example, we can draw neither edge because their presence is not certain when considered individually. To create a TSO violation that would be missed by the baseline algorithm, we can add a similar, mirrored set of nodes such that none of the stores to location A can be ordered first.

To completely verify TSO compliance, we will attempt to determine if there exists a *Total Operation Order* (TOO), which completely orders all operations (loads and stores) in the program, that also satisfies the rest of the TSO axioms. Recall that this TOO corresponds to the stronger version of the Order axiom (which is equivalent to the requirement that only stores be ordered).

A simplistic approach to determining if a valid TOO exists would be to perform a topological sort on the analysis graph after the completion of the baseline algorithm, and check if all the axioms still hold (the same baseline algorithm can be conveniently used to determine the validity of a TOO, as earlier pointed out in Section 4.1). The topological sort effectively creates an arbitrary "tie-break" decision between operations left unordered by

the baseline algorithm. We have found that most often, this sort does not yield a valid order. This is because when we arbitrarily assign an order between a pair of previously unordered operations during topological sort, it often has ordering implications on other unordered operations; this creates conflicts and usually ends up violating the Value axiom. Since a straightforward algorithm based on topological sort does not work, we discuss three techniques in the following sections towards improving the chances of finding a valid TOO. In all cases, we assume the baseline algorithm has inferred all its edges and terminated without cycles in the graph.

4.2.1. Heuristic for topological sort (*Heu*). In our previous work, we ensure that each time a store node is picked by the topological sort, rule R7 is immediately applied to it [11]. An alternative, but equivalent, implementation of this heuristic is to track the *active* store (the store that was most recently picked by the topological sort) for each memory location and allow the topological sort to further pick only a load that reads the value written by the *active* store or by the store preceding the load in program order. When all loads that read the value written by an *active* store have been picked, the store becomes *inactive* and new store can be picked and made *active*. (For SC, this heuristic is similar to the conditions used to determine the validity of frontiers in the $O(n^p)$ backtracking algorithm by Gibbons and Korach [5]. However, an important difference is that their algorithm does not have any notion of initially inferring edges as in our baseline algorithm, and as a result will visit many more invalid paths in the frontier graph).

Time Complexity: A typical topological sort has $O(n+e)$ complexity where n is the number of nodes and e is the number of edges, which is $O(pn)$ in this case (because each node only maintains a vector clock). In addition, this heuristic spends $O(p)$ time to evaluate the selection for the next node. This extra effort is $O(pn)$ and, nevertheless, the total complexity is still $O(pn)$. Note that this time complexity is for a case when the algorithm succeeds in finding a valid TOO. The heuristic may terminate much sooner when a TOO cannot be found.

Although this heuristic is intuitive and fast, we find that it is inadequate; it helps find a valid TOO only when there is relatively low sharing, i.e. *p/a* is small (where *p* is the number of processors and *a* is the number of memory locations) [11]. Section 5 provides more results.

4.2.2. Deriving edges during topological sort (*Deriv*). We can extend the heuristic technique in the previous section thus: Each time a store node is picked by the topological sort, rules R6 and R7 are reapplied iteratively to the whole graph until a new fixed point is reached. Careful implementations can minimize the computation by applying the rules only to the affected nodes. (In our implementations, such optimizations are also applied to the baseline algorithm during iteration.)

173

Time Complexity: Although this heuristic has to go through as many fixed points as the total number of stores which is $O(n)$, the total number of iterations required to apply rules R6 and R7 throughout these $O(n)$ fixed points is still bounded by the total number of possible edges, $O(n^2)$. Therefore, the worst-case time complexity remains $O(pn^3)$. Again, this time complexity is for the case when the algorithm succeeds in finding a valid TOO. It may terminate much sooner when this heuristic fails.

Despite the additional effort spent in deriving more edges, this algorithm's effectiveness in finding a valid TOO is still limited with intense sharing. Nevertheless, in practice, it provides significant improvement in TOO completion rate over the previous heuristic.

4.2.3. Backtracking (*Heu+Back, Deriv+Back*).

Since the above heuristics are only best-effort and had unsatisfactory rates of completion (in which case the analysis is inconclusive and optimistically assumed passing), we decided to implement backtracking on top of both the heuristics described above. When the topological sort gets stuck (no instruction can be picked without violating any TSO axioms), instead of giving up, we backtrack to the last arbitrary tie-break decision made and choose a different operation to order first. Given that a valid Total Store Order will also result in a valid TOO (as pointed out in Section 2 regarding the equivalence of the two different versions of the Order axiom), we can unwind the order directly to the most recent store.

For the heuristic *Heu* in Section 4.2.1, adding backtracking is relatively easy. Adding the feature to the *Deriv* algorithm in Section 4.2.2 is less straightforward because it modifies the graph by deriving additional edges based on ordering decisions made by the topological sort. We maintain our data structures such that we can checkpoint and undo these updates when we need to backtrack and cancel the decision. Edges that are derived after a store is picked by the topological sort will be associated with the store. When we backtrack and undo the picking of a store, we remove all the derived edges associated with it and recompute vector clocks for all the affected nodes.

Time Complexity: By using a similar argument to that which Gibbons and Korach use to explain the bounds on their backtracking algorithm based on searching the frontier graph [5], the worst-case complexity of our backtracking algorithms is also $O(n^p/p^p)$. At each step during backtracking, the additional cost of finding a new fixed point is $O(pn^3)$. This results in $O(n^p/p^p \times pn^3)$ in total. However, in practice, the number and depth of backtracks is small, resulting in small penalty in terms of time over the *Deriv* heuristic in the previous section. In return for this increase in analysis time, we achieve a 100% completion rate when a valid ordering exists which justifies the results of the program.

5. Results

In this section, we present results of our extensions to the baseline analysis algorithm on test results generated from a new multiprocessor system which is actively under test at Sun Microsystems. Our results show that *Deriv+Back* performs very well; it completely analyzes programs with 512K memory operations distributed across 60 processors and finds a valid TOO for each program within 5 minutes. On average, the analysis time is less than 2.6 times that of the incomplete baseline algorithm which may miss errors. Therefore we find that *Deriv+Back* greatly increases our confidence in the correctness of the results generated by the multiprocessor, and allows us to potentially uncover more bugs in the design than was previously possible.

On the other hand, *Heu+Back* (which does not iteratively derive additional edges during the topological sort) does not perform well at all; on all tests except the ones with a small number of processors, it did not finish in a reasonable amount of time. Therefore, we ignore it from further consideration. Also recall that all of the algorithms *Heu*, *Deriv*, and *Deriv+Back* are applied on top of the baseline algorithm, that is after it has reached a fixed point. Applying them directly, without first running the baseline algorithm, we found they were much less effective: the effectiveness of *Heu* and *Deriv* in finding a valid TOO reduced dramatically and the time spent in *Deriv+Back* exploded as the number of backtracks increased substantially. While we studied these variations for completeness, we do not consider them interesting and therefore omit their detailed results from this section.

System under test: We performed the following experiments on an actual multiprocessor system designed and built by Sun Microsystems. The system we ran the test programs on has 60 processor cores. Test threads are bound to different processor cores, and run mostly concurrently since the system is quiet except for background operating system activity. We ran pseudo-random multi-threaded programs with the following instruction mix: 33.3% loads, 33.3% stores, 30% atomic swaps, 1.7% membars, and 1.7% others. We varied the number of threads/processors (p) and the number of memory locations (a) used by the programs, as well as the size of the programs (denoted as n, the total number of memory operations across all processors). The execution results of these programs were saved and later analyzed on a different system based on a previous generation 1.2 GHz Sun's UltraSPARC-III+ processor. For each tuple (n,p,a), 16 different pseudo-random programs were generated, executed, and analyzed. Unless noted otherwise, the presented results are the average over these 16 runs for each tuple. Analysis time is the major factor determining test throughput since the test threads are pre-generated and pre-compiled, and only thread selection is done at runtime. Running the test itself takes on the order of a few milliseconds on a real system.

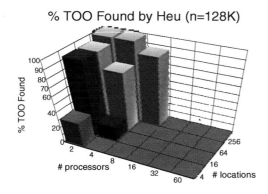

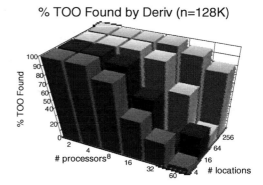

Figure 3. Effectiveness of *Heu* and *Deriv* in finding valid TOO's

While we have also applied our verification methodology to the same system in a pre-silicon software simulation environment, analysis time was not a major concern in that case. Nevertheless having a complete algorithm is useful. In simulation, though we can sometimes deal with the much simpler VTSO-conflict problem - which is in P - if total write order for each location can be observed, in reality, such ordering is often not readily available in the simulation test bench, as a single point of ordering may not exist in complex systems. Besides, software simulators usually scale up to only a few processors and cannot handle large whole-system simulations.

Figure 3 shows the effectiveness of *Heu* and *Deriv* in finding a valid TOO for n=128K. (For larger number of operations, n, their effectiveness decreases as expected.) *Deriv* provides significant improvement over *Heu* but it is still incomplete when data sharing is intense. With backtracking, *Deriv+Back* always finds a valid TOO in our experiments. A key finding is that when backtracking is necessary, the number of backtracks is at most 75, which is small for the large problem sizes used in our experiments, and the algorithm never backtracks more than 1 level each time. This means that the additional overhead due to backtracking is minimal, compared to just running *Deriv*. We also note that the analysis time overhead incurred by *Heu* is virtually constant and minimal, about 10%, while the overhead incurred by *Deriv+Back* is significant and grows with all of p, n, and a. Analyzing the largest test programs in our experiment, with n=512K, p=60, and a=256, takes, on the average, 118% more time than the baseline algorithm for cases that require backtracking (while *Deriv* would take 108% more time for cases not requiring backtracking, just a slightly smaller overhead). With a lower processor count (16 and below), the analysis time overhead is usually less than 80% over the baseline algorithm.

We deem the extra overhead in terms of analysis time worth the extra assurance that the program results are indeed correct, especially for large processor configurations where the errors may be subtle and test methodologies are limited.

Figure 4 shows the effect of n, p, and a on the analysis time. The absolute analysis time of the baseline algorithm and *Deriv+Back* are plotted in Figure 4a and 4c respectively. Figure 4b shows the ratio of the analysis time of *Deriv+Back* over the baseline. Since the graphs are plotted using log scale over the same range on Y-axis, we can view Figure 4c as being the superposition of Figure 4a and 4b. As can be seen, the slope in Figure 4b is less than that in Figure 4a, which means the increasing analysis time seen in Figure 4c are dominated by the increasing analysis time in Figure 4a. This interpretation suggests that our backtracking technique can scale (as long as the baseline algorithm scales).

We also repeated the same experiments using 2 other instruction distributions in the pseudo-random test generator: one biased toward load instructions, with 50% loads and 16% stores, and the other biased toward store instruction, with 50% stores and 16% loads (percentages of other instructions were kept the same). On the average, as the percentage of stores increases, we find that the analysis takes more time. Both the absolute analysis time of the baseline and the slowdown ratio of *Deriv+Back* are affected, as shown in Table 1.

We conjecture that a higher store density requires longer analysis time for *Deriv+Back* because there are potentially more values that are not observed at all, and hence, the baseline algorithm can infer fewer relations which would be helpful for *Deriv+Back* during backtracking. With no loads at all, on the other hand, the analysis would run very quickly because any ordering would be acceptable under TSO axioms. Therefore, we

Table 1. Baseline analysis time and slowdown ratio of *Deriv+Back* for n=256K, averaged over p and a.

	LD-biased	LD-ST equal	ST-biased
Baseline (secs)	14.9	16.5	17.5
Slowdown ratio	1.45	1.73	2.05

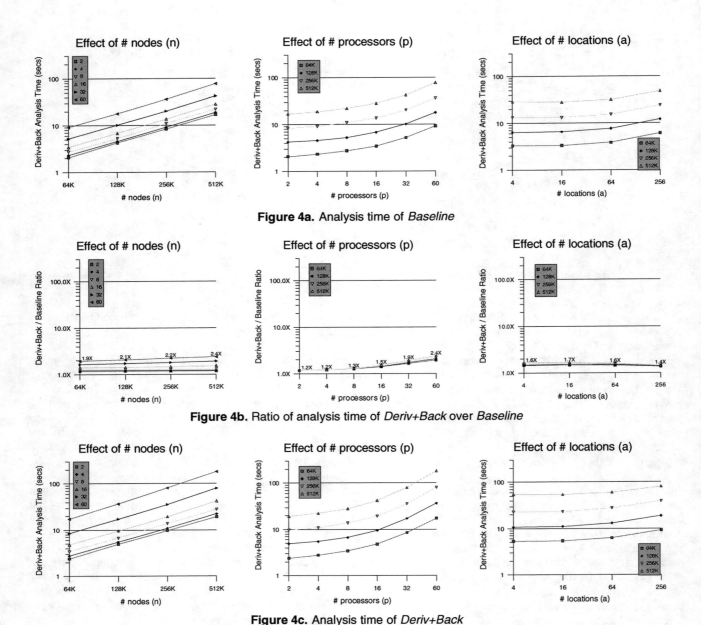

Figure 4a. Analysis time of *Baseline*

Figure 4b. Ratio of analysis time of *Deriv+Back* over *Baseline*

Figure 4c. Analysis time of *Deriv+Back*

Figure 4. Analysis time of *Deriv+Back* vs. *n* (averaged over *a*), *p* (averaged over *a*), and *a* (averaged over *p*)

expect a tipping point, as we bias the test more towards stores, where the runtime starts to decrease.

Although *Deriv+Back* has not discovered any bugs so far in the real system that are missed by the baseline analysis, we tested it with TSO violations based on the examples in Figure 2, and it successfully found the missed cycles, as expected. Being a backtracking algorithm, however, it cannot avoid the exponential analysis time complexity for such cases. We expect to explore other heuristics in order to find a smaller portion of an execution trace that contains the TSO violation.

6. Conclusions and future work

We have described a set of algorithms which can be used to verify whether a test program execution complies with the axioms of the memory consistency model. Our algorithms encompass a range of accuracy and runtime. Faster algorithms may miss errors in return for higher throughput; slower algorithms based on backtracking will not miss errors, but have an additional runtime overhead of 20-160%.

Overall, our findings indicate that backtracking is essential for a good completion rate when no violation exists; however the actual number of backtracks needed even in a large program is relatively small, and the backtracking depth is shallow. Therefore, it is well worth the trade-off to implement backtracking, since it implies only a small overhead compared to algorithms whose completion rate is much lower.

Although we present our algorithms and results based on the TSO and SC memory models, the framework that we have developed is applicable to other memory models including Relaxed Memory Order (RMO) and Transactional Memory.

7. Acknowledgments

We thank the anonymous reviewers for their useful comments, Robert Cypher for many helpful discussions regarding the VTSO problems, and Shrenik Mehta and Durgam Vahia for managerial support.

8. References

[1] S.V. Adve and K. Gharachorloo, "Shared Memory Consistency Models: A Tutorial", *Digital Western Research Laboratory Technical Report*, 1995.

[2] B. Bentley and R. Gray, "Validating The Intel Pentium-4 Processor", *Intel Technology Journal*, 1st Quarter 2001.

[3] H.W. Cain and M.H. Lipasti, "Verifying Sequential Consistency Using Vector Clocks", *Proceedings of the 14th ACM Symposium on Parallel Algorithms and Architectures (SPAA)*, 2002.

[4] J.E. Cantin, M.H. Lipasti, and J.E. Smith, "The complexity of Verifying Memory Coherence", *Proceedings of the 15th annual ACM symposium on Parallel Algorithms and Architectures*, pp. 254-255, ACM, 2003.

[5] P.B. Gibbons and E. Korach, "On Testing Cache-Coherent Shared Memories", *Proceedings of the 6th ACM Symposium on Parallel Algorithms and Architectures (SPAA)*, 1994.

[6] P.B. Gibbons and E. Korach, "Testing Shared Memories", *Siam Journal on Computing*, pp. 1208-1244, August 1997.

[7] K. Gharachorloo, D. Lenoski, J. Laudon et al, "Memory Consistency and Event Ordering in Scalable Shared-Memory Multiprocessors", *Proceedings of the 17th International Symposium on Computer Architecture (ISCA)*, 1990.

[8] S. Hangal, D. Vahia, C. Manovit, J. Lu, and S. Narayanan, "TSOtool: A Program to Verify Multiprocessor Memory Systems Using the Memory Consistency Model", *Proceedings of the International Symposium on Computer Architecture (ISCA)*, 2004.

[9] J. Ludden, W. Roesner, G.M. Heiling et al, "Functional Verification of the POWER4 Microprocessor and POWER4 Multiprocessor Systems", *IBM Journal of Research and Development*, Vol. 46, No. 1, 2002.

[10] A. Landin, E. Hagersten, and S. Haridi, "Race-free Interconnection Networks and Multiprocessor Consistency", *Proceedings of the 18th Annual International Symposium on Computer Architecture (ISCA)*, 1991.

[11] C. Manovit and S. Hangal, "Efficient Algorithms for Verifying Memory Consistency", *Proceedings of the Symposium on Parallelism in Algorithms and Architectures (SPAA)*, 2005.

[12] A. Meixner and D.J. Sorin, "Dynamic Verification of Sequential Consistency", *Proceedings of the 32nd Annual International Symposium on Computer Architecture (ISCA)*, 2005.

[13] D. Marr, S. Thakkar, and R. Zucker, "Multiprocessor Validation of the Pentium Pro Microprocessor", *Proceedings of COMPCON*, 1996.

[14] C. Papadimitriou, "The Serializability of Concurrent Database Updates", *Journal of the ACM*, 26 (1979), pp. 631-653.

[15] M. Plakal, D.J. Sorin, A.E. Condon, and M. Hill, "Lamport Clocks: Verifying a Directory Cache-Coherence Protocol", *Proceedings of the 10th ACM Symposium on Parallel Algorithms and Architectures (SPAA)*, 1998.

[16] P.S. Sindhu, J.M. Frailong, and M. Cekleov, "Formal Specification of Memory Models", *Xerox PARC Technical Report*, December 1991.

[17] S. Taylor, C. Ramey, C. Barner, and D. Asher, "A Simulation-Based Method for the Verification of Shared Memory in Multiprocessor Systems", *Proceedings of IEEE/ACM International Conference on Computer-Aided Design (ICCAD)*, 2001.

[18] D.L. Weaver, T. Germond, Editors, *The SPARC Architecture Version 9*, Prentice Hall, 1994.

Session 6:
Disk and High Performance I/O

Understanding the Performance-Temperature Interactions in Disk I/O of Server Workloads

Youngjae Kim[†]   Sudhanva Gurumurthi[‡]   Anand Sivasubramaniam[†]

[†]Dept. of Computer Science and Engineering
The Pennsylvania State University
University Park, PA 16802
{youkim, anand}@cse.psu.edu

[‡]Dept. of Computer Science
University of Virginia
Charlottesville, VA 22904
gurumurthi@cs.virginia.edu

Abstract

This paper describes the first infrastructure for integrated studies of the performance and thermal behavior of storage systems. Using microbenchmarks running on this infrastructure, we first gain insight into how I/O characteristics can affect the temperature of disk drives. We use this analysis to identify the most promising, yet simple, "knobs" for temperature optimization of high speed disks, which can be implemented on existing disks. We then analyze the thermal profiles of real workloads that use such disk drives in their storage systems, pointing out which knobs are most useful for dynamic thermal management when pushing the performance envelope.

Keywords: Storage System, Disk Drives, Power and Temperature Management.

1 Introduction

A steady growth in the data rate of disk drives has been instrumental in their successful deployment across a diverse range of environments. In addition to data-centric services such as file, web and media servers, transaction processing, etc., disk drive performance is becoming extremely critical for even consumer electronic products such as digital video recorders, personal entertainment and gaming devices. While parallelism using RAID [24] has been effectively employed in server environments for higher bandwidth, the growth in the raw data rate is still very important for single drive performance across all these applications.

The internal data rate (IDR) of the drive is dependent on the linear density, rotational speed, and the platter size. The IDR has been growing at an exponential rate of 40% per-annum over the last fifteen years, due to a combination of brisk growth in linear density and higher rotational speeds (expressed in Rotations-per-Minute or RPM). However, increasing the RPM leads to excessive heat being generated since the viscous dissipation is proportional to nearly the cubic power [7]. In order to ensure that the disk drives adhere to the thermal design constraints when increasing the RPM, the platter size (which is proportional in nearly the fifth power to heat) may need to be reduced. This provides a margin within which the target IDR can be achieved for the same amount of heat by merely shrinking the platters and then compensating for the smaller size by increasing the RPM appropriately.

Designing disks to operate within the thermal design envelope is critical for reliable operation [1]. High temperatures can cause a host of reliability problems, such as off-track writes due to the thermal tilt of the disk stack and actuators, which can lead to corruption of data, or even a complete failure of the device due to a head crash [15]. It may appear that a simple solution to this problem is to provision a more powerful cooling system, since that would facilitate the extraction of heat from the device, thereby reducing its operating temperature. However, such cooling systems are prohibitively expensive [31].

It has been shown that the pace of growth in the linear density is expected to slow in the future, requiring much more aggressive scaling of the RPM to sustain the IDR growth rate [13]. Furthermore, this study showed that such aggressive scaling of the RPM cannot be sustained within the thermal envelope even for very small platter sizes thereby leading to a significant slowdown in the IDR growth rate in the near future. The implication of this is that disks in the future would have to be designed for *average case* thermal behavior rather than the worst case situation, incorporating the characteristics needed for higher performance, such as a higher RPM. However, this design approach can cause the operating temperature to exceed the the thermal envelope at runtime, if we do not incorporate any safeguards. To avoid thermal emergencies, [13] suggested the use of *Dynamic Thermal Management (DTM)*, a philosophy that is being actively investigated in the context of microprocessor design as well [4, 28]. In DTM, the disk is allowed to serve I/O requests as usual. However, if there is an imminent danger of violating the thermal envelope, we dynamically modulate the drive activities to prevent such a situation from occurring.

Designing and optimizing DTM techniques requires a careful analysis of how different drive activities impact the temperature, using real workloads. For instance, if we have a disk operating at a given RPM, how do the seeks in the workload increase the temperature? How far apart do seeks need to be in order to remain within the thermal envelope? Within a seek, how do the different phases - acceleration, coast, deceleration - impact the temperature? Can we modulate the head scheduling or request service schemes for DTM? Given different DTM alternatives, how do we pick one over another for a given set of workload conditions and disk drive parameters?

Such a detailed understanding of the interaction between workload activities and disk drive parameters, and their impact on temperature, requires detailed toolsets that are currently unavailable. Though there are tools such as Disksim [10] which are widely used for performance studies, there is no tool available today to study the temperature of a drive running a real workload. The earlier work in thermal modeling of disk drives [7, 13] has been more intended to study the temperature of drives under steady state conditions for static configurations of different drive parameters, and have not really looked at the temperature during the dynamic execution of a workload.

With these motivations, this paper presents the first integrated performance-thermal simulator to study the temperature of disk drives with real workloads. We profile the thermal behavior of real server workloads and show how the temperature varies during the execution. We also show that the spatial locality (minimizing seek activity) and the temporal separation between the seeks is adequate in these workloads that we can automatically apply a 5,000 RPM boost to their baseline disk configurations without exceeding the thermal envelope. This results in around 21-53% improvement in response times. Higher RPMs mandate more active DTM schemes.

The organization of the rest of this paper is as follows. Section 2 reviews the related work in this area. Section 3 describes our integrated thermal-performance framework, and the microbenchmark evaluations are given in Section 4. The evaluation with real workloads is conducted in section 5 for different drive RPMs. Finally section 6 concludes this paper.

2 Related Work

There have been many prior studies on the power consumption of disk drives [17, 32] and its optimization in mobile/desktop systems. Prediction of idleness is used to spin down the disk to a low power mode during periods of inactivity [21, 8]. [23] uses a combination of prefetching and caching to increase such idleness for more effective power management.

More recently, there has been interest in reducing the disk power consumption in server systems [14, 5]. The problem is more challenging in these environments because the workloads may not have sufficient idleness, and may not tolerate degradation in performance. Further, server disks have quite different characteristics compared to their laptop/desktop counterparts [1], with much larger transition times to/from the low power modes. The solutions for server environments employ multi-speed/DRPM disks [12, 5], which can be used in conjunction with other techniques such as data clustering [25] or cache management [33, 34].

Another approach is to use flash memory (which consumes lower power and is also faster than a disk) to construct a large buffer, to increase disk idleness. In fact, Sam-

sung recently announced a flash based disk that can provide over 16 GB of storage [26]. Such a disk can delay writes to the magnetic disk by accumulating them in the flash buffer and doing a bulk write. Although this solution is good for laptops and desktops, where I/O traffic is lower, it is not easily applicable for servers.

Temperature-aware design is becoming important in the context of microprocessors [28], interconnection networks [27], and storage systems [13] due to its strong correlation to the reliability of components and the high cost of cooling. [7] describes a model of the thermal behavior of a disk drive based on several parameters such as drive geometry, number of platters in the disk stack, RPM, and materials used for building the drive. However, this model [7], and the other closely related work in this area [13], are both studies of the thermal behavior of disk drives (based on different drive parameters) under static conditions, and the behavior has not been previously studied during the dynamic execution of real workloads. There has also been a study on modeling and designing disk arrays in a temperature-aware manner [18].

3 A Framework for Integrated Thermal-Performance Simulation

In order to analyze the thermal behavior of applications (and possibly control it dynamically), we need a framework that can relate activities in the storage system to their corresponding thermal phenomena as the workload execution is in progress. In a real system, this can be achieved by instrumenting the I/O operations and leveraging the thermal sensors [15] that are commonplace in most high-end disks drives today. However, since the objective of this study is to investigate the effect of disk configurations that are not yet available in the market today using highly controlled experiments (without external perturbances), we use a simulation-based approach. In this section, we describe the simulation framework that we have developed to study performance and thermal behavior of storage systems in an integrated manner.

The simulator consists of two components, namely, a *performance model* and a *thermal model*. In our simulator, the performance model we use is Disksim [10], which models the performance aspects of the disk drives, controllers, caches, and interconnects in a fairly detailed manner. Disksim is an event-driven simulator, with the simulated time being updated at discrete events, e.g. arrival of request, completion of seek, etc. Disksim has been extensively used in different studies and has been widely validated with several disk models.

Our thermal simulation model is based on the one developed by Eibeck and Cohen [9]. The sources of heat within the drive include the power expended by the spindle motor (to rotate the platters) and the voice-coil motor (VCM) (moving the disk arms). The thermal model evaluates the temperature distribution within a disk drive from these two sources by setting up the heat flow equations for different components of the drive such as the internal air, the spindle and voice-coil motor assemblies, and the drive base and cover. It uses the finite difference method [20] to calculate the heat flow, and iteratively calculates the temperatures of these components at each time step until it converges to a

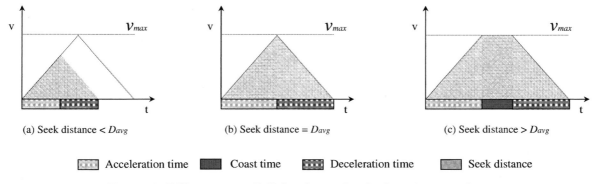

Figure 1. Different possibilities for a physical seek operation.

steady state temperature. Such a simulation model is sometimes referred to as a time-step simulator.

Our integration of these two models is based on the observation that the only two governing factors from the performance model which affect the thermal model include the seek activity (particularly the VCM on and off events) and any RPM changes (if using a multi-speed/DRPM disk). At these points, the performance model invokes the thermal model to iteratively (time-steps) compute the heat flows until the simulated time of the thermal model reaches the simulated time of the next such point in the performance model. In other words, we normally run the performance model for the sequence of incoming I/O requests. Whenever this model incurs a VCM switch from its prior state (i.e. on from off, or vice-versa), it invokes the thermal model with the appropriate VCM state information so that the thermal model can catch up on its time to the time in the performance model, at which point control flows back to the performance model. In the case of a multi-speed disk, this invocation is also done at RPM change events.

Such an integration between the two models requires a careful tuning of the time-step in the thermal model, since it affects both the speed and accuracy of the simulation. A relatively large time-step, as can be expected, can give a faster simulator at the expense of lower accuracy, and a finer granularity would give high accuracy at a slower speed. To evaluate these trade-offs, we ran workloads comparing their temperature profile using different time-step granularities (varying between 100 to 2500 steps between successive I/O events in the performance simulator), with that of a high resolution thermal simulation (60,000 steps/minute). We chose a time step that gave results very close to the high resolution simulation.

3.1 Modeling the Physical Behavior of Disk Seeks

When doing the thermal-performance simulation, one of the activities that needs to be modeled accurately is the dynamics of a physical seek operation. Although the time taken for a seek is already accounted for by the performance model, the mechanical work involved to effect the seek operation has a strong influence on temperature.

The seek time depends on two factors, namely, the inertial power of the VCM assembly and the radial length of the data band being traversed on the platter [11]. The VCM, which is also sometimes referred to as the arm actuator, is used to move the disk arms across the surface of the platters. Physically, a seek involves an acceleration phase, when the VCM is powered, followed by a coast phase of constant velocity where the VCM is off, and then a deceleration phase to stop the arms near the desired track when the VCM is again turned on but the current is reversed to generate the braking effect. This is then followed by a head settling period. For very short seeks, the settle time dominates the overall seek time whereas for slightly longer (intermediate) seeks, the acceleration and deceleration phases dominate. Coasting is more significant for long seeks. We capture the physical behavior of seeks using a Bang-Bang Triangular model [16]. In this model, for any physical seek operation, the time taken for acceleration and subsequent deceleration are equal. To calculate the acceleration/deceleration components, we make the following assumptions:

- The head settle time is approximated as the track-to-track seek time.
- Let V_{max} denote the maximum velocity that is permissible for the head, which is dictated by the characteristics of the VCM assembly and also by the bandwidth of the underlying servo system (needed to accurately position the head over the desired track). We use a V_{max} value of 120 inches/second, which reflects many modern disk drive implementations.
- The average seek distance (D_{avg}) for a large number of random seeks is equal to a seek across $\frac{1}{3}$ of the data zone [3].
- The coast time for an average seek (of this distance D_{avg}) is zero, since that would yield the lowest seek time on the average.

The last three assumptions are essentially used to fix/calculate the acceleration/deceleration of the VCM based on what is needed to bring the head assembly to a maximum velocity (V_{max}) immediately followed by the reverse braking/deceleration to give the lowest possible seek time when the average covered distance is D_{avg}.

Let D_{avg} and T_{avg} denote the distance of $\frac{1}{3}$ of the data zone and the corresponding (average) seek time. Since we are calculating the time only during the movement of the disk arm and not the settling period, T_{avg} is adjusted by subtracting the settle time of a head (i.e., the track-to-track seek time) from the average seek time. We can now calculate the time taken during the acceleration, coast, and deceleration phases of a physical disk seek operation (of distance d) as follows:

- Case $d = D_{avg}$: For a seek operation that needs to traverse a distance of D_{avg} as is shown in Figure 1 (b), the VCM accelerates the actuator from an initial speed of 0, to a maximum velocity V_{max}, and then immediately applies the reverse braking affect which takes the same amount of time as the acceleration, i.e. there is zero coast time and the VCM is on during the entire duration of the seek. We can calculate these durations as $T_{Acc} = T_{Dec} = \frac{D_{avg}}{V_{max}}$.

  So when the requested seek distance d is D_{avg}, the VCM is continuously on for this entire duration of $T_{Acc} + T_{Dec}$.

- Case $d > D_{avg}$: Since the actuator cannot move faster than V_{max}, once it reaches this velocity after the initial acceleration, there needs to be a coast phase (as depicted in Figure 1 (c)) before the deceleration. Note that the VCM is on during the T_{Acc} and T_{Dec} (whose values are the same as in the previous case) phases, with a coast time duration of $\frac{d - D_{avg}}{V_{max}}$ in between when the VCM is off.

- Case $d < D_{avg}$: The distance is lesser than what is needed to reach the maximum velocity for the calculated acceleration above. Consequently, we again only have an acceleration phase followed immediately by the deceleration phase. We can apply the Second Law of Motion to calculate the T_{Acc} and T_{Dec} in this case as $T_{Acc} = T_{Dec} = \sqrt{\frac{2 \times \frac{d}{2}}{Acc}}$.

The on/off states of the VCM are then communicated to the thermal model at the appropriate points as explained earlier.

Validation: In order to validate this model, we calculated the acceleration that is computed by our model, under all the stated assumptions for a Fujitsu AL-7LX disk drive, which is a 2.6" 15,000 RPM disk drive, and compared it to its measured mechanical seek characteristics [2]. Using the drive characteristics, we found the D_{avg} for this disk to be 0.22". The reported value for the acceleration to satisfy the seek time requirement is 220 G (2150 m/s^2), whereas our model calculates it using the D_{avg} to be 253.5 G (2488.1 m/s^2), which is within 15% of the reported value.

3.2 Simulation "Warm-up"

At the beginning of the simulation, all the disks are in a cold state, having the same temperature as that of the outside air. It takes roughly 50 minutes of simulated time before the temperature reaches a steady state. In order to prevent start-up effects from skewing our results, we perform the experiments only after the system has reached the steady state temperature. We literally warm up the disk by running the stand-alone thermal model for the first 150 minutes of simulation assuming that the disks are idle (i.e., the disks are spinning but there are no arm movements). Simulation of the workload is started after this warm-up period.

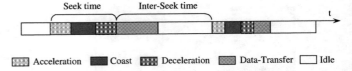

Figure 2. The different physical phases of an I/O operation to a disk.

4 Impact of I/O Activities on Disk Drive Thermal Behavior

In order to understand the thermal behavior of real workloads, we first analyze the impact of various types of I/O activities on the temperature of a disk drive. From the sequence of events shown in Figure 2, we see that the temperature variation of a disk operating at a given RPM depends on the *seek time*, *coast time*, and the *inter-seek time*, pictorially shown in Figure 2. Even though the coast is in turn accounted for in the seek times (i.e. a large coast does translate to a large seek time), we would like to identify this as a separate factor in our studies since its effect counter-acts the acceleration/deceleration effects (a long coast can possibly allow the disk to cool since the VCM is off). A seek operation that accelerates to the maximum velocity, V_{max} and subsequently decelerates without any coast time (i.e. the profile in Figure 1 (b)) generates the maximum heat for any given seek operation. Let us denote this type of seek operation as a *min-coast* seek. Note that the coast is zero even for those seeks with distances less than D_{avg} (Figure 1 (a)), and the term can be viewed to be somewhat of a misnomer, but we refer specifically to the profile in Figure 1 (b) as a min-coast seek.

The inter-seek time is the time between the end of a seek operation and the beginning of another. If inter-seek times are short, then the dissipation of heat from inside the drive during the idle phase between any two seek operations is lower, thereby further increasing the temperature. Although a single seek operation might not create a significant change in the drive temperature, a sequence of such temporally close operations (burstiness) can have a more significant effect.

To summarize, a lower thermal profile can be achieved by one or more of the following:

- Low (possibly zero) seek times, where the acceleration/deceleration durations are low.
- Large coast times, which can possibly outweigh the effects of longer acceleration/deceleration phases.
- Large inter-seek times, allowing the disk to cool between successive accesses.

We next perform a microbenchmark study to investigate the impact of these factors on a disk's temperature. In these microbenchmarks, we vary the inter-seek time (IST) from 0 ms to 8 ms in increments of 2 ms. In addition, we also vary the total seek time by considering discrete values between 0 ms to 5 ms, in discrete steps of 1 ms. We also consider a seek time that corresponds to the min-coast value explained above (which turns out to be 3.38 ms and 3.82 ms for a 3.3" and 3.7" platter sizes respectively). For a given set of values

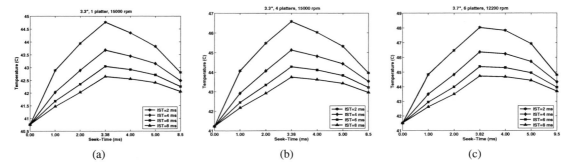

Figure 3. Relationship between seek-time and disk temperature. The highest point for each of the curves corresponds to a min-coast seek.

in this two dimensional design space (inter-seek times and seek times), the microbenchmark introduces a large number of seeks (over a period of 150 minutes) of these specified parameters after initial Warm-up of the thermal state.

In Figure 3, we plot the temperature of some disk drive configurations for various seek-time values (x-axis) for a given inter-seek time. Note that the points in the middle of the seek-time range which usually yield the highest temperatures correspond to "min-coast". The extreme left points correspond to "zero-seek", and the ones on the extreme right correspond to "max-coast".

As expected, the temperature starts going up with non-zero seek times for a given inter-seek time. We see around 2-6 C increase in temperature when going from zero-seek to the min-coast value in these three disk configurations. The duration for which the VCM is active grows linearly with the seek time (until the min-coast value), contributing to the increase in temperature. Beyond the min-coast point, though the VCM is exercised as much in the seeks, the gap (coast) allows the disk to cool a little. Despite this cooling effect, the temperatures for even the full-stroke seeks are still higher than not performing any seeks, suggesting that seek time optimization plays an important role in thermal management as well (and not just for the traditional performance goals).

We find that the inter-seek time has an equally important effect on the thermal behavior. With temporally close (Burst) seeks, the disk does not have as much time to cool, yielding higher temperatures compared to a workload with seeks that are more temporally separated. Further, a smaller inter-seek time amplifies the effects of the individual seek activities. For instance, when we look at the curve for the 2 ms inter-seek time, in Figure 3(a), we see that if we reduce the seek-time by 1 ms from the 2 ms seek-time point, there is nearly a 1.05 C reduction in the temperature. Nearly the same reduction in temperature is also achievable by increasing the inter-seek time by 2 ms. On the other hand, when we see that for the curves with inter-seek times that are longer than 2 ms, the temperature variation becomes less sensitive to the inter-seek times but is affected more by the seek-time.

The rise in the temperature is faster for disks that have more platters (Figure 3(b)) or larger platters (Figure 3(c)), due to the increased viscous heating. This also makes the absolute temperature values in Figure 3(c) the highest due to the nearly fifth-power impact of platter size, and that in

Figure 3(b) higher than the 1-platter configuration, since the number of platters has a linear effect on the viscous dissipation.

We have repeated these benchmarks across different disk/RPM configurations, particularly for those of interest in the latter portion of this paper. Rather than re-draw all the lines, we summarize the temperatures for the (i) zero seek, (ii) min-coast and (iii) max-coast (full-stroke seek), for the considered configurations in Figure 4. In addition, we also show the thermal envelope line (calculated to be 45.22 C using the same techniques described in [13]). The second and third column of graphs shows the thermal profiles for successive increases in the RPM for the same platter size and number of platters shown in the first column.

When we look at the leftmost bar (where the VCM is always on) in each graph on the first column, we find that the temperatures are very close to the thermal envelope, since the cooling system was provisioned to handle this workload scenario. These disk configurations correspond to the baseline case, i.e. they are actual product configurations of prior calendar years when the workload traces were collected. However, we observe that if there are long seek operations (higher coast time), the temperature of the disks are significantly lower than the worst-case. For instance, for the 3.3" 4-platter disk, when coast times are long, there is close to a 7 C drop in the temperature compared to the worst-case. This relative difference in the temperature is also observable for the higher RPMs.

We can also lower the temperature by having much shorter (or even zero) seeks, and the savings is much more pronounced when there is no movement of the arm at all. We see over 8 C temperature drop in the low inter-seek time experiments of the first column when we move from min-coast to zero-seek. We also find that there is a greater amount of temperature reduction for the 3.7" disk compared to the 3.3". This is because the power output of the VCM depends on the platter size and thus has a more significant impact on temperature for the 3.7" drive. When the disk seek-times are very small, increasing the inter-seek time lowers the temperature, although it has a lesser impact as observed earlier in Figure 3. When coast times are high, the inter-seek time has negligible impact on the temperature of the drives.

When we turn our attention to the second column of graphs, where the disk speeds are increased by 5,000 RPM

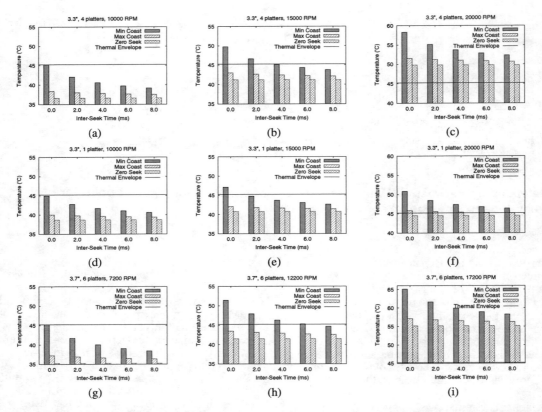

Figure 4. Results of Microbenchmark Study. Each row of graphs shows the steady-state temperature for a disk configuration for various RPMs (in increasing order from left to right). The horizontal line in each graph is the thermal envelope.

from their baseline counterparts in the first column, we find that the min-coast bars (where the VCM is always on) exceed the thermal envelope. However, as we note in these graphs, there is a relatively large difference in temperature between the min-coast and the other two bars, especially at smaller inter-seek times. In fact, these two bars lie within the thermal envelope, suggesting that we can even operate at this higher RPM with an appropriate DTM scheme.

The above results for the 5,000 RPM boost show that zero-seeks definitely give lower temperature than max-coast. Consequently, disk arm scheduling algorithms such as Shortest Positioning Time First (SPTF) can possibly serve to lower the temperature (and not just enhance performance for which it has been intended). However, if the waiting queue of requests is such that the seek distances are not necessarily that low (i.e. the thermal profile is heading more towards the min-coast region), then one may possibly opt for an inverse SPTF algorithm (i.e. Longest Positioning Time First Algorithm), since in this case we may be able to increase the coast times.

However, it is possible that we may reach points when changing the arm scheduling algorithm may not suffice to remain within the thermal envelope. The bars for the 0 ms inter-seek time in Figure 4 (f) give some evidence of this observation, where min-coast exceeds the thermal envelope as well and the zero-seek is fairly close to the envelope.

Getting to the zero-seek value may not be achievable in a real workload, and in this case the DTM option may actually need to increase the inter-seek times (by introducing delays) sufficiently so that the disk may cool between successive requests.

Finally, we notice that in the first and third rows of the last column of graphs, the 10,000 RPM increase from the baseline causes all bars to exceed the envelope. Disk head scheduling and introducing delays are not sufficient to manage the temperature in these cases, and more aggressive techniques such as dynamic RPM modulation [12, 5] may need to be employed for DTM.

5 Thermal Behavior of Real Server Workloads

In the previous section, we identified the salient aspects of I/O behavior at the disk drive level that can affect temperature. Although this study helps us understand the relative importance of the various parameters on the drive temperature, it is important to analyze how real workloads use the disk drives within this broad space.

Workload	Year	# Requests	# Disks	Per-Disk Capacity (GB)	RPM	Platter Diameter (in)	Platters (#)	RAID ?
HPL Openmail [29]	2000	3,053,745	8	9.29	10,000	3.3	1	Yes
OLTP Application [30]	1999	5,334,945	24	19.07	10,000	3.3	4	No
Search-Engine [30]	1999	4,579,809	6	19.07	10,000	3.3	4	No
TPC-C	2002	6,155,547	4	37.17	10,000	3.3	4	Yes
TPC-H	2002	4,228,725	15	35.96	7,200	3.7	6	No

Table 1. Description of workloads and storage system used.

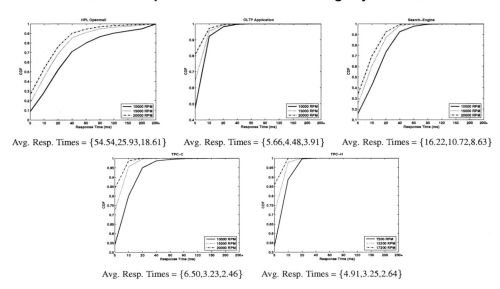

Avg. Resp. Times = {54.54,25.93,18.61} Avg. Resp. Times = {5.66,4.48,3.91} Avg. Resp. Times = {16.22,10.72,8.63}

Avg. Resp. Times = {6.50,3.23,2.46} Avg. Resp. Times = {4.91,3.25,2.64}

Figure 5. Performance impact of faster disk drives for the server workloads. Each graph shows the CDF of the response times for each RPM. The solid curve for each graph shows the performance of the baseline system. The average response times are shown below each graph in the order of increasing RPMs.

5.1 Workloads

In this paper, we use five commercial I/O traces, whose characteristics are given in Table 1, along with details of the storage system (from prior years) on which each trace was collected. Although the disks listed in the Table use platters that are larger and also lower RPMs than those used in drives today (e.g. 2.6" and 15,000 RPM), we tried to be as faithful as possible to the original storage system configurations used for these applications, so as not to skew our observations. In Figure 5 we quantify the performance for each of the workloads in their *baseline* and higher speed configurations by plotting the CDF of the response times when their respective storage systems employ the faster disks. However, we restricted the highest RPM value to 20,000 RPM, which has been shown to be feasible for reliable disk-drive operation [6].

5.2 Thermal Profiles

Figure 6 shows the temperature of the higher RPM disks when running these workloads. For clarity, we look at the thermal profiles across two time granularities. The first column of graphs shows the profiles, for the disks of different RPMs, across the entire simulation of each workload.

Again, in the interest of clarity and space, we show the profiles only for one representative disk in the storage system for each workload. The right column goes for a closer look by plotting just a second at the 50th minute of execution.

We find that a 5,000 RPM increase from the baseline RPM can be easily accommodated within the thermal envelope without having to increase the cooling requirements. The significance of this can be seen by looking at the performance plots in Figure 5, where a 5,000 RPM increase can provide 21%-53% improvement in the response time from the baseline.

In order to better understand why we are still within the thermal envelope, we first dissect the seek time of the workloads into the acceleration, coast, and deceleration components. We histogrammed these values for each workload, into bucket sizes of 1 ms granularities, and associated the value of each bucket with its upper interval. In Table 2 we show the results for the top two seek-time occurrences, since these really dominate the execution. In addition to this, we also show the probability density function (PDF) of the inter-seek times of disk-0 for the workloads in Figure 7. Each graph shows two sets of PDFs, one for the inter-seek times between any two disk seeks (denoted as "All") and another only for the seeks that actually involve a movement of the disk arm (denoted as "Without 0-Seeks"). The latter is used to remove any bias towards the high occurrences of

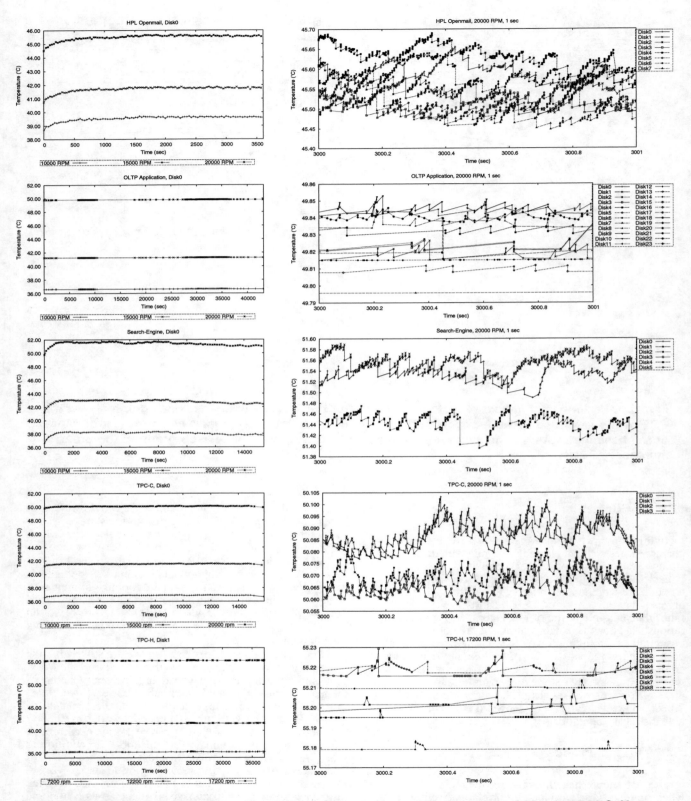

Figure 6. Thermal profiles of the workloads for two time ranges. The thermal envelope is 45.22 C. Note that the scale of the y-axes is different for each graph in order to make the temperature variations as detailed as possible.

0-seeks which do not increase the temperature despite coming temporally close to each other.

From the Table, we see that the bulk of the seeks, across all the workloads, have a duration of 0 ms or 1 ms. Only the Search-Engine and Openmail workloads show seeks that are of duration 2 ms and higher. As we saw in the previous section, if the time taken for a seek is around this 1 ms value, then the heat that is generated is much less than for a min-coast seek. However, the actual temperature of the disk also depends on the inter-seek time value, which is shown in Figure 7. For the OLTP and TPC-H applications, many of the inter-seek times are quite long, especially for the former, where they are in the order of several hundreds of milliseconds. However, between these workloads, we find that TPC-H runs a little cooler than OLTP, despite the latter experiencing about an order of magnitude larger inter-seek times for the majority of the seeks. This is due to the seek-time behavior of the two workloads (shown in Table 2). The vast majority of the seeks in both these workloads are of 0 ms and 1 ms in duration. However, TPC-H is composed of a larger proportion of zero-seek operations compared to OLTP (i.e. there is very good spatial locality in TPC-H). As we saw in Section 4, when inter-seek times are greater than 2 ms, the relative temperature differences for larger values of the inter-seek time become progressively smaller. However, the seek-time still has a strong impact on temperature, especially in the region that is less than the min-coast value. As TPC-H has about 6% more 0 ms seeks than OLTP, its disks experience a lower temperature.

TPC-C shows a temperature profile that is somewhat similar to OLTP but exhibits a different set of characteristics. The bulk of the seek-times in this workload are of 0 ms in duration and the remaining being 1 ms. In particular, we can see from Table 2 that its seek-time distribution is quite comparable to the TPC-H workload. However, there are a significant number of inter-seek times (around 30%) that are less than 10 ms (the "Without 0-Seek" curve in Figure 7(d)). This would cause the temperature to be higher than TPC-H. However, as we have already seen, the differences in the inter-seek time do not play a very dominant role, except for very short values, making the temperature only slightly higher than TPC-H.

The Openmail and Search-Engine workloads exhibit a larger variation in seek-times. There is also significant variation in the inter-seek times between different disks for the Search-Engine workload (as shown in Figure 7(c) for disks 0 and 4). We find that 6.5% of the seeks in Openmail take between 2-3 ms and none between 3-4 ms. 4.7% of the seek operations in the Search-Engine workload have times between 2-3 ms and 14.8% of them are in the range of 3-4 ms. These two workloads also have half their inter-seek times in the 10 ms range. Recall that, as the seek-time increases (until we reach the min-coast point), the acceleration that is required increases as well, causing each seek operation to generate more heat. This phenomenon is observable for these two workloads, where the constituent disks in their respective storage systems experience the highest temperatures for 15,000 RPM. Between these two workloads, Search-Engine has a higher absolute temperature because it uses 4-platter disks (as shown in Table 1), which generates more heat (by a linear factor) than the 1-platter units used by Openmail.

Although we consider both 3.3" and 3.7" disks, we provision sufficient cooling such that all the drives satisfy the thermal envelope of 45.22 C in their baseline configurations. Search-Engine uses 3.3" 4-platter 10,000 RPM disks in its baseline configuration whereas TPC-H uses 3.7" 6-platter 7200 RPM drives. We found that these two configurations are not exactly equivalent from the thermal viewpoint in the sense that the latter can generate more heat than the former, requiring the outside temperature to be slightly cooler. Therefore, if we increase the RPM by 5,000 from their baseline configurations without altering the cooling system, we might expect the heating to be higher for the 3.7" disk by virtue of its larger platter size and number of platters. However, we have seen that the disks used by Search-Engine experience higher temperatures than TPC-H. In fact, the highest temperature that any disk in TPC-H reaches for 12,200 RPM is 41.86 C, compared to 43.15 C for Search-Engine. This is again due to the same factors outlined above, namely, very short seek-times and large idleness, both of which are application dependent.

When we increase the RPM by a further 5,000, we find that all the curves are now above the thermal envelope. As we had seen in the microbenchmark evaluation, the highest temperatures are now experienced by the 3.7" disks used in TPC-H. This was observed in the microbenchmark result in Figure 4(i), where even with inter-seek times of 8 ms and maximum coasting, the temperature of a 3.7" disk is higher than those of the other two, across all the chosen values for the inter-seek time and coast-time. This change in the thermal behavior from lower speeds is because the RPM is now high enough such that it is now the most dominant determinant of the overall drive heat. Although there is still some variation in temperature with workload behavior, even the idle operating temperature is significantly (more than 10 C) above the thermal envelope. Similar trends are observable for the other workloads as well and most of them operate roughly 5 C above the thermal envelope. Since even a 5 C variation in temperature above the thermal envelope can significantly affect reliability [1], it is imperative to apply a DTM technique to manage its temperature.

From the above results, we note the following important observations across the workloads:

- The seek-times are significantly lower than the min-coast value. Even if there are considerable short inter-seek times (over 50% lower than 10 ms in many workloads), the short (or zero-distance) seeks keep the disk cool enough even when there is a 5,000 RPM boost from the baseline. This is achievable with neither an alteration of the cooling system nor by the use of any DTM technique. This is a rather powerful observation since we are pronouncing that the disk could have been provisioned with the 5,000 RPM boost statically and we would have never exceeded the thermal envelope (and gained between 21-53% response time improvement).

- Going for another 5,000 RPM boost does cause the results to violate the thermal envelope especially in the disks with higher and larger platters, regardless of the workload.

- If we do decide to incorporate any DTM (say in the case of Openmail with a 10,000 RPM boost from the baseline), our results also give insights on how we should go about it. With most of the seek-times falling less than 2 ms, SPTF is good enough for a thermal management strategy (we do not need to amplify the

Workload	First Most Frequent Seek-Time				Second Most Frequent Seek-Time			
	Frequency (%)	Seek-Time (ms)	Acceleration Time (ms)	Coast Time (ms)	Frequency (%)	Seek-Time (ms)	Acceleration Time (ms)	Coast Time (ms)
Openmail	46.7	1.0	0.5	0.0	18.6	2.0	1.0	0.0
OLTP	62.5	1.0	0.5	0.0	37.5	0.0	0.0	0.0
Search-Engine	29.4	1.0	0.5	0.0	19.6	2.0	1.0	0.0
TPC-C	58.4	0.0	0.0	0.0	41.6	1.0	0.5	0.0
TPC-H	56.5	1.0	0.5	0.0	43.2	0.0	0.0	0.0

Table 2. Seek-time breakdown of the applications using disks that are 5,000 RPM faster than their baseline values. The deceleration time is not shown since its value is same as that for acceleration.

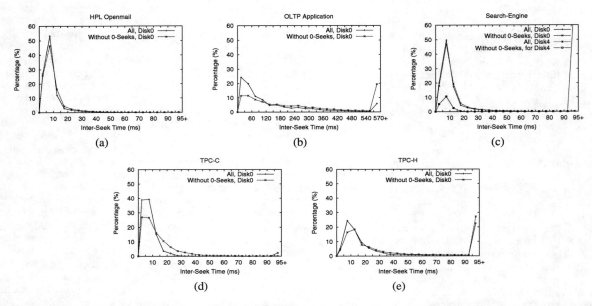

(a) (b) (c)

(d) (e)

Figure 7. Probability Density Function (PDF) of the inter-seek times for the workloads. For each workload, the curve labeled "All" includes disk requests that do not involve a movement of the arm (zero-distance seeks) and "Without 0-Seeks" shows the inter-seek times only between seek operations that actually involve a movement of the arm.

coast times). Rather, extending inter-seek times (by possibly introducing delays) can be more rewarding. Our preliminary investigations [19] of introducing delays between seeks suggest that performance can deteriorate substantially for I/O intensive workloads.

- Finally, at high enough RPMs, one can simply not sustain the workloads without exceeding the thermal envelope. In these cases, neither seek-time optimizations nor delays between requests may be viable DTM choices. One may need to opt for more extensive DTM techniques such as dynamic RPM modulation, and we leave it to future work to explore such issues.

6 Concluding Remarks

This paper has presented the first integrated performance-thermal simulator that can be used to study the temperature of disks executing real workloads. This infrastructure requires a careful modeling of the details of a seek, and we have shown how to account for the heat generated in the acceleration/deceleration phases, and the coast in-between when the disk can possibly cool down. The simulator integrates a discrete-event performance model (Disksim) with a time-step thermal model.

Using this simulator we have conducted detailed microbenchmark studies to understand the temperature relationship to disk level I/O activities. We point out several options for temperature management - reducing seek distances, amplifying coast times, and temporal spacing between seeks - which can be applied even on existing disks. With five real commercial traces, we show that one can obtain a 5,000 RPM boost without having to resort to any explicit thermal management. Above this level, we need to employ DTM to stay below the thermal envelope. We intend to investigate these possibilities in future work.

Acknowledgements

This research has been funded in part by NSF grants 0429500, 0325056, 0130143, 0509234 and 0103583, and an IBM Faculty Award. We wish to thank Erik Riedel and Bob Warren at Seagate Technology for insightful comments leading to the contents of this paper.

References

[1] D. Anderson, J. Dykes, and E. Riedel. More Than An Interface - SCSI vs. ATA. In *Proceedings of the Annual Conference on File and Storage Technology (FAST)*, March 2003.

[2] K. Aruga. 3.5-Inch High-Performance Disk Drives for Enterprise Applications: AL-7 Series. *Fujitsu Science and Technology Journal*, 37(2):126–139, December 2001.

[3] K. Ashar. *Magnetic Disk Drive Technology: Heads, Media, Channel, Interfaces, and Integration*. IEEE Press, 1997.

[4] D. Brooks and M. Martonosi. Dynamic Thermal Management for High-Performance Microprocessors. In *Proceedings of the International Symposium on High-Performance Computer Architecture (HPCA)*, pages 171–182, January 2001.

[5] E. Carrera, E. Pinheiro, and R. Bianchini. Conserving Disk Energy in Network Servers. In *Proceedings of the International Conference on Supercomputing (ICS)*, June 2003.

[6] S. Chen, Q. Zhang, H. Chong, T. Komatsu, and C. Kang. Some Design and Prototyping Issues on a 20000 RPM HDD Spindle Motor with a Ferro-Fluid Bearing System. *IEEE Transactions on Magnetics*, 37(2):805–809, March 2001.

[7] N. Clauss. A Computational Model of the Thermal Expansion Within a Fixed Disk Drive Storage System. Master's thesis, University of California, Berkeley, 1988.

[8] F. Douglis and P. Krishnan. Adaptive Disk Spin-Down Policies for Mobile Computers. *Computing Systems*, 8(4):381–413, 1995.

[9] P. Eibeck and D. Cohen. Modeling Thermal Characteristics of a Fixed Disk Drive. *IEEE Transactions on Components, Hybrids, and Manufacturing Technology*, 11(4):566–570, December 1988.

[10] G. Ganger, B. Worthington, and Y. Patt. *The DiskSim Simulation Environment Version 2.0 Reference Manual*. http://www.ece.cmu.edu/ ganger/disksim/.

[11] E. Grochowski and R. Halem. Technological Impact of Magnetic Hard Disk Drives on Storage Systems. *IBM Systems Journal*, 42(2):338–346, 2003.

[12] S. Gurumurthi, A. Sivasubramaniam, M. Kandemir, and H. Franke. DRPM: Dynamic Speed Control for Power Management in Server Class Disks. In *Proceedings of the International Symposium on Computer Architecture (ISCA)*, pages 169–179, June 2003.

[13] S. Gurumurthi, A. Sivasubramaniam, and V. Natarajan. Disk Drive Roadmap from the Thermal Perspective: A Case for Dynamic Thermal Management. In *Proceedings of the International Symposium on Computer Architecture (ISCA)*, pages 38–49, June 2005.

[14] S. Gurumurthi, J. Zhang, A. Sivasubramaniam, M. Kandemir, H. Franke, N. Vijaykrishnan, and M. Irwin. Interplay of Energy and Performance for Disk Arrays Running Transaction Processing Workloads. In *Proceedings of the International Symposium on Performance Analysis of Systems and Software (ISPASS)*, pages 123–132, March 2003.

[15] G. Herbst. IBM's Drive Temperature Indicator Processor (Drive-TIP) Helps Ensure High Drive Reliability. In *IBM Whitepaper*, October 1997.

[16] H. Ho. Fast Servo Bang-Bang Seek Control. *IEEE Transactions on Magnetics*, 33(6):4522–4527, November 1997.

[17] I. Hong and M. Potkonjak. Power Optimization in Disk-Based Real-Time Application Specific System s. In *Proceedings of the International Conference on Computer-Aided Desi gn (ICCAD)*, pages 634–637, November 1996.

[18] R. Huang and D. Chung. Thermal Design of a Disk-Array System. In *Proceedings of the InterSociety Conference on Thermal and Thermomechanical Phenomena in Electronic Systems*, pages 106–112, May 2002.

[19] Y. Kim, S. Gurumurthi, and A. Sivasubramaniam. Understanding the Performance-Temperature Interactions in Disk I/O of Server workloads. Technical Report CSE-05-007, The Pennsylvania State University, November 2005.

[20] H. Levy and F. Lessman. *Finite Difference Equations*. Dover Publications, 1992.

[21] K. Li, R. Kumpf, P. Horton, and T. Anderson. Quantitative Analysis of Disk Drive Power Management in Portable Computers. In *Proceedings of the USENIX Winter Conference*, pages 279–291, 1994.

[22] C. Nicholson. Improved Disk Drive Power Consumption Using Solid State Non-Volatile Memory. In *Proceedings of the Windows Hardware Engineering Conference (WinHEC)*, May 2004.

[23] A. E. Papathanasiou and M. L. Scott. Energy Efficient Prefetching and Caching. In *Proceedings of the USENIX Annual Technical Conference*, June 2004.

[24] D. Patterson, G. Gibson, and R. Katz. A Case for Redundant Arrays of Inexpensive Disks (RAID). In *Proceedings of ACM SIGMOD Conference on the Management of Data*, pages 109–116, June 1988.

[25] E. Pinheiro and R. Bianchini. Energy Conservation Techniques for Disk Array-Based Servers. In *Proceedings of the International Conference on Supercomputing (ICS)*, June 2004.

[26] Samsung Electronics Develops Solid State Disk Using NAND Flash Technology, May 2005. http://www.samsung.com/PressCenter/PressRelease/PressRelease.asp?seq=20050523_0000123980.

[27] L. Shang, L.-S. Peh, A. Kumar, and N. Jha. Thermal Modeling, Characterization and Management of On-Chip Networks. In *Proceedings of the International Symposium on Microarchitecture (MICRO)*, pages 67–78, December 2004.

[28] K. Skadron, M. Stan, W. Huang, S. Velusamy, K. Sankaranarayanan, and D. Tarjan. Temperature-Aware Microarchitecture. In *Proceedings of the International Symposium on Computer Architecture (ISCA)*, pages 1–13, June 2003.

[29] The Openmail Trace. http://tesla.hpl.hp.com/private software/.

[30] UMass Trace Repository. http://traces.cs.umass.edu.

[31] R. Viswanath, V. Wakharkar, A. Watwe, and V. Lebonheur. Thermal Performance Challenges from Silicon to Systems. *Intel Technology Journal*, Q3 2000.

[32] J. Zedlewski, S. Sobti, N. Garg, F. Zheng, A. Krishnamurthy, and R. Wang. Modeling Hard-Disk Power Consumption. In *Proceedings of the Annual Conference on File and Storage Technology (FAST)*, March 2003.

[33] Q. Zhu, F. David, C. Devraj, Z. Li, Y. Zhou, and P. Cao. Reducing Energy Consumption of Disk Storage Using Power-Aware Cache Management. In *Proceedings of the International Symposium on High-Performance Computer Architecture (HPCA)*, Febuary 2004.

[34] Q. Zhu, A. Shankar, and Y. Zhou. PB-LRU: A Self-Tuning Power Aware Storage Cache Replacement Algorithm for Conserving Disk Energy. In *Proceedings of the International Conference on Supercomputing (ICS)*, June 2004.

High Performance File I/O for The Blue Gene/L Supercomputer

H. Yu, R. K. Sahoo, C. Howson, G. Almási, J. G. Castaños, M. Gupta
IBM T. J. Watson Research Ctr, Yorktown Hts, NY
{*yuh,rsahoo,chowson,gheorghe,castanos,mgupta*}*@us.ibm.com*

J. E. Moreira, J. J. Parker
IBM System & Tech. Group, Rochester, MN
{*jmoreira,jjparker*}*@us.ibm.com*

T. E. Engelsiepen
IBM Almaden Research Ctr, San Jose, CA
engelspn@almaden.ibm.com

R. B. Ross, R. Thakur, R. Latham, W. D. Gropp
MCS, Argonne Nat'l Lab., Argonne, IL
{*rross,thakur,robl,gropp*}*@mcs.anl.gov*

Abstract

Parallel I/O plays a crucial role for most data-intensive applications running on massively parallel systems like Blue Gene/L that provides the promise of delivering enormous computational capability. We designed and implemented a highly scalable parallel file I/O architecture for Blue Gene/L, which leverages the benefit of the hierarchical and functional partitioning design of the system software with separate computational and I/O cores. The architecture exploits the scalability aspect of GPFS (General Parallel File System) at the backend, while using MPI I/O as an interface between the application I/O and the file system. We demonstrate the impact of our high performance I/O solution for Blue Gene/L with a comprehensive evaluation that consists of a number of widely used parallel I/O benchmarks and I/O intensive applications. Our design and implementation is not only able to deliver at least one order of magnitude speed up in terms of I/O bandwidth for a real-scale application HOMME [7] (achieving aggregate bandwidth of 1.8 GB/Sec and 2.3 GB/Sec for write and read accesses, respectively), but also supports high-level parallel I/O data interfaces such as parallel HDF5 and parallel NetCDF scaling up to a large number of processors.

1. Introduction

In recent years, one of the major challenges for computational scientists is to deal with very large datasets while running massively parallel applications on supercomputers. While most computationally intensive challenges are handled by emerging massively parallel systems with thousands of processors (e.g. Blue Gene/L), data-intensive computing with scientific and non-scientific applications still continues to be a major area of interest due to the gap between computation and I/O speed. Crucial for useful performance in a high-performance computing environment is the seamless transfer of data between memory and a file system for large-scale parallel programs.

Blue Gene/L [8] is a new massively parallel computer developed by IBM in partnership with Lawrence Livermore National Laboratory (LLNL). The Blue Gene/L (BG/L) system exploits low power processors, system-on-a-chip integration and a highly scalable architecture putting together up to 65536 embedded dual-processor PowerPC nodes (700 MHz) with high speed interconnects. LLNL's 64K-node BG/L system will deliver up to 360 Teraflops of peak computing power upon completion. BG/L is currently ranked as the world's fastest supercomputer in Top500 list of supercomputers, and represents five of the top ten entities in the list. While impressive scaling results have been obtained up to 32768 nodes [11], there has been relatively few results published on I/O performance for data-intensive applications on BG/L or any other massively parallel system.

A scalable parallel I/O support mainly consists of high-performance file systems and effective parallel I/O application programming interfaces. There have been many efforts developing parallel file systems for supercomputers, such as GPFS (General Parallel File System) [20] for IBM SP systems as well as Linux clusters, PVFS [5] and Lustre [2] for Linux-based platforms. In this work, we leverage GPFS, which is widely used on many large-scale commercial and supercomputing systems for its scalability, stability as well as reliability. Representative parallel file I/O programming interfaces include POSIX I/O interface [16], MPI I/O [19], and high-level abstraction layers such as parallel

Hierarchical Data Format (HDF) [1] and parallel NetCDF (PnetCDF) [17]. Among them, MPI I/O is synonymous with parallel file I/O for scientific computing, because of its wide use and its base on MPI. In addition, MPI I/O supports for relatively rich file access patterns and operations, which allows aggressive optimizations to be integrated.

The primary goal of the paper is to demonstrate the design, integration, and implementation of a hierarchical scalable file I/O architecture for BG/L. Our parallel file I/O solution consists of GPFS at the backend, while the I/O interface is handled through an optimized implementation of MPI I/O. We came across a number of BG/L specific hardware and software requirements while implementing MPI I/O (an optimized port of ROMIO [22]). In particular we evaluate the role of optimization of collective I/O primitives in communication phase, and file-domain partitioning within our implementation. We also characterize the scalability and performance of our BG/L file I/O solution not only for a list of I/O intensive benchmarks, but also real-scale applications as well as high-level libraries.

This paper makes the following contributions:

- We present the design and integration of a hierarchical parallel file I/O architecture for BG/L supercomputer, which delivers I/O performance scaling beyond conventional cluster-based parallel systems. We describe optimizations that contribute to the scalability.

- Quantitatively, we show the need to use MPI I/O collective operations for the scalability of parallel file I/O encountered frequently in real-world applications, usually with non-contiguous and irregular access patterns.

- We report the best bandwidth speedups ever achieved (to the best of our knowledge) for a number of commonly used I/O benchmarks, including an important I/O intensive application, HOMME from NCAR [7].

- Our file I/O solution provides efficient support for well-known high-level parallel file I/O interfaces, parallel HDF5 and parallel NetCDF. We present the first set of results demonstrating the scaling of programs written on these interfaces to a large number of processors.

The rest of the paper is organized as follows. Sec. 2 gives an overview of BG/L architecture from a parallel file I/O perspective. Sec. 3 presents the design of a parallel I/O solution followed by the optimizations carried out for scaling application-level parallel I/O. Sec. 4 describes issues related to our implementation of MPI I/O. Sec. 5 presents a thorough evaluation for the scaling performance of our solution against widely used parallel I/O benchmarks and a real-world application. Finally, we conclude the paper in Sec. 6.

2. Blue Gene/L: A Parallel I/O Perspective

BG/L uses a scalable architecture based on low power embedded processor, and integration of powerful networks,

using system-on-a-chip technology [8]. It uses a hierarchical system software architecture to achieve unprecedented levels of scalability [10]. In this section we describe some of these features we exploit to achieve highly scalable parallel I/O and create an attractive platform for data-intensive computation.

The BG/L core system consists of compute and I/O nodes with compute nodes viewed as computational engines attached to I/O nodes. The compute nodes and I/O nodes are organized into *processing sets* (*pset*), each of which contains one I/O node and a fixed number of compute nodes. Running on simplified embedded Linux, the I/O nodes represent the core system to the outside world as a cluster. In each pset, program control and I/O are accomplished via messages passed among its I/O node and compute nodes over a *collective* network. The I/O related communication among compute nodes and the I/O node in a pset is with little disturbance. BG/L compute nodes and I/O nodes are built out of the same chips, with only differences in terms of packaging and enabled networks. While, the compute node runs a unique, light-weight compute node kernel (CNK), the I/O node provides file service via Linux VFS. I/O related system calls trapped in CNK are shipped to the corresponding I/O node and processed by a console daemon CIOD, thus a POSIX-like I/O interface is supported for user-level compute processes. The separation and cooperation accomplished via the simple function shipping off-loads non-computation related services to the I/O nodes to keep a noise-free state for the compute nodes while achieving superior scalability [11]. In addition, the separation of I/O nodes and compute nodes, together with organizing them into balanced psets and providing almost dedicated communication channels for I/O operations, essentially provide the capability for scalable I/O.

Nevertheless, the scalable I/O capability does not necessarily lead to scalable application-level file I/O. Usually, such applications involve accessing a single file concurrently and with non-contiguous and/or irregular access patterns. While, the rest of the paper describes our effort on meeting the challenge, we first discuss a couple of BG/L features that we have particularly utilized.

The BG/L torus network, connecting the compute nodes, is the primary network for inter-processes communications for its high speed. Specifically, the bandwidth of a single link is close to its designed peak, 175 MB/sec in each direction. For the LLNL machine, the 65,536 compute nodes are organized into a $64 \times 32 \times 32$ three-dimensional torus. At 1.4 Gb/s per torus link, the unidirectional bisection bandwidth of the system will be 360 GB/s. The high bandwidth and high speed of the torus network provides the capability to move large amount of data across the compute nodes.

BG/L-MPI [9] has successfully exploited the rich features of BG/L in terms of the network topology, special purpose network hardware, and architectural compromises. While BG/L-MPI is originally ported from MPICH2 [3], its collective routines have demonstrated superior performance comparing to the original implementation and is close to the peak capabilities of the networks and processors. From an I/O perspective, a scalable implementation of BG/L-MPI provides an effective mean to optimize for concurrent and coordinated file accesses from a large number of processes.

In the following section, we will describe how we leverage BG/L's features such as its capability for scalable I/O, its high-performance interconnects, and its MPI implementation to deliver application-level scalable I/O.

3. A Scalable Parallel I/O Design for BG/L

In this section, we first present our parallel file system solution for BG/L: GPFS. Then, we describe our design steps and consideration to provide MPI I/O support to complement the GPFS-based solution and eventually to meet the I/O demands of applications running on BG/L. Additional implementation details will be discussed in Sec. 4.

3.1. GPFS-Based Solution

GPFS is IBM's parallel, shared-disk file system supporting both AIX- and Linux-based systems [20]. It allows parallel applications' concurrent access to the same files or different files, from nodes that mount the file system. In its latest release, GPFS 2.3 allows users to share files across clusters, which improves the system capacity as well as simplifies system administration. So far, the largest tested GPFS cluster contains 1170 Linux nodes [6], which is more than the I/O nodes of the largest BG/L systems installed so far (e.g., the LLNL 64-rack system has 1024 I/O nodes and the ASTRON [4] 6-rack system has 768 I/O nodes).

Our solution for integrating GPFS and BG/L consists of a three tier architecture (Fig. 1). The first tier of the architecture consists of I/O nodes as GPFS clients, whereas the second tier is an array of NSD (network shared disks) servers. The third tier consists of the storage area network (SAN) fabric and the actual disks. The interconnect between the I/O nodes and the NSD servers are Ethernet, while the connection between the second and third tier can be either fiber channel, fiber-channel switch or Ethernet (iSCSI). The choice of NSD servers, SAN fabric and storage devices depend on the customer requirements. This solution has been fully implemented and the performance evaluation shows that it had successfully explored and utilized the enormous potential I/O bandwidth of BG/L. Later on, we will show that the aggregated read/write at BG/L compute nodes reach 80% and 60% of that the underneath file system can deliver.

GPFS achieves its high throughput based on techniques such as large-block based disk striping, client-side caching,

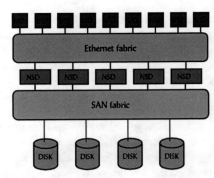

Figure 1. GPFS layout for BG/L

prefetching, and write-behind [20]. In addition, it supports file consistency using a sophisticated distributed byte-range file-locking technique. GPFS has managed to limit the performance side-effect of the file locking operation with an aggressive optimization for block-level data accesses.

Overall, GPFS is highly optimized for large-chunk I/O operations with regular access patterns (contiguous or regularly strided). However, its performance for small-chunk, non-contiguous I/O operations with irregular access patterns (non-constant strided) is less optimized. Particularly, concurrent accesses (from distinct processes) to different file regions in the same GPFS block introduce additional file system activities associated to its file locking mechanism, which can hurt performance. To complement GPFS, we use MPI I/O for I/O operations in scientific applications.

3.2. MPI I/O Design Goals

MPI I/O is the parallel I/O interface specified in the MPI-2 standard [19]. Because of its support for a much richer file access patterns and operations, MPI I/O is better suited for MPI based parallel programs than POSIX I/O interface. Particularly, MPI I/O includes a class of collective I/O operations (enabling a group of processes to access a common file in a coordinated fashion), which provide better flexibility for MPI I/O implementations to optimize I/O, by aggregating/distributing I/O operations transparently.

The general technique for implementing MPI I/O collective operations is by means of providing *collective buffering* [21]. Collective buffering is based on a common experience that the aggregated inter-processor communication speeds are significantly higher than I/O speeds. It rearranges and aggregates data in memory prior to writing to files to reduce the number of disk accesses. For scientific applications (typically with non-contiguous and irregular file access patterns), collective buffering is effective for achieving scalable I/O, particularly for systems without efficient support of asynchronous communication primitive, and exploiting massive parallelism like BG/L. Therefore, we set our design goal of MPI I/O for BG/L as to maximize the performance of MPI I/O collective operations.

To facilitate the design goals, we started our work on MPI I/O from ROMIO [21], an implementation of MPI I/O from Argonne National Laboratory. The primary reason for choosing ROMIO is for it's fully functional MPI I/O implementation (except *data representation*). Further, ROMIO integrated the collective buffering technique into its implementation of collective I/O operations, which allows us to concentrate on performance optimizations. In the following sub-sections, we elaborate our design decisions made in providing a scalable implementation of MPI I/O collective operations for BG/L configured with GPFS.

3.3. The *pset* Organization

I/O systems by nature are much more efficient for contiguous disk accesses than for non-contiguous, or irregular accesses. Particularly, GPFS is highly optimized for large-chunk, regular (contiguous or regularly strided) I/O accesses [20]. Therefore, it is better for the I/O requests from compute nodes to be contiguous.

As stated previously, pset organization of compute and I/O nodes plays a key role for BG/L I/O performance. Exploiting the collective buffering technique, MPI I/O collective operations provide opportunities for the pset structure of BG/L to be communicated, and an optimized file access pattern can be reached. The specific motivations for using pset and collective buffering approach are two folds. First, the best observed I/O performance of a BG/L partition containing multiple psets is often obtained when the I/O load is balanced across all the I/O nodes. Second, we have observed that for the case of a relatively large compute node to I/O node ratio (e.g. 64:1 on LLNL system), the I/O performance of a pset reaches the peak when 8-16 compute nodes perform I/O concurrently, not all the compute nodes.

The implementation of collective buffering in ROMIO (referred as *two-phase I/O*) distinguishes two interleaved phases: an inter-process data exchange phase and an I/O phase [21]. The two-phase I/O first selects a set of processes as I/O aggregators, which partitions the I/O responsibilities for a file. Based on this file partitioning, the in-memory data exchange phase routes the data among all participating processes and the I/O aggregators. In the I/O phase, the I/O aggregators issue read or write system calls to access file data.

In our design, the I/O aggregators are chosen in such a way that they are evenly distributed across the participating psets. Each BG/L node has a personality structure which keeps its run-time configuration data [10]. We utilize the pset configuration information. First, each compute node collects its pset ID, MPI rank. Then, the information of all compute nodes is gathered onto each compute node. Finally, each compute node generates a list of I/O aggrega-

tors so that they are distributed evenly across the psets, and the I/O aggregators from the same pset are contiguous in the list. When one MPI I/O collective routine is called, the collective file access region is computed and the I/O responsibility is distributed across the selected I/O aggregators. For a collective I/O operation with small data amount, a subset of the pre-selected I/O aggregators are used.

Here, the BG/L I/O nodes are not used for I/O aggregation. First, with the same ASIC as the compute nodes, I/O nodes have limited processing power for relative complicated aggregation tasks. Second, the possible communication channels among the I/O nodes are Ethernet and BG/L collective network. Although the collective network can be configured to contain multiple I/O nodes, the bisection bandwidth of the collective network is bounded by 350 MB/sec. The I/O nodes can potentially talk to each other over Ethernet. However, additional communication among I/O nodes through Ethernet may interfere with the file system client-side operations running on the I/O nodes. A comparison of file access operations on compute nodes against that from I/O nodes indicated little performance difference. Hence, having the compute nodes as I/O aggregators potentially provides more flexibility for dealing different BG/L configurations that have different compute nodes to I/O nodes ratio, avoiding a potential bottleneck at the I/O nodes.

3.4. File Domain Partitioning

As mentioned, GPFS block-level file accesses are highly optimized and scalable. Therefore, if a GPFS client node (i.e. BG/L I/O node in our design) only issues data-access requests having large size and aligning to GPFS block boundaries, the scalability of GPFS will be preserved, while successfully meeting the MPI I/O collective operation requirements. ROMIO assigns the I/O responsibilities for a file across the I/O aggregators with a balanced partitioning of the file region defined by the first and last file offsets of the collective operation. It has been reported in [14] that the simple file-partitioning method has various drawbacks and there are multiple ways for its optimization. For the case of GPFS, the main problem of the default file-partitioning method is that it can generate I/O operations only accessing part of GPFS blocks, which will trigger additional file system activities related to file locking.

To investigate the effect of associating the I/O aggregators with file regions align to the GPFS blocks, we wrote a synthetic program that partitions the file domain across processes in an absolutely balanced manner or with additional consideration to align with GPFS blocks. We call the two file partitioning methods as *balanced* and *aligned* file partitioning, respectively. After establish a mapping from file regions to processes, each process performs one contiguous write operation to its designated file region. Here, when ap-

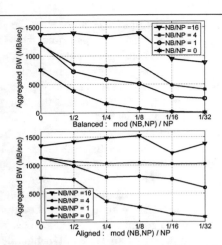

Figure 2. Balanced vs Aligned file partitioning

plying the balanced file partitioning, the neighboring I/O aggregators will compete for the lock of a single GPFS block. On the other hand, when applying aligned file partitioning, load imbalance could be a problem. This way, we will find which hurts performance more between concurrent accesses of a GPFS block and the imbalanced load.

We ran the experiment on an I/O rich BG/L system using 256 compute nodes and 32 I/O nodes (details of the platform is given in Sec. 5.1). Fig. 2 shows the results of the two mapping methods. Here, NB represents the total number of GPFS blocks and NP represents the number of processes. A non-zero value of $X = mod\ (NB, NP) / NP$ indicates that $R = X \times NP$ file blocks will be shared by multiple processes for the balanced partitioning case; for the aligned partitioning case, there will be R processes each of which accesses one additional file block comparing to the other processes. The results indicate that aligned file partitioning outperforms balanced file partitioning and its I/O performance stays flat for most of the cases, except when some of the I/O nodes have no work to do.

Based on the observation, we augmented ROMIO's default file partitioning method to have each I/O aggregator's file domain aligned to GPFS block in both size and offset. The GPFS block size can be reset using an environment variable at run-time, with a pre-set value as 1MB (the maximal file block size currently supported in GPFS). Later on (Sec. 5), we will show that the file-domain partitioning optimization (referred as *Aligned*) has contributed to significant performance improvement.

3.5. Communication Phase Optimizations

For the two phases of MPI I/O collective operations, the performance of file accesses issued by the I/O aggregators are bounded by the POSIX I/O performance on BG/L. However, for certain I/O access patterns (e.g. all processes read-

ing the same data from a file), the inter-process data exchange phase may dominate the overall performance. To address the issue of the communication phase of MPI I/O collective operations, we rely on the BG/L MPI implementation [9] as it has successfully explored and utilized the rich network features of BG/L machine. We tuned the communication phase of MPI I/O collective operations to choose the best performing communication method among BG/L MPI routines. Here, we highlight two optimizations whose benefits are clearly demonstrated in our experiments.

3.5.1. Inter-Process Data Exchange   ROMIO has implemented the communication phase of MPI I/O collective operations by using MPI send/receive functions, which can be further optimized on BG/L. As reported in [9], on BG/L, the optimized collective communication functions usually achieve much higher performance than the point-to-point communication functions. Particularly, the optimized MPI_Alltoall and MPI_Alltoallv can utilize up to 98% of the peak bandwidth of the underneath torus/mesh network for long messages, and their performance scales with the number of compute nodes. Therefore, we have replaced the use of the point-to-point functions in this phase with MPI_Alltoallv. In our experiments, we refer to this specific optimization as *Alltoall*.

3.5.2. Access Range Information Exchange   Prior to the interleaved communication and I/O phases, the two-phase I/O implementation schedules the communication among the I/O aggregators and the processors issuing I/O operations. Here, all processes exchange the information about their I/O requests. This was originally implemented via MPI_Allgather operations so that each process will have the file range information of all the I/O requests. We found that these operations take up to 30% of the time of the collective write operations in a few runs of the BTIO benchmark (see Sec. 5.1 for details). On BG/L, the MPI_Allgather operation is implemented by performing P MPI_Bcast operations, where P is the number of processes in the communicator. On BlueGen/L, for very short messages, MPI_Bcast has high overhead. We replaced the MPI_Allgather with an MPI_Allreduce, which performs much better for short and medium sized messages to gain the MPI benefits. The optimization is referred as *Allreduce* in our experiments.

4. MPI I/O Implementation Issues

Having been ported to a large number of parallel systems [22], ROMIO's portability mainly relies on two features. First, it uses MPI, which allows ROMIO to be ported to most parallel computing platforms that support MPI. Secondly, ROMIO has an intermediate interface called ADIO (Abstract Device Interface for I/O), which hides the implementation details for different file systems and makes it a

Program	Description	From	Used by
IOR	General I/O benchmarking	LLNL	LLNL
NAS BT-IO	NAS BT benchmark with checkpointing	NASA Ames Research Ctr	[21] [14] [25]
coll_perf	ROMIO collective I/O performance test	ANL	[13]
FLASH io_bench	Benchmark for the I/O requirements of FLASH2	U Chicago	[17] [13] [14]
HOMME	High Order Method Modeling Environment	NCAR	[7]

Table 1. Benchmarking programs and applications

relatively easy task for porting and performance tuning on a specific system. To port ROMIO onto a specific system or file system, one only needs to implement a small set of system-dependent functions under ADIO. Most of our development for BG/L MPI I/O that presented in this paper are under the ROMIO ADIO layer. Concentrating on optimizing MPI I/O collective operations, we have overridden ADIO's default implementation for this class of operations.

To provide a complete MPI I/O support, we have augmented CIOD with *fcntl* byte-range file locking functionality, facilitating MPI I/O atomic mode. On BG/L, fcntl byte-range file locking is different from most of the file I/O system calls, as it cannot be realized by simple function forwarding. Specifically, when a file lock is trapped at the compute node kernel and forwarded to the I/O node, the CIOD process is the one that actually issues fcntl for locking a file region. Since CIOD is a user process, the Linux kernel on the I/O node treats all the file locking requests (though from different compute-nodes) as if they are from a single Linux process. This causes a problem when two compute nodes in the same pset (i.e., their I/O requests go to the same I/O node) compete for a lock over the same file region. As a result, both compute-processes will gain access to the file region and the MPI I/O atomic semantic is violated.

To support correct fcntl file locking functionality, we keep the file locking information in CIOD for all the files opened by the computing-processes in the pset. That is, for each opened file, CIOD keeps two lists of byte-range pairs. One list keeps the regions that are locked by compute nodes in the pset, while another list keeps the pending file locking requests. Recall that the protocol between BG/L compute and I/O nodes is blocking, and the fcntl is no exception. For the blocked call of fcntl (e.g. F_SETLKW), we do not want to block the I/O node. In our implementation, CIOD translates all blocked fcntl file locking requests from compute nodes into repeated non-blocking calls. Specifically, in CIOD there is a loop repeatedly querying the devices (tree, Ethernet), and for the denied non-blocking fcntl file locking requests, CIOD re-tries the file-locking requests for every few iterations. This process repeats until a fcntl file locking requests is satisfied. The rest of the implementation is similar to the file locking implementation in Linux kernel [12].

5. Performance Evaluation

In this section we present the evaluation of our scalable parallel I/O solution against a collection of widely used benchmarks and a real application utilizing parallel I/O. We will demonstrate scalable performance resulted from our solution showing that it matches the extraordinary computational power and the corresponding file I/O needs of scientific applications running on BG/L.

5.1. Experiment Setup

We used a two-rack I/O rich BG/L system, containing 2048 compute nodes and 256 I/O nodes. The system has two 512 compute-node partition and one 1024 compute-node partition that mount GPFS on their I/O nodes, and no smaller partitions are configured. To demonstrate scalability, we used mapping files [9] that assigns contiguous MPI ranks to the compute nodes in the same *pset* to keep the compute nodes to I/O nodes ratio as 8:1, when using less than 512 nodes.

The attached GPFS file system contains 32 NSD servers (running on x335 Linux PCs). The system has 8 DS4300 storage manager (aka FAStT600), with each has 4 Fiber Channel connections to 4 NSD servers. The 8 DS4300 together host 448 disks. On the other side, the NSD servers connect to the BG/L I/O nodes via Gigabit Ethernet. Although the aggregated disk bandwidth can be as high as 10 to 20 GB/sec, the performance of the configuration is bounded by the bandwidth from the I/O nodes to the NSD servers (the possible peak bandwidth of the 32 Gb Ethernet links is 4 GB/sec). The GPFS block size is set to 1 MB to maximize the system throughput. The page pool size on I/O nodes is 192 MB (GPFS page pool is used for client-side caching). Currently, the maximum performance for accessing a single file from BG/L compute nodes is about 2.0 GB/sec for write and 2.6 GB/sec for read. The gap between the observed I/O rates from BG/L compute nodes and available bandwidth of the specific configuration (4 GB/sec) are from protocol overheads of TCP, and the data transfer among BG/L compute and I/O nodes.

Table 1 lists five benchmarks and applications we used here for our experiments.

IOR is a parallel file system test code developed at LLNL. It performs parallel writes and reads to/from file(s)

195

using MPI I/O and POSIX operations. It can be configured to access a single file or each process accessing a separate file; use collective/non-collective operations; and perform contiguous or strided accesses, etc. IOR (version 2.8.1) has been used to measure the parallel file system performance for BG/L. Here, we compare the performance of IOR using MPI I/O against using POSIX operations to show that our MPI I/O implementation delivers comparable performance for parallel I/O operations with regular (contiguous or strided) access patterns. We use the rest of the programs to demonstrate the advantage of MPI I/O for I/O with non-contiguous and irregular access patterns. For eliminating possible client-side caching effects at the I/O nodes, we configured each process to do 384 write/read operations, each of which access 1 MB of data.

NAS BT-IO [24], an extension of NAS BT benchmark, simulates the I/O requirement of BT. BT-IO distributes multiple Cartesian subsets of the global dataset to processes using diagonal multi-partitioning domain decompositions. The in-core data structure are three-dimensional arrays and are written to a file periodically. The file access pattern of each process is non-contiguous with non-constant strides. NAS BT-IO's file access pattern is typical among scientific applications, which has been frequently used for performance evaluation of parallel file I/O [21, 14, 25]. BT-IO has three implementations for its file I/O. The *full-mpiio* carries out the I/O using MPI I/O collective routines, while the *simple-mpiio* does the I/O using MPI I/O independent routines, and the *fortran-io* has FORTRAN iterative write statements in a multi-level loop nest. Here, we used NAS input class C (the underneath process topologies are squares). To keep the per-process load constant across runs, we changed the default *problem_size* parameter to have each process access about 3 MB data in each collective I/O call.

coll_perf is a synthetic benchmark in ROMIO [23]. It collectively writes and reads a three-dimensional, block-distributed array to/from a file in a non-contiguous manner. To keep the work (data/file size) of each processor constant, each process accesses 256^3 integer elements, resulting an average I/O of 64 MB per-process.

FLASH I/O benchmark [26] simulates the I/O pattern of the FLASH2 code [15], a parallel hydrodynamics code that simulates astrophysical thermonuclear flashes in two or three dimensions by solving the compressible Euler equations on a block-structured adaptive mesh. The benchmark program is distributed together with the full FLASH2 application and its I/O routines are identical to the routines used by FLASH2. So the performance demonstrated by the benchmark would closely reflect the performance of the full application's I/O performance. The FLASH I/O benchmark recreates the primary data structures in the FLASH2 code and produces a checkpoint file, a plotfile for centered data, and a plotfile for corner data. Same as FLASH2 code,

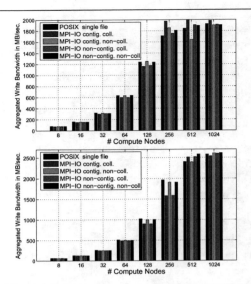

Figure 3. Performance baseline (IOR W/R)

the original version of FLASH I/O benchmark uses parallel HDF5 [1]. In short, the in-core data structure of FLASH I/O benchmark is a block-distributed three-dimensional array, and the file structure is a distribution of the three-dimensional array along the Z-dimension. In its latest distribution, FLASH I/O benchmark includes a version that uses PnetCDF [17]. The benchmark measures the time spent on a collection of I/O and data manipulation operations and then computes the data rate based on these timings. To be consistent with the rest of the performance data shown in this paper, we have instrumented the HDF5 and PnetCDF libraries to time the MPI I/O file access routines (used inside the libraries). Because PnetCDF only uses collective file access routines, we did not collect independent I/O performance for FLASH I/O benchmark. We configured the benchmark for each process to access about 2.5 MB data in each MPI I/O collective operation.

5.2. Performance Baseline

The performance of application-level parallel I/O demonstrated in this paper is bounded by the POSIX I/O performance of our experiment platform, and our first experiment is to establish a performance baseline.

Fig. 3 shows the results from IOR. We ran various configurations of IOR. The *POSIX single file* configuration gives the I/O bandwidth obtained on the system when all processes accessing distinct regions of a common file. The results indicate that the performance scales well (averaging 100 MB per second for each BG/L I/O node) up to about 256 compute nodes (32 I/O nodes), and then flats out. The specific GPFS file system was set up for the purpose of development and the performance shown in Fig. 3 is quite close

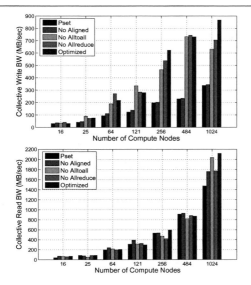

Figure 4. Optimization effects on BT-IO

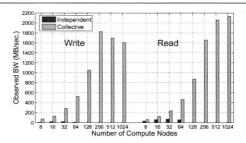

Figure 5. ROMIO coll_perf results

to its capability. We have run most of our experiments up to 1024 compute nodes, and some results show that the performance still grows when 1024 compute nodes are used. This is because MPI I/O performance is different from raw I/O performance. It reflects the MPI communication performance and how the cross-processor communication and the I/O activities interacts. For the MPI I/O related configurations, *contig.* indicates that the accesses from each process are contiguous; *non-contig.* indicates that the accesses are constantly strided; *coll.* indicates that collective I/O operations are used; *non-coll.* indicates that independent I/O operations are used. The corresponding results are fairly close to that of POSIX, which indicate that MPI I/O does not introduce significant overhead (from implementation, byte-range file locking) for simple file access patterns (i.e., having large contiguous chunks as 1 MB). The following sections will show that for irregular file access patterns exposed in benchmarks and applications, MPI I/O becomes the most effective mean for obtaining high-level I/O performance.

5.3. Effects of Optimizations

In this section, we evaluate the effects of different optimizations discussed in Sec. 3 using NAS BT-IO benchmark. We compare five configurations:
- *Optimized* applies all the optimizations from Sec. 3;
- *No Allreduce* applies *Optimized*, except the *Allreduce* optimization (Sec. 3.5.2);
- *No Alltoall* applies *Optimized*, except the *Alltoall* optimization (Sec. 3.5.1);
- *No Aligned* applies *Optimized*, except the *Aligned* optimization (Sec. 3.4).

- *Pset* only applies the optimization that integrates the *pset* structure into the selection of I/O aggregators (Sec. 3.3).

The configurations *No Allreducce*, *No Alltoall*, and *No Aligned* are to show the performance degradations from the best configuration (*Optimized*), when the specific optimizations are not applied.

Fig. 4 gives the results for BT-IO. It shows that using MPI I/O collective routines in general gives the best I/O performance when the number of processes increases. As shown in the graph, among the three optimizations, the aligned file domain partitioning gives the best performance improvement, i.e., while comparing to the best configuration, *No Aligned* gives the most performance degradation for write operations. This is consistent with our synthetic experiment in Sec. 3.4. For the other two optimizations (*Alltoall* and *Allreduce*), it shows that, when they are not applied, the performance degradations scale with the number of processors, which confirms that the optimizations result better scaling. Finally, there is at least three fold speedup for the write operations, when comparing the *Optimized* and the *Pset* configurations.

These optimizations have more significant effects on the write operations than for read, because GPFS' file byte-range locking is not optimized for small-chunk file write operations. In addition, the bandwidth numbers reported in Fig. 4 represent averaged numbers across all the instances of MPI I/O collective operations. We have noticed that there are performance variations across the instances, and we are investigating the issue.

5.4. Benchmark Results

In Fig. 5 and 6, we show performance obtained on two widely used benchmark programs. The results for coll_perf confirm that MPI I/O collective operations on BG/L can deliver scalable performance that is only bounded by the underlying system. Particularly, the poor performance of independent I/O operations states a strong recommendation to use MPI I/O collective routines. For the write results, there is a slight drop of the performance when more than 256 processes are used. We think the performance drop was due to

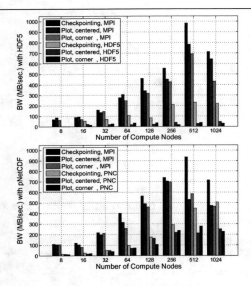

Figure 6. FLASH I/O Benchmark results

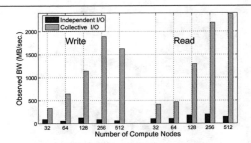

Figure 7. HOMME I/O results

the increasing latency of the inter-process data exchange of the two-phase I/O when the performance of the I/O phase reached the system's capability, and we are working on a thorough investigation of this behavior.

Fig. 6 shows the performance of the FLASH I/O benchmark. We present two sets of results: MPI and HDF5; MPI and PNC (PnetCDF). The legends marked MPI are obtained from our instrumentation inside HDF5 and PnetCDF that measure the wall-time of MPI I/O collective read/write operations. The legends marked with HDF5 or PNC are simply based on the wall-time of the application-level I/O functions. This results show that at the observation level of high-level parallel I/O library routines, our solution delivers up to 240 MB/sec with HDF5, and 500 MB/sec with PnetCDF. The results are about several folds better than similar experiments presented previously for cluster-based parallel file I/O solutions [17]. Here, because the bandwidth numbers are averaged across multiple MPI I/O calls, the results do not match up with those of IOR. Besides the effects similar to coll_perf, the results show that the best performance is reached when using 512 processes, this is because that the data-size was small (averaged 2.5 MB per process per collective call) and hence the I/O phase could not fully explore available bandwidth of the system (e.g., disk accesses are not balanced across a large number of disks) for small scale runs. Nevertheless, the aggregate performance is significant. In addition to scalable MPI I/O performance, the results marked as *Checkpointing, HDF5/PNC* indicate that for the two MPI I/O based high-level interfaces, when observing at the level of their high-level I/O routines, the I/O bandwidth numbers scale up to 256/512 processes.

5.5. Application Results

Finally, we demonstrate the scalability of the file I/O for the HOMME (High-Order Multiscale Modeling Environment) code, a scalable and efficient spectral element based atmospheric dynamical code. The application has been running on BG/L and its scalability and performance (without the I/O part) has been demonstrated with up to 7776 processors [7]. The file I/O part of HOMME deals with checkpointing, restarting from checkpoints and dumping movie files. In addition, each process dumps a movie file where MPI I/O is not used. Since writing to separate files is not interesting from MPI I/O perspective, we did not configure HOMME input file for such operations. The checkpoint/restore part of HOMME is written using MPI I/O independent file access routines in a loop-nest. We have replaced the loop nest containing the MPI I/O independent operations with a MPI I/O collection operation and a file set-view call within the application.

We used an input of simulation on *Aquaplanet* with Emanuel physics [18]. To benchmark its I/O aspect, we have changed the input configuration of checkpoint frequency and simulation steps. The total amount of work was kept constant for all the runs. To evaluate the performance for both write and read, for each data point in the graphs, we invoked the application four times: an initial run with checkpoint only configuration followed by three runs with restart and checkpoint configuration. Each run has 20 time steps with one checkpointing for every 5 time steps. Each checkpoint operation generates a 500 MB file.

Fig. 7 shows the performance of the I/O part of HOMME. Here, we show the performance improvement associated with our modification of changing MPI independent I/O operations to collective operations. The results indicate that for the application, using MPI I/O collective read/write operations delivers I/O performance that is close to the baseline. Overall, we achieved 10-15 folds speedups for the time consuming I/O part of HOMME compared to its original implementation (using MPI I/O independent operations).

Program	BW in MB/sec.	
	Write	Read
LLNL IOR	1,970	2,600
ROMIO collective I/O performance test	1,400	1,800
NAS BT benchmark with checkpointing	870	2,100
FLASH2 I/O benchmark with HDF5	963	
FLASH2 I/O benchmark with PnetCDF	940	
HOMME application from NCAR	1,800	2,300

Table 2. Results summary

6. Conclusions and Future Work

Productivity and performance of today's supercomputing systems have been limited by the I/O bottlenecks due to the inability of existing software layers to scale to the desired level. While impressive computational scaling results have been obtained on massively parallel systems like Blue Gene/L, relatively very few scalable I/O performance results exist for data-intensive applications on such systems.

We address the challenge with a highly scalable file I/O design and implementation which would deliver unprecedented levels of I/O performance for BG/L. By leveraging the benefit of functional partitioning and hierarchical structure of Blue Gene/L system software, our parallel file I/O design, is able to provide scalable file I/O bandwidth far beyond the level of any conventional cluster-based supercomputing systems. The design exploits the scalability of GPFS at the backend and provides effective MPI I/O support (collective operations in particular) as the API for application-level I/O requirements.

We evaluated our design and implementation on an 1-rack Blue Gene/L system against a number of popular benchmarks as well as HOMME [7], a real application. Highlights of our results (the best aggregated bandwidth of MPI I/O collective file access operations running on up to 1024 BG/L compute nodes) are summarized in Table 2. It shows the best bandwidth speedups ever achieved (to the best of our knowledge) for these benchmarks and applications. In addition, for the first time, we demonstrate the scaling for popular parallel I/O interfaces such as parallel HDF5 and parallel NetCDF. to a large number of processors.

While the results presented in this paper are obtained on an I/O rich BG/L system with 1024 compute nodes, our solution is not limited to this configuration. We are investigating the solution on bigger systems. As a continuation to our on-going research we would like to expand API solutions beyond the scope of MPI I/O. We are also investigating the possibility of optimizing across-process data exchange patterns, exploring effective file domain distribution, and addressing potential meta-data scalability.

References

[1] HDF5 home page. URL: *http:// hdf.ncsa.uiuc.edu/ HDF5*.

[2] Lustre scalable storage. URL: *http:// www.clusterfs.com*.

[3] The MPICH and MPICH2 homepage. URL: *http:// www-unix.mcs.anl.gov/ mpi/ mpich*.

[4] LOFAR BlueGene/L Workshop. URL: *http:// www.lofar.org/ BlueGene/*, 2004.

[5] Parallel Virtual File System 2 (PVFS2). URL: *http:// www.pvfs.org/ pvfs2*, 2004.

[6] *GPFS for Linux, FAQ*. URL: *http:// publib.boulder.ibm.com/ clresctr/ windows/ public/ gpfsbooks.html*, 2005.

[7] HOMME on the IBM BlueGene/L. URL: *http:// www.homme.ucar.edu*, 2005.

[8] N. R. Adiga et al. An overview of the BlueGene/L supercomputer. In *SC'02*.

[9] G. Almási et al. Optimization of MPI collective communication on BlueGene/L systems. In *ICS'05*.

[10] G. Almási et al. An overview of the BlueGene/L system software organization. In *Euro-Par'03*.

[11] G. Almási et al. Scaling physics and material science applications on a massively parallel BG/L system. In *ICS'05*.

[12] D. P. Bovet and M. Cesati. *Understanding the Linux Kernel*. O'Reilly and Associated, Inc., 2002.

[13] A. Ching et al. Noncontiguous I/O Accesses Through MPI-IO. In *CCGRID'03*.

[14] K. Coloma et al. Scalable high-level caching for parallel I/O. In *IPDPS'04*.

[15] B. Fryxell et al. FLASH: An adaptive mesh hydrodynamics code for modeling astrophysical thermonuclear flashes. *Astrophysical Journal Supplement*, 2000.

[16] B. Gallmeister. *POSIX.4*. O'Reilly and Assoc., Inc., 1994.

[17] J. Li et al. Parallel netCDF: A High-Performance Scientific I/O Interface. In *SC'03*.

[18] R. D. Loft. Blue Gene/L Experiences at NCAR. in IBM System Scientific User Group meeting (SCICOMP11), URL: *http:// www.spscicomp.org*, 2005.

[19] Message Passing Interface Forum. MPI-2: a message passing interface standand. *High Performance Computing Applications*, 12(1-2), 1998.

[20] F. B. Schmuck and R. L. Haskin. GPFS: a shared-disk file system for large computing clusters. In *FAST'02*.

[21] R. Thakur, W. Gropp, and E. Lusk. Data sieving and collective I/O in ROMIO. In *IOPADS'99*.

[22] R. Thakur, W. Gropp, and E. Lusk. On implementing MPI-IO portably and with high performance. In *IOPADS'99*.

[23] R. Thakur, R. Ross, E. Lusk, and W. Gropp. ROMIO: A High-Performance, Portable MPI-IO Implementation. URL: *http:// www-unix.mcs.anl.gov/ romio/*, 2002.

[24] P. Wong and R. F. V. der Wijingaart. NAS Parallel benchmark I/O v2.4. Technical Report NAS-03-002, NASA Ames Research Center, 2003.

[25] J. Worringen, J. L. Traeff, and H. Ritzdorf. Fast parallel noncontiguous file access. In *SC'03*.

[26] M. Zingale. FLASH I/O benchmark routine. http:// flash.uchicago.edu/ zingale/flash_benchmark_io, 2002.

Session 7:
Industrial Perspective
(Invited Presentation)

Industrial perspectives on Challenges for Next-Generation Computer Systems

Chair: Mazin Yousif
Intel Corporation

The purpose of this session is to present an industrial perspective on the architecture of future platforms, including processors, caches, memory and I/O, and technical challenges and the approaches to resolve them. It is intended to encourage the research community to investigate relevant solutions. In this session, there will be three presentations, as follows:

1. "Platform Design Challenges with Many cores" Raj Yavatkar, Intel Corporation
2. "System IO Network Evolution - Closing Requirement Gaps," Renato Recio, IBM Corporation
3. "The Next Roadblocks in SOC Evolution: On-Chip Storage Capacity and Off-Chip Bandwidth," Philip Emma, IBM Corporation

Raj Yavatkar, Intel Corporation, will focus on the architecture challenges of platform designed with many core processors – processors with large number of internal cores. Challenges for many-core-based platforms include, but not limited to, power management, reliability and balancing processor-memory-I/O bandwidth requirements. Renato Recio, IBM Corporation, will focus on I/O network evolution and how I/O architectures are addressing the requirements gaps including performance, connectivity and power management. Philip Emma, IBM Corporation, discusses system-on-chip evolutions and the challenges to meet networking bandwidth and storage capacity requirements.

Session 8:
Fault-Tolerant Architecture and Security

ReViveI/O: Efficient Handling of I/O
in Highly-Available Rollback-Recovery Servers[*]

Jun Nakano, Pablo Montesinos, Kourosh Gharachorloo[†], and **Josep Torrellas**
University of Illinois at Urbana-Champaign   [†]Google
{nakano, pmontesi, torrellas}@cs.uiuc.edu, kourosh@google.com
http://iacoma.cs.uiuc.edu

Abstract

The increasing demand for reliable computers has led to proposals for hardware-assisted rollback of memory state. Such approach promises major reductions in Mean Time To Repair (MTTR). The benefits are especially compelling for database servers, where existing recovery software typically leads to downtimes of tens of minutes. Unfortunately, adoption of such proposals is hindered by the lack of efficient mechanisms for I/O recovery.

This paper presents and evaluates ReViveI/O, a scheme for I/O undo and redo that is compatible with mechanisms for hardware-assisted rollback of memory state. We have fully implemented a Linux-based prototype that shows that low-overhead, low-MTTR recovery of I/O is feasible. For 20–120 ms between checkpoints, a throughput-oriented workload such as TPC-C has negligible overhead. Moreover, for 50 ms or less between checkpoints, the response time of a latency-bound workload such as WebStone remains tolerable. In all cases, the recovery time of ReViveI/O is practically negligible. The result is a cost-effective highly-available server.

1. Introduction

Highly-available shared-memory servers have to be able to cope with system-level faults. Faults are often transient, such as hardware glitches caused by high-energy particles, or OS panic due to unusual interleavings of software events. There are also permanent hardware faults, which can bring down part of the machine. Fault frequencies are projected to remain high in the future. This is worrisome, given the growing number of businesses with database applications that crucially depend on their servers being up practically all the time.

One approach to attain fault tolerance is to employ extensive self-checking and correcting hardware, often through redundancy and even lock-step execution. This is the approach used by HP's Nonstop Architecture [11] and IBM's S/390 mainframes [33]. Unfortunately, this approach is too expensive for many users.

An alternative approach is to use plain server hardware and support software-based checkpoint and rollback recovery. In such

systems, the operating system [18, 19, 32], virtual machine monitor [5], or application (e.g., the database [8]) periodically checkpoints the state of the machine, virtual machine, or processes, respectively, to safe storage. If a fault is detected, the system rolls back to a state preceding the fault. However, since software checkpointing has significant overhead, checkpoints are typically only taken every few minutes or less frequently. As a result, when a fault occurs, the Mean Time To Repair (MTTR) is significant, and the machine becomes unavailable for a sizable period. For example, the recovery time of Oracle 9.2 on a Solaris server is typically tens of minutes [22].

A second shortcoming of software-based checkpointing appears in workloads where server and clients frequently exchange messages. To correctly support recovery, the server must delay sending messages until after they are checkpointed. If checkpoints are infrequent to minimize overheads, messages suffer long delays.

One way to significantly reduce server MTTR and avoid long message delays is to support *high-frequency* checkpointing (e.g., one every few tens of milliseconds). Several architectures with such support have been proposed [21, 24, 29, 34]. These architectures rely on hardware assistance for checkpointing or for data buffering, logging or replication. For example, ReVive induces about 6% overhead and recovers from the types of faults supported in less than 1 second [29]. Such tiny MTTR boosts machine availability. Moreover, as suggested by the ROC project, it opens up opportunities to lower cost of ownership [27].

Unfortunately, past work on these high-frequency checkpointing architectures has focused on recovering the *memory state* of the machine. It has not fully addressed the problem of rollback recovery in the presence of I/O. When workloads perform I/O, rollback is tricky: how can the server "undo" a disk write or a message send? Can it "redo" it? Unless these issues are addressed, the proposed high-frequency checkpointing solutions are unusable. These issues are also particularly relevant to architectures for transactional memory [10], which rely on the ability to roll back a section of code and then re-execute it.

A known approach to handle I/O in checkpointing systems is to delay the commit of output until the next checkpoint (output commit problem). To accomplish this, Masubuchi *et al.* [21] proposed adding a "virtual" or "Pseudo" Device Driver (PDD) layer between the kernel and the Device Drivers (DD). Disk output requests are redirected to the PDD rather than the DD. The PDD blocks any output-requesting process until the next check-

---

[*]This work was supported in part by the National Science Foundation under grants EIA-0072102, EIA-0103610, CHE-0121357, and CCR-0325603; DARPA under grant NBCH30390004; DOE under grant B347886; and gifts from IBM and Intel.

point [20], after which the output is performed. Masubuchi *et al.*'s design has limitations, such as (i) blocking processes until a checkpoint and (ii) only supporting disk I/O. However, their general method is attractive because it requires no kernel or application modification. It can be built upon to provide efficient I/O undo/redo for high-frequency checkpointing architectures.

1.1. Contribution of This Paper

Our main contribution is the full implementation, testing, and experimental evaluation of *ReViveI/O*, an efficient I/O undo/redo scheme that is compatible with high-frequency checkpointing architectures such as ReVive [29] and SafetyNet [34]. Our work completes the viability assessment of such novel memory-recovery architectures. It is only through a complete implementation that we identify true overheads, relevant ordering constraints, and corner cases. Moreover, we perform a sensitivity analysis of what checkpoint frequencies are required to maintain acceptable throughput and tolerable response times.

We also enhance Masubuchi *et al.*'s approach in two ways. First, the PDD now also supports network I/O. Secondly, the disk PDD, rather than blocking the output-requesting process, quickly buffers the output and returns. After the next checkpoint, the I/O operation is committed in the background. This provides efficient I/O undo/redo.

We installed our ReViveI/O prototype on a Linux 2.4-based multiprocessor server running TPC-C on Oracle, and WebStone on Apache. Our prototype shows that low-overhead, tiny-MTTR recovery of I/O is feasible. Specifically, for 20–120 ms between checkpoints, a throughput-oriented workload such as TPC-C has negligible overhead. In addition, for 50 ms or less between checkpoints, the response time of a latency-bound workload such as WebStone on Apache remains tolerable. In all cases, the recovery time of ReViveI/O is practically negligible. Finally, combining ReVive and ReViveI/O is likely to reduce the throughput of TPC-C-class applications by 7% or less for 60–120 ms checkpoint intervals, while incurring a tiny MTTR of less than 1 second.

Our work is significant in that, with ReVive and ReViveI/O, a shared-memory server can quickly recover from: (i) any hardware (and some software) transient faults in the machine, and (ii) permanent faults that at most take out one node in the machine. Indeed, both the processor/memory state (thanks to ReVive) and the I/O state (thanks to ReViveI/O) are restored to the preceding checkpoint *within 1 second and transparently* to the database. No ongoing database transactions are lost.

There are rare faults for which ReVive cannot restore the processor/memory state, such as the simultaneous permanent loss of multiple nodes. In this case, the fault is not transparent to the database. A few seconds after the machine is rebooted, ReViveI/O brings the I/O state to its correct state at the preceding checkpoint. Then, we simply depend on the normal recovery mechanisms of the database to reconstruct the state from the logs saved on disk.

The overall result is much higher server availability: the majority of faults are recovered from with sub-second MTTR and transparently, while only infrequent faults require the much slower recovery mechanism of the database.

The paper is organized as follows: Section 2 gives background; Sections 3 and 4 present ReViveI/O's architecture and implementation; Section 5 describes our evaluation methodology; Section 6

evaluates ReViveI/O; and Section 7 discusses related work. Note that fault detection is beyond the scope of this paper.

2. Background
2.1. Context of Our Work

The context of our work is shared-memory multiprocessors such as IBM's eServer pSeries p5 595 [14] or HP's Integrity Superdome [12] used as back-end database servers. These servers store the database in local disk subsystems and communicate over networks with many clients. They execute transaction-processing applications similar to TPC-C.

A major issue in these systems is server uptime. Unfortunately, a high-energy particle impact may cause a processor reset, an unusual data race may crash the OS, or a link failure may disconnect a node. In these cases, transactions are typically aborted and the database attempts to recover. Such recovery often renders the server unavailable for tens of minutes [22].

To understand the recovery requirements of these systems, note that I/O is practically limited to disk and network. Moreover, these workloads are typically not latency bound. For example, in TPC-C, 88% of transactions are NewOrder or Payment, which involve the exchange of a single request and response between client and server. IBM's p5 595 reports an average response time of 340 ms for these transactions [37]. Consequently, adding a few tens of ms to each transaction to support a recovery scheme is tolerable.

2.2. Fault Model

We leverage proposed rollback-recovery architectures [21, 24, 29, 34] that support high-frequency checkpointing (ten times or more per second) and, for the fault types supported, are able to recover the *memory state* of the machine before the fault. These schemes typically have low overhead and a tiny MTTR.

As an example, we use ReVive [29] in this paper. Appendix A outlines ReVive. With 100 ms between checkpoints, ReVive has an average execution overhead of 6.3%. Moreover, it recovers from the supported faults in under 1 second. This results in 99.999% availability even with one fault per day.

Specifically, ReVive recovers the memory state of the machine for: (i) transient faults and (ii) permanent faults that at most take out one node in the machine. Although fault detection is beyond the scope of this paper, the implicit assumption is that some mechanism detects these faults within a checkpoint interval. Such short detection latency is more feasible for hardware faults than for software ones. However, there are some software transient faults that are fail fast. For example, Gu *et al.* [9] show that a sizable portion of kernel errors can be detected within 100,000 cycles. Overall, we refer to all these faults, from which ReVive can recover the memory state, as *Memory-Recoverable* (MR) faults.

The other faults, from which ReVive cannot recover the machine's memory state, we call *Non-Memory-Recoverable* (NMR). An example is the simultaneous permanent loss of multiple nodes [29].

In this paper, we also assume that non-volatile storage, namely disks and any closely-attached non-volatile memories (NVRAMs), can only suffer transient faults. They have the appropriate support (e.g., RAID 5) to avoid permanent faults.

With these assumptions, we will show that, for MR faults, we restore both the processor/memory state (thanks to ReVive) and the I/O state (thanks to ReViveI/O) to the preceding checkpoint. The restoration is *transparent* to the database. No ongoing transactions are lost (Figure 1).

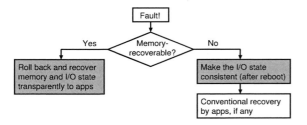

Figure 1. Faults handled by the combination of ReVive and ReViveI/O.

For NMR faults, recovery is not transparent to the database. The machine has to be fixed and rebooted. ReViveI/O then restores the I/O state to its consistent state at the preceding checkpoint. Finally, the conventional recovery mechanisms of the database reconstruct the database state.

2.3. Integrating I/O with Checkpoints

Work on checkpointed message-based distributed systems [7, 17] shows how to support I/O undo/redo under checkpointing. The commit of outputs is delayed until the next checkpoint (output commit problem); only then can the system guarantee that it will not have to roll back to a state prior to issuing the outputs.

To address the output commit problem without kernel modifications, Masubuchi *et al.* proposed the Pseudo Device Driver (PDD) [21] (Figure 2). Disk output requests are redirected to the PDD rather than the Device Driver (DD). The PDD blocks any output-requesting process until the next checkpoint [20], after which the output is performed. The PDD can be considered an extremely thin virtual machine layer for I/O checkpointing.

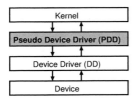

Figure 2. The Pseudo Device Driver software layer.

We enhance Masubuchi *et al.*'s scheme in two ways. First, processes requesting disk writes are not blocked until the next checkpoint. Secondly, we also support network I/O. Kernel, DDs, and server/client applications remain unmodified.

3. Architecture of ReViveI/O

This section describes the organization ReViveI/O, with key ordering issues, overheads, and limitations.

3.1. Description of Operation

We start by examining three properties that we leverage. Then, for readability, we describe ReViveI/O in two steps: first, an initial incomplete solution, and then the complete one.

3.1.1. Properties Leveraged

We leverage three properties to build a low-overhead I/O undo/redo prototype. First, ReVive's ability to roll back the memory state is leveraged to restore PDD consistency after a fault. Specifically, we assign to the PDD a portion of main memory called the *Memory Buffer*. In there, the PDD buffers all the output requests until the next checkpoint; after the checkpoint, the outputs are performed in the background and removed from the buffer. If a fault occurs, ReVive returns the memory state to the previous checkpoint. This automatically makes the PDD consistent: all the output requests in the current checkpoint interval disappear from the Memory Buffer, and all those from the previous checkpoint interval re-appear in the Memory Buffer and are ready to be performed again.

Second, the fact that the output operations under consideration are idempotent (i.e., replayable) is leveraged to allow the recovery scheme to re-perform output operations without hurting correctness. Indeed, disk output operations are trivially idempotent. Network output is idempotent due to the high-level support provided by TCP [36]. With TCP, each packet has a sequence number. If the client receives the same packet twice, TCP sees the same sequence number and discards one of them[1]. Consequently, correctness is not compromised when, after a rollback, the requests in the Memory Buffer force our scheme to re-write the same disk blocks and re-send the same messages.

Finally, properties of the I/O considered are leveraged to not have to buffer any inputs for later "re-consumption" should rollback be needed. Specifically, disk inputs need no buffering because the application will automatically re-issue them if it needs to. For network input, we avoid buffering by again relying on TCP properties. With TCP, packets are acknowledged by the receiver; if the client does not receive an acknowledgment (ACK) from the server within a timeout period, it resends the packet. In our design, ACKs, like all outgoing messages, are delayed by the server until after the next checkpoint.

Consequently, suppose that the server receives an input message, issues an ACK that gets stored in the Memory Buffer, and a fault occurs. Two cases are possible. First, if the fault occurs before the end of the next checkpoint, the rollback removes the effect of the input message from the server, as well as the ACK from the Memory Buffer. In this case, the ACK is not sent and the client will resend the input message. If, instead, the fault occurs after the next checkpoint, the rollback removes neither the effect of the input message from the server, nor the ACK from the Memory Buffer. This case is also correct because the ACK will eventually be sent. In either case, the server does not need to buffer network input.

3.1.2. Initial Incomplete Solution: BufferVolatile

All network and disk output requests issued by the application (*OutReq1* and *OutReq2* in Figure 3-(a)) are transparently intercepted by the PDD and buffered in the Memory Buffer. The buffered information includes the output data and metadata such as the destination block number in the device. After the next

---

[1]The User Datagram Protocol (UDP) does not provide TCP's support to eliminate duplicates. UDP is unreliable by definition, and the application (e.g., NFS over UDP) is responsible for dealing with duplicate and lost packets. Consequently, we only focus on TCP.

checkpoint (*C2* in Figure 3-(a)), the PDD passes the information to the DDs, which perform the output operations (e.g., DMA writes to disk or to the network card) in the background (*OutOp1* and *OutOp2* in Figure 3-(a)).

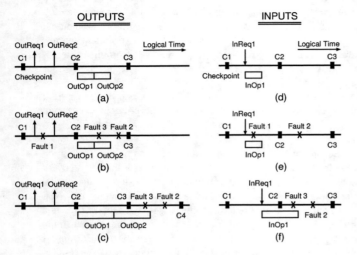

Figure 3. I/O operations and faults in different scenarios. In the figure, *InReq*, *OutReq*, *InOp*, and *OutOp* mean input request, output request, input operation, and output operation, respectively.

Consider now input requests, such as reads from the disk or the network card. On receiving the request (*InReq1* in Figure 3-(d)), the PDD checks if the requested data is in the Memory Buffer. If so, the data is provided. Otherwise, the PDD passes the request to the DD, which performs the operation in the background (*InOp1* in Figure 3-(d)). As indicated in Section 3.1.1, no buffering is needed.

We call this initial solution *BufferVolatile*. With it, if an MR fault (Section 2.2) occurs, the server recovers both memory and I/O states *transparently* to the running application. Consider the four possible timeframes wherein a fault can occur.

1. Fault before the end of the checkpoint that immediately follows the I/O request (*Fault 1* in Figures 3-(b) and (e)). In this case, ReVive rolls back the memory state to the previous checkpoint *C1*. As a result, the Memory Buffer loses any record of output request *OutReq1*. This automatically "undoes" *OutReq1*, as desired. Thus, *OutOp1* is not performed. As for input I/O, since the rollback operation involves resetting the devices, any ongoing input operation such as *InOp1* is aborted.

2. Fault after the end of the checkpoint that immediately follows the I/O request; the I/O is already performed (*Fault 2* in Figures 3-(b) and (e)). ReVive rolls back the memory state to the previous checkpoint *C2*. The only interesting case is for outputs. The Memory Buffer gets restored to the state it had at *C2*, where it contained a record of the output operations to perform. Consequently, the PDD will eventually automatically re-issue *OutOp1* and *OutOp2* to the DDs. This is correct because of the idempotent nature of the I/O in consideration.

3. Like Case 2 but the background I/O is not yet completely performed when the fault occurs (*Fault 3* in Figure 3-(b)). As the system rolls back, the devices are reset and the ongoing I/O

is aborted. Then, all I/O operations (*OutOp1* and *OutOp2*) will eventually be performed again.

4. Special case: Fault in an interval preceded by a checkpoint overlapped with an I/O operation. Sometimes, an I/O operation initiated before a checkpoint extends past it. This is seen for *OutOp2* in Figure 3-(c) and *InOp1* in Figure 3-(f). If a fault such as *Fault 2* or *Fault 3* in these figures occurs, the memory state rolls back to the checkpoint that overlapped with the I/O operation. During the recovery process, the I/O operation (*OutOp2* or *InOp1*) gets killed, since all I/O devices (disk controller and network adapter) get reset. This is discussed in Section 3.3.2. Unfortunately, the rollback would leave the memory state in inconsistent state: while the I/O operation is killed, it is incorrectly marked "in progress", and it is only partially performed.

To solve this problem, after the recovery process rolls back the memory state to the previous checkpoint, the PDD re-issues to the DDs any checkpoint-overlapping I/O operation *from the beginning*. Note that the PDD can find out what are the I/O operations that are (incorrectly) marked "in progress" (*OutOp2* and *InOp1*). Optionally, the PDD can skip re-issuing the network input operations that overlapped with the checkpoint: there is no need to re-initiate the transfer of data from the network adapter to memory because TCP will ensure that incoming packets are retransmitted.

Overall, our *BufferVolatile* scheme ensures database consistency in an environment with MR faults (and/or transient faults in non-volatile storage as per Section 2.2). For example, assume that a client starts a transaction that involves writes to disk (Figure 4-(a)). After the disk PDD has buffered the data and destination block number in the Memory Buffer, the database sends a response message to the client. The message is buffered by the network PDD. After the next checkpoint, the message is sent and the write is issued to the disk. If an MR fault occurs before this checkpoint, *BufferVolatile* will roll back and eventually receive the automatic retransmission of the original request message after the timeout. Moreover, if the PDD observes a transient disk error when it issues the write, it will simply retry until it succeeds. In any case, when the client receives the response message, it can assume that the disk write in the transaction has been committed. Some ordering issues are examined in Section 3.2.

3.1.3. Complete Solutions: Buffer and Rename

BufferVolatile is inadequate if an NMR fault (Section 2.2) occurs, such as the simultaneous permanent loss of multiple nodes. As an example, consider Figure 4-(a) after the second checkpoint. Suppose that an NMR fault occurs after the response to the client is sent but before the disk is updated in the background. ReVive cannot restore the contents of the Memory Buffer and, therefore, re-issue the buffered write to disk. The disk is left in a state that is inconsistent with the information passed to the client. Note that conventional database recovery mechanisms cannot help: the missing write can be a log write, without which the database cannot redo the operation.

To solve this problem, we enhance *BufferVolatile* to ensure that the PDD also saves the output request information in non-volatile "temporary" storage before the next checkpoint. If an NMR fault occurs as in the example just described, we can copy the information from the non-volatile temporary storage to the server disk, and thus make the disk consistent. Then, we can rely on the con-

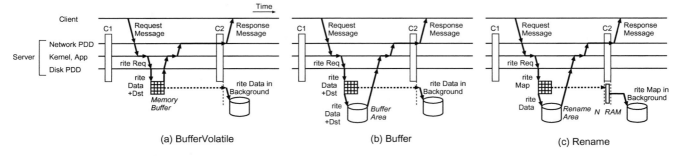

Figure 4. Operation of ReVivel/O. The scenario depicts a transaction with a disk write. NVRAM and *Dst* stand for Non-Volatile RAM and the destination block number, respectively.

ventional mechanisms of the database for recovery, although the downtime will be longer (Figure 1).

We propose two alternative schemes, called *Buffer* and *Rename*, as shown in Figures 4-(b) and (c), respectively. *Buffer* is based on temporarily buffering output request data, and is conceptually simpler. *Rename* is based on renaming the data, and can be more efficient because it requires fewer disk writes. To describe the schemes, we focus on disk I/O because network I/O does not distinguish between the schemes.

In *Buffer*, a disk write request updates the Memory Buffer and a disk buffer area before returning (Figure 4-(b)). The update includes both the data and some metadata such as the destination block number. To speed up this operation, the updates to the disk buffer are done on sequential blocks. Moreover, the disk buffer can be a dedicated small, fast disk, similar to the Disk Caching Disk [13]. After the next checkpoint, all data in the Memory Buffer are copied to their true locations on the main disk. In fault-free conditions, the disk buffer is never read.

In *Rename*, a write request writes the output data to a new disk block in a rename area, and saves the new logical-to-physical block number mapping in the Memory Buffer before returning (Figure 4-(c)). During the checkpoint, the mappings in the Memory Buffer are copied to a small (e.g., 32 MB) Non-Volatile RAM (NVRAM) associated with the disk. Later, the mappings in the NVRAM are committed to disk in the background.

The NVRAM is not a single point of failure. Specifically, there are commodity disk adapters with internal NVRAM where the NVRAM is transparently backed up by an additional copy of the data. An example is IBM's Fast Write Cache [15]. Moreover, transient errors in the NVRAM or associated disk are handled by the PDD retrying the request. Recall that we assume there are no permanent faults in non-volatile storage.

Note that these NVRAMs usually work asynchronously — the data is destaged to the disk only when the NVRAM is getting full or the data has stayed in the NVRAM for a certain time. Therefore, if a fault occurs during a checkpoint, an asynchronous NVRAM could incorrectly write its mappings to disk while we are rolling back to the previous checkpoint. This problem is solved by also storing the original mapping information in the NVRAM, so that if the problem occurs, we can undo the changes of mapping.

An important design issue in *Rename* is the policy for allocating the renamed blocks. One option is to write the new blocks sequentially on a free disk area, just like the log-structured file system (LFS) [31]. With this design, occasional defragmentation

of the disk may be needed. Another option is to map each block to either one of two physically consecutive blocks in the disk as in TWIST [30]. This design requires double disk space for blocks. However, the mapping information per block is only one bit, compared to (typically) 8 bytes for the first design.

With *Buffer* or *Rename*, the disk can always be brought to the state corresponding to the checkpoint immediately preceding the fault, even for an NMR fault. Indeed, consider a disk write request. If the fault happens between the request and the end of the next checkpoint, the contents of the disk buffer are discarded (*Buffer*) or the new mapping information is not written to NVRAM (*Rename*); the main disk remains unmodified and the client is never notified. If, instead, the fault happens after the next checkpoint, a disk update is guaranteed to occur: the data and metadata in the disk buffer (*Buffer*) or the mapping in NVRAM (*Rename*) are used to update the disk.

3.2. Ordering Issues

Our schemes (*Buffer* and *Rename*) change the timing of I/O operations. However, they always satisfy the ordering properties of I/O in databases, which require that logs are fully committed before data is. This is accomplished by updating the Memory Buffer and the disk buffer or rename area in the order that the disk write requests are received. Moreover, after the subsequent checkpoint, all updates are guaranteed to commit to their final storage locations.

As the updates commit after the checkpoint, our schemes do not force disk write serialization across different block addresses. Instead, the data blocks buffered in the Memory Buffer (or mappings in the NVRAM) are written to the final disk location in an overlapped manner. They can even proceed with some re-ordering. Overlapping and re-ordering enables higher performance without affecting correctness. In theory, the performance could be even higher than a system without recovery.

We have seen that in all cases, if a client receives a transaction-completion message (Figure 4), then disk updates are guaranteed to commit. Still, it is possible that the client receives the completion message and sends another request before the server has physically finished the disk writes. Even if this request needs to read the data that is still being written to disk, no race occurs. The reason is that the PDD will automatically redirect the request to the Memory Buffer, which only deallocates an entry when the final disk update is completed.

207

3.3. Overheads and Recovery Latency

3.3.1. Overheads

ReViveI/O increases the latency of network messages because the server PDD does not send packets until after the next checkpoint. In practice, back-end database servers running TPC-C class applications are not particularly latency bound. Adding tens of ms to each transaction to support recovery is tolerable.

However, we tune TCP in two ways. First, since packets now take longer to be acknowledged, we increase the sliding window [36] that buffers yet-to-be-acknowledged packets. There is no danger of buffer overflow because TCP throttles packet sending as a buffer becomes full. Second, since the server PDD sends packets after checkpoints, the packet round trip time becomes more variable. This additional variability disrupts TCP's flow control mechanism. To solve this problem, the server PDD does not send all the packets as fast as it can after a checkpoint; instead, it smooths out the traffic.

ReViveI/O's impact on computation, memory, and disk accesses may also affect application throughput. Consider computation and memory accesses. For each output request, ReViveI/O requires an initial write and a later read to the Memory Buffer (Figure 4). For network I/O, the data written/read is only a pointer to the socket buffer; the actual packet payload is retained in the sliding window elsewhere in memory. For disk I/O, the data written/read is the block data and metadata (*Buffer*), or the mapping only (*Rename*). For *Rename*, the mapping is also written to the NVRAM at checkpoints. In addition, the PDD executes bookkeeping code to manage the Memory Buffer.

For disk accesses, *Buffer* performs two disk writes per write request, although only one is in the critical path (Figure 4-(b)). The one in the critical path is fast because the disk buffer is written sequentially, and it can be a small, fast disk. *Rename* performs two writes on the same disk per request: one for the data and one for the new mapping (Figure 4-(c)). The first one is in the critical path; the second one can be merged with other updates of mappings from the same checkpoint interval. In addition, *Rename* may require periodic disk block compaction.

3.3.2. Recovery Latency

The latency of a recovery depends on the type of fault. Consider first an MR fault. Figure 5 shows a ReVive recovery time-line from [29], for the worst MR fault: the permanent loss of one node at a checkpoint. The latency numbers assume a 100 ms checkpoint interval. On top of the ReVive recovery, the thick up-arrows show the three actions performed by ReViveI/O.

Immediately after fault detection, ReViveI/O resets the I/O devices, namely network card and disk. This operation kills any ongoing DMA, which could overwrite the data being restored in the rollback. This operation is quick — 1 ms or less. It is also device dependent: it involves writing to a special I/O port to reset the network card, and sending a signal to reset the disk controller. It does not require any slow disk access.

After the memory state has been rolled back to the checkpoint, ReViveI/O re-initializes the device drivers (Figure 5). They have been left in an inconsistent state relative to the reset devices. This operation involves updating data structures in memory such as buffers and pointers, and bringing back the device driver's configuration parameters. It typically takes 10 ms or less.

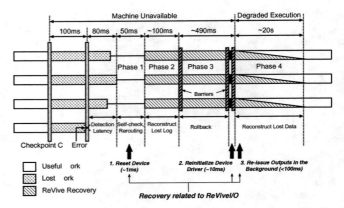

Figure 5. Recovery time-line for the permanent loss of one node at a checkpoint. ReViveI/O actions are shown with thick arrows.

Finally, after application execution has resumed, ReViveI/O performs in the background all the output operations needed to bring the I/O state to the checkpoint immediately preceding the fault. Performing all these operations is easy. Indeed, for *Buffer*, the rolled-back Memory Buffer has an accurate record of all such operations. For *Rename*, the Memory Buffer has the record for the network operations, while the NVRAM has the record of the disk mappings to save. Performing these actions degrades the machine's performance for tens of ms, but does not make it unavailable.

Overall, the three ReViveI/O-related recovery actions negligibly add to the unavailable time and keep the fault transparent to the database.

Consider now an NMR fault. All currently-executing transactions abort and the system is typically rebooted. Before the database can use its own recovery mechanisms, ReViveI/O brings the disk to the state at the checkpoint immediately preceding the fault. This is done as follows: for *Buffer*, the disk output information is recovered from the disk buffer area; for *Rename*, the disk mappings are recovered from the NVRAM. The latency of performing these actions is much smaller than the time required for rebooting or for the database to recover. Therefore, ReViveI/O again adds negligibly to the unavailable time.

Finally, a second fault may occur while recovering. If ReVive can recover the memory state, ReViveI/O re-executes the three actions shown in Figure 5. Otherwise, ReViveI/O brings the disk to a consistent state after reboot as just described.

3.4. Limitations

ReViveI/O has several applicability limitations. First, it is not applicable to latency-critical workloads, such as those with user interaction through graphics, keyboards, or other devices.

ReViveI/O relies on system-level code to intercept I/O requests, buffer them, and perform the operations later. This approach rules out, as they are currently implemented, user-level I/O and I/O coprocessors such as TCP Offload Engines (TOEs). User-level I/O relies on user libraries to perform I/O, eliminating kernel involvement. For example, uncached accesses from user mode to the network interface send messages without involving the kernel. To be able to support schemes similar to ReViveI/O, we would have to add a PDD component to the user libraries

TOEs implement TCP operations in hardware. The kernel is not involved in performing the low-level operations in packet handling. Again, to support schemes similar to ReViveI/O, we would have to modify the TOE hardware to perform the PDD operation, namely buffer the packet for later issue. We would also have to synchronize the processor and the TOE at checkpoints.

We feel that, while user-level I/O and TOEs are interesting alternatives, they are still new technologies with poor standardization and, as a result, are hard to maintain in large server installations. The standard software TCP solution that ReViveI/O supports is overwhelmingly the most popular one.

4. Implementation Aspects

We have implemented a ReViveI/O prototype on a multiprocessor server with two 1.5 GHz AMD Athlon processors, 1.2 Gbytes of memory, two 80-Gbyte IDE disks, and a 1 Gbit ethernet card. One of the two disks is used as a disk buffer. The server runs Linux 2.4. The PDD is about 2,000 lines of C code for the disk and 2,000 for the network. The DDs, the Linux kernel, and the applications remain unmodified.

Note that our server does not have ReVive hardware. Consequently, when needed, we simulate its effect. Specifically, to test recovery, we pretend that a fault occurs immediately after a checkpoint and, therefore, the memory state rolls back instantly. ReViveI/O can then proceed with resetting the devices, re-initializing the DDs and issuing all the buffered outputs. Since the memory state recovery and the I/O state recovery are conveniently decoupled (Figure 5), we can test the correctness of the I/O-related recovery without memory-checkpointing hardware. Under fault-free conditions, we do not model ReVive. However, in Section 6.3, we estimate the combined overhead and availability of ReVive and ReViveI/O.

Except for the ReVive support, we have thoroughly tested the prototype under many workload conditions (e.g., heavy disk writes, frequent small messages, or bulk data transmission) and restart scenarios (e.g., DMA in progress or many pending I/O requests). We also injected different faults that allowed us to test most software paths. In the following, we outline some implementation aspects.

4.1. Support for Disk I/O

ReViveI/O can be designed for disks accessed through a file system or as raw devices. In our prototype, we use a file system. Figure 6 expands Figure 2 showing the interface between kernel, PDD, and disk DD [4] for *Buffer* and *Rename*. The modules in shaded pattern are those added for ReViveI/O: PDD, Memory Buffer, disk buffer or rename area, and NVRAM.

In a conventional system, a read request causes a buffer cache access. If a miss occurs, the low-level DD satisfies the request. In a write, a block is allocated in the buffer cache if it is not already there. The block is updated and marked dirty. Sometime later, the kernel writes it to disk.

With ReViveI/O, such dirty block writes are directed to the PDD. As indicated before, the PDD buffers the information and commits it after the next checkpoint. Although individual DMA operations (e.g., setup, execution, postprocessing) performed by

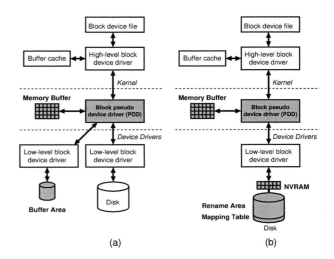

Figure 6. Interface between kernel, PDD, and disk DD for *Buffer* (a) and *Rename* (b).

the low-level DD may not be idempotent, disk writes at the PDD level are idempotent because the PDD triggers these low-level operations as an indivisible operation.

The Memory Buffer is sized based on the machine's total disk bandwidth and the checkpoint interval. The same applies to the NVRAM except that the bandwidth is per disk, since ReViveI/O has one NVRAM per disk. For example, a 100 MB/s disk array in a 100 ms checkpoint interval can consume 10 MB. Consequently, for *Buffer*, a 20 MB Memory Buffer and a 20 MB disk buffer area suffice. For this update rate, *Rename* generates about 20 KB of mappings per checkpoint interval. Consequently, for *Rename*, a 20 MB disk rename area, 40 KB Memory Buffer, and 40 KB NVRAM suffice. Since the checkpoint operation takes about 1 ms [29], an NVRAM built out of battery-backed SRAM has sufficient bandwidth (∼100 MB/s [35]) to load these 20 KB mappings during a checkpoint.

4.2. Support for Network I/O

The kernel does not use the usual interface (e.g., eth0). Instead, it uses the virtual interface provided by the network PDD (say, veth0). The data structure passed between the kernel and the network DD is the socket buffer, which contains the length of the packet, a pointer to the packet, and other fields. When the kernel passes a socket buffer to the PDD, a pointer to it is copied to the Memory Buffer. We copy only the pointer to reduce overhead. After the checkpoint, the socket buffer is passed to the network DD.

When an input packet arrives at the network card, the appropriate handler is triggered in the network DD, which in turn calls the netif_rx function in the kernel to process the packet. TCP would get confused if the kernel sent a packet through veth0 and received the reply from eth0. Consequently, the DD call is routed through a netif_rx function in a special library that changes the device field of the socket buffer to veth0. Neither DD nor kernel are modified.

Workload		Description	I/O
Micro-Benchmarks	RandomWrite	Repeatedly write blocks of a given size to disk. The writes are synchronous and directed to random locations. Size can be set.	Disk
	SequentialWrite	Like RandomWrite but writes are directed to sequential locations.	Disk
	Iperf [16]	Repeatedly send messages of a given size. Size can be set.	Network
Throughput oriented	TPC-C-like on Oracle 9.0.2	32 warehouses, 30 remote clients, no think time, 400-Mbyte database buffer, and 4-Kbyte blocks	Disk and network
Latency bound	WebStone 2.5 with Apache 2.0	Memory resident, variable number of remote clients, no think time, 85 HTML documents of 100 KB on average	Network

Table 1. Workloads used in the evaluation. We use the term "TPC-C-like" because compliance with the specification is not fully checked.

5. Evaluation Methodology

We evaluate the three schemes of Table 2. Of the ReViveI/O approaches, we select *Buffer* for evaluation. *NoRollback* is the unmodified server, which has no provision for I/O undo/redo. *Stall* is a scheme for disk I/O similar to Masubuchi *et al.* [20, 21]. In *Stall*, there is no data buffering; requesting processes are not notified of output I/O completion until the next checkpoint.

Scheme	Description
Buffer	ReViveI/O approach. Supports I/O undo/redo for disk & network I/O.
NoRollback	Unmodified server. No provision for I/O undo/redo.
Stall	Output I/O blocks until next checkpoint. Scheme for disk I/O only. Similar to Masubuchi *et al.* [20, 21].

Table 2. Schemes evaluated.

We run the workloads of Table 1: a throughput-oriented one (TPC-C on Oracle 9.0.2), a latency-bound one (WebStone [38] on the Apache server [1]), and several microbenchmarks.

We experiment with 20-240 ms checkpoint intervals. For each checkpoint interval, we set the TCP sliding window size to buffer all unacknowledged packets at the 1 Gbit ethernet bandwidth, and the Memory Buffer size to hold all the data that can be written to disk. For 80 ms intervals, this is 12 MB for the sliding window and 8 MB for the buffer. The ratio is the same for the other intervals.

6. Evaluation

To evaluate our ReViveI/O prototype, we measure its overhead in fault-free execution (Section 6.1) and the latency of fault recovery (Section 6.2). Then, we project the impact of combining ReViveI/O and ReVive (Section 6.3).

6.1. Execution Overhead

6.1.1. Disk I/O Microbenchmarks

The RandomWrite and SequentialWrite microbenchmarks test worst-case disk I/O conditions. They consist of a loop that synchronously writes blocks of a given size to disk. Consequently, the disk is constantly busy. In our server, one disk can support up to 32 Mbytes/s of write throughput, while the other (used as disk buffer) up to 36 Mbytes/s. With such hardware, Figure 7 shows the resulting system throughput as a function of the size of the blocks written. We consider 20 and 160 ms checkpoint intervals.

We see that the various overheads of *Buffer* (Section 3.3.1) do not reduce throughput relative to *NoRollback* under heavy disk write traffic. In fact, *Buffer*'s throughput is slightly higher than *NoRollback*'s. The reason is that a write request in *Buffer* returns as soon as the data is written to the faster disk *sequentially*, rather

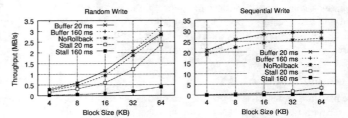

Figure 7. Disk I/O throughput for random and sequential synchronous writes.

than to the other disk randomly (RandomWrite) or sequentially (SequentialWrite).

The checkpoint interval size has little effect on *Buffer*. The reason is that PDD operations have only tiny overhead. Finally, *Stall* delivers a very low throughput; effectively, *Stall* manages only a single synchronous write per thread per checkpoint.

6.1.2. Network I/O Microbenchmark

The Iperf microbenchmark measures the maximum TCP bandwidth. Figure 8 shows the sustained throughput as a function of the message size for two cases: our server sends messages to one client (Unidirectional) and both client and server send messages to each other (Bidirectional). The case where the client sends messages to the server is similar to Unidirectional — messages have the same Round Trip Time (RTT) because the server delays all packets, including ACKs. In this experiment, *Stall* does not apply.

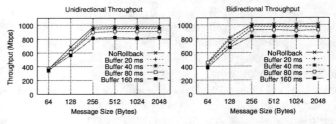

Figure 8. Uni- and bi-directional throughput between one client and the server over 1 Gbit ethernet.

We see that, under these extreme conditions, *Buffer* lowers the throughput relative to *NoRollback*. This is due to PDD overheads (Section 3.3.1) and suboptimal TCP operation in a high-bandwidth, high-latency network. However, the throughput reduction is modest: it ranges from 5% with a 20 ms interval to less than 20% with 160 ms.

Finally, *Buffer* also increases packet RTT. The resulting impact on the response time depends on the application. The impact is tolerable in applications where the server performs substantial work or where the communication pattern involves bulk data transmission. We consider this issue next.

6.1.3. Throughput-Oriented Workload: TPC-C + Oracle

This workload is typical of back-end database servers. The major concern is not response time, but maintaining high throughput. Individual transactions can take significant time, as they typically perform disk I/O in the server. In *Buffer*, this workload exercises both disk and network PDDs.

Figure 9 shows the average TPC-C throughput with different schemes and checkpoint intervals normalized to that in *NoRollback*[2]. The throughput of our moderately tuned *NoRollback* setup is 1561 transactions per minute and its average response time is 612 ms. The figure shows data for *Stall*, and for *Buffer* with disk PDD only and with disk plus network PDDs. To minimize errors, we report conditions of the first 10-minute interval after the database is warmed up and the throughput becomes steady. During that period, we take a measurement every 30 seconds. The figure shows the mean and standard deviation of such measurements.

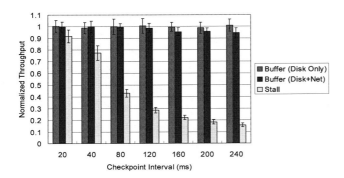

Figure 9. Transaction throughput with different schemes and checkpoint intervals normalized to *NoRollback*. The experiments run with 30 remote clients.

Consider *Stall* first. If we can only tolerate a 5% reduction in throughput, none of the checkpoint intervals shown is acceptable. In contrast, *Buffer* keeps the throughput reduction within 1% up to 120 ms checkpoint intervals. Note that for checkpoint intervals above 120 ms, the throughput reduction comes mainly from network PDD overhead. Interestingly, the average response time does not degrade as we increase the checkpoint interval. In fact, it goes down slightly, decreasing to 590 ms by the time we use 240 ms checkpoint interval. The reason is that long intervals reduce the transaction rate, which in turn diminishes disk contention.

We have repeated the *Buffer* experiments for different numbers of clients and obtained similar results. Figure 10 shows the normalized throughput for a range of checkpoint intervals for 60 and 90 clients. Each bar is normalized to *NoRollback* for the same number of clients. As we increase the number of clients (i.e., more transactions overlap in time), the delay incurred by the network PDD is less visible and, therefore, long checkpoint intervals become more tolerable.

---

[2]Throughput is given in New Order transactions per minute; response time is for New Order transactions as well.

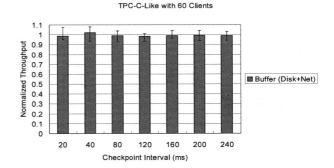

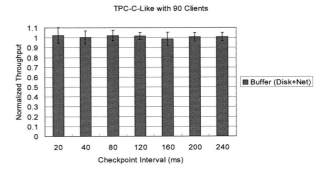

Figure 10. Normalized transaction throughput as a function of the checkpoint interval for different numbers of clients.

Overall, we conclude that in throughput-oriented workloads like TPC-C, and for 20–120 ms checkpoint intervals, our proposed *Buffer* scheme induces very small throughput reductions of up to 1%. In such workloads, the progress of transaction processing typically depends on the rate of synchronous writes issued by the database log-writer process. Our *Buffer* scheme affects such progress minimally.

6.1.4. Latency-Bound Workload: WebStone + Apache

In this workload, multiple remote clients read HTML documents that are memory-resident in the server. Each transaction involves establishing the connection with a three-way handshake, reading a file, and closing the connection. Transactions are short because there is no disk I/O — only the network PDD is exercised. This workload simulates an interactive environment. Consequently, we are interested in response time, measured as the time between requesting the connection until the whole file is received.

Figure 11 shows the response time for different numbers of clients and checkpoint intervals. The figure is organized in numbers of clients. In each group, there are bars for *NoRollback*, and for *Buffer* with different checkpoint intervals. Since there is no disk I/O, the *Stall* scheme is irrelevant. To obtain the data, we run each experiment for 10 minutes, with the server at 100% CPU usage.

We see that the response time quickly increases with the checkpoint interval. With a checkpoint interval T, the response time should increase by $2 \times T$, since we add T to establish the connection and T to get the data (Recall from Section 3.3.1 that the PDD smooths out outgoing messages). This is what we observe with

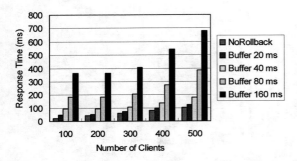

Figure 11. Response time for different numbers of clients and checkpoint intervals.

100 clients. For more than 300 clients and $T \geq 80$ms, contention causes larger increases in the response time.

According to [25], it is acceptable to add up to 100 ms to the response time of a transaction. Consequently, our *Buffer* scheme can be used in the web server measured, as long as the checkpoint interval is ~50 ms or shorter.

6.2. Latency of Fault Recovery

To recover from an MR fault, our schemes perform three actions (Section 3.3.2): reset the devices, re-initialize the DDs and, in the background, perform all the buffered output operations to bring the I/O state to the checkpoint immediately preceding the fault. While our prototype server lacks ReVive hardware, we can measure the recovery latency of ReViveI/O as discussed in Section 4.

We have measured the latency of each part of the recovery for *Buffer*, and listed average values in Table 3. From the table, we see that device reset and DD re-initialization are quick. Note that, to re-initialize the disk DD, we do not need to access the disk to get information such as the number of cylinders and the sector size; these parameters are obtained from the recovered memory. Finally, the third operation takes tens of ms, but it is executed in the background. Overall, compared to the ReVive recovery latency (Figure 5), ReViveI/O adds negligible recovery overhead.

Operation	Duration	
	Disk	Network
Reset device	1 ms	15 μs
Re-initialize device driver	10 ms	60 μs
Re-issue operations in background	$\sim T$	$\sim T$

Table 3. Latencies of the operations needed to recover from an MR fault. T is the checkpoint interval.

If the fault is NMR, *Buffer* only needs to re-issue the buffered output operations. This activity takes several seconds, as *Buffer* has to read data and mappings from the disk buffer. Such latency is negligible compared to the tens of minutes needed to reboot the server and run a database recovery routine after this type of fault.

6.3. Combining ReVive and ReViveI/O: Performance Overheads and Availability

We would like to estimate the impact of combining ReViveI/O and ReVive. In [29], ReVive was evaluated for a checkpoint interval $T = 100$ ms, where each checkpoint took 1 ms. ReVive induced a 6% execution overhead.

We model ReVive as inducing a $c = 1$ ms overhead every checkpoint, and a fixed $r = 5\%$ overhead for the period between checkpoints, independently of T. Therefore, the throughput reduction factor induced by ReVive is $f = \frac{c+(T-c)\times r}{T}$. The response time increase due to ReVive is $t_s \times \frac{f}{1-f}$, where t_s is the time that the transaction spends executing in the server.

Figure 12 takes the impact of *Buffer* on TPC-C throughput (Section 6.1.3) and WebStone response time (Section 6.1.4), and adds the estimated effect of ReVive. We can see that a throughput-oriented workload such as TPC-C keeps the throughput reduction at 7% or below for checkpoint intervals between 60 and 120 ms. Most of the overhead is due to ReVive. On the other hand, the response time increase in a latency-bound workload such as WebStone is practically all due to ReViveI/O. The increase is $2 \times T$, where T is the checkpoint interval (Section 6.1.4).

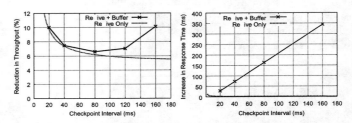

Figure 12. Estimated combined effect of ReVive and ReViveI/O on the throughput of TPC-C (left) and the response time of WebStone (right).

To complete the picture, we compare the availability of *ReVive+Buffer* and *NoRollback*. For the former, we assume that MR and NMR faults are independent and distributed exponentially. As a result, the availability of *ReVive+Buffer* is $1 - \frac{MTTR_{MR}}{MTBF_{MR}} - \frac{MTTR_{NMR}}{MTBF_{NMR}}$. We estimate $MTTR_{NMR}$ as 5 minutes for machine reboot plus 5 minutes for database recovery [22]. We set $MTTR_{MR}$ to 1 second [29]. For *NoRollback*, all faults have the same MTTR, namely $MTTR_{NMR}$.

Figure 13 shows the unavailability as a function of $MTBF_{MR}$. Note that both axes in the figure are logarithmic. For *ReVive+Buffer*, we show two curves: 1:100 assumes that $MTBF_{NMR} = 100 \times MTBF_{MR}$, while 1:1000 assumes that $MTBF_{NMR} = 1000 \times MTBF_{MR}$. For *NoRollback*, both curves are practically the same, and we show only one.

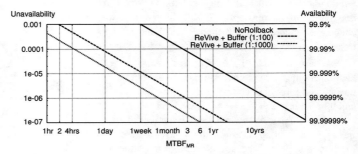

Figure 13. Unavailability as a function of the MTBF of MR faults. The MTBF of NMR faults is set to 100 or 1000 times the MTBF of MR faults (curves 1:100 and 1:1000, respectively).

The figure shows that *ReVive+Buffer* has much lower unavailability than *NoRollback* thanks to its tiny recovery latency for the more common MR faults. For example, for 1-week $MTBF_{MR}$, *ReVive+Buffer* (1:100) has an unavailability of $\sim 10^{-5}$, which corresponds to 99.999% availability, while *NoRollback* has an unavailability of 0.001, which corresponds to 99.9% availability. Overall, *ReVive+Buffer*'s unavailability is 86 and 375 times lower than *NoRollback*'s for 1:100 and 1:1000, respectively.

In summary, *ReVive+Buffer* provides higher availability than conventional systems while delivering slightly lower throughput. We believe that, at least in the applications considered, reducing downtime is much more important than achieving peak throughput while the machine is up.

7. Related Work

Masubuchi *et al.* [21] proposed adding a PDD to the kernel to support disk I/O recovery. Their scheme corresponds to *Stall* in Section 5, which blocks disk writes until the next checkpoint [20]. ReViveI/O differs as follows: (i) instead of blocking, it buffers the data and commits them later in the background, and (ii) it supports network I/O. More importantly, this paper contributed with the full implementation, testing, and evaluation of an efficient I/O undo/redo prototype compatible with solutions such as ReVive [29] or SafetyNet [34].

High-availability machines such as HP's Nonstop Architecture [11] and IBM's S/390 mainframes [33] attain fault tolerance through expensive hardware support, often involving extensive component replication. We seek a less expensive design point.

Sequoia [3] is an SMP where mirrored main memory is considered to be the checkpointed state. When a dirty line is evicted from a cache, a checkpoint is triggered. A checkpoint is also forced every time a processor requests I/O, which is an inefficient approach.

OS- and library-based checkpointing includes UNICOS [18], KeyKOS [19], diskless checkpointing [28], and fault-tolerant Mach [32]. Their checkpoint interval is typically minutes or longer. This results in high MTTR and would induce intolerably long message delays. Some schemes provide disk I/O recovery by journaling, but none addresses network I/O recovery.

Database management systems (DBMS) have their own well-known I/O recovery mechanisms [8]. Checkpoint intervals are in the order of minutes to achieve low enough overheads, and the recovery process takes tens of minutes [22] or more. For example, for System B of [22], targeting a 5-minute database recovery time, incurs 8.2% overhead in throughput. Note that such database recovery time does not include the system recovery time (e.g., repair and reboot), which at least adds minutes. Similarly, targeting a 20-minute database recovery time incurs 6.6% overhead. Also, the fault results in the loss of ongoing transactions. In contrast, for the frequent faults (MR faults), ReVive plus ReViveI/O has three advantages: (i) ongoing transactions are not lost, (ii) the system recovers in less than 1 second, and (iii) applications and kernel need no modification. When a DBMS runs on ReVive with our I/O undo/redo layer, only the infrequent faults (NMR faults) trigger database recovery. Consequently, the DBMS can use lower-overhead checkpointing, at the expense of longer recovery time.

There are cluster options for databases such as Oracle RAC (Real Application Clusters) [26]. These solutions use multiple machines to provide higher system availability. However, to achieve good performance, they require major changes to the database management system and, possibly, to the applications that run on top of it.

Our mechanisms overlap with ideas from other works. Hu and Yang [13] proposed the Disk Caching Disk (DCD), mainly to boost the performance of random disk writes; our disk buffer area is like a DCD for reliability. Several systems, such as the Legato Prestoserve [23] and Baker *et al.*'s scheme [2] have used NVRAM to speed up disk writes; we use NVRAM to speed up writes within checkpoints. Our PDD can be thought of as a thin Virtual Machine (VM) for I/O; VMs have been used for forward error recovery [5] and for post-intrusion replay [6], rather than for rollback recovery of faults.

ReViveI/O is also related to transactional memory systems (TMS) [10]. TMS share similar I/O issues with hardware-based memory checkpointing systems: when a transaction is aborted, TMS need to undo any work done by that transaction, including I/O. On the other hand, there are some differences: (i) TMS do not need to redo I/O after a transaction is aborted, (ii) TMS have less emphasis on durability than memory checkpointing systems because their primary purpose is to support atomicity, not reliability, and (iii) TMS may additionally need some mechanism to detect and track the dependences and conflicts between threads that are induced by I/O operations.

8. Conclusion

The main contribution of this paper is the full implementation, testing, and experimental evaluation of *ReViveI/O*, an efficient scheme for I/O undo/redo that is compatible with high-frequency checkpointing architectures such as ReVive and SafetyNet. In addition, we perform a sensitivity analysis of what checkpoint frequencies are required to maintain acceptable throughput and response times. Overall, this work completes the viability assessment of such novel memory-recovery architectures.

Our ReViveI/O prototype shows that low-overhead, tiny-MTTR recovery of I/O is feasible. For 20–120 ms between checkpoints, the throughput of a throughput-oriented workload such as TPC-C on Oracle decreases by no more than 1%. Moreover, for 50 ms between checkpoints or less, the response time of a latency-bound workload such as WebStone on Apache remains tolerable. In all cases, the recovery time is practically negligible. Moreover, kernel, device drivers, and applications remain unmodified. Finally, the combination of ReVive and ReViveI/O is likely to reduce the throughput of TPC-C-class applications by 7% or less for 60–120 ms checkpoint intervals, while incurring a tiny MTTR of less than 1 second.

Our analysis suggests that support for ReVive plus ReViveI/O makes for a very cost-effective high-availability server. In general, compared to software-based recovery solutions (OS, library, and database), our approach has a higher error coverage, lower overhead, and much smaller MTTR. We estimate that it delivers a 2–3 orders of magnitude reduction in unavailability over a database server that we evaluated. Finally, compared to hardware-intensive solutions such as HP NonStop systems, it is much cheaper while maintaining high availability.

An avenue for future work is to apply our techniques to transactional memory systems. We expect that ReViveI/O can be applied to transactional memory systems by adding support for per-thread output commit and for some dependence/conflict tracking mechanism through the Memory Buffer.

Acknowledgments

The authors would like to thank the members of HP's former Western Research Laboratory and of the I-ACOMA group at the University of Illinois for their helpful comments.

References

[1] Apache. http://www.apache.org/.

[2] M. Baker et al. Non-volatile memory for fast, reliable file systems. In *Proceedings of the 5th International Conference on Architectural Support for Programming Languages and Operating System*, pages 10–22, 1992.

[3] P. Bernstein. Sequoia: a fault-tolerant tightly coupled multiprocessor for transaction processing. *IEEE Computer*, 21(2):37–45, 1988.

[4] D. Bovet and M. Cesati. *Understanding the Linux Kernel*. O'Reilly, 2002.

[5] T. Bressoud and F. Schneider. Hypervisor-based fault-tolerance. In *Proceedings of the 15th ACM Symposium on Operating Systems Principles*, pages 1–11, 1995.

[6] G. Dunlap et al. ReVirt: Enabling intrusion analysis through virtual-machine logging and replay. In *Proceedings of the 5th Symposium on Operating Systems Design and Implementation*, pages 211–224, 2002.

[7] E. Elnozahy et al. A survey of rollback-recovery protocols in message-passing systems. *ACM Computing Surveys*, 34(3):375–408, 2002.

[8] J. Gray and A. Reuter. *Transaction Processing: Concepts and Techniques*. Morgan Kaufmann, 1993.

[9] W. Gu et al. Characterization of Linux kernel behavior under errors. In *Proceedings of the International Conference on Dependable Systems and Networks*, pages 459–468, 2003.

[10] L. Hammond et al. Transactional memory coherence and consistency. In *Proceedings of the 31st Annual International Symposium on Computer Architecture*, pages 102–113, 2004.

[11] HP Integrity NonStop computing. http://www.hp.com/go/integritynonstop.

[12] HP Integrity servers. http://www.hp.com/products1/servers/integrity/.

[13] Y. Hu and Q. Yang. DCD – Disk Caching Disk: A new approach for boosting I/O performance. In *Proceedings of the 23rd International Symposium on Computer Architecture*, pages 169–178, 1996.

[14] IBM System p5 servers. http://www.ibm.com/systems/p/.

[15] IBM Advanced SerialRAID Adapters Technical Reference (SA33-3286-02), September 2000.

[16] Iperf Benchmark. http://dast.nlanr.net/Projects/Iperf/.

[17] D. Johnson. Efficient transparent optimistic rollback recovery for distributed application programs. In *Proceedings of the Symposium on Reliable Distributed Systems*, pages 86–95, 1993.

[18] B. Kingsbury and J. Kline. Job and process recovery in a UNIX-based operating system. In *Proceedings of the Usenix Winter 1989 Technical Conference*, pages 355–364, 1989.

[19] C. Landau. The checkpoint mechanism in KeyKOS. In *Proceedings of the 2nd International Workshop on Object Orientation in Operating Systems*, pages 86–91, 1992.

[20] Y. Masubuchi. Personal communication. Oct. 2003.

[21] Y. Masubuchi et al. Fault recovery mechanism for multiprocessor servers. In *Proceedings of the 27th International Symposium on Fault-Tolerant Computing*, pages 184–193, 1997.

[22] J. Mauro. Tuning Oracle to minimize recovery time. Technical Report 817-4445-10, Sun Microsystems, November 2003.

[23] J. Moran et al. Breaking through the NFS performance barrier. In *Proceedings of the European Unix Users Group Spring*, pages 199–206, 1990.

[24] C. Morin et al. COMA: an opportunity for building fault-tolerant scalable shared memory multiprocessors. In *Proceedings of the 23rd Annual International Symposium on Computer Architecture*, pages 56–65, 1996.

[25] J. Nielsen. *Usability Engineering*. Morgan Kaufmann, 1994.

[26] Oracle Real Application Clusters 10g. Oracle Technical White Paper, May 2005.

[27] D. Patterson et al. Recovery Oriented Computing (ROC): Motivation, definition, techniques, and case studies. Technical Report UCB/CSD-02-1175, UC Berkeley, March 2002.

[28] J. Plank, K. Li, and M. Puening. Diskless checkpointing. *IEEE Transactions on Parallel and Distributed Systems*, 9(10):972–986, 1998.

[29] M. Prvulovic, Z. Zhang, and J. Torrellas. ReVive: Cost-effective architectural support for rollback recovery in shared-memory multiprocessors. In *Proceedings of the 29th Annual International Symposium on Computer Architecture*, pages 111–122, 2002.

[30] A. Reuter. A fast transaction-oriented logging scheme for UNDO recovery. *IEEE Transactions on Software Engineering*, SE-6(4):348–356, 1980.

[31] M. Rosenblum and K. Ousterhout. The design and implementation of a log-structured file system. *ACM Transactions on Computer Systems*, 10(1):26–52, 1992.

[32] M. Russinovich and Z. Segall. Fault-tolerance for off-the-shelf applications and hardware. In *Proceedings of the 25th International Symposium on Fault-Tolerant Computing*, pages 67–71, 1995.

[33] T. Slegel et al. IBM's S/390 G5 microprocessor design. *IEEE Micro*, 19(2):12–23, 1999.

[34] D. Sorin et al. SafetyNet: Improving the availability of shared memory multiprocessors with global checkpoint/recovery. In *Proceedings of the 29th Annual International Symposium on Computer Architecture*, pages 123–134, 2002.

[35] Sun Microsystems. *Sun StorEdge Fast Write Cache 2.0 Configuration Guide*, February 2000.

[36] A. Tanenbaum. *Computer Networks*. Prentice Hall, 2003.

[37] Transaction Processing Performance Council. Top ten non-clustered TPC-C by performance (as of November 2005). http://www.tpc.org/.

[38] WebStone Benchmark. http://www.mindcraft.com/webstone/.

Appendix A: Summarized Operation of ReVive

During fault-free execution, all processors are periodically interrupted to establish a global checkpoint. Establishing a checkpoint involves writing back register and modified cache state to memory. As a result, main memory *is* the checkpointed state at that point. Between checkpoints, the program may modify the memory contents. However, when a line of checkpoint data in main memory is about to be overwritten by a cache eviction, the memory controller saves the line in a log. Later, after the next checkpoint is established, the logs are discarded. At any time, if a fault is detected, the logs are used to restore the memory state to that of the last checkpoint.

To enable recovery from faults that result in lost memory content, ReVive organizes pages from different nodes into parity groups. Each main memory write is intercepted by the memory controller in the node, triggering an update of the corresponding parity bits located in a page on another node. The parity information is used when the system detects a fault in the memory of one node (e.g., permanent loss of a node's memory). Then, the parity bits and data from the remaining nodes' memories are used to reconstruct the lost memory content (both logs and program state). More details are found in [29].

Reducing Resource Redundancy for Concurrent Error Detection Techniques in High Performance Microprocessors

Sumeet Kumar
ECE Department
Binghamton University
Binghamton, NY 13902
skumar1@binghamton.edu

Aneesh Aggarwal
ECE Department
Binghamton University
Binghamton, NY 13902
aneesh@binghamton.edu

Abstract

With reducing feature size, increasing chip capacity, and increasing clock speed, microprocessors are becoming increasingly susceptible to transient (soft) errors. Redundant multi-threading (RMT) is an attractive approach for concurrent error detection and recovery. However, redundant threads significantly increase the pressure on the processor resources, resulting in dramatic performance impact.

In this paper, we propose reducing resource redundancy as a means to mitigate the performance impact of redundancy. In this approach, all the instructions are redundantly executed, however, the redundant instructions do not use many of the resources used by an instruction. The approach taken to reduce resource redundancy is to exploit the runtime profile of the leading thread to optimally allocate resources to the trailing thread in a staggered RMT *architecture. The key observation used in this approach is that, even with a small* slack *between the two threads, many instructions in the leading thread have already produced their results before their trailing counterparts are renamed. We investigate two techniques in this approach (i) register bits reuse* technique that attempts to use the same *register (but different bits) for both the copies of the same instruction, if the result produced by the instruction is of small size, and (ii) reg-ister value reuse* technique that attempts to use the same register for *a main instruction and a distinct redundant instruction, if both the instructions produce the same result. These techniques, along with some others, are used to reduce redundancy in register file, reorder buffer, and load/store buffer. The techniques are evaluated in terms of their performance, power, and vulnerability impact on an* RMT *processor. Our experiments show that the techniques achieve about 95% performance improvement and about 17% energy reduction. The vulnerability of the* RMT *remains the same with the techniques.*

Keywords: Concurrent Error Detection, Reducing Redundancy, Register File, Redundant Multi-threading

1 Introduction

With the current trends in transistor size, voltage and clock frequency, microprocessors are becoming increasingly susceptible to hardware failures. Hardware errors in the current technology are predominantly transient errors [4, 18] that occur randomly due to various reasons such as electromagnetic influences, alpha particle radiations, power supply fluctuations due to ground bounce, crosstalk or glitches, and partially defective components and loose connections. Current trends suggest that transient errors will be an increasing burden for microprocessor designers [23, 11]. Transient hardware errors are troublesome because they elude most of the current testing methods. A popular approach to detect transient errors is to use redundant multi-threading (*RMT*) [14, 6, 4, 19, 1, 13, 15, 16, 21, 22, 7]. In this approach, the same application is run multiple times and the errors are detected by corroborating the redundant results. Studies [22, 7] have shown that a *staggered RMT*, where one thread *slacks* behind the other thread, results in better performance because the trailing thread does not incur many of the branch misprediction and the load miss penalties incurred by the leading thread.

Running multiple threads places a significant pressure on the processor resources, resulting in a considerable performance loss. In this paper, we propose reducing resource redundancy to mitigate the performance impact of *RMT*. In this approach, full instruction redundancy is provided for full error coverage, however, many redundant instructions do not use all the resources used by an instruction. This reduces the pressure on the resources, thus improving performance and reducing energy consumption. In addition, we observed that reducing redundancy in just one resource simply shifts the pressure from the optimally allocated resource to another resource, and does not result in significant performance improvement. Hence, in this paper, we attempt to simultaneously reduce redundancy in multiple resources to achieve significant improvement. The key observation used in reducing the redundancy is that many instructions in the leading thread produce their results before the trailing thread is renamed. This enables us to exploit the leading thread's runtime profile for reducing redundancy in the trailing thread. These techniques are very well suited particularly for a *staggered RMT* execution.

The first technique in this approach — *register bits reuse (RBR)* — exploits the sizes of the results produced by the leading instructions for optimal resource allocation. If the value produced by a leading instruction is narrow, the renamer allocates the same register (as used by the leading instruction) to its trailing counterpart. In this technique, the lower bits of the register hold the leading instruction's result, and the higher bits of the register hold the trailing instruction's result, thus effectively reducing the use of additional registers by the redundant trailing instructions. We also discuss novel ways of defining a narrow width value, which result in a significant number of narrow values (even floating-point values). We extend the *RBR* technique to also reduce the redundant allocation of reorder buffer (ROB) entries to the trailing thread. This is possible because many instructions have exactly the same ROB entry values for the leading and the trailing counterparts when these instructions use the same register mapping. Even with reducing the redundancy in the register file and the ROB, we observed that the load/store buffer (LSB) became a bottleneck for many benchmarks. Hence, we propose a novel technique to reduce the pressure on the LSB and obtain an average performance improvement of about 62%. We also evaluate the techniques in terms of their energy and vulnerability impact and observe an average of about 17% in energy. The vulnerability of the *RMT* remains almost the same.

For the normal-sized results, we investigate *register value reuse (RVR)* technique that exploits data value locality observed in instructions' results. In this technique, if two leading instructions produce the same value, then the trailing counterpart of the second leading instruction is assigned the register of the first leading instruction. This technique further reduces the register file pressure, especially for the floating-point benchmarks, resulting in overall performance improvement of about 96%.

The rest of the paper is organized as follows. Section 2 discusses the background and provides the motivation for our techniques. Section 3 discusses the *RBR* technique. Section 4 presents the experimental results and analysis. Section 5 discusses further enhancements to the *RBR* technique. Section 6 presents sensitivity study for the *RBR* technique. Section 7 presents the implementation details and experimental results for the *RVR* technique. Section 8 presents related work. Finally, in Section 9, we conclude.

2 Background and Motivation

2.1 Background

In this paper, we consider a reliable microprocessor configuration running one redundant thread for concurrent error detection, shown in Figure 1. The threads are fetched independent of each other, using multiple PCs. One thread is always ahead of the other by a few instructions (*staggered* execution) [22]. However, instructions record a bit indicating whether they are leading or trailing instructions. The threads are decoded and renamed concurrently. In the rename stage, different map tables are used for the two threads. Once renamed, the instructions are dispatched to the issue queue, ROB, and load/store buffer (for load and store instructions). The threads are then executed concurrently. The results of the multiple copies of an instruction are compared for error detection when the instructions commit. Since, we use a unified register file, at commit, the instructions also update the backend map-tables. To reduce the register file port requirements for error detection, we use an *additional value buffer*, which also stores the results stored in the register file and from which the values are read for comparison at commit time [7].

The entries for the instructions of the two threads are fixed in the ROB and the LSB, to facilitate finding multiple copies of an instruction at commit. In our processor, only the leading load and store instructions access the memory, which is as-

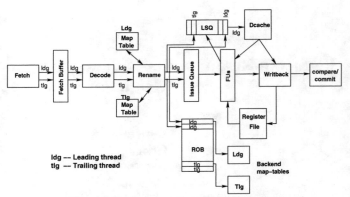

Figure 1. Diagram of a Reliable Processor

sumed to be transient fault tolerant (by using Error Detection and Correction Codes). The value loaded by the leading load instruction is also forwarded to the register allocated to the trailing load instructions, using a separate buffer to store the loaded values [7]. However, the addresses of the loads and the stores (and the value to be stored for the stores) are generated multiple times, and checked during commit for any errors.

Deadlocks are avoided by keeping counters that count the number of trailing instructions in the pipeline. If any resource is full without any trailing instructions, then a potential deadlock is avoided by squashing the younger leading instructions and fetching the trailing ones, irrespective of the *slack* condition. The *slack* between the threads depends on the size of the various buffers (such as ROB, LSB, RF, etc.) provided in the processor. We measured the IPCs with *slacks* of 32, 64, 96, and 128 instructions. We found that the IPC is the best for a *slack* of 64 instructions. For the rest of the paper, we choose an instruction *slack* of 64 instructions between the threads.

2.2 Motivation

Performance degrades because the resources (such as ROB, issue queue, LSB, and register file entries, and dispatch/issue/commit slots) are shared among the threads. To motivate the resource redundancy reduction techniques, we measured the IPCs (presented in Figure 2) of 3 configurations — base single-thread execution (*BST*), base redundant multi-threading with one redundant thread (*RMT*), and *RMT* where the trailing instructions do not consume any registers, LSB, and ROB entries (*RMT-TNR*). The IPC reduces dramatically from *BST* to *RMT*. For *RMT-TNR*, the IPC increases by about 150%, compared to *RMT*. Drop in IPC from *BST* to *RMT-TNR* is due to redundancy in other resources such as the dispatch/issue slots, issue queue entries, etc. An important observation that can be made from Figure 2 is that the difference in IPC of the *RMT* and the *RMT-TNR* configurations is not the same for all the benchmarks. The difference in IPC between the *RMT* and the *RMT-TNR* configurations depends on the IPC of the benchmark and the actual resource pressure observed during program execution. If the IPC is lower, then other shared resources such as the issue queue can also become a bottleneck. If the register/ROB/LSB pressure is lower, then avoiding allocation of these resources (*RMT-TNR*) may not benefit significantly.

As discussed in introduction, it may not be sufficient to reduce the redundancy in just one resource. Figure 3(a) shows

216

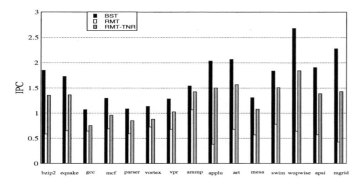

Figure 2. IPCs for 3 configurations showing the benefits from reducing resource redundancy for trailing instructions

the normalized percentage distribution of cycles (out of the total cycles where decode/dispatch was attempted) in which the instructions were stalled due to unavailability of register file, LSB and ROB buffer. When measuring the stalls, if multiple resources are not available, register file is given the highest priority, followed by ROB and then by LSB. The measurements are made when the redundant instructions do not allocate registers (*Rep-NoReg*), ROB entries (*Rep-NoROB*), or LSB entries (Rep-NoLSB). Normalization is performed with respect to the *Rep-NoLSB* configuration. The rest of the hardware parameters are shown in Table 1. As seen in Figure 3(a), if the pressure on a resource is alleviated, the stalls shift from that resource to another. For instance, for gcc, the stalls are due to LSB entries if the trailing instructions are not allocated either ROB entries or registers, and the stalls shift to integer registers if the trailing instructions are not allocated LSB entries. Figure 3(b) further gives the Instructions per Cycle (IPC) count for the four – *Rep-NoReg*, *Rep-NoROB*, Rep-NoLSB, and *RMT-TNR* – configurations. Figure 3(b) shows that the *RMT-TNR* configuration performs better than the other three configurations for most of the benchmarks. For some benchmarks (such as mesa, parser, and vpr), we observed that *RMT-TNR* performed slightly worse, primarily due to a reduction in branch mispredictions and load-alias misspeculations. Figures 3(a) and (b) show that it is imperative to have a comprehensive technique that attempts to reduce the redundancy in multiple resources.

3 Reducing Resource Redundancy

3.1 Reducing Register Redundancy with Register Bits Reuse (RBR)

Previous studies [8, 9, 2] have shown that many narrow-sized data values are produced in a program. Traditionally, values are categorized as narrow only if their leading bits are all zeros or ones. However, this categorization will fail to include most of the floating-point values because of the *IEEE 754* standard used for their representation. Intuitively, for a floating-point value, the least significant portion of the significand may have a higher probability of being all zeros (for instance, a value 0.5). Hence, in our studies, any value whose at least 16 (for a 32-bit word) leading or trailing bits are zeros or ones is categorized as narrow. We observed, there are a considerable number of values with at least 16 trailing zero bits and non-zero bits in the upper 16 bits. For instance, bzip2

had about 10% values with at least 16 trailing zeros. Overall, about 50% of the results could be categorized as narrow.

If a leading instruction produces a narrow result, the result can be compressed into the lower 16 bits of a register. In such a case, the upper 16 bits of the register can be used to store the trailing instruction's result, avoiding a separate register for the redundant trailing instruction. Figure 4 illustrates the working of the *RBR* technique for the instruction i_x that produces a narrow value $0xfa25ffff$. In Figure 4(a), by the time the trailing counterpart of i_x (i_{xR}) is renamed, i_x has already produced a value and stored it in the register P_{10}. When i_{xR} produces the result $0xfa25ffff$, the value stored in the P_{10} is $0xfa25fa25$.

To pass the leading instruction's result's size and its register identifier to the trailing instruction, we use an additional *size bit* for each ROB entry in the leading thread's ROB section (ROBs 1 - N in Figure 4(b)) and an additional *replica pointer* for the ROB (Figure 4(b)). The *size bit* indicates the size of the instruction's result, and the *replica pointer* points to the ROB entry whose trailing instruction will be next renamed. When leading instructions are dispatched, the corresponding size bits are *reset*. Since, the dispatch is in-order, a single port (with multiple bit-lines activated) is enough to *reset* the bits. When a leading instruction produces a narrow result, it *sets* its *size bit*. In this case as well, a single port is enough to set the appropriate bits for all the instructions producing narrow results in a cycle. Hence, the *size bits* bit-vector requires 2 write ports and a single read port. The trailing instructions that are getting renamed in a cycle read the size bits following the bit pointed to by the *replica pointer*. The *rename pointer* is then incremented.

The register to be allocated to the trailing instructions (if their leading counterparts produce a narrow result) can be determined from the ROB entries pointed to by the *replica pointer*. Note that, each ROB entry holds the register identifier used by an instruction to update the *backend map tables* at commit. However, this will necessitate an increase in the number of read ports into the register identifier portion of the ROB. This increase in the number of read ports can be avoided as we will discuss in Section 3.2. If the *size bit* is set, the same register is allocated to the trailing instruction, else another register is sought. The *replica pointer* is updated as the instructions are committed or squashed. Figure 4(b) shows the renaming and register allocation for instructions i_x and i_{xR} that produce a narrow result. Each ROB entry for the trailing instruction is also provided with a *check bit* which is set (at dispatch) if the trailing instruction reuses the register of the leading instruction. The *check bit* is used to guarantee the correct functioning of the *RBR* technique. At commit, the identifiers of the registers allocated to the two instructions are compared and the *check bit* of the trailing instruction is checked. If the register identifiers match and the *check bit* is set, or the register identifiers mismatch and the *check bit* is reset, then the correct operation is assumed. A single *check bit* is enough to detect errors caused by single event upsets (SEUs).

Width, *location*, and *value* bit-vectors (each of size equal to the number of physical registers) are used to appropriately read and write the registers, as shown in Figure 4(c). For a leading instruction's register, the *width* bit is set if the result is narrow, the *location* bit is set if the result has non-significant

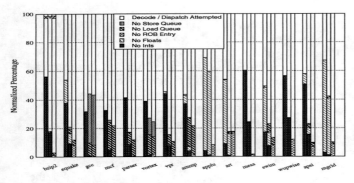

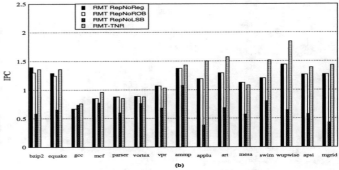

Figure 3. (a) Percentage Distribution of decode/dispatch stalls for (X) No LSB (RepNoLSB); (Y) No ROB (RepNoROB); and (Z) No Register (RepNoReg); (b) IPCs for the different configurations

data in the front, and the *value* bit is set if the non-significant data is all ones. For example, in Figure 4(c), the *width, location*, and *value* bits for $0xfa25ffff$ are "101". To mitigate faulty execution because of errors in these status bits, a *parity bit* is used to detect errors in the *width, location*, and *value* bits. *RBR*'s functions correctly even if a trailing instruction is renamed before the leading instruction generates a narrow result. Since the copies of instructions are committed and squashed simultaneously, the registers used by these instructions are de-allocated simultaneously.

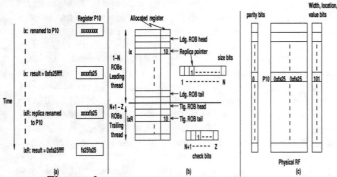

Figure 4. Example Illustrating the *RBR* technique

The *RBR* technique reduces the register file pressure and the energy consumption in the register file, by reducing both the size and the number of values read from and written into the register file. It also reduces the energy consumption in the additional value buffer (refer Section 2.1) because if the *check bit* of the trailing instruction's ROB entry is set, then a single register is read from the additional value buffer.

3.2 Reducing ROB Redundancy with RBR

The ROB entries of the same instruction in the two threads differ only in the register mapping information. The mapping information stored in the ROB entry can only be the current mapping (for checkpointed branch misprediction recovery) or both current and previous mappings (for ROB-walk based branch misprediction recovery). With the *RBR* scheme, it is possible that the ROB entries of the same instruction in the two threads may be the same. We experiment with a more pathological case of ROB-walk based branch misprediction recovery, for which both the current and the previous mappings of an instruction should be the same for their ROB entries to be exactly similar. For instance, if the *definer* and the

redefiner of a register produce narrow results, then the trailing counterpart of the *redefiner* will have exactly the same ROB entry as the leading instruction. ROB allocation for the trailing counterpart can be avoided in this case. To implement this scheme, an additional *map bit* is maintained in the map table for the trailing instructions. If a trailing instruction is using the same mapping as its leading counterpart, then the *map bit* is set. For a trailing instruction, if the *map bit* is set and the current mapping is also the same its leading counterpart, then that instruction is not allocated an ROB entry. On a branch misprediction, all the *map bits* are reset. To further reduce the redundancy in ROB allocation, control type instructions (such as branch and jump instructions) are also allocated a single ROB entry for their leading and trailing counterparts.

This scheme will necessitate that the ROB entries are protected using parity bits, as an error in an ROB entry may not detected because that ROB entry may be used by both the copies of an instruction. The parity bits are generated after rename and before dispatch, in parallel to other pipeline stages. To cover faults that may occur after rename but before parity generation, the ROB entry is written by the leading instruction, whereas the parity bit for the entry is generated for the trailing instruction and written into the *parity bits buffer*. Parity bit generation is required for only those trailing instructions that do not use a separate ROB entry, thus limiting the additional energy as well. Each *parity bit buffer* entry is also provided with a *valid-parity bit* which also signifies whether a separate ROB entry is used by the trailing instruction. At commit, if the *valid-parity bit* is set, then the corresponding parity bit detects errors in the ROB entry. The *map* and *valid-parity* bits may be duplicated to avoid faulty execution on errors in these bits. ROB redundancy reduction will also save energy by reducing the number of writes and reads from the ROB.

Reduction in the ROB entries that are read at commit can facilitate increasing the commit width. However, to limit the increase in ROB read ports (refer Section 3.1), we limit the commit width (from a maximum of four leading and four trailing instructions) to a maximum of four instructions. This will commit four distinct instructions if the copies of all the four instructions share the ROB entries. If only two or three instructions (out of the four instructions) share their ROB entries, then only three distinct instructions can be committed. The determination of the number of instructions to be committed is performed one cycle prior to the commit of the instructions.

3.3 Reducing LSB Redundancy

Traditionally, LSB is implemented in a way that load instructions broadcast their addresses in the store buffer and store instructions broadcast their addresses in the load buffer. These broadcasts are followed by comparisons to detect any load alias misspeculation and store-to-load forwarding. The trailing load and store instructions simply write their addresses (and value for the store instruction) into the LSB entry allocated to them. However, if the leading load and store instructions have already produced their addresses by the time their trailing counterparts are dispatched, then the same broadcast and compare hardware can be used to perform the comparisons for error detection. To detect whether a leading memory instruction has generated its address, a *LSB pointer* similar to the *replica pointer* is used to point to the next memory instruction whose trailing counterpart will be dispatched. On dispatch of trailing memory instructions, if the *valid bits* of the LSB entries of their leading counterparts are set, then the trailing instructions are not allocated LSB entries.

In this technique, a trailing load instruction (whose leading counterpart has already generated its address) generates its address on the store's address generation unit (AGU). This results in its address being broadcasted in the load buffer and compared with the leading counterpart's entry in the load buffer. A trailing store instruction is executed in a similar fashion. In case there is a mismatch in the addresses generated by the two counterparts, the instruction is marked as being faulty. If the leading load instruction has not have generated the address by the time its trailing counterpart is dispatched, the trailing load instruction is made dependent on the leading load instruction to serialize their execution. This is possible because most of the load instructions have a single register operand. If a load instruction has two register operands, then the dispatch is stalled till the leading counterpart produces its address. However, a trailing store instruction is allocated a separate store buffer entry if its leading counterpart has not produced its address. This scheme replaces the write and read of the address of the trailing instructions, with a single broadcast of its address, thus saving energy as well.

This technique may remove all the redundancy in the load buffer due to trailing instructions. However, store instructions also have to store the value in the store buffer entry to support store-to-load forwarding. Hence, allocation of store buffer entries to the trailing store instructions can only be avoided for the instructions that store a narrow value, so that the space for the value can be shared among the instructions from both the threads. Note that, this technique will require *parity* and *valid-parity* bits to protect the store buffer entries' addresses (not the values) once the comparison has been performed.

3.4 Limited RBR

To reduce the additional *width*, *location*, *value*, and *parity* bits required for each register in the *RBR* technique, we propose a *limited RBR* technique where a value is narrow if its significant part is 14 bits or less. In this case, each 32-bit register can either hold a normal value or two narrow values and the duplicated *location* and *value* bits for the two values. The *width* bit has to be provided and duplicated outside of the register to determine the size of the values. In *limited RBR*, the number of additional bits reduce from four to two.

4 Experimental Results

4.1 Experimental Setup

The hardware parameters for the base *RMT* superscalar processor are given in Table 1. Our base pipeline (for the *BST* configuration) consists of 8 front-end stages. For the *RMT* configuration without the *RBR* technique, one pipeline stage is inserted before the commit stage to check the values. For the *RBR* technique, one pipeline stage is inserted after execution and before writeback to check the size of the result values. Another pipeline stage is inserted after the register read to re-construct the correct values from the compressed values read from the register file. Overall, the branch misprediction penalty increases by 1 cycle because of the additional pipeline stage before the register read.

We use a modified SimpleScalar simulator [3], simulating a 32-bit PISA architecture. In our simulator, we use a unified physical and architectural register file. Two registers are allocated to an instruction producing a long or a double result value (requiring 64 bits for representation). For benchmarks, we use 6 SPEC2000 integer (vpr, mcf, parser, bzip2, vortex, and gcc), and 9 FP (wupwise, ammp, swim, equake, applu, art, apsi, mgrid, and mesa) benchmarks. The statistics are collected for 500M instructions after skipping the first 1B instructions.

For the *RBR* technique, the number of ROB, Load buffer, and Store buffer entries for the trailing instructions are reduced to 32, 0, and 5 respectively. The remaining entries are provided for the leading instructions. Note that this distribution of entries may not be the best possible distribution (which can be determined empirically), because the trailing instructions may stall due to too few entries provided for them. We use a single *parity bit* each for the ROB entry, store buffer entry, and the additional status bits in the register file to protect from a single event upset (SEU). The number of *parity bits* can be increased to protect from multi-bit upsets.

4.2 Results

Figure 5(a) shows the IPC results of the *RBR* and *Limited RBR* techniques, compared to *RMT* and *RMT-TNR* configurations. We also experiment with two more configurations – *RMT-Add* and *RMT-Add-Ltd* – where the additional bits required for each structure in the *RBR* technique are used to increase the capacity of the structures in the base *RMT* configuration. For instance, the *width*, *location*, *value*, and *parity* bits are used to increase the number of registers by 16 in the *RMT-Add* configuration and the additional *width* bits increase the number of registers by eight in the *RMT-Add-Ltd* configuration. Depending on the additional bits, the ROB size can be increased by 10 entries. Similarly, the load buffer increases by one entry and the store buffer increases by two entries. Figure 5(b) shows the IPCs of *RBR* and *Limited RBR* compared to *RMT-Add* and *RMT-Add-Ltd*. *Note that an increase in the structures' sizes will signifi cantly impact their access time, which is not affected in the RBR technique, where the bits are used as separate status bits.*

As can be seen from Figure 5(a), IPC difference between *RBR* and *Limited RBR* techniques is negligible. However, *RBR* technique increases the IPC of the *RMT* configuration by about 62% with a maximum reaching 144% for apsi. As

Parameter	Value	Parameter	Value
Fetch/Decode/ Commit Width	8 instructions	FP FUs	3 ALU, 1 Mul/Div
Unified Phy. Register File	128 INT/128 FP entries, 2-cycle acc. lat. 1-cycle inter-subsystem lat.	Int. FUs	4 ALU, 2 AGU 1 Mul/Div
Issue Width	5/3 INT/FP instructions	Issue Queue	96 INT/64 FP Instructions
Branch Predictor	Gshare 4K entries	BTB Size	4K entries, 2-way assoc.
L1 - I-cache	32K, direct-map, 2 cycle latency	L1 - D-cache	32K, 4-way assoc., 2 cycle latency, 2 r/w ports
Memory Latency	100 cycles first word 2 cycle/inter-word	L2 - cache	unified 512K, 8-way assoc., 10 cycles
ROB size	128 leading 64 trailing	Load buffer size Store buffer size	30 leading, 10 trailing 30 leading, 10 trailing

Table 1. Baseline Processor Hardware Parameters for the Experimental Evaluation

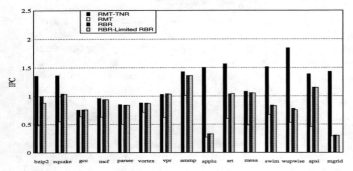 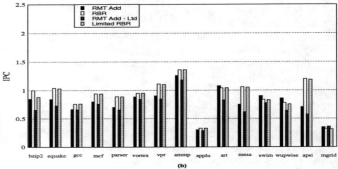

Figure 5. (a) IPCs for *RMT, RMT-TNR, RBR,* and *Limited RBR* configurations; (b) IPCs for *RBR,Limited RBR, RMT-Add, RMT-Add-Ltd* configurations

expected, we observe that the techniques perform better for integer benchmarks, where more narrow values are encountered. The IPC with *RBR* is better than that for *RMT-TNR* for gcc and vpr because the stalls in these benchmarks are almost reduced to that of *RMT-TNR*, because of a high percentage of narrow values. However, lower branch misprediction and load-alias misspeculation gives slightly better results for the *RBR* technique. Figure 5(b) shows that *limited RBR* is significantly better than *RMT-Add-Ltd*, where the additional hardware in *limited RBR* is instead used to increase the size of the structures. However, when the number of registers are increased by 16, *RMT-Add* performs slightly better than *RBR* for art, swim, wupwise, and mgrid because of fewer narrow values encountered in these benchmarks.

The performance improvement obtained from the *RBR* technique is not equal for all the benchmarks, because it depends on the amount by which the pressure is reduced. For the benchmarks that are register constrained, the performance improvement obtained from the *RBR* technique also depends on the type of registers for which the pressure is reduced. For instance, if a benchmark is floating-point register constrained and the techniques reduce the integer register pressure, then the techniques are not expected to be very effective. For instance, consider applu and swim in Figure 6. Figure 6 presents the reduction in register, ROB, and store buffer redundancy. Load buffer redundancy reduction is 100% and hence not shown. The bars in Figure 6 present the percentage of trailing instructions (out of those that require a resource) for which separate allocation of that resource was avoided. For instance,

bar 1 shows the percentage of integer result producing trailing instructions for which integer register allocation was avoided. Applu and Swim are constrained by floating-point registers. The *RBR* scheme is able to save more than 40% of integer registers for these two benchmarks, whereas only about 15% of floating point registers. Hence, *RBR* scheme does not perform that well for these two benchmarks.

Overall, for about 45% of result producing instructions of the trailing thread register allocation was avoided, for about 50% of trailing instructions ROB allocation was avoided, for about 50% of trailing store instructions store buffer allocation was avoided. The absence of the bar for floating-point registers is due to the absence of floating-point instructions.

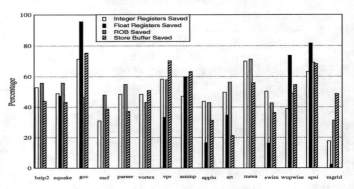

Figure 6. Percentage Savings of Integer and Floating-point registers, ROB and Store buffer entries for the trailing thread with *RBR*

220

4.3 Power Results

We use the cacti tool [17] to perform the energy measurements for the register file, ROB, LSB, and the additional value buffer. For the measurements, we measure the energy consumption for each access and the type of access and multiply it by the number of such accesses obtained from the simulations. Energy consumption in the register file and additional value buffer (*AVB*) will reduce because for many instructions, fewer bit-lines are activated to write and read smaller values from the register file. When instructions that share a single register commit, a single register is read from the *AVB* also saving energy by reducing the number of commit-time reads. However, additional energy is consumed in the additional *width*, *location*, *value* and *parity* bits. Energy consumption in the ROB and LSB is reduced primarily because of fewer writes and reads from these structures. However, some of the energy saved in the LSB is compensated by the additional broadcast and compare for the trailing instructions. Additional energy is also consumed in the ROB and the LSB from *parity* and *valid-parity* bits. Figure 7 shows the percentage savings in dynamic energy consumption (w.r.t *RMT*) obtained in the register file, ROB, LSB, and the additional value buffer, respectively. These measurements also include the energy consumed in the additional bits. As seen in Figure 7, about 10% energy savings is achieved in the register file, about 25% in the ROB, about 30% in the load buffer, about 10% in the store buffer, and about 18% in the additional value buffer. Figure 7 shows that, in general, energy savings is more in integer benchmarks than the floating-point benchmarks, which is expected.

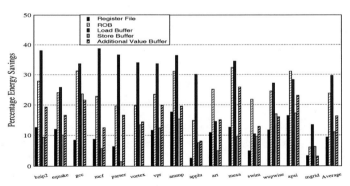

Figure 7. Percentage energy saving in RF, ROB, Load/Store Buffer, and AVB for the *RBR* configuration

4.4 Load Value Buffer

In staggered execution, the values loaded by the leading thread are forwarded to the trailing thread using a load value buffer. The load value buffer size will depend on the average number of load instructions in the *slack*. In the *RBR* technique, if the leading load instruction loads a narrow value by the time its trailing counterpart has been renamed, then the two instructions will share the same register. Hence, to reduce the size of the load buffer required, when a leading load instruction loads a narrow value and its trailing counterpart has not been renamed, the value is replicated in the register and no load value buffer entry is allocated for that value. We call this technique *load value buffer reduction (LVBR)*. The

replica pointer is used to determine whether a trailing counterpart of a leading load instruction has been renamed or not. The trailing load instruction is accordingly notified. For the measurement of the load buffer size required, we measured the average number of load instructions in the slack of 64 instructions for each benchmark. For the *RMT* configuration, the average number of load instructions that require a load buffer entry (across all the benchmarks) is about 30, and with *LVBR* scheme, this number reduces by about 46%.

We performed experiments with a 32-entry load value buffer in the *RMT* configuration, a 32-entry load value buffer in the *RBR* configuration, and a 16-entry load value buffer in the *RBR-LVBR* technique. We observed that the IPC reduction was about 5% in going from *RBR* to *RBR-LVBR* technique. However, the reduction in power consumption in the load value buffer was about 65%. The structure of the load value buffer assumed was a fully associative buffer with a register identifier field and a loaded value field. The trailing load instruction broadcasts the register identifier of the leading load instruction, and on a match reads the value. On a mismatch, the trailing load instruction waits to be woken up by the leading load instruction. The structure and the working of the load value buffer will remain the same in the *RMT* and the *RBR-LVBR* techniques. The reduction in energy consumption is significantly greater than the reduction in size because the savings are achieved from both the reduction in size and accesses.

4.5 Vulnerability Impact of RBR

As discussed in the previous sections, with the addition of *parity bits* and the duplication of selective status bits, the *RBR* will be able to detect all the single event upsets (SEUs) that result in a single bit flip. However, the probability of a multi-bit error in the same ROB entry, store buffer entry, and *width*, *location*, and *value* bits going undetected may increase slightly for the *RBR* technique. In addition, there is a possibility that an error may not be detected if a leading instruction erroneously produces a smaller-sized value, and its trailing counterpart trailing instruction only writes half of its result bits into the upper half of the register. To address this issue, if an instruction marked as producing a small-sized result, produces a normal-sized value, then the error is detected by tagging the instruction as faulty in the ROB.

We measure the vulnerability of the *RMT* architecture in terms of the number of errors that are incurred in the execution of a program. Of course, these errors will be detected in the *RMT* architecture. If all the errors are assumed to be independent of each other, the number of errors will be given by $N_e = P_i \times N_i$, where P_i is the probability of an error in a committed instruction and N_i is the number of committed instructions. N_i remains the same in the base *RMT* and *RMT* with *RBR*. Hence the vulnerability of these two configurations depends on P_i. P_i will be given by $P_i \; \alpha \; P_e \times P_{ip} \times P_{ep}$, where P_e is the probability that an error occurs, P_{ip} is the probability that the instruction i is in the processor when the error occurred, and P_{ep} is the probability that the error occurred in the hardware being used by the instruction i. This equation assumes that all the three events are independent. To first order approximation, P_i will be
$P_i \; \alpha \; A \times C_i/C_t \times 1/W^2 \; \alpha \; C_i/C_t$
where, A is the area of the processor, C_i is the number of

cycles spent by an instruction in the pipeline, C_t is the total cycles taken by the program, and W is the width of the processor. We assume that A almost remains constant when going from *RMT* to *RBR*. Hence, we measured the average number of cycles spent by an instruction in the pipeline and the total cycles spent for executing the code, for the *RMT* and the *RBR* configurations. We observed that the number of cycles for which a committed instruction remains in the pipeline reduces by about 33% for the *RBR* configuration, while the total number of cycles reduce by about 35%, suggesting that the probability of an instruction incurring an error remains almost the same.

5 Violating the Slack

In all the experiments so far, the slack between the leading and the trailing instructions has been fixed at 64 instructions. In such situations, if the leading thread stalls due to unavailability of resources, the trailing thread also stalls even if it had resources available. For instance, a leading instruction stalled because of a filled load buffer can stall a trailing instruction that does not require a load buffer entry. Such cases become much more prominent in the *RBR* technique where the trailing instructions may not even require any additional resources. Hence, we experimented with *RMT* and *RBR* configurations that were allowed to violate the slack condition if the trailing instructions could go forward. Note that the slack is violated only if the leading instructions are stalled. Figure 8 shows that IPCs of the *RMT* and the *RBR* configurations with and without the violating the slack condition. It can be seen from Figure 8, that the performance of the *RMT* configuration does not improve when violation of the slack condition is allowed, whereas, the performance of the *RBR* technique increases by about 7%.

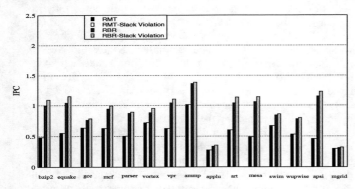

Figure 8. IPCs for *RMT* and *RBR* configurations with and without slack violation

6 Sensitivity Study

In this section, we measure the IPCs of the *RMT* and the *RBR* configurations as the register file size is changed to 96 and 164, the ROB size is changed to 128 and 256, and the Load/store buffers are changed to 32 and 24 entries. In these experiments, all the other hardware parameters remain the same. For instance, when changing the register file size, ROB and LSB are also kept at default values. When ROB size is varied, the difference in the number of leading and trailing entries is maintained at 64 for *RMT*, and the trailing entries are

halved for *RBR*. When the LSB size is varied, the 3:1 ratio in the number of leading and trailing entries is also maintained for *RMT*, and the store buffer entries are halved for *RBR*. Figure 9 presents the integer and floating-point benchmarks' average IPC, as the resource sizes are varied. When the ROB is increased beyond 192 entries, the IPCs of both the *RMT* and the *RBR* configurations remain the same, as ROB is no longer a bottleneck. However, for 128-entry ROB, the average integer IPC reduces slightly for *RMT* whereas it remains the same for *RBR*. When the *LSB* entries are reduced, the *RMT* IPC reduces whereas the *RBR* remains almost the same. As the number of registers are varied from 164 to 128, *RMT* IPC reduces much faster than *RBR* IPC. In fact for the integer benchmarks, the *RBR* IPC almost remains the same. However, when they are reduced from 128 to 96, *RBR* IPC reduces faster than *RMT* IPC. This is because at register file size of 96, registers start to become a bottleneck for the *RBR* technique as well, whereas at register file size of 128, the registers are not much of a bottleneck. This is especially true for the integer benchmarks. For *RMT*, the registers are a bottleneck at both 96 and 128, and hence the decrease in IPC in going from 128 to 96 is not large.

7 Register Value Reuse (RVR)

RBR technique reduces redundancy only if the results generated by instructions are narrow. We investigate *register value reuse (RVR)* technique to reduce redundancy even for normal-sized values. The *RVR* technique can only reduce redundancy in the register file. We also observed that about 19% of the normal results generated by instructions were repeated when considering the previous eight unique normal results. In the *RVR* technique, if a leading instruction produces a normal result that is already present in another register (written to by another leading instruction), then the trailing counterpart of that instruction is renamed to the register already holding the value. Figure 10 explains the *RVR* technique. As seen in Figure 10, instructions i_1, i_x, and i_y generate the same normal result X, where i_1 is the first instruction that generates X. If i_x generates the result by the time i_{xR} (trailing instruction of i_x) is renamed, i_{xR} can be renamed to the register used by i_1 (i. e. $P10$). Note that the leading instruction has already broadcast its register identifier in the issue queue (to wake up dependent instructions) by the time the trailing counterpart is renamed to that register.

The *RVR* technique will not increase the vulnerability of the processor to SEUs. Consider that an error occurs in one of the instructions i_x and i_{xR} in Figure 10, whereas i_y and i_{yR} compute correct results. In *RVR* technique, there are two cases: (i) register used by i_x is not overwritten by i_{yR} by the time i_x and i_{xR} commit, and (ii) register used by i_x is overwritten by i_{yR} by the time i_x and i_{xR} commit. In the first case, the error will be detected when the results of i_x and i_{xR} are compared at commit time. In the second case, if an error occurred in i_{xR}, then the error will again be detected when the results of i_{yR} (which overwrites the result of i_x) and i_{xR} are compared at commit time. If i_x errs (i. e. i_x erroneously produced a result equal to that of i_1 and i_y), the error is again detected when i_{yR} and i_{xR} are compared at commit.

In this paper, we employ the *RVR* technique on top of the *RBR* technique. To compare the result values of different leading instructions and also to forward the register identifiers to

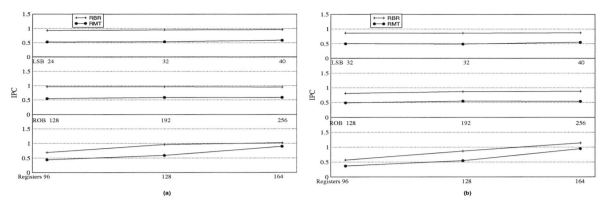

Figure 9. IPCs for *RMT* and *RBR* as the Register File, ROB and LSB sizes are varied for (a) Integer; (b) Floating-Point benchmarks

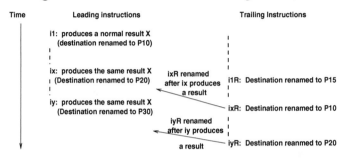

Figure 10. Example Illustrating the Basic Idea behind the *Register Value Reuse* technique

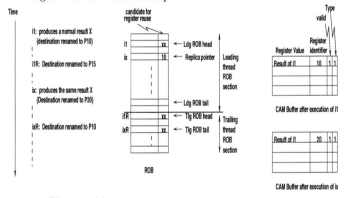

Figure 11. Example Illustrating the *RVR* technique

the trailing counterparts, we use a small CAM (Context Addressable Memory) buffer. The buffer is accessed when the leading instructions produce a value and when a leading redefiner instruction of a register commits. When a redefiner instruction commits, the entry holding the register it redefines is invalidated. When leading instructions produce normal results, unique results are compared with the values in the CAM buffer, and on a match the register identifiers in the ROB (candidate register identifier in Figure 11), and the CAM buffer are updated accordingly. If there is no match, then the least recently filled entry is updated. When a trailing instruction is renamed, it obtains the reuse candidate through the *replica pointer*. Figure 11 illustrates the working of the *RVR* technique when instructions i_1 and i_x produce the same result. When instruction i_1 writes back its result, the CAM buffer is updated with i_1's result. Consequently, when i_x writes the

result, the CAM buffer entry is updated with the register identifier of i_x and the ROB entry of i_x records register P_{10} as a reuse candidate for i_{xR}. To handle register deallocation accurately in the *RVR* technique, 2 *register usage* bit-vectors (each of size equal to the number of physical registers) are used, one for the leading instructions and the other for the trailing. A register is deallocated only when its bit in both the bit-vectors is *reset*. A parity bit-vector is required to protect these two bit-vectors. As explained earlier in the section, any errors in the CAM buffer or the additional bits in the ROB will not result in a faulty detection and the error will be detected. This technique will not hamper in the working of *RBR*.

The only potential problem in this technique will arise if a register gets recorded as a candidate for reuse, but is deallocated and reallocated before it is reused. To handle these situations, we use a *candidate valid* bit-vector (with one bit for each physical register), where the bits are set when a physical register becomes a reuse candidate for reuse and reset when the register is reused. However, if a leading instruction allocates a register with the *candidate valid* bit set, the instruction does not access the CAM buffer even if it produces a normal value. When reusing a register for a trailing instruction, the *candidate valid* bit should be "1", otherwise another register is sought.

Results: In this section, we present the IPC results of *RMT-TNR*, *RBR*, and *RBR+RVR* configurations in Figure 12. We use a fully associative 8-entry CAM structure for *RVR*. As seen in the figure, the *RVR* technique results in further performance improvement, an average of about 20% (over the *RBR* technique), especially for the floating point benchmarks that have a larger percentage of normal values.

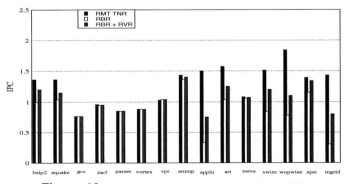

Figure 12. IPCs of *RMT-TNR*, *RBR*, and *RBR + RVR*

8 Related Work

Techniques that simultaneously execute multiple copies of the same instructions have been proposed for concurrent error detection and recovery [14, 1, 13, 15, 16, 21, 22, 7]. Ray, Hoe, and Falsafi [14] use the same superscalar datapath to execute the multiple copies of an instruction for fault-tolerance. Austin proposes a very different fault-tolerant scheme [1] which comprises of an aggressive out-of-order superscalar processor checked by a simple in-order checker processor. The fault-tolerant architectures in [15, 16, 22, 7] use the inherent hardware redundancy in simultaneous multithreading and chip multiprocessors for concurrent error detection. Patel and Fung [13] propose transforming the input operands between redundant computations to expose a persistent fault.

Smolens et. al. [20] study the performance impact of redundant execution. They focus their studies on the issue logic and the ROB, as they do not allocate registers to the trailing instructions. However, their techniques may be susceptible to errors in the pipeline frontend, such as errors in rename.

Packing multiple values in a register has been discussed using speculation techniques for a single threaded by Oguz et. al. [12]. The techniques discussed in this paper are non-speculative because when running the trailing thread at a *slack*, the information from the leading thread is readily available and can be exploited. Exploiting value locality in the register file for a single threaded processor in [2] can be difficult to implement, especially in the presence of exceptions, unless only a small subset of a priori decided values are used. In our proposal, value locality is exploited to avoid redundant register allocation, eliminating many of the implementation difficulties (such as reference counters, updating the renaming of dependent instructions, etc.) when used for a single thread.

Shubhendu, et. al. [10] suggest that "dead" values reduce the vulnerability of an architecture to soft failures. However, they do not explore the possibility of utilizing the "dead" values to improve the performance of a reliable processor.

9 Conclusion

Ensuring reliability in systems using redundant threads place a significant pressure on the processor resources, especially the register file, ROB, and LSB, thus impacting the performance. In this paper, we investigate techniques reduce resource redundancy in Register File, ROB, and LSB. The techniques in this paper are based on a key observation: in *staggered execution*, the leading instructions usually produce their results before their trailing counterparts are renamed. The *register bits reuse* technique allocates a single register to both copies of an instruction, if the result produced by the instruction is narrow. To enhance the number of narrow width values produced in a program, we propose a novel way of defining a narrow value as one that has either leading or trailing zeros or ones. The *RBR* technique is extended to also avoid the redundancy in ROB entries for many trailing instructions. Innovative scheme is also proposed to reuse the load/store buffer hardware to avoid redundancy in LSB entries.

We observed that the *RBR* technique produces about 62% performance improvement over the base *RMT* configuration. The power consumption reduces by about 10-30% in the various hardware structures. We also proposed reusing the regis-

ters for normal values. In this case if two leading instructions produce the same normal result, then the trailing counterpart of the second is renamed to the register used by the first leading instruction. This technique improves the performance to about 95% more than the base case.

References

[1] T. Austin, 'DIVA: a reliable substrate for deep submicron microarchitecture design," *Proc. Micro-32*, 1999.

[2] S. Balakrishnan, et. al., 'Exploiting Value Locality in Physical Register Files," *Proc. Micro-36*, 2003.

[3] D. Burger and T. M. Austin, 'The SimpleScalar Tool Set, Version 2.0," *Computer Arch. News*, 1997.

[4] Compaq Computer Corp., 'Data integrity for Compaq Non-Stop Himalaya servers," *http://nonstop.compaq.com*, 1999.

[5] G. Hinton, et al, 'A 0.18-um CMOS IA-32 Processor With a 4-GHz Integer Execution Unit," *IEEE Journal of Solid-State Circuits*, Vol. 36, No. 11, Nov. 2001.

[6] J. G. Holm, and P. Banerjee, 'Low cost concurrent error detection in a VLIW architecture using replicated instructions" *Proc. ICPP-21*, 1992.

[7] M. Gomaa, et. al., 'Transient-Fault Recovery for Chip Multiprocessors," *Proc. ISCA-30*, 2003.

[8] G. Loh, 'Exploiting data-width locality to increase superscalar execution bandwidth," *Proc. Micro-35*, 2002.

[9] S. Kumar, P. Pujara and A. Aggarwal, 'Bit-Sliced datapath for energy-effi cient high performance microprocessors," *Workshop on PACS*, 2004.

[10] S. Mukherjee, et. al., 'A Systematic methodology to compute the architectural vulnerability factors for a high-performance microprocessor," *Micro-36*, 2003.

[11] S. Mukherjee, et. al., 'A Systematic Methodology to Compute the Architectural Vulnerability Factors for a High-Performance Microprocessor," *Proc. Micro-36*, 2003.

[12] O. Ergin, et. al., 'Register Packing: Exploiting Narrow-Width Operands for Reducing Register File Pressure," *Proc. Micro-37*, 2004.

[13] J. H. Patel, and L. T. Fung, 'Concurrent error detection in ALU's by recomputing with shifted operands," *IEEE Transactions on Computers*, 31(7):589-595, July 1982.

[14] J. Ray, J. Hoe, and B. Falsafi , 'Dual use of superscalar datapath for transient-fault detection and recovery," *Proc. Micro-34*, 2001.

[15] S. Reinhardt, and S. Mukherjee, 'Transient fault detection via simultaneous multithreading," *Proc. ISCA-27*, June 2000.

[16] E. Rotenberg, 'AR-SMT: A microarchitectural approach to fault tolerance in microprocessors," *Proc. 29th Intl. Symp. on Fault-Tolerant Computing Systems*, 1999.

[17] P. Shivakumar, and N. Jouppi, 'CACTI 3.0: An Integrated Cache Timing Power, and Area Model," *Technical Report, DEC Western Research Lab*, 2002.

[18] D. P. Siewiorek and R. S. Swarz, 'Reliable Computer Systems Design and Evaluation," *The Digital Press*, 1992.

[19] T. J. Slegel, et al. 'IBM's S/390 G5 microprocessor design," *IEEE Micro*, 19(2):12-23, March/April 1999.

[20] J.Smolens, et. al., 'Effi cient Resource sharing in Concurrent error detecting Superscalar microarchitectures ," *Proc. Micro-37*, 2004.

[21] K. Sundaramoorthy, Z. Purser, and E. Rotenberg, 'Slipstream processors: Improving both performance and fault tolerance," *In Proc. Micro-33*, December 2000.

[22] T. Vijaykumar, I. Pomeranz, and K. Cheng, 'Transient-fault recovery using simultaneous multithreading," *Proc. ISCA-29*, 2002.

[23] C. Weaver, et. al., 'Techniques to Reduce the Soft Error Rate of a High Performance Microprocessor," *Proc. ISCA-31*, 2004.

InfoShield: A Security Architecture for Protecting Information Usage in Memory

Weidong Shi   Joshua B. Fryman[1]   Guofei Gu

Hsien-Hsin S. Lee   Youtao Zhang[2]   Jun Yang[3]

School of Electrical and Computer Engineering, College of Computing, Georgia Tech
[1]Programming System Lab, Corporate Tech. Group, Intel Corporation
[2]Dept. of Computer Science, University of Pittsburgh
[3]Dept. of Computer Science and Engineering, University of California, Riverside

leehs@gatech.edu   {shiw, guofei}@cc.gatech.edu   joshua.b.fryman@intel.com   zhangyt@cs.pitt.edu   junyang@cs.ucr.edu

ABSTRACT

*Cyber theft is a serious threat to Internet security. It is one of the major security concerns by both network service providers and Internet users. Though sensitive information can be encrypted when stored in non-volatile memory such as hard disks, for many e-commerce and network applications, sensitive information is often stored as plaintext in main memory. Documented and reported exploits facilitate an adversary stealing sensitive information from an application's memory. These exploits include illegitimate memory scan, information theft oriented buffer overflow, invalid pointer manipulation, integer overflow, password stealing trojans and so forth. Today's computing system and its hardware cannot address these exploits effectively in a coherent way. This paper presents a unified and lightweight solution, called **InfoShield**, that can strengthen application protection against theft of sensitive information such as passwords, encryption keys, and other private data with a minimal performance impact. Unlike prior whole memory encryption and information flow based efforts, InfoShield protects the usage of information. InfoShield ensures that sensitive data are used only as defined by application semantics, preventing misuse of information. Comparing with prior art, InfoShield handles a broader range of information theft scenarios in a unified framework with less overhead. Evaluation using popular network client-server applications shows that InfoShield is sound for practical use and incurs little performance loss because InfoShield only protects absolute, critical sensitive information. Based on the profiling results, only 0.3% of memory accesses and 0.2% of executed codes are affected by InfoShield.*

1. INTRODUCTION

The leakage of sensitive information in network servers can result in serious consequences. First of all, any disclosure of credential information such as a login account with password can assist adversaries in gaining privileged accesses to computing facilities. Also, theft of user information such as credit card numbers, social security numbers, and other personal information is a major concern of companies offering online services. The loss in revenue due to cyber vandalism and information theft is in billions of dollars annually [6]. There are many techniques that can be applied by a remote or local adversary to compromise data privacy. These techniques include, but not limited to, password stealing worms/trojan horses [32, 27], memory scans using either legitimate or malicious software [15], theft or destruction of private or system data via buffer overflow exploits [20], as well as stealing sensitive information through altering

memory pointers, data offsets, or array indices [20].

The causes of data privacy violation are diverse, so are the solutions. In fact, there are very few studies in the past that directly address the problems from the aforementioned attacks. In many cases, data privacy often comes as a by-product of safe programming practices using either security analysis tools or an intrinsically safe source language. For example, special compiler and program analysis tools [5, 16, 4] were developed to reduce the risks of buffer overflow and memory reference errors. This approach indirectly mitigates the risk of disclosing sensitive data through these types of exploits. Two particular research areas that directly address the issue of data safety are *access control* and *information flow analysis* [7, 29, 10, 1]. As we will show later, traditional access control approaches do not provide sufficient protection on information safety because the OS-based access control is too coarse-grained. On the other hand, using static information flow analysis to ensure privacy and security of information is sometimes too restrictive [21] for real applications where sharing or disclosing information is mandatory and frequent.

In this paper, we present a new approach, termed *InfoShield*, to protecting the privacy of sensitive information based on *information usage*. As can be readily seen from Internet viruses and spyware, misuse of information is one major threat to information security. Many attacks stem from abnormal or unauthorized usage of information. For example, a password or encryption key must be strictly used for access authentication by the designated functions based on a specific control flow. Any other usage of the information, e.g. memory scan or following a different control flow path, should be considered unsafe and prohibited to prevent a security breach. Specifically, the major contributions of this paper are:

- Addressing the issue of information usage safety and its implications to defending real attacks to information privacy.

- Presenting a novel architecture called InfoShield that enforces proper usage of sensitive data according to program definition or semantics at runtime.

- Proposing lightweight hardware solutions to facilitate and accelerate the process of information usage protection.

The unique characteristics of information usage based protection on data privacy are:

- **Improved data privacy.** The notion of information usage safety is proposed based on vulnerability analysis and exploits to address real threats. Particularly, the usage verification and authorization are performed at runtime on-demand due to the dynamic nature of information usage.

- **Increased enforceability.** The proposed InfoShield is easily enforceable for real software systems where information is frequently shared or disclosed. It leaves the decision of what information can be shared or disclosed to the software developers, therefore avoiding the overprotection problem associated with traditional information flow based protection. It enforces protection on usage of sensitive information by ensuring that the data can only be used in a specific way by the designated program according to pre-defined program semantics.

- **Optimized performance.** InfoShield guarantees proper usage of information at a fine granularity (down to each word in memory). It verifies the usage of information at runtime by replacing some LD/ST operations with security-aware equivalents. Using architectural support, InfoShield can achieve real-time protection of information usage with negligible performance loss.

- **Composable security.** The proposed protection on information usage is orthogonal to other language based schemes on program security. It provides composable security by allowing it to be combined with other techniques such as information flow based protection. For example, static information flow based analysis can be applied first to ensure that a program is written properly and there is no leakage of private information based on program semantics. Then, information usage protection guarantees that information is used exactly as defined, precluding any undesired disclosure of sensitive data.

The remainder of the paper is organized as follows. In Section 2, we discuss threats on information privacy caused by information misuse. Section 3 presents the InfoShield architecture. Section 4 and Section 5 examine security issues and evaluate the performance of InfoShield. Section 6 is an overview of related work, and finally Section 7 concludes the paper.

2. THREAT MODELS

There are many software exploits that can result in disclosure of sensitive information. These exploits can be either launched by remote attackers or local access adversaries.

2.1 Attacks on Information

2.1.1 Memory scan

Memory scanning is one of the most straightforward ways to search for sensitive information stored in either application or kernel memory. If adversaries know the whereabouts of the secret information, their job would be much easier. If adversaries have local access, they can use memory dumping tools that often can access higher privilege memory [15]. For remote exploits, techniques such as memory resident worms, Trojan horses, or malicious dummy kernel drivers can be used. After loading in memory, such malware can periodically scan application or even kernel memory for sensitive information. When found, the malware can send the information out without the knowledge of the data owner. As shown in [15], many important data can be easily recovered by a simple keyword-based scan of memory. For example, the iDefense security advisory [11] documents a number of memory scan attacks for logon credentials applicable to popular network clients including PuTTY ssh2 client, SecureCRT, and AbsoluteTelnet.

There are three basic memory scan techniques that allow adversaries to identify secrets in an application's virtual memory. First, they can search for a pivot string such as "password" or "ssh-connection." The real password and encryption key is often stored at a location with fixed offset from the pivot string [11]. Second, adversaries can run a local copy of the same system and reverse-engineer the likely locations where sensitive data may be stored [15]. Third, entropy-based

analysis can be used to discover encryption keys stored in random places of a server memory [28]. The effectiveness of this technique to break encryption keys has been demonstrated by a commercial key finding tool developed by nCipher [35].

2.1.2 Invalid input

Another technique is to manipulate input data to make the victim application misbehave, disclosing sensitive data (in)voluntarily. For example, the Linux kernel allows a local adversary to obtain sensitive kernel information by gaining access to kernel memory via vulnerabilities in the /proc interfaces. One documented vulnerability with 32- to 64-bit conversions in the kernel [20] allows insecure modification of file offset pointers in the kernel using the file API (such as open and lseek). Through carefully orchestrated manipulation of file pointers, a /proc file can be advanced to a negative value that allows kernel memory to be copied to user space. These vulnerabilities allow a local unprivileged attacker to access segments of kernel memory which may contain sensitive information. A similar example is a flaw in the FreeBSD process file system (GENERIC-MAP-NOMATCH) [20]. In the uiomove system call, a local attacker can set the uio_offset parameter of struct uio to extremely large or negative values, to cause the function to return a portion of the kernel memory, e.g. terminal buffers, which could contain a user-entered password. Aside from the OS kernel itself, device drivers and other vendor-centric software also reside in the kernel space. Vulnerability of these modules can also be exploited. For instance, the Linux e1000 Ethernet card driver had a flaw that unbounded input can be redirected as an input for the *copy_to_user* function, causing kernel memory to be returned (CAN-2004-0535) [20].

2.1.3 Buffer overflow

Buffer overflow [2], a traditional exploit technique, allows attackers to overwrite data in an application's stack or heap with arbitrary data or malicious code. The injected code, if executed, helps the attacker gain access to sensitive information. Adversaries can also elevate their privilege level by running injected code through buffer attacks. A specific form of buffer overflow is the format string attack [26] that exploits any vulnerability of a format specifier (e.g., "%n") in standard C functions. The existence of the format string attack in some cases allows sensitive information to be disclosed without code injection. One example is the documented Mac OS X *pppd* format string vulnerability (CAN-2004-0165) [20]. When *pppd* receives an invalid command line argument, it will eventually pass it as a format specifier to vslprintf(), which can be exploited to read arbitrary data out of *pppd*'s process. When the system is used as a PPP server under certain circumstances, it is also possible to steal PAP/CHAP authentication credentials by exploiting the format string vulnerability without code injection.

2.1.4 Worms and Trojan horses

A large number of worms and Trojan horses are concocted to compromise users or system information [32, 27]. As studies indicate, approximately 90% of Trojan horses found in circulation today are from online services. A significant number of them try to steal sensitive information such as login IDs or passwords. Examples of such Trojans include W32/Eyeveg-B, VBS/LoveLetter.bd, BadTrans.B, and Lirva [27]. These respectively attack online-banking customer accounts, send compromised information to an email address, or steal password by crawling through ICQ, email, or peer-to-peer file sharing systems. Lirva can even disable antivirus and security applications.

The aforementioned exploits on information privacy achieve their goal through misuse of information or through induced software misbehavior. Sensitive information such as passwords and crypto keys should be strictly used only by the designated codes rather than a third party software such as memory scan tools. Memory reference

226

manipulation through invalid input or buffer overflow are obviously abnormal information usage. Note that these kind of exploits cannot be prevented by a simple shutdown of all the output channels. In many cases, the victim software is supposed to disclose certain information. However, through maliciously induced changes on pointers or memory offset, other (sensitive) information is disclosed instead.

2.2 Assumption of Attack Models

Note that InfoShield is designed for an enterprise computing environment, where theft of sensitive user or system information through any attack is a major concern. However, our simple implementation is useful for any domain that has security concerns, such as consumer products. InfoShield is not for countering sophisticated physical or side-channel attacks that require a skill set that exploits bus traffic using a logic analyzer or oscilloscope. We assume that the computing platforms are physically secured. Furthermore, we are only concerned about certain critical information such as credit numbers, social security numbers, passwords, login accounts, encryption keys, etc. Protecting the usage of all data is often unnecessary and too costly. Also note that InfoShield assumes integrity protection on application code, namely, semantics of the application code cannot be arbitrarily changed. This assumption is in fact required by almost all the runtime based information security schemes including dynamic tracking of information flow [31] and proof carrying program execution [22, 23]. Simple solutions based on trusted computing systems such as LaGrande Technology can have programs signed or certificated. Integrity of the signed program code can be verified before it is executed and memory pages of the verified codes are marked write-protected. More rigorous protection on program integrity such as [9] can be also employed to prevent even runtime tampering with code integrity. Code signing itself does not provide protection for data privacy.

3. INFOSHIELD ARCHITECTURE

Under the concept of information usage safety, what can be disclosed or what can be shared is determined by the application and programmers. It is assumed that the program was properly written and audited, such that it shares or discloses only information that should be shared or disclosed. Then InfoShield enforces at runtime that sensitive information is used only in the way defined during program development.

3.1 Information usage safety

In this subsection, we compare the differences among several methods for information safety and address the necessity of information *usage* safety. As mentioned in Section 1, access control provides only a limited coarse-level data protection in memory. Attacks such as injected code, memory scan, or input manipulation cannot be prevented by simple user level or OS based access control. Another concept is *information flow safety* [1, 7, 10, 29]. According to this notion, information is labelled based on its privilege or security level, and an information flow tracking mechanism assures that privilege information does not flow to a channel with lower privilege or lower security levels. Information flow safety is a powerful concept but sometimes becomes too restrictive. For example, an encryption key is considered as a high security level item. Assuming that a user wants to send low privilege information, but prefers to have it encrypted first, then the encrypted data will carry information about the encryption key. The consequence is that the resulting encrypted information should also be considered as a high security and thus unsafe to be shared or disclosed. An alternative concept, called *computational safety* is used to address this problem. According to this concept, a piece of information (although carrying high privilege information) is considered safe to be disclosed if it is computationally infeasible to extract the

sensitive information from the disclosed data. Based on this concept, disclosing or sharing encrypted data is a safe operation if the encryption algorithm can ensure computational safety. Some efforts have been made in the past on finding a middle ground between these two concepts to avoid the problem of overprotection based on traditional information flow analysis [33, 17]. Table 1 summarizes the differences of the three information safety concepts.

However, information flow safety and information usage safety are complementary to each other since they address different aspects of information security. The former can be applied to decide what information is safe to be disclosed by program semantics, while the latter guarantees that no information misuse occurs according to the defined semantics. Note that there are many subtle differences between information flow and information usage. For example, a program may have two components, A and B, with each one disclosing a piece of information, a and b, at the same security level. According to information flow safety, A can also disclose information b. However, based on information usage safety, A cannot disclose b if this operation is not defined according to the program semantics. This prevents malicious exploits on pointers of A to make them point to b.

3.2 Protection on information usage

Here we present a protection scheme for information usage security that uses real-time authorization codes in the application. The necessary program alterations can be generated directly by a security enhanced compiler or by a separate information usage security analysis tool which does binary rewriting.

The basic idea of real-time protection of information usage are: 1) permission to use sensitive information is granted dynamically, exactly according to application semantics; 2) usage of information is dynamically verified to ensure that it conforms with the defined usage; 3) improper access attempts cannot compromise data confidentiality. Integrity of the application information usage is verified throughout the program execution. At the micro level, InfoShield guarantees that:

- Sensitive information is used only in the order defined by the application.
- Sensitive information is used only by the instructions that must use them.
- The user is assured that no misuse of information occurs if no exceptions are raised.

Our proposed implementation of InfoShield defines new architectural instructions for supporting information usage safety. These new operations combine regular access instructions with additional functionality for tracking security state. InfoShield will only protect usage of information in memory, which is sufficient for countering most of the exploits described in Section 2.

Conceptually, the implementation of information usage protection is simple. Consider a hypothetical example where an encryption key is created and then used. At the declaration of the encryption key or its pointer, the programmer annotates the source code that the contents of the key are sensitive. When the storage of the key is created, (e.g. by malloc), the compiler records the returned address with the annotation indicating that it is an address for sensitive data. Prior to passing the pointer to the surrounding code for proper handling, the compiler injects additional instructions to *guard* the data contents. In a separate hardware table, this address of the key is entered along with the PC of the *next* instruction that can access the contents of this address. Every load/store operation checks this table to ensure that no access occurs when the PC is not the designated next-access PC by the compiler. Such violations raise an exception bit for later handling.

Each attempt to use the sensitive information must come from an authorized instruction. Since each instruction authorizes the next in-

Information flow safety [1, 7]	Computational safety [33, 17]	Information usage safety (InfoShield)
The encrypted result is generated using a secret key. All the bits of encrypted result carry details of the key and are considered un-safe to be disclosed	The encrypted result is computationally safe to be disclosed. It is not feasible to extract the key from the encrypted data.	The encrypted result is safe to be disclosed if it is based on correct execution of the function and there is no misuse of the key.

Table 1: Comparison of Information Safety Models

struction dynamically and instruction memory is read-only, no violation can occur. Since every load/store operation must check the security address table, and only compile-time authorized instructions can read/write the data, all non-Trojan attacks are effectively blocked. The only vulnerability is the initial registration of an address to be guarded. However, any preemptive capture of the protected data location will either result in the proper guard instruction failing, or the proper guard instruction taking control over the next-authorized PC field. In either case, no violation of the security occurs such that sensitive information is revealed. The intricacies of handling function calls, register spills, garbage collection, and so forth are detailed later.

3.2.1 Instruction extensions

The security-aware instruction extensions we propose require a limited hardware support in the processor along the lines of a primitive cache or register file with CAM lookup capability as shown in Figure 1. Primarily, a structure that can be indexed like a register file for secure address testing is required. However, the address field in the structure must also be searchable like a CAM. While a full implementation is possible without this unit, performance would be substantially degraded. An overview of the instruction extensions is shown in Table 2, where the fields referenced are from Figure 1.

	Valid	VAddr_Low	VAddr_High	NextPC_Low	NextPC_High
SR_0					
SR_1					
SR_{N-1}					

Figure 1: Security-aware Register (SR) Hardware Table.

There are three principle design axioms that ensure correct operation with negligible performance impact: (a) each Security-Aware (SAx) operation is atomic; (b) programs, including the OS, are in read-only memory pages; and (c) while LD/ST operations may be common, LD/ST operations to sensitive data are rare. To walk through an example, Figure 2(a) is a simple C program snippet, with Figure 2(b) a pseudo-assembly listing for (a). An extension to gcc provides the "secure" attribute on line 1.

In the assembly listing, after the instruction at 0xA004 has executed, no interception of the protected data is possible. Any attempt to take control over a later instruction requires that no prior security aware instruction executed properly. Similarly, any attempt to divulge memory through stack or pointer manipulation will trigger an exception to the application.

Under InfoShield's threat model assumption, a hacker cannot directly modify the original software code (protected with code signing, runtime integrity check and execution only pages). But hackers can send invalid input or hijack control flow. All the SAx instructions of an application form a chain of information usage authorization. Protected sensitive data will not be disclosed through control hijack in the middle of the chain because it violates semantics of SAx instructions. A hacker may insert SAx instruction ahead of an SAx instruction chain. But those illegal SAx instructions will fail the first legitimate SAP instruction, thus no sensitive information will be revealed. Also note that applications always store sensitive data to a memory location after a SAP that declared that location. If a SAP instruction cannot find a matching entry in the SR table, it means that it is the first SAP instruction of a SAx instruction chain. In this case, the first SAP's PC is not checked.

```
                              .org    $0100
_attribute secure long long *key  0x0100  .word   key

                              .org    $1000
                      0x1000

key = malloc(sizeof(long long));  0xA000  call    _malloc        ; r1 = ptr
                      0xA004  add     r2, r1, #8      ;securing 8 bytes
                      0xA008  mov     r3, #0xB00C     ; start of next-valid PCs
                      0xA00C  mov     r4, #0xB014     ; end of next-valid PCs
                      0xA010  sag     r0              ; get next free security slot
                      0xA014  sap     r0, r1, r2, r3, r4  ; enable protection
                      0xA018  mov     r7, r1          ; r7 is the beginning of the
                                                      ; secure data
                      0xA01C  push    r0              ; save r0 for later

                      0xAFFC  pop     r0              ; recall our slot
*key = srand();       0xB000  call    _srand          ; r1 = random data
                      0xB004  mov     r2, #0xC008     ; start of next-valid PCs
                      0xB008  mov     r3, #0xC00C     ; end of next-valid PCs
                      0xB00C  st      r1, [r7]        ; write to the key slot
                      0xB010  sas     r0, r2, r3      ; slide protection window
                      0xB014  push    r0              ; save the slot

                      0xBFFC  pop     r0              ; recall our slot
                      0xC000  mov     r2, #0xD020     ; prepare next valid PC block
                      0xC004  mov     r3, #0xD0A0     ; big switch statement...
                      0xC008  ld      r1, [r7]        ; secure read key val
                      0xC00C  sas     r0, r2, r3      ; slide the protection window
                      0xC010  push    r0              ; save our slot
err = encrypt ( data, *key);  0xC014  call    encrypt         ; make call; r1 S bit set!
         (a)                                (b)
```

Figure 2: (a) Example of C program snippet (b) corresponding security aware assembly code.

3.2.2 Non-restrictive addressing

The security aware extensions (SAG, SAP, etc.) place no restrictions on addressing modes. In particular, there are no specific instructions to load or store data at protected addresses. This is achieved by checking *every* load/store operation against the protected addresses in the SR table by testing the effective (virtual) address. A mechanism for removing this check from the critical path is presented later.

The result of this model is that the security aware extension instructions only manipulate security information, and not data – with the exception of the SAM instruction. The need for the SAM instruction is presented in the garbage collection analysis below. Therefore, all of the standard memory addressing modes – direct, register offset, and so forth – work without modification. Only at retirement time will the security check results be used to accept or reject the results of any load/store operation.

3.2.3 Function calls

Protection of information usage across function calls is also supported. There are two basic methods for handling argument passing. If all programs (and programmers) adhere to a convention that only the address of a sensitive data location is passed as an argument, never the contents, then no further architectural support is necessary. However, considering the large volume of existing software passing arguments by registers for which simple recompilation will not repair, as well as the inability to ensure that programmers always follow safe practices, additional architectural changes will be needed to handle secure usage regardless of programmers' behavior.

First, we extend each register beyond its basic data and control state to include a security aware flag. The flag is an indicator that this specific register was read or written from a registered security aware region. Any other register derived from this register has its security

Instruction	Behavior	Purpose
SAG Rd Set Address Guard	$\exists\, n\ \&\ SR[n].Valid == 0 \Rightarrow$ $\quad RF[Rd] \leftarrow n$ $\quad SR[n].Valid \leftarrow 1$ else $CCR[SX] \leftarrow 1$	Get the first free SR table entry and return else throw an exception
SAP Rd, Ral, Rah, Rpl, Rph Set Address Protection	$\forall\, n,\ \exists\, m \in ((RF[Ral]..RF[Rah])$ $\quad ((SR[n].valid == 1)\ \&$ $\quad (SR[n].VAl \le m \le SR[n].VAhi)) \Rightarrow$ $\qquad Err \leftarrow Err\ |\ SR[RF[Rd]].Valid == 0\ |$ $\qquad \neg[(PC \ge SR[n].PClo)\ |\ (PC \le SR[n].PChi)]$ $CCR[SX] \leftarrow Err$ $SR[RF[Rd]].PClo \leftarrow RF[Rpl]$ $SR[RF[Rd]].PChi \leftarrow RF[Rph]$ $SR[RF[Rd]].Valid \leftarrow 1$ $SR[RF[Rd]].VAlo \leftarrow RF[Ral]$ $SR[RF[Rd]].VAhi \leftarrow RF[Rah]$	Verify that this PC is in the permitted group to setup target protection; if no Err, proceed to set up the valid code window that can access a memory block [Ral:Rah] and set the next-valid instruction PC range to [Rpl:Rph] in SR table
SAS Rd, Rpl, Rph Secure Address Shift	$Err \leftarrow (SR[RF[Rd]].Valid == 0)\ |$ $\quad (PC \le SR[RF[Rd]].PClo)\ |\ (PC \ge SR[Rf[Rd]].PChi)$ $CCR[SX] \leftarrow Err$ $SR[RF[Rd]].PClo \leftarrow RF[Rpl]$ $SR[RF[Rd]].PChi \leftarrow RF[Rph]$	Verify this PC can slide the next-instr window; if ok, set up the valid code window that can access a memory
SAC Rd, #const Secure Address Clear	$Err \leftarrow (SR[RF[Rd]].Valid == 0)\ |$ $\quad (PC \le SR[RF[Rd]].PClo)\ |\ (PC \ge SR[Rf[Rd]].PChi)$ $CCR[SX] \leftarrow Err$ $const == 0 \Rightarrow$ $\quad Mem[SR[RF[Rd]].VAlo..SR[RF[Rd]].VAhi] \leftarrow 0$ $SR[RF[Rd]].PClo \leftarrow 0$ $SR[RF[Rd]].PChi \leftarrow 0$ $SR[RF[Rd]].Valid \leftarrow 0$ $SR[RF[Rd]].VAlo \leftarrow 0$ $SR[RF[Rd]].VAhi \leftarrow 0$	Verify this PC can clear the protections; if ok, do we need to clean memory to prevent leaking of sensitive information? Clear out and free the corresponding entry in SR table, regardless.
SAM* Ras, Rae, Rad Secure Address Move	$\forall\, n,\ \exists\, m \in (RF[Ras]..RF[Rae])$ $\quad (SR[n].valid == 1\ \&\ SR[n].VAlo \le m \le SR[n].VAhi)) \Rightarrow$ $\qquad Err \leftarrow Err\ |\ (SR[n].VAlo \neq RF[Ras])\ |\ (SR[n].VAhi \neq RF[Rae])$ $CCR[SX] \leftarrow Err$ $\forall\, n,\ SR[n].VAlo == RF[Ras] \Rightarrow$ $\quad SR[n].VAhi \leftarrow RF[Rad] + SR[n].VAhi - SR[n].VAlo$ $\quad SR[n].VAlo \leftarrow RF[Rad]$ $\forall\, addr \in [RF[Ras]..RF[Rae]] \Rightarrow$ $\quad Mem[RF[Rad] + (addr - RF[Ras])] \leftarrow Mem[addr]$ $\quad Mem[addr] \leftarrow 0$	Over the start-end source range, be sure it's a perfect match, otherwise throw an exception; for every range match, fix the guard to point to the new addr block for post-move security and then set up the actual Moving protected data, erasing the source

Table 2: Security Aware instruction extensions (*SAx*) that manipulate the SR table. *PC* is the PC of the currently executing instruction. If no error is encountered, the actual instruction behavior is then executed. *RF* denotes the main register file and *Mem* is memory, while *SR* is the security register set and the *CCR* is the condition-code register with the *SX* bit corresponding to a security exception condition, causing a fault. The $\forall$ searching nature suggests the use of CAM cells for the given field in the SR table. *This instruction is only executable from super-user mode (i.e., typically via a kernel syscall).

bits set accordingly (i.e., any xor, add, shift, etc. that uses a "secure" register value automatically becomes "secure" flagged). Any attempt to execute a load/store operation on any register which is annotated as secure enabled requires the same authorization step – namely, passing the security check from the SR table. If this security check fails, then the contents must be encrypted prior to writing to memory.

3.2.4 Register spills, Page tables

One drawback to the enhancement in the register file is the inability for backing up and restoring secure-aware flag during register spills. This is handled by exploitation of the ECC memory bits [25]. The ECC memory bits, which are typically unused, provide approximately one extra bit per machine word. With registers marked "secure", the only way to preserve the integrity of sensitive information is to encrypt the store to memory. However, the encryption process cannot expand the machine word via padding or other methods. Therefore, we propose to use the ECC bit corresponding to each machine word as an *encrypted data* flag. When storing to memory from a secure register to an insecure location, the contents are encrypted with a key embedded in the processor. There may be several such keys used on a random basis to reduce the chance of brute-force attacks. Regardless, during write-out the ECC bit is set. When that memory location is read back, the ECC bit indicates that the contents need to be decrypted *and* that the secure bit in the register file should be set. Otherwise any load from a non-secure memory location resets the security bit in the register file for the destination register.

The exploitation of ECC bits, however, gives rise to the problem of page tables and swapping to disk. In general, the practice of swapping secure or encrypted information to disk should not be encouraged. In the specifics of our InfoShield system, we require that any page that contains secure or ECC-flagged encrypted data must be pinned in memory. Therefore, it cannot be swapped to disk to risk sensitive information disclosure or the loss of the ECC encryption bits that indicate scrambled memory contents.

By presenting an argument where encryption exists internal to the processor, a strong question is whether just encrypting all sensitive data is sufficient without our proposed architectural changes. In reality, just encrypting memory in this manner is vulnerable to a brute force attack, since the contents of memory can still be read. With the restrictions on padding, brute force attacks are possible. Our solution, however, prevents the attacker from even reading the contents of secure memory from the running process, which eliminates the brute force approach. Compromising another process and reading this processes memory is of little use since any other process will not know which memory is encrypted and which memory is not.

3.2.5 Garbage Collection and Block Copy

Many modern languages, as well as older languages with support libraries, provide garbage collection systems. Garbage collection (GC) violates the abstractions introduced here to protect sensitive memory.

By nature, GC tries to walk through all of dynamic memory to facilitate compaction and freeing of bulk heap space. However, with no *a priori* knowledge, GC systems will inadvertently attempt to access or move protected memory, causing security exceptions.

Our solution is via a privileged security-aware *move* instruction (SAM in Table 2). This instruction is capable of moving the contents of protected memory, but is unable to return the contents of protected memory or to alter the next-authorized instruction windows. Its purpose is primarily to support GC algorithms of any type. A typical GC that runs on a security aware platform would have to implement exception handlers to catch security violations (i.e., via *sigaction()* and friends). During GC data movement, any movement that causes the security exception to be returned turns into an iterative per-word movement until the protection region is found and the complete protected region size is determined. Once found, a syscall is made to the OS to request privileged movement of the sensitive data from the old to new address. This movement does alter and update the address range in the SR table, yet it does not impact the authorized PC in the application. While our solution does require minor modifications to any general GC implementation, once implemented it will work for all programs. The same technique is also applicable to secure block copy operations using library routines such as *memcpy()*.

On those architectures supporting complex memory-to-memory copy operations, such as a *string copy or "movs" instruction* in x86, the principle is similar. Such CISC instructions are actually decoded into a series of *μops* to set up a loop and execute individual load/store operations. If any *μop* load/store fails due to a security violation, the re-order buffer is tagged as receiving the security exception for the original *movs* instruction. This in turn can be caught by signal handlers which switch from *movs* to the iterative block copy routines.

3.2.6   Multiple consumers or producers

Certain coding constructions such as virtual tables, switch statements, and function pointer lookups create scenarios where there may exist multiple valid next-target PCs. Even simple code hammocks may try to access sensitive data or create sensitive container in each path, requiring some mechanism for support.

First, we support defining of regions that cover instructions which may access sensitive data. Rather than have several entries, we can define a large window of code that continually operates on sensitive data, when the sensitive information is first put under *guard* a first-next-PC and a last-next-PC may be specified. Second, we support multiple entries in the SR table for a given sensitive address. That is, if address 0xA000 is protected, multiple *SAP* entries may have this address for different consumers of the data. That we support this repetition in the secure register table is the reason the "for all"(∀) constructs exist in Table 2 security extension instructions. In particular, any instruction attempting to register *additional* next-valid PCs must be itself authorized.

3.2.7   Context switching

A potential issue for any security method that uses write-only architectural state as our SR table is handling a context switch. Since no instruction is capable of reading the contents of any SR register field, support for context switching must be moved into the necessary supporting instructions. We expect that every process has a private process space in memory for storing context information. If a unique key exists inside each system, then the hardware may write the SR table to the process space in memory encrypted with the secure key. No additional overhead or management by the OS is required. Since the addresses in the SR table are all virtual, no side effects of operations such as page table modification will impact the security features.

3.2.8   Dynamic or shared libraries

Verification of secure information usage across dynamic libraries

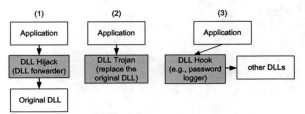

Figure 3: Trojan DLL

is not trivial, since frequently the caller has no precise knowledge of the callee code that will use sensitive information. To make things even worse, systems such as Windows use DLLs heavily for normal execution of applications. This allows third-party DLLs to be inserted or hooked into an application program that can intercept and detect messages communicated between applications and libraries, as well as between different libraries [12]. The types of information that can be intercepted include passwords, account ids, keystrokes, and so forth.

Figure 3 shows three ways of exploiting a typical Windows DLL vulnerability for information theft. First, a malicious DLL that has the same name as a legitimate DLL (such as *wsock32.dll*, the Windows system DLL responsible for network connections) can be injected into user or kernel space. The malicious DLL exports all the symbols of the original DLL and hijacks all calls to the original DLL. It intercepts sensitive information from a hijack before delegating the call to the original DLL function. For example, a worm can install a malicious *wsock32.dll* and rename the original as something else. Then each time after the system is booted, network applications such as IE will call the malicious wsock32 for transmitting passwords, username, credit card numbers, etc. The hijack DLL can examine the data before forwarding them to the original DLL. If sensitive information is found, it may mail it out to an outside email account. Second, an information stealing Trojan can replace or patch the original DLL. The new DLL contains malicious code that can disclose sensitive data to outside world. Examples of such attacks are socket Trojans such as Happy 99 [27] and Hybris [27]. Third, Windows allows arbitrary DLLs to be hooked into an application's memory space [12]. Any malicious DLL downloaded either by an Internet worm or unwillingly invited to the system as a Trojan horse can be hooked into an application's memory space. This DLL will register a callback function for handling sensitive user information. Many password stealing or keyboard input logger trojans are based on the vulnerability of Windows hooks [8].

InfoShield tackles this issue through a sequenced signature verification, which relies on a safe signing/certification of libraries with versioning. During application development, calls to external libraries are annotated with a required library version and the library public key in use at compile-time. This signature and version information is embedded in the application image. During the initialization of the *main()* sequence, all required external libraries are pre-loaded and their OS fingerprints are checked. This process involves the operating system loading and verifying the internal signature of the library, ensuring that no tampering has taken place from what the original developer provided for certification. This OS fingerprint is followed by verifying the developer signature on the library code with the applications' embedded public key.

Within any DLL that manipulates sensitive information, protection is enforced by a *policy* of secure instruction placement within the DLL function body. This policy can easily be enforced by the compilers. The premise to the policy is that as versions of a DLL change, there is no safe *a priori* method for knowing *which* instruction within a DLL function foo will be the first to require security permissions. Therefore, on entry any function that will manipulate sensitive data

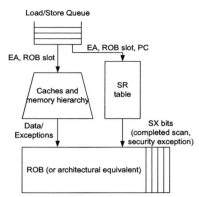

Figure 4: Decoupling SR table check and lazy update of ROB.

must execute as its first instruction the necessary setup for the secure permissions within the body of that function. Therefore, even if the first working instruction that uses sensitive data is moved to a new address during version changes, the external program is unaware and the system operates normally.

Given the condition that DLLs or other shared libraries are signed and certified, applications can seal sensitive data based on the signature/certificate. This simple solution prevents almost all variants of the three exploit scenarios using Trojan or malicious library hooks. For DLL hijacking, the internal application version signatures will fail to match resulting in aborted execution. In the case of DLL replacement, the malicious code module will have a different signature, thus it cannot properly unseal the information since each signature generates a unique key. The third scenario of DLL hooks can also be prevented in a manner similar to the case of DLL hijack.

3.2.9   Critical Path

One potential performance downside in InfoShield is caused by the fact that every load/store operation must check the SR table. This is likely to become the critical path in the memory pipeline. We propose to decouple the SR table check such that it is off the critical path entirely, with the SR check results pushed into the reorder buffer for evaluation at retirement.

Our proposed change is shown in Figure 4. As effective addresses (EAs) are moved into the memory hierarchy for access, the EA and its associated PC (along with the ROB target) are also passed to the SR table. Once the pipelined SR lookup resolves whether the access is valid, it updates the two *SX* bits in the reorder buffer to indicate that checking is complete (bit 0), and whether an exception was generated (bit 1). During retirement, any incidence of a violation in the SX bit causes a fault to be generated. This can then be handled by the OS, or passed to the user for signal handling.

4.   SECURITY ASSESSMENT AND LIMITATION

InfoShield is a novel scheme for protecting usage of sensitive data against local and remote software exploits. It is aimed to counter realistic attacks on disclosing sensitive user or system information through: 1) direct or covert memory scan by malware [15]; 2) invalid input to an application or function call (CAN-2004-0415, CAN-2004-0535, GENERIC-MAP-NOMATCH) [20]; 3) buffer overrun based information theft (CAN-2004-0165)[20], or 4) malicious DLL hooks or API hijacking Trojan [8, 32, 27].

Using special dynamic protection on information usage, InfoShield can enhance the assurance that sensitive data is used, shared or disclosed in the way as defined by application semantics. InfoShield improves protection on data privacy against many documented attacks,

exploits or vulnerabilities. One advantage of InfoShield is that it is compatible with the current software system model. It supports programs or libraries from different sources (sometimes un-trusted) to inter-operate and co-exist in the same memory space. More importantly, InfoShield does not require that every program component in an application's memory space must be benign, exploit-free or bug-free. However, InfoShield does not prevent all the possible attacks or exploits on data privacy, especially information theft using sophisticated physical attacks. Specifically, InfoShield protects sensitive information stored in the memory from

- theft through memory scan
- leakage through function call interception
- unwanted disclosure via hacker induced pointer/index overflow

In reality, there is no silver bullet for solving all the data privacy issues and exploits. It is preferred that a combination of many techniques such as a firewall, safe programming, or information flow analysis with InfoShield be used to prevent cyber theft. Furthermore, InfoShield assumes separate protection on program integrity. It requires that code image is properly signed with digital signature and certified. Given a program that is properly designed, InfoShield ensures that during execution there is no misuse or abnormal use of information caused by many real local or remote exploits. When a process finishes using sensitive data, InfoShield's *erase* operation resets the memory state preventing accidental leakage [3]. The OS can also ensure that memory pages allocated to a user process are properly cleared. InfoShield also assumes that applications are executed in released mode instead of debug mode. Debug mode execution often needs random access to memory that would require break of InfoShield protection. To prevent production application from being executed in debug mode, we extend the signed code image with a special debug mode disable flag. For released software, this flag is set. Since the code image is signed and certified, it is not possible to wiggle the flag without being detected.

5.   EVALUATION AND ANALYSIS

To evaluate the idea of information usage protection and the specifics of InfoShield design, we used a number of network applications that manipulate sensitive user data such as a login password, cryptographic keys, or other credentials. A straightforward implementation of InfoShield can be achieved by extending the ISA and adding necessary compiler support. For evaluation purpose, we manually identify sensitive data based on the application source and annotate the application for emulation-based evaluation. We used a open-source IA32 full system emulator — Bochs [14] which models the entire platform including the network device, VGA monitor, and other devices to support the execution of a complete off-the-shelf OS and its applications. We use the memory tainting technique similar to that in [3]. Different from the objective of [3]'s study that focused on proper cleanses of sensitive information after their lifetime, we focus on the guarantee of proper usage of sensitive data during their lifetime.

We used RedHat distribution of Linux as our target system. We evaluated eight network server/client applications. They are file transfer server (wu-ftp daemon), web server (Apache http daemon), email sever (imap daemon), ftp client, a text based web browser called Lynx, an email client Pine, Openssh daemon (sshd) and Openssh based secure file transfer server (sftp). We manually annotated each application's source code such that sensitive data "live ranges" are explicitly exposed to the Bochs emulator. The implementation is similar to the memory tainting technique in [3]. In addition to memory tainting, we also applied register tainting that keeps track of instructions operating on sensitive data.

5.1   Sensitive Information and Usage Protection

For all the eight applications, we identified the global and local variables for storing the sensitive information and the program codes that operate on the information. To avoid unnecessary over-protection, we consider only the following information as critical sensitive data that requires InfoShield protection,

5.1.1 User password

All Unix and Linux applications use the well-known shadow password authentication approach. On the server side, user passwords are stored in an encrypted format or cryptographically encoded format. This is done by invoking *crypt* function with the input text set to NULL and the key set to be the password. Crypt is a one way hash function. This is an algorithm that is easy to compute in one direction, but very difficult, if not impossible, to calculate in the reverse direction. When a user picks a password, it is cryptographically encoded with crypt along with a salt value. Note that salt itself is not sensitive data. The result, i.e. shadow password, is stored in the hard disk. When a user logs in and supplies a password, the supplied password is cryptographically encoded and then compared with the encoded shadow password loaded from disk. If there is a match, then the user is authenticated. During the authentication process, user's password will reside in the server's memory space and vulnerable to memory scan, pointer overflow, or crypt function interception attacks. We can use InfoShield to ensure that during user password's lifetime, it is only used by the proper authentication routines as defined by the program semantics. Applications can declare the password's memory space as sensitive after it is first time loaded into memory.

5.1.2 Openssh host key

Openssh uses the well-known asymmetric key approach for user authentication. For each server, there is at least a pair of private and public keys. In general, only the private key is considered as sensitive and requires protection. In Openssh implementation, private keys are stored in a global data structure called "sensitive data". Openssh memsets sensitive data to zero after they are no longer needed. To protect private keys from theft during its lifetime, we declare their memory space as sensitive data and apply InfoShield protection. It ensures that only the private key authentication routine can access those keys in the way as defined by the authentication semantics.

5.1.3 AES cryptographic keys

For each data channel, Openssh uses AES standard for encryption and decryption. For each new connection, Openssh daemon will spawn a new child process. The AES keys are stored in each child process's memory space and used for network data encryption/decryption. The AES key's lifetime spans from the beginning to the end of a connection. During this time, it is vulnerable to attacks such as memory scan and invalid pointer/array index exploits. In our evaluation, we declared AES keys as sensitive information. The requirement is that they can only be used by the AES encryption/decryption routines based on the AES implementation. Any other access including access from other part of the Openssh daemon is considered as a protection violation of InfoShield.

Note that we only treat the original password and cryptographic key as sensitive information. Password digests or encrypted passwords or encrypted keys are not considered as sensitive data. In real systems, password digests or encrypted passwords are not treated as secrets and often stored in files that allow public access.

5.2 Analysis of Performance Impact

The performance impact of InfoShield on application execution is very small given that comparing with the whole application, the amount of data and code that handles passwords, cryptographic keys or other sensitive data is small. To verify this projection, we used the memory tainting technique that keeps track how sensitive data is ac-

cessed during its lifetime. The goal is to show that the overall number of memory accesses to the sensitive data and the total number of instructions directly operating on the sensitive data during any sensitive lifetime are both negligible.

In our evaluation, all the applications are tested in real-time with Bochs emulation. We used automatic scripts whenever possible or manual interaction. For OpenSSH, the test consists of connecting to the server, login with authentication, and run a list of popular shell commands. To simulate an ssh server scenario, the test included four concurrent ssh connections. For sftp, the test consists of connecting to the server with authentication, upload and download a set of files. To simulate a server setting, the test used six concurrent sftp connections. Test of wu-ftp server was similar to the sftp test case except it used wu-ftp server instead of the OpenSSH ftp server. For Apache, the Bochs emulated server hosts a website where access to the webpages requires proper user authentication. The test uses wget, a popular command line web page download tool. It automatically supplies download requests with user password and recursively downloads all the web pages from an URL. For imap server (an email server), the test consists of running a python script that automatically connects to the server as a user with password, and retrieves all the emails. For ftp client, the test is similar to the ftp server test with the difference that the client not the server is executed in the emulated platform. Both Pine and Lynx are client applications that require user interaction. Test of Pine consists of connecting to a mail server, supplying password and reading received emails. Test of Lynx consists of connecting to a web server, browsing some webpages that require user authentication. The middle column of Table 3 shows the number of profiled instructions for each application.

Applications	Instruction Count	Sensitive memory blocks required per process
OpenSSH	887803740	18
sftp	1430629493	18
httpd (Apache)	809343773	1
ftpd	575053604	1
imapd	795433147	1
ftp	564446668	1
Pine	656122506	1
Lynx	1189131107	1

Table 3: Dynamic Instruction Count and Sensitive Memory Blocks

With the Bochs emulator, we are able to measure the percentage of accesses to the sensitive information comparing with the total number of regular memory accesses. Figure 5 shows the results. For five of the eight tested applications (ftpd, imapd, ftp client, Pine, and Lynx), the percentage is less than 0.002%. For OpenSSH, the percentage is 0.1% and for sftp, 0.6%. Apache has the highest percentage of 1.8%. One of the contributing factors why Apache has so many accesses than others is that Apache verifies password for each file downloaded from a server. Typically, one webpage may contain hundreds of small files. This leads to frequent access to user password. OpenSSH applications have more frequent access due to the reasons that they use AES to encrypt/decrypt every network packet. The average is 0.3%.

Figure 6 shows the percentage of dynamic instructions that directly operate on sensitive information (load instruction included). For all the tested applications, the percentage is below 1%. For some applications, the number is below 0.001%. The average is 0.2%.

Results in Figure 5 and Figure 6 show that for typical applications, the amount of memory reads and dynamic instructions dealing with sensitive information are both very small. Since InfoShield has performance impact only on the part of application codes that handle sensitive information, its overall performance impact would be very small.

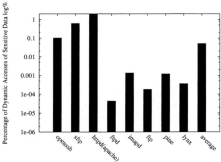

Figure 5: Percentage of accesses to passwords and keys over all memory accesses (log scale of % data).

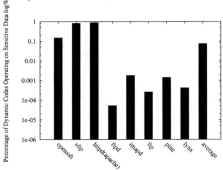

Figure 6: Percentage of dynamic instructions directly operating on sensitive information (log scale of % data).

For all the tested server applications, for each new connection, the server process will spawn a new child process for processing the new connection. The number of sensitive data regions is really small if considered at per-process basis. For shadow password authentication, the number is one (region where plaintext user password is stored). For OpenSSH, the number is six per process. Based on the test result, increasing the number of concurrent connections does not affect the number of sensitive data regions per process as each new connection is handled by a separate child process.

5.3 Sizing the Security Register Table

To determine the number of slots required in the SR Table, as outlined in Section 3.2.1, the same benchmarks were evaluated for their unique contiguous regions of memory that contain sensitive information. The result of this analysis is shown in the third column of Table 3. They suggest that the SR table itself can be kept quite small, less than 32 entries even for complex applications. These values represent the secure regions over the complete dynamic lifetime of an application, and do no consider that not all regions may be active at the same phase of execution. The small requirements for the table also result in faster access and lower power dissipation.

6. RELATED WORK

There are many approaches proposed before to address the protection of information privacy using either software or hardware mechanisms. InfoShield, however, is the first one as to our knowledge that protects dynamic usage of information according to program semantics.

6.1 Proof carrying code

Proof carrying code is a concept that users of a program can verify the safety of a program provided by an untrusted source. Using formal methods and first order logic, the program carries with itself a proof that it will abide with certain clearly-defined safety policies

of the user. The proof can be verified by the user before execution. If the proof can be verified, the user can be convinced that the program is safe to be executed [22]. Proof carrying code has been extensively studied for mobile code security where producers of mobile code provide proofs and consumers of mobile code validates the proof. However, writing proof carrying code program is a daunting task for regular programmers as it requires understanding of formal logic and safety theorem proving. Another issue is that it is not clear whether the proof system is powerful enough to capture all the security constraints of a software system. In contrast, information usage safety is a much simpler concept and protection of information usage as proposed in this paper can be fully automated.

6.2 Information flow analysis

Information flow analysis is a language based technique that addresses the concern on data privacy by clarifying conditions when flow of information is safe. Through information flow analysis [7, 29], it can be enforced that high privilege and high security level information would not flow to channels with low privilege or low security level. Information flow based protection constraints unsafe flow of information. Recently, dynamic tracking of information flow for protecting data privacy using hardware approach is also proposed to confine flow of information in execution time [31]. As we have addressed before, there are many differences between the concept of information flow safety and information usage safety. Unlike information flow safety, information usage safety itself does not restrict sharing and disclosing of information as long as such operations are carried out according to program semantic.

6.3 Safe language based protection

Another language based effort to secure data privacy is strongly typed language that ensures type safe access of private information [13]. For example, a type safe language defines what operations a piece of code can perform on objects or data of a particular type. Type safety can be either enforced statically such as Java or dynamically at run-time. Information usage safety and InfoShield are different from language type safety based protection. Information usage as proposed provides more protection on information because it restricts that the protected information be only used in a specific manner while type safety only ensures that the information is operated by operations that can access the type of data.

6.4 Static language based checks

There are compiler and programming language based techniques that automatically check buffer overflow or memory reference bugs in application source code [5, 4]. Those techniques can mitigate some of the risks of disclosing sensitive data by ensuring that the applications satisfy certain safety standards. However, different from *InfoShield*, they cannot provide real-time safeguard on the access and usage of information.

6.5 Memory reference monitor and Mondrian

Hardware based memory protections such as virtual memory protection, user/supervisor execution levels, process memory space isolation and etc are based on checking the privilege of addresses issued by executing instructions to the memory. As we have addressed, these protections provide only very coarse level protection on memory and they cannot prevent exploits using malicious code residing in the same memory space as the application or exploits that induce misbehavior of the application to disclose sensitive information. Mondrian is a hardware architecture motivated to provide fine-grained access control on memory at small granularity such as word level [34]. The memory state of InfoShield is also fine-grained with each 32-bit dword having its own state. In this aspect, it is similar to Mondrian. But the similarity ends here. Mondrian is not designed to handle many of the exploits or vulnerabilities on data privacy mentioned in this paper.

6.6 Hydra

Hydra [18] was one early object-oriented capability-based system which separated access control mechanism from security policy. Follow up operating system such as KeyKOS [24] also used similar idea of capability. A capability is a token that designates an object and indicates a specific set of authorized actions (such as reading or writing) on that object. Every object in the system was protected and any access required capabilities. InfoShield is very different from Hydra-like capability-based systems. First, Hydra-like systems divide everything into objects and enforce access control on every objects which lead to a system that is too general and complex. InfoShield is a simple and efficient mechanism which only aims to protect critical information in memory. Second, Hydra-like systems only care about the access control of objects, it cannot enforce proper sequences of information usage according to the program definition or semantic in real execution time.

6.7 Tamper resistant systems

Tamper resistant systems using memory encryption [19, 30] are related in the sense that tamper resistant systems also provide data privacy by storing encrypted data in memory. There are many fundamental differences between InfoShield and tamper resistant systems. First, InfoShield is designed for protecting data privacy against many software based exploits and vulnerability without using memory encryption. Overhead of InfoShield is much smaller than [19, 30]. Second, InfoShield enforces information usage safety (information used exactly the way as defined by application) while current tamper resistant systems do not have this notion. It is believed that tamper resistant systems are also vulnerable to exploits of pointer references, array indexes. Also it is not clear how tamper resistant system based software platform supports DLL hooks and tackles trojan horse injection. InfoShield solves these issues without the assumption of memory encryption.

7. CONCLUSION

This paper presents *InfoShield* that provides architectural and programming support to protect usage of sensitive information against many documented attacks and exploits on data privacy including memory scan, pointer/array index manipulation, integer overflow, format string attacks, and password-stealing trojans. By embedding specialized verification and tracking instructions inside the applications, InfoShield is capable of ensuring that secrets such as passwords and access credentials are accessed only in the way as defined by the given application. Such authenticated information usage provides a safer environment for network applications where disclosure of sensitive information due to remote or local software exploits is a major concern. Comparing with prior works on protection of data privacy, InfoShield is a much light-weight alternative and would incur much less performance penalty based on application profiling.

8. ACKNOWLEDGMENT

This work is supported in part by NSF grants CCF-0326396, CCF-0447934, CCF-0430021, CNS-0325536, and a DOE Early CAREER Award.

9. REFERENCES

[1] M. Abadi, A. Banerjee, N. Heintze, and J. G. Riecke. A Core Calculus of Dependency. In *Proceedings of the ACM Symposium on Principles of Programming Languages*, 1999.

[2] Aleph One. Smashing the stack for fun and profit. *Phrack*, 7(49), November 1996.

[3] J. Chow, B. Pfaff, T. Garfinkel, K. Christopher, and M. Rosenblum. Understanding Data Lifetime via Whole System Simulation. In *USENIX Security Symposium*, 2004.

[4] C. Cowan, M. Barringer, S. Beattie, and G. Kroah-Hartman. FormatGuard: Automatic Protection From printf Format String Vulnerabilities. In *USENIX Security Symposium*, 2001.

[5] C. Cowan, C. Pu, D. Maier, H. Hinton, J. Walpole, P. Bakke, S. Beattie, A. Grier, P. Wagle, and Q. Zhang. StackGuard: Automatic Adaptive Detection and Prevention of Buffer-Overflow Attacks. In *USENIX Security Symposium*, 1998.

[6] CyberCrime. http://www.ssg-inc.net/cyber_crime/cyber_crime.html.

[7] D. E. Denning and P. J. Denning. Certification of programs for secure information flow. *Commun. ACM*, 20(7):504–513, 1977.

[8] B. Friesen. Passwordspy - retrieving lost passwords using windows hooks. *http://www.codeproject.com/*.

[9] B. Gassend, G. E. Suh, D. Clarke, M. van Dijk, and S. Devadas. Caches and Hash Trees for Efficient Memory Integrity Verification. In *Proceedings of the Ninth Annual Symposium on High Performance Computer Architecture*, 2003.

[10] N. Heintze and J. G. Riecke. The SLam calculus: programming with secrecy and integrity. In *Proceedings of the ACM Symposium on Principles of Programming Languages*, 1998.

[11] iDefense. http://www.idefense.com/advisory/01.28.03.txt.

[12] I. Ivanov. Api hooking revealed. *http://www.codeproject.com/*.

[13] A. K. Jones and B. H. Liskov. A language extension for expressing constraints on data access. *Commun. ACM*, 21(5):358–367, 1978.

[14] K. Lawton. Welcome to the Bochs x86 PC Emulation Software Home Page. http://www.bochs.com.

[15] A. Kumar. Discovering passwords in the memory. *http://www.infosecwriters.com/text_resources/*, 2004.

[16] D. Larochelle and D. Evans. Statically Detecting Likely Buffer Overflow Vulnerabilities. In *USENIX Security Symposium*, 2001.

[17] P. Laud. Semantics and Program Analysis of Computationally Secure Information Flow. In *Proceedings of the 10th European Symposium on Programming Languages and Systems*, 2001.

[18] R. Levin, E. Cohen, W. Corwin, and W. Wulf. Policy/mechanism Separation in Hydra. In *Proceedings of the ACM Symposium on Operating Systems Principles*, 1975.

[19] D. Lie, C. Thekkath, M. Mitchell, P. Lincoln, D. B. J. Mitchell, and M. Horowitz. Architectual support for copy and tamper resistant software. In *Proceedings of the 9th Symposium on Architectural Support for Programming Languages and Operating Systems*, 2000.

[20] MITRE. http://cve.mitre.org/.

[21] A. C. Myers and B. Liskov. Protecting privacy using the decentralized label model. *ACM Trans. Softw. Eng. Methodol.*, 9(4):410–442, 2000.

[22] G. C. Necula. Proof-carrying code. In *Proceedings of the 24th ACM SIGPLAN-SIGACT symposium on Principles of programming languages*, pages 106–119. ACM Press, 1997.

[23] G. C. Necula and P. Lee. Efficient representation and validation of proofs. In *Proceedings of the 13th Annual IEEE Symposium on Logic in Computer Science*, 1998.

[24] N.Hardy. The keykos architecture. In *Operating Systems Review*, 1985.

[25] F. Qin, S. Lu, and Y. Zhou. SafeMem: Exploiting ECC-Memory for Detecting Memory Leaks and Memory Corruption During Production Runs. In *International Symposium on High-Performance Computer Architecture*, 2005.

[26] Scut. Exploiting format string vulnerabilities. 2001.

[27] SecurityResponse. http://securityresponse.symantec.com/.

[28] A. Shamir and N. van Someren. Playing hide and seek with stored keys.

[29] G. Smith and D. Volpano. Secure Information Flow in a Multi-threaded Imperative Language. In *Proceedings of the Symposium on Principles of Programming Languages*, 1998.

[30] E. G. Suh, D. Clarke, M. van Dijk, B. Gassend, and S.Devadas. AEGIS: Architecture for Tamper-Evident and Tamper-Resistant Processing . In *Proceedings of The Int'l Conference on Supercomputing*, 2003.

[31] N. Vachharajani, M. J. Bridges, J. Chang, R. Rangan, G. Ottoni, J. A. Blome, G. A. Reis, M. Vachharajani, and D. I. August. RIFLE: An Architectural Framework for User-Centric Information-Flow Security. In *Proceedings of the 37th International Symposium on Microarchitecture*, 2004.

[32] VirusLibarary. http://www.viruslibrary.com/.

[33] D. Volpano and G. Smith. Verifying Secrets and Relative Secrecy. In *Proceedings of the Symposium on Principles of Programming Languages*, 2000.

[34] E. Witchel, J. Cates, and K. Asanovic. Mondrian Memory Protection. In *Proceedings of the Int'l Conf. on Architectural Support for Programming Languages and Operating Systems*, 2002.

[35] www.ncipher.com.

Session 9:
Hardware/Software Tradeoffs

CORD: Cost-effective (and nearly overhead-free) Order-Recording and Data race detection *

Milos Prvulovic

Georgia Institute of Technology

http://www.cc.gatech.edu/~milos

Abstract

Chip-multiprocessors are becoming the dominant vehicle for general-purpose processing, and parallel software will be needed to effectively utilize them. This parallel software is notoriously prone to synchronization bugs, which are often difficult to detect and repeat for debugging. While data race detection and order-recording for deterministic replay are useful in debugging such problems, only order-recording schemes are lightweight, whereas data race detection support scales poorly and degrades performance significantly.

This paper presents our CORD (Cost-effective Order-Recording and Data race detection) mechanism. It is similar in cost to prior order-recording mechanisms, but costs considerably less then prior schemes for data race detection. CORD also has a negligible performance overhead (0.4% on average) and detects most dynamic manifestations of synchronization problems (77% on average). Overall, CORD is fast enough to run always (even in performance-sensitive production runs) and provides the support programmers need to deal with the complexities of writing, debugging, and maintaining parallel software for future multi-threaded and multi-core machines.

1. Introduction

In the near future, multi-threaded and multi-core processors will become the dominant platform for general-purpose processing, and parallel software will be needed to effectively utilize them. Unfortunately, non-deterministic ordering of memory accesses across threads makes parallel software notoriously difficult to write and debug. This non-determinism can be intentional or unintentional. Intentional non-determinism increases parallelism, e.g. when threads are allowed to go through a critical section as they arrive, instead of forcing them to enter in a pre-determined order. Unintentional non-determinism is manifested through data races, typically due to missing or incorrect synchronization, and may cause a wide variety of incorrect program behavior. Both kinds of non-determinism make errors difficult to repeat for debugging. Additionally, unintentional non-

---

*This work was supported, in part, by the National Science Foundation under Grant Number CCF-0447783. Any opinions, findings, and conclusions or recommendations expressed in this material are those of the author and do not necessarily reflect the views of the National Science Foundation.

determinism can be manifested only intermittently and be very difficult to detect.

To repeat execution for debugging, the system must record outcomes of races (both intentional and unintentional) that determine the actual execution order at runtime. When a bug is detected, *deterministic replay* for debugging is achieved by replaying these race outcomes. For readability, *order-recording* will be used to refer to the activity of recording race outcomes for later deterministic replay. Note that order-recording proceeds together with normal application execution, while replay occurs only when a bug is found. Typical program execution (especially in production runs) is mostly bug-free, so recording efficiency is a priority.

A runtime manifestation of a synchronization problem can be detected by discovering at least one data race caused by that problem. Data races are conflicting memory accesses [22] whose order is not determined by synchronization [15]. Following this definition, a data race detector tracks synchronization-induced ordering during program execution, monitors conflicting data (non-synchronization) accesses, and finds a data race when conflicting data accesses are unordered according to the already observed synchronization order. Like order-recording, data race detection (DRD) proceeds together with normal application execution, so it should have a low performance overhead and avoid detection of false problems.

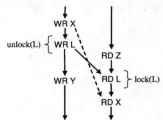

Figure 1. Example execution ordering.

The exact runtime ordering in an execution of a multi-threaded program defines a *happens-before* [11] relationship among memory access events in that execution. For two conflicting memory accesses A and B, either A happens before B ($A \rightarrow B$) or B happens before A ($B \rightarrow A$). Non-conflicting accesses can be concurrent (unordered), or they can be ordered transitively through program order and ordering of conflicting accesses. For example, a two-thread execution is shown in Figure 1. Vertical arrows represent program order within each thread, while diagonal arrows represent ordering of cross-thread conflicts. In this example, WR X → WR L due to program order, WR L → RD L due to a race outcome, transitivity results in WR X → RD L, and WR Y and RD X are concurrent. Note that WR X → RD X is a conflict outcome, but this order is also due to transitivity.

For deterministic replay of this example, only WR L → RD L needs to be recorded, because enforcement of that order also repeats the order of WR X and RD X. However, replay is correct if WR X → RD X is also recorded. Recording either WR Y → RD X or RD X → WR Y (but not both) is also consistent with correct replay, although the accesses are actually concurrent. In fact, replay is correct even if we record WR L → RD Z and then omit the actual race outcome WR L → RD L as redundant. In general, an order-recording mechanism must record a consistent ordering (no cycles) that implies actual race outcomes, but need not precisely detect which accesses conflict or which conflicts are races – when in doubt, any pair of accesses can be treated as a race and its outcome recorded.

Data race detection (DRD) for execution in Figure 1 requires knowledge of which memory accesses are synchronization accesses and which are data accesses. Such knowledge can be obtained, for example, by marking synchronization load/store instructions in synchronization primitives (e.g. *lock*, *unlock*, *barrier* etc.). Using this knowledge, the detector records the ordering introduced by races among synchronization accesses and then looks for conflicting data accesses which are concurrent according to the previously observed synchronization-induced ordering. In Figure 1, when RD L executes the detector finds a conflict with WR L and records WR L → RD L as synchronization-induced ordering. When RD X executes later, the detector finds the conflict with WR X, but also finds that their ordering is a transitive consequence of program order and synchronization. As a result, no data race is detected. It should be noted that a DRD mechanism must track ordering information much more precisely than an order-recorder. If, for example, the detector treats the conflict between WR X an RD X as a race, a problem is reported where in fact there is none. Similarly, a false problem is reported if the detector believes that WR Y and RD X conflict.

Both order-recording and data race detection can track access ordering and discover races using *logical time* [11]. Memory locations can be timestamped with logical timestamps of previous accesses, and each thread can maintain its current logical time. When a memory location is written to, its timestamps are compared to the current logical time of the writing thread. On a read access only the write timestamps are compared because at least one of the accesses in a conflict must be a write [22]. If the thread's logical time is greater than the location's timestamp, the two accesses are already ordered and no race is recorded or detected. If the location's timestamp is greater than the thread's logical time, or if they are unordered, a race is recorded and, in case of data accesses, a data race is found; the thread's logical time is then updated to reflect this newly found ordering.

Tracking and detection of races for order-recording need not be very precise, so scalar logical clocks can be used and multiple memory locations can share a timestamp. Scalar clocks result in losing much concurrency-detection ability, while coarse-grain timestamps result in detection of false races between accesses to different locations that share a timestamp. However, such imprecision does not affect correctness of order-recording, so it can be implemented simply and with a very low performance overhead [26].

In contrast, it has been shown [24] that data race detection requires vector clocks [9] and per-word vector timestamps for all shared memory locations, to avoid detection of false data races and detect all real data races exposed by causality of an execution. Such clocks have been used in software tools [20], but often result in order-of-magnitude slowdowns which preclude always-on use. This has lead to data race detection with hardware-implemented vector clocks in ReEnact [17]. However, ReEnact still suffers from significant performance overheads, scales poorly to more than a few threads, and has a considerable hardware complexity.

In this paper we find that, in most cases, a dynamic occurrence of a synchronization problem results in several data races, where detection of any one of these races points out the underlying synchronization problem. Based on this observation, we describe several key new insights that allow data race detection to be simplified and combined with an order-recording scheme. The resulting combined mechanism, which we call CORD (Cost-effective Order-Recording and Data race detection), is similar in complexity to order-recording schemes, but also provides practically useful data race detection support which reports no false positives and detects on average 77% of dynamic occurrences of synchronization problems.

To achieve the simplicity of CORD, we employ scalar clocks and timestamps, keep timestamps only for data in on-chip caches, and allow only two timestamps for each cached block. To avoid detection of numerous false data races due to out-of-order removal of timestamps from on-chip caches, CORD uses our novel main memory timestamp mechanism, which is fully distributed and has negligible cost and performance overheads. In contrast, ReEnact requires complex version combining and multi-version buffering mechanisms of thread-level speculation (TLS) for this purpose. In terms of timestamp storage, CORD uses on-chip state equal to 19% of cache capacity and supports any number of threads in the system. In contrast, vector timestamps used in prior work require the same amount of state to support only two threads, with state requirements growing in linear proportion to the number of supported threads.

To improve data race detection accuracy of CORD, we investigate typical data race scenarios which are not detected using basic scalar clocks. We find that many data races are missed because scalar clocks are often unable to capture the difference between clock updates due to synchronization and due to other events. To alleviate this problem, we propose a new clock update scheme that often succeeds in capturing this difference and, as a result, improves the problem detection rate of scalar clocks by 62% without any significant increase in complexity or performance overheads.

In terms of performance, CORD has negligible overheads: 0.4% on average and 3% worst-case on Splash-2 benchmarks. These overheads are much lower than in prior work [17], mostly because CORD avoids the use of multi-version buffering and large vector timestamps and, as a result, uses on-chip cache space and bus bandwidth more efficiently.

The rest of this paper is organized as follows: Section 2 presents the CORD mechanism, Section 3 presents our experimental setup, Section 4 presents our experimental results, Section 5 discusses related work, and Section 6 summarizes our conclusions.

2 The CORD Mechanism

This section briefly reviews the background and definitions for order recording and data race detection. We then describe an ideal data race detection scheme and several considerations that limit the accuracy of practical schemes. Finally, we present the CORD mechanism, its main memory timestamp mechanism, its new clock update scheme, and some additional practical considerations.

2.1 Conflicts, Races, and Synchronization

Two accesses from different threads *conflict* if at least one of them is a write and they access the same memory location [22]. Conflicting accesses are *ordered* if their order follows from the order of previously executed conflicting accesses, otherwise they are *unordered*. An unordered conflict is also called a *race* [15], and all ordering across threads is determined by races outcomes. Because any memory access may potentially participate in one or more races, it is difficult to reason about parallel execution unless some programming convention is followed. To establish such a convention, *synchronization races* are distinguished from *data races*. Synchronization races occur between accesses *intended* to introduce ordering among threads. Accesses performed to lock/unlock a mutex are examples of synchronization accesses, and races between them are carefully crafted to introduce the intended ordering (e.g. mutual exclusion for a mutex). *Data races* occur between data (non-synchronization) accesses. An execution in which all data accesses are ordered by synchronization and program order is said to be *data-race-free*. Finally, if all possible executions of a program are data-race-free, the program itself is data-race-free or *properly labeled* [1].

Most parallel programs are intended to be properly labeled. However, this property is difficult to prove because all possible runs of a program must be taken into account. A more common approach is to test the program with a tool that detects data races at runtime [3, 4, 6, 8, 10, 16, 19, 20, 21]. If no data races are found in test runs, the program is assumed to be properly labeled. Unfortunately, a synchronization defect may be manifested through data races only under conditions that are not included in test runs. Such problems remain in deployed software and cause seemingly random occurrences of crashes and erroneous results (*Heisenbugs*). Continuous data race detection (DRD) would eventually pinpoint these synchronization problems, and deterministic replay would allow these and other bugs to be debugged effectively.

2.2 Ideal Support for Order-Recording and Data Race Detection (DRD)

The ideal mechanism accurately identifies all races and correctly determines their type (synchronization or data). Race outcomes can then be recorded for deterministic replay and data races can be reported as bugs. This ideal race identification can be accomplished by timestamping each memory access. Upon a new access to a location, the thread's current logical time is compared to timestamps of previous conflicting accesses. To determine whether there is a conflict, the mode of each access (read of write) must also be recorded. Because the current access (e.g. a write) may conflict and have a race with many past accesses (e.g. reads) to the same variable, many timestamps per memory location must be kept to detect all races. In general, the number of timestamps per location and the number of locations for which timestamps must be kept can not be determined a priori. However, hardware support for unlimited access history buffering is impractical due to space limitations and due to performance overheads caused by numerous timestamp comparisons on each memory access.

The format of logical clocks and timestamps also poses a challenge for hardware implementation. Ideally, a comparison of two timestamps exactly indicates their current *happens-before* relationship, and a race is found when the comparison indicates that the accesses are concurrent. Logical vector clocks [9] are a classical scheme that accurately tracks the happens-before relationship. A vector clock or timestamp has one scalar component for each thread in the system, and it has been shown [24] that, if N threads may share memory, no clocking scheme with fewer than N scalar components can accurately capture the happens-before relationship. Unfortunately, hardware implementation of vector clocks is very problematic: fixed-size clocks and timestamps can be managed and cached relatively simply, but limit the number of parallel threads in the system. Conversely, variable-size clocks and timestamps would be very difficult to manage, store, and compare in hardware.

2.3 Realistic Access History Buffering

A practical hardware implementation of order-recording and DRD must have limited access history buffering requirements. To do this, we must allow false alarms, allow real races to sometimes be missed, or both. False alarms in production runs trigger costly debugging and error-reporting activities and inconvenience the user, so we need a scheme free of false alarms. As a result, our limited access history buffering will come at at the cost of missing some real data races.

First, we limit the number of timestamps kept for each shared memory location. However, we do not simply keep a few most recently generated timestamps for each location, because then a thread that frequently accesses a shared location can "crowd out" other threads' timestamps. When that happens, a synchronization problem will only be detected if accesses from the frequent-access thread are involved. As a result of this consideration, we keep the last read and the last write timestamp for each <location,thread> pair. This follows existing work in debugging parallel programs, which indicates that beyond the first race for a manifestation of a problem, additional data races yield little additional insight into the problem [5, 14, 15, 17, 20]. With this per-thread approach, replacement decisions for access history entries are also simplified, because each thread's processor can locally make its replacement decisions.

Our second simplification is to keep access histories only for locations that are present in the caches of the local processor. As discussed in Section 1, a timestamp should be associated with each word to prevent detection of false races. However, such per-word timestamps would result in a significant increase in cache complexity and affect cache hit times. For example, per-word vector timestamps, each with four 16-bit components, represent a 200% cache area overhead.

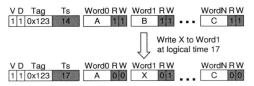

Figure 2. With only one timestamp per line, a timestamp change erases the line's history (CORD state shown in gray).

We reduce the chip-area overhead by keeping a per-line timestamp. To avoid detection of false data races, we still associate the line's timestamp with individual words by keeping two bits of per-word state. These bits indicate whether the word has been read and/or written with the line's timestamp. This effectively provides per-word timestamps, but only for accesses that correspond to the line's latest timestamp. However, a problematic situation is shown in Figure 2. It occurs when one word is accessed with a new timestamp (17 in our example). This timestamp replaces the old one and results in clearing all existing access bits. Note that before this latest access all words were effectively timestamped (in both read and write modes) with the old timestamp (14 in our example). This is a typical situation because spatial locality eventually results in setting access bits for most words. However, a timestamp change erases this history information and setting of access bits begins from scratch. To alleviate this problem, we keep two latest timestamps per line and two sets of per-word access bits, so the old timestamp and its access bits can provide access history for words that are not yet accessed with the newest timestamp. Our evaluation shows (Section 4.3) that with two timestamps per line we see little degradation in DRD ability, compared to an unlimited number of timestamps per word. Note that even a single timestamp, without per-word access bits, suffices for correct order-recording.

With 4x16-bit vector timestamps four threads can be supported, and with 64-byte cache lines the chip area overhead of timestamps and access bits is 38% of the cache's data area. Next, we describe how 16-bit scalar clocks can be used to reduce this overhead to 19%, regardless of the number of threads supported.

2.4 Using Scalar Logical Time

Real systems may have many more threads than processors, so much larger (and more expensive) vector timestamps are needed. Since only data race detection (DRD) benefits from these vector timestamps, it is difficult to justify the on-chip area and the performance overhead associated with maintaining, updating, and comparing very large vector clocks.

To avoid these cost and scalability problems, CORD uses scalar timestamps (integer numbers) for both order-recording and DRD. We start with classical Lamport clocks [11], which are designed to provide total ordering among timestamped events. A Lamport clock consists of a sequence number and a thread ID. To determine the ordering of two logical times, their sequence numbers are compared first and the clock with the lower sequence number is assumed to happen before the one with the higher sequence number. Ties are broken using thread IDs [1]. When a thread accesses a memory location, the thread's current logical clock is compared to the timestamps of conflicting accesses in the location's access history. If a comparison indicates that the thread's access happens after the history access, the conflict is assumed to be already ordered by transitivity. When the clock-timestamp comparison indicates that the thread's access happens before the timestamp's access, a race is found and the thread's clock is updated to reflect the race outcome. This update consists of setting the clock's sequence number to be equal to one plus the timestamp's sequence number. Finally, each access has a unique timestamp because the thread's clock is incremented after each access to a shared memory location.

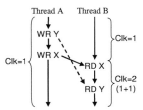

Figure 3. Data race on X results in an update of Thread B's clock. This update prevents detection of data race on Y.

For order-recording and data race detection (DRD), total ordering of accesses is not needed – DRD actually works better with clocks that can express concurrency. Consequently, we can eliminate tie-breaking thread IDs and use a simple integer number as a logical clock. A race is now found when the thread's current clock is less than *or equal to* the timestamp of a conflicting access in the access history. To reflect the new ordering, the thread's logical clock is then incremented to become one plus the timestamp. For order-recording, these clock updates eliminate recording of redundant ordering. They also allow the simple recording format we use (Section 2.7.1). In DRD, we

---

[1]If thread IDs are also equal, the two clocks belong to the same thread and program order defines their happens-before relationship

note that clock updates are needed on every synchronization race found, to prevent later detection of false data races. Updates on data races, however, may prevent detection of other data races because they can appear "synchronized" by a prior data race. Figure 3 show one such situation. The race on variable X is detected and the clock of Thread B is updated. As a result, the race on variable Y is not detected because Thread B's clock, when it reads Y, is already larger than Y's write timestamp. Fortunately, if synchronization bugs are not manifested often (a mostly data-race-free execution), such "overlapping" races are very likely caused by the same synchronization problem. The problem is detected by detecting any one of the races it causes, and when the problem is repaired all its races would be eliminated. As a result of these considerations, we choose to perform clock updates on all races.

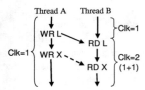

Figure 4. Data race on X is missed if Thread A's clock is not incremented after a write to synchronization variable L.

Lamport clocks are incremented on every "event" (in our case, every shared memory access). Clocks that advance so quickly would need to be large (e.g. 64-bit) to prevent frequent overflows, so we increment our clocks only on synchronization writes. These increments are needed by our DRD scheme to differentiate between pre-synchronization and post-synchronization accesses. Figure 4 shows an example in which Thread B reads the synchronization variable L and updates its clock to succeed L's write timestamp of 1. If Thread A's clock is not incremented after the synchronization write, its write to X is also timestamped with a logical time of 1, which is lower than Thread B's clock of 2 when it reads X. As a result, the (real) data race on X is not detected. If Thread A's clock was incremented after its write to synchronization variable L, the race on X would be detected. Due to this consideration, we increment a thread's clock following each synchronization write. However, clock increments on reads and non-synchronization writes are unnecessary and would harm DRD (see Figure 5).

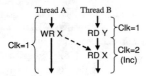

Figure 5. Data race on X is missed if Thread B's clock is incremented after it reads Y.

2.5   Main Memory Timestamp

We want to avoid timestamping words or even blocks in main memory. However, a race can not be identified if it involves a location without any timestamps. Figure 6 shows an example of this problem, where synchronization variable L is displaced from the cache after it is written in Thread A. As a result, when Thread B reads L it has no timestamp to compare against. If Thread B simply ignores this situation, replay is incorrect because the recorded ordering (which follows the thread's clock) now indicates that Thread B reads L before Thread A writes it. Neglecting a synchronization race (Figure 6) also results in detection of a false data race on X.

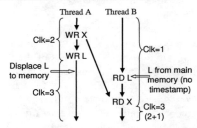

Figure 6. Synchronization on L is missed without memory timestamps, resulting in incorrect order-recording and detection of false data race on X.

Our solution is to keep one read and one write timestamp *for the entire main memory*. Main memory timestamps are updated when a per-line timestamp and its access bits are removed to make room for a newer timestamp. If any of the access bits indicates a read access to any word, the line's timestamp overwrites the memory read timestamp if the line's timestamp is larger. The memory write timestamp is similarly updated if any per-word write access bit is set and the line's timestamp is larger than the memory write timestamp. Effectively, the entire main memory becomes a very large block that shares a single timestamp, which allows correct order-recording.

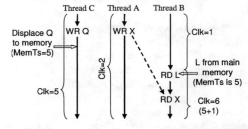

Figure 7. Displacement of Q to memory in Thread C leads Thread B to update its clock when it reads lock L from memory, resulting in a missed data race on X.

However, the many-words granularity of main-memory timestamps prohibits precise data race detection. Figure 7 shows an example in which the main memory timestamp is updated on a write-back of Q in Thread C. Thread B then reads a synchronization variable L from memory, updates Thread B's logical clock using the main memory timestamp, and consequently misses the data race on variable X. We note that Thread B must perform a clock update because it can not determine whether or not the memory write timestamp corresponds to a write-back of variable L. Because false positives are more damaging in production runs than undetected races, and because order-recording also benefits from clock updates using memory timestamps, in CORD we choose to perform such clock updates even at the cost of missing some data races. Finally, if variable L in Figure 7 were not a synchronization variable, when Thread B reads it from memory and compares its clock against the main memory timestamp, the comparison would indicate that L is involved in a data race (which is not true). Fortunately, we can simply ignore (and not report) any data race detections that used a main memory timestamp. This may result in missing a real data race through memory, but avoids reporting false ones.

Maintaining the two main memory timestamps is relatively easy in a small-scale system with snooping - each cache can maintain its own copy the two main memory timestamps. When a cache line or its oldest access history entry is displaced, its timestamp is compared to the local main memory timestamp. If this results in changing the local main memory timestamp, a special memory timestamp update transaction is broadcast on the bus (or piggy-backed to the write-back, if there is one). Other processors can then update their own memory timestamps. A straightforward extension of this protocol to a directory-based system is possible, but in this paper we focus on systems (CMPs and SMPs) with snooping cache coherence.

We note that ReEnact [17] performs data race detection (DRD) without timestamping main memory at all. However, ReEnact uses thread-level speculation (TLS) support with special version combining mechanisms to avoid detection of false races when synchronization through memory is missed. Also, like our new main memory timestamps, ReEnact's approach misses all real data races through non-cached variables. Consequently, our new main memory timestamps provide the same order-recording and DRD capabilities without the complexity and performance overheads of TLS.

2.6 Sync-Read Clock Updates Revisited

As described in prior sections, our CORD mechanism correctly records execution order for deterministic replay, avoids detection of false data races, and detects some data races. Still, we find that many injected manifestations of synchronization problems were undetected, and identify three main reasons for missing them. First, some data races involved accesses that are too far apart to be detected using only in-cache timestamps with limited access histories. Any architectural mechanism that does not individually timestamp main memory locations and limits in-cache access histories would suffer from this problem, but to our knowledge this paper is the first to quantify it (Section 4.3). Second, some data races were missed because scalar clocks can not precisely capture the ordering across threads. This problem is quantified in Section 4.4. The third class of missed data races is described below, together with a new clock update mechanism that vastly improves their detection.

In some of the applications we study, synchronization writes occur at about the same rate in all threads. As a result, a thread's current scalar clock tends to be larger than timestamps of variables accessed earlier by other threads. Figure 8 shows an example of this problem. In this example, only data races that involve nearly simultaneous pairs of accesses (e.g. the race on

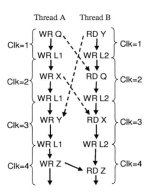

Figure 8. Synchronization writes on L1 nd L2 update thread's clock, so they appear synchronized and data races on Q, X, and Y are missed. Only nearly-simultaneous data races (like the one on X) are detected.

Z) are detected. This problem would be eliminated if we eliminate clock increments on synchronization writes, but then many other data races would be missed (Section 2.4).

Our solution to this problem is to increase the "window of opportunity" for data race detection when logical clocks and timestamps are compared. Two accesses are normally considered synchronized if the logical clock of the second one is larger than the timestamp of the first one. However, in general we can require the timestamp of the second access to be larger by at least D for the two accesses to be considered synchronized. If $D > 2$, all data races in Figure 8 would be detected.

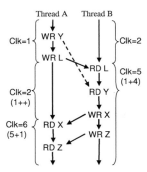

Figure 9. Sync-read on L creates a clock difference of $D = 4$, while other clock updates and clock increments use a difference of one. This allows correct treatment of the synchronized conflict on Y, detection of a data race on X, and even detection on a data race on Z.

Of course, synchronization reads must now update the thread's clock to be at least D larger than the synchronization variable's latest write timestamp. All other updates and clock increments continue to use an increment of one. An example of this behavior is shown in Figure 9, where the synchronization read in Thread B is updated to be $D = 4$ larger than the lock's write timestamp, but Thread A's clock is incremented by only one following that write. When the race on X is found, Thread B's clock is updated to be larger by only one than X's timestamp. This last update allows the order-recorder to avoid redundant recording of the race on Y, but this race is still detected by our data race detection (DRD) scheme. Note that the order-recorder can still omit races in which the second access has a clock greater than the timestamp of the first access. If such a difference is less than D, the accesses can still be treated as transitively ordered, but the DRD mechanism can detect a data race because it knows that this ordering is not through synchronization. The change in D, therefore, directly affects only the DRD scheme and allows it to detect more data races without detecting false positives.

2.7 Implementation Details

2.7.1. Format for Order-Recording. The processor chip contains two registers, which contain physical memory addresses of the next available location in the execution order log and of the end of the region reserved for the log. In our experiments we reserve sufficient log space for the entire application run, but if this space does run out, an exception is triggered to save the log or allocate more space.

When a thread's clock changes, it appends to the log an entry that contains the previous clock value, the thread ID and the number of instructions executed with that clock value. We use 16-bit thread IDs and clock values and 32-bit instruction counts, for a total of eight bytes per log entry. To prevent instruction count overflow, the thread's clock is simply incremented when its instruction count is about to overflow. This happens rarely, is compatible with correct order-recording, results in no detection of false data races, and has a negligible impact on detection of real races.

Our deterministic replay orders the log by logical time and then proceeds through log entries one by one. For each log entry, the thread with the recorded ID has its clock value set to the recorded clock value, and is then allowed to execute the recorded number of instructions. Note that during recording, if conflicting accesses have the same logical clock, we update the clock of one of the accesses. As a result, only non-conflicting fragments of execution from different threads can have equal logical clocks, in which case they can be replayed in any order. Optimizations are possible to allow some concurrency in replay, but this is a secondary concern because the replay occurs only in debugging when a problem is found.

2.7.2. Clock Comparisons. A memory access instruction results in an attempt to find the requested variable in the local cache. If the variable is not found, a bus request, tagged with the processor's current logical clock, is sent to fetch the block from memory or another cache. Snooping hits in other caches result in data race checks. Data responses are tagged with the data's timestamp and result in a clock update on the requesting processor. Memory responses use the main memory timestamps instead.

If the processor's access is a cache hit, both timestamps for the in-cache block can be lower than the current logical clock. In that case, the lower of the two timestamps and its access bits are removed (potentially causing a main memory timestamp update) and the new timestamp takes its place, with all access bits

reset to zero. An access that finds the corresponding access bit to be zero results in broadcasting a special *race check request* on the bus. This request is similar in effect to a cache miss, but without the actual data transfer. We also maintain two *check filter* bits per line that indicate when the entire line can be read and/or written without additional race check requests. As a result, each race check request actually results in the entire line being checked. A race on the particular word being accessed results in normal order-recording and data race detection activity. Absence of any potential conflicts for the entire line results in a permission to set one or both of the check filter bits. Note that our race check requests only use the less-utilized address and timestamp buses and cause no data bus contention.

Our clock comparisons are performed using simple integer subtractions (when $D > 1$) and comparisons. A timestamp comparison for order-recording can use a simple comparator, while for data race detection with $D > 1$ we need a subtracter and then a comparator. With two timestamps per cache block, each snooping hit and cache access results in two subtractions and four comparisons, which are easily handled by simple dedicated circuitry. We note that main memory itself is oblivious to our CORD scheme – our main memory timestamps are kept and compared on-chip.

2.7.3. Synchronization. Our scheme must distinguish between synchronization and data accesses, because they require different treatment: data race checks should only be done for data accesses, while synchronization accesses result in clock updates. To tell synchronization and data accesses apart, we rely on modified synchronization libraries that use special instructions to label some accesses as synchronization accesses. A similar approach is used in other data race detection work [6, 10, 17, 19, 20, 21].

2.7.4. Thread Migration. A practical data race detection (DRD) mechanism must allow a thread to migrate from one processor to another. However, such migration might cause false alarms in a DRD scheme because the timestamps of the thread remain on its previous processor and appear to belong to another thread. Since our logical clocks are not incremented on each memory access, an access by a migrated thread can find the data in the cache of its original processor, timestamped with the same timestamp, and with access bits that indicate a "conflict". As a result, a data race is falsely detected.

This problem is eliminated by simply incrementing the clock of a thread by D each time it begins running on a processor. With this simple modification, the self-race problem can no longer occur because new execution is "synchronized" with prior execution on the other processor. This can allow some data races to occur undetected, but thread migration occurs far less frequently than other clock updates. In our experiments, no data races are missed solely due to clock increments on thread migration. We note that a vector-clock scheme would suffer from the same thread migration problem, and that our "synchronize on migration" solution also applies to vector-clock schemes.

2.7.5. Clock Overflow. We use 16-bit logical clocks and timestamps, to reduce the cache area overhead. These clocks can overflow and result in order-recording problems (missed races) or false positives in DRD. Fortunately, we find that we can use a sliding window approach with a window size of $2^{15} - 1$. This approach requires a slight modification in our comparator circuitry and requires elimination of very stale timestamps to prevent them from exiting the window. For this purpose, we use a cache-walker that uses idle cache ports to look up timestamps of in-cache blocks and trigger eviction of very old ones. During each pass, the walker also determines the minimum (oldest) timestamp still present in the cache. This minimum timestamp is kept by each cache and used to stall any clock update that would exceed the sliding window size. In our experiments no such stalls actually occur, because the cache walker is very effective in removing very old timestamps before they become a problem. Another concern is that removal of these old timestamps might prevent our DRD scheme from detecting some races. However, in our experiments we find that removed timestamps are much lower than current clock values in all threads, so for reasonable values of D no races can be detected with these old timestamps anyway.

2.7.6. Recovery from Synchronization Problems. CORD's order-recording mechanism can be combined with a check-pointing mechanism to allow automated analysis and recovery from detected synchronization problems. Possible approaches for such recovery are to use pattern matching to identify and repair the dynamic instance of the problem [17], or to use conservative thread scheduling to serialize execution in the vicinity of the problem [27]. However, such recovery is beyond the scope of this paper, which focuses on cost-effective support for data race detection and order-recording.

3 Experimental Setup

3.1 Simulation Environment

We use a cycle-accurate execution-driven simulator of 4-processor CMP with private L1 and L2 caches. The 4-issue, out-of-order, 4GHz processor cores are modeled after Intel's Pentium 4. They are connected using a 128-bit on-chip data bus operating at 1GHz, and the processor chip is connected to the main memory using a 200MHz quad-pumped 64-bit bus. Round-trip memory latency is 600 processor cycles, and the on-chip L2 cache-to-cache round-trip latency is 20 cycles. All other parameters, such as branch predictors, functional units, etc. represent an aggressive near-future design.

Because we use relatively small input sets for our applications, we use reduced-size caches to preserve realistic cache hit rates and bus traffic, using Woo et al. [25] as a reference. Each L2 cache is only 32KB and each L1 cache is 8KB in size. This reduced cache size also yields a realistic evaluation of data race detection accuracy, which would benefit from the numerous timestamps available in larger caches.

In our evaluation of performance overhead, the processor consumes data values on cache hits without waiting for a CORD timestamp comparison. Thus, we do not model any additional cache hit latency for CORD, but we do model bus and cache contention due to race check requests and the (rare) retirement

delay for each instruction whose CORD race check is still in progress when the instruction is otherwise ready to be retired.

3.2 Applications

To evaluate our CORD mechanism, we use Splash-2 [25] applications. These applications and the input sets we use are listed in Table 1. We note that some of these input sets are reduced from the default Splash-2 input sets. The reason for this is that, with our *Ideal* configuration, we keep (and check for data races) the entire history of accesses for every word the application accesses, and recycle a history entry only when it is guaranteed not to have any more races. This results in enormous memory space requirements - in some applications the simulation uses hundreds of megabytes even with the reduced input sets we use. In Radiosity, even with the test input set, simulation of *Ideal* runs exceeds the 2GB virtual address limitation.

App.	Input	App.	Input
barnes	n2048	cholesky	tk23.0
fft	m16	fmm	2048
lu	512x512	ocean	130x130
Radiosity	-test	radix	256K keys
raytrace	teapot	volrend	head-sd2
water-n2	216	water-sp	216

Table 1. Applications evaluated and their input sets.

3.3 Order-Recording

We performed numerous tests, with and without data race injections, to verify that the entire execution can be accurately replayed. Our order logs are very compact and in all applications require less than 1MB for the entire execution.

We note, however, that our system currently does not include checkpointing or I/O recording capabilities, so it can only replay an entire execution and requires manual replay of its inputs. This is not a problem in Splash-2 applications, in which the only inputs are files, but can be a problem in interactive applications. Checkpointing and I/O recording are largely orthogonal to the order-recording mechanism, and our CORD mechanism can be used with existing mechanisms for checkpointing and/or I/O replay, such as RecPlay [20], FDR [26], ReVive [18], BugNet [13], Flashback [23], etc. Our order-recording (and data race detection) results in negligible performance overheads (Section 4.1), so combined scheme's overhead would mostly depend on the checkpointing and I/O recording scheme.

3.4 Data Races

Several Splash-2 applications already have data races that are discovered by CORD. Almost all are only potential portability problems, but at least one is an actual bug. All of these existing races can be removed by simple changes in the code and without much performance degradation, and most of the problems can be discovered even on very small input sets. Overall, these existing problems can be found by existing software tools and repaired before the software actually ships. In this paper, our goal is continuous testing in production runs. Therefore, we evaluate the effectiveness of each configuration in detecting those elusive synchronization problems that escape testing, remain in production codes, are manifested sporadically, and offer only rare opportunities for detection.

We model this kind of error by injecting a single *dynamic instance* of missing synchronization into each run of the application. Injection is random with a uniform distribution, so each dynamic synchronization operation has an equal chance of being removed. When a synchronization instance to be removed is chosen, it is removed in a manner that depends on the type of synchronization. For mutex synchronization, we ignore a dynamic instance of a call to the "lock" primitive and the corresponding call to "unlock". For flag (condition variable) synchronization, we ignore a single call to the flag "wait" primitive. Barrier synchronization uses a combination of mutex and flag operations in its implementation and each dynamic invocation of those mutex and flag primitives is treated as a separate instance of synchronization. This treatment of barriers results in more difficult detection than if an entire call to "barrier" is ignored – removing a single such call results in thousands of data races, one of which is virtually certain to be found. This would defeat our intent to model elusive, difficult to detect errors.

It is important to note that each of the error injections described above is performed in a separate simulation run to let us tell whether each injected error was detected. For each configuration we perform between 20 and 100 injections per application. The number of injections depends on the application because, somewhat surprisingly, in several applications most dynamic instances of synchronization are redundant - they result in no new cross-thread ordering and their removal creates no data races. Figure 10 shows the percentage of injections that actually resulted in an data races, as detected by the *Ideal* configuration which detects all dynamically occurring data races. We also check and confirm that program outputs are indeed correct in all injection runs for which *Ideal* finds no data races. Further analysis reveals that, in most of these injections, we removed a dynamic instance of a critical section protected by a lock that was previously held by the same thread, in which case the removed synchronization introduces no new cross-thread ordering. This finding further stresses the importance of always-on detection, because it indicates that synchronization defects in the code may become detectable only infrequently.

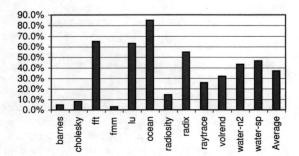

Figure 10. Percentage of injected dynamic instances of missing that resulted in at least one data race.

Since many injection runs result in no detectable data races, for some applications the number of runs with data races is too small to allow us to draw per-application conclusions, despite a large number of injection runs and thousands of processor-hours of simulation time. For example, we perform 100 injection runs per configuration in fmm, but get only 3 errors. However, our results still yield significant insight when comparing the configurations. This is especially true for averages across all applications, which are based on more than a hundred manifested errors per configuration.

4   Experimental Evaluation

In this section we evaluate our new CORD scheme, first its performance overhead and then its usefulness in detecting synchronization problems. Our order-recording is active in all experiments and we present no separate evaluation of its performance overhead because the overhead of the entire CORD mechanism is already negligible. Also, no separate evaluation is presented for the effectiveness of the order-recorder, because it always enables fully accurate replay.

4.1   Performance Overhead

Figure 11 shows the execution time with CORD, relative to a machine without any order-recording or data race detection support. We see that CORD imposes a very low performance overhead, 0.4% on average with a maximum of 3% for Cholesky. The increased overhead in Cholesky is primarily due to the increased on-chip address/timestamp bus contention. This bus is ordinarily less occupied than the data bus, so it runs at half the frequency of the data bus. Frequent synchronization in Cholesky results in many timestamp changes, which cause bursts of timestamp removals and race check requests on subsequent memory accesses. This, in turn, increases the contention for the address/timestamp bus.

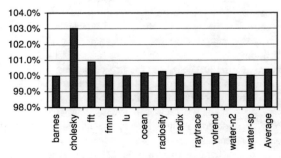

Figure 11. Execution time with *CORD* relative to the *Baseline* which has no order-recording and no DRD support.

4.2   Data Race Detection

We use two criteria to compare effectiveness of data race detection (DRD) schemes. One criterion for DRD effectiveness is the actual *raw data race detection rate*, defined as the number of data races detected. The other criterion we call *problem detection rate*. The main purpose of a DRD mechanism is to find dynamic occurrences of synchronization problems. When such an occurrence is found, it can be replayed, analyzed, and the problem repaired. As a result, the problem detection rate is defined as the number of runtime manifestations of synchronization errors for which at least one data race is detected. Our experience in debugging parallel software indicates that usefulness of a DRD mechanism is mostly dependent on its problem detection rate, so it serves at the main evaluation criterion for CORD's effectiveness. Raw data race detection rates are also presented to provide additional insight.

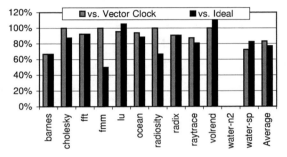

Figure 12. Problem detection rate.

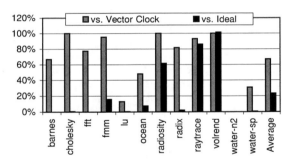

Figure 13. Raw data race detection rate.

Figure 12 shows CORD's problem detection rate, relative to the problem detection rate of a CORD-like scheme that uses vector clocks. On average, our decision to use scalar clocks results in detecting only 83% of the problems that would be detected with vector clocks. We also note that in water-n2 CORD finds none of the problems, although several are found by the Ideal scheme and some are found by a vector-clock scheme. This stresses the fact that the choice between vector clocks and scalar clocks is a tradeoff and not a trivial decision. In our case, we target a cost-effective hardware implementation, in which case our scalar clocks offer an excellent tradeoff between cost, performance, and problem detection rates. Figure 12 also compares CORD's problem detection to that of the *Ideal* configuration, which uses unlimited caches, unlimited number of history entries per cache line, and vector clocks. We see that our simple, implementable, and high-performance CORD scheme still detects the majority (77% on average) of all problems detected by an ideal data race detection scheme.

In Figure 12, CORD finds 18 problems for Volrend, two more than the ideal scheme. This seemingly contradictory result is due to the non-deterministic nature of parallel execution.

Our fault injector randomly generates a number N and then injects a fault into N-th dynamic instance of synchronization for each configuration. However, fault injections for *CORD* and for *Ideal* are performed in different runs, so the Nth instance of synchronization in one run may be different from the Nth instance in the other run. Execution order in different configurations changes mainly due to different cache hit/miss scenarios (Ideal's L2 cache is infinite and always hits).

Figure 13 shows CORD's effectiveness in detecting raw data races. Again, the results are relative to the vector-clock scheme and the Ideal scheme. An interesting trend can be observed by comparing Figures 12 and and 13. We see that CORD's ability to detect raw data races is significantly diminished (only 20% of Ideal). However, there seems to be little clustering of data races that CORD does and doesn't find. As a result, for a problem that causes several data races there is a large probability that one of those races will be detected. This finding indicates that the choices we made when simplifying CORD's hardware mechanisms (limited access histories and buffering, scalar clocks) have largely resulted in sacrificing the less valuable raw data race detection capability, but still retain much of the more useful problem detection capability.

4.3 Impact of Limited Access Histories on Data Race Detection (DRD)

To gain better insight into tradeoffs of designing a DRD mechanism, we now evaluate how access history limitations alone affect the effectiveness of a DRD scheme. The *Ideal* configuration uses vector clocks, unlimited caches, and an unlimited number of access history entries per cache block. The *InfCache* configuration still uses vector clocks and unlimited caches but limits the number of timestamps per block to two. The *L2Cache* configuration uses vector clocks, but with our default L2 cache size and two timestamps (with their per-word access bits) per line, and *L1Cache* maintains two vector timestamps and their access bits per line only in our L1 caches. Problem detection rates of these schemes are shown in Figure 14. Few problems are missed due to a limited number of timestamps per cache line, and limiting access histories to the L2 cache results in a small additional loss of problem detection. A severe limitation (*L1Cache*) degrades problem detection significantly, although most problems are detected even then.

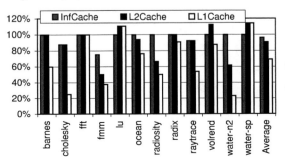

Figure 14. Problem detection rate with limited access histories and buffering limitations.

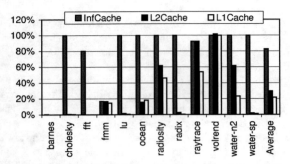

Figure 15. Raw data race detection rate with limited access histories and buffering limitations.

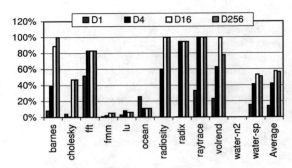

Figure 17. Raw data race detection with different logical clock mechanisms.

Figure 15 shows raw data race detection rates for the same four configurations. We see that most races are missed in *L2Cache* and *L1Cache*, and even an unlimited cache with only two timestamps per line misses 18% of all data races.

Overall, these results indicate that it is possible to effectively detect synchronization problems with a limited number of available timestamps and timestamped memory locations, although raw data race detection rates diminish when the number of timestamped locations is limited. We also find that a severely constrained system (*L1Cache*) has considerably worse problem detection rate than a moderately constrained one.

4.4 Impact of Clock Limitations

In this section we evaluate the impact of clocking limitations on the effectiveness of data race detection. All configurations used in this evaluation use two timestamps per line in L1 and L2 caches. The results are all relative to a scheme that uses vector clocks (the *L2Cache* configuration in Section 4.3). We show a CORD configuration without additional sync-read clock updates described in Section 2.6 ($D = 1$), and CORD configurations with sync-read clock updates of $D = 4$, $D = 16$, and $D = 256$.

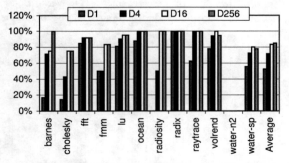

Figure 16. Synchronization problem detection with our scalar clocks.

Figures 16 and 17 show the results for problem detection and raw data race instruction. We observe that, compared to vector clocks, scalar clocks with $D = 1$ result in a major loss of raw data race detection ability, but only a moderate loss of problem detection capability. We also find significant improvement in

both problem detection and raw data race detection as D increases up to 16. For values of D beyond 16, we see additional improvement only in barnes.

5 Related Work

Much work has been done in software tools and methods for order-recording and detection of data races or serializability violations such as RecPlay [20], Eraser [21], ParaScope [6], and others [3, 4, 8, 10, 16, 19, 27]. All of these schemes, especially those that detect data races or serializability violations, suffer from significant performance overheads. Low-overhead order-recording hardware has been proposed by Xu et al. [26], but without DRD support. Hardware has also been proposed for detection of races that violate a consistency model [2], or for specifically structured programs [3, 12]. A more recently proposed hardware mechanism, called ReEnact [17], supports both order-recording and DRD but uses vector clocks, thread-level speculation support, and multi-version caches. The complexity of this mechanism is considerable and performance overhead are non-negligible, mainly due to multi-version buffering which reduces the effective cache capacity by storing different versions of the same block in the same cache, and also due to large vector timestamps that increase bus traffic. However, vector clocks used by ReEnact allow detection of 22% more instances of synchronization problems than scalar clocks used in our CORD mechanism.

Finally, different clocking schemes are discussed and compared in prior work [7, 24], but mostly in the context of distributed systems and without considerations related to hardware constraints. Scalar clocks used there are not limited in size, are updated and compared differently than in our CORD scheme, and do not employ our $D > 1$ sync-read clock increments.

6 Conclusions

This paper presents our new Cost-effective Order-Recording and Data race detection (CORD) mechanism. This mechanism is comparable in cost to existing order-recording schemes and considerably less complex than prior hardware support for data race detection. CORD also has a *negligible performance overhead* of 0.4% on average and 3% worst-case across Splash-2 benchmarks. Still, CORD records the execution order for *ac-*

curate deterministic replay, and *detects most dynamic manifestations of synchronization problems* (77% on average) in our problem-injection experiments.

We also quantitatively determine the effect of various limitations and enhancements in our CORD mechanism. Realistic buffering limitations result in missing 9% of synchronization problems. Note that these limitations are present in prior architectural schemes for data race, detection but their effect was not quantified. The additional transition from classical vector clocks to our scalar clocks, which are needed to reduce complexity and scale to more than a few threads, results in missing an additional 17% of synchronization problems. Finally, we find that our optimizations of the clock update scheme result in finding 62% more problems than a naive scalar clock update scheme.

We conclude that, with a careful quantitative approach, hardware for detection of most (77% in our experiments) synchronization problems can be achieved at a very low cost, without false alarms, and with a negligible performance overhead (0.4% on average in our experiments). Furthermore, the same hardware also records execution ordering for deterministic replay. This combined CORD mechanism is simple enough to be implementable, is fast enough to run always (even in performance-sensitive production runs), and provides the support programmers need to deal with the complexities of designing and supporting parallel software for future chip-multiprocessors and multi-threaded machines.

References

[1] S. V. Adve and M. D. Hill. Weak ordering - a new definition. In *17th Intl. Symp. on Computer Architecture*, pages 2–14, 1990.

[2] S. V. Adve, M. D. Hill, B. P. Miller, and R. H. B. Netzer. Detecting Data Races on Weak Memory Systems. In *18th Intl. Symp. on Computer Architecture*, pages 234–243, 1991.

[3] K. Audenaert and L. Levrouw. Space efficient data race detection for parallel programs with series-parallel task graphs. In *3rd Euromicro Workshop on Parallel and Distributed Processing*, page 508, 1995.

[4] J.-D. Choi, K. Lee, A. Loginov, R. O'Callahan, V. Sarkar, and M. Sridharan. Efficient and Precise Datarace Detection for Multithreaded Object-Oriented Programs. In *ACM SIGPLAN 2002 Conf. on Prog. Lang. Design and Implementation*, pages 258–269, 2002.

[5] J.-D. Choi and S. L. Min. Race Frontier: Reproducing Data Races in Parallel-Program Debugging. In *3rd ACM SIGPLAN Symp. on Principles & Practice of Parallel Programming*, pages 145–154, 1991.

[6] K. D. Cooper, M. W. Hall, R. T. Hood, K. Kennedy, K. S. McKinley, J. M. Mellor-Crummey, L. Torczon, and S. K. Warren. The ParaScope Parallel Programming Environment. *Proc. of the IEEE*, 81(2):244–263, 1993.

[7] K. De Bosschere and M. Ronsse. Clock snooping and its application in on-the-fly data race detection. In *third Intl. Symp. on Parallel Architectures, Algorithms, and Networks (I-SPAN)*, pages 324–330, 1997.

[8] A. Dinning and E. Schonberg. An empirical comparison of monitoring algorithms for access anomaly detection. In *second ACM SIGPLAN Symp. on Principles and Practice of Parallel Programming*, pages 1–10, 1990.

[9] C. Fidge. Logical Time in Distributed Computing Systems. *IEEE Computer*, 24(8):23–33, 1991.

[10] R. Hood, K. Kennedy, and J. Mellor-Crummey. Parallel program debugging with on-the-fly anomaly detection. In *1990 Conf. on Supercomputing*, pages 74–81, 1990.

[11] L. Lamport. Time, Clocks, and the Ordering of Events in a Distributed System. *Communications of the ACM*, 21(7):558–565, 1978.

[12] S. L. Min and J.-D. Choi. An Efficient Cache-Based Access Anomaly Detection Scheme. In *4th Intl. Conf. on Arch. Support for Prog. Lang. and Operating Sys.*, pages 235–244, 1991.

[13] S. Narayanasamy, G. Pokam, and B. Calder. BugNet: Continuously Recording Program Execution for Deterministic Replay Debugging. In *32nd Intl. Symp. on Computer Architecture*, 2005.

[14] R. H. B. Netzer and B. P. Miller. Improving the accuracy of data race detection. In *third ACM SIGPLAN Symp. on Principles and Practice of Parallel Programming*, pages 133–144, 1991.

[15] R. H. B. Netzer and B. P. Miller. What are race conditions?: Some issues and formalizations. *ACM Letters on Prog. Lang. and Systems*, 1(1):74–88, 1992.

[16] D. Perkovic and P. J. Keleher. A Protocol-Centric Approach to On-the-Fly Race Detection. *IEEE Trans. on Parallel and Distributed Systems*, 11(10):1058–1072, 2000.

[17] M. Prvulovic and J. Torrellas. ReEnact: Using Thread-Level Speculation Mechanisms to Debug Data Races in Multithreaded Codes. In *30th Intl. Symp. on Computer Architecture*, pages 110–121, 2003.

[18] M. Prvulovic, Z. Zhang, and J. Torrellas. ReVive: Cost-Effective Architectural Support for Rollback Recovery in Shared-Memory Multiprocessors. In *29th Intl. Symp. on Computer Architecture*, pages 111–122, 2002.

[19] B. Richards and J. R. Larus. Protocol-based data-race detection. In *SIGMETRICS Symp. on Parallel and Distributed Tools*, pages 40–47, 1998.

[20] M. Ronsse and K. De Bosschere. RecPlay: A Fully Integrated Practical Record/Replay System. *ACM Trans. on Computer Systems*, 17(2):133–152, 1999.

[21] S. Savage, M. Burrows, G. Nelson, P. Sobalvarro, and T. Anderson. Eraser: A Dynamic Data Race Detector for Multi-Threaded Programs. *ACM Trans. on Computer Systems*, 15(4):391–411, 1997.

[22] D. Shasha and M. Snir. Efficient and Correct Execution of Parallel Programs that Share Memory. *ACM Trans. on Prog. Lang. and Systems*, 10(2):282–312, 1988.

[23] S. Srinivasan, C. Andrews, S. Kandula, and Y. Zhou. Flashback: A Light-weight Extension for Rollback and Deterministic Replay for Software Debugging. In *Usenix technical conference (USENIX)*, 2004.

[24] C. Valot. Characterizing the Accuracy of Distributed Timestamps. In *1993 ACM/ONR Workshop on Parallel and Distributed Debugging*, pages 43–52, 1993.

[25] S. C. Woo, M. Ohara, E. Torrie, J. P. Singh, and A. Gupta. The SPLASH-2 Programs: Characterization and Methodological Considerations. In *22nd Intl. Symp. on Computer Architecture*, pages 24–38, 1995.

[26] M. Xu, R. Bodik, and M. D. Hill. A 'Flight Data Recorder' for Enabling Full-System Multiprocessor Deterministic Replay. In *30th Intl. Symp. on Computer Architecture*, pages 122–135, 2003.

[27] M. Xu, R. Bodk, and M. D. Hill. A Serializability Violation Detector for Shared-Memory Server Programs. In *ACM SIGPLAN 2005 Conf. on Prog. Lang. Design and Implementation (PLDI)*, 2005.

Software-Hardware Cooperative Memory Disambiguation

Ruke Huang, Alok Garg, and Michael Huang
Department of Electrical & Computer Engineering
University of Rochester
{hrk1,garg,michael.huang}@ece.rochester.edu

Abstract

In high-end processors, increasing the number of in-flight in-structions can improve performance by overlapping useful process-ing with long-latency accesses to the main memory. Buffering these instructions requires a tremendous amount of microarchitectural re-sources. Unfortunately, large structures negatively impact proces-sor clock speed and energy efficiency. Thus, innovations in effective and efficient utilization of these resources are needed. In this paper, we target the load-store queue, a dynamic memory disambiguation logic that is among the least scalable structures in a modern micro-processor. We propose to use software assistance to identify load instructions that are guaranteed not to overlap with earlier pend-ing stores and prevent them from competing for the resources in the load-store queue. We show that the design is practical, requiring off-line analyses and minimum architectural support. It is also very effective, allowing more than 40% of loads to bypass the load-store queue for floating-point applications. This reduces resource pres-sure and can lead to significant performance improvements.

1 Introduction

To continue exploiting device speed improvement to provide ever higher performance is challenging but imperative. Simply trans-lating device speed improvement to higher clock speed does not guarantee better performance. We need to effectively bridge the speed gap between the processor core and the main memory. For an important type of applications that have never-ending demand for higher performance (mostly numerical codes), an effective and straightforward approach is to increase the number of in-flight in-structions to overlap with long latencies. This requires a commen-surate increase in the effective capacity of many microarchitectural resources. Naive implementation of larger physical structures is not a viable solution as it not only incurs high energy consumption but also increases access latency which can negate improvement in clock rate. Thus, we need to consider innovative approaches that manages these resources in an efficient and effective manner.

We argue that a software-hardware cooperative approach to re-source management is becoming an increasingly attractive alterna-tive. A software component can analyze the static code in a more global fashion and obtain information hardware alone can not ob-tain efficiently. Furthermore, this analysis done in software does not generate recurring energy overhead. With energy consumption being of paramount importance, this advantage alone may justify the effort needed to overcome certain inconvenience to support a cooperative resource management paradigm.

In this paper, we explore a software-hardware cooperative ap-proach to dynamic memory disambiguation. The conventional hardware-only approach employs the load-store queue (LSQ) to keep track of memory instructions to make sure that the out-of-

order execution of these instructions do not violate the program se-mantics. Without the a priori knowledge of which load instructions can execute out of program order and not violate program seman-tics, conventional implementations simply buffer all in-flight load and store instructions and perform cross-comparisons during their execution to detect all violations. The hardware uses associative arrays with priority encoding. Such a design makes the LSQ proba-bly the least scalable of all microarchitectural structures in modern out-of-order processors. In reality, we observe that in many appli-cations, especially array-based floating-point applications, a signif-icant portion of memory instructions can be statically determined not to cause any possible violations. Based on these observations, we propose to use software analysis to identify certain memory in-structions to bypass hardware memory disambiguation. We show a proof-of-concept design where with simple hardware support, the cooperative mechanism can allow an average of 43% and up to 97% of loads in floating-point applications to bypass the LSQ. The re-duction in disambiguation demand results in energy savings and re-duced resource pressure which can improve performance.

The rest of the paper is organized as follows: Section 2 provides a high-level overview of our cooperative disambiguation model; Sec-tions 3 and 4 describe the software and hardware support respec-tively; Section 5 discusses our experimental setup; Section 6 shows our quantitative analyses; Section 7 summarizes some related work; and Section 8 concludes.

2 Resource-Effective Memory Disambiguation
2.1 Resource-Effective Computing

Modern high-end out-of-order cores typically use very aggressive speculations to extract instruction-level parallelism. These specu-lations require predictors, book-keeping structures, and buffers to track dependences, detect violations, and undo any effect of mis-speculation. High-end processors typically spend far more transis-tors on orchestrating speculations than on the actual execution of individual instructions. Unfortunately, as the number of in-flight in-structions increases, the effective size of these structures has to be scaled up accordingly to prevent frequent pipeline stalls. Increasing the actual size of these resources presents many problems. First and foremost, the energy consumption increases. The increase is espe-cially significant if the structure is accessed in an associative manner such as in the case of the issue queue and the LSQ. At a time when energy consumption is perhaps the most important limiting factor for high-end processors, any change in microarchitecture that re-sults in energy increase will need substantial justifications. Second, larger physical structures take longer to access, which may translate into extra cycles in the pipeline and diminish the return of buffer-ing more instructions. Therefore, we need to innovate in the man-agement of these resources and create *resource-effective* designs. Whether the speculative out-of-order execution model can continue to exploit technology improvements to provide higher single-thread performance is to a large extent determined by whether we can effectively utilize these resources.

Much research has been done in microarchitectural resource management such as providing two-level implementations of register files, issue queues, and the LSQ [2–4,11,16,23,27]. This prior research focuses on hardware-only approach. A primary benefit of hardware-only approaches is that they can be readily deployed into existing architectures and maintain binary compatibility. However, the introduction of software to gather information has many advantages over a hardware-only approach. First, a software component can analyze the static code in a more global fashion and obtain information hardware alone can not (efficiently) obtain. For instance, a compiler can easily determine that a register is dead on all possible subsequent paths, whereas in hardware, the same information would be highly inefficient to obtain. Thus, a hardware-software *cooperative* approach can achieve better optimization with lower overall system complexity. Second, even if certain information is practical to obtain via hardware look-ahead, there is a recurring energy overhead associated with it, possibly for every dynamic instance of some event. With the increasing importance of energy efficiency, we argue that a cooperative approach to resource management (or optimization in general) is a promising area that deserves more attention.

A cooperative approach does raise several new issues. One important issue is the support for a general-purpose interface to communicate information between the software and hardware components *without creating compatibility obligations*. Although this is a different topic altogether and an in-depth study is beyond the scope of this paper, we note that this could be achieved through decoupling the architected ISA (instruction set architecture) and the physical ISA and rely on binary translation between the two. Such virtualization of ISA is feasible, well understood, and tested in real-world products [15]. In Figure 1, we illustrate one example system where the hardware can directly execute un-translated "external" binaries as well as translated internal ones. In such a system, different implementations are compatible at the architected ISA level but *do not* maintain compatibility at the physical ISA level. Thus, necessary physical ISA changes to support certain optimization can be easily removed when the optimization is no longer appropriate such as when superseded by a better approach or when it prevents/complicates a more important new optimization. In our study, we assume such support to extend the physical ISA is available.

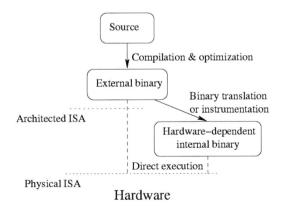

Figure 1. Instruction set architecture support for low-level software-hardware cooperative optimization.

2.2 Cooperative Memory Disambiguation

In this paper, we look at a particular microarchitectural resource, the LSQ used in dynamic memory disambiguation. For space constraint, we do not detail the general operation of the LSQ [10, 26]. Because of the frequent associative searching with wide operands (memory addresses) and the complex priority encoding logic, the LSQ is probably the least scalable structure in an out-of-order core. Yet, *all* resources need to scale up in order to buffer more in-flight instructions. In Figure 2, we show the average performance improvements of increasing the load queue (LQ) size from 48 entries in the otherwise scaled-up baseline configuration (see Section 5). In contrast, we also show the improvement from doubling the number of functional units and issue-width (16-issue) and from doubling the width throughout the pipeline (decode/rename/issue/commit). Predictably, simply increasing issue width or even the entire pipeline's width has a small impact. In contrast, increasing LQ size has a larger impact than doubling the width of the entire processor, which is far more costly. In floating-point applications, this difference is significant. Ironically, these applications tend to have a more regular memory access pattern and in fact do not actually have a high demand for dynamic memory disambiguation.

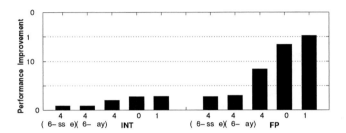

Figure 2. Average performance improvement for SPEC Int and SPEC FP applications as a result of increasing issue width, entire processor pipeline width, or the LQ size.

We envision a *cooperative memory disambiguation* mechanism which uses software to analyze the program binary and, given implementation details, annotate the binary to indicate to hardware what set of memory operations need dynamic memory disambiguation. The hardware can then spend resources only on those operations. In this paper, we focus on load instructions and identify what we call *safe loads*. These instructions are guaranteed (sometimes conditionally) not to overlap with older in-flight stores and hence do not need to check the store queue (SQ) when they execute and do not need an LQ entry. This saves energy needed to search the SQ associatively and reduces the pressure on the LQ.

Using a binary parser, we identify two types of safe loads. First, read-only loads are safe by definition. We use the parser to perform extended constant propagation in order to identify addresses pointing to read-only data segments. Second, in the steady state of loops, any pending stores come from the loop body. In those loops with regular array-based accesses, we can relatively easily determine the relationship between the address of a load and those of all older pending stores. We can thus identify loads that can not possibly overlap with any older pending stores, given architecture details, which determine the number of in-flight instructions. Load identified as safe will be encoded differently by the binary parser and handled accordingly by the hardware.

In addition to identify safe loads statically, we also use software and hardware to cooperate in identifying safe loads dynamically.

We use the same binary parser to identify safe stores that are guaranteed not to overlap with future loads (within a certain scope). Safe stores thus identified can indirectly lead to the discovery of more safe loads at runtime: at the dispatch time of a regular (unsafe) load, if all in-flight stores are safe stores, the load can be treated as a safe load. In the following, we will discuss the algorithms we use in the parser and the hardware support needed.

3 Static Analysis with Binary Parsing

We use a parser based on `alto` [20] and work on the program's binary. If the source code or an information-rich intermediate representation (*e.g.*, [1]) is available, more information can be extracted to identify safe loads more effectively. Without a sophisticated compiler infrastructure, our analysis presented in this work is much less powerful than the state-of-the-art compiler-based dependence analysis or alias analysis. However, this lack of strength does not prevent our proof-of-concept effort to show the benefit of a cooperative approach to memory disambiguation: a more advanced analysis can only improve the effectiveness of this approach.

Our parser targets two types of memory accesses: load from read-only data segments and regular array-based accesses. We emphasize that the goal of using static memory disambiguation is to reduce the unnecessary waste of LSQ resources: to remove those easily analyzable accesses from competing for the resource with those that truly require dynamic disambiguation. Therefore, we do not expect to reduce LSQ pressure for *all* applications. In fact, it is conceivable that for many applications, the parser may not be able to analyze a majority of the read accesses.

3.1 Identifying Read-Only Data Accesses

By definition, read-only data will not be written by stores and therefore, a load of read-only data (referred to as a read-only load hereafter) does not need to be disambiguated from pending stores. To study the potential of identifying read-only loads, we experiment with statically linked Alpha COFF binary format. In this format, there are a few read-only sections storing literals, constants, and other read-only data such as addresses. These sections include `.rconst`, `.rdata`, `.lit4`, `.lit8`, `.lita`, `.pdata`, and `.xdata`. The global pointer (GP), which points to the starting point of the global data section in memory, is a constant in these binaries. The address ranges of read-only sections and the initial value of GP are all encoded in the binary and are thus known to the parser. Since our goal is to explore the potential of cooperative resource management, our effort is not about addressing all possible implementation issues given different binary conventions, or non-conforming binaries. Indeed, when cooperative models are shown to be promising and subsequently adopted in future products, new conventions may be created to maximize their effectiveness.

Knowing the locations of the read-only sections, we can identify static load instructions whose runtime effective address is guaranteed to fall into one of the read-only sections. If a load uses GP as the base address register, it is straightforward to determine whether it is a read-only load. However, to determine if a load using another register as the base is read-only or not, we need to perform data-flow analysis. Our analysis is very similar to constant propagation. The difference is that a register may have different incoming constant values but all point to the read-only sections. In normal constant propagation, the register is usually considered unknown, whereas for our purpose, we know that if a load instruction uses this register as the base *with a zero offset* it is a safe load.

In our algorithm, a register can be in four different states: no

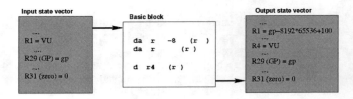

Figure 3. An example of register state propagation via symbolic execution. `lda` and `ldah` are address manipulation instructions equivalent to add with a literal.

information (NI), value known (VK), value is an address in read-only sections (RO), and value unknown (VU). Except for the GP and ZERO registers, whose value we know at all time, all other registers are initialized to NI. After initialization, we symbolically execute basic blocks on the work list, which is set to contain all the basic blocks at the beginning. During the symbolic execution, only when an instruction is in the form of adding a literal (*i.e.*, $R_i = R_j + literal$) and the source register's state is VK do we set the state of destination register to VK and compute the actual value. In all other cases, the destination register's state is assigned VU (see example in Figure 3).

When joining all predecessors' output vectors to form a basic block's input state vector, a register is VK only if its state in all incoming vectors is VK and the value is the same (normal constant propagation rule). Additionally, a register can be in state RO if in all predecessor blocks it either has a state of RO or has a state of VK and the value points to a read-only section. Otherwise, the register's state is set to VU. Any change in a basic block's input state puts it in the work list for another round of symbolic execution. Essentially, our algorithm is a special constant propagation algorithm with a slightly different lattice as shown in Figure 4. Thus, termination can be similarly proved. Once the data-flow process converges, we perform another pass of symbolic execution for each basic block to determine which load instruction is a read-only load.

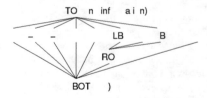

Figure 4. Lattice used in the special constant propagation algorithm. LB and UB indicate the lower and upper address bound of a read-only section. Only one address pair is shown.

In this analysis, we assume the availability of a complete control flow graph with help from the relocation table in the binary [20]. When the table is not embedded in the binary, we can adopt a number of different approaches with different tradeoff between implementation complexity and coverage of read-only loads. On the conservative side, we can do address propagation only within basic blocks or none at all (*i.e.*, identifying only read-only loads with GP as the base register). In a more aggressive implementation, we can profile the application to find out destinations of indirect jumps. We can use the information to augment the control flow. In such a profile-based implementation, as a runtime safety net, a wrapper for all the indirect jumps is employed to detect jumps to destinations not seen before [8]. When such a jump is detected, the runtime system can disable the optimization for the current execution and record the new destination so that the parser can fix the binary for future runs.

3.2 Identifying Other Safe Loads

During an out-of-order program execution, loads are executed eagerly and may access memory before an older store to the same location has been committed, thereby loading stale data from memory. In theory, any load could load stale data and thus the LSQ disambiguates all memory instructions indiscriminately [10, 26]. In practice, however, out-of-order execution is only performed in a limited scope. If the load instruction is sufficiently "far away" from the producer stores, in a normal implementation, we can *guarantee* the relative order. For example, if there are more dynamic store instructions between the producer store and a consumer load than the size of the SQ, then by the time the load is executed, we can guarantee that the producer store has been committed. Notice that the software component in the cooperative optimization model is part of the implementation and therefore can use implementation-specific parameters such as the size of the re-order buffer (ROB) and the SQ. With this knowledge of the processor, we can deduct which stores can still be in-flight when a load executes. We can then analyze the relationship between a load and only those stores. When a load does not overlap with these stores, it is a safe load. To make the job of analyzing all possible prior pending stores tractable, we target loops.

Scope of analysis We only consider loops that do not have other loops nested inside or any function calls/indirect jumps. Additionally if a loop overlaps with a previously analyzed loop, we also ignore it. When a loop has internal control flows, the number of possible execution paths grows exponentially and the analysis becomes intractable. To avoid this problem, we can form traces [14] within the loop body and treat any diversion from the trace as side exits of the loop (which we did in an earlier implementation). This, however, does not significantly increase the coverage of loads in the applications we studied. For simplicity of discussion, we stick with the more limited scope: inner loops without any internal control flows. Note that the loop can still have branches inside, only that these branches have to be side exits. In our study, this scope still covers a significant fraction of dynamic loads (63% for floating-point applications).

In the *steady state* of these loops, only different iterations of the loop will be in-flight. For every load, the maximum number of older in-flight instructions is finite due to various resource constraints and can be determined as $min(C(S_{ROB}), C(S_{SQ}), ..)$, where $C(S_r)$ is the maximum capacity of in-flight instructions when resource r's size is S_r. The set of store instances a load needs to disambiguate against can be precisely determined given the loop body. For convenience, we refer to this set as the disambiguation store set (DSS) hereafter. For example, if the ROB has n entries, the DSS of a load is at most all the stores in the preceding n instructions from the load. If the parser can statically determine that the load does not conflict with any store instance in the DSS then the load is safe in the steady state. Before reaching this steady state, however, a load can be in-flight together with stores from code sections prior to the loop, outside the scope of the analysis. For this initial transient state, we revert to hardware disambiguation to guarantee memory-based dependences. We place a marker instruction (mark_sq in the example shown later in Figure 7) before the loop and any identified safe load will be treated by the hardware as a normal load until all stores prior to the marker drain out of the processor. The design of the hardware support is discussed in Section 4.

Symbolic execution Intuitively, strided array access is a frequent pattern in many loops. With strided accesses, the address at any particular iteration i can be calculated before entering the loop and therefore whether a load overlaps with the stores from the DSS can also be known before entering the loop. Thus, we can generate condition testing code to put in the prologue of the loop. This prologue computes conditions under which a load does not overlap with any stores in its DSS for *any* iteration i. We can then allow the load to become a conditional safe load based on the generated condition. Conditional safe load can be implemented via condition registers reminiscent of predicate registers (Section 4).

To identify these strided accesses and derive the expressions of the address, we use an ad hoc analysis that symbolically executes the loop and tracks the register content. When an address register's state converges to a strided pattern, we can derive its value expression, and hence the steady-state address expression.

Each entry of the symbol table contains a $Base$ and an $Offset$ component ($r_i = Base + Offset$). We use symbols $\_R0$, $\_R1$, ..., and $\_R30$ to represent the loop inputs: the initial values of registers r0 through r30 upon entering the loop (r31 is the hardwired zero register in our environment). Thus the table starts with ($r_i = \_R_i + 0$) as shown in Figure 5. The symbolic execution then propagates these values through address manipulation instructions. To keep the analysis simple and because we are interested in strided access only, we only support one form of address manipulation instructions: add-constant instructions (or ACI for short). This type includes instructions that perform addition/subtraction of a register and a literal (*e.g.*, in Alpha instruction set: lda, ldah, some variations of add/sub with a literal operand, etc.) and addition/subtraction of two registers but one is loop-invariant. When such an instruction is encountered, the source register's $Base$ and $Offset$ component is propagated to the destination register with the adjustment of the constant (literal or the content of a loop-invariant register) to $Offset$. Any other instructions (*e.g.*, load) would cause the $Base$ of destination register to be set to UNKNOWN. Therefore, at any moment, a register can be either UNKNOWN or of the form ($\_R_i + const$).

To further clarify the operations, we walk through an example shown in Figure 5. The figure shows some snapshots of the register symbolic value table *before* executing instructions ①, ②, and ③. In iteration 0, $r3$'s value is initial value $\_R3 + 0$. After instruction ①, which loads into $r3$, its symbolic value becomes UNKNOWN. However, after instruction ⑤, the value becomes known again, in the form of $\_R2 + 8$. To detect strided accesses and compute stride, the symbolic value of the address register (shaded entries in Figure 5) in one iteration is recorded to compare to that of the next iteration. In iteration 0 and 1, $r3$'s values at instruction ① do not "converge" because of the two different reaching definitions. However, in iteration 1 and 2, the values converge to $\_R2 + const$ (with different constants). Since every register used in the loop can have up to two reaching definitions (one from within the loop which is essentially straight-line code and another from before the loop), it may take several iterations for a register to converge. In certain cases, where there is a chain of cyclic assignments, there may not be a convergence. Therefore, our algorithm iterates until the $Base$ component of all registers converge or until we reach a certain limit of iterations (100 in this paper).

Once the $Base$ component converges at *each point* of the loop (*i.e.*, after symbolic execution of every instruction, the destination register's $Base$ is the same as in the prior iteration at the same pro-

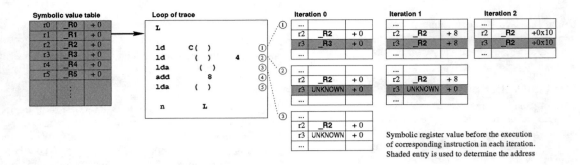

Figure 5. Example of symbolic execution. The register symbolic value is expressed as the sum of an initial register value (*e.g.*, _R1) and a constant (*e.g.*, +0x10). In this example, we show that the first load renders register r3 to become UNKNOWN. This makes the second load un-analyzable. However, register r3 is always known before the execution of the first load, which makes it analyzable. `ld` is a load, `addq` is a 64-bit add, `lda` is an address calculation equivalent to adding constant, and `bne` is a conditional branch.

gram point), no "new" propagation of *Base* is done and therefore the *Base* component of all registers stays the same in subsequent iterations. After convergence, the only change to the symbolic table is that of the *Offset*, and only an ACI (whose source register's *Base* is not UNKNOWN) changes that. The set of ACIs in the entire loop are fixed and always add the same constants, and therefore the change to the *Offset* in the symbol table will be constant for each entry.

Before the base address register of a load converges, the address can have transient-state expressions. In the example shown in Figure 5, the first load's effective address (r3+0xC) can be _R3+0xC or _R2+0xC+8 * *i* (*i* = 1, 2, ...). When generating conditions, we make sure all possibilities are considered. We also note that for *any* load to be safe, *all* stores in the loop have to be analyzable.

Condition generation After the address expressions are computed, we analyze those of the loads against those of the stores and determine under what conditions a load never accesses the same location as any store in the DSS. Since each static store may have multiple instances in a load's DSS, we summarize all locations accessed by these store instances as an address range. Given a strided load, we find out the condition that the load's address falls outside all address ranges for all static stores. Such a range test is a sufficient but not necessary condition to guarantee the safety of the load. The pseudo code of this algorithm is shown in Figure 6. We use *i* to indicate any iteration. The conditions generated have to be loop-invariant (*i.e.*, independent of *i*) since they will be tested in the prologue of the loop once for the entire loop. Therefore, when the loads and stores have different strides, our algorithm would not compare them. To remove this limitation, one could apply other tests such as the GCD test or the Omega test [22].

We now show a typical code example based on a real application in Figure 7-(a). In this loop, there are 17 instructions, two of them stores. In our baseline configuration, DSS membership is limited by the 32-entry SQ. Then, in the steady state, there can be at most 16 outstanding iterations. In this particular example, every load has the same set of 32 dynamic store instances in its DSS. Also, none of the loads or stores has transient-state address. In iteration *i*, the (quad-word aligned) address range of these store instances is $[\_R11 + (i-16)*16, \_R11+(i-1)*16+8]$ and the address of $Ld1$ is $\_R3+16*i$. ($\_R11$ and $\_R3$ are the initial values at loop entrance of register r11 and r3 respectively.) If the address of $Ld1$ falls outside the range, $Ld1$ becomes a safe load. The condition for that is $(\_R3 + 16 * i < \_R11 + (i-16)*16)$ **OR** $(\_R3+16*i > \_R11+(i-1)*16+8)$.

```
foreach l in {all static loads with stride}
    cs[l] = { }        // initial condition set empty
    foreach s = {all static stores}
        // find out range of static instances of s in l[i]'s DSS
        j = min n, s[n] ∈ DSS(l[i])
        k = max n, s[n] ∈ DSS(l[i])
        [r_lb, r_ub] = Address range of {s[j] ... s[k]}

        // Load l's current iteration address or its transient-
        // state addresses can not overlap with the address
        // range of outstanding instances of store s or its
        // transient-state addresses
        cs[l] = cs[l] ∪ (Addr(l[i]) > r_ub||Addr(l[i]) < r_lb)
        cs[l] = cs[l] ∪ (TrAddr(l) > r_ub||TrAddr(l) < r_lb)
        cs[l] = cs[l] ∪ (Addr(l[i]) ≠ TrAddr(s))
        cs[l] = cs[l] ∪ (TrAddr(l) ≠ TrAddr(s))
    end
    Simplify conditions in cs[l]
end
```

Figure 6. Pseudo code of the algorithm that determines the condition for a strided load to be safe. $l[i]$ ($s[j]$) indicates the dynamic instance of l (s) in iteration i (j). DSS($l[i]$) is $l[i]$'s disambiguation store set.

After solving the inequalities, we get $(\_R3 - \_R11 + 8 > 0)$ **OR** $(\_R3 - \_R11 + 256 < 0)$. Likewise, we can compute the condition for $Ld2$ to be safe: $(\_R3 - \_R11 + 16 > 0)$ **OR** $(\_R3 - \_R11 + 264 < 0)$. The two conditions can be combined into one: $(\_R3 - \_R11 + 8 > 0)$ **OR** $(\_R3 - \_R11 + 264 < 0)$. The addresses of $Ld3$ and $Ld4$ are $\_R11 + 16 * i$ and $\_R11 + 8 + 16 * i$. They can be statically determined to be safe, without the need for runtime condition testing. So they are assigned a special condition register CR_TRUE (Section 4). Figure 7-(b) shows the resulted code after binary parser's analysis and transformation. To be concise, we only show pseudo code of condition evaluation.

Pruning and condition consolidation In the most straightforward implementation, every analyzable load has its own set of conditions and allocates a condition register. Optionally, we can perform profile-driven pruning. Using a training input, we can identify conditions that are likely to be true and those that are not. This al-

```
0x120033140: ldl r31, 256(r3)        ;    prefetch
0x120033144: ldt f21, 0(r3)          ; Ld1
0x120033148: lda r27, -2(r27)        ;    r27 <- r27-2
0x12003314c: lda r3, 16(r3)          ;    r3 <- r3+16
0x120033150: ldt f22, -8(r3)         ; Ld2
0x120033154: ldt f23, 0(r11)         ; Ld3
0x120033158: cmple r27, 0x1, r1      ;    compare
0x12003315c: lda r11, 16(r11)        ;    r11 <- r11+16
0x120033160: ldt f24, -8(r11)        ; Ld4
0x120033164: lds f31, 240(r11)       ;    prefetch
0x120033168: mult f20, f21, f21      ;
0x12003316c: mult f20, f22, f22      ;
0x120033170: addt f23, f21, f21      ;
0x120033174: addt f24, f22, f22      ;
0x120033178: stt f21, -16(r11)       ; St1
0x12003317c: stt f22, -8(r11)        ; St2
0x120033180: beq r1, 0x120033140     ;
```

(a) Original code

```
New_loop_entry: mark_sq
                if(r3-r11+8>0) or (r3-r11+264<0) then
                    cset CR0, 1

0x120033140: ldl r31, 256(r3)
0x120033144: sldt f21, 0(r3), [CR0]; safe load with
             :                   ; cond. reg. CR0
0x120033150: sldt f22,-8(r3), [CR0]
0x120033154: sldt f23, 0(r11), [CR_TRUE]
             :
0x120033160: sldt f24, -8(r11), [CR_TRUE]
             :
             :
0x120033178: stt f21, -16(r11)
0x12003317c: stt f22, -8(r11)
0x120033180: beq r1, 0x120033140
```

(b) Transformed code

Figure 7. Code example from application *galgel*.

lows us to transform unlikely safe loads back to normal loads and thus eliminate unnecessary condition calculation. Perhaps a more important implication of profiling is condition consolidation. Since the remaining safe loads' conditions tend to be true, we can "AND" them together to use fewer condition registers. In the extreme, we can use only one condition register and thus make it the implied condition (even for the unconditional safe loads). Furthermore, we can limit the types of safe load to a few common cases. These measures together will reduce the (physical) instruction code space needed to support our cooperative memory disambiguation model. The tradeoff is that fewer loads will be treated as safe at runtime. We study this tradeoff in Section 6.

Finally, we note that the address used in the parser is virtual address and if a program deliberately maps different virtual pages to the same physical page, the parser can inaccurately identify loads as safe. In general, such address "pinning" is very uncommon: none of the applications we studied does this. In practice, the parser can search in the binary for the related system calls to pin virtual pages and insert code to disable the entire mechanism should those calls be invoked at runtime.

Bypassing load through identifying safe stores Like loads, stores can also be "safe" if it is guaranteed not to overlap with any *future* in-flight loads. In this paper, we identify safe stores in order to indirectly discovery more safe loads. If there is an unanalyzable store in a loop, usually none of the loads may be safe because the DSS of any load is very likely to contain at least one instance of the unanalyzable store. However, the DSS is defined very conservatively and in practice, when a load is brought into the pipeline, usually only a subset of these store instances in the DSS are still in-flight. If this subset does not contain any instance of unanalyzable

stores, then the load may still be safe. If we can identify and mark safe stores that do not overlap with future in-flight loads, then at runtime when a normal load is dispatched while there are only safe stores in-flight, we can guarantee that the load will not overlap with any single store. Consequently, we do not need any further dynamic disambiguation and therefore can re-encode the load as a safe load.

The algorithm to identify safe stores mirrors the above-mentioned algorithm to identify safe loads: (1) Instead of finding a load's DSS, we find a store's DLS (disambiguation load set), which contains loads *later* than the store; (2) For a store to be safe, all *loads* in the loop have to be analyzable; (3) Since a safe store is only "safe" with respect to loads within the loop, we place a marker (mark_sq) upon the *exit* of the loop. As before, an in-flight marker indicates transient state, during which period all loads are handled as normal loads.

4 Architectural Support

Encoding safe loads For those safe loads identified by software, we need a mechanism to encode the information and communicate it to the hardware. There are a number of options. One possibility is to generate a mask for the text section. One or more bits are associated with each instruction differentiating safe loads from other loads. The mask can be stored in the program binary separate from the text. During an instruction cache fill, special predecoding logic can fetch the instructions and the corresponding masks and store the internal, predecoded instruction format in the I-cache. A more straightforward approach is to extend the *physical* ISA to represent safe loads and modify load instructions *in situ*, in the text section. Since we use a binary parser, this extension of the physical ISA does not affect the architected ISA (Section 2). Our study assumes this latter approach.

Conditional safe loads When the parser transforms a normal load into a safe load, there is a condition register associated with it. Only when the condition register is true will the safe load instruction be treated as safe. The architectural support needed includes (a) a few single-bit condition registers, similar to predicate registers, (b) a special instruction (cset) that sets a condition register, and (c) a safe load instruction (sld) that encodes the condition register used. At the dispatch time of an sld instruction, if the value of the specified condition register is false, the safe load will be treated just like a normal load and placed into the LQ. Since the sld instructions after a cset instruction (in program order) can be dispatched before the cset has set the condition (at the execution stage), the condition register is conservatively reset (set to false) when the cset instruction is dispatched. Alternatively, we can flash-reset all condition registers when dispatching the marker (mark_sq) instruction. A special condition register CR_TRUE is dedicated for unconditional safe loads. It can be set to true either explicitly by a cset or implicitly when a mark_sq is dispatched.

SQ marker The analyzer places a mark_sq instruction to indicate the scope of the analysis: all the dynamic stores older than the marker are outside the scope of the analysis and can overlap with subsequent loads. Therefore, even though the condition register's value may be true, conditional safe loads still need to be treated as normal loads until the stores older than the marker drain out of the SQ. By that time, future safe loads can be dispatched as safe loads (if the condition is satisfied).

While conceptually a marker can be a special occupant of an SQ entry, in a real implementation, we use an extra (marker) bit associated with each entry to represent a scope marker: when a mark_sq instruction is dispatched, the marker bit of the youngest valid entry in the SQ (if any) is set. This bit is cleared when that entry is recycled. This design allows two practical advantages. First, we do not waste an SQ entry just to store a marker. Second, and more importantly, the special processing of multiple markers in the SQ is simpler. It is possible that more than one marker appears in the SQ, and only when all markers drain out of the SQ can we let conditional safe loads to bypass the LQ. With the marker bits, it is easy to detect if all markers are drained: any bit that is set pulls down a global signal line. A high voltage in the line indicates the lack of in-flight marker.

Indirect Jumps Though exceedingly unlikely, it is possible that the control flow transfers into a loop through an indirect jump without going through the prologue where the analyzer places the SQ marker and condition testing instructions. To ensure that we do not incorrectly use an uninitialized condition register, we flash-clear all condition registers (including CR_TRUE) when an indirect jump instruction is dispatched.

Safe stores In terms of instruction encoding and the use of condition registers, safe stores are no different from safe loads. However, the handling of safe stores is quite different: because our purpose of identifying them is to further increase the number of safe loads, we are only interested in when the SQ contains just safe stores. The hardware implementation is simple: any entry with a valid, normal (unsafe) store can pull down a global signal line. When this signal is high, we can dynamically dispatch a regular load as a safe one. Of course, software-identified safe stores are safe only within the scope of the analysis (loop). When a loop terminates, the hardware needs to be notified. This is handled by the same SQ marker mechanism described above: when a marker is in-flight, the hardware treats all loads as normal loads. We note that a degenerate form of this mechanism is to dispatch a load as a safe load when there is no in-flight stores at all. This mechanism can be implemented purely in hardware without any software support.

In contrast to the simple support needed in our design, safe stores could be exploited to reduce the pressure of SQ but would require more extensive hardware support. Very likely, we need to split the functionalities of SQ and implement a FIFO queue for buffering and in-order committing of stores and an associative queue for disambiguation and forwarding. Perhaps the more challenging aspect of the design is that we need to ensure that when the scope of analysis (in our case loops) is exited, the identified safe stores from the loop have to participate in the disambiguation/forwarding process with loads from after the exit.

Support for coherent I/O Moving a load out of the LQ prevents the normal monitoring by the coherence and consistency maintenance mechanism. Therefore, the design requires additional support to function in a multiprocessor environment, which is the subject of our on-going work. We note that in a uni-processor environment, if the system provides coherent I/O, there is also the need to monitor load ordering to enforce write serialization, an implicit requirement of coherence. Maintaining write serialization is often done by monitoring the execution of load instructions to detect violations: two loads to the same location executed out of program order and separated by an invalidation to the same location (caused by a DMA transfer). However, invalidations due to DMA transfers are exceedingly infrequent compared to stores issued by the processor. Consequently, we can use a separate, light-weight mechanism such as hash tables to keep track of load ordering involving safe loads, thereby avoiding undue increase of LQ pressure. We studied ways to keep track of memory addresses of safe loads. For brevity, we leave the details in [12].

5 Experimental Setup

To evaluate our proposal, we perform a set of experiments using the SimpleScalar [6] 3.0b tool set with the Wattch extension [5] and simulate 1 billion instructions from each of the 26 SPEC CPU2000 benchmarks. We use Alpha binaries.

We made a few simple but important modifications to the simulator. First, we do not allocate an entry in the LQ for loads to the zero register (R31). These essentially prefetch instructions are safe loads that do not need to participate in the dynamic disambiguation process as they do not change program semantics. We note that in our baseline architecture, the LQ only performs disambiguation functions. Buffering information related to outstanding misses is done by the MSHRs (miss status holding registers). If we allocate LQ entries for prefetches, we would exaggerate the result by increasing the pressure on the LQ unnecessarily and quite significantly, since the heavily optimized binaries (compiled using -O4 or -O5) include many prefetches, around 20% of all loads. Second, to model high-performance processors more closely, we simulate speculative load issue (not blocked by prior unresolved stores) and store-load replay. The simulated baseline configuration is listed in Table 1.

Processor core	
Issue/Decode/Commit width	8 / 8 / 8
Issue queue size	64 INT, 64 FP
Functional units	INT 8+2 mul/div, FP 8+2 mul/div
Branch predictor	Bimodal and Gshare combined
- Gshare	8192 entries, 13 bit history
- Bimodal/Meta table/BTB entries	4096/8192/4096 (4 way)
Branch misprediction latency	10+ cycles
ROB/LSQ(LQ,SQ)/Register(INT,FP)	320/96(48,48)/(256,256)
Memory hierarchy	
L1 instruction cache	32KB, 64B line, 2-way, 2 cycle
L1 data cache	32KB, 64B line, 2-way, 2 cycle
	2 (read/write) ports
L2 unified cache	1MB, 64B line, 4-way, 15 cycles
Memory access latency	250 cycles

Table 1. Baseline system configuration.

6 Evaluation

Percentage of safe loads identified The most important metric measuring the effectiveness of our design is the percentage of instructions that bypass the LQ. In Figure 8, we present a breakdown of these safe loads based on their category: (a) read-only loads (ROL), (b) statically safe loads (SSL): loads (other than read-only load) that are encoded as safe loads by the parser and dispatched as safe loads, (c) dynamically safe loads (DSL): normal loads dispatched as safe because all pending stores in the SQ are safe, and (d) degenerate dynamically safe loads (DDSL): normal loads dispatched as safe because the SQ is empty at that time. In Figure 9 we show the number of safe stores identified.

As we can see from Figure 8, in floating-point applications, a significant portion of the loads are safe, suggesting the effectiveness of the cooperative approach. As can be expected, the parser identifies a larger portion of safe loads in floating-point applications than in integer applications. In three applications, about 80% or more loads are dispatched as safe. Even targeting just read-only loads, we can still mark up to 20% of loads as safe.

We can also see that there is only a small portion of dynamically safe loads although Figure 9 shows an average of 30% and up to 98% of stores in floating-point applications are safe. Apparently, we need a very significant number of safe stores to get a sufficient amount of DSL. In applications *applu* and *mgrid*, we do observe a

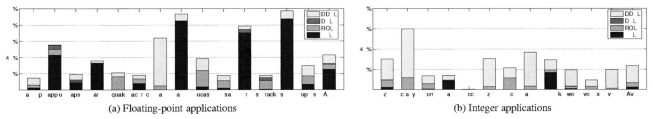

(a) Floating-point applications   (b) Integer applications

Figure 8. The breakdown of dynamic load instructions dispatched as safe.

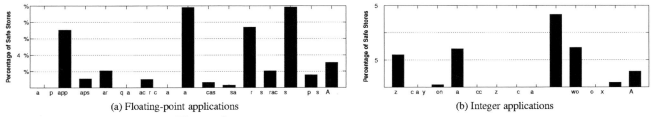

(a) Floating-point applications   (b) Integer applications

Figure 9. The percentage of store instructions that are safe.

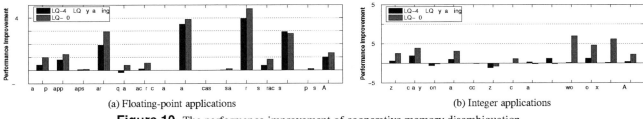

(a) Floating-point applications   (b) Integer applications

Figure 10. The performance improvement of cooperative memory disambiguation.

notable fraction of DSL correlated with the high percentage of safe stores. However, in *galgel* and *swim*, the memory access pattern is very regular. So much so, that more than 90% of loads are statically safe loads, subsuming most would-be dynamically safe loads.

In addition, we see that the percentage of degenerate dynamically safe loads is quite small in floating-point applications, suggesting that only targeting these loads is unlikely to be very effective.

Overall, these results show the effectiveness of cross-layer optimizations, where information useful for optimization in one layer can be hard to obtain in that layer (*e.g.*, hardware), but is easy to obtain in another layer (*e.g.*, compiler, programming language). With simple hardware support, our cooperative disambiguation scheme filters out an average of 43% and up to 97% of loads from doing the unnecessary dynamic disambiguation or competing for related resources.

	Not Safe		Safe		
	A	B	C	D	E
INT	9.2%	10.2%	12.9%	4.0%	40.0%
FP	7.7%	6.6%	13.5%	3.7%	25.6%

Table 2. Breakdown of loads not dispatched as safe.

Finally, in Table 2, we show the breakdown of the dynamic load instructions not identified as safe, including: (A) those that actually read from an in-flight store; (B) those that read from a committed store that is in the load's disambiguation store set (this category excludes those loads dynamically identified as safe – DSL or DDSL); (C) those that are analyzed by the parser but not marked as a safe load; (D) those that are dispatched in the transient state when a marker is still in-flight; and (E) those that are outside the scope of analysis. Loads in categories C, D, and E do not read from any stores in their DSS. In categories A and B, the parser correctly keeps

the load instructions regular, whereas in categories C, D, and E, a more powerful parser may be able to prove some of them safe. We see that to further enhance the effectiveness, we can target category E by broadening the scope of analysis. For example, with the capability to perform inter-procedural analysis, we can handle loops with function calls inside.

Performance impact Reducing resource pressure ameliorates bottleneck and allows a given architecture to exceed its original buffering capability, which in turn increases exploitable ILP. However, quantifying such performance benefit is not entirely straightforward: reducing the pressure on one microarchitectural resource may shift the bottleneck to another, especially if the system is well balanced to start with. Thus, to get an understanding of how effective cooperative disambiguation can be, we experiment with a baseline configuration where other resources are provisioned more generously than the LQ. In Figure 10, we show the performance improvement obtained through LQ bypassing in this baseline configuration. For comparison, we also show the improvement obtained when the LQ size is significantly increased to 80 entries.

For some applications, we can clearly observe the correlation between the percentage of loads bypassing the LQ and the performance improvement. For example, the three floating-point applications that have about 80% or more loads bypassing the LQ (*galgel*, *mgrid*, and *swim*) obtain a significant performance improvement of 29-40%. In general, the effect of identifying safe loads to bypass LQ brings the performance potential of a much larger LQ without the circuit and logic design challenges of building a large LQ.

Clearly, increasing the LQ size only increases the *potential* of performance improvement. Indeed, integer applications in general do not show significant improvement when the LQ size is increased. For a few applications, performance actually degrades. This is possible because, for example, the processor may forge ahead deeper

255

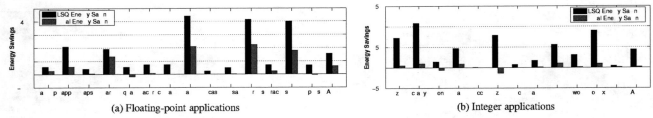

Figure 11. The energy savings of cooperative memory disambiguation.

on the wrong path and creates more pollution in the cache. We can also see this degradation in the configuration with an 80-entry LQ. Through instrumentation, however, we can identify loops whose overall performance was negatively affected after transforming regular loads to safe loads. We verified that changing these safe loads back to regular ones eliminates all the performance degradation. Predictably, such a feedback-based pruning has an insignificant impact on other applications.

Energy impact In Figure 11, we show the energy impact of our optimization. Specifically, we compute the energy savings in the LSQ and throughout the processor. Energy savings in the LSQ mainly come from the fact that safe loads do not search the SQ. Note that our cooperative memory disambiguation does not reduce energy spent by store instructions accessing the LSQ or the clock power in the LSQ. Thus even with close to 100% loads bypassing the LQ in some applications, the energy savings in the LSQ is less than half. The processor-wide energy savings are mainly the byproduct of expedited execution as according to our Wattch-based simulator, the energy consumption of the LQ and SQ combined is only about 3%. This is also reflected in the results of some applications. For example, in *equake*, *eon* and *gzip*, the total energy savings are negated because of the slowdown. Again, after we apply the feedback-guided pruning mentioned above, the slowdown is eliminated, the performance and energy consumption stay almost unchanged as only a small number of loads still bypass the LQ.

Consolidation of condition registers In the above analysis, we assume we have a sufficient number of condition registers, therefore each conditional load instruction uses its own condition register. In our application suite, at most 14 such registers are needed. As explained before, for implementation simplicity, we may choose to use fewer or even just one (implied) condition register. When we limit the number of condition registers to two, we observe no noticeable performance impact for any application we studied. With only one condition register, a naive approach is to set it to the "AND" of all conditions. This creates some "pollution" as one unsatisfied condition prevents all loads in the same loop from becoming safe loads. However, we found that even when we use the naive approach to share the sole condition register, only 3 applications show performance degradation compared to using unlimited number of condition registers: *ammp* (-2.5%), *applu* (-5.9%), and *art* (-15.3%). The rest of the applications show no observable impact. Intuitively, a feedback-based approach can help reduce the impact of condition register deficiency. We found that even simple pruning can be very effective: by filtering out the loads whose condition is never satisfied in a training run, we eliminated the performance degradation of *ammp* and *applu*. However, with such a small set of applications to study, we can not draw many general conclusions.

Overhead of condition testing code Finally, we also collect statistics on the actual performance overhead incurred because of executing condition-testing instructions for safe loads. The overhead turns out to be very small. On average, it is about 0.2% of

the total dynamic instructions. The maximum overhead is only 1.6%. This overhead can be further reduced by applying profile-based pruning. It is worth mentioning that the offline analysis incurs very little overhead too. On a mid-range PC, our parser takes between 1 and 16 seconds analyzing the suite of applications used. The average run time is 3 seconds.

7 Related Work

To increase the number of in-flight instructions, the effective capacity of various microarchitectural resources need to be scaled accordingly. The challenge is to do so without significantly increasing access latency, energy consumption, and design complexity. There are several techniques that address the issue by reducing the frequency of accessing large structures or the performance impact of doing so. Sethumadhavan et al. propose to use bloom filters to reduce the access frequency of the LSQ [25]. When the address misses in the bloom filter, it is guaranteed that the LQ (SQ) does not contain the address, and therefore the checking can be skipped.

A large body of work adopts a two-level approach to disambiguation and forwarding. The guiding principle is largely the same. That is to make the first-level (L1) structure small (thus fast and energy efficient) and still able to perform a large majority of the work. This L1 structure is backed up by a much larger second-level (L2) structure to correct/complement the work of the L1 structure. The L1 structure can be allocated according to program order or execution order (within a bank, if banked) for every store [2, 11, 27] or only allocated to those stores predicted to be involved in forwarding [4, 23]. The L2 structure is also used in varying ways due to different focuses. It can be banked to save energy per access [4, 23]; it can be filtered to reduce access frequency (and thus energy) [2, 25]; or it can be simplified in functionality such as removing the forwarding capability [27].

Most of these approaches are hardware-only techniques and focus on the *provisioning* side of the issue by reducing the negative impact of using a large load queue. Every load still "rightfully" occupies some resource in these designs. Our approach, on the other hand, addresses the *consumption* side of the issue: loads that can be statically disambiguated do not need redundant dynamic disambiguation and therefore are barred from competing for the precious resources. We have shown that in some applications, a significant percentage of loads are positively identified as safe. With increased sophistication in the analysis methods, we expect an even larger portion to be proven safe. When only provisioning-side optimizations are applied, these loads will still consume resources. Additionally, our design is a very cost-effective alternative. It incurs minimal architectural complexity and does not rely on prediction to carry out the optimization, thereby avoids any recurring energy cost for training or table maintenance. Finally, because we are addressing a different part of the problem, our approach can be used in conjunction with some of these hardware-only approaches.

Memory dependence prediction is a well-studied alternative to address-based mechanisms to allow aggressive speculation and yet avoid penalties associated with squashing [9, 17–19]. A key insight of prior studies is that memory-based dependences can be predicted without depending on actual address of each instance of memory instructions and this prediction allows for stream-lined communication between likely dependent pairs. Detailed studies between schemes using dependence speculation and address-based memory schedulers are presented in [19]. A predictor to predict communicating store-load pairs is used by Park et al. to filter out loads that do not belong to any pair so that they do not access the store queue [21]. To ensure correctness, stores check the LQ at commit stage to ensure incorrectly speculated loads are replayed. They also use a smaller buffer to keep out-of-order loads (with respect to other loads) to reduce the impact of LQ checking for load-load order violations.

Value-based re-execution presents a new paradigm for memory disambiguation. In [7], the LQ is eliminated altogether and loads re-execute to validate the prior execution. Notice that the SQ and associated disambiguation/forwarding logic still remain. Filters are developed to reduce the re-execution frequency [7, 24]. Otherwise, the performance impact due to increased memory pressure can be significant [24].

Finally, a software-hardware cooperative strategy has been applied in other optimizations [13, 28]. In [13], a compile-time and run-time cooperative strategy is used for memory disambiguation. If instruction scheduling results in re-ordering of memory accesses not proven safe by the static disambiguation, it is done speculatively through a form of predicated execution. Code to perform runtime alias check is inserted to generate the predicates. In [28], compiler analysis helps significantly reduce cache tag accesses.

8 Conclusions

In this paper, we have proposed a software-hardware cooperative optimization strategy to reduce resource waste of the LSQ. Specifically, a software-based parser analyzes the program binary to identify loads that can safely bypass the dynamic memory disambiguation process. The hardware, on the other hand, only provides support for the software to specify the necessity of disambiguation. Collectively, the mechanism is inexpensive since the complexity is shifted to software and it is effective: on average, 43% of loads bypass the LQ in floating-point applications, and this translates into a 10% performance gain in our baseline architecture.

Our technique demonstrates the potential of a vertically integrated optimization approach, where different system layers communicate with each other beyond standard functional interfaces, so that the layer most efficient in handling an optimization can be used and pass information on to other layers. We believe such a *cooperative* approach will be increasingly resorted to as a way to manage system complexity while continue to deliver system improvements.

Acknowledgments

This work is supported in part by the National Science Foundation through grant CNS-0509270. We wish to thank the anonymous reviewers for their valuable comments and Jose Renau for his help in cross-validating some statistics.

References

[1] V. Adve, C. Lattner, M. Brukman, A. Shukla, and B. Gaeke. LLVA: A Low-level Virtual Instruction Set Architecture. In *International Symposium on Microarchitecture*, pages 205–216, San Diego, California, December 2003.

[2] H. Akkary, R. Rajwar, and S. Srinivasan. Checkpoint Processing and Recovery: Towards Scalable Large Instruction Window Processors. In *International Symposium on Microarchitecture*, pages 423–434, San Diego, California, December 2003.

[3] R. Balasubramanian, D. Albonesi, A. Buyuktosunoglu, and S. Dwarkadas. Memory Hierarchy Reconfiguration for Energy and Performance in General-Purpose Processor Architectures. In *International Symposium on Microarchitecture*, pages 245–257, Monterey, California, December 2000.

[4] L. Baugh and C. Zilles. Decomposing the Load-Store Queue by Function for Power Reduction and Scalability. In *Watson Conference on Interaction between Architecture, Circuits, and Compilers*, Yorktown Heights, New York, October 2004.

[5] D. Brooks, V. Tiwari, and M. Martonosi. Wattch: A Framework for Architectural-Level Power Analysis and Optimizations. In *International Symposium on Computer Architecture*, pages 83–94, Vancouver, Canada, June 2000.

[6] D. Burger and T. Austin. The SimpleScalar Tool Set, Version 2.0. Technical report 1342, Computer Sciences Department, University of Wisconsin-Madison, June 1997.

[7] H. Cain and M. Lipasti. Memory Ordering: A Value-based Approach. In *International Symposium on Computer Architecture*, pages 90–101, Munich, Germany, June 2004.

[8] A. Chernoff, M. Herdeg, R. Hookway, C. Reeve, N. Rubin, T. Tye, S. Yadavalli, and J. Yates. FX!32: A Profile-Directed Binary Translator. *IEEE Micro*, 18(2):56–64, March/April 1998.

[9] G. Chrysos and J. Emer. Memory Dependence Prediction Using Store Sets. In *International Symposium on Computer Architecture*, pages 142 –153, Barcelona, Spain, June–July 1998.

[10] Compaq Computer Corporation. *Alpha 21264/EV6 Microprocessor Hardware Reference Manual*, September 2000. Order number: DS-0027B-TE.

[11] A. Gandhi, H. Akkary, R. Rajwar, S. Srinivasan, and K. Lai. Scalable Load and Store Processing in Latency Tolerant Processors. In *International Symposium on Computer Architecture*, Madison, Wisconsin, June 2005.

[12] A. Garg, R. Huang, and M. Huang. Implementing Software-Hardware Cooperative Memory Disambiguation. Technical report, Electrical & Computer Engineering Department, University of Rochester, December 2005.

[13] A. Huang, G. Slavenburg, and J. Shen. Speculative Disambiguation: A Compilation Technique for Dynamic Memory Disambiguation. In *International Symposium on Computer Architecture*, pages 200–210, Chicago, Illinois, April 1994.

[14] W. Hwu, S. Mahlke, W. Chen, P. Chang, N. Warter, R. Bringmann, R. Ouellette, R. Hank, T. Kiyohara, G. Haab, J. Holm, and D. Lavery. The Superblock: An Effective Technique for VLIW and Superscalar Compilation. *Journal of Supercomputing*, pages 229–248, 1993.

[15] A. Klaiber. The Technology Behind Crusoe™ Processors. Technical Report, Transmeta Corporation, January 2000.

[16] A. Lebeck, J. Koppanalil, T. Li, J. Patwardhan, and E. Rotenberg. A Large, Fast Instruction Window for Tolerating Cache Misses. In *International Symposium on Computer Architecture*, pages 59–70, Anchorage, Alaska, May 2002.

[17] A. Moshovos, S. Breach, T. Vijaykumar, and G. Sohi. Dynamic Speculation and Synchronization of Data Dependences. In *International Symposium on Computer Architecture*, pages 181–193, Denver Colorado, June 1997.

[18] A. Moshovos and G. Sohi. Streamlining Inter-operation Memory Communication via Data Dependence Prediction. In *International Symposium on Microarchitecture*, pages 235–245, Research Triangle Park, North Carolina, December 1997.

[19] A. Moshovos and G. Sohi. Memory Dependence Speculation Tradeoffs in Centralized, Continuous-Window Superscalar Processors. In *International Symposium on High-Performance Computer Architecture*, pages 301–312, Toulouse, France, January 2000.

[20] R. Muth, S. Debray, S. Watterson, and K. De Bosschere. alto: A Link-Time Optimizer for the Compaq Alpha. *Software: Practices and Experience*, 31(1):67–101, January 2001.

[21] I. Park, C. Ooi, and T. Vijaykumar. Reducing Design Complexity of the Load/Store Queue. In *International Symposium on Microarchitecture*, pages 411–422, San Diego, California, December 2003.

[22] W. Pugh. The Omega Test: a Fast and Practical Integer Programming Algorithm for Dependence Analysis. *Communications of the ACM*, 35(8):102–114, August 1992.

[23] A. Roth. A High-Bandwidth Load-Store Unit for Single- and Multi- Threaded Processors. Technical Report (CIS), Development of Computer and Information Science, University of Pennsylvania, September 2004.

[24] A. Roth. Store Vulnerability Window (SVW): Re-Execution Filtering for Enhanced Load Optimization. In *International Symposium on Computer Architecture*, Madison, Wisconsin, June 2005.

[25] S. Sethumadhavan, R. Desikan, D. Burger, C. Moore, and S. Keckler. Scalable Hardware Memory Disambiguation for High ILP Processors. In *International Symposium on Microarchitecture*, pages 399–410, San Diego, California, December 2003.

[26] J. Tendler, J. Dodson, J. Fields, H. Le, and B. Sinharoy. POWER4 System Microarchitecture. *IBM Journal of Research and Development*, 46(1):5–25, January 2002.

[27] E. Torres, P. Ibanez, V. Vinals, and J. Llaberia. Store Buffer Design in First-Level Multibanked Data Caches. In *International Symposium on Computer Architecture*, Madison, Wisconsin, June 2005.

[28] E. Witchel, S. Larsen, C. Ananian, and K. Asanovic. Direct Addressed Caches for Reduced Power Consumption. In *International Symposium on Microarchitecture*, pages 124–133, Austin, Texas, December 2001.

LogTM: Log-based Transactional Memory

Kevin E. Moore, Jayaram Bobba, Michelle J. Moravan, Mark D. Hill & David A. Wood

Department of Computer Sciences, University of Wisconsin–Madison
{kmoore, bobba, moravan, markhill, david}@cs.wisc.edu
http://www.cs.wisc.edu/multifacet

Abstract

Transactional memory (TM) simplifies parallel programming by guaranteeing that transactions appear to execute atomically *and in* isolation. *Implementing these properties includes providing data* version management *for the simultaneous storage of both new (visible if the transaction commits) and old (retained if the transaction aborts) values. Most (hardware) TM systems leave old values "in place" (the target memory address) and buffer new values elsewhere until commit. This makes aborts fast, but penalizes (the much more frequent) commits.*

In this paper, we present a new implementation of transactional memory, Log-based Transactional Memory *(LogTM), that makes commits fast by storing old values to a per-thread log in cacheable virtual memory and storing new values in place. LogTM makes two additional contributions. First, LogTM extends a MOESI directory protocol to enable both fast conflict detection on evicted blocks and fast commit (using lazy cleanup). Second, LogTM handles aborts in (library) software with little performance penalty. Evaluations running micro- and SPLASH-2 benchmarks on a 32-way multiprocessor support our decision to optimize for commit by showing that only 1-2% of transactions abort.*

1. Introduction

The promise of plentiful thread support from chip multiprocessors is re-energizing interest in *transactional memory (TM)* [14] systems, implemented in software only [12, 13, 18, 27] or, our focus, in hardware (with some software support) [2, 11, 14, 25]. TM systems must provide transaction *atomicity* (all or nothing) and *isolation* (the partially-complete state of a transaction is hidden from other transactions) [9]. Providing these properties requires data *version management* and *conflict detection*, whose implementations distinguish alternative TM proposals.

Version management handles the simultaneous storage of both *new* data (to be visible if the transaction *commits*) and *old* data (retained if the transaction *aborts*). At most one of these values can be stored "in place" (the target memory address), while the other value must be stored "on the side"

(e.g., in speculative hardware). On a store, a TM system can use *eager version management* and put the new value in place, or use *lazy version management* to (temporarily) leave the old value in place.

Conflict detection signals an overlap between the *write set* (data written) of one transaction and the write set or *read set* (data read) of other concurrent transactions. Conflict detection is called *eager* if it detects offending loads or stores immediately and *lazy* if it defers detection until later (e.g., when transactions commit).

The taxonomy in Table 1 illustrates which TM proposals use lazy versus eager version management and conflict detection.

TCC. Hammond et al.'s *Transactional Memory Coherence and Consistency (TCC)* [11] uses both lazy version management and lazy conflict detection, similar to the few *database management systems (DBMSs)* that use optimistic concurrency control (OCC) [16]. TCC buffers stores at the processor's L1 cache and overwrites the L2 cache and memory only on commit. TCC detects conflicts with a pending transaction only when other transactions commit (not when data is first stored).

LTM. Ananian et al.'s *Large Transactional Memory (LTM)* [2] uses lazy version management and eager conflict detection. LTM keeps the old value in main memory and stores the new value in cache, coercing the coherence protocol to store two different values at the same address. Repeated transactions which modify the same block, however, require a writeback of the block once per transaction. On cache overflows, LTM spills the new values to an in-memory hash table. In contrast to TCC, LTM uses eager conflict detection invoked when conflicting loads or stores seek to execute. LTM conflict detection is complicated by the cache overflow case. When the controller detects a potential conflict with an overflowed block, it must walk the uncacheable in-memory hash table before responding (and possibly aborting).

VTM. Rajwar et al.'s *Virtual Transactional Memory (VTM)* [25] also combines lazy version management with eager conflict detection. Memory always holds old values. On cache overflows, VTM writes the new (and a second copy of

Table 1: A Transactional Memory (TM) taxonomy

		Version Management	
		Lazy	**Eager**
Conflict	**Lazy**	OCC DBMSs [16] Stanford TCC [11]	none
	Eager	MIT LTM [2] Intel/Brown VTM [25] (on cache conflicts)	CCC DBMSs [6] MIT UTM [2] *LogTM [new]*

old) values to an in-memory table (XADT). VTM does not specify version management when data fits in cache, but rather recommends other proposals [2, 11, 14, 24, 30].

UTM. Ananian et al.'s *Unbounded Transactional Memory (UTM)* [2] proposes using both eager version management and eager conflict detection. This follows the example of the vast majority of DBMSs that use *conservative concurrency control (CCC)* [6]. UTM's implementation is complex, however, and even Ananian et al. appear to abandon it (without evaluation) in favor of advocating LTM.

Ideally, transactional memory should use eager version management and eager conflict deflection, because:

- Eager version management puts new values "in place," making commits faster than aborts. This makes sense when commits are much more common than aborts, which we generally find.

- Eager conflict detection finds conflicts early, reducing wasted work by conflicting transactions. This makes sense, since standard coherence makes implementing eager conflict detection efficient (as LTM and VTM find).

To this end, we propose *Log-based Transactional Memory (LogTM),* which we argue makes eager conflict detection and eager version management practical in a TM system built on a multiprocessor with private caches kept coherent with a directory protocol. LogTM implements eager version management by creating a per-thread *transaction log* in cacheable virtual memory, which holds the virtual addresses and old values of all memory blocks modified during a transaction. LogTM detects in-cache conflicts using a directory protocol and read/write bits on cache blocks (like many other proposals). LogTM novelly extends the directory protocol (e.g., with a "sticky-M" state) to perform conflict detection even after replacing transactional data from the cache. In LogTM, a processor commits a transaction by discarding the log (resetting a log pointer) and flash clearing the read/write bits. No other work is needed, because new values are already in place and, in another innovation, LogTM lazily clears "sticky" states. On abort, LogTM must walk the log to restore val-

ues. We find aborts sufficiently rare that we use a trap handler to perform them in (library) software. For ease of implementation, the processor whose coherence request causes a conflict always resolves the conflict by waiting (to reduce aborts) or aborting (if deadlock is possible). Currently, LogTM does not permit thread movement or paging within transactions, as do UTM and VTM.

Contributions: In developing LogTM, we make the following contributions:

- We develop and evaluate a TM system that uses eager version management to store new values "in place," making commits faster than aborts. On commit, no data moves (even when transactions overflow the cache).

- We efficiently allow cache evictions of transactional data by extending a MOESI directory protocol to enable (a) fast conflict detection on evicted blocks and (b) fast commit by lazily resetting the directory state. LogTM does *not* require log or hash table walks to evict a cache block, detect a conflict, or commit a transaction, but works best if evictions of transactional data are uncommon.

- We handle aborts via a log walk by (library) software with little performance penalty, since simulation results with micro- and SPLASH-2 benchmarks on Solaris 9 confirm that aborts are much less common than commits.

2. LogTM: Log-based Transactional Memory

LogTM builds upon a conventional shared memory multiprocessor: each processor has two (or more) levels of private caches kept coherent by a MOESI directory protocol [5]. This section describes LogTM's eager version management (Section 2.1), eager conflict detection (Section 2.2), and other specifics (Section 2.3 and Section 2.4).

2.1. Version management

A defining feature of LogTM is its use of *eager version management*, wherein new values are stored "in place," while old values are saved "on the side." LogTM saves old values in a *before-image log*, like most DBMSs [6]. Specifically, LogTM saves old values in a *per-thread log in cacheable virtual memory*. On creation, each thread allocates virtual memory for its log and informs the LogTM system of its start and end. On a store within a transaction, LogTM hardware appends to the log the virtual address of the stored block and the block's *old* value. To suppress redundant log writes, LogTM augments the state of each cached block with a *write (W)* bit [2, 11, 14] that tracks whether a block has been stored to (and logged). Redundant log entries may still arise in the (uncommon) case that a block with the W bit set gets both written back to mem-

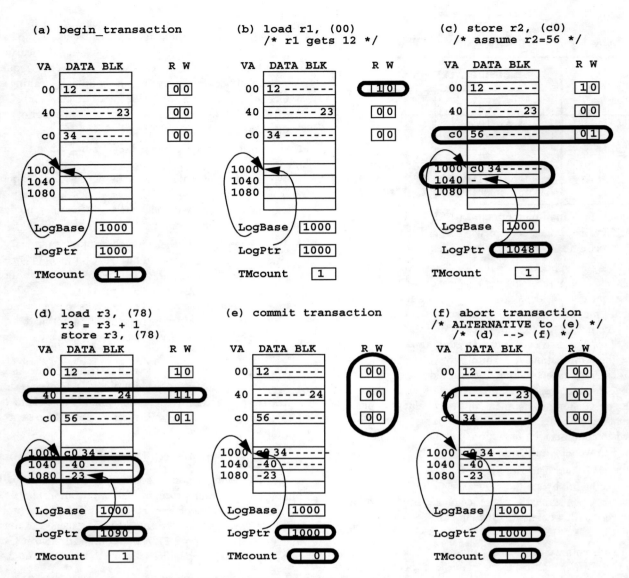

Figure 1. Execution of a Transaction with Two Alternative Endings

Part (a) displays a logical view of a thread that has just begun a transaction by incrementing its TMcount. We assume that the thread's log begins at virtual address (VA) 1000 (all numbers in hexadecimal), but is empty (LogPtr=LogBase). LogTM divides the virtual address (VA) space into data blocks whose value in this example is given as a two-digit word and seven dashes (for the other eight-byte words of a 64-byte block). Each data block has associated read (R) and write (W) bits. Circles indicate changes from the previous snapshot. Section 2.2 explains the purpose of the R bits.

Part (b) shows a load from virtual address 00 setting the block's R bit.

Part (c) shows a store to virtual address c0 setting the block's W bit and logging its virtual address and old data (34 --------).

Part (d) shows a read-modify write of address 78 that sets the block's R and W bits and logs its virtual address (40) and old data (------- 23).

Part (e) shows a transaction commit that decrements TMcount, and, because TMcount is now zero, resets LogPtr and R and W bits.

Part (f) shows an alternative execution where, after part (d), something triggers a conflict that results in abort. The abort handler restores values from the log before resetting the TMcount, LogPtr, and R/W bits.

ory and re-fetched in the same transaction (due to a subtle interaction with conflict detection (Section 2.2)).

Writing log entries generates less overhead than one might expect. Log writes will often be cache hits, because the log is cacheable, thread private, and most transactions write few blocks. A single entry micro-TLB effectively pre-translates the log's virtual address. A small hardware log buffer reduces contention for the L1 cache port and hides any L1 cache miss latencies. Since the log is not needed until abort time, these writes can be delayed in a hardware log write buffer and either discarded on a commit, or performed on an abort or when resources fill. Processors with the ability to buffer four blocks would avoid almost all log writes for most of our workloads (Section 3.3).

The principle merit of LogTM's eager version management is fast commits. To commit, a LogTM processor flash clears its cache's W bits and resets the thread's log pointer (to discard the transaction's log).

A drawback of eager version management is that aborts are slower. To abort, LogTM must "undo" the transaction by writing old values back to their appropriate virtual addresses from the log before resetting the W bits. Since a block may be logged more than once, "undo" must proceed from the end of the log back to the beginning (last-in-first-out). Section 2.3 describes LogTM's conflict handler interface that allows abort sequencing to be done by (library) software.

To make LogTM more concrete, Figure 1 and its caption "animate" a transaction on LogTM (a-d) with two alternative endings: commit (e) and abort (f).

2.2. Conflict detection

Conceptually, LogTM performs eager conflict detection in several steps: (a) the requesting processor sends a coherence request to the directory, (b) the directory responds and possibly forwards the request to one or more processors, (c) each responding processor examines some local state to *detect* a conflict, (d) the responding processors each *ack* (no conflict), or *nack* (conflict) the request, and (e) the requesting processor *resolves* any conflict (see Section 2.3).

For in-cache blocks, LogTM follows others [2, 11, 14] to augment each cache block with a read (R) bit (see Figure 2), as well as the W bit discussed above. LogTM sets the R bit for each block read during a transaction (see Figure 3-b) and flash clears all R bits, along with the W bits, when a transaction ends. LogTM only sets an R bit for valid blocks (MOESI states: *Modified (M), Owned (O), Exclusive (E),* or *Shared (S))* and a W bit for blocks in the M state. This ensures that standard directory protocols will properly forward all potentially-conflicting requests to the appropriate processor(s) for conflict detection. As illus-

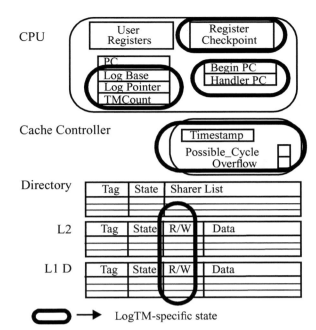

Figure 2. LogTM hardware overview: the circled areas indicate added state for LogTM in the processor, caches and cache controller.

trated in Figure 3-c, after receiving a request from the directory, a processor checks its local state to detect a possible conflict.

A contribution of LogTM is its graceful handling of conflict detection even after transactions overflow the cache. The key step is extending the directory protocol to forward all potentially conflicting requests to the appropriate processors, even after cache replacements. The process works as follows: a processor P replaces a transactional block and sets a per-processor overflow bit (like VTM's XADT overflow count), the extended directory protocol continues to forward potentially conflicting requests to P, which nacks to signal a (potential) conflict. Thus, LogTM conservatively detects conflicts with slightly-augmented coherence hardware. LogTM's solution does *not* require a data structure insertion for a cache replacement (like LTM, UTM, and VTM), a data structure walk to provide a coherence response (LTM), or data structure clean up at commit (LTM, UTM, and VTM).

Specifically, if processor P replaces *transactional* block B (i.e., B's R or W bit is set) the directory must continue to forward processor Q's conflicting requests to P. LogTM's replacement behavior depends on B's valid MOESI state:

M. P replaces B using a transactional writeback, transitioning the directory to a new state "*sticky-M@*P" (Figure 3-d). When Q requests B, the directory in "sticky-M@P" forwards the request to P. P has no record of B, but infers the (potential) conflict from the forwarded request (Figure 3-e).

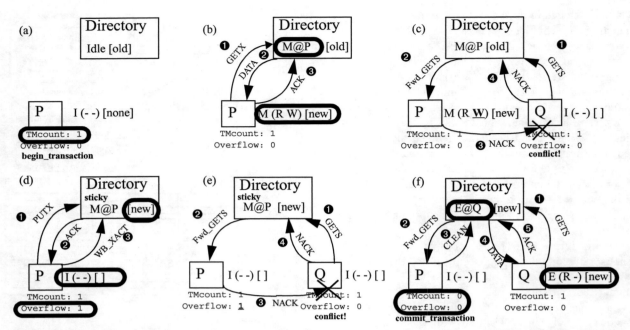

Figure 3. LogTM Conflict Detection Examples: in-cache detection (a)-(c), and out-of-cache detection (d)-(f). This example illustrates LogTM's conflict detection (but elides version management). The example shows the state for one block at the directory and in processors P's and Q's private caches. Processor P writes the block and replaces it in a transaction that eventually commits (f). The state of the block includes the cache state and R/W bits in caches and an owner or sharer list at the directory. In addition to the state for the block, each processor maintains a TMcount and an overflow bit.

(a) Begin transaction: Processor P begins a transaction, incrementing its TMcount; the block is valid at the directory only.

(b) P stores the block: Not finding the block in its cache, P sends a get exclusive (GETX) request to the directory (step ❶). The directory responds with data (the "old" version of this block). When the data arrives, the store completes creating the "new" version of the data and setting the R and W bits for the block in P's cache (step ❷). P sends an ACK to the directory to confirm that it received the data (step ❸).

(c) In-cache transaction conflict: In step ❶, Q issues a get-shared (GETS) request to the directory. In step ❷, the directory forwards the request to P. In step ❸, P detects the conflict (the W bit is set) and nacks the request. When Q receives the NACK, it resolves the conflict (not shown). Q sends a NACK to the directory to signal that its request has completed unsuccessfully (step ❹).

(d) Cache overflow: In step ❶, P informs the directory that it intends to update the data value at memory (currently [old]) by sending a put-exclusive (PUTX) request; In step ❷, the directory acknowledges the request (ACK). In step ❸, P writes the new data back to memory (WB_XACT) and sets its overflow bit. After the writeback, the block is in state I at P, but P remains the owner of the block at the directory (the "sticky-M" state); memory has the new data.

(e) Out-of-cache conflict: In step ❶, Q re-issues its request from part (c), which the directory again forwards to P (step ❷). Upon receiving a forwarded request for a block not present in its cache, P checks its overflow bit. In step ❸, since the overflow bit is set, P assumes a conflict, and nacks Q's request, signalling a conflict. As in (c), Q sends a NACK to the directory to signal that its request has completed unsuccessfully (step ❹).

(f) Lazy clear of the sticky-M state: P commits its transaction by decrementing its TMcount. Since TMcount is now zero, P flash clears the R and W bits in its cache and resets the overflow bit. The block is still in the sticky-M state at the directory. In step ❶, Q once again retries its request, which is again forwarded to P by the directory (step ❷). This time, P's overflow bit is clear. In step ❸, P responds indirectly by sending a clean-up (CLEAN) message to the directory. This message informs the directory that it has valid data, which it sends to Q (step ❹). Finally, Q informs the directory that its load completed successfully and the block is left in state E@Q (step ❺).

S. P silently replaces B, leaving P in the directory's sharer list. Conceptually, we consider the directory in "*sticky-S*" but the actual state is unchanged. When Q requests B exclusively, the directory naturally forwards invalidations to all sharers, enabling P to detect the (potential) conflict.

O. P writes B back to the directory, which adds P to the sharer list. When Q requests B exclusively, behavior is the same as for the S replacement above.

E. P behaves the same as the O replacement above. Alternatively, P could silently replace E state blocks, but on a forwarded request it must assume it was previously in M, resulting in more false conflicts.

LogTM makes commits very fast: a committing processor just resets its overflow bit, log pointer, and flash clears its cache's R and W bits. The processor does not walk data structures to find replaced blocks (like LTM and VTM), but instead *lazily* clears the sticky states. This means that processor Q's request for block B may be forwarded to processor P even after P has committed the transaction that overflowed.

Coherence requests forwarded by "sticky" directory states are only potential conflicts. Forwarded requests that arrive while P is not in a transaction clearly result from a "stale" sticky state from an earlier transaction. The same is true if P is in a transaction, but has not overflowed (overflow = 0). In both cases, P clears the "sticky" state by sending a CLEAN message to the directory. The directory then responds to processor Q's request with the already valid data (Figure 3-f). False conflicts only arise when processor Q accesses (writes) a block in "sticky-M@P" ("sticky-S@P") *and* processor P is currently executing a later transaction that has also overflowed. Processor P must conservatively assume that the "sticky" state originated during the current transaction and represents an actual conflict (Figure 3-e).

LogTM's approach of lazily cleaning up sticky states makes the most sense if transactions rarely overflow the cache (as in our current benchmarks). If overflow occurs more frequently, LogTM's single overflow bit can be replaced by a more accurate filter (e.g., a per-set bit [2] or Bloom filter [25]). If overflows become the norm, other approaches may be preferred.

A subtle ambiguity arises when a processor P fetches a block B in "sticky-M@P" during a transaction. This case could arise from a writeback and re-fetch during the *same* transaction, requiring only that P set the R and W bits. Alternatively, the writeback could have occurred in an *earlier* transaction, requiring that P treat this fetch as the first access to B (and thus log the old value on the first store). LogTM handles this case conservatively, having P set B's R and W bits and (perhaps redundantly) logging B's old value.

Table 2: LogTM Interface

User Interface

`begin_transaction()` Requests that subsequent dynamic statements form a transaction. Logically saves a copy of user-visible non-memory thread state (i.e., architectural registers, condition codes, etc.).

`commit_transaction()` Ends successful transaction begun by matching `begin_transaction()`. Discards any transaction state saved for potential abort.

`abort_transaction()` Transfers control to a previously-registered conflict handler which should undo and discard work since last `begin_transaction()` and (usually) restarts the transaction.

System/Library Interface

`initialize_transactions(Thread* thread_struct, Address log_base, Address log_bound)` Initiates a thread's transactional support, including allocating virtual address space for a thread's log. As for each thread's stack, page table entries and physical memory may be allocated on demand and the thread fails if it exceeds the large, but finite log size. (Other options are possible if they prove necessary.) We expect this call to be wrapped with a user-level thread initiation call (e.g., for P-Threads).

`register_conflict_handler(void (*) conflict_handler)` Registers a function to be called when transactions conflict or are explicitly aborted. Conflict handlers are registered on a per-thread basis. The registered handler should assume the following pre-conditions and ensure the following post-conditions if the transaction aborts:

Conflict Handler Pre-conditions: Memory blocks written by the thread (a) have new values in (virtual) memory, (b) are still isolated, and (c) have their (virtual) address and pre-write values in the log. If a block is logged more than once, its first entry pushed on the log must contain its pre-transaction value. The log also contains a record of pre-transaction user-visible non-memory thread state.

Abort Post-conditions: If conflict resolution resulted in abort, the handler called `undo_log_entry()` to pop off every log entry then called `complete_abort(restart)`

Low-Level Interface

`undo_log_entry()` Reads a block's (virtual) address and pre-write data from the last log entry, writes the data to the address, and pops the entry off of the log.

`complete_abort(bool restart)` Ends isolation on all memory blocks. Either restores thread's non-memory state from last `begin_transaction()`, and resumes execution there, or returns to conflict handler to handle error conditions or switch user-level threads.

2.3. LogTM specifics

Interface. Table 2 presents LogTM's interface in three levels. The *user interface* (top) allows user threads to *begin*, *commit* and *abort* transactions. All user-level memory references between begin and commit are part of a transaction executed with *strong atomicity* [3]—i.e., atomic and isolated from all other user threads whether or not they are in transactions. The system/library interface (middle) lets thread packages initialize per-thread logs and register a handler to resolve conflicts (discussed below). Conflicts may result in transaction abort, which LogTM handles in software by "undoing" the log via a sequence of calls using the low-level interface (bottom). In the common case, the handler can restart the transaction with user-visible register and memory state restored to their pre-transaction values. Rather than just restart, a handler may decide to execute other code after rolling back the transaction, (e.g., to avoid repeated conflicts).

Operating System Interaction. LogTM's model is that transactions pertain to user-visible state (e.g., registers and user virtual memory) being manipulated by user threads running in a single virtual address space on top of a commercial operating system (OS). Currently, the OS operates outside of user-level transactions. Thus, the OS never stalls or aborts due to user-level transactions, but cannot currently use transactions itself.

The current LogTM implementation still has considerable OS limitations. LogTM transactions may only invoke the trivial subset of system calls with do not require an "undo," such as *sbrk* invoked by *malloc* and SPARC TLB miss traps. LogTM does not currently handle transactional data that is both paged out and paged back in within the same transaction, or thread switching/migration, as do UTM and VTM.

Processor Support. LogTM extends each processor with a transaction nesting count (TMcount) and log pointer (shown in Figure 2). TMcount allows the first, outer transaction to subsume subsequent, inner transactions. The processor also implements the user-level instructions *begin*, *commit* and *abort* to directly support the LogTM interface. Instruction *begin* increments the TMcount. If the processor was previously not in transaction mode (i.e., TMcount = 0), it checkpoints the thread's architectural registers to a shadow register file. Although logically part of the log, lazy update semantics effectively allow register checkpoints to remain in the shadow copy indefinitely. Instruction *commit* decrements TMcount. If now zero, the processor commits the outermost transaction, resetting the overflow bit and flash clearing the cache's R and W bits. Instruction *abort* triggers a trap to the software conflict handler, which aborts the transaction. On completion of the abort, the handler resets the TMcount, overflow bit, and log pointer.

Conflict Resolution. When two transactions conflict, at least one transaction must stall (risking deadlock) or abort (risking live-lock). The decision can be made quickly, but myopically, by hardware, or slowly, but carefully, by a software contention manager [26]. Ultimately, a hybrid solution might be best, where hardware seeks a fast resolution, but traps to software when problems persist.

Recall that when a LogTM processor Q makes a coherence request, it may get forwarded to processor P to *detect* a conflict. P then responds to Q with an ack (no conflict) or a nack (conflict). If there is a conflict, processor Q must *resolve* it on receiving the nack. Q could always abort its transaction, but this wastes work (and power). Alternatively, Q may re-issue its request (perhaps after a backoff delay) in the hope that P had completed its conflicting transaction. Q cannot wait indefinitely for P, however, without risking deadlock (e.g., if P is waiting on Q).

To guarantee forward progress and reduce aborts, the current LogTM implementation logically orders transactions using TLR's distributed timestamp method [24]. LogTM only traps to the conflict handler when a transaction (a) could introduce deadlock and (b) is logically later than the transaction with which it conflicts. LogTM detects potential deadlock by recognizing the situation in which one transaction is both waiting for a logically earlier transaction and causing a logically earlier transaction to wait. This is implemented with a per-processor `possible_cycle` flag, which is set if a processor sends a nack to a logically earlier transaction. A processor triggers a conflict only if it receives a nack from a logically earlier transaction while its `possible_cycle` flag is set.

2.4. Generalizing LogTM

LogTM implementations may also relax some of the concrete assumptions made above. First, Section 2.2 describes LogTM using a system with private cache hierarchies and full-mapped directory protocol. The LogTM approach extends easily to a *chip multiprocessor* (CMP) where the shared L2 cache tracks where blocks are cached in per-core L1 caches, effectively acting as a directory. Second, the LogTM implementation uses the directory to filter coherence requests when transactions overflow. Alternative LogTM implementations could use other coherence protocols (e.g., snooping), extended with appropriate filters to limit false conflicts. Third, LogTM uses hardware to save user-visible register state and restore it on transaction abort (Section 2.3). This could also be done by the compiler or run-time support.

Finally, the current LogTM implementation uses timestamps to prioritize transactions and resolve conflicts. This simple, but rigid policy may result in convoys (e.g., if a transaction gets pre-empted) or priority inversion (e.g., if a logically earlier transaction holds a block needed by a higher priority, but logically later transaction). Future work will investigate having the (software) conflict handler invoke an application-level contention manager that implements more flexible policies. To do this, LogTM needs a few additional mechanisms, such as allowing a processor P to abort another thread's transaction, particularly one that is not actively running on a processor.

Table 3. System model parameters

	System Model Settings
Processors	32, 1 GHz, single-issue, in-order, non-memory IPC=1
L1 Cache	16 kB 4-way split, 1-cycle latency
L2 Cache	4 MB 4-way unified, 12-cycle latency
Memory	4 GB 80-cycle latency
Directory	Full-bit vector sharer list; migratory sharing optimization; Directory cache, 6-cycle latency
Interconnection Network	Hierarchical switch topology, 14-cycle link latency

Because LogTM stores the old values in the user program's address space, these mechanisms appear possible. A sufficiently robust software contention manager may also obviate the low-level timestamp mechanism.

3. Evaluation

This section describes the simulation of LogTM and a baseline system using spin locks (Section 3.1) and compares them using a microbenchmark (Section 3.2) and parallel applications from the SPLASH-2 suite [32] (Section 3.3).

3.1. Target System & Simulation Model

LogTM and the baseline system share the same basic SPARC/Solaris multiprocessor architecture, summarized in Table 3. Each system has 32 processors, each with two levels of private cache. A MOESI directory protocol maintains coherence over a high-bandwidth switched interconnect. Though single-issue and in-order, the processor model includes an aggressive, single-cycle non-memory IPC. The detailed memory system model includes most timing intricacies of the transactional memory extensions.

Some TM systems advocate special transactional load instructions for data likely to be stored soon [14]. This support avoids obtaining read permission and then later write permission (with implications on both traffic and conflicts). The LogTM implementation obtains a similar effect using a *write set predictor* that tracks the addresses of 64 blocks recently loaded and then stored within a transaction.

The simulation framework uses *Virtutech Simics* [17] in conjunction with customized memory models built on *Wisconsin GEMS* [19, 31]. Simics, a full-system functional simulator, accurately models the SPARC architecture but does not support transactional memory. Support for the LogTM interface was added using Simics "magic" instructions: special no-ops that Simics catches and passes

```
for(i=0; i<10000; ++i){
    begin_transaction();
        new_total = total.count + 1;
        private_data[id].count++;
        total.count = new_total;
    commit_transaction();
    think();
}
```

Figure 4. Shared-counter microbenchmark (main loop)

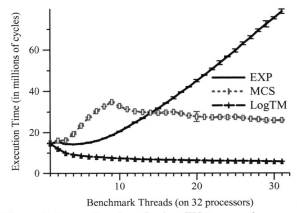

Figure 5. Execution time for LogTM transactions, test-and-test-and-set locks with exponential backoff (EXP) and MCS locks (MCS).

to the memory model. To implement the *begin* instruction, the memory simulator uses a Simics call to read the thread's architectural registers and create a checkpoint. During a transaction, the memory simulator models the log updates. After an abort rolls back the log, the register checkpoint is written back to Simics, and the thread restarts the transaction.

3.2. Microbenchmark Analysis

This section uses a shared-counter micro-benchmark to show that LogTM performs well under high contention, despite frequent conflicts. Figure 4 illustrates a simple, multi-threaded program that generates high contention for a shared variable. Each thread repeatedly tries to atomically fetch-and-increment a single shared counter and update some private state with a random think time between accesses (avg. 2.5 μs). This delay generates opportunities for parallelism and allows improved performance with multiple threads.

For comparison, the `begin_transaction()` and `commit_transaction()` calls translate to test-and-test-and-set locks with exponential backoff (EXP), MCS locks [21], or LogTM transactions (LogTM). Figure 5 displays the execution times for 10,000 iterations of the shared

Table 4. SPLASH-2 Benchmarks and Inputs

Benchmark	Input	Synchronization Methods
Barnes	512 bodies	locks on tree nodes
Cholesky	14	task queue locks
Ocean	contiguous partitions, 258	barriers
Radiosity	room	task queue & buffer locks
Raytrace-Base	small image (teapot)	work list & counter locks
Raytrace-Opt	small image(teapot)	work list & counter locks
Water N-Squared	512 molecules	barriers

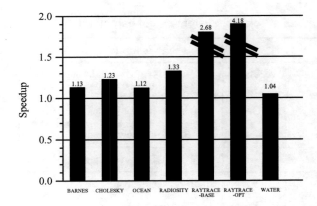

Figure 6. SPLASH performance comparison: execution time of "transactionized" SPLASH benchmarks on LogTM normalized to the performance of the benchmarks with lock-based synchronization on the baseline system

counter micro-benchmarks for varying number of threads. For locks, results confirm that MCS locks are slower than EXP with little contention (less than 15 threads), but faster under high contention.

In contrast, the LogTM implementation fulfills the potential of transactional memory by always performing better than either lock implementation and consistently benefiting from more threads. Moreover, more detailed analysis (not shown) reveals that, for this simple micro-benchmark, LogTM never wastes work by aborting a transaction, but rather stalls transactions when conflicts occur.

3.3. SPLASH Benchmarks

This section evaluates LogTM on a subset of the SPLASH-2 benchmarks. The benchmarks described in Table 4 use locks in place of, or in addition to, barriers. The results show that LogTM improves performance relative to locks.

The LogTM version of the SPLASH-2 benchmarks replaces locks with `begin_transaction()` and `commit_transaction()` calls. Barriers and other synchronization mechanisms are not changed. The SPLASH-2 benchmarks use PARMACS library locks, which use test-and-test-and-set locks but yield the processor after a pre-determined number of attempts (only one for these experiments). Raytrace has two versions: Raytrace-Base and Raytrace-Opt, which eliminates false sharing between two transactions.

Figure 6 shows the speedup from using LogTM transactions versus locks for the SPLASH-2 benchmarks, running 32 user threads on a 32-way multiprocessor. All LogTM versions are faster than the lock-based ones. Some speedups are modest (Water 4% faster, Ocean 12%, and Barnes 13%). Other speedups are good (Cholesky 23% and Radiosity 33%). Finally, Raytrace speedup is "off scale" with Raytrace-Base speeding up 2.7x and Raytrace-Opt 4.2x!

These speedups occur because LogTM (and other TM systems) enable *critical section parallelism* (an oxymoron) by allowing multiple threads to operate concurrently in the same critical section. For example, LogTM allows an average of 3.2 concurrent threads in Raytrace-Base's most frequently-executed critical section, as measured by dividing the sum of each thread's cycles in the critical section by the total cycles when one or more threads was in the critical section. Raytrace-Opt increases the critical section parallelism to 5.5. In contrast, lock-based critical section parallelism is always one.

LogTM makes two central design decisions that assume that commits occur much more frequently than aborts. First, by writing new values in place, eager version management makes commits faster than aborts. Second, LogTM traps to software to handle conflicts and abort transactions. The results in column four of Table 5 support these decisions: only 1-2% of transactions end in an abort for all benchmarks, except Barnes, in which 15% of transactions abort.

LogTM makes aborts less common by using stalls to resolve conflicting transactions when deadlock is not possible (Section 2.3). Column three of Table 5 shows the fraction of transactions that stalled before committing, while column four gives the fraction that aborted. The fraction of transactions that conflicted with at least one other transaction is the sum of columns three and four. For several benchmarks (e.g., Cholesky, Radiosity, and Raytrace-Opt), LogTM stalls transactions 2–5 times more often than it aborts them. Raytrace-Base stalls nearly 25% of all transactions!

266

Table 5: Selected transactional data

Benchmark	# Trans.	% Stalls	% Aborts	Stores/Trans.	% Read-Modify-Writes
Barnes	3,067	4.89	15.3	5.50	27.9
Cholesky	22,309	4.54	2.07	1.68	82.3
Ocean	6,693	0.30	0.52	0.112	100
Radiosity	279,750	3.96	1.03	1.64	82.7
Raytrace-Base	48,285	24.7	1.24	1.96	99.9
Raytrace-Opt	47,884	2.04	0.41	1.97	99.9
Water	35,398	0.00	0.11	1.98	99.6

Table 6: Cumulative distribution of write set sizes (in 64-byte blocks)

Benchmark	% < 4	% < 8	% < 16	% < 32	% < 64	Max
Barnes	44.5	85.7	95.0	95.3	100	55
Cholesky	100	100	100	100	100	3
Ocean	100	100	100	100	100	1
Radiosity	97.0	99.6	99.6	100	100	67
Raytrace-Base	100	100	100	100	100	3
Raytrace-Opt	100	100	100	100	100	3
Water	100	100	100	100	100	2

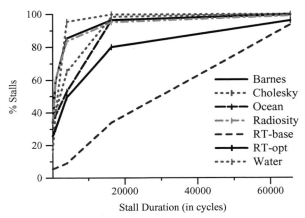

Figure 7. Stall distribution

Stalling a transaction wastes less work than aborting it, but represents lost opportunity. A potential third alternative is to switch to another thread, perhaps making progress on another transaction. Such an action requires additional enhancements to LogTM, such as the software contention manager discussed in Section 2.4. Figure 7 presents the cumulative stall distribution (in cycles) and shows that while many stalls are shorter than a typical software context switch, the distribution has a heavy tail. An enhanced LogTM implementation might stall for a while in hardware before trapping to a software contention manager to possibly abort and switch threads.

The Raytrace-Base stall behavior also reveals a limitation of TM systems that build on cache coherence: *Reducing false sharing with TM is even more important that reducing it with locks.* With TM, false sharing creates (apparent) conflicts that can stall or abort entire transactions. Raytrace-Opt eliminates most false sharing in Raytrace-Base by moving two global variables (ray identifier

and free list pointer) to different blocks. This optimization improved the lock-based Raytrace's performance a little and LogTM Raytrace's a lot (due to eliminating conflicts between a frequent but short transaction that accesses the ray identifier and a less frequent but long transaction that accesses the free list pointer). LogTM shares this limitation with other transactional memory implementations [2, 14, 25], except TCC [11], which optionally tracks transactions' read and write sets at word or byte granularity.

These experiments also alleviate two concerns about LogTM's eager version management. First, LogTM must read a data block before writing it to the log. This read is extra work if the data would not otherwise be read. Fortunately, the final column of Table 5 shows that (except for Barnes) most data blocks are read before written within a transaction. Thus, LogTM does not usually add the cost of an additional read. Second, writing LogTM's log could significantly increase cache write bandwidth. Fortunately, because the log does not need to be valid until an abort occurs, a LogTM implementation could use a *k-block log write buffer* to elide log writes for transactions that write k or fewer blocks (Section 2.1). Table 6 shows the cumulative distribution of transaction write-set size. A four-entry buffer eliminates all log writes for committed transactions in Cholesky, Ocean, Raytrace, and Water and all but 3% for Radiosity. A 16-entry buffer eliminates all but 0.4% of Radiosity's writes and all but 5% of Barnes's.

4. Discussion and Related Work

We developed and evaluated *Log-based Transactional Memory (LogTM)* that (a) always stores new values "in place," to make commits faster than aborts, (b) extends a MOESI directory protocol to enable fast conflict detection and transaction commits, even when data has been evicted from caches, and (c) handles aborts in software, since they are uncommon. LogTM is most-closely related to TCC,

LTM, UTM, and VTM, but we see substantial differences in both version management and conflict detection.

TCC. Whereas TCC version management keeps new data in a speculative cache until commit, when they are written through to a shared L2 cache, LogTM can operate with writeback caches and generates no traffic at commit. In TCC's lazy conflict detection, other transactions learn about transaction T's conflicting store when T commits, not earlier when the store is executed. In contrast, LogTM uses eager conflict detection to detect conflicts when the store is executed to facilitate earlier corrective action.

LTM. Like LogTM, LTM keeps new data in cache when it can. However, when a transaction overflows a set in the cache, LTM stores new values in an uncacheable in-memory hash table. On commit, LTM copies overflowed data to its new location. In contrast, LogTM allows both old and new versions to be cached (often generating no memory traffic) and never copies data on commit. Whereas an LTM processor must search a table in uncacheable memory on an incoming request to any set that has overflowed a block during the transaction, a LogTM processor needs check only local state allowing it to respond immediately to a directory request.

UTM. Like LogTM, UTM version management stores new values in place and old values in a log. UTM's log is larger, however, because it contains blocks that are targets of both loads and stores, whereas LogTM's log only contains blocks targeted by stores. UTM uses this extra log state to provide more complete virtualization of conflict detection, allowing transactions to survive paging, context switching and thread migration. UTM's conflict detection must, however, walk the log on certain coherence requests, and clean up log state on commit, while LogTM uses a simple directory protocol extension (that does not even know the location of the log) and uses lazy cleanup to optimize commits.

VTM. VTM takes most in-cache TM systems and adds a per-address-space virtual mode that handles transactions after cache evictions, paging, and context switches. In this mode, VTM performs version-management lazily (in contrast to LogTM's eager approach). Both virtualized VTM and LogTM do eager conflict detection, but VTM uses low-level PAL or micro-code, while LogTM continues to use coherence hardware. In contrast to VTM (and UTM), however, LogTM handles (infrequent) cache evictions, but not paging or context switches.

In addition, other work informs and enriches recent work on (hardware) TM systems. Early TM work showed the way, but exposed fixed hardware sizes to programmers [14, 15, 30]. The 801 minicomputer [4] provided lock bits on memory blocks for conflict detection. Thread-level speculation work developed version management and con-flict detection mechanisms for a different purpose: *achieving serial semantics* [1, 7, 8, 10, 22, 28, 29, 33, 34]. In fact, both Garzarán et al. [7] and Zhang et al. [33, 34] use the mechanism of undo logs for this different purpose. Others speculatively turn explicit parallel synchronization (e.g., locks) into implicit transactions when resources are sufficient [20, 23, 24], but fall back on explicit synchronization otherwise. Finally, many researchers seek all software TM solutions [12, 13, 18, 27].

5. Conclusions and Future Work

LogTM is a promising approach to providing hardware (assisted) transactional memory. LogTM optimizes for the expected common case of small (i.e., in-cache) transactions, yet efficiently supports dynamically infrequent large transactions. LogTM also optimizes for the expected common case that transactions commit, using eager version management and software abort handling.

Looking forward, LogTM presents several challenges and opportunities. Challenges include the need for better virtualization to support paging, context switches, and other operating system interactions without undue runtime overhead or complexity. This work also identifies the challenge that false sharing presents to all TM systems based on cache coherence. Opportunities include generalizing LogTM to a true hardware-software hybrid where hardware implements mechanisms and software sets policies. LogTM's log structure also lends itself to a straight-forward extension to nested transactions. Finally, LogTM is implemented in a full-system simulation environment and is available under GPL in the GEMS distribution [19].

6. Acknowledgments

This work is supported in part by the National Science Foundation (NSF), with grants CCF-0085949, CCR-0105721, EIA/CNS-0205286, CCR-0324878, as well as donations from Intel and Sun Microsystems. Hill and Wood have significant financial interest in Sun Microsystems. The views expressed herein are not necessarily those of the NSF, Intel, or Sun Microsystems.

We thank Virtutech AB, the Wisconsin Condor group, and the Wisconsin Computer Systems Lab for their help and support. We thank Zoran Radovic for help configuring our benchmarks. We thank Alaa Alameldeen, Brad Beckmann, Ben Liblit, Mike Marty, Mark Moir, Dan Nussbaum, Ravi Rajwar, Dan Sorin, Min Xu, the UW Computer Architecture Affiliates, and the Wisconsin Multifacet project for their helpful feedback on this work.

7. References

[1] Haitham Akkary and Michael A. Driscoll. A Dynamic Multithreading Processor. In *Proc. of the 31st Annual IEEE/ACM Intl. Symp. on Microarchitecture*, pages 226–236, Nov. 1998.

[2] C. Scott Ananian, Krste Asanovic, Bradley C. Kuszmaul, Charles E. Leiserson, and Sean Lie. Unbounded Transactional Memory. In *Proc. of the Eleventh IEEE Symp. on High-Performance Computer Architecture*, Feb. 2005.

[3] Colin Blundell, E Christopher Lewis, and Milo M.K. Martin. Deconstructing Transactional Semantics: The Subtleties of Atomicity. In *Workshop on Duplicating, Deconstructing, and Debunking (WDDD)*, Jun. 2005.

[4] Albert Chang and Mark F. Mergen. 801 Storage: Architecture and Programming. *ACM Trans. on Computer Sys.*, 6(1), Feb. 1988.

[5] David E. Culler and J.P. Singh. *Parallel Computer Architecture: A Hardware/Software Approach*. Morgan Kaufmann Publishers, Inc., 1999.

[6] K. P. Eswaran, J. N. Gray, R. A. Lorie, and I. L. Traiger. The Notions of Consistency and Predicate Locks in a Database System. *Communications of the ACM*, 19(11):624–633, 1976.

[7] María Jesús Garzarán, Milos Prvulovic, Victor Viñals, José María Llabería, Lawrence Rauchwerger, and Josep Torrellas. Using Software Logging to Support Multi-Version Buffering in Thread-Level Speculation. In *Proc. of the Intl. Conference on Parallel Architectures and Compilation Techniques*, Sep. 2003.

[8] Sridhar Gopal, T.N. Vijaykumar, James E. Smith, and Gurindar S. Sohi. Speculative Versioning Cache. In *Proc. of the Fourth IEEE Symp. on High-Performance Computer Architecture*, pages 195–205, Feb. 1998.

[9] J. Gray, R. Lorie, F. Putzolu, and I. Traiger. Granularity of Locks and Degrees of Consistency in a Shared Database. In *Modeling in Data Base Management Systems, Elsevier North Holland, New York*, 1975.

[10] Lance Hammond, Mark Willey, and Kunle Olukotun. Data Speculation Support for a Chip Multiprocessor. In *Proc. of the Eighth Intl. Conference on Architectural Support for Programming Languages and Operating Systems*, pages 58–69, Oct. 1998.

[11] Lance Hammond, Vicky Wong, Mike Chen, Brian D. Carlstrom, John D. Davis, Ben Hertzberg, Manohar K. Prabhu, Honggo Wijaya, Christos Kozyrakis, and Kunle Olukotun. Transactional Memory Coherence and Consistency. In *Proc. of the 31st Annual Intl. Symp. on Computer Architecture*, June 2004.

[12] Tim Harris and Keir Fraser. Language support for lightweight transactions. In *Proc. of the 18th SIGPLAN Conference on Object-Oriented Programming, Systems, Languages and Application (OOPSLA)*, Oct. 2003.

[13] Maurice Herlihy, Victor Luchangco, Mark Moir, and William Scherer III. Software Transactional Memory for Dynamic-Sized Data Structures. In *Twenty-Second ACM Symp. on Principles of Distributed Computing, Boston, Massachusetts*, Jul. 2003.

[14] Maurice Herlihy and J. Eliot B. Moss. Transactional Memory: Architectural Support for Lock-Free Data Structures. In *Proc. of the 20th Annual Intl. Symp. on Computer Architecture*, pages 289–300, May 1993.

[15] Tom Knight. An Architecture for Mostly Functional Languages. In *Proc. of the ACM Conference on LISP and Functional Programming*, pages 105–112, 1986.

[16] H. T. Kung and J. T. Robinson. On Optimistic Methods for Concurrency Control. *ACM Transactions on Database Systems*, pages 213–226, Jun. 1981.

[17] Peter S. Magnusson et al. Simics: A Full System Simulation Platform. *IEEE Computer*, 35(2):50–58, Feb. 2002.

[18] V. J. Marathe, W. N. Scherer III, and M. L. Scott. Adaptive Software Transactional Memory. Technical Report 868, Computer Science Department, University of Rochester, 2005.

[19] Milo M.K. Martin, Daniel J. Sorin, Bradford M. Beckmann, Michael R. Marty, Min Xu, Alaa R. Alameldeen, Kevin E. Moore, Mark D. Hill, and David A. Wood. Multifacet's General Execution-driven Multiprocessor Simulator (GEMS) Toolset. *Computer Architecture News*, 2005.

[20] José F. Martínez and Josep Torrellas. Speculative Synchronization: Applying Thread-Level Speculation to Explicitly Parallel Applications. In *Proc. of the Tenth Intl. Conference on Architectural Support for Programming Languages and Operating Systems*, pages 18–29, Oct. 2002.

[21] John M. Mellor-Curmmey and Michael L. Scott. Algorithms for Scalable Synchronization on Shared-Memory Multiprocessors. *ACM Transactions on Computer Systems*, 9(1):21–65, 1991.

[22] Milos Prvulovic, María Jesús Garzarán, Lawrence Rauchwerger, and Josep Torrellas. Removing Architectural Bottlenecks to the Scalability of Speculative Parallelization. In *Proc. of the 28th Intl. Symp. on Computer Architecture*, pages 204–215, Jul. 2001.

[23] Ravi Rajwar and James R. Goodman. Speculative Lock Elision: Enabling Highly Concurrent Multithreaded Execution. In *Proc. of the 34th Annual IEEE/ACM Intl. Symp. on Microarchitecture*, Dec. 2001.

[24] Ravi Rajwar and James R. Goodman. Transactional Lock-Free Execution of Lock-Based Programs. In *Proc. of the Tenth Intl. Conference on Architectural Support for Programming Languages and Operating Systems*, Oct. 2002.

[25] Ravi Rajwar, Maurice Herlihy, and Konrad Lai. Virtualizing Transactional Memory. In *Proc. of the 32nd Annual Intl. Symp. on Computer Architecture*, Jun. 2005.

[26] W. N. Scherer III and M. L. Scott. Advanced Contention Management for Dynamic Software Transactional Memory. In *24th ACM Symp. on Principles of Distributed Computing*, Jul. 2005.

[27] Nir Shavit and Dan Touitou. Software Transactional Memory. In *Fourteenth ACM Symp. on Principles of Distributed Computing, Ottawa, Ontario, Canada*, pages 204–213, Aug. 1995.

[28] G.S. Sohi, S. Breach, and T.N. Vijaykumar. Multiscalar Processors. In *Proc. of the 22nd Annual Intl. Symp. on Computer Architecture*, pages 414–425, Jun. 1995.

[29] J. Gregory Steffan and Todd C. Mowry. The Potential for Using Thread-Level Data Speculation to Facilitate Automatic Parallelization. In *Proc. of the Fourth IEEE Symp. on High-Performance Computer Architecture*, pages 2–13, Feb. 1998.

[30] Janice M. Stone, Harold S. Stone, Philip Heidelberger, and John Turek. Multiple Reservations and the Oklahoma Update. *IEEE Parallel and Distributed Technology, Systems, & Applications*, 1(4):58–71, Nov. 1993.

[31] Wisconsin Multifacet GEMS http://www.cs.wisc.edu/gems.

[32] Steven Cameron Woo, Moriyoshi Ohara, Evan Torrie, Jaswinder Pal Singh, and Anoop Gupta. The SPLASH-2 Programs: Characterization and Methodological Considerations. In *Proc. of the 22nd Annual Intl. Symp. on Computer Architecture*, pages 24–37, Jun. 1995.

[33] Ye Zhang, Lawrence Rauchwerger, and Josep Torrellas. Hardware for Speculative Run-Time Parallelization in Distributed Shared-Memory Multiprocessors. In *Proc. of the Fourth IEEE Symp. on High-Performance Computer Architecture*, Feb. 1998.

[34] Ye Zhang, Lawrence Rauchwerger, and Josep Torrellas. Hardware for Speculative Parallelization of Partially-Parallel Loops in DSM Multiprocessors,. In *Proc. of the Fifth IEEE Symp. on High-Performance Computer Architecture*, Jan. 1999.

Session 10:
Multi-Threaded Systems

The Common Case Transactional Behavior of Multithreaded Programs

JaeWoong Chung, Hassan Chafi, C. Cao Minh, Austen McDonald, Brian Carlstrom
Christos Kozyrakis, Kunle Olukotun

Computer Systems Laboratory
Stanford University
{jwchung, hchafi, caominh, austenmc, bdc, kozyraki, kunle}@stanford.edu

Abstract

Transactional memory (TM) provides an easy-to-use and high-performance parallel programming model for the upcoming chip-multiprocessor systems. Several researchers have proposed alternative hardware and software TM implementations. However, the lack of transaction-based programs makes it difficult to understand the merits of each proposal and to tune future TM implementations to the common case behavior of real application.

This work addresses this problem by analyzing the common case transactional behavior for 35 multithreaded programs from a wide range of application domains. We identify transactions within the source code by mapping existing primitives for parallelism and synchronization management to transaction boundaries. The analysis covers basic characteristics such as transaction length, distribution of read-set and write-set size, and the frequency of nesting and I/O operations. The measured characteristics provide key insights into the design of efficient TM systems for both non-blocking synchronization and speculative parallelization.

1. Introduction

With most hardware vendors shipping chip-multiprocessors (CMPs) for the desktop, embedded, and server markets [15, 16, 24], mainstream applications must become concurrent to take advantage of the multiple cores [38]. Traditionally, programmers have associated locks with shared data in order to synchronize concurrent accesses. However, locks have well-known software engineering issues that make parallel programming too complicated for the average developer [39]. The programmer must choose between the easy-to-use coarse-grain locking that leads to unnecessary blocking and the scalable fine-grain locking that requires complex coding conventions to avoid deadlocks, priority inversion, or convoying.

Moreover, lock-based code does not automatically compose and is not robust to hardware or software failures.

Transactional Memory (TM) [14] provides an alternative model for concurrency management. A TM system operates on shared data using sequences of instructions (transactions) which execute in an atomic and isolated manner [8]. Transactional memory simplifies parallel programming by providing non-blocking synchronization with easy-to-write, coarse-grain transactions by virtue of optimistic concurrency [17]. It also allows for speculative parallelization of sequential code [9]. Furthermore, transactional code is composable and robust in the face of failures.

The significant advantages of the TM model have motivated several proposals for hardware-based [29, 23, 2, 25] or software-only [34, 12, 13, 22, 31, 32] implementations. Some proposals advocate continuous transactional execution in parallel systems [10, 18]. The various TM designs suggest different tradeoffs in the mechanisms used to track transactional state and detect conflicts, the size and location of buffers, and the overheads associated with basic operations. At this point, however, there is not enough transaction-based software to properly evaluate the merit of each proposal. System designers need transactional code to tune their TM designs to the common case behavior of real applications. At the same time, application developers are waiting for efficient and complete TM system before they port a significant volume of applications to the new concurrency model.

This paper attempts to break the deadlock. We study a wide range of existing multithreaded applications and analyze the likely common-case behavior of their future transactional versions. The basic premise of our approach is that the high-level parallelism and synchronization characteristics in an application are unlikely to change significantly regardless of the mechanism used to manage them (locks or transactions). Our study involves 35 multithreaded programs from a wide range of applications domains, written in four parallel programming models. To define transaction boundaries in the source code, we examine the primitives used for concurrency control in each parallel model and re-cast their meaning in a transactional context for both non-blocking synchronization and speculative parallelization. Then, we trace and analyze each application to measure basic characteristics such as the transaction length, the read-set and write-set size, and the frequency of nested transactions and I/O operations. The characteristics provide key insights into the common case support necessary to implement an efficient TM system.

The major observations from our analysis are:

- Transactions are mostly short. Hence, the fixed overheads associated with starting and ending transactions must be minimized. Short transactions also allow us to handle interrupts and context switches efficiently without the need for complex hardware mechanisms for TM virtualization.

- The read-sets and write-sets for most transactions fit in L1-sized buffers. However, read-/write- set buffering in L2-sized buffers is necessary to avoid frequent overflows on the longer transactions, especially in the case of speculative parallelism. If L2 caches can store transaction read-/write- sets, complex hardware mechanisms for TM virtualization can be replaced by simple, software-only alternatives.

- When used for non-blocking synchronization, many transactions access a large number of unique addresses compared to their length. Hence, the overhead of buffering, committing, or rolling back per unique address must be minimized. This issue is not aggravated when transactions are used continuously or when they support speculative parallelization.

- Nested transactions occur in system code but rarely in user code. Since the nesting depth is low, hardware support for nested transactions can be limited to a couple of nesting levels.

- I/O operations within transactions are also rare. The observed I/O patterns are easy to handle through I/O buffering techniques.

The rest of the paper is organized as follows. Section 2 summarizes transactional memory and discusses the major design tradeoffs that motivate this study. In Section 3, we present our experimental methodology for analyzing multithreaded applications within a transactional context. Section 4 and 5 present our analysis results when transactions are used for non-blocking synchronization and speculative parallelization respectively. We conclude the paper in Section 6.

2. Transactional Memory

2.1 Transactional Memory Overview

With transactional memory, programmers define atomic blocks of code (transactions) that can include unstructured flow-control and any number of memory accesses. A TM system executes atomic blocks in a manner that preserves the following properties: a) *atomicity*: either the whole transaction executes or none of it; b) *isolation*: partial memory updates are not visible to other transactions; and c) *consistency*: there is a single order of completion for transactions across the whole system [14]. TM systems achieve high performance through optimistic concurrency [17]. A transaction runs without acquiring locks, optimistically assuming no other transaction operates concurrently on the same data. If that assumption is true by the end of its execution, the transaction commits its updates to shared memory. If interference between transactions is detected, then the transaction aborts, its updates so far are rolled back, and it is re-executed from scratch.

A TM system must implement the following mechanisms: (1) *speculative buffering* of stores (*write-set*) until the transaction commits; (2) *conflict detection* between concurrent transactions; (3) *atomic commit* of transaction stores to shared memory; (4) *rollback* of transaction stores when conflicts are detected. Conflict detection requires tracking the addresses read by each transaction (*read-set*). A conflict occurs when the write-set of a committing transaction overlaps with the read-set of an executing transaction. The mechanisms can be implemented either in hardware (HTM) [29, 23, 2, 25] or software (STM) [34, 12, 13, 22, 31, 32]. HTM minimizes the overhead of the basic mechanisms, which is likely to lead to higher performance. STM runs on stock processors and provides implementation flexibility.

HTM systems implement speculative buffering in the processor caches using a store-buffer [29, 23] or an undo-log [2, 25]. A store-buffer allows for truly non-blocking TM but defers all memory updates until the transaction commits. An undo-log accelerates commits by updating shared memory as the transaction executes, but has slower aborts, incurs per access overheads, and introduces blocking and deadlock issues. Since caches have limited capacity and buffer/log overflow is possible, some HTM systems [2, 30] provide elaborate hardware mechanisms to extend the buffer/log into virtual memory (space virtualization). The same mechanisms can be used to context switch a thread in the middle of a transaction if an interrupt occurs (time virtualization). Read-sets are also tracked in caches and conflicts are detected using the cache coherence protocol. Transaction roll-back requires flushing the transaction write-set and read-set from caches.

STM systems implement buffering, conflict detection, commit, and abort entirely in software using runtime primitives. Apart from defining transaction boundaries, STM requires a runtime call at least once per unique address read or written in a transaction so that read-set and write-set can be tracked. Again, speculative buffering can be implemented using a write-buffer [12] or an undo-log [32]. For conflict detection, the STM runtime can either acquire read-write locks during the transaction execution (faster detection) or acquire write locks only and validate the version of all read data before commit (reduced interference at increased commit overhead) [12]. Read-set and write-set tracking can be at the granularity of words, cache-lines, or objects. Commit and abort require walking through the structures that track read-set and write-set to validate, copy, or roll back values, depending on the implementation approach. Buffer/log overflow cannot occur with STM as it operates on top of the virtual memory system.

I/O calls within transactions [11] as well as the semantics and support for nested transactions are topics of active research for both HTM and STM systems.

2.2 Design Challenges & Application Characteristics

It is clear from the above overview that the design of a transactional memory system involves a large number of implementation decisions. As it is common with all systems, the guiding principle for making such decisiosn will be "*make the common case fast*". Designers will look at the common values for basic characteristics of transactional applications to select the right implementation approach for the TM mechanisms, to size buffer components, and to tune the overhead of basic operations. In this section, we review the basic application characteristics for transactional memory and the implementation aspects they interact with.

Transaction Length: Short transactions make it difficult to amortize fixed overheads for starting and committing transactions. On the other hand, long transactions may run into interrupts and require time virtualization support. Long transactions are also more likely to cause rollbacks. This study measures the distribution of transaction lengths in instructions.

Read-set and Write-set Size: The common read-set and write-set sizes dictate the necessary capacity for the buffer used to track them. They also determine the frequency of buffer overflows and whether a fast mechanism is necessary for space virtualization. The granularity for tracking read- and write-sets is also important in order to balance overheads against the frequency of rollbacks due to false sharing. This study measures the distribution of read-/write- sets in words, cache lines, and pages.

Read-/Write- Set to Transaction Length Ratio: The ratio determines if any overhead per unique address read or written in each transaction can be easily amortized. Hence, it helps the designer tune the overhead of basic operations like log update, validateion of a read, and the commit or abort of a store.

Nesting Frequency: The frequency and depth of nested transactions determines the necessary support for nesting in HTM systems. It is also important to understand the potential performance cost from flattening nested transactions, a common approach in current TM designs.

I/O Frequency within Transactions: Non-idempotent I/O within a transaction can be difficult to handle as it cannot be rolled back. Moreover, delaying I/O until the transaction commits may lead to system deadlock. This study does not implement a specific solution, but characterizes the frequency and type of I/O operations within transactions.

In measuring the above application characteristics, it is important to understand that transactions can be used in multiple ways. The original goal for TM has been to provide *non-blocking synchronization* in multiprocessor systems by implementing transactions on top of ordinary cache coherence protocols [14]. Lately, there have been proposals to build TM systems for *continuous transaction execution* to further simplify parallel hardware and software [10, 18]. Finally, the TM mechanisms can support speculative parallelization of sequential code [9]. This study measures application characteristics under all three TM use scenarios.

3. Experimental Methodology

To provide detailed insights into the common case transactional behavior of real programs, we study a large set of existing multithreaded applications. This section describes the experimental methodology, which includes application selection, defining transaction boundaries in multithreaded code, and a trace-based analysis that extracts the characteristics discussed in Section 2.2.

3.1 Multithreaded Applications

Table 1 presents the 35 multithreaded applications we used in this study. The applications were parallelized using four parallel programming models: Java threads [4], C and Pthreads [19], C and OpenMP [28], and the ANL parallel processing macros [21]. Java is increasingly popular and includes multithreading in the base language specification. OpenMP is a widely adopted model based on high-level compiler directives for semi-automatic parallelization. Pthreads is a widely available multithreading package for POSIX systems. Finally, the ANL macros were designed to provide a simple, concise, and portable interface covering a variety of parallel applications. We use the Java, Pthreads, and ANL applications to study the use of transactions for non-blocking synchronization (29 applications). We use the

Prog. Model	Application	Problem Size	Source	Domain/Description
Java	MolDyn	2,048 Particles	JavaGrande	Scientific / Molecular Dynamics
	MonteCarlo	10,000 Runs	JavaGrande	Scientific / Finance
	RayTracer	150x150 Pixels	JavaGrande	Graphics / 3D Raytracer
	Crypt	200,000 Bytes	JavaGrande	Kernel / Encryption and Decryption
	LUFact	500x500 Matrix	JavaGrande	Kernel / Solving NxN Linear System
	Series	200 Coefficients	JavaGrande	Kernel / First N Fourier Coefficients
	SOR	1,000x1,000 Grid	JavaGrande	Kernel / Successive Over-Relaxation
	SparseMatmul	250,000x250,000 Matrix	JavaGrande	Kernel / Matrix Multiplication
	SPECjbb2000	8 Warehouses	SPECjbb2000	Commercial / E-Commerce
	PMD	18 Java Files	DaCapo	Commercial / Java Code Checking
	HSQLDB	10 Tellers, 1,000	DaCapo	Commercial / Banking with hsql database
Pthreads	Apache	20 Worker Threads	Apache	Commercial / HTTP web server
	Kingate	10,000 HTTP Requests	SourceForge	Commercial / Web proxy
	Bp-vision	384x288 Image	Univ. of Chi.	Machine Learning / Loopy Belief Propagation
	Localize	477x177 Map	CARMEN	Robotics / Finding a Robot Position in a Map
	Ultra Tic Tac	5x5 Board, 3 Step	SourceForge	AI / Tic Tac Toe Game
	MPEG2	640x480 Clip	MPEG S.S.G.	MultiMedia / MPEG2 Decoder
	AOL Server	20 Worker Threads	AOL Website	Commercial / HTTP web server
OpenMP	Equake	380K Nodes	SPEComp	Scientific / Seismic Wave Propagation Simulation
	Art	640x480 Image	SPEComp	Scientific / Neural Network Simulation
	CG	1400x1400 Matrix	NAS	Scientific / Conjugate Gradient Method
	BT	12x12x12 Matrix	NAS	Scientific / CFD
	IS	1M Keys	NAS	Scientific / Large-scale Integer Sort
	Swim	1,900x900 Matrix	SPEComp	Scientific / Shallow Water Modeling
ANL Macros	Barnes	16K Particles	SPLASH-2	Scientific / Evolution of Galaxies
	Mp3d	3,000 Molecules, 50 Steps	SPLASH	Scientific / Rarefied Hypersonic Flow
	Ocean	258x258 Ocean	SPLASH-2	Scientific / Eddy Currents in an Ocean Basin
	Radix	1M Ints., Radix 1024	SPLASH-2	Kernel / Radix Sort
	FMM	2,049 Particles	SPLASH-2	Kernel / N-body Simulation
	Cholesky	TK23.0	SPLASH-2	Kernel / Sparse Matrix Factorization
	Radiosity	Room	SPLASH-2	Graphics / Equilibrium of Light Distribution
	FFT	256K points	SPLASH-2	Kernel / 1-D version of the radix-N2 FFT
	Volrend	Head-Scaledown 4	SPLASH-2	Graphics / 3-D Volumn Rendering
	Water-N2	512 molecules	SPLASH-2	Scientific / Evolution of System of Water Molecules
	Water-Spatial	512 molecules	SPLASH-2	Scientific / Evolution of System of Water Molecules

Table 1: The 35 multithreaded applications used in this study.

six OpenMP applications to study the use of transactions for speculative parallelization.

The selected programs cover a wide range of application domains. Apart from scientific computations, the list includes commercial applications (web servers, web proxies, relational databases, e-commerce systems), graphics, multimedia, and artificial intelligence programs (machine learning, robotics, games). These important application domains are good targets for current and future parallel systems as they operate on increasing datasets and use seemingly parallel algorithms.

We obtained the applications from a variety of sources. Eight of the Java programs are from the JavaGrande benchmark suite [35], while the remaining three are from the DaCapo benchmark suite [6] and the SPECjbb2000 benchmark [36]. The OpenMP applications are from the SPEComp [37] and the NAS [27] benchmark suites. All ANL applications were obtained from the SPLASH and SPLASH-2 benchmark suites [40]. The Pthreads applications come from various sources: the Apache Software Foundation (Apache [3]), SourceForge.net (Kingate and Ul-

tra Tic-Tac-Toe), the University of Chicago (BP-vision [7]), the CMU Carmen project (Localize [41]), and the MPEG Software Simulation Group (Mpeg2 [26]). The variety of sources also implies variability in parallelization quality. While commercial programs such as Apache or benchmark suites are likely to be thoroughly optimized, other programs may not be fully tuned. We believe that measuring transactional behavior in the presence of such variability is actually good as both expert and novice developers will be coding for CMPs in the near future. Hence, we did not attempt further optimizations on any of the applications.

3.2 Transaction Boundaries

Our analysis is based on the premise that the high-level parallelism and synchronization patterns are unlikely to change when applications are ported from lock-based programming models to transactional models. After all, these patterns depend heavily on the algorithm and on the programmer's understanding of the algorithm. Hence, we create transactional versions of the applications by mapping

TM System Case	Abstract Threading Primitive	Transaction Mapping	Transaction Type
Non-blocking Synchronization	Lock	BEGIN	Critical
	Unlock	END	Critical
	Wait	END-BEGIN	Critical
Continuous Transactions	Thread Create/Entry	BEGIN	Non-critical
	Thread Exit/Join	END	Non-critical
	Notify	END-BEGIN	Non-critical
	I/O	END-BEGIN	Non-critical
Speculative Parallelization	Parallel Iteration Start	BEGIN	Critical
	Parallel Iteration End	END	Critical

Table 2: The mapping of multithreading primitives to transaction BEGIN and END markers.

the threading and locking primitives in their code to BEGIN and END (commit) markers for transactions. The mapping is performed merely for the purpose of introducing transaction boundaries in the execution trace generated by running the original multithreaded code. Automatically translating lock-based primitives to transactions (lock elision) and running the new code on a TM system is not always safe [5].

Table 2 summarizes the mapping between multithreading primitives in the application code and transaction boundaries. For brevity, we abstract out the differences between similar primitives in the four programming models. For example, the abstract primitive *Lock* represents the opening bracket on a `synchronized` block in Java, the `LOCK()` macro in ANL, the `pthread_*lock()` calls in Pthreads (regular, read, and write locks), and the opening bracket of the `CRITICAL/ATOMIC` pragmas and the `omp_locks()` call in OpenMP. Overall, we identified nine abstract primitives that must be mapped to transactions. Our mapping considers three TM uses: the sporadic use of transactions for non-blocking synchronization, the continuous use of transactions, and the use of transactions for speculative parallelization.

For systems that use TM for non-blocking synchronization, we map *Lock* and *Unlock* primitives to BEGIN and END transaction markers. These markers define nested transactions if locks are nested in the application code. We assume a closed-nesting model, where the stores of an inner transaction are committed to shared memory only when the outer-most transaction commits. We also mark I/O statements within transactions but these markers do not affect the transaction boundaries. The Java conditional `wait` construct (`java.lang.Object.wait()`) is an interesting case. Java requires that a thread obtains a monitor before it calls `wait`, hence `wait` statements are typically made within a `synchronized` block. When `wait` is called, the thread releases the monitor. When the thread resumes after a matching notify, the thread re-acquires the monitor. To reflect this properly, we map `wait` to an END marker (end previous transaction) and a BEGIN marker (start new

transaction) pair.

For systems that execute transactions continuously, there is no code execution outside transactions [10, 18]. Again, *Lock*, *Unlock*, and `wait` primitives are mapped to BEGIN and END transaction markers. We call the corresponding transactions *critical* as they must be executed atomically under all circumstances. The difference in this case is that even the code between END and BEGIN markers defined by locks must execute as a transaction. We call these transactions *non-critical* as the TM system could freely split them into multiple transactions by introducing commits to reduce buffer pressure or for other optimizations without loss of atomicity. Thread create/entry primitives define BEGIN markers for non-critical transactions, while thread exit/join primitives define END markers for non-critical transactions. I/O statements outside of critical transactions split the current non-critical transaction into two. In other words, each I/O primitive is mapped to a non-critical transaction END followed by a non-critical transaction BEGIN.

For the use of transactions for speculative parallelization, we cast parallel loops defined through OpenMP pragmas as speculative parallel loops. The beginning and end of an iteration in a parallel loop define the BEGIN and END markers respectively for critical transactions. I/O statements within the iterations are marked but they do not affect transaction boundaries.

The transaction markers that correspond to each primitive in the multithreaded code were inserted in the following way. For Java applications, we modified the just-in-time compiler in the Jikes RVM [1] to automatically insert the markers. The SPLASH-2 applications were also annotated automatically by modifying the ANL macros. For the OpenMP and Pthreads applications, we inserted markers in the source code manually.

3.3 Trace-based Analysis

Once the transaction markers were in place, we executed the applications on a PowerPC G5 workstation and collected a detailed execution trace using `amber`, a tool in Apple's Computer Hardware Understanding Development (CHUD) suite. All tracing runs used 8 threads. The trace includes all instructions executed by the program (memory and non-memory). However, when a multithreading primitive is invoked (e.g. Lock or Unlock), the transactional marker is emitted in the trace instead of the actual code that corresponds to the primitive.

We analyzed the traces using a collection of scripts to extract transactional characteristics such as transaction length, read-set and write-set sizes, read-set and write-set to transaction length ratio, frequency of I/O, and frequency of nesting. The read-set and write-set sizes were measured in three granularities: 4-byte words, 32-byte cache lines, and 4-

Kbyte pages. The read-set (write-set) to transaction length ratio is calculated by dividing the read-set (write-set) size by the number of instructions in each transaction. We perform such calculations on individual transactions before calculating averages. For nested transactions, our scripts use a stack to push and pop transactional contexts according to BEGIN and END markers.

3.4 Discussion

Our methodology has certain limitations that require further discussion. First, it is possible that when the applications are re-written for transactional memory and executed on a TM system, some of the measured characteristics may change. However, the existing multithreaded versions provide good indicators of where parallelism exists and where synchronization is needed in the corresponding algorithms. Hence, we expect that transactional behavior will at least be similar.

Our analysis measures transactional characteristics that are largely implementation independent. For example, we do not attempt to measure the number of buffer overflows in a specific HTM system. Instead, we provide the distribution of read-set and write-set sizes from which one can easily calculate the percentage of transactions that will overflow for a given buffer size.

Our methodology cannot evaluate the frequency of transaction rollbacks for a given application. Such an analysis is difficult to make outside of the scope of a specific TM implementation (number of processors, timing of instruction and communication events, transaction scheduling approach, conflict management techniques, etc.). Nevertheless, our study indicates the potential cost of rollbacks: the amount of work wasted is on the average proportional to transaction length; the overhead of the rollback with an undo-log is proportional to the write-set size; etc.

For practical reasons, we use a single dataset for each application. For the applications evaluated for non-blocking synchronization (Pthreads, Java, ANL), synchronization is used only when a thread accesses potentially shared data. Hence, excluding the percentage of time spent in transactions, the rest of the transactional characteristics will probably be similar with different datasets. For applications evaluated for speculative parallelization, the characteristics will remain unchanged if inner-loops are parallelized, but can vary significantly with the data-set if outer-loops have been chosen for parallelization. Our analysis does not separate between truly shared and fully private addresses in the read-sets and write-sets. An optimizing compiler may be able to classify some addresses as thread private, which in turn allows the TM implementation to avoid tracking them for conflict detection.

| Application | Length in Instructions | | | |
	Avg	50th %	95th %	Max
Java avg	5949	149	4256	13519488
sparsematmult	2723	41	34987	53736
series	7756	97	43250	524636
Pthreads avg	879	805	1056	22591
mpeg2	93694	101327	167267	347339
ANL avg	256	114	772	16782
fft	157	157	157	157
radix	9	9	9	9

Table 3: The distribution of critical transaction lengths in instructions.

4. Analysis for Non-blocking Synchronization

This section presents our analysis results for the case of using transactions for non-blocking synchronization with the Java, Pthreads, and ANL applications. For each characteristic analyzed, we first present the application results and then describe a set of basic insights these results provide into building efficient TM systems. We focus mostly on critical transactions but we also comment on non-critical transactions, which are important for systems that execute transactions continuously. Throughout the section, we present tables and figures with averages taken over whole application groups (e.g. the average of all Java programs). We also present the most interesting outliers alongside the averages. Outliers are not included in the group average.

4.1 Transaction Length

Table 3 presents the distribution of critical transaction length in number of instructions. Most transactions tend to be small with 95% of them including less than 5,000 instructions. However, the distribution exhibits a long tail, and a small number of transactions become quite large. ANL applications have the shortest transactions as they are optimized for scalability (infrequent and short atomic regions). The same behavior is observed with Pthreads programs, particularly Apache which is a well-tuned commercial program. Mpeg2 is the only exception as it uses a lock during the whole operation on a video frame slice. Most Java programs exhibit short transactions on the average but have a long distribution tail. The longer transactions are partly due to the applications themselves and partly due to the long critical regions used in Jikes RVM for scheduling, synchronization, class loading, and memory management.

We do not present the length of non-critical transactions due to space limitations. They are typically longer, but they can be split at arbitrary places to avoid any issues associated with their length.

Observations: The high frequency of very short transactions (150 instructions or less) implies that the overheads associated with TM mechanisms such as starting or committing a transaction must be very low. Otherwise, the overheads may cancel out any benefits from non-blocking synchronization. This can be a significant challenge for STM systems which use runtime functions at transaction boundaries. For HTM systems, fast register checkpointing will be necessary to keep the transaction start overhead low. Alternatively, HTM systems will require compiler help to avoid checkpointing all registers on transaction starts.

The frequency of short transactions has implications on time virtualization for HTM systems. The UTM [2] and VTM [30] systems propose that I/O or timer interrupts cause a transaction to be swapped out by saving its transactional state (read-/write- set) in special overflow buffers in virtual memory. The state is restored when the transaction resumes later. Given the overhead of saving/restoring state and that 95% of transactions include less than 5,000 instructions, an alternative approach makes sense. On an interrupt, we should initially wait for one of the processors to finish its current transaction and assign it to interrupt processing. Since most transactions are short (150 instructions), this will likely happen quickly. If the interrupt is a real-time one or becomes critical, we should rollback the youngest transaction and use its processor for interrupt handling. Re-executing some portion of a short transaction is faster than saving and restoring state in virtual memory buffers. Saving and restoring should be reserved only for the very long transactions that span multiple OS quanta (tens of millions of instructions). Our data suggest that this case is extremely rare hence it should be handled in software, using OS-based techniques [33, 20], without the complicated hardware structures discussed in [2] and [30].

4.2 Read-Set and Write-Set Sizes

Figure 1 presents the distribution of read-set and write-set sizes for critical transactions. For 95% of transactions, the read-set is less than 4 Kbytes and the write-set is less than 1 Kbyte. However, we must also consider that large read-/write- sets are typically found in longer transactions. Figure 2 presents the normalized time spent on transactions with read-/write- sets of a specific size. We assume that time is proportional to the transaction length. For read-sets, a 52-Kbyte buffer is needed to cover 80% or more of the transaction execution time for most applications. For write-sets, a 30-Kbyte buffer is sufficient for 80% of the transaction execution time of most applications with the exception of hsqldb. Hsqldb includes some long JDBC connections that execute large SQL queries. We should also note from Figures 1 and 2 that read-set and write-set sizes do not exceed 128 Kbytes. Our analysis also indicates that there is

Application	Read-Set		Write-Set	
	Words/Line	Lines/Page	Words/Line	Lines/Page
Java avg	1.7	3.7	1.7	4.3
Pthreads avg	2.0	3.8	3.5	8.5
ANL avg	2.1	6.8	2.3	7.9
sparsematmul	1.3	1.7	2.1	3.0
mpeg2	7.8	71.2	2.3	7.9

Table 4: The number of words used per line and lines used per page for the transaction read-sets and write-sets.

significant overlap between read- and write-sets. The ratio of their intersection divided by their union is typically 15% to 30%. If both sets are tracked in a unified buffer such as a data cache, large overlaps reduce the pressure on buffer capacity.

Transaction read- and write-sets can be tracked at the granularity of words, cache lines, or memory pages. Coarser granularity tracking reduces overheads but may lead to unnecessary work due to loss of accuracy. Table 4 shows the number of words used per line and the number of lines used per page when the read-/write- sets are tracked at line and page granularity respectively. Words are 4 bytes, lines are 32 bytes, and pages are 4 Kbytes. For most applications, only 2 out of 8 words per cache line in the read-set are actually used. For write-sets, the ratio is at 3 words used per cache line. For the case of page granularity, less than 10 cache lines from the 128 per page are actually used in the read-/write- sets. Mpeg2 is the only exception in both cases as it exhibits very good spatial locality in its read-set and write-set accesses.

Observations: Figure 2 shows that transaction read-sets and write-sets are often too large to fit in small side-buffers as in the original HTM design [14]. However, they are within the capacity of processor caches, which can be modified to track transaction's read-sets and write-sets. The majority of transactions fit in an L1 cache (16 to 32 Kbytes) but support at the L2 cache (128 Kbytes to Mbytes) is needed to avoid overflows for the few long transactions. With read-/write- set tracking in L2 caches, overflows will be extremely rare events. Hence, complex hardware mechanisms that allow read-/write- sets to overflow in virtual memory [2, 30] will hardly ever get used. Instead, it is preferable to have a simple virtualization mechanism that is completely software based. In the rare event of a read-/write- set that exceeds the L2 capacity, an exception is raised and the system executes the transaction using OS-based transactional mechanisms that operate on top of the virtual memory system without any hardware limitations [33, 20].

Tracking read-/write- sets at cache line granularity [29, 2, 25] leads to significant accuracy loss and may lead to performance inefficiencies: unnecessary rollbacks due to false

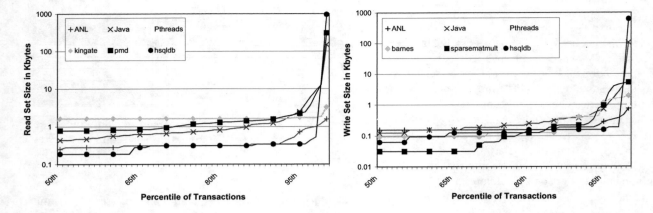

Figure 1: The cumulative distribution of read-set (left) and write-set (right) sizes in Kbytes.

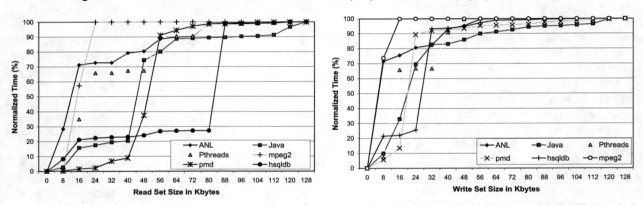

Figure 2: Normalized time spent in transactions with different read-set (left) and write-set (right) sizes.

sharing as well as logging (buffer space waste) or committing (badwidth waste) more than two times the amount of necessary data. Word granularity tracking can eliminate these issues [23]. Page granularity tracking is simply too wasteful to allow for good performance for most of applications.

4.3 Read-/Write- Set Size to Transaction Length Ratio

Hardware and software TM systems perform basic operations for each word in the read- or write- set: log an old value in the undo-log, commit the new value to shared memory, validate a read value before commit, restore old value at abort, etc. The overheads of such operations can be hidden if they can be amortized across a large number of instructions in the transaction. Figure 3 presents the distribution of write-set size (in words) to the transaction length (in instructions) ratio for critical transactions. A ratio of 50% means that the transaction stores to a unique new address every two instructions. The ratio is roughly 10% for most transactions but some of them go as high as 25%. The reason for the high ratios is that these applications perform all updates to shared data in critical sections. For non-critical

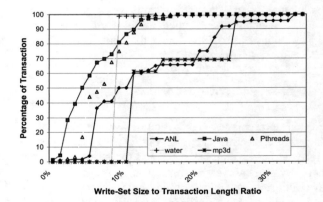

Figure 3: The write-set size (in words) to transaction length (in instructions) ratio for critical transactions.

transactions, the write-set size to transaction length ratio is typically below 10%. The reason is the lower frequency of stores altogether and higher temporal locality for stores. For the read-set size to transaction length ratio, we observed similar statistics. Many critical transactions exhibit ratios of 15% up to 30%. Non-critical transactions have substantially

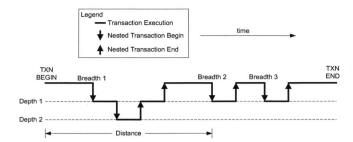

Figure 4: The definition of depth, breadth, and distance for nested transactions.

Application	% Trans. with IO	% Trans. with Wr IO	% Trans. with Rd IO	% Trans. with Rd & Wr IO
water-spatial	5.3	0.0	5.3	0.0
moldyn	0.4	0.4	0.0	0.0
raytracer	0.4	0.4	0.0	0.0
crypt	0.4	0.4	0.0	0.0
series	0.3	0.3	0.0	0.0
sor	0.4	0.4	0.0	0.0
pmd	0.5	0.5	0.0	0.0
kingate	1.3	0.0	1.3	0.0
mpeg2	20.0	20.0	0.0	0.0

Table 6: I/O frequency in critical transactions.

lower ratios.

Observations: The high read-/write- set to instruction length ratios signal potential problems for various TM implementations. For HTM systems using a store buffer, the latency of writing all stores to shared memory at commit time may be difficult to hide. Hence, double-buffering techniques may be necessary to avoid the slowdown [10]. For HTM systems using an undo-log, log updates can be frequent and may require a separate port into the cache hierarchy to avoid stalls. For STM systems, the overhead from lock acquisition for stores and locks or version validation for loads may be difficult to hide if read- and write- sets are tracked at fine granularity.

On the other hand, the above results suggest that systems that support continuous transactional execution do not suffer any additional inefficiencies because of non-critical transactions. The latency of mechanisms for logging, committing, validating, or rolling back transactional data is a bigger issue with critical rather than non-critical transactions.

4.4 Transaction Nesting

Nested transactions may occur in transactional programs when they call library code that uses transactions internally. Nested transactions also allow programmers to avoid expensive rollbacks when potential conflicts are limited within a small portion of a large transaction. A major question for HTM implementations is how much nesting support to provide through fast hardware. To explore this issue, we define four characteristics of nested transactions in Figure 4. Depth refers to the level of nesting at which a transaction executes (number of parents in the nested call graph). Breadth refers to the number of nested calls each transaction makes (number of immediate children in the nested call graph). Distance is the number of instructions between the beginning of a transaction and the beginning of one of its children.

Table 5 presents the nesting characteristics for applications that exhibit nesting in more than 1% of their trans-

actions. It is immediately obvious that nesting is not widespread. Most programmers avoid nested synchronization either because it is difficult to code correctly with current models or because of the obscure performance implications. Most programs in Table 5 are Java applications, where nesting synchronization occurs in the Jikes RVM code to support class loading (tree-like class loader) and just-in-time compilation. Nesting depths of 1 and 2 are the most frequent and the average breadth is 2.2.

Observations: It is difficult to draw general conclusions on nesting from our analysis. For the specific applications, one may be able to eliminate the need for nesting support by recoding the Java virtual machine. For HTM systems that automatically flatten nested transactions, the penalty for a conflict in the inner transaction that leads to an outermost transaction rollback will be proportional to the transaction distance. For the Java programs we studied, the mean distance is quite high (140,000 instructions on the average). For implementations that provide full support for nested transactions, it seems that two levels of nesting support will be sufficient. Such nesting support includes the ability to track read-/write- sets and detect conflicts independently for three transactions. The same hardware resources can be used for double-buffering to hide commit overheads [23]

4.5 Transactions and I/O

I/O operations within a critical transaction can be problematic. Input data from external devices must be buffered in case the transaction rolls back. Output data must also be buffered until the transaction commits. If a single transaction performs both input and output operations, deadlocks can occur through the I/O system. Table 6 shows the percentage of critical transactions that include I/O operations. Most applications have few critical transactions with I/O, which is natural because a long I/O operation is unattractive, and usually unnecessary, within a application-level critical section[1]. Mpeg2 and Water_spatial are the exceptions. The Mpeg2 algorithm holds a lock while reading a slice from the

---

[1]We do not consider any critical sections in the operating system code necessary to implement I/O operations.

Application	% Trans with Nesting	Nesting Depth (% of Nested Trans)			Nesting Breadth (% of Total Trans)			Mean Distance
		1	2	>2	1	2	>2	
moldyn	22	16	42	41	13	7	3	291889
montecarlo	14	99	0	0	0	0	14	2784
raytracer	14	36	41	23	7	4	3	99262
crypt	18	45	37	19	11	3	4	56211
lufact	18	39	38	23	11	3	5	87913
series	14	40	51	8	7	2	4	68782
sor	16	48	4	48	9	3	4	75400
sparsematmult	13	87	11	2	6	1	6	10440
specjbb	9	63	35	2	1	4	4	58855
pmd	17	19	30	52	8	4	5	659871
hsqldb	1	3	97	0	0	0	1	6538826
bp-vision	4	100	0	0	4	0	0	165
localize	2	100	0	0	2	0	0	641

Table 5: The nesting characteristics of critical transactions.

video stream. Water_spatial's output operations use a lock to print to the console. No transactions attempt to execute both an input and an output operation.

With non-critical transactions, I/O handling is easy as we can split transactions in any way necessary (immediately before and after any I/O statement).

Observations: I/O is unlikely to be a serious roadblock to transactional memory. I/O is rare within critical transactions and the deadlock scenario that cannot be handled by buffering I/O does not occur in practice.

5. Analysis for Speculative Parallelization

Apart from facilitating non-blocking synchronization, TM allows for speculative parallelization of sequential programs [9]. Speculative parallelization provides an attractive programming model as it eliminates the burden of developing a provably correct parallel program. Instead, the programmer merely identifies potentially parallel regions in sequential code. Hardware executes these regions optimistically in parallel and resolves dynamically any dependencies based on the sequential semantics of the original code. Nevertheless, using TM for speculative parallelism may lead to significantly different common case behavior than that presented in Section 4. To identify the major trends, we study the six OpenMP applications in Table 1 after remapping the iterations from parallel loops in OpenMP into critical transactions for speculative parallelization. In other words, we assume an OpenMP-like, directive-based model for speculative loop parallelization.

Table 7 presents the transaction length statistics. The applications fall into two categories: those with specula-

Application	Length in Instructions			
	Avg	50th %	95th %	Max
equake	244	9	1134	40750634
art	70062948	71978851	74117449	74824088
is	129	3	3	19844217
swim	62130	68467	91296	91296
cg	521	6	691	18949151
bt	40796	8106	35531	13091051

Table 7: Transaction length statistics for speculative parallelization.

tive parallelism in inner loops (Equake, Is, Cg) that leads to short transactions and those with speculative parallelism from outer loops (Art, Swim, Bt) that leads to significantly longer transactions. For Art in particular, transactions include tens of millions of instructions. Figure 5 presents the transaction read-set and write-set distributions. Applications with long transactions generate significantly larger read-sets and write-sets than those in Section 4 (200 Kbytes to 2 Mbytes). On the other hand, all speculatively parallelized applications exhibit low read-/write- set to transaction length ratios (10% or less) due to high temporal locality in large transactions. None of these applications include noticeable nesting or I/O operations within critical transactions.

Observations: The main conclusion is that using TM for speculative parallelization requires larger buffers to track read-sets and write-sets. L1-sized buffers can be too small for several applications and may lead to frequent overflows. If L1-sized buffers are used, fast TM virtualization techniques will be critical. On the other hand, L2-sized buffers

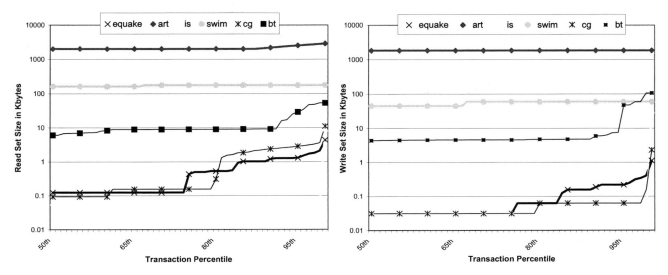

Figure 5: The cumulative distribution of read-set (left) and write-set (right) sizes for speculative parallelization.

are sufficient to eliminate overflows for most applications. Alternatively, one can conclude that speculative parallelization with TM suggests parallelizing the inner loops instead of the outer loops, as in the conventional wisdom with current systems. Since the read-/write- set to transaction length ratios are lower than with non-blocking synchronization, the use of TM for speculative parallelization does not place any additional requirements on the mechanisms for buffering, commit, and rollback.

6. Conclusions and Future Work

We studied a set of existing multithreaded applications in order to characterize their common case behavior with transactional memory systems. The analysis involves mapping parallelism and synchronization primitives in the source code to transaction boundaries. We measure basic characteristics such as the distribution of transaction lengths, read-set and write-set sizes, and the frequency of nested transactions and I/O operations. These characteristics provide key insights into the design of efficient TM systems for both non-blocking synchronization and speculative parallelization.

Our analysis indicates the following trends. Most transactions are small, hence the fixed overheads associated with starting and ending transactions must be minimized. Interrupts and contexts switches can be handled with simple software mechanisms. The read-sets and write-sets for most transactions fit in L1 caches. Long transactions, particularly from speculative parallelization, require read-/write-set buffering in the L2 cache as well. Since L2 overflows will be rare, complex hardware mechanisms for TM virtualization are unnecessary and should be replaced by

software-only alternatives. Continuous transaction execution and speculative parallelization with transactions do not require lower overheads per address read or written than what is needed for non-blocking synchronization. Nested transactions occur mostly in system code and limited hardware support is likely to be sufficient. I/O operations within transactions are also rare. The observed I/O patterns are easy to handle through I/O buffering techniques.

Acknowledgments

This research was sponsored by the Defense Advanced Research Projects Agency (DARPA) through the Department of the Interior National Business Center under grant NBCH104009. The views and conclusions contained in this document are those of the authors and should not be interpreted as representing the official policies, either expressed or implied, of the Defense Advanced Research Projects Agency (DARPA) or the U.S. Government.

Additional support was also available through NSF grant 0444470.

References

[1] B. Alpern and S. Augart. The Jikes Research Virtual Machine Project: Buliding an Open-source Research Community. *IBM Systems Journal*, Nov. 2005.

[2] C. Ananian, K. Asanović, B. Kuszmaul, C. Leiserson, and S. Lie. Unbounded Transactional Memory. In *the 11th Intl. Symposium on High-Performance Computer Architecture*, Feb. 2005.

[3] The Apache HTTP Server Project. http://httpd.apache.org/.

[4] K. Arnold, J. Gosling, and D. Holmes. *The Java Programming Language, 3rd Edition*. Addison-Wesley, 2002.

[5] C. Blundell, E. Lewis, and M. Martin. Deconstructing Transactional Semantics: The Subtleties of Atomicity. In *The 4th Workshop on Duplicating, Deconstructing, and Debunking*, June 2005.

[6] The DaCapo Benchmark Suite. http://www-ali.cs.umass.edu/DaCapo/gcbm.html.

[7] P. Felzenszwalb and D. Huttenlocher. Efficient Belief Propagation for Early Vision. In *the IEEE Conference on Computer Vision and Pattern Recognition*, June 2004.

[8] J. Gray and A. Reuter. *Transaction Processing: Concepts and Techniques*. Morgan Kaufmann, 1993.

[9] L. Hammond, B. D. Carlstrom, V. Wong, B. Hertzberg, M. Chen, C. Kozyrakis, , and K. Olukotun. Programming with transactional coherence and consistency. In *the 11th Intl. Conference on Arch. Support for Programming Languages and Operating Systems*, Oct. 2004.

[10] L. Hammond, V. Wong, M. Chen, B. D. Carlstrom, J. D. Davis, B. Hertzberg, M. K. Prabhu, H. Wijaya, C. Kozyrakis, and K. Olukotun. Transactional memory coherence and consistency. In *the 31st International Symposium on Computer Architecture*, June 2004.

[11] T. Harris. Exceptions and Side-effects in Atomic Blocks. In *the Workshop on Concurrency and Synchronization in Java Programs*, July 2004.

[12] T. Harris and K. Fraser. Language Support for Lightweight Transactions. In *18th Conference on Object-Oriented Programming, Systems, Languages, and Applications*, Oct. 2003.

[13] M. Herlihy, V. Luchangco, M. Moir, and W. Scherer. Software Transactional Memory for Dynamic-sized Data Structures. In *the 22nd Symposium on Principles of Distributed Computing*, July 2003.

[14] M. Herlihy and J. Moss. Transactional Memory: Architectural Support for Lock-Free Data Structures. In *the 20th Intl. Symposium on Computer Architecture*, May 1993.

[15] R. Kalla, B. Sinharoy, and J. Tendler. Simultaneous Multithreading Implementation in POWER5. In *the 15th Hot Chips 15 Symposium*, August 2003.

[16] P. Kongetira, K. Aingaran, and K. Olukotun. Niagara: A 32-Way Multithreaded Sparc Processor. *IEEE MICRO*, 25(2), Mar. 2005.

[17] H. T. Kung and J. T. Robinson. On Optimistic Methods for Concurrency Control. *ACM Transactions on Database Systems*, 6(2), June 1981.

[18] B. Kuzmaul and C. Leiserson. Transactions Everywhere. MIT LCS Research Abstract, 2003.

[19] B. Lewis and D. Berg. *Multithreaded Programming with Pthreads*. Prentice Hall, 1998.

[20] D. Lowell and P. Chen. Free Transactions with Rio Vista. In *the 16th symposium on Operating Systems Principles*, Oct. 1997.

[21] E. Lusk and R.Overbeek. *Portable Programs for Parallel Processors*. Holt, Rinehart and Winston, Inc., 1987.

[22] V. Marathe, W. Scherer, and M. Scott. Adaptive Software Transactional Memory. In *the 19th Intl. Symposium on Distributed Computing*, Sept. 2005.

[23] A. McDonald, J. Chung, H. Chafi, C. Minh, B. Carlstrom, L. Hammond, C. Kozyrakis, and K. Olukotun. Characterization of TCC on Chip-Multiprocessors. In *the 14th Intl. Conference on Parallel Architectures and Compilation Techniques*, Sept. 2005.

[24] C. McNairy. Montecito: The Next Product in the Itanium Processor Family. In *the 16th Hot Chips Symposium*, Aug. 2004.

[25] K. Moore, J. Bobba, M. Morovan, M. Hill, and D. Wood. LogTM: Log Based Transactional Memory. In *the 12th Intl. Conference on High Performance Computer Architecture*, Feb. 2006.

[26] MPEG Software Simulation Group. http://www.mpeg.org/MSSG/.

[27] NASA Advanced Supercomputing Parallel Parallel Benchmarks. http://www.nas.nasa.gov/Software/NPB/.

[28] OpenMP Application Program Interface, Version 2.5. http://www.openmp.org/, May 2005.

[29] R. Rajwar and J. Goodman. Transactional Lock-Free Execution of Lock-Based Programs. In *the 10th Intl. Conference on Arch. Support for Programming Languages and Operating Systems*, October 2002.

[30] R. Rajwar, M. Herlihy, and K. Lai. Virtualizing Transactional Memory. In *the 32nd Intl. Symposium on Computer Architecture*, June 2005.

[31] M. Ringenburg and D. Grossman. AtomCaml: First-Class Atomicity via Rollback. In *the 10th Intl. Conference on Functional Programming*, Sept. 2005.

[32] B. Saha, A. Adl-Tabatabai, R. Hudson, C. Cao Minh, and B. Hertzberg. A High Performance Software Transactional Memory System For A Multi-Core Runtime. Technical report, Intel Inc, 2005.

[33] M. Satyanarayanan et al. Lightweight Recoverable Virtual Memory. *ACM Transactions on Computer Systems*, 12(1), Feb. 1994.

[34] N. Shavit and S. Touitou. Software Transactional Memory. In *the 14th Symposium on Principles of Distributed Computing*, Aug. 1995.

[35] L. Smith, J. Bull, and J. Obdrzalek. A Parallel Java Grande Benchmark Suite. In *the Supercomputing Conference*, Nov. 2001.

[36] The SPEC jbb2000 Benchmark. http://www.spec.org/jbb2000/.

[37] SPEC OpenMP Benchmark Suite. http://www.spec.org/omp/.

[38] H. Sutter. The Concurrency Revolution. *C/C++ Users Journal*, 23(2), Feb. 2005.

[39] H. Sutter. The Trouble with Locks. *C/C++ Users Journal*, 23(3), Mar. 2005.

[40] S.Woo, M. Ohara, E. Torrie, J. P. Singh, and A. Gupta. The SPLASH-2 Programs: Characterization and Methodological Considerations. In *the 22nd Intl. Symposium on Computer Architecture*, June 1995.

[41] S. Thrun, D. Fox, W. Burgard, and F. Dellaert. Robust Monte Carlo Localization for Mobile Robots. *Artificial Intelligence*, 128(1-2):99–141, 2001.

Speculative Synchronization and Thread Management for Fine Granularity Threads

Alex Gontmakher* †Avi Mendelson Assaf Schuster Gregory Shklover
Technion, Israel Institute of Technology   †Intel Labs, Haifa, Israel
{gsasha,assaf,gkovriga}@cs.technion.ac.il   avi.mendelson@intel.com

Abstract

Performance of multithreaded programs is heavily influenced by the latencies of the thread management and synchronization operations. Improving these latencies becomes especially important when the parallelization is performed at fine granularity.

In this work we examine the interaction of speculative execution with the thread-related operations. We develop a unified framework which allows all such operations to be executed speculatively and provides efficient recovery mechanisms to handle misspeculation of branches which affect instructions in several threads.

The framework was evaluated in the context of Inthreads, a programming model designed for very fine grain parallelization. Our measurements show that the speedup obtained by speculative execution of the threads-related instructions can reach 25%.

1   Introduction

Modern processors use a complex of ILP-enhancing mechanisms, such as speculation and multithreaded execution. When combined carefully, these mechanisms complement and amplify each other [28]. However, the mechanisms may interfere and hurt each other's performance. Moreover, the lower the locking granularity, the more significant the performance impact of synchronization [30].

In this work, we investigate the interaction of control speculation with thread management and synchronization instructions. We develop a general framework that enables speculative execution of such instructions and provides an efficient mechanism for misspeculation recovery. The framework, based on identifying and keeping track of the interactions between instructions of different threads, provides a common mechanism that handles speculative execution of synchronization, thread starting and even thread

*This work was supported in part by a research grant from Intel Israel

termination. The case of thread termination involves peculiar side effects due to its reverse effect on speculation, as described in Section 3.1.

We apply the framework to *Inthreads* [6], a lightweight threading model that allows parallelization at a resolution comparable to that of speculative execution. Due to the low parallelization granularity, Inthreads programs are highly sensitive to synchronization latency and benefit from the speculative execution of thread-related operations.

The rest of this paper is organized as follows. In Section 2 we develop the framework of speculative execution of thread management and synchronization instructions. In Section 3 we apply the framework to Inthreads. Section 4 discusses the implementation and Section 5 presents the results of the experimental evaluation. Finally, Section 6 describes the related work and Section 7 concludes the paper.

2   Multithreaded Speculative Execution Model

Modern processors use a variety of mechanisms for improving the computation parallelism. Two such mechanisms are *speculative execution*, intended to improve instruction-level parallelism, and *multithreading*, aimed at thread-level parallelism. Usually, these mechanisms operate at different levels and are orthogonal. However, in case of low granularity parallelization, the synchronization may stand in the way of efficient speculative execution.

For an example, consider the program in Figure 1. When the program is executed serially, branch prediction may allow the processor to execute as many iterations in parallel as the hardware can accommodate. However, in the case of parallelized code, the presence of synchronization limits the number of iterations that can be issued speculatively: since a mutex affects execution of other threads' instructions, it is dangerous to enter the mutex before the `if` has been resolved. As a result, in each thread, the `if` must be resolved before the next `if` can be issued. Therefore, the number of iterations that can proceed in parallel is at most one per

Sequential code	Thread t_k of $\mathbb{T}$
```for(i=0; i<N; i++){ if(d[i%K].val>i) { d[i%K].count++; } } ```	```for(i=k; i<N; i+=T){ if(d[i%K].val>i) { MUTEX_ENTER d[i%K].count++; MUTEX_LEAVE } } ```

Figure 1. Low granularity parallelization example

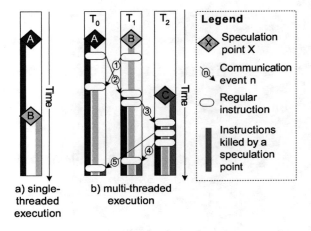

Figure 2. Speculation models for single-threaded and multithreaded execution

active thread, potentially leading to lower ILP than that of the serial, but speculative, code.

To realize the potential of both speculation and multithreading, we must enable speculative execution of instructions that involve communication between threads, such as interactions between instructions involved in a synchronization or between instructions accessing a shared variable. In order to recover from misspeculation, we must keep track of all the *communication events*, and take care of all the instructions, from all the threads, that have been affected by the misspeculated instruction.

Examples of communication events are transfer of a value through a shared variable or an interaction between synchronization instructions. For the purposes of this section, it is enough to note that a communication event consists of a pair of interacting instructions, a *producer* one providing some information to a *consumer* one.

The speculation model of *sequential computation* is linear, as shown in Figure 2a: if an instruction is misspeculated, all the following instructions are squashed. In contrast, the speculation model of *multithreaded computation* is non-linear. Consider the execution in Figure 2b with threads T_0, T_1 and T_2, three speculation points A, B and C, two communication events, 1 and 2, between T_0 and T_1, two events, 3 and 4, between T_1 and T_2, and a communication 5 from T_2 to T_0. It is impossible to arrange the instructions so that all the instructions following a speculation point are those affected by it. For example, A and B are independent, and neither of them should precede the other.

Another observation is that misspeculation recovery is timing sensitive. Consider the misspeculation recovery of B. The misspeculation propagates to T_2 along event 3, squashing the instructions following the consuming instruction of event 3. As a result, the producing instruction of event 4 is squashed, and therefore, the consuming instruction of 4 must be squashed as well. However, that instruction may have been already squashed since it follows B in the program order of T_1, and the pipeline may already contain the instructions for the correct execution path after B. In that case, the processor would squash instructions on the correct execution path. The problem becomes more

acute when misspeculation is propagated through longer sequences of events, such as the sequence of 2, 3 and 5 that would result from misspeculation of A.

A straightforward, albeit expensive, approach to this problem would require stopping the front-end during the propagation of branch misprediction. Our approach, described below, performs the recovery in one step without the need for propagation.

2.1 Speculative Execution Framework

The definitions in this section are conceptually similar to the *happens-before relation* defined by Lamport [14] and the related notion of *vector clocks* by Mattern [18]. These works are developed for distributed processors over a not necessarily in-order medium. Furthermore, the feasibility of bounded timestamps is shown in [5, 7, 11], although system is not truly distributed and thus is simpler.

Our framework is defined over a set of threads rather than processors, and directly models the control speculation and the interactions between instructions. The framework can be applied to an architecture by identifying the possible interactions, and handling them as described in Section 2.2. In Section 3.1 we apply the framework to Inthreads.

Let $\mathbb{T}$ be the set of threads supported by the processor. We model the program as a set of instructions organized in *program orders* for each thread $t \in \mathbb{T}$. We denote that instruction i belongs to the program order of thread t by $tid_i = t$. The program order defines a *full order* for instructions of each thread. We denote that instruction i precedes instruction j in the program order by $i \prec j$.

Execution of the program proceeds through *sliding windows* of instructions. There is one sliding window W_t for each thread t. W_t operates as a FIFO: instructions are *intro-*

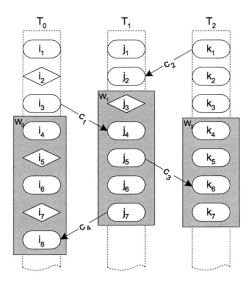

Figure 3. Example execution with speculation and communication events

duced at one end and *retired* at another. $W_t(\tau)$ denotes the contents of W_t at time τ and $W(\tau) = \bigcup_{t \in \mathbb{T}} W_t(\tau)$.

Instructions are classified into *plain* and *speculation point* ones. The speculation point instructions are introduced as *unresolved*. When resolved, a speculation point instruction can be found to be *misspeculated*, in which case all the following instructions must be squashed. We denote the set of speculation point instructions by $\mathbb{S}$ and the set of currently unresolved ones by $\mathbb{S}_?(\tau)$ (clearly, $\mathbb{S}_?(\tau) \subseteq \mathbb{S} \cap W(\tau)$). Also, we define $\mathbb{S}_?(\tau, t) = \mathbb{S}_?(\tau) \cap W_t(\tau)$.

Some instructions participate in *communication events*. A communication event c consists of two instructions, the *producing* one $\vec{c}$ and the *consuming* one $\vec{c}$ ($c = (\vec{c}, \vec{c})$). c introduces a *dependency*: if $\vec{c}$ is squashed, then $\vec{c}$ must be squashed as well. $i \rightsquigarrow j$ denotes that j depends on i through some chain of dependencies. We denote the set of communication events by $\mathbb{C}$.

In the example in Figure 3, $\mathbb{S} = \{i_2, i_5, i_7, j_3\}$, $\mathbb{S}_?(\tau) = \{i_5, i_7, j_3\}$, and $\mathbb{C} = \{c_1 = (i_3, j_4), c_2 = (k_1, j_2), c_3 = (j_5, k_6), c_4 = (j_7, i_6)\}$.

Each instruction i has a *timestamp*, ts_i. The timestamps are assigned independently for each thread, in such a way that $ts_i < ts_j \Leftrightarrow i \prec j$. A *timestamp vector*, tsv_i, defines the latest instruction in each thread t that i depends on:

$$tsv_i(t) = \begin{cases} max_{c \in \mathbb{C}_P(i)} ts_{\vec{c}}, & t \in \mathbb{T} \setminus \{tid_i\} \\ ts_i, & t = tid_i \end{cases},$$

where $\mathbb{C}_P(i)$ is the set of instructions that affect i through a chain of communication events $c_1, \ldots, c_n$:

$$\mathbb{C}_P(i) = \left\{ c : \begin{array}{l} \exists_{c_1, \ldots, c_n \in \mathbb{C}}, c = c_1 \wedge \vec{c}_n \prec i \wedge \\ \forall_{j \in \{1 \ldots n-1\}} (\vec{c}_j \prec \vec{c}_{j+1}) \end{array} \right\}.$$

The value of tsv_j can be used to determine if j depends on a given instruction i:

$$i \rightsquigarrow j \Leftrightarrow ts_i \leq tsv_j(tid_i)$$

When a speculation point instruction b is found to be mispredicted, we need to squash all the instructions $\{i \in W(\tau) : tsv_i(tid_b) > ts_b\}$. Consequently, the set of speculative instructions at time τ is $\{i \in W(\tau) : \exists_{b \in \mathbb{S}_?(\tau)} tsv_i(tid_b) > ts_b\}$.

In the example in Figure 3, $tsv_{j_4} = [3, 4, 1]$, $tsv_{j_2} = [\varnothing, 2, 1]$, $tsv_{k_6} = [3, 5, 6]$ and $tsv_{i_8} = [8, 7, 1]$. If j_3 is mispredicted, checking the tsv reveals that both i_8 and k_6 must be squashed. The speculative instructions (i.e., those that might be squashed) are i_8 in T_0, $j_4 \ldots j_7$ in T_1 and, because of communication event c_3, $k_6 \ldots k_7$ in T_2. Note that j_2 is not speculative, since no unresolved speculation point instructions precede k_1.

In the remainder of this section, we will develop efficient ways for computing the set of speculative instructions and for performing misspeculation recovery.

First, if an instruction i preceded by i' does not take part in a communication event, then $tsv_i(t) = tsv_{i'}(t)$ for any thread $t \neq tid_i$. Therefore, in recovering from a misspeculation from a speculation point b, the earliest squashed instruction in every thread except tid_b must be an instruction that takes a consumer part in a communication. As a result, it is sufficient to just scan the instructions in $\mathbb{C} \cap W(\tau)$ in order to determine which instructions must be killed as a result of misspeculation. In addition, it is sufficient to compute tsv only for the communicating instructions.

Second, we note that since the timestamps are monotonically increasing in each thread, we need to scan only the earliest unresolved speculation point in each thread in order to determine which instructions are speculative.

To summarize, the determination of speculative instructions and the misspeculation recovery are performed in the following way. First, we compute the set of earliest speculation points in each thread by scanning all the currently unresolved speculation point instructions:

$$\mathbb{S}_\mathbb{E}(t) = ts_b : b \in \mathbb{S}_?(\tau, t) \wedge \nexists_{b' \in \mathbb{S}_?(\tau, t)} b' \prec b$$

Using $\mathbb{S}_\mathbb{E}$, we can determine whether a given communication instruction $\vec{c}$ is speculative:

$$spec_{\vec{c}} = \exists_t \mathbb{S}_\mathbb{E}(t) < tsv_{\vec{c}}(t)$$

285

Now we can compute the timestamps of the earliest speculative communication instructions in each thread:

$$\mathbb{C}_{\mathbb{E}}(t) = ts_{\searrow\atop\tilde{c}} \; : \; \begin{array}{l} c \in \mathbb{C} \cap W_t(\tau) \wedge spec_{\searrow\atop\tilde{c}} \\ \wedge \not\exists_{\tilde{c}_1 \prec \tilde{c}} : spec_{\searrow\atop\tilde{c}_1} \end{array}$$

With $\mathbb{S}_{\mathbb{E}}$ and $\mathbb{C}_{\mathbb{E}}$, we can determine whether instruction i is speculative by checking that $ts_i \geq \mathbb{S}_{\mathbb{E}}(tid_i) \vee ts_i \geq \mathbb{C}_{\mathbb{E}}(tid_i)$. The speculative instructions may not be retired even if their execution is completed.

When a speculation instruction b is found to be misspeculated, we determine the set of instructions to be squashed in the following way. For each thread, we scan the communication instructions to determine the earliest squashed one:

$$\mathbb{C}_{\mathbb{E}}^{\mathbb{S}\mathbb{Q}}(b, t) = ts_{\searrow\atop\tilde{c}} \; : \; \begin{array}{l} c \in \mathbb{C} \cap W_t(\tau) \wedge \\ tsv_{\searrow\atop\tilde{c}}(tid_b) > ts_b \wedge \\ \not\exists_{\tilde{c}_1 \prec \tilde{c}} : tsv_{\searrow\atop\tilde{c}_1}(tid_b) > ts_b \end{array}$$

Instruction i must be squashed during the recovery of b if $ts_i \geq \mathbb{C}_{\mathbb{E}}^{\mathbb{S}\mathbb{Q}}(b, tid_i)$.

Finally, the computation of tsv is performed according to its definition by scanning the instructions in $\mathbb{C} \cap W(\tau)$.

Returning to the execution in Figure 3, the computations would proceed in the following way: $\mathbb{S}_{\mathbb{E}} = [5, 3, \varnothing]$, $\mathbb{C}_{\mathbb{E}} = [8, 4, 6]$, exactly as in the original definitions. If j_3 is misspeculated, then $\mathbb{C}_{\mathbb{E}}^{\mathbb{S}\mathbb{Q}}(j_3) = [8, 4, 6]$, implying that the instructions squashed in addition to the instructions following j_3 in T_1 are i_8, k_6 and k_7.

2.2 Handling Communication Instructions

For each instruction i that can potentially take part in a communication event, we must choose one of the two alternative implementations:

- *Issue i speculatively.* In this case, we need to dynamically determine the instructions that participated in a communication with i. The tsv for these instructions must be updated accordingly to enable proper recovery.

- *Delay i until it becomes non-speculative.* Naturally, the instruction that participates in communication with i will not be able to issue before i. On the positive side, squashing of i cannot affect instructions from other threads, and thus the tsv of the instruction receiving the communication need not be updated.

3 Speculation in the Inthreads Model

The Inthreads model is based on a fixed number of threads running over shared registers in the context of a single SMT thread. The model provides an extremely

lightweight threading mechanism: the fixed number of threads allows for thread management to be performed entirely in hardware. In addition, the shared registers provide a straightforward and efficient communication mechanism: a value can be transferred by writing it into a register in one thread and reading it from the same register in another.

Each thread has a thread ID (tid) which is determined at thread creation. The *main thread*, identified by $tid = 0$, is always active, while other threads can be started and terminated on demand. Three instructions control the starting and stopping of threads: inth.start, inth.halt and inth.kill. inth.start creates a new thread with a given tid at a given address. To terminate itself, a thread issues an inth.halt instruction. inth.halt is executed synchronously, guaranteeing that all the instructions preceding it will complete. One thread can kill another by issuing an inth.kill instruction.

The synchronization mechanism consists of a set of binary semaphores stored in *condition registers* controlled by three instructions: cond.wait, cond.set and cond.clr. A cond.wait checks whether a given condition is set. If it is, the condition is cleared; otherwise the issuing thread is stalled until some other thread performs a cond.set to that condition. If several cond.wait instructions accessing the same condition are issued in parallel, only one of them will proceed. A cond.set sets the given condition. If there was a cond.wait suspended on the same condition, the cond.wait is awakened and the condition remains cleared. Finally, a cond.clr clears the given condition.

The programming model is described in detail in [6]. A similar architecture, although using a dedicated namespace for shared registers, is described by Jesshope [12].

3.1 Communication Events in the Inthreads Model

A *Synchronization* event occurs between a cond.set and a cond.wait that accesses the same condition. Synchronization events are relatively easy to detect, as the number of synchronization instructions that must be concurrently in flight is low (see Section 5). cond.wait and cond.clr instructions never take a producer part in communication, and can be executed speculatively with no need for recovery.

A *Variable value transfer* event occurs between any instruction writing a value to a variable (whether in a register or at some memory location) and a subsequent instruction reading the value from that variable.

In contrast to the communication through synchronization, communication through regular variables is harder to detect: any two instructions can potentially communicate, and moreover, communication between memory instructions can be detected only after the addresses for both instructions have been computed.

The Inthreads architecture handles the communication

through variables at the architecture level. To this end, the Inthreads-parallelized programs are required to be *data-race-free* [1], i.e., to ensure that any two instructions that access the same location are separated by synchronization. As a result, recovery of synchronization instructions implies correct squashing of all instructions involved in shared-variable communication.

A *Thread starting* event results from the communication between an inth.start and the first instruction of the started thread. Thread starting events are handled similarly to the synchronization ones. The only difference is that the instruction receiving the communication does not belong to a specific instruction type, but is just the first instruction started by the thread. For this, we hold a *tsv* for every thread, as if the whole thread receives the communication.

A *Thread killing* event occurs between an inth.kill and the first killed instruction of the target thread. While an inth.kill does not supply any "real" information, it does interact with the killed thread since the instructions following the inth.kill should not interact with the ones killed by it.

The situation is further complicated by the fact that inth.kills have a reverse effect on speculation: the instructions in the target thread are squashed only if the inth.kill is not misspeculated. Therefore, it is not sufficient to delay execution of an inth.kill until it becomes non-speculative, as instructions following it might interact with the target thread. Moreover, since an inth.kill terminates other instructions, recovery would be considerably more complex than just killing the dependent instructions. As a result, in this work we consider the inth.kill instructions as communication events, but execute them only non-speculatively.

4 Implementation

In principle, the architecture of Inthreads is quite similar to SMT—both architectures execute multiple independent instruction streams on a shared execution core. Therefore, the microarchitecture re-uses most of the mechanisms present in SMT processors, such as multiple fetch units, multiple ROBs, shared physical register file and functional units and so on (a notable exception is the *Register Allocation Table* (RAT), which is shared between threads in an Inthreads processor). Therefore, we take the SMT microarchitecture as a basis, and only describe the design of the thread management mechanisms.

The mechanisms that support Inthreads execution are outlined in Figure 4. The pipeline includes an additional stage, *Instruction Wait*, which implements delaying instructions of the threads which waiting on a condition. The delayed instructions are stored in the per-thread *Wait Buffers* (WBs). The WBs read the state of condition variables from the *Available Conditions* line to determine which instructions can be released.

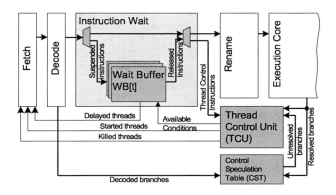

Figure 4. Inthreads microarchitecture outline

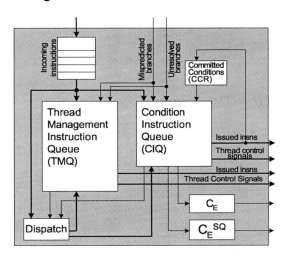

Figure 5. Thread Control Unit

The *Thread Control Unit* (TCU), described in Section 4.1, orchestrates the execution of the threads on the processor. The *Condition Speculation Table* (CST) is used to keep track of the unresolved branch instructions. The computations performed by the TCU and the CST correspond to the multithreading speculation model developed in Section 2 and the Inthreads-specific details in Section 3.

4.1 Thread Control Unit

The TCU, depicted in Figure 5, is used to 1) carry out the side effects of the synchronization and thread management instructions, 2) compute which instructions are speculative, and 3) control the squashing of dependent instructions in all the threads in response to a mispredicted branch.

The TCU holds the instructions in two queues, *CIQ* for the synchronization instructions and *TMQ* for the thread management instructions. Both CIQ and TMQ keep *tsv* of all the contained instructions. The CIQ and TMQ receive

Parameter	No threads	Inthreads
Pipeline Length	8	9
Supported threads	N/A	8
Fetch policy	8 per cycle	ICOUNT2.8
Branch predictor	bimodal	
L1I size	64KB	
Logical Registers	64GP+64FP	
Physical Registers	512GP,512FP	384GP,384FP
ROB size	512	128*8
Issue Queue size	80	
Memory Queue size	40	
Functional units	6 Int,6FP,4 Branch	
Max outst. misses	16	
Max unresolv. branches	16	
Max active synch insns	16	
Memory ports	2	
L1D size, latency	64KB, 1 cycle	
L2 size, latency	1MB, 20 cycles	
Memory latency	200	

Table 1. Basic processor parameters

from the CST the timestamps $\mathbb{S}_E$ of the currently unresolved branches and use them to determine which of the instructions they contain are non-speculative and can be issued. In addition, the CIQ and TMQ receive information on branch mispredictions, in order to control the squashing of instructions from different threads.

Execution of synchronization instructions in the CIQ involves the computation of the currently available conditions, which are used by the WBs to determine which cond.wait instructions can be released. The *Committed Conditions register* (CCR) holds the committed state of the condition variables. The value of the CCR is fed into the CIQ, which updates it according to the synchronization instructions (cond.wait and cond.clr instructions clean the corresponding bit, and cond.set instructions set it). When instructions are issued from the CIQ, they update the corresponding conditions in the CCR.

5 Evaluation

We have extended the SimpleScalar-PISA model [3] with the Inthreads-related extensions. The basic processor is modelled with a 8-stage pipeline, and the Inthreads-enabled variant has one more stage for synchronization functionality. Fetching was managed by the ICOUNT policy [29]. Table 1 summarizes the parameters.

We assume that the instructions dispatched to the TCU execute in as few as two cycles: one to compute the *tsv*, and one cycle to issue the instruction if it is ready. The logic involved in the TCU is similar to that of the Issue Queue, while the number of instructions held in the TCU is significantly lower: in our experiments there was no measurable effect to increasing the TCU size over 16 instructions.

Still, we measured the effect of increasing the TCU latency, shown in Figures 7 and 8.

The evaluation is based on three benchmarks from the SPEC2K suite [8]: 179.art, 181.mcf and 300.twolf, and four programs from the MediaBench suite [15]: Adpcm encode, Adpcm decode, G721 and Mpeg2. As a measure of the programs' run time we used the number of clock cycles reported by the simulator.

We denote the speculation settings with three letters, one for each speculation mechanism from those described in Section 3.1. For example, TFF means that the speculative execution of synchronization instructions was turned on, and speculative value transfer between variables and speculative thread starting was turned off.

5.1 Microbenchmark

To explore the performance behavior of the speculation mechanisms, we have implemented a microbenchmark with a tunable frequency of thread management events. The benchmark contains two nested loops. The inner loop consists of four independent sequences with heavy branching. The inner loop size, or the *iteration size* of the outer loop, determines the frequency of the synchronization, thread creation and termination events. The number of iterations of the outer loop determines the total number of such events.

The results are summarized in Figure 6. The first row of the graphs shows the speedup in comparison with the serial code, while the second one displays just the speedup that results from turning on speculation. The third row displays the percentage of squashed instructions.

The first three columns plot the performance for a fixed iteration size and varying number of iterations. The speedup remains relatively stable, except at a small number of iterations due to uneven branch prediction. Predictably, the speedup grows with the iteration size as the speedup caused by parallelization overcomes the thread management overhead. A more interesting effect is the growth in the additional speedup that results from speculation (row 2). Speculative execution of thread instructions allows different iterations of the outer loop to proceed in parallel, which is more important with a larger iteration size where the difference in the amount of work performed by the threads grows.

The rightmost three columns of Figure 6 show the behavior of parallelization for a given number of iterations of the outer loop. We can see that the speculation reaches its potential only with a relatively large number of iterations.

Finally, Figure 7 shows the effect of the latency of the TCU on performance. For the smallest possible parameters, a 14-cycle latency cancels out the benefits of parallelization. With larger parameters, the communication becomes less frequent, and the code is less sensitive to the latency.

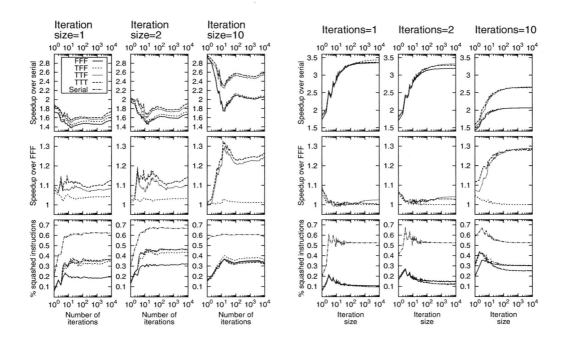

Figure 6. Behavior of the microbenchmark at various size options

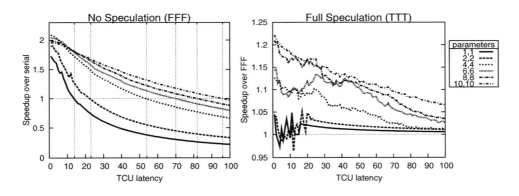

Figure 7. Speedup of the microbenchmark as a function of the TCU latency

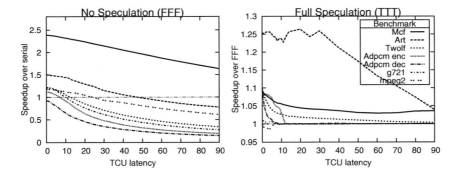

Figure 8. Performance of SPEC and Mediabench benchmarks under varying TCU latency

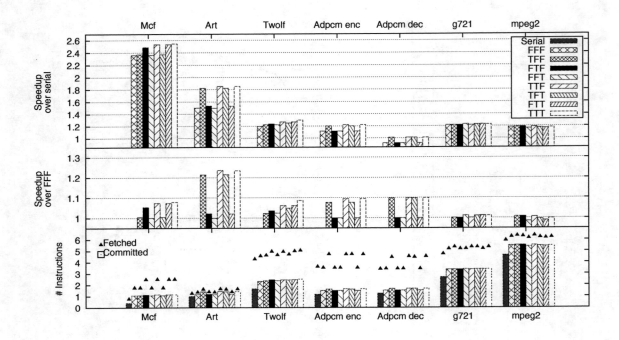

Figure 9. Performance of SPEC and Mediabench benchmarks with speculative execution

5.2   SPEC2000 and Mediabench

The benefit of speculative execution depends on the amount of time saved by earlier execution of thread-related instructions and the frequency of such instructions. Table 2 shows the frequencies and average age of the cond.set and inth.start instructions, measured from the time they enter the TCU and until they are issued.

The results of applying speculative execution of thread-related instructions to the benchmarks are summarized in Figure 9. The first row shows the overall speedup, and the second one—the speedup increment caused by speculation.

Mcf parallelizes consequent iterations that communicate heavily. This communication is sped up when executed speculatively, explaining the sensitivity of Mcf to speculative variable transfer. Art uses very fine grain synchronization, and thus receives most improvement from speculation on synchronization instructions. Both Art and Mcf perform thread starting relatively unfrequently, and therefore do not benefit from speculation in thread starting.

In contrast, Twolf uses threads to parallelize small independent sections of code with heavy branching, and benefits from all the forms of speculative execution.

Both Adpcm programs split the execution into portions executed by threads arranged in a virtual pipeline, using synchronization at a low granularity. As a result, execution is sped up by speculative synchronization.

Both g721 and mpeg2 are barely affected by the speculation, albeit for opposite reasons. In g721, the hard-

Benchmark	cond.set		inth.start	
	Age	Freq	Age	Freq
Mcf	41	0.018	7.0	0.003
Art	32	0.04	391	0.000019
Twolf	4.4	0.057	3.3	0.014
Adpcm enc.	6.3	0.059	2.0	0.000029
Adpcm dec.	2.4	0.061	3.0	0.000031
G721	3.7	0.05	3.1	0.012
Mpeg2	1.5	0.014	9.1	0.014

Table 2. Average ages and frequencies of thread-related instructions

to-predict branches are executed just before synchronization, resulting in poor speculation success rate. In contrast, mpeg2 has long non-speculative sequences, obviating the need for speculative synchronization.

The effect of the TCU latency is shown in Figure 8. Mcf and Art are least sensitive due to the relatively long age of the synchronization instructions. The speedup of adding speculation to thread-related operations, shown in Figure 8b, decreases with the latency when it grows larger than the benefit of speculation. It is interesting to note that the speculation speedup for Mcf almost does not decrease with latency. The reason is that when the latency grows, additional parallelism is achieved by an increase in the number of iterations that execute in parallel.

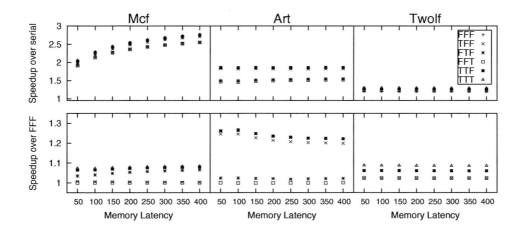

Figure 10. Performance of SPEC benchmarks under varying memory latency

Finally, for the SPEC benchmarks we have measured the effect of memory latency on speedup, shown in Figure 10. While the overall speedup may be sensitive to memory, the additional benefit of speculation remains almost constant.

6   Related Work

Synchronization operations are often redundant and can be ignored speculatively. Examples are *Speculative Synchronization* [17], *Transactional Memory* [9] and *Speculative Lock Elision* [21]. In contrast, just speed synchronization up by executing it speculatively. This avoids the need to detect collisions, and also allows speculation in other thread operations, like starting and terminating.

Thread Level Speculation issues threads derived from a serial program, speculating on a fact that the threads will turn out to be independent. In *Multiscalar processors* [24], the program is partitioned into speculative tasks that execute concurrently while observing data dependencies. *Speculative multithreaded processors* [16] and *Dynamic multithreading processors* [2] generate threads at control speculation points. In those works, the threads are usually very small, often with limited control flow. In contrast, the mechanisms in our work apply to general threads and provide a unified mechanism for speculation of both synchronization and thread management instructions. Other works in this area are [10, 13, 19, 20, 25, 26, 27].

The high cost of branch misprediction has prompted several works that aim at reducing the penalty by retaining those instructions that would execute in the same way regardless of the branch outcome [4, 22, 23]. Our approach can be seen as achieving about the same in software by speculatively starting threads with dependencies marked up by communication instructions.

7   Conclusion

This work provides a unified framework for speculative execution of multithreading-related instructions, including both synchronization primitives and instructions for starting and killing of threads. The framework can be applied to a given architecture by identifying the interactions between instructions of different threads.

The Inthreads architecture has four types of interactions: synchronization, data transfer through variables, thread starting and thread termination. All the types except for data transfer are linked to specific instructions and are easy to detect. The transfer through variables is handled by requiring the programs to be data-race free. As a result, misspeculation recovery of synchronization instructions implies correct recovery shared variable communication.

An additional aspect of this work is that our speculation mechanisms, due to the sharing of the processor resources among several threads, provide a good trade-off between the performance improvement and the increase in the percentage of squashed instructions. This implies that the techniques can be used for improving the power efficiency. We plan to explore this issue in depth in our future work.

References

[1] S. V. Adve and J. K. Aggarwal. A unified formalization of four shared-memory models. *IEEE Trans. Parallel Distrib. Syst.*, 4(6):613–624, 1993.

[2] H. Akkary and M. A. Driscoll. A dynamic multithreading processor. In *Proceedings of the 31st annual ACM/IEEE international symposium on Microarchitecture*, pages 226–236. IEEE Computer Society Press, 1998.

[3] D. Burger, T. M. Austin, and S. Bennett. Evaluating future microprocessors: The SimpleScalar tool set. Technical Re-

port CS-TR-1996-1308, University of Wisconsin-Madison, 1996.

[4] R. Desikan, S. Sethumadhavan, D. Burger, and S. W. Keckler. Scalable selective re-execution for edge architectures. In *Proceedings of the 11th international conference on Architectural support for programming languages and operating systems*, pages 120–132, New York, NY, USA, 2004. ACM Press.

[5] D. Dolev and N. Shavit. Bounded concurrrent time-stamp systems are constructible. In *Proceedings of the twenty-first annual ACM symposium on Theory of computing*, pages 454–466, New York, NY, USA, 1989. ACM Press.

[6] A. Gontmakher, A. Schuster, A. Mendelson, and G. Shklover. Inthreads —a new computational model to enhance ILP of sequential programs. Technical Report CS-2005-16, Technion, Israel Institute of Technology, 2005.

[7] S. Haldar and P. Vitányi. Bounded concurrent timestamp systems using vector clocks. *J. ACM*, 49(1):101–126, 2002.

[8] J. L. Henning. Spec cpu2000: Measuring CPU Performance in the New Millennium. *Computer*, 33(7):28–35, 2000.

[9] M. Herlihy and J. E. B. Moss. Transactional memory: architectural support for lock-free data structures. In *Proceedings of the 20th annual international symposium on Computer architecture*, pages 289–300, New York, NY, USA, 1993. ACM Press.

[10] K. Hiraki, J. Tamatsukuri, and T. Matsumoto. Speculative execution model with duplication. In *Proceedings of the 12th international conference on Supercomputing*, pages 321–328, New York, NY, USA, 1998. ACM Press.

[11] A. Israeli and M. Li. Bounded time-stamps. In *Proceedings of the 28th Annum Symposium on Foundations of Computer Science*, pages 371–382, 1987.

[12] C. Jesshope. Scalable instruction-level parallelism. In *3rd and 4th Intl. Workshops on Computer Systems: Architectures, Modelling and Simulation*, pages 383–392, July 2004.

[13] T. A. Johnson, R. Eigenmann, and T. N. Vijaykumar. Min-cut program decomposition for thread-level speculation. In *Proceedings of the ACM SIGPLAN 2004 conference on Programming language design and implementation*, pages 59–70, New York, NY, USA, 2004. ACM Press.

[14] L. Lamport. Time, clocks, and the ordering of events in a distributed system. *Commun. ACM*, 21(7):558–565, 1978.

[15] C. Lee, M. Potkonjak, and W. H. Mangione-Smith. Mediabench: a tool for evaluating and synthesizing multimedia and communicatons systems. In *Proceedings of the 30th annual ACM/IEEE international symposium on Microarchitecture*, pages 330–335, Washington, DC, USA, 1997. IEEE Computer Society.

[16] P. Marcuello, A. Gonzalez, and J. Tubella. Speculative multithreaded processors. In *Proceedings of the International Conference on Supercomputing (ICS-98)*, pages 77–84, New York, July 13–17 1998. ACM press.

[17] J. F. Martínez and J. Torrellas. Speculative synchronization: applying thread-level speculation to explicitly parallel applications. In *Proceedings of the 10th international conference on Architectural support for programming languages and operating systems*, pages 18–29, New York, NY, USA, 2002. ACM Press.

[18] F. Mattern. Virtual time and global states of distributed systems. In *Proceedings of the International Workshop on Parallel and Distributed Algorithms*, pages 215–226, 1989.

[19] C.-L. Ooi, S. W. Kim, I. Park, R. Eigenmann, B. Falsafi, and T. N. Vijaykumar. Multiplex: unifying conventional and speculative thread-level parallelism on a chip multiprocessor. In *Proceedings of the 15th international conference on Supercomputing*, pages 368–380, New York, NY, USA, 2001. ACM Press.

[20] I. Park, B. Falsafi, and T. N. Vijaykumar. Implicitly-multithreaded processors. In *Proceedings of the 30th annual international symposium on Computer architecture*, pages 39–51, New York, NY, USA, 2003. ACM Press.

[21] R. Rajwar and J. R. Goodman. Speculative lock elision: enabling highly concurrent multithreaded execution. In *Proceedings of the 34th annual ACM/IEEE international symposium on Microarchitecture*, pages 294–305, Washington, DC, USA, 2001. IEEE Computer Society.

[22] E. Rotenberg and J. Smith. Control independence in trace processors. In *Proceedings of the 32nd annual ACM/IEEE international symposium on Microarchitecture*, pages 4–15, Washington, DC, USA, 1999. IEEE Computer Society.

[23] A. Roth and G. S. Sohi. Register integration: a simple and efficient implementation of squash reuse. In *Proceedings of the 33rd annual ACM/IEEE international symposium on Microarchitecture*, pages 223–234, New York, NY, USA, 2000. ACM Press.

[24] G. S. Sohi, S. E. Breach, and T. N. Vijaykumar. Multiscalar processors. In *Proceedings of the 22nd annual international symposium on Computer architecture*, pages 414–425, New York, NY, USA, 1995. ACM Press.

[25] G. S. Sohi and A. Roth. Speculative multithreaded processors. *Computer*, 34(4):66–73, Apr. 2001.

[26] Y. Solihin, J. Lee, and J. Torrellas. Using a user-level memory thread for correlation prefetching. In *Proceedings of the 29th annual international symposium on Computer architecture*, pages 171–182, Washington, DC, USA, 2002. IEEE Computer Society.

[27] J. G. Steffan, C. B. Colohan, A. Zhai, and T. C. Mowry. A scalable approach to thread-level speculation. In *Proceedings of the 27th annual international symposium on Computer architecture*, pages 1–12, New York, NY, USA, 2000. ACM Press.

[28] S. Swanson, L. K. McDowell, M. M. Swift, S. J. Eggers, and H. M. Levy. An evaluation of speculative instruction execution on simultaneous multithreaded processors. *ACM Trans. Comput. Syst.*, 21(3):314–340, 2003.

[29] D. M. Tullsen, S. Eggers, and H. M. Levy. Simultaneous Multithreading: Maximizing On-Chip Parallelism. In *Proceedings of the 22th Annual International Symposium on Computer Architecture*, 1995.

[30] D. M. Tullsen, J. L. Lo, S. J. Eggers, and H. M. Levy. Supporting fine-grained synchronization on a simultaneous multithreading processor. In *Proceedings of the Fifth Annual International Symposium on High-Performance Computer Architecture*, pages 54–58, Jan 1999.

Efficient Instruction Schedulers for SMT Processors

Joseph J. Sharkey, Dmitry V. Ponomarev

Department of Computer Science
State University of New York
Binghamton, NY 13902 USA
{jsharke, dima}@cs.binghamton.edu

Abstract

We propose dynamic scheduler designs to improve the scheduler scalability and reduce its complexity in the SMT processors. Our first design is an adaptation of the recently proposed instruction packing to SMT. Instruction packing opportunistically packs two instructions (possibly from different threads), each with at most one non-ready source operand at the time of dispatch, into the same issue queue entry. Our second design, termed 2OP_BLOCK, takes these ideas one step further and completely avoids the dispatching of the instructions with two non-ready source operands. This technique has several advantages. First, it reduces the scheduling complexity (and the associated delays) as the logic needed to support the instructions with 2 non-ready source operands is eliminated. More surprisingly, 2OP_BLOCK simultaneously improves the performance as the same issue queue entry may be reallocated multiple times to the instructions with at most one non-ready source (which usually spend fewer cycles in the queue) as opposed to hogging the entry with an instruction which enters the queue with two non-ready sources. For the schedulers with the capacity to hold 64 instructions, the 2OP_BLOCK design outperforms the traditional queue by 11%, on the average, and at the same time results in a 10% reduction in the overall scheduling delay.

1. Introduction and Motivation

Simultaneous Multithreading (SMT) is an effective technique to increase the throughput of a traditional superscalar processor via the simultaneous sharing of the key datapath components among multiple threads [41,42]. The shared resources typically include the issue queue, the pool of physical registers, the execution units and the caches. Such sharing elevates the pressure on these resources and increases their utilization, necessitating the use of a larger number of entries in these components to realize the full performance potential afforded by SMT. Unfortunately, the additional complexities that are incurred by the implementation of these larger structures may exacerbate the critical timing paths and negatively

impact the processor's cycle time. As a careful balance must be found between the instruction-level parallelism (ILP) and the cycle time to achieve maximum performance, it is important to reduce the complexity of these critical resources without significantly impacting the ability to extract the ILP or impeding the design scalability.

One such critical datapath structure that experiences elevated pressure due to sharing in an SMT processor is the issue queue (IQ). Figure 1 shows how the processor throughput scales with the size of the IQ for both the superscalar and the 4-threaded SMT machines, based on our simulations (details of our simulation framework are presented in Section 2). Results are shown in the form of the commit IPC improvements over the respective baseline with a 32-entry IQ. The trends clearly indicate that the performance of a superscalar machine (depicted by the bars on the left) increases only slightly as the number of entries in the IQ is increased beyond 32. On the average across the full set of SPEC 2000 benchmarks, the difference between the performance of the processors with 32-entry and 256-entry IQs is only 9%. The situation is, however, quite different for an SMT machine, where four threads execute simultaneously and much more pressure is exerted on the IQ. On the average, there is a 32% IPC difference as the IQ size increases from 32 to 64 entries, an additional 35% if the IQ size is 128 entries, and a further 11% for the 256-entry IQ.

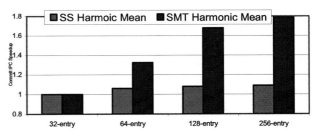

Figure 1: Average performance improvements for superscalar and 4-way SMT machines for various IQ sizes with respect to the corresponding baseline machine with 32-entry IQs.

Thus, SMT machines require very generously sized IQs to realize their full performance potential. However, it is well documented in the recent literature that the wakeup and selection operations associated with the IQ lie on the critical timing path in modern microprocessors [21,27,39] and the delays of both increase proportionally with the number of entries in the IQ. Consequently, increasing the number of entries beyond a certain limit may negatively impact the processor's clock frequency. Largely due to these constraints, even modern processor implementations use rather modestly sized IQs. It is therefore important to investigate techniques that can provide the illusion of larger scheduling windows without physically enlarging the IQ.

All of the existing solutions for optimizing the IQ efficiency on SMT processors do so indirectly by controlling the quality of instructions that are fetched into the pipeline from multiple threads, e.g. ensuring that none of the threads clog the issue queue. For example, the I-Count fetching policy [41] gives priority to threads with fewer not-yet-executed instructions already in the pipeline. Some optimizations to the I-Count policy that further increase the efficiency of the IQ useage have also been proposed in the literature. Fundamentally, these solutions attempt to avoid clogging the queue with instructions that reside there for a large number of cycles before being issued. For example, FLUSH [40], FLUSH++ [11] and the Data Miss Gating technique of [14] combine I-count with a special treatment of threads that experienced misses in various levels of the cache hierarchy. While all these mechanisms are effective to some extent, their inherent limitation lies in the reliance on information that is available at the time of instruction fetch. However, much more effective and precise control can be exercised over the IQ usage if these fetch-centric approaches are augmented with some dynamic register-specific information about the instructions, which is readily available after the register renaming stage. Specifically, we show that the instructions with two non-ready source operands at the time of dispatch (we assume an ISA with two source operand instructions for this study) spend a significantly larger number of cycles in the IQ than other instructions, and most of these cycles are spent waiting for the arrival of the first source. If such instructions are kept outside of the IQ until one of the source operands becomes available, then the pressure on the IQ will be greatly reduced and the performance will improve. All previous proposals do not make use of such information and treat all instructions equally, regardless of the number of ready source operands at the time of dispatch.

The focus of this paper is to consider the mechanisms that augment the existing fetch-centric approaches with dynamic microarchitectural information to obtain more effective control of *how* and *when* the instructions are placed in the IQ. To this end, we propose several solutions. First, we extend the previously introduced instruction packing mechanism [34,35] to SMT. Instruction packing opportunistically places two instructions into the same IQ entry provided that each of these instructions has at most one non-ready source operand at the time of dispatch. We show that the percentage of instructions entering the scheduling window with two non-ready source operands is smaller on an SMT machine than it is on a superscalar, and therefore instruction packing is more amenable to SMT processors. Secondly, we take these ideas one step further and completely disallow the dispatch of instructions with two non-ready source operands. This design (called 2OP_BLOCK in the rest of the paper) reduces the scheduler complexity as the capability to support the instructions with 2 non-ready source operands is not needed. Furthermore, 2OP_BLOCK improves the performance as the same IQ entry may be reallocated multiple times to instructions with at most one non-ready source (which tend to spend fewer cycles in the queue) rather than clogging the entry for a long time with one instruction that has two non-ready sources.

The main contributions and the key results of this paper are:

- We show that from the scalability perspective, instruction packing is much more effective on multi-threaded machines than it is on superscalars. For example, instruction packing applied to a 64-entry queue increases the performance by 21% on a 4-way SMT, while the performance of a superscalar only increases by 5%.

- We propose a scheduler design for SMT (called 2OP_BLOCK) where the dispatching of instructions with two non-ready source operands is disallowed and the corresponding threads are blocked. Such a design significantly reduces the scheduler's complexity and its delay (since the capability to support two operand instructions is not required) and at the same time provides higher instruction throughput compared to both the similarly sized instruction packing scheduler as well as the traditional scheduler.

- We show that, for schedulers with the capacity to hold 64 instructions, the 2OP_BLOCK design outperforms the traditional queue by 11% in terms of IPC, on the average, and at the same time provides a 10% reduction in the overall scheduler delay and significantly reduced design complexity.

The rest of the paper is organized in the following way. We present our simulation methodology in Section 2. We review instruction packing, as proposed for reducing the power consumption in superscalar architectures, in Section 3. Section 4 describes our scheduler designs for SMT processor. Results are presented and discussed in Section 5. We review the related work in Section 6 and offer our concluding remarks in Section 7.

2. Simulation Methodology

For estimating the performance impact of the schemes described in this paper, we used M-Sim [37]: a significantly modified version of the Simplescalar 3.0d simulator [5] that supports the SMT processor model. M-Sim implements separate models for the key pipeline structures such as the issue queue, the reorder buffer, and the physical register file; it also explicitly models register renaming. In the SMT model, the threads share the IQ, the pool of physical registers, the execution units and the caches, but have separate rename tables, program counters, load/store queues and reorder buffers. Each thread also has its own branch predictor. The details of the studied processor configuration are shown in Table 1. In the baseline SMT model, the I-Count fetch policy [41] was implemented and fetching was limited to two threads per cycle.

Table 1: Configuration of the simulated processor.

Parameter	Configuration
Machine width	8-wide fetch, 8-wide issue, 8-wide commit
Window size	issue queue – as specified, 48 entry load/store queue, 96–entry ROB
Function Units and Lat (total/issue)	8 Int Add (1/1), 4 Int Mult (3/1) / Div (20/19), 4 Load/Store (2/1), 8 FP Add (2), 4 FP Mult (4/1) / Div (12/12) / Sqrt (24/24)
Physical Registers	256 integer + 256 floating-point physical registers
L1 I–cache	64 KB, 2–way set–associative, 128 byte line
L1 D–cache	32 KB, 4–way set–associative, 256 byte line
L2 Cache unified	2 MB, 8–way set–associative, 512 byte line, 12 cycles hit time
BTB	2048 entry, 2–way set–associative
Branch Predictor	2K entry gShare, 10-bit global history per thread
Pipeline Structure	5-stage front-end (fetch-dispatch), scheduling, 2 stages for register file access, execution, writeback, commit.
Memory	64 bit wide, 200 cycles access latency

We simulated the full set of SPEC 2000 integer and floating point benchmarks [18], using the precompiled Alpha binaries available from the Simplescalar website [5]. We skipped the initialization part of each benchmark using the procedure prescribed by the Simpoints tool [38] and then simulated the execution of the following 100 million instructions. For multithreaded workloads, we stopped the simulations after 100 million instructions from any thread had committed.

Our multithreaded workloads contain a subset of the possible combinations of the simulated benchmarks. In selecting the multithreaded workloads, we first simulated all benchmarks in the single-threaded superscalar environment and used these results to classify them as low, medium, and high ILP, where the low ILP benchmarks are memory bound and the high ILP benchmarks are execution bound.

In total, we simulated 12 4-threaded workloads, two from each of the following six categories: 1) 4 low-ILP programs; 2) 4 medium-ILP programs; 3) 4 high-ILP programs; 4) 2 low-ILP and 2 high-ILP programs; 5) 2 medium-ILP and 2 high-ILP programs; 6) 2 medium-ILP and 2 low-ILP programs. All workloads are described in detail in Table 2.

Table 2: Simulated multi-threaded workloads

Classification	Mix	Benchmarks
4 LOW ILP	Mix 1	mcf, equake, art, lucas
	Mix 2	twolf, vpr, swim, parser
4 MED ILP	Mix 3	applu, ammp, mgrid, galgel
	Mix 4	gcc, bzip2, eon, apsi
4 HIGH ILP	Mix 5	facerec, crafty, perlbmk, gap
	Mix 6	wupwise, gzip, vortex, mesa
2 LOW ILP + 2 HIGH ILP	Mix 7	mcf, equake, mesa, vortex
	Mix 8	parser, swim, crafty, perlbmk
2 LOW ILP + 2 MED ILP	Mix 9	art, lucas, galgel, gcc
	Mix 10	parser, swim, gcc, bzip2
2 MED ILP + 2 HIGH ILP	Mix 11	gzip, wupwise, fma3d, apsi
	Mix 12	vortex, mesa, mgrid, eon

We used several metrics for evaluating the performance of the multithreaded workloads throughout this paper. The first metric is the total throughput in terms of the commit IPC rate. However, this metric does not accurately reflect changes that favor a thread with high IPC at the expense of significantly hindering a thread with low IPC [25, 41]. Therefore, we also present the "fairness" metric of "harmonic mean of weighted IPCs" [25, 41], which accounts for individual per-thread performance.

For estimating the delays of the various schedulers, we developed hand-crafted and highly-optimized VLSI layouts of the IQ. Layouts were designed in 0.18m 6-metal layer TSMC process using Cadence design tools.

3. Instruction Packing

In this section, we briefly describe instruction packing as proposed for superscalar machines in [34,35] to provide sufficient background for the rest of the paper. Figure 2(a) shows the format of an IQ entry used in traditional designs. The following fields comprise a single entry: a) entry allocated bit (A), b) payload area (opcode, FU type, destination register address, literals), c) tag of the first source, associated comparator (tag CAM word 1, hereafter just tag CAM 1, without the "word") and the source valid bit, d) tag of the second source, associated comparator (tag CAM 2) and source valid bit, and e) the ready bit. The ready bit, used to raise the request signal for the selection logic is derived by AND-ing the valid bits of the two sources.

If at least one of the source operands of an instruction entering the IQ is ready at the time of dispatch, the tag CAM associated with this operand's slot remains unused. To exploit this idle tag CAM, instruction packing [34,35] shares one issue queue entry between two such instructions. With instruction packing, an entry in the IQ can hold one or two instructions, depending on the number of ready operands in the stored instructions at the time of dispatch. The key difference between instruction packing and the previously proposed Tag Elimination mechanism of [15] is that the queue partitioning into the entries with various numbers of comparators is done dynamically in the former scheme and statically in the latter.

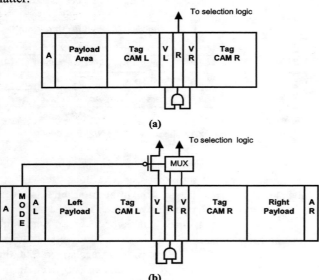

Figure 2: Formats of a traditional IQ entry (a) and an entry of the IQ that supports instruction packing (b)

Figure 2(b) shows the format of an issue queue entry that supports instruction packing. Each IQ entry is comprised of the "entry allocated" bit (A), the ready bit (R), the mode bit (MODE) and the two symmetrical halves: the left half and the right half. The structure of each half is identical, so we will use the left half for the subsequent explanations.

The left half of each IQ entry contains the following fields:

• Left half allocated (AL) bit. This bit is set when the left half-entry is allocated.

• Source tag and associated comparator (Tag CAM). This is where the tag of the non-ready source operand for an instruction with at most one non-ready source is stored.

• Source valid left bit (VL). This bit signifies the validity of the corresponding source operand connected to the comparator in this half of the entry, similar to traditional designs. This bit is also used to indicate if the instruction residing in a half-entry is ready for selection (as explained later)

• Payload area. The payload area contains the same information as in the traditional design, namely: opcode, bits identifying the FU type, destination register address, and literal bits. In addition, the payload area contains the tag of the second source. Notice that the tag of the second source does not participate in the wakeup, because if an instruction is allocated to a half-entry, the second source must be valid at the time of dispatch. Compared to the traditional design, the payload area is increased by the number of bits used to represent a source tag.

The process of instruction wakeup remains exactly the same as in the traditional design for an instruction that occupies a full IQ entry (i.e. enters the queue with two non-ready register sources). Here, the ready bit (R) is set by AND-ing the valid bits of both sources. For instructions that occupy half of an IQ entry, the wakeup simply amounts to setting of the valid bit corresponding to the source that was non-ready when the instruction entered the IQ. The contents of the source valid bits are then directly used to indicate that the instruction is ready for selection (the validity of the second source is implicit in this case).

An increase in the complexity of the selection logic is avoided by sharing one request line between the R and the VR bits. The shared request line is raised if at least one of the bits (the R or the VR) is set. The R and the VR bits are both connected to the shared request line through a multiplexer, which is controlled by the "mode" bit of the IQ entry (Figure 2(b)). In order to avoid additional delays during instruction issue (due to the ambiguity in the location of register tags needed to start the register file read access), the following solution is used. When an instruction with two non-ready sources is allocated to the IQ, the tag that is connected to the left half comparator is also replicated in the payload area storage for the second tag in the right half. As a result, both tags will be present in the right half of the queue, so these tags can be simply used for register file access, without regard for the IQ entry mode.

More details describing this technique can be found elsewhere [34,35]. In the next section, we discuss the application of instruction packing to SMT processors and show that it is an even more effective technique for those machines.

4. Scheduler Designs for SMT

This section describes our proposed designs to maximize the scheduling efficiency of SMT processors.

4.1. Instruction Packing on SMT

Our first step is to simply apply instruction packing to the SMT machine. As follows from the discussions in Section 3, the effectiveness of instruction packing directly depends on the percentage of instructions that enter the scheduling window with two non-ready sources: the lower this percentage is, the better the trade-offs are that can be realized by packing.

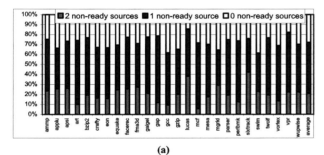

(a)

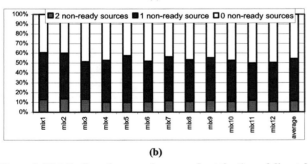

(b)

Figure 3: Distribution of non-ready operands at the time of dispatch in superecalar (a) and SMT (b) machines for 32-entry IQs.

Figure 3 presents the percentage of instructions that are dispatched with 0, 1 and 2 non-ready source operands for both superscalar (top graph) and SMT (bottom graph) processors. While about 21% of the instructions are dispatched with 2 non-ready sources on a superscalar machine, this percentage drops to 11% on a 4-threaded SMT configuration. It is not surprising that the percentage of such instructions is lower on an SMT machine than it is on a superscalar. The fundamental reason behind this lower percentage is that each thread runs relatively slower on SMT, which in turn increases the likelihood of a source operand being produced before the consuming instruction is dispatched. As a result, fewer instructions

require a full-width entry in the instruction packing scheduler on SMT, allowing for a more efficient use of the available comparators.

Figure 4 compares the performance achieved by using various configurations of the traditional schedulers as well as the schedulers supporting instruction packing for both superscalar (SS) and SMT processors. When comparing the different scheduler designs throughout the paper, we adopt the following notation. Each particular scheduler is referred to as *N-Scheme*, where *N* refers to the maximum number of instructions that the scheduler can hold simultaneously (or its capacity), and *Scheme* refers to the scheduling mechanism that is in use (traditional, packing or 2OP_BLOCK). For example, *64-traditional* refers to the traditional issue queue with 64 entries and *64-packing* refers to the scheduler that supports instruction packing and has a capacity to hold up to 64 instructions. Note that in terms of the logic presented in Figure 2(b), such a scheduler will only have 32-entries in the traditional sense, and each of these entries will support up to two instructions. In practice, the maximum number of instructions held by this scheduler is often less than 64, because some instructions occupy full-sized entries. Note further that this terminology is different from that used in our previous work [34, 35].

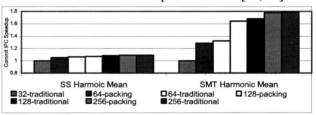

Figure 4: Performance of instruction packing on superscalar (SS Harmonic Mean) and 4-way SMT (SMT Harmonic Mean) machines for various IQ configurations.

While instruction packing provides some benefits for a superscalar machine (the set of bars on the left), the advantages are generally limited to the schedulers of smaller sizes, because the superscalar's performance is virtually insensitive to the IQ size if that exceeds 32 entries on our simulation framework. In contrast, one can observe that on an SMT machine, instruction packing continues to be a very effective technique even for much larger schedulers, as there are significant IPC improvements when the IQ size is increased in the baseline SMT case up to at least 256-entry queues. For SMT processors, a 32-entry IQ represents a large performance bottleneck - the difference between the performance of the machines with a 32-entry IQ and a 64-entry IQ is 32% on the average.

In all of the cases considered and depicted in Figure 4 (the set of bars on the right), the performance of the *N-packing* scheduler comes within a few percentage points of the performance of the *N-traditional* scheduler. This is not surprising, as almost 90% of the instructions (see Figure 3(b)) can be actually packed within the IQ entries and do not require a separate entry of their own. Specifically, the *64-packing* scheduler achieves IPC within 3% of the *64-traditional* scheduler. Results of a similar nature are achieved for other IQ sizes.

While achieving essentially the same performance levels as the traditional queue with the same maximum capacity, instruction packing significantly reduces the access delays and therefore presents a more attractive solution to scaling the dynamic scheduling logic than simply increasing the number of entries in the queue. The reduced amount of associative logic in the packing scheduler results in a drastic reduction of the wakeup access delays compared to the traditional designs of similar capacity. Even though the delays of the selection logic are slightly increased (due to the extra MUX), the overall reduction in the scheduling delays is still substantial. Specific delays of instruction packing schedulers are presented elsewhere [35], the important result to note at this point is that the difference in the scheduling delay between *N-traditional* and *2*N-traditional* designs is roughly twice as much as the difference in the delay between *N-traditional* and *2*N-packing* schedulers. Therefore, simply applying instruction packing to a traditional queue achieves almost the same maximum capacity and the same performance as doubling the queue but with significantly less additional delay.

4.2. 2OP_BLOCK: Blocking Instructions with 2 Non-ready Source Operands

To motivate our next technique, we first present the microarchitectural-level statistics related to the number of cycles that the instructions spend in the 32-entry IQ of the SMT processor as a function of the number of non-ready register source operands at the time of instruction dispatch. Figure 5 shows this data.

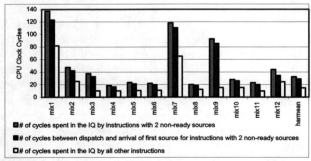

Figure 5: Number of cycles spent by the instructions in the IQ.

The leftmost set of bars in Figure 5 depicts the number of cycles spent in the IQ by the instructions which enter the queue with two non-ready register sources. On average, such instructions wait 33 cycles before being issued. The next set of bars shows the average number of cycles elapsed between the dispatch of such instructions into the queue and the arrival of the first source. It is interesting to observe that most of the cycles are spent waiting for the first-arriving source operand. After that, the instruction typically issues very fast (in 4 cycles on the average). Finally, the third set of bars in Figure 5 shows the number of cycles spent in the queue by all other instructions (the ones that enter with at least one register source ready or have no more than one such source in the first place). As can be seen, the instructions encapsulated by the third bar spend significantly fewer cycles in the queue – they reside in the queue for only 15 cycles as opposed to 33 cycles spent in the queue by the instructions that enter with 2 non-ready sources.

We now examine how to exploit the statistics presented in Figure 5 to increase the efficiency of the SMT scheduling logic. First, we observe that the SMT environment opens up an additional dimension for maximizing the performance and efficiency of instruction scheduling. Specifically, when one of the threads is expected to supply instructions which will spend a large number of cycles in the IQ before being selected for execution, the dispatching of instructions from that thread can be temporarily suspended. In contrast to the single-threaded execution in a superscalar processor, such thread suspension will not result in performance degradation if the supply of instructions from other threads can be sustained.

Existing techniques partially take advantage of this opportunity by controlling the order in which instructions are fetched from multiple threads [11, 40, 41]. However, these policies are limited to the information available at the time of instruction fetch. However, in a typical deeply-pipelined machine, the number of stages between the fetch and dispatch (i.e., insertion into the IQ) can be significant (we assume 5 such stages in our simulations). As a result, the specific situation that led to the decision not to fetch from a certain thread can be completely reversed by the time the fetched instructions actually reach the IQ. Furthermore, additional dynamic microarchitectural information about the instruction (i.e. the status of its physical registers) is readily available after register renaming. Consequently, if the final decision regarding which instructions to place into the IQ is postponed until after the register renaming stage, then the information presented in Figure 5 can be directly exploited by not dispatching instructions with two non-ready source operands into the queue, but instead blocking the dispatching from such a thread until one of the operands becomes ready.

Following these observations, we propose a design, where the instructions can only enter the scheduling window if they have no more than one non-ready register source operand, i.e. will only require one comparator. All instructions with two non-ready operands (and their corresponding threads) will stall until one of the sources becomes ready. In the rest of the paper, we refer to this design as 2OP_BLOCK.

While generally the two design targets of improving the performance and reducing the complexity are at odds with each other, the 2OP_BLOCK scheduler, surprisingly, achieves both of these goals at the same time. The scheduler complexity is reduced, because each entry in the IQ can be reduced to have only one set of comparators. A more non-intuitive result is the increased IPC performance compared to a similarly-sized traditional IQ. Despite the fact that the dispatch stage can be completely blocked in some cycles (when all threads have their oldest non-dispatched instructions with two non-ready source operands at the same time), higher overall performance is still realized, even for fairly sizable IQs, because the queue is utilized much more efficiently. Specifically, the same IQ entry can be reused multiple times by the instructions with at most one non-ready source operand instead of allowing a single instruction with two non-ready sources to clog the entry for a long time. Since the instructions with two non-ready sources are likely to wait for a long time in the IQ anyway, it is more beneficial for performance to have them wait at the dispatch stage, freeing up the valuable space in the scheduler for other instructions which are likely to be issued faster (such as the instructions from other threads which enter with some of their source operands ready).

Notice that while one thread is blocked, the other threads can continue processing through the front end as long as they do not encounter instructions with two non-ready sources. Since typically the thread processing is split in the front end (e.g. each thread uses its own rename table), it is easy to block only the progress of one specific thread. Every cycle when the instructions from this particular thread are considered for dispatching, the ready bits associated with the source operand registers of the blocked instruction are re-examined. If one of these registers becomes ready, the thread is unblocked and further fetches, renames, and dispatches from that thread resume. Notice that such checking of the ready bits is nothing unique to our scheme; such checks are routinely performed in the baseline machine to determine the status of the source register operands before the instruction is moved into the IQ.

4.3. Synergy of 2OP_BLOCK with Instruction Packing and Timing Issues

While the 2OP_BLOCK scheduler can be described and implemented completely independently of instruction packing (as presented in the previous section), additional advantages, primarily from the timing and power

perspectives, can be realized if the physical layout of the IQ which supports instruction packing (and is shown in Figure 2b) is leveraged. In this section, we describe the synergistic advantages of instruction packing and 2OP_BLOCK.

The 2OP_BLOCK mechanism simplifies the instruction packing scheduler of Figure 2(b) in a number of ways. First, as only instructions with at most one non-ready operand are present in the scheduler, both the multiplexer and the p-device that drive the request signals to the select logic are no longer needed. Second, the MODE bit, the A bit, and the R bit can be removed. Furthermore, the AND gate (shown at the bottom of Figure 2b) is not required as the readiness of the instruction is manifested by the ready bit of a single operand. Finally, the capability to search several allocation bits in parallel in the course of setting up the IQ entries is no longer necessary. The resulting combination of 2OP_BLOCK and the instruction packing scheduler is also less complex than the traditional scheduler because of the use of fewer comparators, shorter tag busses, and the absence of the AND gates to drive the final match signal. It is important to understand - that the IPC advantages of the 2OP_BLOCK design come only because of the more efficient usage of the queue and have nothing to do with the underlying circuitry (such as instruction packing logic). The instruction packing logic only provides additional advantages in terms of lower access delay and power dissipation.

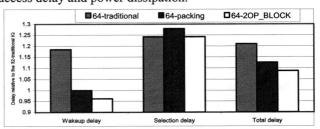

Figure 6: Circuit delays of various scheduler configurations (relative to the 32-traditional design).

We now examine the delays of the 2OP_BLOCK scheduler (which uses the simplified IQ layout derived from instruction packing, as described above) and compare it to that of the traditional IQ as well as the IQ supporting a full-fledged implementation of instruction packing (as presented in Figure 2b). Figure 6 presents the wakeup, selection, and overall delays for various schedulers with the maximum capacity of 64 instructions relative to the traditional scheduler design with 32 entries. As seen from the graph, for the same capacity, the 2OP_BLOCK design has the lowest overall delay, which is 9.5% smaller than the delay of the 64-traditional queue and 3.5% smaller than the delay of the full-fledged packing queue. Compared to packing, this delay reduction comes from two main sources. The wakeup delay is reduced because the AND gate used to drive the final match signal in both traditional and instruction packing designs has been eliminated (this is also the reason why the wakeup delay of *64-2OP_BLOCK* is somewhat smaller than the wakeup delay of the *32-traditional* design). Secondly, the selection delay is reduced because of the elimination of the multiplexer.

The 2OP_BLOCK scheduler, as presented thus far, results in substantial performance losses if only a single thread is executed. For the system where the single thread performance is important and it is a frequent occasion when only a single thread is running, a better design point could be to use the full-fledged instruction packing logic to implement the queue and dynamically switch between the packing mode and the 2OP_BLOCK mode depending on the number of active threads. The switch between the two modes is a simple manner of changing instruction dispatch to allow or disallow the instructions with 2 non-ready sources to enter the scheduler. As we show in the results section, 2OP_BLOCK outperforms instruction packing for 4-threaded workloads, but the opposite is obviously true for a single thread. This switch between the packing mode and the 2OP_BLOCK mode can even be done dynamically, depending on the program phases and corresponding microarchitectural statistics. Such statistics may include instruction issue rates, cache miss rates, branch misprediction rates, etc. The investigation of the specific triggers to drive the transition between the packing and the 2OP_BLOCK mode is beyond the scope of this paper, and is left for future work. Using the instruction packing circuitry from Figure 2(b) in conjunction with the 2OP_BLOCK design is especially attractive because, as seen in the results presented by Figure 6, the increase of the circuit delay is very small if the full-fledged packing is implemented as opposed to the simplified logic that does not support the instructions with two non-ready source operands.

5. Results and Discussions

As mentioned previously, when we compare the performance of different schedulers, the sizes of the IQ are measured in terms of the maximum number of instructions that may be present in the queue simultaneously. Specifically, an *N-traditional* IQ holds up to N instructions; an *N-2OP_BLOCK* scheduler can store up to N instructions, each with at most one non-ready source; and an *N-packing* scheduler can hold up to N-instructions (if all the instructions have at most one non-ready source), but typically holds fewer than N instructions due to the presence of some instructions with two non-ready source operands.

Figure 7 presents the IPC improvements of various scheduler designs considered in this paper with the total capacity of 64 instructions. The results are shown as relative improvements over the baseline IQ with 32 entries. On the average across all simulated workloads, the performance gains with respect to the *32-traditional* design are 21%, 24% and 30% for *64-packing*, *64-traditional* and *64-2OP_BLOCK* schedulers respectively. It is interesting to observe that the 2OP_BLOCK design outperforms the traditional scheduler of the same capacity in all simulated mixes, except for mixes 9 and 12. On the average, *64-2OP_BLOCK* outperforms *64-traditional* scheduler by 11%. Some mixes show especially large gains, up to 34% on mix 1.

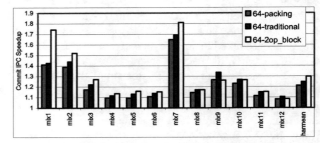

Figure 7: Speedups (in terms of throughput IPC) over the 32-traditional IQ for various scheduler designs.

Figure 8 presents similar results in terms of the fairness metric (which is a harmonic mean of weighted IPCs). Here, the relative difference between the various schedulers is somewhat smaller, but still the 2OP_BLOCK design outperforms the traditional queue on all but two mixes (mix 9 and mix 12) as well as on the average. On the average, the performance of the *64-2OP_BLOCK* is better than the performance of *64-traditional* design by 5% according to the fairness metric.

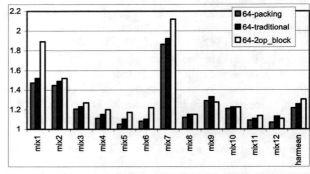

Figure 8: Fairness improvements (in terms of harmonic mean of weighted IPC) over the 32-traditional IQ for various scheduler designs.

While the 2OP_BLOCK scheduler disallows all instructions with two non-ready operands from entering the scheduling window, the thread-level parallelism present in SMT designs naturally allows such limitations to be overcome. Even as the dispatch from one thread may be stalled, dispatch from other threads may continue.

Our results show that 2OP_BLOCK is effective when the percentage of cycles in which the dispatch of all threads is stalled due to the presence of instructions with 2 non-ready sources is rather small. In these cases, the advantages of 2OP_BLOCK scheme outweigh its potential limitations.

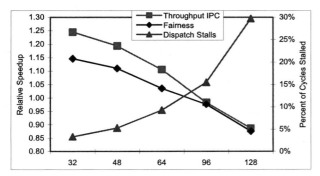

Figure 9: Speedups of the *N-2OP_BLOCK* scheduler over the *N-traditional* scheduler in terms of both throughput IPC and harmonic mean of weighted IPC (axis on the left) and the percentage of cycles in which the dispatch is stalled for all threads (axis on the right) for schedulers of various sizes.

Figure 9 presents the scalability analysis of the 2OP_BLOCK scheduling logic. Results show the relative performance increase of the 2OP_BLOCK scheduler compared to the traditional scheduler of the same total capacity for various sizes of the IQ and are presented in terms of both throughput IPC and the fairness metric (y-axis on the left) and the percentage of cycles in which the dispatch was stalled because the oldest not-yet-dispatched instructions from all threads had both of their source operands in the non-ready state (y-axis on the right). As seen from the graph, the 2OP_BLOCK design outperforms the traditional queue for up to 96-entry schedulers. Note that the gains are especially high for smaller schedulers: for example, the *32-2OP_BLOCK* IQ outperforms the 32-entry traditional IQ by as much as 25% on the average across all simulated mixes according to the throughput IPC metric and by 15% according to fairness metric. As the size of the traditional queue increases beyond 96 entries, the dispatch stalls introduced by 2OP_BLOCK start to dominate its advantages and the resulting performance is actually lower than that of the traditional designs. In particular, the percentage of cycles during which the supply of instructions completely stops because all threads have instructions with two non-ready source operands increases dramatically as the IQ size is increased beyond 96-entries. These stalls prevent the 2OP_BLOCK design from fully utilizing the entries for very large IQs, resulting in the performance degradation compared to the traditional queue of the same capacity. Essentially, at large IQ sizes, the extent to which 2OP_BLOCK relieves the IQ pressure is minimal (because the IQ itself is less of a bottleneck), but instead

additional dispatch stalls are introduced. The percentage of cycles when all threads are simultaneously blocked at dispatch due to the conditions imposed by 2OP_BLOCK increases significantly with larger scheduling windows, as seen in Figure 9. This is because a larger number of non-executed instructions buffered in the scheduler increases the number of non-ready registers.

Finally, we briefly discuss the implications of the proposed designs on the power consumption. It has been shown in [34,35] that instruction packing achieves a significant reduction in the power dissipation of the scheduling logic for superscalar machines – in fact, power reduction was the primary goal of those works. Naturally, these results still hold true for SMT if we compare similarly sized instruction packing and traditional schedulers. The 2OP_BLOCK scheduler results in slightly more power reduction even compared to the instruction packing scheduler. This is because some logic (such as the AND gate, the allocation bit vectors, etc) is eliminated. However, this power reduction is expected to be small (within a few percentage points) because the scheduling power is dominated by the dissipations expended in the course of wakeup tag broadcasts as well as within the logic of the selection tree. None of these components are affected by the 2OP_BLOCK scheduler compared to instruction packing. For more detailed power-related comparisons between the instruction packing and the traditional scheduler, we refer the readers to [34,35].

6. Related Work

Various fetching policies have been proposed in the literature to ensure to supply the instructions for building the most efficient execution schedules. The I-Count [41] gives fetching priority to the threads with fewer not-yet-executed instructions. One deficiency the I-Count is that it does not effectively handle situations where the instructions pile up in the IQ following an L2 cache miss. As a result, the IQ entries are occupied by such instructions for a long time. Several optimizations of I-Count have been proposed to address this deficiency. STALL [40] prevents the thread from fetching further instructions if it experienced an L2 cache miss. FLUSH [40] extends STALL by squashing the already dispatched instructions from such a thread, thus making the shared IQ resources available for the instructions from other threads. FLUSH++ [11] combines the benefits of STALL and FLUSH and uses the cache behavior of threads to dynamically switch between these two mechanisms. The Data Gating techniqueue of [14] avoids fetching from threads that experience an L1 data miss. Predicitive Data Gating goes one step further and avoids fetching from the thread if it is predicted (during the early stage) that a cache miss will soon occur. While all these mechanisms are effective to various degrees, they do not exploit dynamic microarchtiectural information about the instructions available after register renaming. In this paper, we show that additional benefits can be realized if such information is considered.

Several works proposed specific optimizations for the SMT processors. El-Moursy and Albonesi [14] explored new front-end policies that reduce the required integer and floating point issue queue sizes in SMT architectures. Their techniques limit the number of non-ready instructions in the queue from each thread and also block further instruction fetching from a thread if that thread experiences an L1 cache miss. As a result, the queue occupancy is reduced significantly (by about 33%) for the same level of performance. In [33], a partitioned version of the oldest-first issue policy is proposed, where separate issue queues are used to buffer the instructions from different threads. In [32], the effect of partitioning the datapath resources, including the issue queues, across multiple threads is discussed. In [10], a more fine grained dynamic control over SMT resources is proposed.

Researchers have proposed several ways to reduce the complexity and the power consumption of the issue logic in superscalar processors. Dynamic adaptation techniques [2,6,7,17,29] partition the queue into multiple segments and deactivate some segments periodically, when the applications do not require the full issue queue to sustain the commit IPCs. The issue queues used in the SMT processors are generally less amenable to such optimizations, because the occupancy of the queue is typically high as it is shared among multiple threads. Energy-efficient comparators, which dissipate energy predominantly on a tag match were proposed in [30, 31]. Also in [30], the issue queue power was reduced by using zero-byte encoding and bitline segmentation. All these techniques can be naturally applied to the SMT processor without any changes. In [20], the associative broadcast is replaced with indexing to only enable a single instruction to wakeup.

The observation that many instructions are dispatched with at least one of their source operands ready is not new – it was used in [15], where the scheduler design with reduced number of comparators was proposed. In that scheme, some IQ entries have two comparators, others have just one comparator, and yet others have zero comparators. While the work of [15] statically partitions the queue into the groups of entries with various numbers of tag comparators, instruction packing achieves this partitioning dynamically, thus it can better adjust to the characteristics of the executing programs and results in lower performance degradation, as shown in [35].

In [22], the tag buses were categorized into fast buses and slow buses, such that the tag broadcast on the slow bus takes one additional cycle. While the technique proposed in [22] can be trivially adapted to SMT, the design proposed in this paper (2OP-BLOCK scheme, in particular) completely eliminates the second set of comparators and therefore obviates the need to perform last-tag speculation and maintain fast and slow wakeup buses. The capacitive loading on all tag buses is reduced, because half of the comparators are offloaded from every tag bus.

Several techniques have been proposed to pipeline the scheduling logic on a superscalar machine into separate wakeup and selection cycles without commensurate degradation in the IPCs [21,39]. Other proposals have introduced new scheduling techniques with the goal of designing scalable dynamic schedulers to support a very large number of in-flight instructions [3, 12, 23, 24, 28]. Brown et al. [4] proposed to remove the selection logic from the critical path by exploiting the fact that the number of ready instructions in a given cycle is typically smaller than the processor's issue width. The technique of [4] is less likely to be applicable to SMT as the number of ready instructions increases.

Scheduling techniques based on predicting the issue cycle of an instruction [1,8,9,16,19,24,26,36] remove the wakeup delay from the critical path and remove the CAM logic from instruction wakeup, but need to keep track of the cycle when each physical register will become ready. In [13], the wakeup time prediction occurs in parallel with the instruction fetching. Future research is needed to determine the effectiveness of these techniques on an SMT processor.

7. Concluding Remarks

We examined several mechanisms for improving the scalability, reducing the complexity and delays and increasing throughput of the instruction schedulers in multi-threaded processors. We demonstrated that the instruction packing – a technique to pack multiple instructions into the same issue queue entry – is more effective on an SMT than it is on a superscalar. This is because the percentage of instructions that enter the scheduling window with 2 non-ready register source operands on a 4-way SMT is significantly lower than on a superscalar machine (11% vs. 21%).

We then proposed the 2OP_BLOCK scheduler – a scheduling technique that completely disallows the dispatch of instructions with 2 non-ready sources, thus significantly simplifying the IQ logic. This mechanism works well for SMTs, because it often allows the reuse of the same IQ entry multiple times for the instructions with no more than one non-ready source rather than tying up the entry with an instruction with 2 non-ready sources (which typically spend a longer time in the queue). For the schedulers with the capacity to hold 64 instructions, 2OP_BLOCK outperforms the traditional design by 11%

on the average, and at the same time results in 10% reduction in the overall scheduling delay.

In summary, the proposed designs improve the scalability, reduce the complexity and the delays, and/or increase the throughput of the dynamic instruction scheduling logic in SMT machines. Additionally, power dissipation can also be reduced, as smaller schedulers can be used to meet the same performance targets.

8. Acknowledgements

We would like to thank Pavel Vasek and the anonymous reviewers for their useful comments on earlier drafts of this paper. We would also like to thank Oguz Ergin for his assistance with the use of Cadence design tools.

9. References

[1] J. Abella, A. Gonzalez. "Low-Complexity Distributed Issue Queue." in Proc. 10th International Symposium on High Performance Computer Architecture (HPCA), 2004.

[2] P. Bose, et al. "Early Stage Definition of LPX: a Low Power Issue-Execute Processor." in Proc. Workshop on Power-Aware Computer Systems, 2002.

[3] E. Brekelbaum et al. "Hierarchical Scheduling Windows." in Proc. of the International Symposium on Microarchitecture (MICRO), 2002.

[4] M. Brown, et al. "Select-Free Instruction Scheduling Logic." in Proc. of the 34th International Symp. on Microarchitecture (MICRO), 2001.

[5] D. Burger, T. Austin. "The SimpleScalar tool set: Version 2.0." Tech. Report, Dept. of CS, Univ. of Wisconsin-Madison, June 1997 and documentation for all Simplescalar releases.

[6] A. Buyuktosunoglu, et al. "A Circuit-Level Implementation of an Adaptive Issue Queue for Power-Aware Microprocessors." in Proc of Great Lakes Symposium on VLIS, 2001.

[7] A. Buyuktosunoglu et al. "Energy-Efficient Co-adaptive Instruction Fetch and Issue." in Proc. International Symposium on Computer Architecture (ISCA), 2003.

[8] R. Canal, A. Gonzalez. "A Low-Complexity Issue Logic." in Proc. International Conference on Supercomputing (ICS), 2000.

[9] R. Canal, A. Gonzalez. "Reducing the Complexity of the Issue Logic." in Proc. of the Int'l Conference on Supercomputing (ICS), 2001.

[10] F. Cazorla, et al. "Dynamically Controlled Resource Allocation in SMT Processors." in Proc International Symposium on Microarchitecture, 2004.

[11] F. Cazorla, et al. "Improving Memory Latency Aware Fetch Policies for SMT Processors." in Proc International Symposium on High Performance Computing, 2003.

[12] A. Cristal, et al. "Out-of-Order Commit Processors." in Proc. of the International Symposium on High Performance Computer Architecture (HPCA), 2004.

[13] T. Ehrhart, S. Patel. "Reducing the Scheduling Critical Cycle using Wakeup Prediction." in Proc. International Symposium on High Performance Computer Architecture (HPCA), 2004.

[14] A. El-Moursy, D.Albonesi. "Front-End Policies for Improved Issue Efficiency in SMT Processors." in Proc. International Symposium on High-Performance Computer Architecture (HPCA), 2003.

[15] D. Ernst, T. Austin. "Efficient Dynamic Scheduling Through Tag Elimination." in Proc. Int'l Symp on Comp. Architecture (ISCA), 2002.

[16] D. Ernst, et al. "Cyclone: a Broadcast-free Dynamic Instruction Scheduler with Selective Replay." in Proc. International Symposium on Computer Architecture (ISCA), 2003.

[17] D. Folegnani, A. Gonzalez. "Energy-Effective Issue Logic." in Proc International Symposium on Computer Architecture (ISCA) 2001.

[18] J. Henning, "SPEC CPU2000: Measuring CPU Performance in the New Millennium", in the Transactions of IEEE Computer, 33(7):28-35, July 2000.

[19] J. Hu, et al. "Exploring Wakeup-Free Instruction Scheduling." in Proc. International Symposium on High Performance Computer Architecture (HPCA), 2004.

[20] M. Huang et al. "Energy-Efficient Hybrid Wakeup Logic." in Proc International Symp. on Low-power Electronics Design (ISLPED), 2002.

[21] I. Kim , M. Lipasti. "Macro-Op Scheduling: Relaxing Scheduling Loop Constraints.", in Proc. International Symposium on Microarchitecture (MICRO), 2003.

[22] I.Kim, M.Lipasti. "Half-Price Architecture." in Proc International Symposium on Computer Architecture (ISCA), 2003.

[23] A. Lebeck et al. "A Large, Fast Instruction Window for Tolerating Cache Misses." in Proc. International Symposium on Computer Architecture (ISCA), 2002.

[24] Y. Liu, et al. "Scaling the Issue Window with Look-Ahead Latency Prediction." in Proc. International Conf on Supercomputing (ICS), 2004.

[25] K. Luo, et al. "Balancing Throughput and Fairness in SMT Processors." in Proc International Symposium on Performance Analysis of Systems and Software, 2001.

[26] P. Michaud, et al. "Data-Flow Prescheduling for Large Instruction Windows in Out-of-Order Processors." in Proc. International Conference on High Performance Computer Architecture (HPCA), 2001.

[27] S. Palacharla, et al. "Complexity-Effective Superscalar Processors." in Proc. of the Int'l Symp. on Computer Architecture (ISCA), 1997.

[28] S. Raasch, et al. "A Scalable Instruction Queue Design Using Dependence Chains." in Proc of International Symposium on Computer Architecture, 2002.

[29] D. Ponomarev, et al. "Reducing Power Requirements of Instruction Scheduling Through Dynamic Allocation of Multiple Datapath Resources." in Proc. International Symposium on Microarchitecute (MICRO), 2001.

[30] D. Ponomarev, et al. "Energy-Efficient Issue Queue Design." in IEEE Transactions on VLSI Systems, November 2003.

[31] D. Ponomarev, et al. "Energy-Efficient Comparators for Superscalar Datapaths," IEEE Transactions on Computers, July 2004.

[32] S. Raasch et al. "The Impact of Resource Partitioning on SMT Processors." in Proc. PACT, 2003.

[33] B. Robatmili et al. "Thread-Sensitive Instruction Issue for SMT Processors." Computer Architecture News, 2004.

[34] J. Sharkey, et al. "Reducing Delay and Power Consumption of the Wakeup Logic through Instruction Packing and Tag Memoization." in Proc. of the 4th Workshop on Power-Aware Computer Systems, 2004.

[35] J. Sharkey, et al. "Instruction Packing: Reducing Power and Delay of the Dynamic Scheduling Logic." in Proc. of the International Symposium on Low Power Electronics and Design (ISLPED), 2005.

[36] J. Sharkey, D. Ponomarev. "Instruction Recirculation: Reducing Power and Delay of the Dynamic Scheduling Logic." In Proc. ACM/IEEE Euro-Par Conference, 2005.

[37] J. Sharkey. "M-Sim: A Flexible, Multi-threaded Simulation Environment." Tech. Report CS-TR-05-DP1, Department of Computer Science, SUNY Binghamton, 2005.

[38] T. Sherwood, et al. "Automatically Characterizing Large Scale Program Behavior." Proc. ASPLOS, 2002.

[39] J. Stark, et al. "On Pipelining Dynamic Instruction Scheduling Logic" in Proc. International Symposium on Microarchitecture (MICRO), 2000.

[40] D. Tullsen, et al. "Handling Long-Latency Loads in a Simultaneous Multi-threaded Processor." in Proc of International Symposium on Microarchtiecture, 2001.

[41] D. Tullsen, et al. "Exploiting Choice: Instruction Fetch and Issue on an Implementable Simultaneous Multithreading Processor." in Proc International Symposium on Computer Architecture, 1996.

[42] D. Tullsen, et al. "Simultaneous Multithreading: Maximizing on-chip Parallelism." in Proc of International Symposium on Computer Architecture, 1995.